THOUGHT AND KNOWLEDGE
An Introduction to
Critical Thinking

THOUGHT AND KNOWLEDGE

An Introduction to Critical Thinking

SECOND EDITION

DIANE F. HALPERN

*California State University,
San Bernardino*

LAWRENCE ERLBAUM ASSOCIATES, PUBLISHERS

1989   Hillsdale, New Jersey   Hove and London

Lawrence Erlbaum Associates, Inc., Publishers
365 Broadway
Hillsdale, New Jersey 07642

Library of Congress card number: 89-17163
ISBN 0-8058-0294-0
ISBN 0-8058-0295-9 (pbk.)

Printed in the United States of America
10 9 8 7 6 5 4 3 2

To
Sheldon, my husband, and
Evan and Joan, my children—
for their support, encouragement, and love

Contents

Preface to the First Edition

During the last century, psychologists have sought to understand how we think and know about the world around us. As they have gathered information to answer these questions, many have wondered if we could use our knowledge about the way that the mind works to help people improve how they think. It seems clear that we can. The purpose of this book is to apply the research and theories of cognitive psychology to the development of critical thinking skills. It's sort of a user's guide to an immensely complex and highly efficient information processor—the human mind. Because it was written from the perspective of a cognitive psychologist, it can also serve as an introduction to the general area of cognitive psychology.

Traditionally, instruction in how to think has been a neglected component in American education. Students were more often taught what to think than how to think. Education has primarily been concerned with presenting students with the "facts" on a wide variety of topics—the "knowing that"—while offering little on how to utilize this information or how to discover facts on their own—the "knowing how." Domerque (cited in Parnes, Noller, & Biondi, 1977, p. 52) summarized this situation well when he said, "Some people study all their life, and at their death they have learned everything except to think."

I recently had a conversation with a senior partner of a large firm, during which he lamented the current state of recent law school graduates. He complained that although they could recite the relevant laws, they didn't know how to think. Complaints like this one have been raised by many people in almost every discipline. Consider, for example, the A+ student who could recite in order each of the major Chinese dynasties, yet had no idea what a dynasty was. More importantly, it never occurred to him to ask about the meaning of this term, as he had never made it a habit to be mindful of his thoughts or to monitor his own thought processes for understanding. Perhaps vignettes like these that demonstrate the need for critical thinking instruction shouldn't be surprising, since students are rarely given explicit instruction on how to improve their thinking. Modern educators have recognized that this gap exists and have begun instituting courses with the primary objective of teaching students how to improve their thinking. Most students, teachers, and administrators will agree that this is an idea whose time is long overdue.

It is my hope that you, the reader, will take something very valuable away with you after reading this book. You should be able to think more clearly about any topic, recognize muddy thinking, whether your own or someone else's, monitor what you know and, more importantly, what you don't know, and improve your memory, problem solving, decision making, reasoning, and creative thinking skills. These are lofty objectives, yet ones that can be achieved with a little hard work. Current and relevant examples of each thinking skill have been utilized throughout the book. Many of them may be immediately applicable in your own life. I hope that you'll find this book to be informative, worthwhile, and fun.

ACKNOWLEDGMENTS FOR THE FIRST EDITION

Many people have assisted in the preparation of this book. Mr. Jack Burton, Vice President, Lawrence Erlbaum Associates, Inc., has guided me through the publication process with tact and wisdom. In the process, he has become an admired and respected friend. Dr. George Mandler at the University of California, San Diego has read and reread the manuscript, offering expert advice and practical good sense. His wise counsel has been very much appreciated. My dear "aunt," Dr. Katharine D. Newman, now retired from the English Department at West Chester State College, has not only commented on the manuscript, offering helpful suggestions and corrections, but has also served as a life-long role model. She has influenced greatly the course of my life. Dr. Susan Nummedal at California State University, Long Beach, has afforded me the benefit of her expertise with helpful suggestions on the manuscript and has given me support and encouragement with this project. It is deeply appreciated. Dr. Dorothy Piontkowski at San Francisco State University provided several useful insights, especially on Chapter II, The Relationship Between Thought and Language. I would also like to thank an "anonymous philosopher" for comments on the Reasoning Chapter. Ms. Sandi Guideman, production editor, deserves special thanks for all of her help in "pulling the book together" and contributing to its format.

The people most responsible for this text are my husband, Sheldon, and my children, Evan and Joan. Sheldon has read and commented on the entire manuscript, suffered through low points in the writing, encouraged me throughout this project and in almost every endeavor in my life. Evan and Joan have helped in numerous ways, but mostly by just being there and taking pride in my accomplishments. Thanks to all of you.

Diane F. Halpern

Preface to the Second Edition

As the comedians like to say, "There's good news and there's bad news." The bad news is that developing the attitude and skills of a critical thinker will require patience and work. The good news is that there is substantial evidence that with hard work, determination, and the right learning experiences, most people can improve the way they think. It's certainly an objective worth working toward. This is a skills-oriented text with frequent examples of each "thinking skill" for the reader to follow. Occasionally, relevant research and theories are presented to provide the reader with a background in the psychology of thinking. Because this is an introductory text, it does not attempt to provide exhaustive coverage of all possible topics. I hope that this book will spark your interest and lead you to explore the topics in greater depth. The suggested readings at the end of each chapter can serve as guideposts for finding out more about the most fascinating of all human activities: the thinking process.

Many of the major concepts that are presented appear in several places throughout this book because basic thinking skills are broadly applicable in a variety of situations. This should also serve as an aid in learning them; research in learning and memory has shown that when information is learned in a variety of contexts, it is easier to remember and utilize, and makes transfer more likely.

Each chapter has been written to "stand alone" so that the chapters can be read in any order, with the exception of the last chapter, which consists mainly of applications of the thinking skills that are presented in the preceding chapters. Use the outline at the beginning of each chapter to establish a framework for the material. Paying attention to headings and subheadings will help you to organize hierarchically the information.

It is important to work through each sample problem to gain experience with each of the skills presented. Reread difficult sections and paraphrase (restate in your own words) each section. Chapter summaries are provided to serve as a recall cue and memory aid for the information in each chapter. Review the key terms and concepts and be sure that you can answer the end-of-the-chapter questions. Each chapter ends with problems so that you can apply the skills presented in that chapter. In addition, a glossary of terms is provided at the end of every chapter.

Think up your own problems that are like the ones presented in this book, and be sure to keep alert for ways to apply these skills to your life. Read billboards and textbooks critically. Think about your school problems. Examine letters to newspaper editors with care. In short, develop the attitude of a critical thinker. I can't imagine any endeavor more exciting or worthwhile!

One of the goals of this text is to increase the reader's awareness of her or his own thinking process. In order to achieve this goal, the reader will have to work through numerous participatory exercises. As you read through this book, you'll become aware of the ways that language influences thought, learn some strategies for approaching and solving problems, develop the skills needed to reason clearly and make sound decisions, understand how hypotheses are tested and how to use probabilities, learn what to do to help you remember, understand the concept and measurement of intelligence, enhance your ability to think creatively, and apply this knowledge to a wide range of situations.

The first chapter was written to provide a theoretical background and rationale for the book. The remaining chapters of this book are loosely organized around five broad themes. The first is remembering (chapter 2), which includes acquiring, storing, and accessing knowledge about the world. Remembering is sometimes considered a "lower level" skill, but it is a basic one, as the totality of all that we know rests upon the ability to acquire and retrieve information. The second major theme concerns using natural (everyday) language to make sound conclusions about the nature of the world (chapters 3, 4, and 5). This includes determining what to believe and evaluating the strength and validity of evidence, especially when we are presented with persuasive appeals. The third major theme concerns creating knowledge from experience (chapters 6 and 7). This includes determining cause and effect and covariance relationships among variables and dealing with uncertainty. Generating and evaluating solution paths is the fourth theme (chapters 8, 9, and 10). Decision making, problem solving, and creativity are the topics presented in that section. The fifth theme is probably best described as "putting Humpty together again" (chapter 11). Thinking skills are presented in relative isolation and in "clean" examples in the earlier chapters in the book. In real life, thinking is a much murkier business that requires multiple skills in combination and in sequences that soon get rather complicated. The last chapter is an applications chapter in which the types of exercises are closer to those that people encounter in real life, with a special emphasis on the kinds of thinking problems that students are faced with in college.

It has been said that the head remembers what it does. Markle (1977) has claimed that the first axiom of learning is, "It is not what is presented to the student but what the student is led to do that results in learning" (p. 13). I doubt that very much has ever been learned in a passive manner. So, get involved with the material, work the exercises, discuss them with others, raise questions, and enjoy yourself. Thinking is not a spectator sport! Nutritionists warn that you are what you eat. I believe instead that you are what you think.

ACKNOWLEDGMENTS FOR THE SECOND EDITION

This book has benefitted greatly from the thoughtful comments of many wonderful colleagues. My sincere appreciation goes to Dr. Richard Block of Montana State University, Dr. Gregory Kimble of Duke University, Dr. David Riefer of California State University, San Bernardino, and Dr. Robert Sternberg of Yale University. Their suggestions and insights have been invaluable. Thanks to all of you for sharing your time and thoughts with me and with the readers.

Special thanks also to my good friend Robert Perine, a talented artist and creative author, who designed the cover of this book.

Diane F. Halpern

1 Thinking: An Introduction

> *Many people would sooner die than think.*
> *In fact they do.*
> —Bertrand Russell

"Think about it!" How many times have you heard this phrase or said it yourself? Look around you. Watch a student solving a calculus problem, or a programmer

1

"debugging" a computer program, or a politician arguing that the Strategic Defense Initiative will not work. Watch a child absorbed in a fairy tale, or an architect designing a skyscraper, or a senior citizen planning to live on a fixed income. What are they doing that makes their faces appear so serious, so quizzical—so much like Rodin's famous statue, "The Thinker," which appears on the cover of this book? They are all "lost in thought," yet lost seems like a strange word to describe the process of thinking—maybe "finding knowledge in thought" would be a more appropriate phrase.

THE NEED FOR CRITICAL THINKING SKILLS

Although the ability to think critically has always been important, it is imperative for the citizens of the 20th and 21st centuries. For the first time in the history of the human race, we have the ability to destroy all life on Earth. The decisions that we make as individuals and as a society regarding the economy, conservation of natural resources, and the development of nuclear weapons will affect future generations of all people around the world. We are also called on to make decisions on a wide range of important local and personal topics. For example, in

GRIN AND BEAR IT   by Lichty & Wagner

Courtesy of NAS, INC.

6-15

"Fifty cents for my thoughts?"

a recent election, voters had to decide if they favored or opposed an increase in property taxes, the construction of a canal that would divert water from one part of the state to another, mandatory AIDS testing for criminals, and a rent control ordinance, in addition to deciding which candidate they preferred for diverse political offices including governor, state treasurer, county commissioner, and trustee of the local library system. Consumers need to decide if the nitrates in their hot dogs are carcinogens, if the public school system is providing an adequate education, and whether health plans that allow you to choose your physician are preferable to plans that do not allow this flexibility. Because every citizen is required to make countless important decisions, it may seem obvious that, as a society, we should be concerned with the way these decisions are made. Surprisingly, it is only within the last 10 to 15 years that educators, politicians, and the general public have begun to address this topic in a serious manner.

Several recent national reports have shown that instruction that is designed to improve the thinking process is desperately needed. The United States has been described as a "nation at risk" because we are failing to provide students with the most essential component of education—instruction that fosters the development of the ability to think (National Commission of Excellence in Education, 1983). Steen (1987) summarized the results of a recent international study on mathematical reasoning with this ominous warning: "Indeed, as the 'back-to-basics' movement has flourished in the last 15 years, the ability of U.S. students to think (rather than to memorize) has declined accordingly" (p. 251). The Education Commission of the States reached a similar sobering conclusion in its 1982 report: "The pattern is clear: the percentage of students achieving higher order skills is declining" (cited in Baron & Sternberg, 1987, p. x). These sentiments were echoed in a report by the American Association of Medical Colleges (1984), who concluded that ". . . students are not prepared as critical and quantitative thinkers and clinical problem solvers either when they enter or graduate from medical school" (p. 125).

If the conclusions of national and international study groups don't convince you of the need for critical thinking instruction, consider this: Most people will finish their formal education between the ages of 18 and 22. Today's young adults are expected to have the longest average life span in the history of the world, with most living into their 70s and many living into their 80s and 90s. We can only guess what life will be like in the years 2040 and 2050 or beyond, years that many of you who are reading this book will live through. One likely guess is that many of today's young adults will be working at jobs that currently don't exist and dealing with technologies that dwarf the imagination of present-day science fiction writers. What do they need to learn during their first two decades of life that will prepare them for the remaining 50+ years?

A forward-looking education must be built on the twin foundations of knowing how to learn and knowing how to think clearly about the rapidly proliferating information with which we will all have to contend. I have an inexpensive modem attached to my home computer that I can use to access virtually all of the research articles in a major university library, the contents of dozens of daily newspapers, airline flight schedules, several encyclopedia services, the Dow Jones Index, a pharmaceutical reference guide, college catalogues for thousands of colleges, government publications, movie reviews, and much more. All of this information is available in the comfort of my own home with only a few minutes of "search time" on the computer. The problem has become knowing what to do with the deluge of data. The information has to be interpreted, digested, learned, and applied or it is of no more use on my desk than it is on a library shelf. If we cannot think intelligently about the myriad of issues that confront us, then we are in danger of having all of the answers, but still not knowing what they mean.

Despite what may seem to many to be an obvious need in higher education, it is only in recent years that educators have been concerned with designing educational programs to improve the thinking process. It's difficult to imagine any area where the ability to think clearly is not needed. Yet, few of us have ever received explicit instructions in how to improve the way we think. Traditionally, our schools have required students to learn, remember, make decisions, analyze arguments, and solve problems without ever teaching them how. There has been a tacit assumption that adult students already know "how to think." Research has shown, however, this assumption is not warranted. Psychologists have found that only 25% of 1rst-year college students possess the skills needed for logical abstract thought—the type of thought needed to answer "what would happen if . . ." questions and to comprehend abstract concepts (McKinnon & Renner, 1971).

Thought and Knowledge

This is a book about thought and knowledge and the relationship between these two constructs. It's about thinking in ways that allow us to use previous knowledge to create new knowledge. Everything we know and everything everyone else knows, that is all existing knowledge, was created by someone. When we learn Euclidean geometry, we are learning about knowledge created by the great mathematician, Euclid. Similarly, other eminent inventions and insights, like the wheel, shoes, video games, toilet paper, $E = mc^2$, and the "discovery" of America, all represent knowledge created by people. Knowledge is not something static that gets transferred from one person to another like pouring water from one vessel to another. It is something much more dynamic. Of course, it's silly to think that we should all start from "scratch" and begin by recreating the wheel. We build on the knowledge created by others to create new knowledge.

We also create knowledge every time we learn a new concept. The newly acquired information is used to construct our own internal knowledge structures.

These knowledge structures, or **schemata,** are our personal internal representations about the nature of the world. When we recombine them in new ways with other schemata, we are creating new knowledge. This idea was expressed more eloquently by Resnick (1985), when she said: "Knowledge is no longer viewed as a reflection of what has been given from the outside; it is a personal construction in which the individual imposes meaning by relating bits of knowledge and experience to some organizing schemata" (p. 130).

A Working Definition of Critical Thinking

The term **critical thinking** is used to describe thinking that is purposeful, reasoned, and goal directed. It is the kind of thinking involved in solving problems, formulating inferences, calculating likelihoods, and making decisions. The "critical" part of critical thinking denotes an evaluation component. Sometimes the word "critical" is used to convey something negative, as when we say, "The situation is critical." But, evaluation can and should be a constructive consideration of positive and negative attributes. When we think critically, we are evaluating the outcomes of our thought processes—how good a decision is or how well a problem is solved. Critical thinking also involves evaluating the thinking process—the reasoning that went into the conclusion we've arrived at or the kinds of factors considered in making a decision. Critical thinking is also called **directed thinking** because it focuses on obtaining a desired outcome. Daydreams, night dreams, and other sorts of thinking that are not engaged in for a specific purpose are not subsumed under the critical thinking category; neither is the type of thinking that underlies our daily routinized habits, which, although goal directed, involve very little conscious evaluation, such as getting up in the morning, brushing our teeth, or taking the usual route to school or work. These are examples of the kind of thinking called **nondirected thinking.**

The focus of this book is on the development and improvement of those skills that characterize clear, precise, purposeful thinking. It is a practical book, based primarily on applications of cognitive psychology to memory, reasoning, problem solving, creativity, intelligence, language, and decision making.

Although psychology has been concerned with the way people think for much of its 100+ years of existence as an academic discipline, cognitive psychology, the branch of psychology that is concerned with thought and knowledge, has virtually dominated the field of psychology over the last 15 years. Psychologists have been concerned with learning about the skills and strategies used in problem solving, reasoning, and decision making and the way these abilities relate to intelligence. All of this interest in human thinking processes has given birth to a new area of psychology that has come to be known as **cognitive process instruction.** Its goal is to utilize the knowledge we have accumulated about human thinking processes and mechanisms in ways that can help people improve how they think. For example, by examining correct and incorrect responses in a variety of situations, psychologists have found that most people's spontaneous and intuitive approaches to problems are frequently wrong. Furthermore, they can often predict when an incorrect response will be made either because of the nature of the problem or because of biases that a problem solver may bring to the problem. This knowledge is already being put to use to solve a host of applied problems that range from providing military personnel with map-reading skills to designing "user-friendly" (easy to use) computer programs.

Learning How to Think: Can It Be Done?

The answer to this question is a somewhat qualified, "No." Every one of us already knows how to think. It's something we've done, most often without thinking much about it, from birth. It comes as naturally as breathing. On a more positive and relevant note, although it may not be possible to teach someone *how* to think, it is possible to improve the way someone thinks.

It may seem that if I'm concerned with improving the way people think, then I should be able to offer a good definition for the term "thinking," especially because I've already defined critical thinking as one type of thinking. This turns out to be a difficult task. Consider the definition and question offered by Bourne, Ekstrand, and Dominowski (1971):

> Thinking is a complex, multifaceted process. It is essentially internal (and possibly nonbehavioral), involving symbolic representations of events and objects not immediately present, but is initiated by some external event (stimulus). Its function is to generate and to control overt behavior. This expression seems straightforward enough, a reasonable working hypothesis. But is it? (p. 5)

Most people would agree that thinking is complex and that it guides our behavior. In addition, thinking is dynamic; it's something we do. Thinking involves going "beyond the information given" (Bruner, 1957). We take new information, combine it with information stored in memory and end up with something more than and different from what we started with. It's also private, in that no one else can know about our thoughts unless we choose to communicate them. Furthermore, thinking is so private that no one has direct conscious awareness of her or his own thinking processes. As Mandler (1975) reminded us, we usually have no knowledge of how we think; we only know the products of our thoughts. The problem of adequately defining "thinking" shouldn't prevent us from finding ways to improve it. After all, as Munson (1976) astutely observed, "The truth is that not a whole heck of a lot about a complicated subject can be learned from a definition of it" (p. 3).

Changing How People Think: Should It Be Done?

The whole idea of influencing the way people think may seem scary. It suggests terms like "mind control" and "propaganda," or perhaps even a "Big

Brother,'' like the one in Orwell's chilling novel *1984*, who knew what you were thinking. When Orwell wrote his book (in 1949), he was writing about the horrors of a society 35 years into the future. Although 1984 (the year) is recent history, the topic, "thinking," is still very much on the minds of educators and students, but for reasons opposite from those expressed by Orwell. Learning the skills of clear thinking can help everyone to recognize propaganda and thus not fall prey to it, to analyze unstated assumptions in arguments, to realize when there is deliberate deception, to consider the credibility of an information source, and to think a problem or a decision through in the best way possible.

When I discuss the topic of critical thinking with students and other people I come in contact with, I am sometimes told that "it's all a matter of opinion" and that everyone has a right to his or her own opinion. I certainly agree that we all have the "right" to our own opinions, but some "opinions" are better than others. If, for example, you believe that heavy alcohol consumption is good for pregnant women, you had better be able to back up this belief with sound reasoning. (There isn't any.) (More precise definitions of the terms "opinion" and "belief" are presented in chapter 5.) The opposite belief, that pregnant women should drink very little, and preferably no alcohol at all, can be supported with carefully controlled laboratory studies that document the deleterious effect of alcohol on a developing fetus. Similarly, we also need to be aware of the numerous attempts to change how we think about an array of topics so that we can evaluate and interpret the messages we receive.

Let's consider some examples of the need to think critically in a variety of contexts. A good place to start is with commercials. Sponsors pay substantial sums for the opportunity to persuade customers to purchase their products. An advertising campaign is rated as successful if more of the product is sold after the advertisement is run (on television, radio, billboards, newspapers, etc.), and the additional sales more than cover the cost of the advertisement. One of my favorite examples is a cigarette advertisement. As you undoubtedly know, every cigarette advertisement in the United States must carry messages like this one: "Warning: The U.S. Surgeon General has determined that cigarette smoking is dangerous to your health." It would seem that this message would conjure up visions of hacking coughs, stained teeth, and lung cancer, and thus reduce the effectiveness of any cigarette advertisement. To counter the surgeon general's warning, many cigarette advertisements show smokers in natural outdoor surroundings with crystal lakes, clear blue skies, and tall, green pine trees. One cigarette advertisement reads, "Come to where the clean is." Have you ever stopped to consider the association of cigarette smoking and the beauty of an outdoor scene? Does cigarette smoking seem healthier when it is associated with beautiful people in beautiful settings? One new brand of cigarettes is called "Malibu." The advertisements depict the soft white sand and foamy blue ocean at Malibu Beach in California, which is probably the ultimate setting for "beautiful people." I don't know how many people have been influenced by this advertisement. (The cigarette company refused to disclose figures and would say only that the ad campaign is doing well.) It is reasonable to assume, however, that because the advertisement has been used so frequently, it is persuading people to smoke the brand of cigarettes being advertised.

Another example of the need for critical thinking comes from a conversation I once had with a cab driver. Our conversation got around to the way laundry products are advertised. He told me that he never paid any attention to advertisements and that they had no affect on his decision about which product to buy. He went on to say that he always buys the blue liquid detergent that is good at getting out "ring around the collar." Do you see the inconsistency in his statements? Although he believed that he was not allowing the advertising claims to influence him, in fact, they were directly determining his buying habits. I doubt if many people worried about "ring around the collar," "waxy yellow build-up on their kitchen floor," "fresh-smelling carpets," or "soft elbows" before commercials told us that we were remiss and socially undesirable unless we attended to these details. The unstated assumption in these commercials is that the "problems" they raise (e.g., dark lines on the inside neck portion of shirts, or floors that aren't as clear as new ones) are important ones that can be remedied if you purchase the advertised products. The cab driver, for example, accepted the problem as a valid concern and then purchased the advertised product without any conscious awareness of the ways his thoughts and behaviors had been influenced.

In a recent political campaign, one candidate told voters that he was opposed to waste, fraud, pollution, crime, and overpaid bureaucrats. This speech was followed with loud cheering and applause. What's wrong with his speech? He never really said anything. I've never heard any candidate claim to be *for* waste, fraud, pollution, crime, or overpaid bureaucrats. Voters should have asked him to be more explicit about his goals, how he would accomplish them, and where the money would come from to finance his plans.

The following problem was posed to 9-year-olds in the United States: "Joan bought three boxes of pens. What else do you need to know to find out how many pens she bought?" (Solorzano, 1985). Only 35% of the youngsters realized that the missing information was how many pens were in each box. Here is a problem that was presented to a large sample of 13-year-olds: "An army bus holds 36 soldiers. If 1,128 soldiers are being bussed to their training site, how many busses are needed?" (Chance, 1986, p. 26). Most of the students tested had no trouble carrying out the computations. The problem came in using the answer in a meaningful way. Many rounded the answer they received to the nearest whole number and concluded that 31 busses were needed. Others gave a decimal answer (31.33) or showed the remainder from their long division. The problem was not one of basic computational skills, but of thinking about the kind of answer that the problem required and using a strategy that was different from one that was taught in school, namely rounding "up" to the next highest whole number rather than rounding to the nearest whole number.

EMPIRICAL EVIDENCE THAT THINKING
CAN BE IMPROVED

*When you offer someone a penny for his thoughts, you
usually don't expect to get a bargain.*

—Beardsley (1950, p. x)

If you've been thinking critically about the idea of improving how you think, then you've probably begun to wonder if there is any evidence that thinking can be improved. Although there has been some debate about whether it is possible to produce long-lasting enhancement in the ability to think effectively (Block, 1985; Glaser 1984; Resnick, 1983), we now have a considerable body of evidence that thinking skills courses have positive effects that are transferable to a wide variety of situations. At least five qualitatively different forms of outcome evaluations for thinking courses have been conducted, all of which are generally supportive of the idea that the ability to think critically can be improved:

1. Evaluations of Programs Designed to Enhance Thinking Skills. Venezula leads the world in its commitment to improving the thinking skills of its citizens. A major component of this effort has been the design and development of a program of critical thinking instruction for use in their schools. Psychologists from Venezuela and the United States devised 60 lesson plans dealing with topics such as ordering and classifying events, understanding language, verbal reasoning, problem solving, decision making, and inventive or creative thinking. Fifty-six of these lessons were presented in several seventh-grade classes. Other comparable classes were designated as nontreatment control classes. Results obtained from hundreds of students showed that the students who received specific thinking instruction outperformed control subjects on standardized tests of thinking skills. They also showed greater gains in orally presented arguments and in answering open-ended essay questions (Herrnstein, Nickerson, de Sanchez, & Swets, 1986; Schoenfeld, 1987; Walsh, 1981).

Although no other thinking skills program has received the extensive testing and scrutiny that the Venezuela project is undergoing, positive results have been reported for other programs as well. In Chance's (1986) review of several other programs, he concluded that good thinking is a skill that can be taught and that thinking is best taught by direct and systematic instruction.

2. Student Self-Reports. A second approach to answering the question of whether people can learn to improve how they think is to ask the students who have completed a thinking skills course. Although it is important to consider students' perceptions about their own thinking abilities, there are obvious problems with student self-reports. Students may report that they have learned to think better when, in fact, they have not or, conversely, that they have not improved when they really have. Despite this problem, it is comforting to know that the overwhelming majority of students report that they have made substantial gains in their thinking ability after completing a thinking skills course (e.g., Block & Taylor, 1984; Dansereau et al., 1979; Wheeler, 1979).

3. Gains in I.Q. Scores.   Although the relationship between critical thinking and intelligence is considered in a later section in this chapter, it is relevant to note here that one way of measuring thinking improvement is with gains in IQ points on standardized intelligence tests. The underlying rationale is that people should become more intelligent when they think better and that gains in intelligence will be reflected in higher IQ scores. One of the pioneers in this area is Moshe Rubinstein, who has developed a long-running course at UCLA to teach students the skills of critical thinking. An educator at a mid-western university who has adopted Rubinstein's program reported that 82.4% of the students who have taken his course scored higher on a test of intelligence than they did before the course began (Rubinstein, 1980). Detterman and Sternberg (1982) have also presented substantial additional support for the notion that IQ scores can be increased as a result of thinking skills instruction.

4. Cognitive Growth and Development.   Other evidence that thinking skills can be improved with instruction that is specifically designed for this purpose is presented by Fox, Marsh, and Crandall (1983). They found that college students who had been taught general problem-solving skills showed significant gains in measures of cognitive growth and development; whereas, a control group of college students who had not received the problem-solving training did not show significant gains.

5. Expert-Like Mental Representations.   One of the most recent and theoretically advanced means of exploring course-related changes in thinking ability is to examine the underlying structure of cognitive skills and knowledge. It is one method of studying the way people think about and organize information. This is related to the notion of the internal representation of knowledge, or schemata, that was presented earlier. The idea behind this sort of investigation is that when people become better thinkers about a topic, their internal representations of the topic-related knowledge will become similar to the internal representations of experts in that field. In other words, novices will come to think more like the experts.

In a recent attempt to improve thinking skills, Schoenfeld and Herrmann (1982) taught college freshmen and sophomores either general techniques of problem solving or ''structural programming,'' which involved an orderly way to solve nonmathematical problems using the computer. Students who received the general strategy instruction approached mathematical problems in ways that were similar to the approaches used by professors of mathematics. The general strategy approach demonstrated substantial improvement in problem-solving scores, whereas those in the computer course showed little improvement over the scores they had obtained before taking the course.

There are numerous other examples (e.g., see Cyert, 1980; Halpern, 1987a, 1987b; Lochhead & Clement, 1979) that all point to the same conclusion: Better thinking can be learned with appropriate instruction.

Exotic Learning

There are no quick and easy crash programs that will make you a competent thinker overnight, despite some unscrupulous claims that you can think better instantly without really trying. One article in a supermarket-checkout-line "newspaper" claimed that pregnant women could make their as yet unborn children more intelligent by listening to fine music and reading classical literature during their pregnancy. Other ludicrous schemes for better thinking include breathing into paper bags and subliminal learning, or learning without awareness. A large-scale study by The National Academy of Sciences concluded that there is no scientific evidence to support the claim that biofeedback, "neurolinguistic programming," or other chemical "super learning" techniques can improve your thinking (Gillette, 1987; Hostetler, 1988).

Transfer of Training

The real goal of any instruction to improve thinking is **transfer of training.** What I mean by "transfer" is use of critical thinking skills in a wide variety of contexts. The whole enterprise would be of little value if these skills were only used in the classroom or only on problems that are very similar to those presented in class. Ideally, critical thinking skills should be used to recognize and resist unrealistic campaign promises, circular reasoning, faulty probability estimates, weak arguments by analogy, or language designed to mislead whenever and wherever they are encountered. Critical thinkers should be better able to solve (or offer reasonable solutions to) real-world problems, whether it's the problem of nuclear war or how to set up a new video recorder. These skills should also be long lasting and useful for the many decades of critical thinking that most of us face. Admittedly, these are lofty goals, but they are important ones. The best way to promote the kind of transfer I'm advocating is with the conscious and deliberate use of the skills that you learn in a wide variety of contexts. Students can actively enhance transfer by looking for instances that call for critical thinking skills and using them.

THINKING ABOUT THINKING

A moment's thought would have shown him. But, a moment is a long time, and thought is a painful process.

—A. E. Housman

Thinking as a Biological Process

Researchers from many fields have spent their lifetimes trying to understand what people do when they think. Brain researchers are interested in understanding how the brain and other parts of the nervous system work. Every time you have a thought, feel an emotion, or receive information through your senses, your nervous system is involved. If you could examine your own brain, you would, no doubt, be surprised to find that it looks like a giant mushy walnut with the consistency of a soft-boiled egg. There is nothing in its appearance to even suggest that it is the foundation of human thought. Brain researchers study the brain in their attempt to unravel the mystery of the human mind.

The human brain has remained essentially unchanged since the dawn of modern history, yet, during that time, we have developed advanced technologies that include the ability to visit distant planets and have more than doubled the average expected life span. What has changed is "the information that is going into the brain and the process it receives" (Machado, cited in Walsh, 1981, p. 640). It is the ability to learn and to think that has changed the world.

Although brain researchers have discovered fascinating links between the biology (and anatomy) of the brain and intellectual skills, there is still much to learn. As a discipline, brain research is still in its infancy and thus, at present, has little to contribute to the development of our ability to think critically. Because we are certainly not able to control the chemical and neural processes in any direct way, the biological approach has little to suggest about how to improve the way we think. Current science fiction notions about brain transplants, pills to make us smarter, or miracle foods that prolong neural life still remain in the realm of late-night movies and Saturday afternoon matinees.

Thinking as Imagery and Silent Speech

Thinking is the talking of the soul with itself.
—Author Unknown
Found in a Fortune Cookie

Psychologists at the beginning of the century believed that thinking was comprised of mental images. Later in the century, other psychologists hypothesized that thinking was simply a form of "silent speech," much like talking to yourself without vocalization. In order to test these hypotheses, psychologists would ask subjects to describe what they did when responding to certain questions. Let's try some examples. As you answer each of the following questions, try to be aware of what you did when you "thought about it."

1. How many windows are in your living room?
2. What does your mother look like?
3. What letter comes after N in the alphabet?
4. Name a word that rhymes with "shoe."
5. How much is 2 + 3?
6. Can you define "critical thinking?"

As you answered these questions, were you aware of the use of images and/or words? Most people find that when they are asked to describe some concrete

THE FAMILY CIRCUS®   By Bil Keane

12-2

Copyright 1982
The Register and Tribune
Syndicate, Inc

"Thinking is when the picture is in your head
with the sound turned off."

object, like the number of windows in their living room or their mother, they are aware of picture-like images. In fact, it seems almost impossible to answer these questions without generating an internal representation or utilizing **imagery** in some way. Can you describe your mother or anyone else without creating an image? Questions like 3 or 4, which involve the order of letters in the alphabet and the sounds of words, usually require an individual to silently recite the items. (Did you sing "l-m-n-o-p" to yourself in order to answer Question 3?) When answering questions like 5 and 6, people are often unable to say how they arrived at an answer. (By the way, if you answer to Question 6 was "no," go back and reread the beginning sections in this chapter.) Most people feel that the answers just seemed to "pop into their heads" without any conscious awareness of the "medium" or "stuff" of thought.

Currently, research psychologists are debating whether the "true" medium of thought involves imagery or sentence-like propositions or both. For most people, the question is moot, as almost everyone reports that, at least under some circumstances, they are aware of both mental images and "silent speech" during the thought process. Most of the time, however, we have little or no conscious awareness of what happens when we think.

Sometimes, thinking can be improved if we "work at" generating an image or using speech-like thought. Albert Einstein often credited his ability to solve difficult problems to his extensive use of imagery. The most famous use of imagery was recorded by the chemist Kekule. He knew that if he could understand the structure of a benzene molecule he would have hit upon one of the most important discoveries in organic chemistry. Kekule knew that most chemical molecules are long strands of atoms, and that the structure of a benzene molecule had to be different. In order to solve this problem, Kekule practiced generating visual images that might help him to find the right one. His hard work was rewarded when the historic answer came to him this way (Kekule, quoted in Koestler, 1964):

> Again the atoms were gamboling before my eyes . . . My mental eye . . . could now distinguish larger structures . . . all twining and twisting in a snakelike motion. But look! What was that! One of the snakes had seized hold of its own tail, and the form whirled mockingly before my eyes. As if by a sudden flash of lightning I awoke.

The image of a snake biting its own tail led Kekule to the discovery that the benzene molecule was structured as a closed ring and not like strands of the other molecules. Thus, he was able to use visual imagery to direct his thoughts about a complex topic.

Words also serve to direct and stimulate thought. Although it may be obvious that thoughts are usually communicated with language, it is also true that language helps to generate thoughts. The generative role of language can be seen in an experiment by Glucksberg and Weisberg (1966). There is a classic problem in the psychology literature that was originally devised by Duncker (1945). In this problem, subjects are required to attach a candle to a wall so that it can be lit. They are given a candle, a box of matches, and some thumbtacks. Stop now and think how you would go about solving this problem if you were given only these materials (see Fig. 1.1). Don't go on until you've thought about it.

The best solution is to dump the matches from their box, tack the box to the wall and set the candle in the box. Most subjects have difficulty with this task

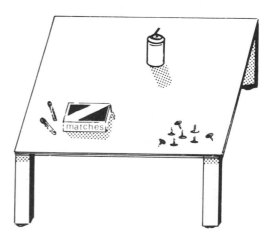

FIG. 1.1. Using only the materials shown in this figure, how would you attach the candle to the wall so that it can be burned?

because they fail to think of the box as part of the solution—they see it as a "box of matches." Glucksberg and Weisberg had people solve this problem under one of two conditions. The items were either labeled ("box," "tacks," "candle," and "matches") or they were not labeled. Subjects in the labeled condition solved the problem in about 1 minute, whereas those in the unlabeled condition took an average of 9 minutes. The labels directed their attention to the relevant items and changed the way the subjects solved this problem.

Let's consider a somewhat different example of the way language directs thought. There is a popular riddle that goes something like this:

> A young boy and his father went for a Sunday drive. A drunken driver swerved in front of their car, killing the father on impact. The young boy was rushed to the nearest hospital where the chief of neurosurgery was summoned to perform an operation. Upon seeing the boy, the chief of neurosurgery cried out, "I can't operate on him, he's my son!" How is this possible?

When I've posed this riddle to students, some of their answers included: "The chief of neurosurgery is the boy's stepfather"; "The real father didn't die"; and "It's impossible." Have you guessed the answer? The answer is that the chief of neurosurgery is the boy's mother. The reason for the difficulty is that in our society, terms like "chief of neurosurgery" lead us to consider only males. The words we use can determine the kinds of thoughts we think. (This concept is developed more fully in chapter 3.)

Have you ever listened to two professionals in the same field discussing their work? Most professionals have highly developed specialized terms to communicate their thoughts. Often, these specialized terms also serve to guide the way the professionals think. Consider these words by Bross (1973):

> How did the surgeon acquire his knowledge of the structure of the human body? . . . It has taken hundreds of dissections to build up the detailed and accurate picture of the structure of the human body that enables the surgeon to know where to cut. A highly specialized sublanguage has evolved for the sole purpose of describing this structure. The surgeon had to learn this jargon of anatomy before the anatomical facts could be effectively transmitted to him. Thus, underlying the "effective action" of the surgeon is an "effective language." Learning this anatomical language was a prerequisite to the transmission of the factual information that is needed here for effective action. (p. 217)

Thus, as the author pointed out, technical jargons not only facilitate communication among professionals, they are an inherent part of the development of ideas in a specialized discipline.

The use of jargon can serve as an efficient shorthand for communication among professionals. Specialized terms, however, can also serve as a barrier that keeps laypersons from understanding. Have you ever gone to a physician and found you were unable to communicate with him or her because you didn't understand the technical terms he or she used? A physician with a clear understanding of the problem should be able to communicate the nature of your problem in plain language. Beware of anyone who scatters terms indiscriminately or uses them as labels for simple phenomena.

A friend of mine once went to an allergy specialist who, after extensive tests, announced that my friend had "chronic rhinitis." Although she found this diagnosis alarming, with further questioning, she learned that this means "runny nose,"—a diagnosis she could have made by herself.

Preferred Modes of Thought

Even though most people report that they are aware of the use of imagery and silent speech, at least some of the time, there is good evidence that individuals have **preferred modes of thought.** That is, some people seem to think more fluently or easily with one of these types of internal representation than the other. Suppose that I were giving you directions to a building on a college campus. Consider the two types of directions shown in Fig. 1.2. Do you prefer the map that conveys information in a spatial array or the verbal directions (e.g., "Take the second left after you pass Lake Avenue")? There also seems to be individual differences in preferred sensory modes. Some students report that they comprehend difficult material best when they read it; others prefer to listen to difficult material.

There is more than just anecdotal evidence in support of the notion that people have preferred modes of thought. Gardner (1983) wrote an award-winning book in which he described "multiple intelligences." There is abundant evidence that some people prefer to think "spatially," whereas others prefer a verbal mode of thought (Clarkson-Smith & Halpern, 1983; Halpern, 1986). There are also some tasks that are particularly well suited for a particular thinking mode. Imagery, for example, is usually a better strategy when dealing with spatial problems like those commonly encountered in geometry, the building trades, and architecture. Deliberately switching from one mode to another is often a critical thinking strategy. I return to this notion several times throughout this book. I suggest that you write out in words the procedures and solutions to mathematics and science problems and use imagery and spatial techniques when comprehending complex prose. Comprehension and problem solving can often be enhanced with the deliberate use of different thinking modes. Even if you are particularly proficient with one mode, it is good to develop less preferred modes.

Thinking as Human Information Processing

A currently popular approach to understanding human thought utilizes computers to model the ways humans think. One approach that psychologists and others

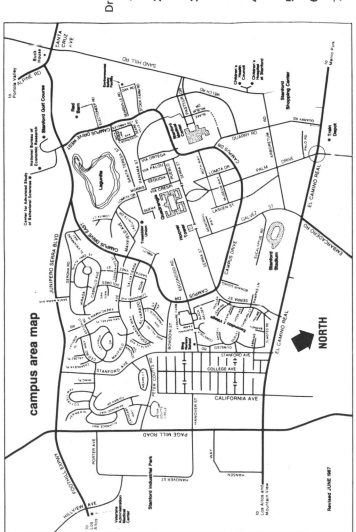

Driving Directions:

1. Take Embarcadero Road exit from the Bayshore Freeway.
2. Make a right at the exit (South) and continue straight for approximately two miles.
3. When you cross El Camino Real the street name changes to Galvez Street. Continue on Galvez to the next large street which is Campus Drive.
4. Make a left on Campus Drive. (This is a curvy street. Follow it around as it curves to the right.)
5. Make a right onto Mayfield Avenue.
6. Take the first right which is Lagunita Drive.
7. Park in the second lot on the left.

FIG. 1.2. Preferred Modes of Thought. Consider the map and the verbal driving directions presented above. If you had to choose between these two information formats, which would you prefer?

17

concerned with computer models of thought (engineers, linguists, medical personnel) have taken is to program a computer so that the processes and strategies it uses in solving a problem are similar to those used by humans. Thus, programs are written that can simulate or imitate human thought. This approach is called **computer simulation.** One problem with this approach is that we need to have very good ideas about the ways humans think in order to tell a computer to do it the same way.

One way of finding out how people think is to ask them to say out loud everything that they consciously thought about as they solved a problem. In this way, experimenters collect **thinking aloud protocols,** which are verbatim records of what the subject says he or she is doing while working on a problem. We have already tried something like this earlier in the chapter, using very simple questions. Let's try it with a more complex problem. As you work through this problem, say aloud every thought you have while working on the problem. It's important that you try to say all of your thoughts out loud. Your false starts, mistakes, repetitions, and so on, are all valuable in understanding how you think.

Here's the problem: Your friend has invited you to a birthday party. She has a square cake that she wants to share equally among the seven guests and herself. Using only three cuts with a knife, how would you cut the cake into eight equal slices?

Stop now, and recite out loud how you would go about solving this problem. If you have a tape recorder available, tape your think-aloud protocol so that you can analyze the thought processes you reveal in the protocol when you're finished. If you don't have a tape recorder, find a friend who is willing to take detailed notes of what you're saying. This gives you the added advantage of having someone with you to discuss your thinking process.

It's important to stop here and say out loud what you're thinking as you go about trying to solve this problem. If you go on reading before you've tried to think aloud, you don't get to eat any of the cake.

Most people find that they try several combinations of three slices before they hit upon the correct answer or give up. Imagery is often useful as you try to think about solutions to this problem because of the spatial nature of the problem. (The correct answer involves slicing the cake into quarters with two cuts, then placing the cake on its edge and slicing through the middle of the cake.) After collecting data from many subjects, a computer can be programmed (given a set of instructions in a computer language) to ''think'' about similar problems the way people do. If the simulation is successful, then the computer would also make the same mistakes that people make. Now that you've gotten the idea of think-aloud protocols, try it again with the next problem (from Hayes, 1982):

"Given Jug A, which contains 9 quarts; Jug B, 42 quarts; and Jug C, 6 quarts, measure out exactly 21 quarts" (p. 65).

Stop now, and verbalize aloud how you go about solving this problem. Be sure to say everything that you're thinking, even if it doesn't seem relevant. As before, you'll find the process more interesting if you can tape your responses so that you can review them later. Don't go on until you've tried to solve this problem.

Compare your protocol with the one presented here. Did you try the same problem-solving strategy used by the 37-year-old lawyer who answered this way?

> OK, I want to, uh, see what is the highest number that will go into 21, of those 3 numbers. A, B, and C . . . 42 is too high, uh, 9 will go into 21 twice . . . and leaves a remainder of, uh, 3 . . . that doesn't work, uh . . . I, uh, will then take 6; 6 will go into 21, 3 times . . . that's no good; it leaves a remainder of 3 . . . If I make it twice, that's 12; that will leave a remainder of 9 quarts that I can use A. That's 9 quarts, so I've got two of the C's, the 6 quarts, and one of the A's. That's 9 quarts.

Sometimes these attempts to describe the thinking process are written out instead of being said aloud, which led to the more general term **thought protocol analysis.** Psychologists study thought protocols to understand how people think. In **protocol analysis,** the protocol is broken down into segments so that each segment can be analyzed separately. Sometimes psychologists have theories about the processes involved and try to confirm or disconfirm them with the protocol. Other times, the purpose of the analysis is exploratory.

Thought protocols have proven to be useful in both understanding thinking processes and improving them. Thomas Good, an authority on research in mathematical education, has found that mathematics students learn best when the teachers actively work with them and model out loud the problem-solving process. It seems that when teachers think out loud they provide "a structure and a way of thinking about the information . . . so [students] can better understand relationships" (Cordes, 1983, p. 7). One way to improve thinking is to analyze the thought protocols of experts and then model your own thinking processes after them. This modeling technique has been found to be a useful aid in developing the thinking processes of novices. It is also useful to examine these records of your thinking in order to identify problems like the failure to consider certain types of information or other slips.

Artificial Intelligence

The term **Artificial Intelligence** (AI) is sometimes used to refer to the way computers solve problems when there has been no attempt to simulate or mimic human behavior. In AI, the programmed instructions to the computer may be very different from the way humans solve the same problem.

Have you ever played chess with a computer? Many computer programs are designed to simulate the moves that humans make. Other chess programs take advantage of the vast "memory" of the computer and have it evaluate the consequences of several different possible moves. Several chess programs can consider between 5,000 and 50,000 possible combinations of moves (Berliner, 1977). Several years ago, it was predicted that world chess championships would all be won by computers. This has not happened. Our best human chess players can still beat the computers with regularity—a fact that makes most of us human beings very happy.

Computer simulation and AI are more than toys. They can be used to guide military and economic decisions and to provide tentative answers to questions like, "What would happen if . . . ?" They also can infer information that is not specifically stated. For example, suppose that I told you that Jerome wanted to make an omelette. He noticed that he was out of butter and went to the market to buy some. Given only this information, answer the following question. Did Jerome have eggs in his house? Undoubtedly, you said, "Yes," because he only went to buy butter, he must have eggs. You can't make an omelette without eggs; and if he had been out of eggs, he would have also bought them at the store. Sophisticated computer programs can also make this inference. They can infer the truth about information not given (e.g., he must have eggs in the house) in much the same way that we humans do.

Computers have also been used to "talk" to people, much as some psychotherapists do. There is a type of psychotherapy called Rogerian therapy (named for Carl Rogers, its creator), in which the therapist rephrases the client's message. A famous computer program (Weizenbaum, 1966) does exactly the same thing. Here is an example of a "conversation" between a Rogerian computer therapist named Eliza and a human client. The conversation took place via typed message on a computer keyboard.

Patient: Men are all alike.
  Eliza: In what way?
Patient: They're always bugging us about something or other.
  Eliza: Can you think of a specific example?
Patient: Well, my boyfriend made me come here.
  Eliza: Your boyfriend made you come here.
Patient: He says I'm depressed much of the time.
  Eliza: I am sorry to hear you are depressed.
Patient: It's true. I am unhappy.
  Eliza: Do you think coming here will help you not to be unhappy?
Patient: I need some help, that much seems certain.
  Eliza: What would it mean to you if you got some help?
Patient: Perhaps I could learn to get along with my mother.
  Eliza: Tell me more about your family.

Does this seem like an ordinary session between a patient and a psychotherapist? The therapist, Eliza, is a computer. If you examine her contributions to the conversation, you'll realize that she really doesn't add much. Eliza is programmed to respond to certain key phrases (e.g., "I feel . . .") by paraphrasing the words that come after them or by adding noncommittal "filler" phrases.

Can Computers Think?

The answer to the question of whether or not computers can think is tied to the way we choose to define thinking. If thinking is defined as a human activity that is dependent on the neural structure of the brain, then, by definition, computers would not qualify. Suppose we don't rule out a priori the notion that computers can think. How would you go about answering this question? The late A.M. Turing (1950) suggested a test for deciding if a computer can think. Appropriately, it's called **Turing's Test.** Suppose that you are sitting alone in a room with a typewriter keyboard. You can type in any question you want, and the typed message will go to two different rooms. In one of these rooms there is a person; in the other there is a computer. Each will send its answer back to you, again via typewriter keyboard. You can ask any question that you want except, "Are you a computer or a human?" According to Turing's Test, if you can't tell from the messages you receive which is the person and which is the computer, then it has been demonstrated that computers can think. What do you think about Turing's Test?

Most people find that they are unwilling to conclude that a computer can think just because they couldn't distinguish the computer's answer from a human's answer. After all, is mimicking thought the same as thinking? If a magician can fool you into believing that he has created a rabbit from thin air, it doesn't mean that he really has. Suppose I designed a robot that would come to your front door every day and take your dog for a walk. The end result would be the same as if a person had walked the dog, but would you be willing to conclude that the robot had exercised its muscles? Just because the end product is the same, it doesn't follow that the process was the same.

On the other hand, consider the following line of reasoning. The most famous mathematical treatise of the 20th century, *Principia Mathematica,* was written in 1925 by Whitehead and Russell. All of us should agree that these outstanding mathematicians were exceptional thinkers. More recently, the information that was known prior to Whitehead and Russell's mathematical discoveries was fed into a computer that rapidly proceeded to derive most of the same theorems that these famous mathematicians had derived. When this intellectual feat was accomplished by humans, it was hailed as extraordinary thinking. Are we then also obliged to label the same feat in the same way when it is done by a computer? Whitehead and Russell's contribution is impressive because they had to select relevant information and ignore other information in order to devise their mathematical treatise. Part of their genius was recognizing which information was relevant. The computer was given all of the needed information, making the computer-generated solutions much less creative and impressive than the task accomplished by these brilliant mathematicians.

Of course, computers and humans differ in many basic ways. Their underlying hardware—neural patterns for humans, electronic circuits for computers—are different. And, of course, humans reproduce themselves, whereas computers rely on humans for their production. It could be argued that computers don't really think because they rely on programs to tell them what to do; however, a similar argument could be made for humans because they rely on their experiences, genetic programs, and input from other humans to tell them what to do. In any case, premonitions of a world ruled by computers like Hal in the movie *2001: A Space Odyssey* still remain in the realm of science fiction.

INTELLIGENCE AND THINKING SKILLS

> *Far be from us the dangerous novelty of thinking.*
> —Address by Ferdinand VII of Spain to The University of Cervera
> (19th Century)

One of the most frequently asked questions concerning thinking skills instruction is whether learning to be a critical thinker will make someone more intelligent. In its more generic form, the question is really about the relationship between the ability to think clearly and intelligence.

The Nature of Intelligence

> *Solving problems is the specific achievement of intelligence.*
> —George Polya

Intelligence is one of the most controversial topics in psychology. It is a basic topic in thinking, because intelligence is the "stuff" of thought. You can conceptualize intelligence as the raw material from which thoughts are made. It is difficult to imagine a context in which intelligence isn't manifested or needed. The term "intelligence" is used commonly in everyday language. Most people believe that they are at least about average or above average in intelligence (Brim, 1966). (Despite Garrison Keillor's assurances to the contrary, you should realize that this is mathematically absurd, because most people can't be above average.)

Psychologists continue to debate exactly what the term "intelligence" *should* mean (Perkins, Lochhead, & Bishop, 1987). Think for a minute about your own definition of intelligence. A dictionary won't be much help, because dictionaries define difficult multifaceted concepts like intelligence with a few simple words. When Robert Sternberg (1982a), a psychologist known for his research on understanding the concept of intelligence, asked people to list the characteristics of an intelligent person, the following answers were frequently given: "reasons logically and well," "reads widely," "keeps an open mind," and "reads with high comprehension." Most people share these intuitive notions of intelligence.

Sternberg's (1981) own definition of intelligence is concerned with the way people approach novel tasks. He believes that little can be learned about intelligence by watching someone perform well-learned tasks. For example, if you are already proficient at long division, then analyzing your performance on long division problems won't reveal much about your intelligence. If, however, you are unfamiliar with long division problems, then examining the way you go about solving them and the kinds of answers you formulate will reveal a great deal about your intelligence. Thus, the ability to handle novel tasks and situations is a key element in Sternberg's definition. Sternberg (1981) has said: "It is not merely the ability to learn and reason with new concepts but the ability to learn and reason with new kinds of concepts. . . . intelligence is in large part the ability to acquire and reason with new conceptual systems" (p. 4).

An Example

Sternberg (1981) has called novel tasks **nonentrenched tasks.** These are tasks that are unfamiliar, and thus can be used to understand the nature of intelligence. One such task is a *projections task*. Individuals who work on projection tasks are required to make predictions about what will be true in the year 2000. If this task seems strange, don't worry, because nonentrenched tasks should be very different from the other kinds of tasks you've encountered in the past.

Consider the following example (adapted from Sternberg, 1981):

Four types of persons live on the planet Kyron.

A **plin** is a person who is born a child and remains a child throughout her or his life span.

A **kwef** is a person who is born an adult and remains an adult throughout her or his life span.

A **balt** is a person who is born a child but becomes an adult during the course of her or his life span.

A **pros** is a person who is born an adult but becomes a child during the course of her or his life span.

This task involves using the preceding information to answer questions about what is true in the year 2000. A person can be described as she or he physically appears: ♀ (a child) or ♀ (an adult) or with one of the four terms: "plin," "kwef," "balt," or "pros." The physical description is always correct, because it merely reflects what is physically true when you make your observations. However, verbal descriptions that are made in the present may be wrong, because they require an implication about the future appearance of a person. For example, if you describe a person as a plin in the present, you are saying that he now appears as a child and that you expect him to also appear as a child in the year 2000. Your belief about the future appearance is only a guess that may be right or wrong. When you make verbal descriptions in the year 2000, there will no longer be any uncertainty, because you will know at that time both the physical appearance in the present and in the year 2000. Thus, verbal descriptions made in 2000 must be correct.

To make these problems even more complicated, sometimes you will be given information that is inconsistent. For example, suppose that a person is born a kwef and is a plin in the year 2000. If a person were born a kwef, we would be certain that he was an adult at birth. If he is a plin in 2000, then we would also be certain that he was born a child and remained as a child in 2000. Because these two pieces of information are inconsistent (he or she could not appear as both a child and an adult at birth), you would have to select I (for inconsistent) as the correct answer. These problems will become clearer as we proceed with some examples. Be sure to work through each example, because most people find that this is a difficult task.

Example 1: A person is born a plin and is a plin in the year 2000.

You now need to select an answer that reflects what is true in the year 2000. The person is described as a plin at birth (born a child and expected to be a child in 2000) and in 2000, thus the physical description in 2000 is the small stick figure. You'd indicate your answer by circling the small stick figure that follows.

⚲ (a child)   ⚲ (an adult)   **I** (inconsistent information)

Example 2: A person is born a plin and is an ⚲ in 2000.

Circle the correct answer:

                    plin   balt   **I**

The verbal description "plin" signifies that the person was born a child and was expected to remain a child. In the year 2000, he appeared as an adult, thus, the correct answer is balt (someone who is born a child and becomes an adult). The verbal description at birth was wrong, because he grew into an adult instead of remaining a child.

Example 3: A person is born an ⚲ and is a kwef in 2000.

Circle the correct answer:

           웃   웃   **I**

You should have circled the large figure, because the kwefs are born adults and are adults in the future, so this person must be an adult in 2000.

Example 4: A person is born a 웃 and is a kwef in 2000.

Select the correct answer:

           웃   웃   **I**

In this example, the person is born a child, but is described verbally as a kwef (born an adult and remains an adult) in 2000. This is not possible. The correct answer is **I** for inconsistent information.

Example 5: A person is born a 웃 and is a 웃 in 2000.

Select the correct answer:

           balt   plin   pros

Because the person is described physically as a child at birth and as an adult in 2000, the correct verbal description is balt (born a child, becomes an adult).

If you were able to solve these problems (most people find them difficult), then you had to think in a new way. The idea of some adults growing into children is, to say the least, novel. Another example of Sternberg's non-entrenched tasks is presented at the end of this chapter.

The definitions of intelligence that we've considered so far include the "person-on-the-street's" notion of intelligence, which includes traits like common sense and open mindedness, and one expert's opinion that the ability to master new kinds of tasks constitutes intelligence. Another definition of intelligence was offered by E. G. Boring (1932) "Intelligence is what the tests test" (p. 35). The "tests" he was referring to are, of course, intelligence tests. The way psychologists have measured intelligence has had a direct effect on the way they have come to think about intelligence.

The Measurement of Intelligence

As you can imagine, the measurement of intelligence has proven to be a difficult task. The underlying idea is that intelligence exists, and because it exists, it exists in some quantity (in each individual), and because it exists in some quantity, it can be measured. The only difficulty with this line of reasoning is: How?

There is an obvious need to be able to quantify or measure intelligence.

Historically, intelligence tests were designed for a very practical reason. In the early part of this century, the French government realized the need to know which children should get regular classroom instruction and which should get remedial or accelerated instruction. Alfred Binet and Theodore Simon were given the job of designing a test that could be used to place children in the appropriate educational setting. Modern intelligence tests are still used for this purpose.

Binet and Simon soon realized that the type of question that an intelligent 4-year-old can answer correctly is very different from the type of question that an intelligent 8-year-old can answer correctly. Thus, they devised a test with items that varied in difficulty for each age level.

Sample Test Items

The tests designed in France by Binet and Simon have been revised many times. The most popular revision was undertaken by Lewis Terman, a psychologist at Stanford University. Terman's revision of the earlier intelligence test is commonly referred to as the Stanford-Binet. Another popular battery of intelligence tests was written by David Wechsler. He authored two separate tests, the Wechsler Intelligence Scale for Children (WISC) and Wechsler Adult Intelligence Scale (WAIS), designed for adults over 15 years of age. Wechsler's intelligence tests yield three IQ scores—one based on Verbal test items, one based on Performance test items, and one based on all of the test items, called Full Scale IQ. Following are some test items written to be similar to the ones found in the WAIS (Jensen, 1980):

Verbal Test Items
1. At what temperature does water freeze?
2. Who wrote The Republic?
3. Why is gold worth more than copper?
4. How many inches are there in $3\frac{1}{2}$ feet?
5. If six men can finish a job in 3 days, how many men would be needed to finish it in 1 day?
6. In what way are sperm and ovum alike?
7. Repeat a series of digits after the test administrator recites them. For example, a test taker would hear "8175621" and then repeat the digits either in the same order they were given or in reverse order.
8. Explain the meaning of strange.
9. Explain the meaning of adumbrate.

Performance Test Items
Test Takers are asked to:
10. Translate the numerals 1 to 9 into code symbols (e.g., 1 = ,[2 =], 3 = #, etc.).
11. Tell what is missing from familiar objects or scenes (e.g., a clock without hands).

12. Use wooden cubes painted red and white to duplicate a design shown on cards.
13. Arrange a series of cartoons into a logical sequence.
14. Assemble jigsaw puzzles. (pp. 144–145)

The actual test items vary in difficulty and are presented in increasing difficulty within each type of test. The IQ score that an individual receives is determined by calculating how many questions she or he answered correctly relative to the average person in the standardization group.

As you can see from these items, intelligence is measured with a variety of questions. The general-knowledge verbal questions tap information that most people would be expected to learn as a member of our society. For most of us, answering questions about the temperature at which water freezes involves only memory retrieval. Some of the more difficult ones, like "Who wrote The Republic?" would obviously favor those with a good academic background. Abstract reasoning about the nature of supply-and-demand is needed to answer the question "Why is gold worth more than copper?" The ability to use numbers as well as the knowledge that there are 12 inches in 1 foot is needed to answer the fourth question. The answer to question number 6 is difficult, because the differences between sperm and ovum may be more salient than their similarities. Of course, you also need to know what these terms mean. Repeating a series of digits forward and backward requires good memory skills. If you practice the memory aids (mnemonics) discussed in chapter 2, you can go off the top of the scale on this question. The eighth and ninth questions are standard vocabulary questions.

The performance items are more difficult to categorize. Because most of the tests are timed, speed is an important factor in determining performance IQ. Changing numerals to code symbols involves a careful balance of speed and accuracy in order to finish as many numeral-to-code transformations as possible with few errors. Question 11 tests the subject's knowledge of common objects. The ability to duplicate designs is a spatial ability. Arranging a series of cartoons in a logical sequence requires the test taker to generate hypotheses about the actions depicted. It's necessary to be able to see a whole object from its parts, a spatial ability, to put jigsaw puzzles together.

Learning To Be Intelligent

Thus far, we have considered several different notions of what it means to be intelligent and some of the problems in determining how intelligent someone is. Because this text is concerned with thinking and getting you to learn how to improve your thinking, it seems reasonable to return to the question posed at the beginning of this section: "Will learning to be a critical thinker make you more intelligent?" An increasing number of psychologists are answering this question with a "yes."

One contemporary view of intelligence is that it is not a single unitary construct. Rather, it is made up of component parts. Sternberg (1985a) has a three-component theory of intelligence that he calls a **Triarchic Theory of Intelligence.** (Triarchic means three parts.) According to this view, intelligence is comprised of (1) **metacomponents,** which are used to plan, evaluate, and monitor how we are thinking; (2) knowledge acquisition components which include the ability to utilize information we have in memory as well as the information provided in the environment; and (3) performance components, which are the thinking skills we use throughout this book. All of these components can be learned, developed, and improved. These three components determine the degree to which an individual can deal with novelty. Whenever you are faced with an unfamiliar task (e.g., fitting in at a new job, solving a calculus problem, caring for a newborn), the efficiency, accuracy, and speed at which you perform the task depends on how well you plan and monitor your progress, how well you acquire the information needed, and your ability to select and apply an appropriate thinking skill or strategy. There will always be some people who are more intelligent than others. There are individual differences and limits on how well each of us can think and reason. But we all also have some amount of undeveloped potential and can make substantial gains in these areas. Even though we can't all be Einstein, we can all learn to think more intelligently.

Sternberg is not alone in his belief that intelligence is comprised of skills that can be enhanced with training (de Groot, 1983; Nickerson, 1986; Perkins, 1985). Sadler and Whimbey (1985), pioneers in the area of thinking skills improvement, echoed these sentiments when they defined intelligence as "a complex of skills" (p. 44). The same basic idea can be seen in de Groot's (1983) definition of intelligence as a mental program consisting of heuristics and in Nickerson's (1987) advice to teachers that they teach for tactics. Skills, strategies, heuristics, and tactics are all different words for the same idea—learnable components of intelligent thought. One of my favorite definitions of critical thinking was published almost 30 years ago (1960) and comes very close to this contemporary notion of intelligence as learnable skills: "Critical thinking then is the process of evaluation or categorization in terms of some previously accepted standards . . . this seems to involve attitude plus knowledge of facts plus some thinking skills" (Russell, cited in d'Angelo, 1971, p. 6). In short, Russell's equation is:

$$\text{Attitude} + \text{Knowledge} + \text{Thinking Skills} = \text{Intelligent Thinking}$$

A Paradox

Gregory (1981) believes that the current notions of intelligence are paradoxical or contradictory because they incorporate the following three propositions, which are logically inconsistent

1. Intelligence is not supposed to be increased by education.
2. Abilities are supposed to be increased by education.
3. Intelligence is measured by abilities. (p. 296)

The paradox he is posing is, in simpler language: How can anyone claim that intelligence is unaffected by education and then measure intelligence by asking someone about things that are typically learned in school? If we think of intelligence as the knowledge you have stored somewhere in your head, then surely some experiences will allow you to acquire more knowledge than others. If we think of intelligence as the ability to solve novel problems, then experience and instruction in solving many types of problems should improve your proficiency at novel problem-solving tasks.

One way to resolve the intelligence paradox is by changing the first assumption and allowing the possibility that intelligence can be increased by education. After all, isn't this how young children increase in intelligence?

A CRITICAL THINKING ATTITUDE

All our dignity lies in thought.
—Blaise Pascal (1623–1662)

No one can become a better thinker just by reading a book. An essential component of critical thinking is developing the attitude of a critical thinker. Good thinkers are motivated and willing to exert the conscious effort needed to work in a planful manner, to check for accuracy, to gather information, and to persist when the solution isn't obvious and/or requires several steps.

Performance–Competence Distinction

Very often, there is an important distinction between what people *can* do and what they actually do. This is called the **performance–competence distinction.** It is of no value to learn a variety of critical thinking skills if you never use them. Developing a **critical thinking attitude** is as important as developing thinking skills. Many errors occur not because people can't think critically, but because they don't. One of the major differences between good and poor thinkers, and correspondingly between good and poor students, is their attitude.

Characteristics of Critical Thinkers

1. Willingness to Plan.   I've watched thousands of students (literally) take exams. There are always some students who begin to write as soon as the exam hits their desk.

They just plow ahead and begin writing before they begin thinking. Not surprisingly, the results are a disoriented jumble that often bears little relation to the questions being asked. When asked a question in class, they will often answer with the first idea that comes to mind. These students need to learn to check their impulsivity and plan their response. (I talk more about how to plan in the next section.) They should be outlining or diagramming the structure of a response before they begin to write. Planning, the invisible first step in critical thinking, is essential. With repeated practice, anyone can develop the **habit of planning.**

2. Flexibility.   In a classic old book, Rokeach (1960) talked about rigidity and dogmatism as the characteristics of a "closed mind." A person with a closed mind responds negatively to new ideas by stating, "That's the way I've always done it." By contrast, an attitude of flexibility is marked by a willingness to consider new options, try things a new way, reconsider old problems. An open-minded person is willing to suspend judgment, gather more information, and attempt to clarify difficult issues.

3. Persistence.   Baron (1987), in an excellent essay on the significance of attitudes, emphasized the importance of persistence to academic success. A closely related attitude, the willingness to start or engage in a thoughtful task is equally important. Some people look at a seemingly difficult task and opt not to even begin the thinking process. They're defeated at the start. Others will start working on a task and stop before its completed. Good thinking is hard work that requires diligent persistence. It can make you as tired as any physical labor, but it can be much more rewarding.

4. Willingness to Self-Correct.   We all make mistakes. Instead of becoming defensive about errors, good thinkers learn from them. They utilize feedback and try to figure out what went wrong and to recognize the factors that led to the error. Ineffective strategies need to be recognized and abandoned in order to improve the thinking process.

A major difficulty in developing an attitude of critical thinking is that many people don't realize when they're acting impulsively or thinking rigidly. McTighe (1986) described the problem this way:

> Students seemed satisfied with their initial interpretation of what they had read and seemed genuinely puzzled at requests to explain or defend their points of view. Few students could provide more than superficial responses to such tasks, and even the better responses showed little evidence of well-developed problem solving strategies or critical thinking skills.

An early study of thinking attitudes (Bloom & Broder, 1950) examined individual differences in the thinking processes of college students. Although this study is an old one, many of their conclusions remain valid today.

College students were tested on a series of reasoning problems. They were required to think aloud so that their thinking processes could be mentioned. Here is a sample item. (Assume that these statements are true):

> Any action that impedes the war effort of the United States should be made illegal.
> All strikes impede the war effort of the United States.

Conclusions: (pick one)
- A. All strikes should be made illegal.
- B. Some restrictions should be placed on the right to strike, but it would be unwise to make them all illegal.
- C. Some strikes should be made illegal.
- D. Unjustifiable strikes should be made illegal.
- E. None of the foregoing conclusions follows.

Don't worry if you're having difficulty answering this question. Reasoning problems like this one are discussed in detail in chapter 4. (The correct answer is A.)

Bloom and Broder compared the kinds of answers given by poor thinkers to those who answered correctly and found several important differences. The students who performed poorly utilized "one-shot" thinking instead of the extended sequential thinking processes of the good thinkers. The poor thinkers were willing to allow gaps in their knowledge to exist. There were basic differences in the *attitude* of the good and poor thinkers. The poor thinkers rushed through the instructions or skipped them altogether. They were passive rather than active in their approach to the problems. When the problems were difficult, they utilized only a few clues to answer the questions or guessed at an answer. They failed to break down complex problems into their constituent parts. In short, they failed to plan, responded impulsively and rigidly, and never realized that improvement was needed.

The researchers developed a remedial course to improve these students' performance. Students were given experts' think-aloud protocols for model solutions. They were taught how the correct answer was obtained, not merely the correct answer. The researchers reported significant success with this program.

Metacognition

> *Ultimately, it is not we who define thinking, it is thinking that defines us.*
> —quote from Carey, Foltz, & Allan *Newsweek,* February 7, 1983.

Metacognition refers to what we know about what we know, or, in more formal language, our knowledge about knowledge. It seems that most people have little awareness of the nature or even the existence of the thinking processes that underlie their judgments, beliefs, inferences, and conclusions about complex issues (Nisbett & Wilson, 1977).

There are many experimental examples of how little we know about the variables that influence our thinking. I'll demonstrate this point with one of my favorites. Researchers (Wilson & Nisbett, 1978) asked consumers in a large bargain store to select which of four pairs of nylon pantyhose they preferred. The stockings were hung on a rack above the researcher's table. The consumers examined the weave, the heel, and the toe. Very few had difficulty making a choice. The stocking in the left-most position was preferred by 12% of the consumers; the one to its right by 17%; the next one to the right by 31%; and the right-most stocking by 40%. This indicates that there were clear preferences among the shoppers. This is especially interesting in light of the fact that the four stockings were identical. Position alone accounted for the consumer preferences, yet none of the consumers indicated that position influenced his or her decision. People are simply not aware of the variables that affect how they think.

Being Mindful

In order to develop basic thinking skills, it is necessary to direct your attention to the processes and products of your own thoughts. You need to become consciously aware of the way you think and to develop the habit of examining the end products of your thought processes—the solution you've arrived at, the decision you've made, the inference that you believe to be true, or the judgment you've formulated. In short, you need to become mindful or aware of how and what you are thinking. **Being mindful** requires a self-conscious concern for and evaluation of the thinking process.

Consider what happens when a student in mathematics or the sciences learns to rely on formulas that she or he does not understand. The student may be able to substitute numbers for the algebraic symbols, then work through the appropriate arithmetic and arrive at the correct answer without ever understanding the principles involved or the meaning or importance of the answer.

Students in the sciences and in mathematics are taught a technical jargon. Too often, they believe that scattering these terms in a discussion is evidence that they understand the concepts, when in fact their understanding of the phenomena involved is shallow and consists mainly of the ability to label events.

Griffiths (1976) raised an interesting question when he asked: "Physics teaching: Does it hinder intellectual development?" (p. 81). Griffiths answered the question by noting that the way physics is currently taught, with vocabulary drills and reliance on formulas, prevents students from learning how to reason or think critically about the issues. In studying how students think about physics problems, Griffiths (1976) found that; "In many instances, when a conflict was apparent between the predicted results and the experimental evidence, a technical term was imposed to explain the discrepancy" (p. 84). Here is one of his student's responses to a classic problem involving an inclined plane. "You have to calculate it. You must set all forces to zero, then sum all the forces acting on the body equal to zero, then solve it for what it really means" (p. 84). You don't need to know anything about physics to realize that this student is in trouble. He has acquired a meaningless vocabulary and has not acquired the ability to think in a cogent way. More troublesome than the student's lack of knowledge in this case is the fact that he doesn't know that he doesn't know. He has not developed the ability to monitor his knowledge and recognize the difference between scattering terms and understanding concepts. He has no awareness or self-monitoring process for his own knowledge.

Consider the following example: Working alone, Stacy can mow her front lawn in 2 hours, whereas it takes her sister Carole 4 hours. How long will it take them to mow the lawn if they work together? Many students routinely apply the well-known formula for finding an average. They add 2 + 4 and divide by 2, concluding that it will take them an average of 3 hours if they work together. Few students stop to realize that this is an unreasonable answer, because it implies that it will take them longer if they work together than it would if Stacy were working alone! Why are students misled into thinking that this is the correct answer? I believe that they have been overly trained to rely on rote applications of formulas. They have not learned to stop and think about the kind of answer they should expect (e.g., a number less than 2); nor have they learned the skills of working through a problem. They have never learned the importance of being mindful. (In case you've been working on this problem and want to check your answer, the correct answer is 1 hour and 20 minutes.)

Another way that thinking may be discouraged in educational settings is in the kinds of examinations that are used to assess learning. Too often, learning is measured solely with fill-in-the-blank, true–false, and multiple-choice questions that are concerned only with recitations of previously presented material. It is possible for students to be able to place the correct word in the correct blank while not understanding very much about the topic.

One of contemporary psychology's best-known spokespersons is B. F. Skinner. In 1968, Skinner stated:

> It has been said that an education is what survives when a man has forgotten all he has been taught. Certainly few students could pass their final examinations even a year or two after leaving school or college. What has been learned of permanent value must therefore not be the facts and principles covered by examinations but certain other kinds of behavior often ascribed to special abilities. Far from neglecting these kinds of behaviors, careful programming reveals the need to teach them as explicit educational objectives. (pp. 89–90)

I believe that, in this passage, Skinner was arguing for specific instruction on how to think instead of the usual instruction in what others have thought. Like many other people, I believe that this is an idea whose time is long overdue.

Perhaps one of the most poignant examples of the way that education has not fostered thinking skills is presented by Carpenter (1981). She presented college students with a novel problem devised by the Swiss psychologist, Jean Piaget. (See chapter 11 for additional Piagetian tasks.) Students were given a small container of water, a large, heavy wooden block, and a small, light wooden block. Their task was to determine if either or both blocks would float and to explain their results. They found that the large, heavy block floated, whereas the small, light one did not. When faced with the task of explaining the results, the college students assumed that they ought to know the answer and tried to remember formulas and terms. The college students who had taken several science courses brought in the terms "center of gravity," "specific gravity," and "surface tension." They were unwilling to test the situation or to explore the materials that were provided. In general, they were unable to generate testable hypotheses. This may be symptomatic of the discomfort that many college students feel with science and mathematics courses. (The correct answer concerns the relationship between weight and area.)

The college students' approach to the problem can be sharply contrasted to the one used by sixth-grade children when they were presented with the same task. The sixth-graders manipulated the materials and revised their hypotheses as they tested the relevant variables of size and weight. Unburdened with technical jargon or the expectancy that this problem could be solved best with a formula, the sixth-graders were more likely to generate testable hypotheses and to manipulate the materials in order to solve the problem than were their college counterparts!

A FRAMEWORK FOR THINKING

Unfortunately, there is no simple "how to" formula that can be used in every situation that calls for critical thought. You already know about the importance of planning, but knowing that it's important to plan is of little value if you don't know how to plan. Consider the following advice about wilderness survival (Vancouver Community Business Directory, 1987):

Wilderness Survival
Things you must *not* do:
- Wear brand new boots
- Leave an open fire unattended
- Panic. If you meet trouble, stop and think.

I'm sure that the first two recommendations are excellent, but I'm less sure about the value of telling someone to think without any instructions about how to go about it. Following is a general, all-purpose framework, or guide, that can be used to direct the thinking process. It's not a sure-fire guarantee to good thinking (there are none), but it is a way of getting started and ensuring that the **executive processes** needed in thinking—planning, monitoring, and evaluating—are being used in a reflective manner. You can probably guess why these are called executive processes. They function like the "boss" in a busy office by directing the flow of work and deciding where to put the available resources. The framework is a series of questions, some of which may be repeated several times during the thinking process, that are general enough to be useful in a wide variety of applications, including reasoning from premises, analyzing arguments, testing hypotheses, solving problems, estimating probabilities, making decisions, and thinking creatively. Although the framework will remain the same for all of these thinking tasks, the actual skills used will vary somewhat with the nature of the task. The proposed framework is an adaptation of the problem-solving procedures originally proposed by the brilliant mathematician and scholar George Polya in 1945. Polya's model is presented in chapter 9 (Problem Solving).

As you progress through each of the following chapters in this book, you will gain experience in applying this framework in different contexts and different knowledge domains. The thinking skills you acquire as you work through this book will transfer to other contexts if you acquire the habit of *using* the framework. The purpose of presenting the framework now is to provide an introduction and overview of what's to come. It's an easy-to-use guide that, through repeated practice, should become automatic. The following questions will be used to guide the thought process.

1. What Is the Goal?

Critical thinking was defined earlier in this chapter as being purposeful and goal directed. The first step in improving thinking is to be clear about the goal or goals. Real-life problems are messy. Sometimes there are multiple goals, and sometimes we'll return to this question several times, as our understanding of the goal will often change after we've worked on it for a while. A clearly articulated goal will provide direction to the thinking process. In the course of thinking about real-world problems, you may need to change direction, but it's still important to provide some focus. After all, if you don't know where you're going, you can never be sure if you've arrived.

There is a large variety of possible goals. Goals can include deciding among a set of possible alternative solutions, generating a solution where there is none, synthesizing information, evaluating the validity of evidence, determining the probable cause of some event, considering the credibility of an information source, and quantifying uncertainty.

Are you making a decision about whether or not to have a heart transplant or what flavor ice cream to select from the corner store? Impulsive thinking about ice cream flavors is not a bad thing; impulsive thinking about life and death decisions is. Everything we do in life doesn't require critical thought. The way you identify the goal should help you plan the time and effort required by the situation.

2. What Is Known?

This is the starting point for directed thinking. Although this may seem fairly straightforward now, when we actually use this framework on real problems, you'll find that you may have to return to the "knowns" several times. Some information will be known with certainty, other information may be only probably true or partially known. This step will also include recognizing gaps in what's known and the need for further information gathering.

3. Which Thinking Skill or Skills Will Get You to Your Goal?

Once you have some idea of where you are (the knowns or givens) and where you're going (the goal or purpose), you're better able to plan goal-directed thinking processes. Knowing how to get from where you are to where you want to be is the power of critical thinking. These are the thinking skills or strategies that have been alluded to throughout this chapter. Just as there are many different possible goals, there are many different strategies for attaining them. Let's consider the "thinking is like a map" analogy a little further, because it can help to clarify some abstract concepts by making them more concrete. Suppose you are about to go on a trip to visit two old friends. One has become a Buddhist monk and lives high on a mountaintop in the Himalayas. The other has become a surfing champion and is living on the beautiful island of Hawaii. You'd have to use a different method of travel to reach each destination, one time scaling a mountain, the other deciding between a plane or boat. Similarly, you'll have to use different thinking skills with different types of thought problems.

This step will involve generating and selecting the appropriate strategy to reach the goal. If you've given any thought to how you will reach a Himalayan mountaintop (I'm assuming that this is a novel thought for most of you), you'll start to generate several options. You'll probably have to cross an ocean, which means deciding between a plane or boat of some sort, and then travel by train and/or car, and then travel by foot and/or animal (which one?). Of course, you'll probably need a guide. And what are the vaccination requirements for someone traveling to Tibet? Oh yes, will you need a visa? I think you've gotten the idea by now that traveling to a Himalayan mountain top is a lot like other quests for knowledge. It will take time and careful planning. By contrast, your trip to visit your surfer friend will be easier and cheaper. Some problems are like that.

4. Have You Reached Your Goal?

I've taught statistics for nearly 10 years now. I must have asked students if they've checked their work as often as I've said my name. A concern with accuracy is probably the biggest predictor of success. Does your solution make sense? Did you get to your mountaintop in Tibet or are you on an anthill in Iowa?

Was your goal the right one or should it really have been "where shall I travel this summer?" If it really should have been the latter goal, then you can forget Tibet and consider Paris or Japan or the rugged beauty of Newfoundland. What have you learned on the way that you can use again?

A Skills Approach

Critical thinking skills are those strategies for finding ways to reach a goal. The actual skills and ways to evaluate and generate them are presented in the subsequent chapters. This is what critical thinking instruction is all about. Critical thinking instructions is predicated on two assumptions: (1) that there are clearly identifiable and definable thinking skills that students can be taught to recognize and apply appropriatcly, and (2) if recognized and applied, students will be more effective thinkers. Intellectual skills, like physical skills, require specific instruction, practice in a variety of contexts, feedback, and time to develop. So, please get comfortable, prepare for some hard work, and enjoy this book.

CHAPTER SUMMARY

1. It is imperative that citizens of the 20th and 21st centuries think critically, yet recent tests have shown that only 25% to 50% of 1rst-year college students have the skills needed for logical thought.

2. Critical thinking was defined as thinking that is purposeful, reasoned, and goal directed.

3. There is considerable empirical evidence that cognitive skills can be learned in specific courses designed to teach them.

4. Although it is possible to view thinking as a biological process, this perspective will not be helpful in devising ways to improve thinking.

5. People report that thinking sometimes seems to rely on visual imagery and sentencelike propositions. There are individual differences and task differences in the use of these modes of thought.

6. Thought-process protocols are used to understand and improve human thought. In computer simulation, they are used to write computer programs that mimic human thought.

7. Many contemporary psychologists conceptualize intelligence as made up of component parts that include knowledge acquisition and utilization, executive process, and skills. These components can all be improved and developed with instruction.

8. Developing a critical thinking attitude is as important as developing the skills of critical thinking. The skills are useless if they are not used.

9. Researchers have found many differences between good and poor thinkers. The poor thinkers had a poorer attitude toward the reasoning problems that they were asked to solve. They were more likely to skip the instructions, work hastily, and guess at the answers. With intensive instruction, they showed considerable improvement.

10. Metacognition refers to people's knowledge of their own thought processes. We often have little conscious awareness of how we think. Self-monitoring your thought processes is one way to improve how you think.

11. A general all-purpose framework for thinking was presented. It consists of four questions that should be asked whenever you're faced with a critical-thinking task. It will serve as a guide for the thinking process.

12. Remember, you are what (and how) you think! Have fun with this book.

Terms to Know

You should be able to define the following terms and concepts. If you find that you're having difficulty with any term, be sure to reread the section in which it is discussed.

Schemata. Internal representation of knowledge. The way we organize our knowledge about the world.

Critical Thinking. Thinking that is purposeful, reasonable, and goal directed. Also known as *directed thinking*. Compare with nondirected thinking.

Nondirected Thinking. Daydreams, night dreams, and other sorts of thinking that are not engaged in for a specific purpose or do not involve the use of critical thinking skills. Compare with directed (or critical) thinking.

Thinking. An often unconscious, dynamic private "activity" that involves combinations of information stored in memory so that we end up with something more than and different from what we started with.

Cognitive Process Instruction. Instruction based on cognitive theories and research that is designed to help people improve how they think.

Transfer of Training. The spontaneous use of skills that are learned in one context in a different context.

Imagery. The use of an internal picture-like representation while thinking.

Preferred Modes of Thought. Individual preferences for different types of internal representations.

Human Information Processing (HIP). A model of human thinking that uses the flow of information through a computer as an analogy of human thought. Like a computer, we take in information from the environment (input), process the information, and then output information.

Computer Simulation. Computer programs that are written to simulate or imitate human thought, and thus may use processes and strategies that are similar to the ones people use in solving problems.

Thinking Aloud Protocols. Verbatim records of what a subject says she or he is doing while solving a problem. They are used to formulate models of how people think.

Thought Process Protocols. Written descriptions by a person thinking about a topic that describe the thinking process.

Protocol Analysis. Thought process protocols are broken into segments and analyzed in ways that help psychologists understand and describe the process of thinking.

Artificial Intelligence (AI). The attempt to develop intelligent systems with use of computer programs, without attempting to simulate human thought processes.

Turing's Test. A test to determine if computers can think. According to A.M. Turing, if people can't determine if responses to their questions have come from a human or a computer, then it has been demonstrated that computers can think.

Intelligence. A general cognitive aptitude. Most people believe that it is manifested in the ability to reason logically and well and the ability to read with high comprehension.

Nonentrenched Tasks. R. Sternberg's term for novel tasks that can be used to assess intelligence by noting how people go about solving them.

Triarchic Theory of Intelligence. Three-part theory of intelligence in which the three parts are metacomponents or planning and monitoring, knowledge acquisition, and performance (R. Sternberg).

Metacomponents. The oversight or executive functions of thinking which include directing attention, being planful, and assessing progress.

Performance–Competence Distinction. Distinction between what people are capable of doing (competence) and what they actually do (performance).

Critical Thinking Attitude. The willingness to plan, flexibility in thinking, persistence, and willingness to self-correct. It is not possible to be a critical thinker without this sort of attitude.

Habit of Planning. The repeated and automatic use of plans.

Metacognition. Our knowledge about our memory and thought processes. Colloquially, what we know about what we know.

Being Mindful. The conscious and deliberate use of critical thinking skills.

Executive Processes. The oversight or planning and monitoring processes in thinking.

Chapter Questions

Be sure that you can answer the following questions:

1. How is critical thinking defined in this chapter? Can you come up with a better definition for this term?

2. Why was the author critical of the political candidate who opposed waste, fraud, pollution, crime, and overpaid bureaucrats? Shouldn't we be concerned with these issues?

3. List several different types of evidence that thinking can be improved with instruction.

4. Opponents of critical thinking instruction sometimes say that it's not needed because everyone has a right to his or her own opinion. How did the author respond to this comment? What is your response?

5. How do biologists study thinking?

6. Explain the idea that thinking is done with images and/or verbal statements. Give an example of each.

7. In what important ways are humans and computers similar? What are the important differences?

8. How can the analysis of thought-process protocols help psychologists understand how people think? How can they be used to improve the thinking process?

9. What points were raised in this chapter when trying to decide if computers think?

10. The answer to the question of whether intelligence can be improved with instruction depends on how intelligence is defined. What are the components of intelligence, and can they be improved with appropriate learning experiences?

11. What are some differences in the way good and poor thinkers solve reasoning problems? What are the attitudinal characteristics of good thinkers?

12. Explain the notion that critical thinkers are "mindful." What is it that they are mindful of?

Exercises

1. A Nonentrenched Task

The following task was adapted from Sternberg (1981). It is a projection task that is similar to the one discussed in this chapter. Because you have already had some experience with projection tasks, it's not a truly novel task.

This task involved determining the color of a circle in the year 2000. A circle can be described as it physically appears: ○ or ●. It can also be described verbally with one of four color words: White, Black, Whack, and Blite. A circle is defined as White if it appears white both in the present and in 2000. A circle is defined as Black if it appears black both in the present and in 2000. A circle is defined as Whack if it appears white in the present and black in 2000. A circle is defined as Blite if it appears black in the present and white in 2000.

Your task is to use the information given to answer questions about what is true in the year 2000. Physical descriptions (○ or ●) are always correct, because they merely reflect how the circle appears when the observation is made. Verbal descriptions made in the present carry implications about the future that may or may not be correct. For example, if a circle appears black (●) in the present, it could either remain black, and thus be labeled "Black," or it could change to white, in which case it would be labeled "Blite." Thus, verbal descriptions made in the present require a guess about the future. Verbal descriptions made in the year 2000 are always correct, because there is no longer any uncertainty about present or future events.

As in the example presented earlier in this chapter, sometimes inconsistent information will be given. In this case, select I (for inconsistent information) as the correct answer.

Question 1.1

A circle is Black at the present, and Black in 2000. Circle the correct answer.

○   ●   I

(This is an easy problem that is presented as a warm-up. The answer must be ●.)

Question 1.2

A circle is Black at the present, and White in 2000. Circle the correct answer.

I   ●   ○

Question 1.3
A circle is Black at the present, and Blite in 2000. Circle the correct answer.

I   ●   ○

Question 1.4
A circle is ● at the present, and White in 2000. Circle the correct answer.

○   ●   I

Question 1.5
A circle is ○ in the present, and Whack in 2000. Circle the correct answer.

○   ●   I

Question 1.6
A circle is White in the present, and ● in 2000. Circle the correct answer.

Whack   Black   I

Question 1.7
A circle is Blite in the present, and ● in 2000. What is the circle in 2000?

I   Blite   Black

Question 1.8
A circle is ○ in the present, and ● in 2000. Circle the correct answer.

Blite   White   Whack

SUGGESTED READINGS

There are many fine books that can serve as an introduction to critical thinking and the psychology of thinking. If you're interested in the use of visual imagery to improve how you think, you'll enjoy Arnheim's (1971) *Visual Thinking* and McKim's (1980) *Thinking Visually: A Strategy Manual for Problem Solving*.

One of the older classic "thinking books" is Flesch's (1951) *The Art of Clear Thinking*. Every chapter in this clever book begins with quotable quotes from the famous and not so famous. Another classic in the field is *New Think: The Use of Lateral Thinking in the Generation of New Ideas* by DeBono (1968). A historical overview is presented by Johnson (1972) in *A Systematic Introduction to the Psychology of Thinking*.

A large and somewhat rambling book that reflects on the nature of thought is *The Act of Creation* by Koestler (1964). My personal favorite for a nonscientific introduction to thinking is *The Mind's Best Work* by Perkins (1981). It's an interesting book filled with strange illustrations and thoughtful questions. It is good food for thought.

A review article that presents some of the most recent psychological perspectives in this area is aptly titled "Thinking" by Erickson and Jones (1978). An old classic with a contemporary flavor is Bartlett's (1958) book *Thinking: An Experimental and Social Study*. If you are interested in the earlier work in the area of thinking, a good source for this is *The Psychology of Thinking* by Bourne, Ekstrand, and Dominowski (1971).

If you're interested in the way education has responded to psychology's views of thinking, you'll find the collection of papers in *Problem Solving and Education: Issues in Teaching and Research,* edited by Tuma and Reif (1980), *Cognitive Process Instruction: Research on Teaching Thinking Skills,* edited by Lochhead and Clement (1979), and *Thinking and Learning Skills,* edited by Lochhead and Clement (1979), and *Thinking and Learning Skills, Vol. 1,* edited by Segal, Chipman, and Glaser (1985), to be informative.

The psychological literature on intelligence is enormous. One of the major controversies is addressed in a book edited by Rubinstein and Slife (1982): *Taking Sides: Clashing Views on Controversial Psychological Issues.* "Is Intelligence Inherited?" is one of the issues they have considered. An article written by Jensen answered this question with a "Yes," and an article written by Whimbey answered "No." Jensen expanded his position in his 1981 book, *Straight Talk About Mental Tests,* and in a more technical book written in 1980, *Bias in Mental Testing.* Lucid presentations of the "no" position can be found in Kamin's (1974) *The Science and Politics of I.Q.* and Whimbey's (1976) *Intelligence Can Be Taught.* A collection of current papers on intelligence can be found in the book edited by Detterman and Sternberg (1982), *How and How Much Can Intelligence Be Increased?* An advanced treatment of intelligence appears in Gregory's (1981) *Mind in Science.* General references on intelligence can be found in Cattell's (1971) classic text, *Abilities: Their Structure, Growth and Action,* Resnick's (1976) edited volume *The Nature of Intelligence,* and Sternberg and Detterman's (1979) edited book *Human Intelligence: Perspective on Its Theory and Measurement.*

An educational program that was developed to raise IQ scores has been written by Samson (1975). It can be found in his book *Thinking Skills: A Guide to Logic and Comprehension.* This is essentially a workbook with exercises graded in difficulty. A similar workbook that is also recommended is Whimbey and Lochhead's (1982) *Problem Solving and Comprehension (3rd ed.).* The most recent and theoretically advanced of the texts designed to improve intelligence is Sternberg's (1986a) skills development book, *Intelligence Applied.* This book reflects Sternberg's work as a consultant to the Venezuela intelligence enhancement project that was described earlier.

A philosophical overview on intelligence testing and its political ramifications can be found in a controversial book by Gould (1981), *The Mismeasure of Man.* The stern rejoinder to Gould and media treatment of the intelligence controversy entitled "I.Q. Testing and the Media" was written by Herrnstein. It appeared in *The Atlantic Monthly* in 1982.

2 Memory: The Acquisition, Retention, and Retrieval of Knowledge

Contents

Many years ago, I read a story about a beautiful young woman who, because of a terrible fear of growing old, made an interesting deal with the Devil. She agreed to sell her soul to him. In return, he promised that she would spend her old age in complete happiness. The Devil kept his promise. When the woman grew old, she became totally senile. Her old age was spent in the memories of her youth, visiting with friends who had long since died, totally oblivious of life around her. The memory of this story has stayed with me for a long time. I wonder if she would have made this deal if she had known that her happiness would be bought with senility and would consist of a life among her memories. I would like to be able to tell you who wrote this story and give you the title, so that you can read it for yourself, but I can't. I've forgotten where I read it. Although I believe that I can remember accurately many of the details of the story, I can't remember where I read it.

MEMORY AS THE MEDIATOR OF COGNITIVE PROCESSES

How wonderful, how very wonderful the operations of time, and the changes of the human mind! . . . If any one faculty of our nature may be called more *wonderful than the rest, I do think it is memory.*
—Austen, 1922

Ulric Neisser (1982), a cognitive psychologist, once asked, "What do we use the past for?" (p. 13). This may seem like a strange question, but a good way to begin our quest to understand memory is by examining its function. According to Neisser, we use the past to define ourselves. If you are a fan of the soap operas, you'll recognize this as one of the favorite themes. Soap opera plots often involve memory loss (amnesia) for one of the protagonists. The usual sequence of events consists of a sudden blow to the head of a leading man or woman followed by a peculiar loss of memory in which the identity of family members is forgotten. Although this is rare in real life, it does point out the essential role of memory. It tells you who you are, where you're from, and where you're going. Try to imagine what life would be like if you had no memory. For most of us, this is a frightening thought. Our memories are our most valuable possession. I don't know anyone who would sell the memories he or she has accumulated over a lifetime, no matter how much money was offered. Life without memory is unfathomable.

All intelligent systems (e.g., humans, computers, dogs, cockroaches) have the ability to learn and remember. These abilities play a crucial role in all of our lives. Most importantly, they are inevitable consequences of living. For humans, the ability to learn and remember well often determines the quality of life, economic status, and sometimes even survival. Because the ability to think clearly depends, in large part, on how well we can utilize past experiences, memory is a central topic in developing thinking skills. In this chapter, we consider current views of how memory works, why forgetting occurs, and ways to improve memory.

All thinking skills are inextricably tied to the ability to remember. As you proceed through the chapters in this book, you will repeatedly find evidence of the pervasive influences of memory on how and what we think. Consider, for example, the perception of risk. Psychologists have found that hazards that are unusually memorable, such as a recent disaster or a sensationalized depiction in a film (e.g., *Jaws, The China Syndrome*), distort people's perception of risk. Most people rate dramatic causes of death like earthquake or shark attack as many times more likely than they actually are, whereas less memorable causes of death are routinely underestimated (Lichtenstein, Slovic, Fischoff, Layman, & Combs, 1978).

Another example of the centrality of memory to the thinking process can be seen in decision making by juries. The jury process is at the heart of the U.S. legal system. It is one of our most cherished rights as citizens. A randomly selected group of strangers is cloistered in a small room for the sole purpose of evaluating evidence pertaining to the guilt or innocence of an accused. The synthesis, analysis, and weighing of evidence that is often contradictory is a complex cognitive process that, like all cognitive processes, depends on what is remembered. In a simulated study of how juries reach decisions, Reyes, Thompson, and Bower (1980) varied the vividness (and, therefore the memorability) of the evidence provided during a mock trial. In half of the cases, the prosecution presented the more vivid information; in the other half, the defense presented the more vivid information. Judgments of guilt paralleled the differential recall of the prosecution and defense arguments. When the information that favored the defendant was more vivid, he or she was more likely to be acquitted (found not guilty), and when the information that favored the plaintiff was more vivid, the defendant was more likely to be found guilty. The "jurors" based their decision about guilt or innocence on the information that was available to them. The vivid information was more memorable, more available, and therefore was more likely to be utilized in the jury deliberations. The influence of the availability of information in decision making is considered again in chapter 8.

LEARNING AND MEMORY

The relationship between learning and memory involves the passage of time. Let's clarify this with an example. It is reasonable to expect that, during a college career, students will take many, many exams. When you finish reading this section of the book, you should be able to answer a question like: "What is the relationship between learning and memory?" If you write the correct answer on an exam, your professor will infer that, sometime before the exam, you learned the relevant material and that you remembered it. Learning and memory are always inferred. No one can ever observe you learning or remembering. These activities are inferred from some behavior. A friend can watch you while you move your eyes across the lines of print that appear in a book propped up in front of you, but she or he can't see you learn. In the example presented here, writing the correct answer on an exam is the behavior that allows the inference that learning and memory have occurred. Learning and memory are **hypothetical constructs,** hypothetical terms that have been made up to help psychologists study and understand the mind and, thus, they have been called "convenient fictions." Learning and memory are like perception, motivation, thirst, sex drives, hallucinations, and many other terms, in that they have no external physical reality. They are only known by inference, and they are helpful in understanding the processes of the mind.

Learning and memory are usually inferred together. If I asked you what notable event occurred in Calgary, Canada, in 1988, and you answered correctly, then I would infer that you learned and remembered that Calgary was the site of the 1988 Winter Olympics. If you are unable to answer this question, then either: (a) you never learned the facts in question; or (b) you learned them, but forgot them.

The Time Line

The relationship between learning and memory is a temporal one (time-based) and is depicted on the time line in Fig. 2.1. Something happens at Time 1 that we call learning. Following Time 1 is an interval that can be as short as a few thousandths of a second or as long as a lifetime. Retention of information during this time interval is attributed to memory, but indexed by retrieval. At Time 2 (some time after Time 1), the individual exhibits some behavior, like correctly answering an exam question, that allows us to infer that the material was both learned and remembered.

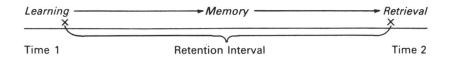

Learning		Memory		Retrieval
X				X
Time 1		Retention Interval		Time 2

Example:

Learning	Memory	Retrieval
Study your textbook	During the retention interval (time between learning and retrieval) you engage in other activities— e.g., eat dinner, sleep, eat breakfast	Answer exam question correctly

FIG. 2.1   A time-line depicting the relationship among learning, memory, and retrieval.

HUMAN INFORMATION PROCESSING

Psychologists often use the word "acquisition" instead of "learning" to denote the process of adding new information to memory. Part of the reason that the terms have changed is that we have changed the way we think about these topics. Psychologists have always borrowed from the most advanced technology of each time period to create a model of how the mind "must" work. Early in this century, when indoor plumbing became widely available, some psychologists suggested that the mind must work like a plumbing system, with thoughts traveling through conduits or pipes (this could irreverently be referred to as the "your mind is like a toilet" metaphor). Later, when large switchboards were developed that could transmit telephone calls to many centers at once, this served as the model of the mind. Currently, the most advanced technology we have is the computer, and many psychologists have been quick to point out parallels between the way humans think and the way computer programs (software) process information. Like a computer, we take in information, process it, and send information out. Thus, the term **Human Information Processing** (HIP) refers to the idea that humans and computers have many functional similarities. These are shown in more detail in Fig. 2.2.

Many psychologists believe that if we think about humans as information processors, similar in function to highly sophisticated computer programs, then we can use this metaphor to understand human memory and thought. It is important to point out here that they're using the computer as a **model** of human thought processes. A model is an "as if" statement—that means we can think about the human mind as if it were a computer. No one believes that the neurons, blood vessels, and brain tissue of the human brain are similar to the hardware (electronic registers) of the computer. The simile that your mind is like a computer applies only to the processes both of them go through in understanding and solving problems. Proponents of the HIP view say that the human information processing model has proven useful in understanding memory and thinking. Those who are opposed to it point out that there are too many differences— people are emotional, machines are not; people are adaptable, machines are rigid; people can create other people and machines, machines cannot. Although these differences are important enough to cause some researchers to abandon this model, it has been a dominant theme in recent research on human memory.

Because our ability to think is viewed as similar to the computer's ability to process information, the first stage of this process is usually called input, or **acquisition,** to keep it consistent with computer terminology.

The interval between acquiring some information and the time when you remember it is called the **retention interval.** The act of remembering something is called **retrieval.** In order to understand memory, we examine each of these three components of human information processing in turn.

Computers:

Central Processing Unit

Input	(inside the computer)	Output
Takes in information from card readers, computer terminals or other input device →	Operates on the information to perform desired tasks, e.g., arithmetic	→ Sends information out over terminals, printers or other output device

People:

Brain—A Human Central
Processing Unit

Input	(inside the person)	Output
Takes in information through eyes, ears, skin, nose, mouth, etc. →	Operates on the information to perform desired tasks, e.g., arithmetic	→ Sends information out via hands (writing), mouth (speaking), etc.

FIG. 2.2. Human Information Processing Model. Computers are used as an analogy for understanding human thought and memory processes.

Acquisition

> A poster of Farrah Fawcett-Majors in a red bathing suit sold over 12 million copies, thus becoming the best-selling poster of all time. One spin-off of this success story is the marketing of Farrah look-alike dolls, clad in a similar red bathing suit, that is "recommended for girls over three years old."

Unless you already knew this, you have just acquired new information. You can answer questions that you couldn't answer a few moments ago. You are a changed person.

You may have heard the term "information explosion," which refers to the tremendous increase in the amount of information we have to deal with in contemporary society—information that has to be acquired, retained, and retrieved if we are to function in an increasingly technical world. Consider, for example, the documentation that soldiers have to master in order to learn and perform maintenance on MI tanks. There are more than 40,000 pages of instructions, and the tools required for maintenance could fill a large truck (Brooks, Simutis, & O'Neil, Jr., 1985). The soldiers who are responsible for MI tanks need to know how to learn and recall large amounts of technical information in order to perform well at this highly complex task.

We are surrounded every moment by more information than we could possibly acquire. Stop some friends some time during the day and ask them to close their eyes. Ask them questions about the room they're in (like which pots are on the stove, if they're in the kitchen) or the book they're reading (like whether there are headings on the page they're reading or what is shown on the book cover) or the person they're with (like does a friend part his or her hair on the side or down the middle). You'll be surprised how much of this potentially available information is not known. We are selective about the nature of the information we acquire.

Attention

One of the primary determinants of what we know is what we attend to. Think back to the last time you were at a large, noisy party with people standing around in small groups talking to each other.

Imagine that you're standing with two acquaintances discussing the weather. There are several small groups of people standing nearby who are also carrying on conversations. If someone near you, but not talking to you, mentions your name or something of interest (e.g., "Did you hear the latest news about Debbie and Stanley? . . ."), this will attract your attention. If, however, the same person standing at the same distance from you, speaking in the same voice is discussing tree blight, you probably would never notice, unless you have a special interest in tree blight. Think about what will happen to the conversation about the weather that you've been engaged in. If your answer is "Not much," you're correct. When you switched your attention to the more interesting conversation, you lost most of the meaning of the original conversation. If, at this point, the person who has been talking to you suddenly stops and asks, "What do you think about it?", you'd have to give an embarrassed explanation, because you would have no knowledge of her or his conversation.

The scenario described here is called the **cocktail party effect.** Most people can think of an episode where something similar to this has happened to them. It demonstrates several basic properties of attention.

1. If you don't pay attention, you won't acquire information. Let's consider the scenario a little more closely. When you were attending to the weather conversation, you knew very little or nothing about the other conversations around you. When you switched your attention to the more interesting conversation, you could not say what was happening in the weather conversation. Thus, attention will be a major concept in what gets remembered, because it determines what gets into the human information system.

2. There are limitations on your ability to process information. All of the conversations going on around you are not processed.

3. There are individual differences in what is attended to. If you had no interest in

"the latest news about Debbie and Stanley," but found the weather fascinating, then you would not have switched your attention and could have responded with more than a sheepish grin to the question, "What do you think about it?"

Experimental Studies. Researchers, of course, don't go to cocktail parties to study attention. (They go for other purposes.) The cocktail party effect is studied in the laboratory with a technique called **dichotic listening.** In the dichotic listening technique, subjects wear headphones that are similar to the ones that come with stereo equipment. Different messages are heard over each earphone. You can try this out for yourself, to see what it's like, by getting two friends to stand on either side of you and having them read aloud, simultaneously, from different books. Try attending to only one message. How much did you remember from that message? How much did you remember from the message you weren't attending to?

When experiments like this were conducted in laboratories under controlled conditions (e.g., volume was controlled and subjects were required to repeat the message to which they were attending to be certain that they really were attending to the appropriate message), researchers found that little was remembered from the nonattended message, although subjects could recall gross properties like whether the voice changed from a man's to a woman's and when there was no message at all (Cherry, 1953; Moray, 1959; Treisman, 1964). The gist, or theme, of the nonattended message was lost, whereas subjects could remember a great deal of the message to which they were attending.

If you're interested in knowing more about memory so that you can improve your own, then you'll have to pay attention to attention. Many people complain that they forget the names of people soon after they've been introduced. It is likely that they never paid attention to the name at the time of introduction. If information is not acquired, then it can never be remembered. When meeting someone, it is a good idea to repeat the person's name aloud to be certain that you've heard it correctly and to be certain that you've paid attention. You need to develop the habit of monitoring your attention. If your eyes are moving across a text, but your mind is somewhere else, you need to be consciously aware of the fact that you're not attending so that you can redirect your effort to the material to be learned. It's been said that a good politician remembers names. This is also true of successful salespeople, teachers, waiters, and waitresses. Even if you'll never be a politician, salesperson, teacher, or waiter or waitress, it is a good social skill that is well worth the effort.

In case you're unimpressed with the rule that unless you attend to something you won't know it, let's try a demonstration. Most people will admit that they like money and have worked hard to earn it and have spent it countless times. In Fig. 2.3, there are several drawings of a penny. Only one is correct. If you're like most people, you won't be able to recognize the correct penny because you never attended to its details. Although you've dealt with pennies numerous

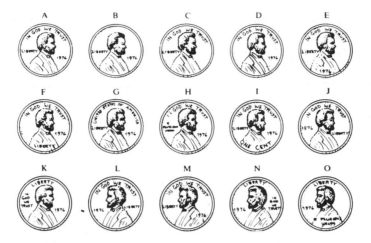

FIG. 2.3. Fifteen drawings of a U. S. penny. Which one is correct? (From Nickerson & Adams, 1979).

times, you learned only enough of the details to tell it apart from other coins. You probably never acquired a detailed memory of pennies. To find the "correct" answer, check it with a real penny, but be certain that you attend to all of the details carefully. If you're still dubious, try drawing a telephone dial from memory. Few people find that they know which numbers and letters go together, yet we've all dialed telephones thousands of times. The moral is simple: Without attention there will be little memory.

The need to pay attention in school should be obvious. John Holt, a respected educator and author of the book *How Children Fail* (1964) believes that many children fail in school because they don't pay attention. Think about how your mind sometimes seems to wander when reading textbooks or during lectures. Most students are not even aware when they're not paying attention. It should be obvious by now that in order to develop better memory skills, you will also have to develop attention skills.

Retention

> *The art of remembering is the art of thinking. . . . our conscious effort should not be so much to* impress *or* retain *(knowledge) as to* connect *it with something already there.*
>
> —William James

The term "retention" is sometimes used synonymously with memory. Unfortunately, this term suggests that memory is like a vast storage tank or library where memories are stored and something like miniature pictures of events are retrieved when we recall an occasion. This notion of memory is wrong. Some psychologists divide the memory system into two or more "types," which are differentiated on the basis of the length of the retrieval interval and the amount of information that they can retain.

One type of memory system covers retention intervals from about 2 seconds to somewhere between 30 seconds and 1 minute. Because this is a relatively short time period, it is called **short-term memory.** All the rest of memory, from 1 minute to a lifetime, is called **long-term memory.**

Many people feel that memories that last only a matter of seconds are not only quantitatively but also qualitatively different from memories that are older. Think of looking up a telephone number in the phone book for a friend you've just met. You find the number, "876-7317," and repeat it to yourself as you walk across the room to dial. If you get a busy signal or if someone interrupts you with a question, or if you trip over the cat, the number is forgotten and you need to look it up again. This certainly seems qualitatively different from the process you go through in remembering your own phone number and those of your close friends and family, whose phone numbers you've known a long time. Furthermore, although you can remember one new phone number as you walk across the room, you can't remember two new 7-digit numbers. (Try it—you'll find that there are too many digits). Compare this with your memory for items you already know. Think of all the words you know, all of the people you can recognize, all of the book plots you can remember. It seems as if your long-term memory is limitless in the number of items it can retain.

Despite the intuitive notion that the distinction between short-term and long-term memory is useful, some psychologists prefer the idea of one memory system. Whether there are one, two, or three memory systems is not as important for a thinking course as understanding what happens to the information that is stored in memory and what we can do to improve our ability to remember.

The Constructive Nature of Memory

Many of the popular notions that people hold about memory are wrong. For example, in a story by the famous mystery writer Agatha Christie, the witness to a crime had her memory of it "covered over" by a series of events that followed the crime so that she was unable to remember what happened. As the years passed and the witness grew old, the distracting and confusing information was forgotten until only the "true" memory remained. The notion of how our memory works makes for great fiction, but is a wrong account of what psychologists have learned about memory.

Prior Knowledge

Your ability to learn and remember new material depends on what you already know. You certainly wouldn't take an advanced course in nuclear physics if you never had a basic course in physics. However, you probably never realized that prior knowledge, the information you already know, influences how you think and how you remember new information in almost any context. You can read a passage about a familiar topic more quickly than you can read a passage of (objectively) comparable difficulty regarding an unfamiliar topic, because your prior knowledge about a known topic facilitates comprehension. Later in this book, I consider the differences between novices and experts in how they solve problems. The expert is better able to comprehend a problem and to remember important aspects of the problem because of his or her prior knowledge of the field.

Stereotype and Prejudice.   An interesting experimental demonstration of the idea that prior knowledge influences what people will remember was conducted by two psychologists, Snyder and Uranowitz (1978). Two groups of college students served as subjects. Students in both groups read the same story about a woman named Betty. The story contained information about her life. Among the information presented was the fact that she occasionally dated men. Up to this point, everything was the same for the students in both groups. After reading the story, one group of students was told that Betty had become a lesbian, whereas the other group of students was told that she was leading a heterosexual lifestyle. The question of interest was whether this would influence what they remembered about Betty's life story. One week later, all of the students returned to the laboratory to answer questions about the story they had read. They were asked many questions. The critical question was:

In high school, Betty:
(a) occasionally dated men
(b) never went out with men
(c) went steady
(d) no information provided

Can you guess the results of this experiment? The group of students who were told that Betty is now a lesbian were much more likely to "remember" that she never went out with men (b) as the correct answer than the group of students who were told that Betty is a heterosexual. Those students believed that they remembered something that hadn't occurred. Their prejudices and beliefs about lesbians caused them to remember events that never transpired.

In an experiment that was designed to determine how sex-role stereotypes influence memory (Halpern, 1985), high school students were given dull, boring stories to read about the life of a main character who was either a male ("David") or a female ("Linda"). The events described in the story were those commonly engaged in by both women and men. Female high school students who read stories with Linda as the protagonist remembered the story better than other female students who read the same story with David as the protagonist, whereas male high school students remembered the story better when David was the protagonist. It seems that the high school students were able to identify with the main character when his or her sex was the same as their own, and this resulted in better memory for the details of the story. In addition, errors in memory were biased toward conformity with sex-role stereotypes.

Our beliefs about lesbians, women, men, and other groups, especially racial and ethnic groups, exert strong influences on what we will remember about members of these groups. People may honestly believe that they are recalling something that, in fact, never occurred, because their beliefs about what must have happened bias how they recall the events.

Experiments like the ones just described have important implications for understanding the nature of prejudice. Let's return to the earlier example and suppose that Betty was a real person whom you knew while growing up. There may be many things that you can remember about Betty. You now learn that she is a lesbian. Suppose further that you have a stereotype of lesbians as women who drive trucks, crush beer cans with one hand, and hate all men. Because this stereotype, like most, contains very little truth about any hypothetical "average" lesbian, you would be forced either to change your stereotype or to change what you remember about Betty. It seems that it is our specific memories that change; whereas, the more abstract memory information underlying our stereotypes resists change. You might selectively remember information like the fact that she always liked to play basketball and forget other information about Betty that is inconsistent with your stereotype, like the fact that she also liked to cook and plant flowers. Allport (1954), in a classic book on prejudice, wrote, "It is possible for a stereotype to grow in defiance of *all* evidence. . . ." (pp. 189–190).

Inference and Distortion

Memory is malleable. Our memory depends on how we encoded or interpreted events, not on the events themselves. What we remember changes over time. When our knowledge and experience change, our memories also change (Bartlett, 1932). There are additions made to memories so that we remember events that never occurred and deletions made so that we forget other events that did. Often, people cannot distinguish between their own thoughts and their perceptions (Johnson & Raye, 1981). Have you ever wondered, "Did she really say that or did I think she said that?" At your next high school or college reunion, get together with friends to remember old times. You may be surprised to find that the same events are remembered differently by each of you, and each will have memories that others don't have.

Eyewitness Testimony.   Seeing is believing, or at least most people believe it is. Nowhere is this adage held as strongly as in our legal system. Very often, eyewitness testimony, the testimony of someone who saw a crime being committed, is the determining factor between a conviction and an acquittal. Defendants with credible, plausible alibis have been convicted by an eye witness's identification. Should we be placing so much faith in the accounts given by eye witnesses?

If we use the theoretical framework provided earlier, then recall of the event depends on acquisition, retention, and retrieval. Information can never be recalled correctly unless it was attended to at the time it occurred. This would not seem to be a problem if we're interested in memory for a crime, because it would seem to demand our attention. In fact, witnesses and victims fail to notice many important details because of a narrowing of attention that occurs under stress. If there is a gun or other weapon used during the crime, then the victim focuses on the weapon. Other details that are needed for correct identification, like whether the assailant had a moustache, may go unnoticed (Loftus, 1979).

There are many alterations of the memory of the event that occur during the retention interval, which, in this case, is the time between the crime and the recollection of it at trial. Discussions of the crime after it occurred can be incorporated into memory so that the individual may honestly believe that he or she is recalling the crime, although what he or she is recalling is a discussion of the crime.

Events that occur at retrieval can also influence memory. For example, the way a question is asked can lead to a particular answer. The legal system has recognized this possibility and consequently doesn't allow an attorney to ask his or her "own" witness "leading" questions. The "line-up" is another example of the way retrieval events can influence what is remembered. Suppose you are in a 24-hour convenience store at night, when a tall, Oriental man bursts in and holds up the cashier at gunpoint. Five days later, you're asked to come to the police station to identify the assailant from a line-up. The line consists of one old woman, a 14-year-old White boy, two young Black men, and one tall Oriental man. The chances of selecting the Oriental man are obviously greater than if the line-up contained five different tall Oriental men. Furthermore, we also know that cross-racial identification tends to be poorer than interracial identification (the idea that "they all look alike"), so unless you too are Oriental, this hapless man is even more likely to be "remembered" as the robber. Because events that occur during the retention interval influence recall, the line-up can actually hinder recall. Once a person is selected from the line-up as the assailant, he will look even more familiar at the trial. The victim may, indeed, be remembering him, but he may look familiar because he was seen in the line-up.

A notorious example of the fallibility of human memory was seen in a highly publicized case involving a Catholic priest who was positively identified as an armed robber by several different witnesses. The trial ended abruptly when a much younger and taller man confessed, offering details of the crime that could only have been known by the real robber, because they were never publicized. The witnesses had not lied. Each honestly believed that he or she remembered seeing the priest as the robber. It is important to realize that although memory can sometimes be astonishingly accurate, it can also be astonishingly wrong.

Meaningfulness

Information that is highly meaningful will be remembered better than information that has little meaning to you. To demonstrate this, look at A, B, and C in Fig. 2.4 for a few seconds, then cover the figures and reproduce them from memory. Try this now.

You probably remembered some parts of the figures shown in Fig. 2.4, but didn't remember them perfectly. Suppose I now tell you that Fig. 2.4A is a

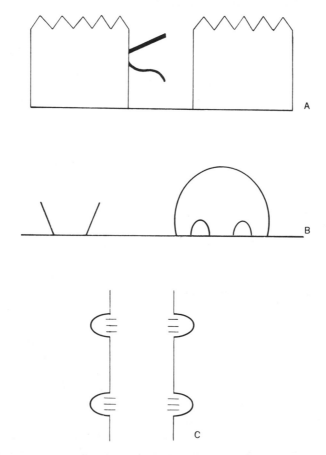

FIG. 2.4.   A demonstration of the effect of meaningfulness on memory. Look at these figures for a few seconds, then cover them and reproduce them from memory. (Figs. A and B are adapted from Osgood, 1953. Fig. C is adapted from Hanson, 1958).

soldier walking his dog behind a picket fence (Do you see the dog's tail and the end of the soldier's rifle?), and that Fig. 2.4B is a washerwoman scrubbing the floor (Do you see her water bucket and the bottoms of her shoes?). If you recognized Fig. 2.4C as a bear behind a tree, then you drew it more accurately than if it seemed more like abstract art. Making the figures meaningful will enhance how well they are remembered. You can test this with friends by telling them what the figures are, uncovering them briefly, and then comparing how much your friends remembered to your own drawings.

Your elementary school teachers recognized the role that meaning plays in memory when they told you to "read for meaning." We can add meaning to information by elaborating on it. For example, when you are learning something, try to relate it to something that you already know. Put the topic in context or make your own summarization of the information. It seems that comprehension and memory go together, and anything that improves comprehension will also improve memory. In a clever demonstration of this, two psychologists (Brans- ford & Johnson, 1972) presented college students with the following passage to read. Read it for yourself and then see how much you can remember:

> The procedure is actually quite simple. First you arrange things into different groups depending on their makeup. Of course, one pile may be sufficient depending on how much there is to do. If you have to go somewhere else due to lack of facilities that is the next step, otherwise you are pretty well set. It is important not to overdo any particular endeavor. That is, it is better to do too few things at once than too many. In the short run this may not seem important, but complications from doing too many can easily arise. A mistake can be expensive as well. The manipulation of the appro- priate mechanisms should be self-explanatory, and we need not dwell on it here. At first the whole procedure will seem complicated. Soon, however, it will become just another facet of life. It is difficult to foresee any end to the necessity for this task in the immediate future, but then one never can tell.

You probably did not remember very much of this passage. I also doubt that you found it very understandable.

I'd like you to read the passage again, this time keeping the title "Washing Clothes" in mind. It should seem much more memorable because the title provided a context or a framework for understanding the passage. When infor- mation is provided before you read a text or learn about a topic, you are better able to assimilate the incoming information. The **advance organizers,** which is the term for the preliminary information, act as a guide or framework that helps the learner to anticipate information and to relate it to other topics.

We seldom remember anything verbatim, that is, in the exact words that were spoken or read. Most of our memory is for **gist,** or interpretation of the meaning of the message. If a student ever answered an examination question with the exact words that I had spoken in class or that the student had read from the text, I'd be worried. I'd think that the student probably didn't understand the material and hadn't learned it in a meaningful way. Let's try another demonstration of the influence of meaningfulness on memory. Read and remember the following passage (Bransford & Johnson, 1973):

Watching a Peace March From the Fortieth Floor

The view was breathtaking. From the window one could see the crowd below. Everything looked extremely small from such a distance, but the colorful costumes could still be seen. Everyone seemed to be moving in one direction in an orderly fashion, and there seemed to be little children as well as adults. The landing was gentle, and luckily the atmosphere was such that no special suits had to be worn. At first there was a great deal of activity. Later, when the speeches started, the crowd quieted down. The man with the television camera took many shots of the setting and the crowd. Everyone was friendly and seemed glad when the music started.

What did you remember from this passage? Most people forget the sentence starting with, "The landing was gentle . . ." Most people who read this try to understand what it is saying about a peace march. The "landing sentence" is incomprehensible in this context, so it is often forgotten. When college students were told that the title was "Space Trip to an Inhabited Planet," the "landing sentence" was almost always remembered. Thus, what people remember depends on the meaning that is extracted. This is also another demonstration of the fact that memory is dynamic and integrative. It is not a static copy of the world; rather, it changes over time with additions and deletions that relate to prior and subsequent knowledge.

Meaningfulness can account for some individual differences in memory. Have you ever wondered how a good poker or pinochle or chess player is able to remember which cards have been played or which moves have been made? In a classic study of chess players' memories for the positions of chess pieces on a board, deGroot (1966) found that chess masters could remember chess positions that had actually occurred in a game after looking at the board for only 5 seconds. Novice chess players had much more difficulty in remembering where the chess pieces had been. Does this mean that really good chess players have extraordinary memories? To answer this question, de Groot placed the pieces randomly on the board and asked master and novice players to view the board for 5 seconds and then recall the positions of the pieces. In the random placement condition, both groups performed about the same. It seems that the master players remembered more than the novices only when the board positions were highly meaningful to the chess masters and, consequently, were remembered quite accurately.

It seems likely that good card players remember which cards have already been played because each hand is highly meaningful to them. For example, John Moss (a pseudonym for the author of *How to Win at Poker,* 1950) described a series of possible hands that a player can be dealt along with several possible cards that could be drawn. It would be easy for him or another poker shark to remember a ''four of diamonds in the hole with a four of hearts, six of diamonds and ace of spades exposed. He could remember this as a single familiar hand, whereas a novice player would have to remember four separate cards. For the good players, this hand would represent a single chunk in memory. Reducing a large number of items to a single item to be remembered is called **chunking.** (No, it is not a brand of Chinese food.) It is a subtle and ubiquitous memory process. It allows us to recall whole sentences instead of words and whole words instead of letters. As material becomes increasingly meaningful, we can reduce the number of items that need to be remembered. Master chess players and card players seem to have this memory advantage.

Look quickly at the row of letters and numbers presented next, and then cover them and try to remember as many as you can:

IB	MF	BI	TW	AJ	FK
816	44	93	62	51	69	41

The reason that you probably had difficulty with this task is that the information is not chunked or grouped into meaningful units. Suppose I reorganize the letters by changing the spacing but not their order. They now become IBM, FBI, TWA, JFK. You should have no difficulty remembering all of the letters now. The amount of information hasn't changed, but the cognitive demand has. It is much easier to recall information that it chunked into meaningful units. Consider the row of numbers. Suppose I tell you that this series, if regrouped, is the sequence 9^2, 8^2, 7^2, and so on. Again, by relating the input to what's known to make it meaningful, a difficult memory task can be made trivial.

The notion that meaning is important in memory is raised again, later in this chapter, when we consider strategies for improving memory.

Retrieval

What is your mother's maiden name? Unless you happened to be sitting here thinking about your mother's name, the name seemed to ''pop'' into your mind. The answer must have been stored in some way that allowed it to be retrieved with a simple question. In fact, it seems almost impossible not to remember your mother's maiden name when you are asked this question. Who was Gerald Ford's vice presidential running mate during his bid for the presidency in 1976? For many people, this is a difficult question to answer. (The answer is Robert Dole.) Certainly you once knew the answer, but over the years, it has been forgotten. Forgetting, or retrieval failure, can be a frustrating experience for everyone. If you want to be able to think effectively, you must be able to retrieve information that is stored in memory when it is needed. How can we understand the retrieval process when it works so well sometimes and so poorly other times?

Forgetting

One of the major theories of forgetting is that events interfere with each other in memory. This is called the **interference theory of forgetting.** Suppose that you are studying French and Spanish in college. You'd probably find that you sometimes get them confused, because what you've learned about one language "interferes" with what you've learned about the other. In general, the more similar two events are (or, in this case, languages), the more interference there will be. By knowing this, can you think of a way to reduce interference and improve memory? In the example just given, one way would be to take the courses in different semesters to minimize the interference, or, at least, one course early in the morning and the other in the evening. By keeping the French and Spanish courses as separate as possible, you can reduce some of the interference.

Organization

"Clean up your room!" I don't think that there is a person alive who hasn't heard (or spoken) these words. The idea that "you'll never be able to find anything in this mess" may also apply to how you store information in memory, although the similarity between memory and a messy room is obviously a gross oversimplification. Organization, however, does make it easier to find a pair of socks that match and easier to retrieve information from memory.

I'd like to demonstrate this point with two lists of words. Read one list, at a rate of approximately one word per second, cover the list and write down as many of the words as you can remember, then repeat this process with the second list.

Girl
Heart
Robin
Purple
Finger
Flute
Blue
Organ
Man
Hawk
Green
Lung
Eagle
Child
Piano

Stop now, cover the preceding list, and write down as many words from this list as you can remember.

Now read the next list, cover it, and then write down as many of the words that you can remember from this list.

Green
Blue
Purple
Man
Girl
Child
Piano
Flute
Organ
Heart
Lung
Finger
Eagle
Hawk
Robin

Stop now, cover the preceding list, and write down as many words from this list as you can remember.

Undoubtedly, you recalled correctly more words from the second list than from the first. You may not have realized that the lists were identical except for the order in which the words were presented. You might expect that you did better the second time because you already had a chance to practice the words once. This is true. The additional time spent studying the words can partially account for the improvement in recall. But, most of the improvement on the second list came from the organization that was provided by presenting words in categories. Research has shown that when lists of words are presented in categories, recall of material was two to three times better than when the same list of words was randomly presented (Bower & Clark, 1969). When words are presented in random order, as in the first list, recall is improved when subjects have enough time to generate their own categories (Bousfield, 1953).

You can apply this memory principle by organizing material that you need to learn. If you are learning a classification system for a biology course or the properties of metals for a course in science, study one group or category at a time. See how the groups relate, and note similarities and differences within and between categories. Impose a structure or organization on the material to be learned. Interrelate the items so that they become coherent. I present several strategies for organizing complex prose passages in the next chapter. Organizational strategies are as important in the recall of prose passages as they are in the recall of lists.

Retrieval Cues

Did you ever smell a particular perfume and remember someone you know who used to wear it? Perfume commercials would have us believe that the memory of your perfume will keep you constantly on his (or her) mind. Have you ever heard a song on the radio and then thought about the time you first heard it? ("They're playing our song.") Where did these memories come from? Something in the environment acted as a retrieval cue so that the memory was brought into conscious awareness.

Let's try a demonstration of the powerful effect retrieval cues can have on memory. Following is a list of words I'd like you to read through. Go through the list once at a rate of approximately one word per second, or have someone read them aloud to you. See how many words you can remember:

Winter
Green
Foot
Pencil
Sweater
Jupiter
Chicago
Bible
French
Violin
Lunch
Russia
Collie
Spaghetti
Thirtysomething
Newsweek

Stop now; cover the preceding list, and see how many of the list items you can recall in any order. Be sure to try this exercise before you go on. **Don't look back at the list when you are finished.**

If you didn't remember all 16 words, I'd like you to think about the items you forgot. What happened to them? Are they permanently lost, or could you remember them with the proper retrieval cues?

Here is a list of cues. See how many of the "forgotten" words you can recall:

A season of the year
A color

A part of the body
A writing instrument
An article of clothing
A planet
A name of a city
A type of book
A language
A musical instrument
A meal
A country
A breed of dog
A food
A television show
A magazine

Certainly, you can remember many more of the items on the list with the appropriate retrieval cues, and this improvement can't be attributed simply to guessing. Generating your own cues while you are trying to learn something, in order to facilitate recall, is one good way to improve memory. The cues interact with information in memory to make it more accessible so that it can be more readily remembered.

Many of the strategies to improve memory "work" by providing retrieval cues. Have you ever had the frustrating experience of struggling with an exam question and then remembering the answer *after* you handed in your paper? The fact that you may have the knowledge needed in a situation does not guarantee that access to that knowledge will occur. Retrieval cues help us to locate relevant information that is stored in memory; they allow us to use what we know. The ability to access stored knowledge is an "important hallmark of intelligence" (Bransford, Sherwood, Vye, & Rieser, 1986).

EMOTIONS AND MEMORY

One of the major criticisms of drawing parallels between the way humans think and remember and the way computers do is that human emotion is an integral part of the human process, and there is no computer counterpart for emotion. There are several ways that emotions influence our ability to think and remember.

Periodic Review

Most people over 30 years of age have heard the question, "Where were you when you heard that President Kennedy was shot?" This was a favorite topic of conversation for many years. It was often the opening line for a couple on their first date (before it was replaced with "What's your sign?"), and it remained a favorite theme for English term paper assignments. Emotionally charged events, both negative and positive, are often rehearsed, whereas everyday events are largely ignored. This periodic review may make the event seem more memorable, but, in fact, you may be remembering your own account of the event rather than the event itself.

An interesting example of the way **periodic review** influences memory for an emotional event can be found in an autobiographical account by the world-famous developmental psychologist, Jean Piaget. He remembered most clearly the following (Piaget, 1962):

> I was sitting in my pram, which my nurse was pushing in the Champs Elysees, when a man tried to kidnap me. I was held in by the strap fastened around me while my nurse bravely tried to stand between me and the thief. She received various scratches, and I can still see vaguely those on her face. Then a crowd gathered, a policeman with a short cloak and a white baton came up, and the man took to his heels. I can still see the whole scene, and can even place it near the tube station. (footnote, pp. 188)

Piaget's childhood and early adulthood passed with the memory of the attempted kidnapping. Later, the former nurse wrote to his parents to say that she had been converted to the Salvation Army. She wanted to confess her past sins and return the watch she had been given as a reward for saving their baby's life. She had made up the entire episode. Piaget's vivid memory of the event was really a memory of the stories he had been told about it. "Many real memories are doubtless of the same order" (Piaget, 1962, p. 188).

As seen in the preceding quote from Piaget, memory changes over time. Stored information becomes integrated with subsequently acquired information. Incoming information is evaluated and integrated serially over time (Anderson, 1986). The result is often a surprisingly vivid "memory" for an event that did not occur or was very different from the way it is remembered.

Anxiety and Stress

> *"The horror of that moment,"* the King went on, *"I shall never, never forget!"*
> *"You will though,"* the Queen said, *"if you don't make a memorandum of it."*
> —Lewis Carroll (*Through the Looking-Glass,* 1872)

What is the influence of extremely negative emotions on memory and thought? If you suffer from severe test anxiety, you already know the answer to this question. Almost everyone becomes somewhat anxious before a test. A moderate amount of anxiety may actually improve performance; however, extreme anxiety adversely affects recall and clear thought. People who become overwhelmed with anxiety during tests find that they can't concentrate while they are preparing their response to the questions. Sometimes, they even have difficulty reading the questions.

Consider how you feel when you are excited, angry, or afraid. Your heart rate accelerates; your face may become flushed or pale; your stomach seems to tighten; and you may begin to perspire. Simple, well-learned tasks, like tying your shoes, won't be affected much by extreme emotions, but difficult tasks like answering exam questions will. A graph of the relationship between level of stress or arousal and efficiency of performance is shown in Fig. 2.5. The ascending portion of the curve shows that performance tends to improve as arousal increases; the descending portion of the curve shows that when arousal is greater than some optimal level, performance declines.

Students who suffer from extreme test anxiety often report that instead of thinking about the questions on the exam, their minds are occupied with thoughts of impending failure. It seems that, among other things, negative emotions

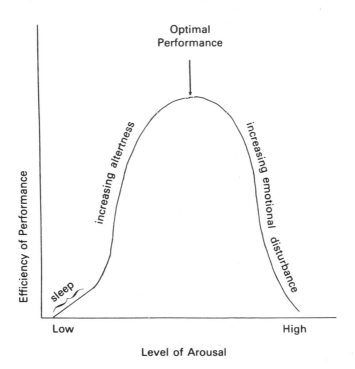

FIG. 2.5. The relationship between level of arousal and efficiency of performance is an "inverted-U-shaped" curve.

generate extraneous thoughts so that the individual finds himself or herself unable to concentrate on the task he or she is supposed to be working on. Most colleges and universities have counseling centers to help students who suffer from extreme test anxiety. One of the best ways to prevent or reduce test anxiety is by establishing a personal history of successful test taking. If you practice the strategies for improving memory, you may be able to reduce test anxiety to a more manageable level. The adage "nothing succeeds like success" is appropriate here.

In a test of the effect of stress on memory (Baddeley, 1972), servicemen were told that it may be necessary to crash-land the plane in which they were traveling. To make this seem real, they were asked to fill out forms to indicate who would get their personal property in the event of death. They were then told that they would need to take a test to see how well they remembered their emergency instructions. The men were told that this might be needed for their heirs to collect the insurance in the event of their death, because it was a way of documenting their preparedness for disaster. Thus, the men were given a test with the belief that they might soon crash and die. They made many more mistakes under these stressful conditions than a control group that took the same test without stress. (Psychologists have to wrestle with the ethical problems in research of this sort. Is such research justifiable on the grounds that countless lives can be saved if we understand how memory and thought functions change under stress and if we can use this knowledge to improve performance?)

Rape victims and other victims of violent crimes often report similar memory lapses, although usually for memory of the event itself. They would like to be able to recall the event clearly, because it would be helpful in apprehending their assailant and because it might be therapeutic. It is not unusual for victims to blame themselves for their attack (I should have been more careful; I should have known better, etc.) and then blame themselves for their inability to recall it in detail. If they knew that memory failures were normal under these circumstances, then at least some of the self-blame could be alleviated.

Repression

Sigmund Freud, the father of a major branch of psychological thought, called **psychoanalysis,** believed that highly emotionally charged events are forgotten because, if they were remembered, we would be flooded with overwhelming emotions that we might not be able to handle. According to Freudian theory, the traumatic event is **repressed** unconsciously (without our awareness) and can be remembered only with appropriate psychotherapy. *Psychotherapy* is a general term that refers to the use of the principles of psychology to alleviate emotional problems or mental disorders. (The term "psychoanalysis" has two meanings. It refers to Freud's theories about psychology and to the form of psychotherapy he developed.)

Bower (1981) reformulated how the emotions experienced during psycho-therapy can trigger memory for previously forgotten events. As an example, he used the case of Sirhan Sirhan, the man who assassinated Robert Kennedy in Los Angeles in 1968. Sirhan had no memory for the emotionally charged event. To help him remember, Bernard Diamond, a forensic psychiatrist (a lawyer who is also a psychiatrist) placed Sirhan under hypnosis:

> Under hypnosis, as Sirhan became more worked up and excited, he recalled pro-gressively more, the memories tumbling out while his excitement built to a crescen-do leading up to the shooting. At that point, Sirhan would scream out the death curses, "fire" the shots, and then choke as he reexperienced the Secret Service bodyguard nearly throttling him after he was caught. On different occasions, while in a trance, Sirhan was able to recall the crucial events, sometimes speaking, other times recording his recollections in automatic writing, but the recall was always accompanied by great excitement. (Bower, 1981, p. 129)

The case of Sirhan Sirhan demonstrates **state-dependent memory;** events that occur in one emotional state are remembered best when the individual is in the same emotional state. Imagine a couple undergoing psychotherapy for mar-riage problems. When they are happy, they seem to remember the good aspects of their marriage, but, when they are unhappy, the bad memories from their marriage predominate. Can you understand how psychotherapy can help some-one remember emotional events? The therapist can induce a particular mood by the kinds of questions he or she poses. Suppose further that the husband—we'll call him Michael—saw his father hit his mother when he was very young. This can be a frightening and confusing experience for a child; and later in life, Michael is unable to recall this event. His therapist can ask him questions about other frightening experiences that occurred during his childhood that he is able to remember, thus making Michael's mood similar to the one he experienced when the forgotten event occurred. The congruity between his present emotional state and the one he was in when the event occurred can facilitate recall. Thus, a skilled therapist can help Michael remember his father's deed. The therapist could also use this knowledge to help Michael understand why he is afraid to show anger toward his wife. Successful retrieval of his memory, which has been hidden since Michael's childhood, could aid Michael in improving his relation-ship with his wife.

The basic idea is that mood can serve as a retrieval cue. When an emotion is aroused, information that was stored with that emotion is more easily accessible. The process of making something easier to remember by presenting subjects with something else (in this case, a mood that is similar to the one experienced at the time of the event) that is associated with it is called **priming.** As stated at the beginning of this chapter, the thinking process relies on what is remembered. One way to influence what gets remembered and the way in which new information is evaluated is to change one's mood. Bower (1987) found that subjects judged an ambiguous facial expression as either happy or sad depending on their own mood. Personal and social judgments are also influenced. When people are happy, they describe themselves as competent, self-assured, outgoing, and "highly esteemed with bright prospects." By contrast, when they are sad, the same people describe themselves in more negative terms—less capable, less successful, less self-esteem.

I'd like to end this section with a note of caution about a topic I raised earlier—hypnosis. It may have been useful in helping Sirhan Sirhan to remember the events surrounding the murder of Robert Kennedy, but it can also produce inaccurate recall. Memory is not a permanent unchanging storage of information, and what is remembered can be influenced by subtle suggestions made during hypnosis. Six states now bar witnesses who have been hypnotised from testifying at trials because their memory may have been altered during hypnosis. On the other hand, some police departments feel that hypnosis is a valuable tool for obtaining information that would not be available without its use. A prudent conclusion about hypnosis is that, although it may make some memories more accessible for recall, they are not necessarily accurate ones. The use of hypnosis as a memory aid is likely to remain a major controversy for many years.

METAMEMORY

The term **metamemory** refers to one's personal knowledge of his or her own memory system. It seems that much of the difference between good and poor learners can be attributed to metamemory. Bransford (1979) has summarized this:

> . . . (E)ffective learners know themselves what they need to know and do in order to perform effectively; they are able to monitor their own levels of understanding and mastery. These active learners are therefore likely to ask questions of clarification and more efficiently plan their study activities. Such activities are quite different from passively accepting (yet momentarily actively processing) the particular information that a person or text presents. (p. 248)

This quote from Bransford brings up the important concept of active learning. Very little, if anything, can be learned passively. This general rule supports the research that was cited earlier, demonstrating the need to monitor the learning process. You need to actively deal with material if you want to remember it. Good learners know when they understand the material and when they do not understand it; poor learners don't seem to notice the difference. Good learners know what they have to do to facilitate learning. These are the executive processes that keep the learner mindful of what and how much is being learned. For example, good learners may spontaneously link new information to information previously learned or think of possible applications for the new materials they are learning. As you read this paragraph, you may be applying this learning "device" by noting the similarity of this concept with one you learned in the section entitled organization, that imposing additional organization on material by activities like these will result in improved comprehension.

An interesting study (Whimbey, 1976) has shown that students who are having academic problems in college approach their text assignments differently from good students. The less successful college students read difficult material straight through, without seeming to notice when they didn't understand the material and without rereading the difficult sections. Good students know these strategies. Most importantly, Whimbey found that he could improve performance for the poorer students by teaching them how to organize the material and how to become aware of what they were understanding and what they weren't. Too often, college students and others believe that they know some material because they've read or heard it. They're surprised to find that they can't answer basic questions about the material they supposedly knew.

MNEMONICS

In a recent episode of the popular children's television show "Sesame Street," Bert and Ernie, two lovable Muppets, discussed an intriguing memory phenomenon. Bert noticed that Ernie had tied a piece of string around his finger to help him remember something. In fact, Ernie tied string around each of his eight fingers (apparently, Muppets have eight fingers) to be really sure that he didn't forget. After some prompting from Bert, Ernie recalled that the string was supposed to help him remember he should buy more string, as they had run out of string.

Although this example is humorous, it illustrates some fundamental assumptions and problems encountered by humans (and Muppets) in dealing with their memory. The wide range of activities from tying a string around one's finger to the more elaborate procedures presented later are called **mnemonic devices.** According to Loftus and Loftus (1976), "A mnemonic device is a technique (often referred to as a memory trick) for organizing information so that it can be more easily remembered" (p. 64). Mnemonics relate to the ways that information is processed so that the material that is being learned is easily recalled. Norman (1976) has said, "they teach the user to pay attention and to learn how to organize" (p. 131). Mnemonics can be used to optimize memory. Many students use mnemonic devices to prepare for exams, and some of the techniques are so common that we usually don't think of them as mnemonics.

During the summers when I was in college, I worked as a waitress at a resort in the Catskill Mountains of New York. The resort had a night club with the usual array of singers, dancers, jugglers, and animal acts. (The kitchen help was not allowed to attend the night club, so, of course, we sneaked in often.) One particular act that amazed me was a memory act by Harry Lorayne. He went around the audience recalling people's names. His memory seemed limitless. I was also surprised at how much the audience enjoyed his performance, and that an amazing memory would qualify as a night club act. Harry Lorayne later wrote two books on this topic (Lorayne, 1975; Lorayne & Locus, 1974). The mnemonic principles he used are presented here, along with several others.

The mnemonics are based on a few simple memory principles. They all force you to pay attention to the items to be remembered. They provide a meaningful context for unrelated items. The user is often required to organize the material and to use the mnemonic as an efficient retrieval cue. The use of mnemonics also requires metacognitive monitoring—keeping track of what you know. They are intentional strategies, ones that you can use when you decide that you want to remember something. Thus, from what you've already learned about memory earlier in this chapter, you can see that mnemonics are not mere theatrical tricks. They work because they represent applications of basic principles of memory.

We all employ memory aids everyday. The most common aids are **external memory aids,** such as the sticky notes that have recently become popular, calendars in which we write appointments and other activities that we want to remember, timers to remind us to turn off the stove, and shopping lists. Mnemonics that are designed top help us retrieve information from memory are called **internal memory aids.** There are five basic types of internal memory aids: keywords and images, rhymes, places, first letters, and narrative stories. Each is discussed in turn followed by some guidelines for selecting the appropriate mnemonic for the type of material to be learned.

Keywords and Images

The following demonstration was presented as an anecdote by Donald Norman (1976). I have used it as a class demonstration many times, and students are always surprised at how well it works. The use of this mnemonic depends on first learning **keywords** that serve as "hooks" for information that is learned later. In this case, the keywords are in the form of a simple poem to learn. Spend a minute or two learning this poem (Norman, 1976):

One is a bun,
Two is a shoe,
Three is a tree,
Four is a door,
Five is a hive,
Six are sticks,

Seven is heaven,
Eight is a gate,
Nine is a line, and
Ten is a hen. (p. 134).

Do you have this memorized? If not, go over the poem again.

Now, I'm going to present a list of words to be remembered. You have to form an image or association between the listed items and the items in the poem you just learned. For example, the first item on the list is ashtray. Imagine an ashtray with a bun in it, since the bun was the first item in the poem. You could imagine something like a large hamburger bun sitting in a dirty ashtray. Read the items on the list one at a time, allowing enough time to form an image.

1. ashtray
2. firewood
3. picture
4. cigarette
5. table
6. matchbook
7. glass
8. lamp
9. shoe
10. phonograph

Now, cover the list of words and answer the following questions:

What is number eight?

What number is cigarette?

If your experience was like the one that Norman described or the ones my students report, then you've been surprised to find that the answers were easily available.

In this case, you learned a list of rhyming keywords and then used imagery to relate the words to be learned to the keywords. Research has shown that images are best when they're interacting (e.g., the bun is in the ashtray and not just next to it; Bower, 1970a), and when they are vivid and detailed (the bun that I was imaging was a hamburger bun and the ashtray was glass; Bower, 1972). The deliberate use of both verbal and imagery modes of thought was introduced in chapter 1. We use this strategy again in chapters 9 and 10 (problem solving and creativity).

A more sophisticated keyword system is the **phonetic system.** It can be used to remember words or numbers. The basic principle is to associate a consonant sound with a digit. It is an old system, developed by Loisette in 1896.

Consider the following pair of digits with consonant sounds:

Digit	Consonants
0	S or Z or soft C
1	T or D or TH
2	N
3	M
4	R
5	L
6	SH or J or CH or soft G
7	K or hard G or hard C or Q or NG
8	F or V
9	B or P

As you might have guessed, there is a mnemonic system to learn mnemonic system:

1=T	T has one vertical stroke
2=N	N has two vertical strokes
3=M	M looks like a 3 when it is rotated sideways
4=R	R is the fourth letter in the word fouR
5=L	L is equal to 50 in Roman Numerals
6=Soft G or J	G looks like the number 6
7=Hard C or K	7 looks like a key
8=F	The lower case f looks like the number 8
9=P or B	P looks like the number 9 when it is rotated
0=Z or S	zerO

How do you use this keyword system? Notice that vowels are not assigned to digits. They are supplied as needed to make up words. Suppose your friend moves to a new home and you need to remember his or her new phone number. You could repeat it over and over again, hoping that, by rehearsal, the number would eventually be learned, or you could use the phonetic system. It's important to remember here that we're interested in the sound of words and not the spelling. Suppose your friend's new phone number is 641-7132. Try to transform this into words with the phonetic system. How about changing 641 into ShiRT, 71 into CaT, and 32 into MaN. As you can see, the vowels are added to make words, but can easily be deleted when you need to phone your friend. You could then form an image of a man wearing a shirt with a large picture of a widely grinning cat, which will help you recall the words you created from the phone number.

Once you have learned the phonetic alphabet, you can use it to remember any sequence of numbers. You could finally learn your social security number, student identification number, bank account number, and all of the other numbers that haunt our lives. The advantage of this technique comes from transforming the numbers, which are abstract and therefore difficult to remember, into a comprehensive unit. The obvious disadvantage is that it requires some preliminary work in order to learn the phonetic system; however, once it's learned, it's yours to use for life. It's an investment well worth making, because it is a flexible mnemonic strategy that will be useful in many contexts.

Images can also be used alone (without keywords). They are especially advantageous when you want to remember names and faces. This is the technique that Harry Lorayne (1975) uses. Change the names you want to remember to a concrete noun; pick out a distinctive feature of the face and image the two as interacting. He suggests that you pay special attention to cheeks, lips, facial lines, forehead, nose, eyebrows, and eyes. For example, if you meet Ms. Silverstein and you notice that she has wide-set eyes, you could image a silver beer mug (stein) between her eyes. Mr. Dinter could be changed to dinner and an entire dinner could be imaged on his large forehead. Try this at the next party you attend. You'll find it fun, and you may surprise yourself with your new abilities.

A keyword mnemonic system has been developed especially for learning a second language (Atkinson, 1975). Suppose you are learning French and are faced with the following three vocabulary words with their English translations to learn:

French	English
homme	man
etoile	star
legume	vegetable

Students begin by generating their own keywords. The keyword should sound like the foreign vocabulary word. Thus, for the word homme, I'd generate "home," for etoile, I'd use "a towel," and for legume, I'd use "lagoon."

The second step makes use of imagery by linking an image of the keyword with the correct translation of the foreign word. I'd visualize a man entering a large home, a towel with a star painted on it, and vegetables floating in a lagoon. (It's best when the items are interacting.) When the foreign words *homme, etoile,* and *legume* are encountered, students would then automatically recall the images and retrieve the correct translations.

Atkinson claims that, as facility with the foreign language develops, the need to remember the images diminishes, and students can extract the intended meaning without the use of imagery. Students who are taught to use this method consistently recall more correct English translations (72% compared with 46%) than students who use the usual rote rehearsal method of repeating the words until they "stick." Furthermore, this method seems to work best when students generate their own keywords and images. The need for active participation in learning is a general rule.

Rhymes

We also use rhymes to help us remember. For example, there are few people who haven't heard: "I before E, except after C," or "Thirty days hath September, April, June, and November."

Answer this question quickly. What letter comes after N? Most people find that they need to sing that portion of the alphabet (l, m, n, o, p) to answer this question. Like rhymes, the rhythm established in songs help to deter forgetting.

Rhymes are useful when order is important, because mistakes in order will usually destroy the rhyme. Notice that the first keyword poem I presented relied on keywords, images, and rhymes (one is a bun, etc.). This is an especially easy mnemonic to use, probably because several mnemonic devices are employed in the same poem to guard against forgetting.

Method of Places

Before I describe how "places" works as a mnemonic device, I'd like you to remember my back-to-school shopping list. Read the list through slowly once, then see how many items you can recall:

Pencils
Ruler
Notebook
Marking pens
Compass
Tape
Paper
Scissors
Sharpener
Reinforcements
Tablet
Glue

How many items on this list did you remember?

Now I'll show you how the **method of places** (or method of loci) could improve your recall for this list. Pick a familiar route, like the one from your house to school. Now imagine each of the items on this list placed somewhere along this route. The pencils could be very tall and form a fence around your front lawn, the ruler could be sitting across your car, the notebook could be the stop sign at your corner, and so on. Try this now with the back-to-school shopping list just presented. Once the images are formed, you should be able to remember every item by "mentally walking through" your route and noticing the items you've imagined along the way.

I once went to an introductory lesson for a very expensive memory improvement course. The method of places was the demonstration they used to convince potential students that the course was valuable. For months afterward, I received letters in the mail asking me if I "forgot" to send my money and to register for their course. The expensive (there are no cheap ones) memory improvement courses teach the same methods presented in this chapter. They have no magic secrets that are unavailable in the psychology literature.

The method of places had an interesting history that was described by an English Historian (Yates, 1966). According to the story, it was first used by a Greek poet named Simonides. He had been paid by a rich nobleman to chant a lyric poem at a banquet. (There were no televisions or video games or Pac-people to provide entertainment in ancient Greece.) He used half of the poem to praise the nobleman who hired him; the other half of the poem was devoted to the twin gods, Pollux and Castor. The nobleman was outraged by this because he wanted the entire poem to consist of praise of himself. Angrily, he told Simonides that he would only pay him half the amount that they had agreed upon. Simonides, he said, could collect the rest of the money from the twin gods he had praised. Later that evening, in the middle of dinner, a messenger told Simonides that two men were waiting outside to see him. When he went outside, no one was there. During his absence, the roof caved in on the nobleman and his banquet guests, who were crushed beyond recognition. Simonides was able to help the relatives claim the appropriate bodies by remembering where they had been sitting at the banquet table. He mentally "walked" around the table, using imagery to remember where each guest had been sitting. It seems that the invisible callers had paid well for their half of the poem. This is reportedly the first use of the method of places.

The Greeks, who were famous for giving long speeches from memory, have left us with many tips on how to best use this method. For example, the same route can be used repeatedly for different lists, but we should be careful not to put more than one item at the same place (Ross & Laurence, 1968). They also suggested that the places should not be too much alike (e.g., don't use only stop signs along your route) and that they should not be too brightly lit (or there will be glare) nor too dimly lit (or the objects will be difficult to see). This is a good method to use when events need to be remembered in a particular order, because the route can be mentally traversed forward or backward.

First Letters

First-letter mnemonics are probably most commonly used in preparing for tests. To use this technique, take the first letter of each term to be learned, insert vowels and other letters if necessary, and make a word. When you need to remember the list, you recall the word you formed and then use each letter as a retrieval cue for each item on the list. Many of us learned to remember the names of the Great Lakes as HOMES (Huron, Ontario, Michigan, Erie, and Superior). If you never learned this before, you'll never forget it again.

The first letter mnemonic organizes unrelated terms into a single word. You already know how important good organization is for memory. I can remember using this technique when I was a college student. The class had been told to be prepared to answer a long essay question that was to be written during an in-class exam. There were six points that I wanted to make in the essay, and I wanted to be sure that I included all of them in order. I took the first letter of each of the points, made up a word using these letters and used this word to help me remember all of the points for the exam. (It worked well.) This technique is also especially useful when you have to speak in front of people without notes. Select one word that can stand for each point you want to make and use the first letter of each word to form a single retrievable word. Even though good speeches may appear unrehearsed, good speakers practice with techniques like this one. It helps them to present their speech in a confident and professional manner.

A related mnemonic that doesn't fit clearly into any of the categories is the one used to recall the value of pi. I'm presenting it in this section because, even though it doesn't involve first letters, it is a letter-based technique. Read the following sentence: *May I have a drink, alcoholic of course.* By counting the letters in each word, you can read off the digits for pi, which are 3.1415926. It is easier to remember a single meaningful sentence than it is to recall eight digits.

Narrative Stories

The **narrative stories** mnemonic method was demonstrated by Bower and Clark (1969). They presented college students with lists of words to remember. The students were told to remember the words by constructing a narrative story that contained all of the words in the list. In addition, they were told to visualize the story they were constructing. (The combined use of verbal and imagery strategies should be a familiar theme by now.) The students were given 12 different lists, each containing 10 words. They remembered an average of over 90% of the 120 words (recall followed each list). A control group of college students, who were given the same lists of words to remember, but were not given the narrative stories instructions, remembered an average of less than 20% of the 120 words. Surprisingly, the students rarely intruded a nonlist word that was part of the story into their recall.

Two sample stories from Bower and Clark's (1969) study are presented here. The list words are typed in capital letters:

A LUMBERJACK DARTed out of a forest, SKATEd around a HEDGE past a COLONY of DUCKs. He tripped on some FURNITURE, tearing his STOCKING while hastening toward the PILLOW where his MISTRESS lay.

A VEGETABLE can be a useful INSTRUMENT for a COLLEGE student. A carrot can be a NAIL for your FENCE or BASIN. But a MERCHANT of the QUEEN would SCALE that fence and feed the carrot to a GOAT. (pp. 181–182)

Mnemonic Principles

Mnemonic devices can be powerful aids for memory. They are also somewhat paradoxical, because it seems that, to remember better, you need to remember more. Consider the narrative-stories mnemonic just presented. To use this method, you are required to remember not just the words in the list, but an entire story as well. The first-letter mnemonic requires that you remember the new word you created with the first letters as well as each of the words. The keyword systems require that you learn a keyword system like the phonetic alphabet system, and the rhymes present you with a song or poem to be learned. They each necessitate work. Acquiring a good memory means working at it, but it is work that pays off in life-long dividends. There are literally hundreds of studies that demonstrate that the deliberate use of mnemonics improves recall (McCormick & Levin, 1987).

Let's try to develop a mnemonic that could help you to remember the five types of mnemonics. First, let's review what they are: keywords and images, rhymes, method of places, narrative stories, and (first) letters. Although you could use the method of places and image each of these terms along a route, or weave them into a narrative story, or associate them with a keyword, or make up a poem, my choice for a list like this one is the first-letter mnemonic. Start by listing the first letter of each term: K, R, M, NS, L. You can modify the first-letter technique by using each letter to begin a word in a sentence, because incorporating these letters in a single word may be difficult. Try it. The sentence one of my students came up with is "Kind Round Men Never Sing Lyrics." Use imagery also to aid recall. Imagine a round (fat) man with a kind face who doesn't sing well. Make your images detailed and vivid. (Can you see his round tummy and hear his very off-key lyrics?) If you're asked to recall the five mnemonic devices, you can list each one, and by remembering the name of each, all of the information you've learned about them should also be easily retrieved.

Many people find it difficult to remember how to spell the word "mnemonics." Another student suggested this one: *M*emory *N*ever *E*xplains *MON*ey and *I*ce *C*ream *S*andwiches. Be sure to think about this mnemonic. You should never have difficulty spelling this word correctly again.

Remembering Events

Very often, we need to remember events rather than lists or related concepts. Much of the work that has been done in the area of event memory has been conducted by psychologists trying to assist victims and witnesses of crime with recall of the criminal activity. We can borrow the mnemonic techniques that they use to improve memory.

The Cognitive Interview

"Information is the lifeblood of a criminal investigation" (Stewart, 1985, p. 1). How can eyewitnesses to an event be helped to remember what happened so that they can provide law enforcement officers with the needed information? One way to improve the quantity and quality of what gets remembered is with the use of a mnemonic for events known as the **cognitive interview** (Geiselman & Fisher, 1985). The cognitive interview is based on principles derived from cognitive psychology about how information is organized and the types of retrieval cues that can work to prime recall. It seems that the unflappable Sargeant Friday from the old television show "Dragnet" was wrong when he asked for, "just the facts, ma'am." The accuracy and completeness of recall is improved by elaboration, especially about objects and activities that occurred near the crime in time or space. Geiselman and Fisher (1985) have found that recall for events can be enhanced by using the following strategies:

1. Start by recalling ordinary events that occurred before the target event (i.e., the crime). Visualize the circumstances. Think about layout of the room, weather, traffic flow, or any other aspect of the scene. Think about your mood at the time.

2. Be as complete as possible in your recall. Don't edit your report or exclude something because you think that it might not be important.

3. Recall the event in both forward and backward order, or start from the middle and recall both forward and backward in time from some central incident.

4. Change your perspective. Try to recall the event as though you were some other person such as a spectator (real or imaginary) or the perpetrator of a crime.

There are additional techniques that can be useful for recall of specific types of information. If you are trying to remember the physical appearance of someone, does someone else whom you know come to mind? Why? In what ways are they similar? If you can't recall a name, recite the alphabet to see if a particular letter can "jog" your memory. Sometimes, partial information, like the number of syllables in a name, can be recalled. If numbers are involved (e.g., a license plate), try to recall the number of digits or some physical characteristic of the digits, like their size or color.

The techniques of the cognitive interview can be used anytime you need to remember an event. For example, suppose that there has been a recent rash of burglaries in your neighborhood. Suppose further that you hid a valuable piece of jewelry as a deterrent to theft, but you later realize that you can't remember where you hid it. Or, more commonly, suppose you can't remember where you left your car keys. This can be a very frustrating type of forgetting. In this case, you would try to retrace your steps and try to recall the last time you used them. Systematic and deliberate use of these techniques should be helpful in recall.

BIASES IN MEMORY

All of the mnemonics, or strategies for remembering, presented thus far in this chapter have been concerned with the deliberate use of memory strategies. Much of what we remember was acquired incidentally, that is without the use of a conscious, deliberate scheme. If you go to the movies, you can later recall the plot and the actors as well the name of the theater you were sitting in, without deliberately creating images or using rhymes. It's fortunate that we don't always have to work at remembering.

Unfortunately, our memories are subject to certain biases. All items stored in memory are not equally likely to be recalled. One type of bias that was already discussed is the effect of stereotypes. Stereotypes alter memory in predictable ways. The influence of stereotypes is just one instance of a more general bias to remember more easily information that confirms our hypotheses than information that contradicts them (Beyth-Marom, Dekel, Gombo, & Shaked, 1985). We also know that there is a recall advantage to information that is well known, familiar, prominent (generally important or personal), recent, vivid, and dramatic.

I return to biases in memory several times throughout this book. You can take advantage of these operating principles of memory in two ways. First, you could use them to improve memory by considering information that you want to remember and making it familiar, prominent, and so on. Second, and more important, you can be aware of the ways your memory is likely to be biased and deliberately attempt to debias your recollections. Ask yourself questions like, "What is the evidence for a less favored view" or, "Is there less dramatic support for the other side of a controversy?"

APPLYING THE FRAMEWORK

A general framework for thinking was presented in chapter 1. Let's see how we can apply it to the topic of memory.

1. *What is the goal?* At least three different types of thinking goals involve memory. The first is how to acquire (learn) something so that it can more readily be recalled at a later time. This is an **encoding (or acquisition) goal.** A second type is a **retrieval goal,** in which the desired outcome is recall of some item that was previously stored. Finally, there is a **debiasing goal.** This involves examining your recall for evidence of bias so that you can correct for it.

The first step in applying the framework is to determine what the appropriate goal is for a given situation.

2. *What is known?* This is a question about where you're starting from. Is there a list of foreign vocabulary words sitting in front of you that you have to learn? Can you remember seeing your wallet this morning, but can't remember what you did with it after that? Can you remember most of the battles fought in Europe during the 19th century, but can't get the order straight? Different skills would be used in each of these situations. By paying careful attention to what is known or given, you can use this information as a guide for selecting the appropriate skill for each situation.

3. *Which thinking skill or skills will get you to your goal?* Several different strategies to improve memory were presented in this chapter. You have to select among them for one that is most likely to help you attain your goal. The selection is based the nature of the goal, what is known, and how much effort you are willing to put into goal attainment. For example, if your goal is to remember the names of the people you meet during a business meeting or during the course of interviewing with many different people, you would select Harry Lorayne's imaging technique for associating names and faces. Formulas in chemistry and math can be learned with the phonetic alphabet system. You could use the method of places for subject areas like history and social sciences, where knowing the correct sequence of events is crucial to understanding them.

The following memory skills were presented in this chapter. Review each skill and be sure that you understand how to use each one.

- monitoring your attention
- developing an awareness of the influence of stereotypes and other beliefs on what we remember
- making abstract information meaningful as an aid to comprehension and recall
- using advance organizers to anticipate new information
- organizing information so that it can be recalled more easily
- generating retrieval cues at both acquisition and retrieval
- using emotional states as one type of retrieval cue
- monitoring how well you are learning
- using external memory aids
- employing keywords and images, rhymes, places, first letters, and narrative stories as internal memory aids
- applying the cognitive interview techniques
- developing an awareness of biases in memory

4. *Have you reached your goal?* Suppose that you selected the keyword mnemonic for foreign language learning to learn a list of technical terms in a course in physics. You go through the list, generate familiar English words that sound like the ones you're trying to learn, and so on. (You cleverly adapted the technique for use with words that may as well be from a foreign language as far as you're concerned.) The effort doesn't stop there. Go over the list "cold" (without your notes and with their definitions covered). Do you know the words? If not, go through the technique as many times as needed to pass this

quality assurance test. As mentioned in chapter 1, parts of this framework may have to be reiterated. You may need to select a different mnemonic if the first one isn't getting you to your goal. Try singing the words and their definitions. Use them in a narrative story in which you can utilize context to clarify meaning. This step calls for careful monitoring of progress, persistence, and flexibility until you find a strategy that works.

CHAPTER SUMMARY

1. Memory was described as the mediator of cognitive processes, because all of our thoughts depend on the ability to use what we have stored in memory.

2. The human information processing approach uses a computer analogy to understand human memory.

3. Like a computer, people acquire, retain, and retrieve information.

4. It is important to attend to information that you want to learn.

5. Our memories are not perfect true "copies" of events that have occurred. Prior knowledge, subsequent knowledge, stereotypes, and meaningfulness of the material all influence what will be remembered.

6. Memory can be improved with appropriate retrieval cues and good organization.

7. Emotions like anxiety and stress can either improve memory because of periodic review or hinder memory because of the distractions they provide.

8. Mnemonics improve recall because they utilize the basic memory principles of attention, organization, meaningfulness, and chunking. The mnemonics presented were keywords and images, rhymes, method of places, narrative stories, and first letters. (Remember: *K*ind *R*ound *M*en *N*ever *S*ing *L*yrics.)

9. Memory for events can be improved with the cognitive interview technique.

10. Our memories are biased in predictable ways. Examine recall for the possible influence of biases related to confirmation of a favored hypothesis, or for information characteristics such as being well known, familiar, prominent, recent, vivid, and/or dramatic.

Terms to Know

You should be able to define or describe the following terms and concepts. If you find that you're having difficulty with any term, be sure to reread the section in which it is discussed.

Hypothetical Constructs. Terms like "learning," "memory," and "perception" that are used as labels for the theoretical processes that underlie human thought and behavior.

Human Information Processing (HIP). A model of human thinking that uses the flow of information through a computer as an analogy of human thought. Like a computer, we take in information from the environment (input), process the information, and then output information.

Model. An "as if" statement. Models of human thought processes are used to help psychologists understand how the mind works.

Acquisition. Used to describe learning in the human information processing model. Also known as *encoding*, or putting information into memory.

Retention Interval. The time interval between the acquisition of new information (learning) and its retrieval.

Retrieval. The act of recalling or remembering information that had been previously acquired (learned).

Cocktail Party Effect. Information that is being attended to will be remembered, whereas information that is not being attended to will be forgotten or never learned. Phenomenon is named for the way people switch their attention among different simultaneous conversations at large parties.

Dichotic Listening. A laboratory procedure that is used to study attention. Individuals wear headphones with different messages coming into each ear. They are asked to attend to only one message and are tested for their memory of the unattended message.

Short-Term Memory. Refers to the limited capacity memory system that "stores" memories that last up to approximately one minute. Also called *working memory*. Compare with long-term memory.

Long-Term Memory. The memory system that retains information over long retention intervals—perhaps as long as a lifetime. Compare with short-term memory.

Gist. The interpretation or meaning of a message.

Chunking. A memory process in which a number of related items are stored and retrieved as a unit in order to facilitate memory.

Interference Theory of Forgetting. A theory of how we forget that attributes forgetting to "interference" or displacement of the to-be-remembered items by other material that has been previously or subsequently learned.

Periodic Review. Memories for highly emotional events are often retrieved and retold many times. The frequent retrieval of these memories can alter how they are remembered.

Psychoanalysis. Refers to Sigmund Freud's theory of psychology and to the form of psychotherapy he developed.

Repression. According to Freudian theory, the inability to recall traumatic events is mediated by an unconscious process that won't allow the memory to become conscious because it would overwhelm the individual.

State-Dependent Memory. The ability to recall certain events is facilitated when individuals are in a mood or drug state at recall that is similar to the one they were in at acquisition.

Metamemory. A person's knowledge about his or her own memory system; for example, knowing that you have to repeat a series of digits in order to maintain them in memory.

Mnemonics. Memory aids or techniques that are utilized to improve memory.

External Memory Aids. The deliberate use of lists, timers, calendars, and similar devices to remind an individual to do something.

Internal Memory Aids. Mnemonic devices or memory aids that rely on plans or strategies to make retrieval easier and more likely.

Keywords. A mnemonic device or memory aid in which a previously learned list of words or rhymes serve as associates or "hooks" for the to-be-remembered items.

Phonetic System. A mnemonic device in which a consonant sound is associated with a digit. When a string of numbers is to be remembered, it is converted into a meaningful word using the associated consonants and supplying vowels as needed.

Method of Places. (Also known as method of loci.) A mnemonic device or memory aid in which a familiar route is selected, and the to-be-remembered items are imaged at intervals along the route. At recall, the individual "mentally traverses" the route to retrieve the items.

First-Letter Mnemonics. A mnemonic device or memory aid in which the first letters of each word to be learned are combined into a single word.

Narrative Stories. A mnemonic device or memory aid in which the words to be remembered are incorporated in a meaningful story.

Cognitive Interview. A technique for recalling events that uses principles of cognitive psychology to guide the retrieval process.

Chapter Questions

Be sure that you can answer the following questions:

1. Why should a book on critical thinking skills begin with a chapter on memory?

2. What is the relationship between learning and memory? (You should have expected this question.)

3. Why are learning and memory called hypothetical constructs?

4. The human information processing model is predicated on the idea that people and computers are similar in many important ways. What are the similarities? What are some important differences between humans and computers that weaken the model?

5. Name and explain some basic properties of attention. Why is it an important concept in memory?

6. Two different types of memory were discussed in your text. Name and briefly describe each. Be sure to give the appropriate retention interval for each type of memory.

7. How can stereotypes and prejudices influence what we remember? Describe an experimental study that supports this view.

8. What does it mean to say, "memory is malleable."

9. There are several ways that emotions can affect memory. How can they improve memory? How can they diminish it?

10. What were the results of the research that tested servicemen's memory for emergency information under extremely stressful conditions? Why is it important to know this?

11. How can the concept of state-dependent memory be used to explain why some events that normally aren't available can be recalled during psychotherapy?

12. How can the development of a good metamemory improve your academic performance?

13. How do mnemonic devices work? List and describe five different types of mnemonics.

14. Which cognitive principles are used in the cognitive interview? Describe a situation in which this technique would be useful.

Exercises

Try out the memory skills you've learned in this chapter.

1. If you are currently learning a second language, use the keyword technique for second language learning (Atkinson, 1975) to learn your foreign vocabulary for the next month. You may find that it's fun to change the way you usually study, and you should be able to improve your memory for the foreign language terms.

2. Learn the phonetic alphabet system and use it to remember the important numbers in your life. B. F. Anderson (1980) suggested that you use this system to astound your friends. The next time you're at a party, go around the room assigning different 4-digit numbers to each person there, and demonstrate that you can remember each person's number at the end of the evening or at any time in the future. You can do this by giving each person the 4-digit number that translates into her or his name. Thus, Katharine would be given the number 7142 (KTHRN in the phonetic number alphabet); Robert would be given 4941 (RBRT); and Charles would be given 6450 (CHRLS).

Use the phonetic system for the following numbers: 415-452-8766; 8297; 16-32-12.

3. Now that you understand the importance of attention for memory and thought, try to become aware of the times when your attention wanders from a task. With some effort, you can learn to pay attention. You may be surprised at all that you've missed. The next time you take a walk, notice the colors of the flowers, the shades of raindrops, the expressions of children. Some believe that artists attend to these things that most of us miss.

4. Organize your notes so that topics that belong together are placed near each other. Divide your study material into units that can be studied in one block of time. Look for the structure in the material you're learning and interrelate the items so that you can "see the whole picture."

5. Go to your local courthouse and see part of a trial. (Traffic court works well for this purpose.) What are some possible memory biases in the testimony given by eyewitnesses?

6. Use the mnemonics described in this chapter to help you prepare for exams. Be sure that you understand the material you're learning.

7. There are many popular memory games. For example, one game involves planning for a trip. Each person tells what she or he will pack and must also remember what the previous players are packing. Use imagery so that for each item you can visualize it along with the person's face who named the item. You'll be sure to win first prize, unless someone else in the room is also using an imagery mnemonic.

8. Be aware of common notions of memory that are presented in books, on television, and in movies. Most show memory as a passive storage tank that can be accessed with the

appropriate tools. Few present the view that memory is dynamic and changes as the individual changes. Discuss these topics with friends and family to see what they think about memory.

9. Try to remember something that happened to you in your childhood and then compare that memory with the account given by a parent or older child you were with at that time. Compare the similarities and discrepancies in your memories. What are some principles that you've learned in this chapter that could account for the differences?

10. Learn how to generate your own retrieval cues. Loftus (1980) suggested that if you go the supermarket without a shopping list, you can remember what items are needed by going through categories such as dairy, spices, meats, and cleaning supplies. You can use categories as retrieval cues in a variety of situations. Did you ever have the frustrating experience of knowing that you have to call someone, but don't remember who? Try to recall by systematically going through categories—family, friends from school, employer, and so on.

11. For the following tasks, indicate the type of goal involved and one or more mnemonics that would be useful for the situation described:

a. studying for a physiology exam that involves learning Latin names for body parts

b. remembering where you left your car at the time you park it

c. remembering where you left your car hours later when you realize that you can't find it

d. considering all of the factors in deciding whether to spend Spring break in Florida with friends or with your kid sister in Saskatchewan

e. helping a friend remember a joyous childhood experience

f. learning the part for a lead role in a school play

g. learning a random list of digits in the order in which they were presented

h. learning the value of pi to 12 decimal places

i. recalling where you were on New Year's eve

12. Find a willing family member, friend, or classmate and help him or her remember what he or she was doing at exactly 5:00 p.m. last Monday.

SUGGESTED READINGS

There are several good books that discuss the memory phenomena presented here. I recommend Klatsky's (1980) *Human Memory: Structures and Processes (2nd ed.),* Baddeley's (1976) *The Psychology of Memory,* and Zechmeister and Nyberg's (1982) *Human Memory: An Introduction to Research and Theory* for easy-to-read, comprehensive reviews of most of these topics. You may also find the book *Memory: Surprising New Insights Into How We Remember and Why We Forget* by E. Loftus (1980) to be an interesting account of some of the more intriguing aspects of memory, but you should realize that it is not intended for a college audience; and you may find her treatment of some of the topics to be too simplistic. E. Loftus is also the author of several other excellent texts in this area of memory. If your interest was piqued by the section on eyewitness testimony, then I suggest that you read her 1979 book entitled *Eyewitness Testimony,* which is a pleasant meld of memory theory, research, and law.

A classic leading text in the area of *Human Information Processing* is one by that name

(2nd ed., 1977) by Lindsay and Norman. Even though it is over a decade old, it can still serve as a fascinating introduction to this field. It was written with a student audience in mind.

There are several good accounts of mnemonic devices. A collection of articles with extensive commentary on this and related topics was compiled by Norman in *Memory and Attention: An Introduction to Human Information Processing* (2nd ed., 1976). As the title implies, it also contains a section on attention, which deals largely with theories and models of attention. A detailed and influential study of mnemonics was published by a Russian, Luria. His book, *The Mind of a Mnemonist* (1968) provided an indepth account of a man with a "supernormal" memory. McDaniel and Pressley (1987) have edited a recent collection of papers in their book entitled, *Imagery and Related Mnemonic Processes*.

The mnemonist Harry Lorayne has written two books that have also been popular in this area. They are *The Memory Book* (1974) by Lorayne and Lucus and *Remembering People* (1975) by Lorayne. An interesting account of some research on the method of places and other memory phenomena is presented by Crovitz in *Galton's Walk: Methods for the Analysis of Thinking, Intelligence and Creativity* (1970).

If you're interested in memory for everyday events, then you'll want to consult Neisser's (1982) edited volume *Memory Observed,* Gruneberg and Morris' (1979) edited volume *Applied Problems in Memory,* and Seamon's (1980) *Human Memory: Contemporary Readings.*

A recent update on the fascinating area of mood and memory can be found in Bower's (1987) article, "Commentary on mood and memory." Beyth-Marom, Dekel, Gombo, and Shaked (1985) provided numerous examples of the way memory can bias decisions in a book they wrote for Israeli teenagers to help them learn how to make sound judgments, *An Elementary Approach to Thinking Under Uncertainty.*

3   The Relationship Between Thought and Language

Contents

There is an old story about three umpires that goes something like this:

> Three umpires were unwinding at a local pub after a very tough day. All three had endured abusive shouts like, "Kill the Umpire" and had had numerous offers for new pairs of eyeglasses. After a few mugs of brew, they began discussing how they decide to call balls and strikes. The first umpire, Jim, explained that it was really quite simple. "I simply call them as I see them."
>
> Donnie, the second umpire, disagreed when he said, "I see them as I call them."
>
> Neil, the third umpire emphatically shook his head in disagreement with the other two. "You're both wrong," he said, slurring his words somewhat. "They don't even exist until I call them."

Neil had a good point. Whether a ball whizzing past home plate is a ball or strike depends on what the umpire labels it. The words he uses both interpret and define reality.

THOUGHT AND LANGUAGE

How do you express your thoughts in words and sentences? How influenced are you by your particular language? You will have difficulty answering these questions, because you use both so automatically and because you have conscious awareness of the way your thoughts give rise to the words you use to express them. In fact, if you try to monitor your speaking process, you'll find yourself stuttering and interfering with the fluid speech that you normally create so easily. It's as though speech emerges automatically and preformed. Conscious attention directed at the process tends to interfere with it.

Psycholinguistics

> *Communication is primarily an exercise in thinking.*
> —Pitt and Leavenworth (1968, p. viii)

Psycholinguistics is the field of psychology that is concerned with how we acquire and use language. Language is a complex cognitive activity that all normal humans perform with skill and apparent ease. As speakers, we select the words we want to use and produce them in a grammatically correct form. As listeners, we use the information in another's utterance in order to share the expressed thoughts. What do we know about the way speakers and listeners share thoughts through the medium of language?

Underlying Representation and Surface Structure

> *Language appears to be simply the clothing of naked thought.*
> —Miller (1972, p. 43)

The comprehension of language is a process in which the message is used to construct a representation of the information referred to in the message (Resnick, 1985). The sequence of sounds that we produce must correspond to our intended meaning if we are to communicate successfully. The "sender" and the "receiver" also must share a common knowledge of word meanings and grammar.

Because language is always incomplete, the receiver must rely on prior knowledge, context, and other cues to comprehension in order to construct a correct representation.

Psychologists who are concerned with the way people use and understand language divide language into two structures, or types of representations. The **underlying representation** of language refers to the meaning component of language—it's the thought you want to convey. **Surface structure** refers to the sounds of the verbal expression that you use. The problem in producing language is deriving surface structure from the underlying representation, whereas the problem in comprehending language is getting from the surface structure back to the speaker's (or writer's) underlying representation.

A communication is "successful" when the underlying representation constructed by the receiver matches the underlying representation of the sender. The receiver's representation of the meaning is constructed over time, because language is a sequential process with words uttered or read one after the other. All strategies for improving comprehension involve ways of building representations so that they will most nearly match the one intended by the sender. It is the representation of knowledge about the world, the "architecture of the cognitive system," (Bower & Cirilo, 1985) that mediates comprehension.

When language is ambiguous, the surface structure can have more than one meaning or underlying representation. Some examples of ambiguous sentences are:

- Visiting professors can be boring. (This can be interpreted to mean either that it is boring to visit the homes of professors or that it is boring when professors visit campus.)

- They are kissing fish. (This can be interpreted to mean either that they are a variety of fish called "kissing fish," or that they are a variety of fish who kiss, or that at least two people have their mouths in the fish bowl and are engaging in the somewhat kinky behavior of kissing fish.)

- He cooks carrots and peas in the same pot. (I won't explain the two possible interpretations.)

Each of these sentences is ambiguous, because there is a single surface structure (the sound of the sentence) and at least two possible underlying representations or interpretations. Clear communications are unambiguous. With only a little effort, an ambiguous statement can be made clear so that it corresponds to only one underlying representation. For example, the first sentence can be made unambiguous with simple changes:

It is boring to visit professors.
or
Visiting professors are boring.

Analogy and Metaphor

Midway between the unintelligible and the commonplace, it is metaphor which most produces knowledge.

—Aristotle (Rhetoric III, 1410b)

One exception to the rule that the words used to convey a message should correspond to their intended meaning is the use of analogy and metaphor. (The English grammatical distinction among analogy, metaphor, and simile is not considered here, because it is irrelevant in this context.) If I tell you that "Myrtle is a hard headed woman," the literal translation is not the one intended. In this case, the receiver must use his or her knowledge about the referent topic (hard surfaces) and "map" the relevant knowledge onto his or her knowledge of Myrtle. Although you certainly have never met Myrtle, and you may never have heard the expression "a hardheaded woman," you can probably tell me that she is a stubborn, strong-willed person. You came to this understanding by taking your knowledge of hard surfaces, selecting characteristics of hard surfaces that might be relevant to a description of a person, and transferring that knowledge to what you already know about Myrtle.

Analogies are pervasive in human thought. Whenever we are faced with a novel situation, we seek to understand it by reference to a known familiar one. When we think by analogy, we map the underlying structure of a known topic onto the target or unknown topic. This mental process is known as "structure mapping" (Gentner & Gentner, 1983). Structure mapping assumes network-like representations of concepts in memory in which underlying structural relationships and surface attributes (physical characteristics) are coded along with each concept. For example, when we read that an atom is like a miniature solar system, the implication is that the solar system and the atom have similar relationships among their component parts—smaller bodies revolving around a larger one in fixed path patterns. Surface similarity (e.g., the sun is hot and large and contains burning gases) is not implied.

All analogies and metaphors state that two concepts are alike in some way. Good analogies have similar underlying structures even when the topics are highly dissimilar. They maintain much of their underlying structure in the transfer from base (known) to target (unknown) domains; surface features are of minimal importance. Poor analogies are ones in which only surface or superficial characteristics are similar. If I said that Myrtle is like milk because they both start with the letter *m*, this would be a very poor analogy. Whenever you encounter an analogy, you need to consider the nature of the similarity relationship. Are the two concepts similar in their underlying structure so that relevant information about one concept can be mapped onto the other concept, or is the similarity superficial or trivial?

We frequently use analogies to persuade someone that *X* is analogous to *Y*, therefore what is true for *X* is also true for *Y*. A good example of this sort of "reasoning by analogy" was presented by Bransford, Arbitman-Smith, Stein, and Vye (1985). They told about a legal trial that was described in the book, *Till Death Us Do Part* (Bugliosi, 1978). Much of the evidence presented at the trial was circumstantial. The attorney for the defense argued that the evidence was like a chain and, like a chain, it was only as strong as its weakest link. He went on to argue that there were several weak links in the evidence; therefore, the jurors should not convict the accused. The prosecutor also used an analogy to make his point. He argued that the evidence was like a rope made off many independent strands. Several strands can be weak and break, and you will still have a strong rope. Similarly, even though some of the evidence was weak, there was still enough strong evidence to convict the accused. (The prosecutor won.)

Can you see how the use of analogies can guide how we think? In the trial example, different sorts of outcomes depend on which of the analogies you found more compelling. Let's consider an easier example. At a meeting of county administrators, several people who were receiving welfare argued that there should be welfare recipients on the county board. They argued that welfare recipients were in the best position to understand the problems of life on welfare. One of the board members said that that was an absurd proposition. He argued that having welfare recipients on the county board was like putting residents of an insane asylum on the committee that makes the rules for the asylum. What do you think of this analogy? In what ways are people on welfare like the residents of an insane asylum? How are they different? Are they different in ways that makes the board member's conclusions invalid? The insane are unable to think rationally, by definition. This is not true for the poor. I don't believe that this was a good analogy, and I would not have been persuaded by it.

In addition to being powerful persuasive devices, analogies have also been found to be useful tools in the comprehension and recall of scientific passages (Halpern, 1987a; Hansen & Halpern, 1987). When students read technical passages that contained good analogies to familiar topics, they scored higher on tests of comprehension and recall than a control group of students that read the same passage without the analogy. Analogies are useful thinking strategies in many different contexts. The deliberate use of analogies as an aid to solving problems and enhancing creativity is discussed in later chapters.

WORDS AND THEIR MEANINGS

Language: Tool or Master of Thought?

> *Learn a new language and get a new soul.*
> —Czech proverb

We use language not only to convey our thoughts, but also to mold and shape them. Language and thought are inextricably related concepts that exert mutual influences on each other. Some psychologists believe that language, at least in part, influences thought. The hypothesis that the language we use affects how we think is called the **Sapir-Whorf hypothesis of linguistic relativity** or, more informally, the Sapir-Whorf hypothesis (Sapir, 1960; Whorf, 1956).

"How do I know what I mean until I see what I say?" (Miller, 1972, p. 43). In a humorous way, this question examines the relationship between thought and language. Although it seems clear to most people that our thoughts influence the language that we use, it is sometimes more difficult to understand the reciprocal nature of the relationship. Anthropologists and psychologists have studied whether people who speak different languages also think somewhat differently. Perhaps you have had the experience of translating a passage from one language to another and had difficulty conveying exactly the same meaning. Jokes are a good example of this. Ethnic jokes that are told in their native language frequently lose their humor when they are told in translation. Could this indicate that ways of thinking, as reflected in language, differ across cultures?

Some chilling implications of the Sapir-Whorf hypothesis appeared in George Orwell's (1949) classic book, *1984.* In *1984,* he wrote about a repressive society

Senior Citizen   Old Man   Golden Ager

FIG. 3.1.   The words we use influence how we think. Compare the different thoughts that are evoked by the terms "senior citizen," "old man," and "golden ager."

that was able to control the thoughts of its citizenry by redefining some words and removing others from the language. By gaining control of the language, this futuristic society dictated which thoughts were possible and which were not.

The Orwellian example is an extreme interpretation of the Sapir-Whorf hypothesis that language absolutely determines thought. According to this view, if a term does not exist within a language, speakers do not have the corresponding thought. Do you believe that if the word "love" didn't exist in our language, then people wouldn't be able to feel this emotion? Most people would disagree with the strong form of the Sapir-Whorf hypothesis. Cross-cultural research that has examined the way different languages influence thought has not supported the strong version of the Sapir-Whorf hypothesis (Berlin & Kay, 1969; Rosch, 1977). A weaker version of the Sapir-Whorf hypothesis is that language influences, but does not determine, thinking. As an example of this, consider the following terms carefully and decide if each evokes a somewhat different thought: senior citizen; old man; golden-ager. Did each term connote a different thought? Did you think about a different type of person with each word? Most people agree that they did. (See Fig. 3.1.)

The Direction and Misdirection of Thought

All words are pegs to hang ideas on.
—Henry Ward Beecher (1812–1887) *Proverbs from Plymouth Pulpit*

Emotional Language, Labeling, and Name Calling

The same event can be described in several different ways. Yet, the words we use to describe an event are not interchangeable in the meaning they convey. Language that is highly emotional has a different effect on readers and listeners than more mundane ways of conveying the intended meaning. This is the weaker version of the Sapir-Whorf hypothesis: although language may not *determine* thought, it directs—and sometimes misdirects—it. Consider the heated debate between those who are for and those who are against abortion. The faction opposed to abortion realized that it is better to be for something than against something and therefore decided to call their stance "pro-life." On the other side, those who favored abortion certainly didn't want to be called "anti-life" and decided to label their stance "pro-choice." They hoped that people would think differently about a position that is "pro-choice" than they would about one that is "anti-life." Of course, the position hasn't changed—only its label, or name, has changed, but presumably, the way the position is labeled influences how people think about it. One "pro-lifer" told a colleague that the best way to win a debate on this topic is to use frequently the words "kill" and "baby" in the same sentence (Kahane, 1980). The juxtaposition of these two words is sure to bring about an emotional response.

Another example of the deliberate choice of words to create a carefully planned impression concerns the "rewriting" of history. All history texts (indeed, everything) were written by someone with a particular point of view. Recently, the word "aggression" was taken out of Japanese history books that described World War II invasions. Do the same descriptions of an act seem "better" in some sense when they are not modified by the word "aggressive?" The contemporary Japanese historians who asked for this deletion apparently think so. It is clear that emotionally laden words influence how people think.

Copi (1986) described a 1948 study (Chase) in which people were asked if they agreed or disagreed with several different statements. Consider your own response to the following two statements about the appropriate role of a news reporter in delivering the news: "Some people say it is better to explain our point of view as well as give the news." Agree or Disagree? "Some people say it is better to include some propaganda as well as give the news." Agree or Disagree? When subjects read the first statement, 42.8% agreed with it. As you can probably guess, many fewer agreed with the second statement (25.7%). The difference between the two statements was in the exchange of the term "propaganda" for "give their own views." "Propaganda" is an emotionally charged term. Its use in this sentence swayed how many people thought about the topic. (Propaganda is discussed in chapter 5, "Analyzing Arguments.")

When you want to influence how people think, choose your words carefully. You also need to be aware of the ways that others attempt to manipulate your thoughts by the labels they use. The deliberate use of words designed to create a particular attitude or foster certain beliefs is called **semantic slanting.** The meaning (semantics) is slanted so that the listener's thoughts will be directed in some way. It's fairly easy to find examples of this around election time when issues and groups label themselves with favorable terms and label others with negative terms (name calling). During a recent election, a group called "Citizens for Sane Laws" opposed a proposition, whereas another group called "Citizens for Better Government" favored it. The political advertisements continued to broadcast these group names and the message to vote "No on 10" or "Yes on 10," depending on who financed the advertisement. Very little meaningful information was ever given on the merits or problems of the proposition. Be wary of attempts to influence your thinking through the use of positive and negative labels, especially on the important issues that concern social and political policies.

Ambiguity, Vagueness, and Equivocation

The thinking process can also be misled when words are imprecise and/or misused. Words are ambiguous when they can have multiple meanings, depending on context, and the appropriate meaning is unclear in a given context. The problem here, as in the sentences described earlier, is one of determining the intended meaning or underlying representation. A good example of this was provided by von Oech (1983). According to von Oech, J. Edgar Hoover, the former director of the FBI, was reviewing a typed copy of a letter he had dictated to his secretary. He didn't like the margin widths she had used for the letter and wrote, ''Watch the borders'' on the letter and asked her to retype the letter and send copies to top FBI agents. For the next two weeks, FBI agents were put on special alert along the Canadian and Mexican borders.

Another humorous example of **ambiguity** was provided by Fogelin (1987). Compare the following two sentences:

Mary had a little lamb; it followed her to school.

Mary had a little lamb; and then a little broccoli.

The word ''had'' is ambiguous. It is used to mean ''owned'' in the first sentence and ''ate'' in the second sentence. Its meaning is not clarified until the second half of each sentence is read. A clever example of ambiguity can be found in the title of a popular book by Phyllis Chesler (1972), *Women and Madness*, in which she meant madness to mean both anger and insanity.

Whereas ambiguous words have multiple meanings; vague words have imprecise meanings. **Vagueness** refers to a lack of precision in a communication. If your friend Valerie told you to bake a cake in a hot oven, you'd probably ask her how hot it should be. In this context, the word ''hot'' is too vague and needs to be specified further. Similarly, if you were told that your blind date for tonight is overweight, you'd want to know how much overweight. A communication is vague if it does not specify enough details for its intended purpose.

There is legislation in California that requires that warning notices be posted in all places where the public may come in contact with cancer-causing chemicals. The sign that was designed for gas stations is shown in Fig. 3.2.

As you can see, the new signs are too vague to be of value. There is no information about the level of risk, or the likelihood of developing cancer, or how

FIG. 3.2.   An example of vagueness. California law requires that warning signs be posted in all places where consumers come in contact with cancer-causing chemicals. Signs like this one are being used at all gas stations. The information they convey is too vague to be meaningful.

Warning

Detectable amounts of chemicals known to the State of California to cause cancer, birth defects, or other reproductive harm may be found in and around this facility.

long you would have to be exposed to these chemicals to reach some level of risk. This is a clear example of a deliberately unclear communication. The gasoline companies were opposed to this law and have registered their complaint by posting the required signs but not providing the public with interpretable information.

The problem of vagueness is often one of borderline cases. For example, when does an *erotic* film become *pornographic,* or when does a *fetus* become a *baby?* The way we answer these questions has important consequences. Evaluative terms, like "successful," "rich," "difficult," "bad," "progress," and "late," are vague. At what point does someone become *rich* or *bald* or *old?* What do movie ads mean when they use vague terms like "acclaimed" and "hit"?

Vague expressions are often used to express degrees of belief. Examples of this include the terms *probably, maybe,* and *certainly.* Reliance on such vague expressions can lead to misunderstandings and bad decisions (Beyth-Marom et al., 1985).

Equivocation occurs when the meaning of a word is changed in the course of the same discussion. Consider the following "line of reasoning": (Reasoning is considered more fully in chapter 4.)

1. Man is the only rational animal.
2. No woman is a man.
3. Therefore, no woman is rational. (Damer, 1987).

The meaning of the word "man" changed from the first to the second sentence. In the first sentence, "man" stood for all of humanity—both female and male. In the second sentence, it was used as a sex-specific term, with females conveniently omitted. This is an example of equivocation.

Hedging

Hedging occurs when a statement is asserted with something less than complete certainty. A hedge is often an introductory phrase in a sentence or paragraph. If I started a statement with "It is arguable that . . . ," I would be hedging. Vague and imprecise terms for degree of belief, which were discussed in the previous section, are sometimes used as hedges. Suppose you meet with your stock broker. In telling you about some stock that she or he wants you to buy, your broker says, "It is likely that this stock will double in value within the next year." The use of "it is likely" protects her or his statement. Your broker can't guarantee that it will double or even increase in value; therefore, she or he needs to hedge when discussing the purchase. There is nothing inherently wrong with hedging. Almost all reports of research contain some hedge (e.g., "Most researchers agree''). Hedging becomes a problem when the receiver hears "it is likely that," but translates or utilizes the information as "it is definite that." A popular television commercial for a high-fiber cereal probably could win an award for "most hedging in one sentence." It goes something like this: "Research findings *suggest* that a high fiber diet *may* reduce the risk of *some* kinds of cancer." Now that's hedging.

Etymology, Definitions, and Reification

These three terms all concern word meaning. **Etymology** is the study of word origins. It's often interesting to learn how language evolved and developed. But, it is wrong to conclude that a word has a particular meaning or nuance based on the word from which it was derived. Consider, for example, the use of the word "gay" to refer to homosexual men. The word is commonly used today to denote pride and other positive attributes of male homosexuals. The origin of the word was quite different. The word "gay" was derived from a definition meaning "wanton and licentious." It would be wrong to conclude that gays are therefore wanton and licentious. Language is a living thing, and word definitions evolve and change. Returning to a word's origins to find its contemporary meaning is like studying the writings of Karl Marx to understand modern communism.

Although word meanings change, it is not true that a word can mean anything that you want it to. There is an advertisement in a large city newspaper for a plastic surgeon who "specializes in nose reduction, breast enlargement and reduction, liposuction, baggy eyes, weak chins, face lifts, and saddlebag thighs." This surgeon claims to do it all. How then, can he claim to be a "specialist?" The word is being misused to convey the idea that he has great depth of knowledge and experience in *all* aspects of plastic surgery. If he can perform many types of plastic surgery, he is a generalist. By definition, he can't specialize in everything.

Reification is a somewhat more difficult concept to explain. Reification occurs when something abstract is given a name and then treated as though it were a concrete object. An example should help here. Consider the Freudian notion of the "ego." According to Freudian theory, it is that portion of the personality that deals with reality. It is an abstract concept that was developed by Freud. Sometimes, therapists forget that it is an abstract concept and start treating it as though it were tangible. If a surgeon said he wanted to operate on your ego, you should run quickly from his office. The ego is not something that can be cut or physically altered, because it is an abstract concept, not a physical body part. This is an example of reification.

Bureaucratese and Euphemism

Two language barriers to comprehension are bureaucratese and euphemism. **Bureaucratese** is the use of formal, stilted language that is often unfamiliar to people who lack special training. The same information can be expressed better

jargon

with simpler terms. Bureaucratese is different from the use of precise technical terms that may be needed in specialized disciplines; in bureaucratese, the style and language hinders our understanding instead of aiding it. The legal profession is often guilty of bureaucratese. I once read a legal document that began with the term "Witnesseth." Of course, I questioned what meaning was being conveyed with the use of this term, which is standard on many legal forms. The answer was, "very little." It could have been deleted altogether or replaced with "Notice" or "Read this document," both of which would have been more meaningful than the obscure, "Witnesseth."

Euphemism is the substitution of a desirable term for a less desirable or offensive one. The result is often a loss of communication. Euphemism is common in hospital and medical facilities where bodily functions need to be discussed. Hospital personnel may ask a patient if he has "voided his bladder." Many patients do not realize that this refers to urination. In fact, it has been shown that a majority of patients do not understand the language that is commonly used in their interactions with medical staff. Many do not understand words like "malignant," "benign," "terminal," and "generic." Imagine a solemn physician telling a patient that she is "terminal," with the patient then brightly inquiring when she'll get better. It is easy to see how the use of euphemisms can lead to misunderstandings. Euphemisms abound in advertisements of all sorts. Do "bathroom tissue" and "feminine hygiene products" seem more desirable and glamorous than toilet paper and menstrual pads? Euphemisms often obscure the intended meaning. Although polite speech is a necessary rule of society, euphemistic terms that are not commonly used interfere with the communication of ideas, and thus should be avoided.

Framing With Leading Questions, Negation, and Marked Words

Framing occurs when a question is asked in a way that suggests what the correct response should be. The reader is "led" into assuming a particular perspective, or point of view. Consider the following problem (from Tversky & Kahneman, 1981):

> Imagine that the U.S. is preparing for the outbreak of an unusual disease, which is expected to kill 600 people. Two alternative programs to combat the disease have been proposed. Assume that the exact scientific estimate of the consequences of the programs are as follows:
>
> If Program A is adopted, 200 people will be saved.
> If Program B is adopted, there is ⅓ probability that 600 people will be saved, and ⅔ probability that no people will be saved. (p. 453)
>
> Which of the two programs would you favor?

Now consider the same problem, and select between the following two programs (Tversky & Kahneman, 1981):

If Program C is adopted, 400 people will die.
If Program D is adopted there is ⅓ probability that nobody will die, and ⅔ probability that 600 people will die.

Which of these two programs would you favor?

When this problem was presented to college students, 72% of those given the first set of choices selected Program A, whereas 78% of those given the second set of choices selected Program D. Look closely at the choices. Program A and C are effectively identical—they differ only in that A is described in terms of the numbers of lives saved, whereas C is described in terms of the number who will die. Program B and D are also identical, differing only in the language used to describe the outcomes. The percentage of people who prefer each alternative differs significantly, depending on the language used to describe each alternative. This is an important result, showing that human judgments and preferences can be readily manipulated by changes in the way questions are asked or framed. If I tell you that a new medical treatment has a 50% success rate you will be more likely to endorse its use than if I tell you that it has a 50% failure rate. The only difference is whether the information was presented in a positive (success rate) frame or a negative (failure rate) frame (Halpern & Blackman, 1985; Halpern, Blackman, & Salzman, in press).

Another example of the influence of language on thought comes from a study by Loftus (1975). Forty people were asked questions about their headaches. A key question was posed in one of two ways: "Do you get headaches frequently, and, if so, how often?" or "Do you get headaches occasionally, and, if so, how often?" (p. 561).

Can you anticipate the results of this study? The respondents who answered the first question reported an average of 2.2 headaches per week, whereas those who answered the second question reported an average of .7 headaches per week. It seems that if people are asked questions with the word "frequently," they will believe that they have experienced more headaches than if they are asked the same question with the word "occasionally." Note that, although this example does not seem to contain any deliberate attempts to mislead or direct respondents' answers, the changes in wording have accomplished exactly that end. Pay careful attention to the way that questions are posed. Always consider if slight changes in the language used would result in different responses.

"When did you stop beating your wife?" There is another example of a framed, or leading question, because the assumption that you beat your wife is inherent in it. Salespeople know that leading questions can be good for business. If I were showing you some household items, a good sales technique would be to ask, "How many will you take?" The assumption here is that the sale is made, and it is only a matter of how many you will buy, not whether you will or will not buy.

Advertisers and merchants like to price their wares in uneven amounts, like $19.99 and $24.95. Have you ever wondered why they don't simplify matters and price garments to the nearest dollar so that $19.99 would be labeled $20.00 and $24.95 would become $25.00? They believe that consumers will think that $19.99 is considerably less than $20.00. The frame, or perspective, being induced here is one of considering the price as "less than $20.00." Of course, the one cent difference is negligible, but it does seem to change how people think about the price.

Another way of leading listeners to a particular outcome is with the use of **marked words.** A word is marked when it is the less commonly used end of some continuum. Again, an example should help to clarify this concept. If I want to know about someone's height, I would ask, "How tall is he?" Would you think it was odd if I asked, "How short is he?" Short is the marked end of a height continuum ranging from short to tall. If I asked how short someone is, you would assume that I was expecting an answer that was near the short end, whereas no such bias would be present if I asked how tall someone is. Similarly, if I asked how old someone is, there would be no bias. If I asked how young someone is, you'd believe that I was expecting a response that was relatively young. In this example, young is the marked, or less commonly used, end of an age continuum.

Listeners can also be framed or misled with **negation.** Suppose you read that a prominent politician is not a drunk. Suppose further that this is absolutely true; he or she is not a drunk. Most people would infer that there was some question about his or her sobriety and the truth of the assertion. The pragmatic function of negation is to deny something that is plausible (Carroll, 1986). Thus, listeners will infer the plausibility of that which was denied. Richard Nixon hadn't considered this psycholinguistic principle when he uttered the now famous words, "I am not a crook." Most people took this to mean that it is plausible that he is a crook.

A sentence with two negations, known as **double negation,** is usually a difficult way of communicating a positive. Think about the following two sentences:

It's not true that he didn't steal the wallet.

He stole the wallet.

Although both sentences have the same meaning, in that they both communicate affirmative information about someone's guilt, they are not identical in their effect on the listener. The first is more obviously a protest against some statement that he didn't steal the wallet. Statements containing negation are also, in general, more difficult to comprehend. This aspect of negation is discussed in chapter 4, "Reasoning."

COMPREHENSION: THE REASON FOR LANGUAGE

Language is the first medium of the rational mind.
—Ferguson (1981, p. 120)

A student once told me that, although she really wanted to understand the material in her textbook, she found that the information "went in one eye and out the other." In other words, it "didn't stick" or seem to involve her brain at all. She was unable to understand or remember the material. We can all sympathize with her, because we've all had this experience at one time or another. Comprehension failure often result from the language used to express an idea and not from the difficulty of the idea itself. Good teachers know how to communicate complex ideas so that they can be easily understood, whereas poor teachers could talk or write for days without conveying the ideas to their students. The purpose of language is communication of ideas. The goal is to transfer the thoughts that reside in the mind of the speaker or writer to that of the listener or reader. Language is the vehicle or mode for the transfer of ideas. Comprehension occurs when the listener arrives at the intended meaning. Comprehension is the goal of communication; the reason for language. We've all heard the familiar complaint "Nobody understands me," representing an obvious failure in communication. Either the speaker didn't make himself or herself clear or the listener was insufficiently sensitive to the meaning in the message or, somewhere along the transmission route, the message went astray, much like excessive static over telephone wires. The next section is concerned with the ways that meaningful information can be clearly transmitted.

Rules for Clear Communication

"When I use a word," Humpty Dumpty said, in a rather scornful tone, "it means just what I choose it to mean—neither more or less."

"The question is," said Alice, "whether you can make words mean so many different things."

"The question is," said Humpty Dumpty, "which is to be master—that's all."

—Lewis Carroll
Through the Looking Glass

In order to communicate effectively, you need to know a great many things: What is the purpose of the communication? What are your listener's characteristics? That is, what is your listener's age and social status? How much does the listener know or want to know about the topic? The answers to all of these questions shape the nature of communication. Without giving much thought to

101

them, we implicitly change the way we speak or write, depending on how we answer these questions. Communication is governed by rules that we all obey, although you may never have consciously considered them.

Rule 1: Tell Listeners What You Believe They Want to Know

Consider how you would answer a simple question like, "Where do you live?" If I met you in Europe and asked you this question, you would probably respond, "In the United States." If I asked you this question in New York, you would respond with the name of a state, like, "In Pennsylvania." If I asked you the same question on your college campus, you might respond, "In the dorms." If I asked you this question while we were in the dorms, you might respond, "In Wing D, Room 331." The same question could be asked each time, yet you would give a different answer that depended on the context of the question and what you thought I wanted to know. The level of information you choose to convey depends on the purpose of the communication.

Rule 2: Don't Tell Listeners What They Already Know

In the first chapter, I began by introducing the topic of thinking and the need for the development of critical thinking skills. You probably did not think that this was unusual. Suppose I started every chapter in this book the same way. You would not only think that this was unusual, you would also question my mental status.

When you present information to an audience, you balance the amount of new information that you present with the old or already known information. If you present too much new information at once, listeners will be lost and will not be able to extract the intended meaning; if you present too much old or known information, listeners will be bored. The relative proportion of old information to new information is known as the **given/new distinction** (Clark & Haviland, 1977). The ratio of given, of known, information to new information is a determinant of the difficulty of a communication. If a passage (spoken or written) contains too much new material for a listener or reader, it will be difficult to comprehend. No one would take an advanced course in biochemistry without first obtaining the requisite background in biology and chemistry. The educational process, if successful, fosters the transformation of new information into the students' systems of known information.

Rule 3: Vary the Style of Your Communication, Depending on the Knowledge, Age, and Status of the Listeners

Suppose you are an expert computer programmer that has been given the task of describing the operations of a computer center to a group of visitors. You would vary the way you convey the necessary information for each of the following: a group of politicians; a third-grade class from an elementary school; your history professor, a close friend, or an expert programmer from another university.

Your communication would be more or less technical, depending on what you believe your listener knows about the topic. You might tell the politicians about the high costs of maintaining a computer center; the third-grade class might simply be told about the general use of computers; you might explain to your history professor how computers can be used in research; your close friend might be told that you feel you're being underpaid; and the visiting programmer might be told about the capacity of the computers and the steps you've taken to prevent the spread of computer "viruses."

The readability of text (or ease with which spoken language is understood) depends, in large part, on the match between the text and the reader. The reason so many of us find income tax and legal documents so difficult is that they are written by and for accountants and lawyers—people with highly differentiated underlying representations of the topics referred to in these documents. The rest of us have to make many more inferences and a greater number of memory searches to understand the concepts because our underlying representations of these concepts are relatively sparse. This is why, whenever we're engaged in communication, it is important to consider the characteristics of the reader or listener. This is a more formal way of saying that the beliefs, knowledge, and expectations of the intended audience for a communication should determine how much detail goes into a communication and which words are used. The difficulty of a text does not reside in the text itself, but in the reader–text interaction.

Rule 4: Tell the Truth

When we communicate with each other, it is assumed that the information being conveyed is truthful. This is an imperative for meaningful communication. Of course, sometimes, people lie. How do you process information when you believe that the speaker is lying? All components of the communication are scrutinized. In general, the communication process breaks down when the listener suspects that the speaker is violating this rule.

Rule 5: Use a Simple, Straightforward Style

Mark Twain said this best when he said, "Eschew surplusage." Information is transmitted best when simple and precise language is used. Some people think that use of multisyllabic words and intricate sentence structures is a sign of intelligence. This is not true. It is a far more difficult task to express complex thoughts in simple language than to express simple thoughts in complex language. The transformation of our private thoughts into easily understood language is the benchmark of human cognition.

Rule 6: Utilize Manner and Context to Clarify Meaning

Meaning depends not only on the words that we use, but also on the context and the manner we use to convey it. Have you ever tried to explain to someone why it is funny when Steve Martin says, "excu-u-u-se me?" The humor is not in the words themselves, but in the way he says them. We often rely on intonation, hesitations, and nonverbal behaviors to clarify intended meanings. Often, these secondary clues will negate a verbal expression. Have you ever had the experience of having someone say, "I'll be happy to do that for you" in a manner that clearly showed that she or he was most unhappy?

Context is a critical aid for comprehension. "The food is on the table" can be an invitation to eat or a simple descriptive statement, depending on the context. Context is also used to decide which of two possible meanings is the intended meaning for ambiguous sentences. The intended meaning of "They are kissing fish" is usually straightforward when spoken in context.

One way that context directs comprehension is by influencing the way we process incoming language. In a classic study of context effects (Warren & Warren, 1970), subjects were asked to repeat a simple six-word sentence. All subjects heard the same five words at the start of the sentence, but different groups of subjects heard a different sixth word. This is what they heard:

> "The *eel was on the axle"
>   shoe"
>   orange"
>   table"

The "*" at the beginning of the word "eel" marks a place in the sentence where the speaker coughed, so the resulting sound was "eel." Subjects who heard the sentence ending with "axle" believed that the word "eel" had been "wheel." Similarly, the subjects who heard the sentence ending with shoe believed that "eel" had been "heel." The subjects who heard the sentence ending with "orange" believed that they had heard "peel," and the subjects that heard "table" believed that they had heard "meal." Subjects' beliefs about what they had heard depended on the context that was presented after they had heard the word. Thus, their interpretation of a sound pattern was determined by subsequently presented context clues. It was the context that gave meaning to the "eel" sound pattern.

Figure 3.3 demonstrates a parallel effect in visual perception. You'll find that you have no difficulty reading any of the words in Fig. 3.3. Now look carefully at the letters that make up the words. The "H" in "the" is the same form as the "A" in "cat," yet you may not have noticed this unless I pointed it out to you. Similarly, the way we perceive the other "inky" letters depends on the rest of the letters that make up the word context. Context provides strong cues that guide the way we construct knowledge about the nature of the world.

TAE CAT
RED
SROT
EISH
DEBT

FIG. 3.3. Examples of the way context influences meaning. (Adapted from Rumelhart, D. E., McClelland, J. L., & the PDP Research Group (1986). *Parallel Distributed Processing.* Cambridge: The MIT Press, p. 0).

Context is also utilized to provide meaning to other cognitive activities like judging and evaluating. Parducci (1968) asked subjects to decide how bad it is to "pocket the tip which the previous customers left for the waitress." Half the subjects were asked to judge this event along with the following mild infractions: stealing a loaf of bread from a store when you are starving; playing poker on Sunday; cheating at solitaire. The other half of the subjects were asked to judge the same event (pocketing the tip that the previous customers left for the waitress) along with the following infractions: spreading rumors that an acquaintance is a sexual pervert; putting your deformed child in the circus; murdering your mother without justification or provocation.

Taking a waitress' tip was judged to be a more serious offense when it was presented along with milder infractions than when it was presented among a list of serious infractions. The event (pocketing a tip) was exactly the same in each case, and the wording was identical. Changes in the context in which it was presented created changes in the way it was evaluated. Context is an important determinant of the meaning we assign to events.

Implications and Inference

Communication depends as much on information that is implied as it does on the words that are explicitly stated. Comprehension of meaningful material will always require the listener or reader to make inferences by going beyond the words uttered. Consider this very simple three-sentence story:

Matt inherited a great deal of money.
Bertha loves diamonds and furs.
Bertha married Matt.

Although very little factual information was provided, it is a meaningful story. Readers infer that Bertha married Matt for his money and that she will use his money to buy diamonds and furs. All communication requires the receiver to fill in gaps between given bits of information to understand intended meanings. In the first chapter of this book, one definition of thinking was "going beyond the information given." Understanding language by making inferences is a prime example of this definition of thinking.

The Role of Inference in Advertisements

When you produce speech, the intended meaning is implied, or suggested, by the words you use, the context in which it is embedded, and verbal and nonverbal expressions. It is possible to say one thing while communicating something quite different. This technique is often used by advertisers who want to persuade you to buy their products but have legal restrictions on the kinds of statements they can make.

A recent television commercial for American Express Traveler's Cheques goes something like this:

> "Oh, no, we've lost our travelers cheques! What will we do?" (Couple wrings their respective hands at point, obviously looking distressed.)
> The voice of a distinguished actor comes on, "What kind were they?"
> Distressed couple responds, "American Express."
> The distinguished actor calmly reassures them, "Good thing you have American Express Travelers Cheques. You can get a refund at their conveniently located office across the street."
> The now-smiling couple walk off the screen to the tune of "Don't leave home without them."

Other traveler's check companies have complained about this advertisement, because it implies that people who lose other brands of traveler's checks may not get a refund. Notice that, although this is never stated, it is a reasonable inference from the information offered.

Perhaps you're familiar with a popular advertisement for Listerine, a brand of mouthwash. A middle-class mother bundles her children in warm clothing while discussing colds and flus. She earnestly states how much she dislikes "scratchy sore throats" and "runny noses." To keep her family healthy, she sees that they eat right, get plenty of rest and exercise, and "gargle with Listerine." Of course, she never says that Listerine will prevent or cure colds. This would be a false claim, because there is no evidence that it does. Yet, this information is implied. Studies with fictitious commercials have shown that viewers do infer from advertisements like this one that mouthwash will protect against colds (Harris, 1977).

Carefully selected words in advertisements are used to create an inference that something is true when it is not. Airlines and other businesses often boast that, "Nobody beats our fares." They expect that readers will infer that this means that they have the lowest fares. Of course, they never state that they have the lowest fares, because that would be false. Nobody beats their fares because virtually all of the fares are the same. They could have said, "Our fares are exactly the same as our competitors." But, if they said it that way, it would not mislead readers into believing that they have the lowest fares. Always consider the distinction between linguistic message and the inference you draw from it.

When you start reading and listening critically to advertisements, you may be surprised to find appalling attempts to create impressions that can change beliefs. It is instructive to read the advertisements for supposed weight-loss products (e.g., cellulite creams, sauna suits, herbal wraps, vitamins, magic formula pills). Even the ubiquitous "before and after" photos are designed to create the inference that you will lose "30 or more pounds in two weeks" while eating anything you want and without "tedious" exercise.

Moreover, Harris (1977) found that people remember the implied meaning of a message, and not the actual statements that were made. If you have already read the chapter on the development of memory skills, this shouldn't be surprising to you. Meaningful information is more easily remembered than non-meaningful information. People remember the meaning, or gist, of the message and not the actual words that were spoken. We rarely remember statements verbatim. Thus, our memory of events depends on the interpretations we give them when they occur.

Strategies for Comprehension

What can you do to enhance your ability to comprehend? There are a number of comprehension strategies or skills that are designed to help make information that is presented in natural (everyday) language more understandable. These strategies act as aids in discovering, retaining, and utilizing the information in speech and written prose. They all involve ways of building a meaningful representation that matches the one used by the "sender."

The process of comprehension may be best described with an analogy. Imagine that a friend has a large jungle gym (child's climbing toy) in his or her back yard, and that he or she is giving it to you as a present. Because it is too large to transfer in its assembled state, you need to take it apart in order to move it to your home. Once you get it home, you need to reassemble the toy. In order to do this, you have to identify which part is the base and then add component parts to it. When it is reassembled, it should look the same as it did in your friend's yard.

The same is true of comprehension. If your friend has a complex knowledge structure in his or her head, he or she would transfer the information to you via language. You would have to identify the main ideas (or base) in order to build your own mental representation. You would also have to understand the relationships among the parts of the information so that you can graft them onto the main ideas in the correct way. Comprehension is attained when your knowledge structure "looks the same as" the one your friend has in his or her head. In other

words, you would both have the same underlying representation for the transferred information. All comprehension strategies are activities that aid in the
transfer of underlying structures. They provide guides for identifying main ideas
and determining the relevance of various components of the message. They assist
the comprehender in discovering the underlying relationships among the constituent parts of the message.

What do you do when you comprehend a passage? Most people respond that
they have no idea what they do to aid their understanding, yet they can say what
they do when they study. As previously stated, any cognitive activity that aids
comprehension will also aid memory, so any effective comprehension strategy is
also a memory strategy.

Some of the most commonly used study aids are the poorest. Notably, the
practice of underlining ("highlighting") words and phrases in texts is one of the
least efficient ways of enhancing comprehension and recall, because it is a
relatively passive activity that requires very little cognitive involvement. It is
possible to "paint" your entire text with a bright highlighter and still be unable
to state a single fact from the book. All of the strategies that "work" require
learners to deal with the structure of the underlying relationship and to be mindful of the nature of the mental representation they are constructing.

Questioning and Paraphrase

There have been numerous demonstrations of the beneficial effects of posing
questions to oneself as part of the learning process. Palincsar & Brown (1984),
for example, found that when students are required to formulate relevant questions for their peers, they are better able to comprehend new passages than a
control group of students who never practiced posing questions. The best known
technique for studying from text is based on the process of asking good questions
about the material being read and then demonstrating comprehension by answering the questions. Several studies have shown that when students generate and
answer their own questions about a text, comprehension and recall improves
(Heiman & Slomianko, 1986).

One of the best-known methods based on the combination of questioning and
paraphrase is **SQ3R,** which stands for Survey, Question, Read, Recite, Review
(Adams, Carnine, & Gersten, 1982; Robinson, 1946). The first thing to do when
you begin reading complex text is to Survey the chapter (or some other manageable unit of text). When you survey, you look at section headings and subheadings to gain an overview of what you will be reading about. This will allow you
to anticipate related topics as you read. It also forms a skeletal framework for the
mental representation you will be building that can be used to interpret and
organize incoming information. Before you read each section (approximately
one or two pages is usually a good length), turn the section heading into a
Question. For example, the main heading for this section of text is "strategies

for comprehension." A good question that you should be able to answer when you finish this section is, "What are some strategies for comprehension, and how do they work?" If you can't answer this question, with the book closed, when you finish this section, then you do not know the information presented. A good question for this subsection on "questioning and paraphrase" is, "How are questioning and paraphrase used to improve comprehension?"

The first of the three **R**s is "*R*ead." Reading is the third step; it is not the first thing you do when learning from text. It is often useful to take notes at this time. In order for these notes to be beneficial, they need to be a **paraphrase** or restatement—*in your own words*—of the information. The "*R*ecite" portion is the answering of the questions you previously posed. This needs to be done without reference to the book or your notes. It is too easy to believe that you know the material when it is sitting in front of you, only to later discover that you really don't "own" it when you are away from the book or your notes. At this point, you need to monitor the quality of your response by assessing how well you can answer the questions. It's a good idea to recite the answer out loud or to write out an answer. Cognitive psychologists know that practice at recall improves later recall (e.g., Hansen & Halpern 1987). If you can't answer the questions, you need to go back and recycle. Reread the section, reconsider the questions you've posed, review the structure of the information. The final **R** is for *R*eview. Go over the material again. Psychologists call this **overlearning.** Recall becomes increasingly automatic with overlearning.

Graphic Organizers

An oft-repeated theme in this book is to utilize both verbal and imagery, or spatial-like, strategies as thinking aids. **Graphic organizers** (sometimes called concept maps) are spatial arrays that require learners to attend explicitly to the underlying structure in a passage. Mayer (1987) has called the deliberate use of graphic organizers "structure training techniques" because they force the learner to focus on the structure of a text. There are several varieties of graphic organizers, but all of them use spatial representations to make efficient use of the information in a text.

Linear Arrays.   Sometimes, the best way to understand a topic is to represent the information in a **linear array.** This is useful when the information presented is fairly linear, or straight-line-like, in its structure. An example of this would be a very simple "line" of causal reasoning: The girl hit the boy. He started to cry. The teacher heard the boy's cry. She ran into the room. She punished the girl. The girl was sent to the principal's office. And so on.

This rather boring story is a straightforward sequence of events that followed each other in a strict temporal ordering. A simple linear representation would adequately capture all of the relevant information.

- girl hit boy
- boy cried
- teacher arrived
- teacher punished girl
- girl to principal's office
- and so on

Another example of when a modified linear array would be a good choice of representation is in representing any parts or processes that are aligned linearly in

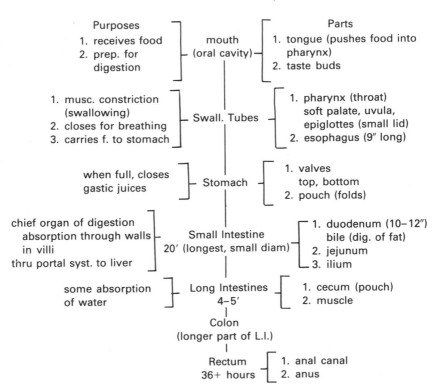

FIG. 3.4.   Modified linear array depicting the purposes and parts of the digestive system. Adapted from Vaughan (1984).

the physical world. Vaughan (1984) taught medical students how to utilize graphic organizers when learning from medical texts. The digestive system is aligned in a fairly linear manner, beginning with the mouth and ending with the rectum. Students who read about the digestive system listed the parts of the digestive system in linear order and noted along with each part its purposes in the digestive process and its components. The resulting linear array is shown in Fig. 3.4. Vaughan reported that the medical students who learned to use graphic organizers like this one showed significant improvement in their comprehension of medical school texts.

Hierarchies.   Most of the information we deal with is considerably more complex that simple linear chains. An alternative structural form for information is that of **hierarchies,** or tree structures, in which information is organized around class inclusion rules. Class inclusion rules are those rules in which something is a part of or a type of something else. Examples of class inclusion rules are the classification of toes as part of the foot and roses as a type of flower. Information of this sort can usually be categorized into levels with higher levels dividing into lower levels, according to some rule. Biological classification systems are a good example of hierarchically organized information. Bower (1970b) studied organizational factors in memory, using hierarchically arranged information about minerals. Consider Fig. 3.5, which depicts this hierarchy. Bower found that, when subjects organized information this way, they had significantly better recall than a group of control subjects. Furthermore, he found that when a "node" or branch of the hierarchy was forgotten, subjects failed to recall the entire portion of the "tree" that was below it. I return to these results later in this book, in

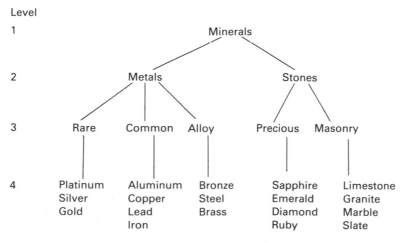

FIG. 3.5.   Hierarchy of minerals. An example of a hierarchical graphic organizer. Adapted from Bower (1970b).

chapter 9, "Problem Solving." Hierarchies, or tree diagrams, are sometimes used as problem-solving aids.

Networks. The relationships among ideas in a communication are not usually based on simple class inclusion rules. Concepts can be related to each other in numerous other ways, and it is the depiction of the correct relationship among concepts that is central to all graphic organizing techniques. Networks are graphic organizers in which several different types of relationships are made explicit. Much of the work in this area has been conducted by Dansereau and his colleagues and is presented in an edited book by Holley and Dansereau (1984).

When students learn the technique of networking, they are taught to focus on and identify six different types of relationships, or links, among concepts (Holley, Dansereau, McDonald, Garland, & Collins 1979). Two of these relationships are the class inclusion rules of hierarchies: X is a part of Y, and X is a type of Y. The third relationship is called a "leads to link." This type of relationship occurs whenever X leads to Y. The other three relationships, or links, are analogy (X is like Y), characteristic (X is a characteristic or feature of Y), and evidence (X is evidence that Y occurred). These six relationships are described more fully in Table 3.1.

As you can see from Table 3.1, networking requires students to consider the nature of the relationships among concepts in a text and then to categorize them into six different possible types. Once this is done, the relationships are depicted in a networklike array with all of the relationships labeled. An example of a completed network is shown in Fig. 3.6. The network shows the relationships among concepts in a nursing text on wounds. Look carefully at this figure. "Types of wounds" and the "process of healing" are *parts* of the discussion of wounds. "Open," "closed," "accidental," and "intentional" are *types* of wounds. In the process of healing, the "lag phase" *leads to* the "fibroplasia phase," which *leads to* the contraction phase. "Soft, pink, and friable" is *a characteristic of* tissue continuity. The other two types of relationships, analogy and evidence, are not used in this network.

Identification and use of these six types of relationships (or links) and their combination in a unified network requires considerable practice. This is an effortful strategy that, like some of the mnemonic techniques, pays off once it is well learned. Holley et al. (1979) found that, when subjects were well trained with this technique, they performed significantly better on subsequent tests than control students who did not learn this technique, with the biggest improvement for students with low grade point averages. It seems that the students who were doing very well in school were already attending to the relationships among concepts; therefore, it was the poorer students who benefitted most from explicit instruction and practice in identifying, labeling, and diagramming the relationships among concepts.

TABLE 3.1
Six Types of Links Used in Networks[a]

Type	Example	Structure	Key Words
Part of link	hand |p finger	*Hierarchy*—the lower node is part of the higher node	is a part of is a segment of is a portion of
Type of/ example of link	school |t private	*Hierarchy*—the lower node is an example of the higher node	is a type of is in the category is an example of is a kind of three procedures are
Leads to link	practice |l perfection	*Chain*—the object of the higher node leads to or results in the lower node	leads to results in causes is a tool of produces
Analogy link	school_a_factory	*Cluster*—the content of one node is analogous to the other node	is similar to is analogous to is like corresponds to
Characteristic link	sky_c_blue	*Cluster*—the content of one node is a trait of the other node	has is characterized by feature is property is trait is aspect is attribute is
Evidence link	broken_e_x-ray arm	*Cluster*—the content of one node is evidence for the other node	indicates is illustrated by is demonstrated by supports documents is proof of confirms

[a]This table is adapted from Holley et al. (1979).

Matrices.   When the material to be comprehended involves comparisons of several topics along a number of dimensions, a **matrix** is the representation of choice. (The word "matrices" is the plural of matrix.) Suppose, for example, that you are reading a passage about wars. The purpose of the passage is to compare and contrast various antecedent conditions of war and to consider their effect. Suppose further that the wars being considered are the Revolutionary War, World War I, World War II, The Korean Conflict, and the Vietnam Conflict. In order to understand the nature of these U. S. wars, you need to

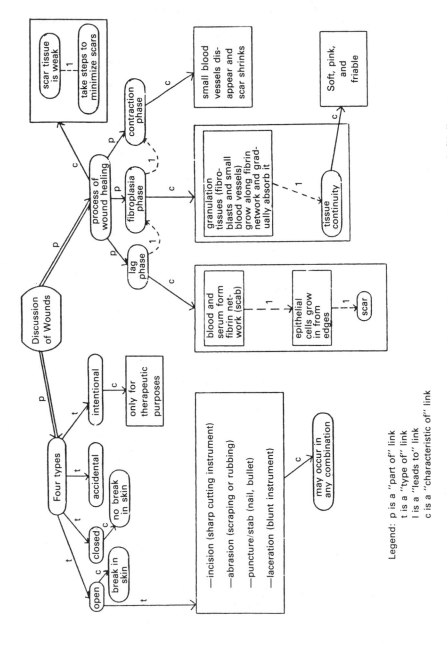

FIG. 3.6. Example of a network of a chapter from a nursing text on wounds (Holley et al., 1979). (Reprinted with permission from Academic Press.)

Legend: p is a "part of" link
t is a "type of" link
l is a "leads to" link
c is a "characteristic of" link

114

TABLE 3.2
Example of a Matrix Graphic Organizer

	War				
	Revolutionary War	*World War I*	*World War II*	*Korean Conflict*	*Viet Nam Conflict*
Major precipitating events					
U.S. justification for the war					
"Other side" justification for the war					
Number of lives lost—each side					
Major battles					
Resolution					
Types of weapons					
Relationship to later war, if any					

organize the information so that commonalities and distinctions will emerge. A suggested matrix for this information is shown in Table 3.2.

By filling in the empty cells in Table 3.2, certain categories of information can readily be compared. A coherent "pattern" of information about these wars can then be extracted. The framework can be applied to other wars involving other countries to determine, for example, if there are universal commonalities for all wars.

Flow Charts.   Sometimes the content of a passage is best described as a series of actions, with the specific action to be taken dependent on some previous circumstance. A relevant example of this sort of passage is instructions for selecting the appropriate graphic organizer for a passage. In general, the "rules" generally fit the format: "If X is true, then do Y. If X is not true, then do Z." A good representation for these decisional rules is a flow chart. **Flow charts** are particularly useful when the passage contains explicit, logical, and sequential instructions. As you probably know, they are used by computer programmers when the programmers are planning the sequence of operations that a computer must perform in order to accomplish a task.

Flow charts use a variety of symbols for their notational system. A few of these symbols are:

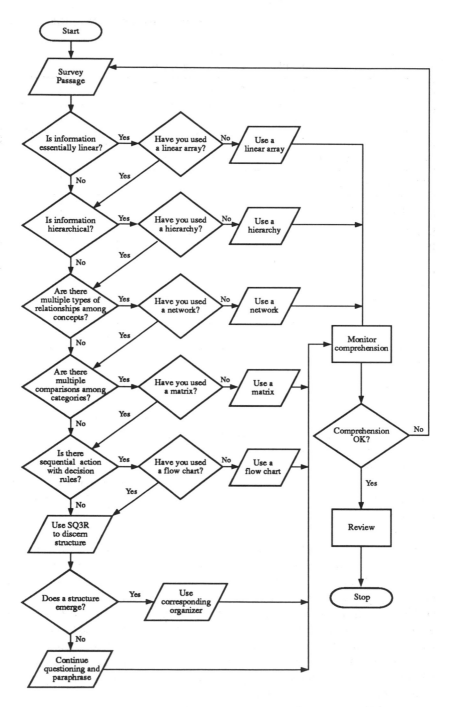

FIG. 3.7. Flow chart for deciding which graphic organizer is best suited for the comprehension of a specific text.

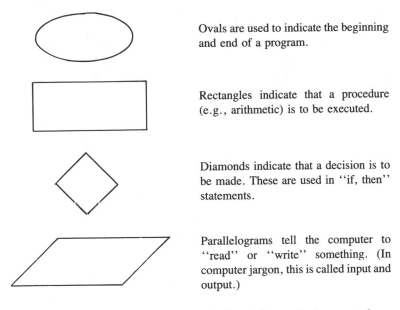

Ovals are used to indicate the beginning and end of a program.

Rectangles indicate that a procedure (e.g., arithmetic) is to be executed.

Diamonds indicate that a decision is to be made. These are used in "if, then" statements.

Parallelograms tell the computer to "read" or "write" something. (In computer jargon, this is called input and output.)

One of the benefits of using flow charts is that it forces the learner to be very clear and explicit about the nature of decisions and the sequence of steps.

A flow chart for selecting the appropriate strategy for comprehension is depicted in Fig. 3.7.

General Guidelines and Principles

All of the strategies for comprehension require learners to monitor their understanding of the information. They are all active cognitive strategies that facilitate the construction of meaningful representations. The graphic organizers offer ways to transform text into explicit spatial representations that display relationships among concepts. They all make abstract concepts more concrete. Like all good cognitive strategies, they require the learner to relate new information to prior knowledge in a way that makes knowledge retrieval (remembering) most efficient. And, like many of the other thinking skills presented in this book, they require effort and must be practiced in order to be useful. It is not enough to read about them. They have to be used in a variety of situations to ensure transfer.

Although most of this chapter has been concerned with the process of comprehension—that is, going from surface structure to underlying structure—many of the principles can be used in language production or going from underlying structure to surface structure. The task of writing involves transforming your internalized meaning into words. Many people have difficulty with writing because they find that this is a difficult translation. Graphic organizers can be terrific aids in the writing process. Suppose you were to write an essay about

Acquired Immune Deficiency Syndrome (AIDS). You could begin the planning process by considering the kinds of links employed in networking (type of, part of, leads to, evidence for, characteristics of, and analogy). What "types of" people are most and least at risk? What is the "evidence for" AIDS (laboratory tests, symptoms)? What are the "characteristics of" at-risk groups or risky activities? Some people have called for quarantine, which is "analogous to" the way the way society has responded to other dread diseases. Once you have considered the information you want to present, the relationship among the facts can be depicted in a network. The network offers a nonlinear alternative to outlines when planning the writing process. Thus, by "running comprehension strategies backward," they can be used to produce language (spoken or written) instead of their more usual role in comprehending language.

APPLYING THE FRAMEWORK

1. *What is the goal?* The thinking goal addressed in this chapter is how to enhance comprehension when the medium for communication is natural language. A more formal way of saying the same thing is that the goal is to create an accurate underlying representation from the surface structure provided in speech and written text.

2. *What is known?* This step requires determining where you are before selecting the appropriate thinking skill. Are you in a situation in which there is likely to be deliberate attempts to bias your thinking on an issue (e.g., consumer decisions, political rhetoric)? Do you have a text containing information that you will soon be tested on?

3. *Which thinking skill or skills will get you to your goal?* The skills presented in this chapter are those involved in comprehending language. As with every list of skills, users need to monitor their comprehension to determine what is and what isn't being understood. The process of skill use often requires trying a different skill if the one being used is not promoting understanding. The following comprehension skills were presented in this chapter. Review each skill and be sure that you understand when and how to use each one.

- recognizing and defending against the inappropriate use of emotional language, labeling, name calling, ambiguity, vagueness, hedging, and arguments by etymology
- developing the ability to detect misuse of definitions, reification, euphemism, and bureaucratese
- understanding the use of framing with leading questions, negation, and marked words
- using analogies appropriately, which includes examining the nature of the similarity and its relationship to the conclusion
- employing questioning and paraphrase as a skill for text comprehension
- selecting and using graphic organizers (linear arrays, hierarchies, networks, matrices, flow charts)

4. *Have you reached your goal?* Have you been monitoring your understanding? Can you paraphrase a passage with the book closed? Did you systematically consider all of the ways that we can be misled with language that were presented in this chapter?

CHAPTER SUMMARY

1. Psycholinguistics is the branch of psychology that is concerned with understanding how people produce and comprehend language.

2. Psychologists view language as comprised of two components or levels: a meaning component (underlying representation) and a speech sound component (surface structure).

3. Language is ambiguous when a single surface structure has two or more possible underlying representations.

4. Language and thought exert mutual influences on each other with our thoughts determining the language we use and, in turn, the language we use reshaping our thoughts.

5. Six rules of communication were presented. Every time we attempt to communicate with others, we utilize these rules to determine what information we will convey and how to express the information.

6. Language comprehension requires that the listener make many inferences. The kinds of inferences we make depends on context, manner, and the words selected to convey the message.

7. There are many ways that words can be used to deliberately mislead the listener. Several ways that the choice of words can influence thought were presented.

8. Strategies to improve the comprehension of text were described. They all require learners to attend to the structure of the information and to make the relationships among concepts explicit.

Terms to Know

You should be able to define or describe the following terms and concepts. If you find that you're having difficulty with any term, be sure to reread the section in which it is discussed.

Psycholinguistics. The branch of psychology that is concerned with the production, comprehension, and usage of language.

Underlying Representation. The meaning component of language. It's the thought that you want to convey with an utterance. Compare with surface structure.

Surface Structure. The sounds of an utterance or the outward appearance of a language expression. Compare with underlying representation.

Sapir-Whorf Hypothesis of Linguistic Relativity. The hypothesis that language, at least in part, determines or influences thought.

Semantic Slanting. The deliberate use of words designed to create a particular attitude or foster certain beliefs.

Ambiguous. An utterance is ambiguous when it can have more than one meaning or underlying representation.

Vagueness. A lack of precision in a communication. A communication is vague if it does not specify enough details for its intended purpose.

Equivocation. A change in the meaning of a word in the course of the same discussion.

Hedging. An assertion that is made with less than complete certainty.

Etymology. Reference to the origin of a word in order to determine its meaning.

Reification. Occurs when an abstract concept is given a name and then treated as though it were a concrete object.

Bureaucratese. The use of formal, stilted language that is often unfamiliar to people who lack special training.

Euphemism. The substitution of a desirable term for a less desirable or offensive one.

Framing. Occurs when a question is asked in a way that suggests what the correct response should be. The reader is "led" into assuming a particular perspective or point of view.

Marked Words. Words that connote a bias when they appear in a question (e.g., poor, dumb, or small). When asked "How poor is he," it is presumed that the response will be toward the poor extreme and not toward the rich extreme.

Negation. The use of denial to imply that a fact is plausible.

Double Negation. The use of two negations in the same sentence. The net result is an afffirmative statement that is difficult to comprehend.

Given/New Distinction. The ratio of known (given) information to new information in a communication. It is a primary determinant of the difficulty of a communication.

SQ3R. A strategy for comprehension that requires the use of questioning and paraphrase. The letters stand for **S**urvey, **Q**uestion, **R**ead, **R**ecite, and **R**eview.

Paraphrase. Restating ideas in your own words.

Overlearning. Reviewing material after it is learned so that recall becomes automatic.

Graphic Organizers. The use of spatial displays to organize information. Also known as *concept maps*.

Linear Arrays. A graphic organizer in which information is presented in a list format.

Hierarchies. A type of graphic organizer that uses a tree structure. Most useful when information is organized according to class inclusion rules.

Networks. Graphic organizers in which types of relationships among concepts are depicted.

Matrix. A rectangular array that is useful when the information presented involves comparisons along several dimensions.

Flow Charts. A graphic organizer that depicts specific actions to be taken when these actions depend on previous circumstances.

Chapter Questions

Be sure that you can answer the following questions:

1. Explain the relationship between underlying representation and surface structure. Why has the gap between them been called the ''problem'' of producing and comprehending language?

2. What is the Sapir-Whorf hypothesis of linguistic relativity?

3. Distinguish between the strong and weak forms of the Sapir-Whorf hypothesis. What do you think about the truth of each of these forms?

4. Experimental studies were presented to demonstrate empirically how slight changes in wording can cause substantial differences in the way people think. Describe two of these studies.

5. What are some circumstances when it is particularly important to consider the way choice of words influences thought?

6. What's wrong with interpreting the meaning of a word by reference to its origin?

7. How do you decide which strategy to improve comprehension should be used?

8. What general cognitive principles are common to all of the strategies for improving comprehension?

Exercises

Identify possible attempts to mislead how you think in the following statements. Determine if any of the following are being used: ambiguity, vagueness, emotional terms, equivocation, etymology, framing, bureaucratese, euphemism, reification, negation, and marked adjectives. Explain your answers. Which ones are not necessarily misleading, but might be, depending on context?

1. Why should I have to learn about analyzing arguments to determine if they are clear? Aren't there too many arguments in the world already?

2. One possible conclusion from the research is that learning thinking skills may improve your intelligence.

3. This song is a big hit in Mexico.

4. Why would you want to be friends with a queer?

5. The best way to overcome shyness is by retraining your personality.

6. Druggies hits a higher level of pain relief.

7. Only future YUPPIES would attend that snooty private school.

8. The word ''education'' comes from ''educe,'' which means to bring out. When we educate someone we should be trying to bring out the information that he or she already knows.

9. Pursuant to our agreement and attached hereto is the codicil. (A codicil is an amendment to a will.)

10. Have your stomach pains been accompanied by increased flatulence?

11. You're so vain!

12. How bad are the Giants this season?

13. Did you see the car run the stop sign?

14. This ground beef is 75% fat free. *framing*
15. This ground beef is 25% pure fat. *framing*
16. Coke is it! *vague*
17. All patriotic Canadians will agree. *framing*
18. I don't know which of them is worse. *marked*

Consider and comment on the following analogies. How good are they? In what ways are the two topics that are being compared similar and dissimilar? What is the purpose of the analogy?

19. You'd go to an orthopedist if you broke your arm, so why not go to a love doctor when you break your heart?

20. It is completely legal to drink alcohol and smoke cigarettes, both of which are known to have serious effects on one's health. Yet, marijuana is not legalized, and its effects on health are not as well documented as alcohol and smoking. Therefore, marijuana should be legalized.

21. Comprehension is like moving a jungle gym from your friend's yard to your own. (Refer back to the text for the rest of this analogy.)

22. Jealousy is a green-eyed monster.

23. My love is like a red, red rose.

24. Why should the children of faculty members attend the university free? We don't send the children of politicians or public school teachers to school without cost.

25. Listed below are several kinds of text. Which graphic organizer would you use to depict the underlying relationships? Why? (There may be more than one correct answer.)
    a. a complex "who done it" type mystery story
    b. an essay on the effects of geography on the type of economy that develops in a region
    c. a manual on the repair of automobiles
    d. a description of a chemical chain reaction
    e. a classification of wild plants endogenous to Tasmania
    f. a "how-to" manual for deep sea diving

26. Use questioning and paraphrase for the information provided in this chapter. Write out the questions and respond to them.

27. Use a graphic organizer to depict the information presented in the chapter on memory (Chapter 2).

28. Use the strategies for comprehension in your other class work. If you're not taking any other classes, apply them to a lengthy newspaper or magazine article.

29. List at least five situations that would require the deliberate use of strategies for comprehension.

30. Draw a flow chart of the information provided in this paragraph:

    In the event of fire, you should feel the door. If it is hot, remain in your room with the door closed. If the door is cool, open the door carefully and look for smoke in the hall. If there is smoke, remain in your room with the door closed. If there is no smoke, proceed to the exit. (Black & Black, 1985, p. 193)

SUGGESTED READINGS

An excellent and easy-to-read text in psycholinguistics is Clark and Clark's (1977) *Psychology and Language: An Introduction to Psycholinguistics.* It is highly recommended for anyone who wants to learn more about this area of psychology. A more recent text on this topic that is also recommended is Carroll's (1986) *Psychology of Language.* Slobin's (1974) slim text, appropriately titled *Psycholinguistics,* is also a good starting place for an introduction to the field.

A somewhat rambling book that is difficult to classify is Brown's (1958) *Words and Things.* It's provocative reading on the wide range of topics that concern language. Pollio, Barlow, Fine, and Pollio (1977) have compiled an interesting series of papers on the psychology of language in their book with the intriguing title, *Psychology and the Poetics of Growth.*

An interesting book that describes the interpersonal aspects of communication is Adler, Rosenfeld, and Towne's (1980) *Interplay: The Process of Interpersonal Communication.* It is easy reading. Two texts that view the relationship between thought and language from the perspective of an English professor are *Word, Self, Reality: The Rhetoric of Imagination* by Miller (1972) and *Good Reasons for Writing* by Barry (1983).

The best collection of papers on the use of graphic organizers is Holley and Dansereau's (1984) edited volume *Spatial Learning Strategies.* In fact, theirs is the only edited collection that I know of on this subject. Holley et al.'s (1979) journal article entitled, "Evaluation of a hierarchical mapping technique as an aid to prose processing" describes the use of networks and presents empirical evidence for their effectiveness as an aid to comprehension.

4 Reasoning: Drawing Deductively Valid Conclusions

Contents

As far as Joan's opponent was concerned, the debate wasn't going well. It was clear from the sea of nodding heads and sounds of "uh huh" and "yeah" that Joan was scoring points and convincing the audience, whereas he seemed to be losing support every time he spoke. He wasn't surprised; he had been warned. Joan had studied reasoning and now knew how to make people believe anything. Soon, she would have everyone convinced that the war was justified and what was wrong was right. The way she was going, she could probably make people believe that day was night. It certainly wasn't fair, but what can you expect from someone who studied reasoning?

This fictional vignette was taken from a real-life incident. I was present at a debate where one debater accused the other of cheating by using reasoning. At the time, I thought that this was pretty funny, because I had come to think of reasoning as an important critical thinking skill—the sort of skill that you would use to make valid conclusions when dealing with information that is complex and emotional. To the losing side of this debate, it was a trick. Trick, skill, or strategy, reasoning is the best way to decide whom and what to believe.

LOGICAL AND PSYCHOLOGICAL

The trick, of course, is to reason well. It isn't easy and it isn't automatic.
—Kahane (1980, p.3)

Reasoning is often taken to be the hallmark of the human species. Colloquially, reasoning tells us "what follows what." When we reason, we use our knowledge about one or more related statements to determine if another statement, the conclusion, is correct. A **conclusion** is an inferential belief that is derived from other statements. The ability to reason well is a critical-thinking skill that is crucial in science, mathematics, law, forecasting, diagnosing, and just about every other context you can imagine. In fact, I can't think of an academic or "real world" context in which the ability to reason well is not of great importance.

When we reason logically, we are following a set of rules that specify how we "ought to" derive conclusions. **Logic** is the branch of philosophy that explicitly states the rules for deriving valid (correct) conclusions. A conclusion is **valid** if it necessarily follows from some statements called *premises*. Conclusions that are not in accord with the rules of logic are **illogical.** Although we maintain that the ability for rational, logical thought is unique to humans, all too often we reach invalid or illogical conclusions. This fact has led Hunt (1982) to award "A flunking grade in logic for the world's only logical animal" (p. 121).

Psychologists who study reasoning have been concerned with how people process information in reasoning tasks. The fact is that, in our everyday thinking, the psychological processes quite often are not logical. In a classic paper on the relation between logic and thinking, Henle (1962) noted that, although everyday thought does not generally follow the formal rules of logic, people use their own imperfect rules. If we were not logical, at least some of the time, we wouldn't be able to understand each other, "follow one another's thinking, reach common decisions, and work together" (p. 374). To demonstrate this point, stop now and work on one of the problems that Henle (1962) posed to her subjects in one of her studies:

A group of women were discussing their household problems. Mrs. Shivers broke the ice by saying: "I'm so glad we're talking about these problems. It's so important to talk about things that are in our minds. We spend so much of our time in the kitchen that, of course, household problems are in our minds. So it is important to talk about them." (Does it follow that it is important to talk about them? Give your reasoning.) (p. 370)

Do not go on until you decide if it is valid to conclude that Mrs. Shivers is correct when she says that it is important to talk about household problems. Why did you answer as you did?

When Henle posed this problem to graduate students, she found that some arrived at the wrong answer (as defined by the rules of logic); whereas, others arrived at the right answer for the wrong reasons. Consider the following answer given by one of her subjects: "No. It is not important to talk about things that are in our minds unless they worry us, which is not the case" (p. 370). Where did this subject go wrong? Instead of deciding if the conclusion followed logically from the earlier statements, she added her own opinions about what sorts of things it is important to talk about. Thus, although the answer is incorrect as evaluated by the standard rules of logic, it is correct by the subject's own rules. Consider this answer: "Yes. It could be very important for the individual doing the talking and possibly to some of those listening, because it is important for people to 'get a load off their chest,' but not for any other reason, unless in the process one or the other learns something new and of value" (p. 370). This time, the subject gave the correct answer, but for the wrong reasons. This subject, like the first one, added her own beliefs to the problem instead of deriving her conclusions solely on the basis of the information presented. Henle has termed this the **failure to accept the logical task.** It seems that in everyday use of reasoning, we don't determine if a conclusion is valid solely on the basis of the statements we're given. Instead, we alter the statements we're given according to our beliefs and then decide if a conclusion follows from the altered statements. We function under a kind of "personal logic," in which we utilize our personal beliefs about the world to formulate conclusions about related issues.

Inductive and Deductive Reasoning

> *Actual thinking has its own logic; it is orderly, reasonable, reflective.*
> —Dewey (1933)

A distinction is often made between inductive and deductive reasoning. (See chapter 6 for a related discussion of this topic.) In **inductive reasoning,** observations are collected that support or suggest a conclusion. For example, if every person you have ever seen has only one head, you would use this evidence to support the conclusion (or hypothesis) that everyone in the world has only one head. Of course, you can't be absolutely certain of this fact. It's always possible that someone you've never met has two heads. If you met just one person with two heads, your conclusion must be wrong. Thus, with inductive reasoning, you can never *prove* that your conclusion or hypothesis is correct, but you can disprove it.

When we reason inductively, we collect facts and use them to provide support or disconfirmation for conclusions or hypotheses. It's how we discover what the world is like. Lopes (1982) described induction this way: "Scientists do it; lay people do it; even birds and beasts do it. But the process is mysterious and full of

© King Features Syndicate, Courtesy KFS, INC.

paradox . . . induction cannot be justified on logical grounds" (p. 626). We reason inductively, both informally in the course of everyday living, and formally in experimental research. For this reason, hypothesis testing is sometimes described as the process of inductive reasoning. When we reason inductively, we generalize from our experiences to create beliefs or expectations. Sometimes, inductive reasoning is described as reasoning "up" from particular instances or experiences in the world to a belief about the nature of the world.

In **deductive reasoning,** you would begin with statements known or believed to be true, like "everyone has only one head," and then conclude or infer that Karen, a woman you've never met, will have only one head. This conclusion follows logically from the earlier statement. If we know that it is true that everyone has only one head, then it must also be true that any specific person will have only one head. This conclusion necessarily follows from the belief; if the belief is true, the conclusion *must* be true. Deductive reasoning is sometimes described as reasoning "down" from beliefs about the nature of the world to particular instances. Rips (1988) has argued that deduction is a general-purpose mechanism for cognitive tasks. According to Rips, deduction "enables us to answer questions from information stored in memory, to plan actions according to goals, and to solve certain kinds of puzzles" (p. 117).

Although it is common to make a distinction between inductive and deductive reasoning, the distinction may not be a particularly useful description of how people reason in real life. In everyday context, we switch from inductive to deductive reasoning in the course of thinking. Our hypotheses and beliefs guide the observations we make, and our observations, in turn, modify our hypotheses and beliefs. Often, this process will involve a continuous interplay of inductive and deductive reasoning. Thinking in real-world contexts almost always involves the use of multiple types of thinking skills.

SYLLOGISTIC REASONING

Nothing intelligible ever puzzles me. Logic puzzles me.
—Lewis Carroll (1887)

Syllogistic reasoning is a form of reasoning that involves deciding whether or not a conclusion can properly be inferred from two or more statements. One type of syllogistic reasoning is categorical reasoning. **Categorical reasoning** involves **quantifiers,** or terms that tell us how many. Quantifiers are terms like "all," "some," "none," and "no." The quantifiers indicate how many items belong in specified categories.

A **syllogism** usually consists of two statements that are called **premises** and a third statement, called the **conclusion.** In categorical syllogisms, quantifiers are used in the premises and conclusion. The task is to determine if the conclusion follows logically from the premises.

The premises and conclusion of a syllogism are classified according to **mood.** There are four different moods, or combinations of positive and negative statements with the terms "all" or "some." The four moods are:

Mood	Abstract Example	Concrete Example
Universal Affirmative	All A are B.	All students are smart.
Particular Affirmative	Some A are B.	Some video games are fun.
Universal Negative	No A are B.	No smurfs are pink.
Particular Negative	Some A are not B.	Some democrats are not liberals.

As you can see from this table, a statement is universal if it contains the terms "all" or "no"; it is particular if it contains the term "some"; it is negative if it contains "no" or "not"; and it is affirmative if it is not negative. Thus, it should be easy to classify the mood of any statement by searching out the key terms.

Several syllogisms are presented here. Each consists of two premises and a conclusion. Work through each syllogism and decide if the conclusion is valid (V) or invalid (I). In order to be valid, the conclusion must *always* be correct, given its premises. If you can think of one way that the conclusion could be false when the premises are true, then it is invalid. Don't go on until you have worked through these syllogisms.

1. Premise #1   All A are B.
   Premise #2   All B are C.
   Conclusion   All A are C.   V or I

2. Premise #1   Some A are B.
   Premise #2   Some B are C.
   Conclusion   Some A are C.   V or I

3. Premise #1   All A are B.
   Premise #2   Some B are C.
   Conclusion   Some A are C.   V or I

4. Premise #1   No A are B.
   Premise #2   All B are C.
   Conclusion   No A are C.   V or I

5. Premise #1   No A are B.
   Premise #2   No B are C.
   Conclusion   No A are C.   V or I

6. Premise #1   All zaks are creb.
   Premise #2   All creb are bips.
   Conclusion   All zaks are bips.   V or I

7. Premise #1   Some flubs are gluck.
   Premise #2   Some gluck are chez.
   Conclusion   Some flubs are chez.   V or I

8. Premise #1   All vox are thed.
   Premise #2   Some thed are hef.
   Conclusion   Some vox are hef.   V or I

9. Premise #1   No crim are bub.
   Premise #2   All bub are glot.
   Conclusion   No crim are glot.   V or I

10. Premise #1   No zevs are hip.
    Premise #2   No hip are crep.
    Conclusion   No zevs are crep.   V or I

11. Premise #1   All boys are athletes.
    Premise #2   All athletes are muscular.
    Conclusion   All boys are muscular.   V or I

12. Premise #1   Some lawyers are honest.
    Premise #2   Some honest people pay taxes.
    Conclusion   Some lawyers pay taxes.   V or I

13. Premise #1   All judges are wise.
    Premise #2   Some wise people are liberals.
    Conclusion   Some judges are liberals.   V or I

14. Premise #1   No teenagers are happy.
    Premise #2   All happy people are rich.
    Conclusion   No teenagers are rich.   V or I

15. Premise #1   No professors are cool.
    Premise #2   No cool people are punk.
    Conclusion   No professors are punk.   V or I

According to the rules of logic, it should not matter if the syllogisms are presented in abstract terms of *A*s and *B*s, nonsense terms like "zev" and "creb," or meaningful terms like "lawyers" and "cool." The logical rules for deciding if a conclusion can be validly inferred from the premises remain the same. We're really saying "All _____ are _____." It should make no difference how we fill in the blanks; any letters, nonsense or meaningful words, or even fancy pictures should be handled in the same way. However, from a psychological perspective, there are important content differences. Did Syllogisms #6 to #10 seem easier to you than #1 to #5? Did the last five syllogisms seem the easiest? Did you realize that the same five syllogisms were used in each set with only the content words changing? I return to the "problem" of content in a later section, when I discuss common errors.

Determining If a Conclusion Is Valid

How did you go about deciding if the conclusions were valid? There are two different types of strategies that can be used with syllogisms to determine if a conclusion follows from its premises. If you've been reading the chapters in order, then you know that a common approach to improving thinking is the deliberate use of both spatial and verbal strategies. The same two approaches apply here. First, I present a spatial method for testing conclusions, then I provide some verbal rules that can also be used. Either method will "work," but you'll probably find that you prefer one method over the other.

Circle Diagrams

One way of determining if a conclusion is true is with the use of circle diagrams that depict the relationships among the three terms (A, B, C, or whatever we used to fill in the blanks). The degree to which the circles overlap depicts the inclusion or exclusion of the categories. Look very carefully at Fig. 4.1.

The four moods that statements in syllogisms can have are listed in the left-hand column of Fig. 4.1. Next to each statement are circle diagrams that are correct depictions of the relationships in the statement.

There are several different methods of drawing diagrams to depict the relationships among the terms in a syllogism. One of these methods is known as **Venn Diagrams,** named for the 19th-century English mathematician and logician who first introduced them. These are the same diagrams that you probably used in mathematics classes if you ever studied set theory. A second method of diagramming relationships is known as **Euler Diagrams.** According to popular lore, this method was devised by Leonard Euler, an 18th-century Swiss mathematician, who was given the task of teaching the laws of syllogistic reasoning to a German princess. Because the princess was having difficulty understanding the task, Euler created a simple procedure that could be used to understand the relationships among the terms and to check on the validity of inferences. A third method is called the "Ballantine method," because of its use of three overlapping circles. In all of these methods, circles are used to indicate category membership. The differences among these methods is not important here, and the general strategy of checking conclusions with circle drawings is referred to as **circle diagrams.** If you've learned a different method of circle diagrams in another context (e.g., a class on set theory or a logic class), then continue to use that method as long as it works well for you.

Let's draw circle diagrams to depict the relationships in Syllogisms #1, #6, and #11. The same diagram will work for these three syllogisms, because they are identical except for the content words.

Premise #1 states that "All A are B." Look at Fig. 4.1. There are two different ways of drawing circles that are correct interpretations of this relationship.

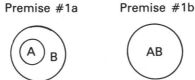

Premise #1a

Premise #1b

The A circle is in the B circle.

A and B are the same circle.

Universal Affirmative All A are B. (All angels are bald.)	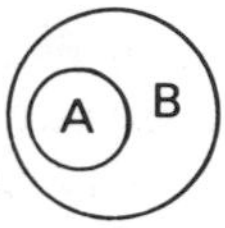 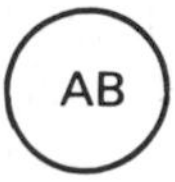 All A are B, *and* All A are B, *and* some B are not A. all B are A.

Particular Affirmative
 	
Some A are B.
(Some angels are bald.)
	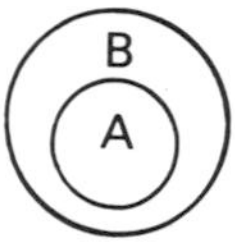 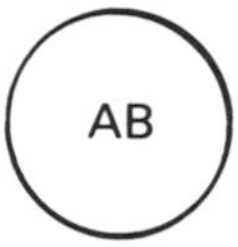 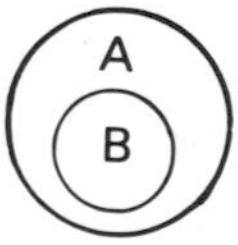 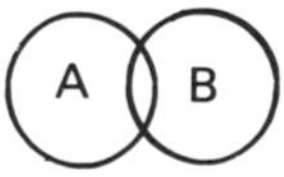
	
	All A are B, *and* All A are B, *and*
	some B are not A. all B are A.
	
	All B are A, *and* Some A are B
	Some A are not B. *and* some B are A.
	    Also some A are not B,
	    and some B are not A.

Universal Negative No A are B. (No angels are bald.)	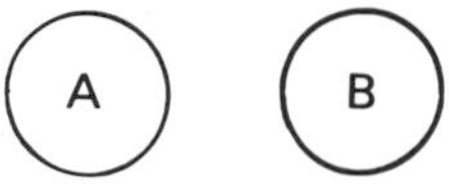 No A are B, and no B are A.
Particular Negative Some A are not B. (Some angels are not bald.)	  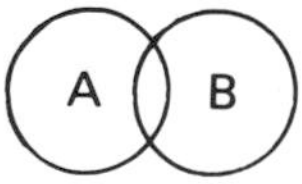 No A are B, and All B are A, *and* no B are A. some A are not B. Some A are B, and some B are A. Also some A are not B, and some B are not A.

FIG. 4.1. Circle diagrams depicting correct interpretations of the premises used in syllogisms. Note that "all" can have two correct interpretations, "some" can have four correct interpretations, "no" has one correct interpretation, and "some–not" can have three correct interpretations.

In the diagram on the left, the circle that has the letter A inside of it stands for all things that are A. This circle is inside the B circle to indicate that everything that is A is B. This diagram shows a situation in which "All A are B, and some B are not A." Using the more concrete language of Syllogism #11, this diagram depicts the situation in which "All boys are athletes, but there are athletes who are not boys." The diagram on the right is also a correct interpretation of "All A are B," but it represents a different interpretation of the A–B relationship. In this figure, "All A are B, and all B are A." Using the language of Syllogism #11, this translates to "All boys are athletes, and all athletes are boys." According to this depiction, everyone who is an athlete must also be a boy. Either of these diagrams is correct, given the information that "All A are B." It is important to consider both interpretations of this relationship.

Let's go on and consider the second premise in Syllogism #1, which is identical to the second premise in Syllogisms #6 and #11. Again, this premise is the universal affirmative mood and will look the same as the preceding figures, except that we changed the letters.

Premise #2a   Premise #2b

The B circle is in   B and C are the
the C circle.   same circle.

Given these four figures, two possible correct depictions of Premise #1 and two possible correct depictions of Premise #2, how do we use them to determine if the conclusion is valid? Start by drawing the relationships in the conclusion. This should be fairly easy because, in this example, the conclusion is also universal affirmative.

Conclusion: All A are C.

The A circle is in   A and C are the
the C circle.   same circle.

Now, to check the validity of the conclusion, draw *all* combinations of diagrams for Premise #1 and diagrams for Premise #2. Let's do this systematically, first putting together Premise #1a with Premise #2a, then Premise #1a with Premise #2b, then Premise #1b with Premise #2a, and finally Premise #1b with Premise #2b.

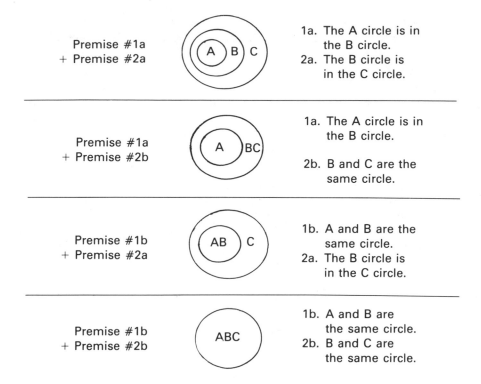

| Premise #1a
+ Premise #2a | | 1a. The A circle is in
the B circle.
2a. The B circle is
in the C circle. |

| Premise #1a
+ Premise #2b | | 1a. The A circle is in
the B circle.

2b. B and C are the
same circle. |

| Premise #1b
+ Premise #2a | | 1b. A and B are the
same circle.
2a. The B circle is
in the C circle. |

| Premise #1b
+ Premise #2b | | 1b. A and B are
the same circle.
2b. B and C are
the same circle. |

Look at the four correct circle diagrams that result from combining all possible interpretations of the two premises. Check each one. Is it always true that "All A are C?" I hope that you can see that the answer is "yes." In all four diagrams, the circle with A is either inside the circle with C or it is the same circle as the C circle.

Suppose that the conclusion had been, "All C are A." Is this a valid conclusion, given the premises? To answer this question, look at the diagrams that resulted from all combinations of the premises. If you can find one diagram in which this is false, then the conclusion in invalid. Can you find any? The first three conclusion diagrams depict relationships in which there are some C that are not A, thus this conclusion would be invalid.

The problem with using circle diagrams comes in drawing all possible combinations of the premises in order to check the validity of the conclusion (Guyote & Sternberg, 1981). Sometimes, there are as many as 33 different possible combinations. Fortunately, we really don't always have to draw all of them. As soon as you draw one combination in which the conclusion is false, you can stop there because you've already shown that the conclusion does not necessarily follow from the premises.

A list of steps for checking the validity of conclusions with circle diagrams is shown in Table 4.1. Stop now and look over the steps. Refer back to them as we work through the rest of the syllogisms.

TABLE 4.1
Steps for Determining the Validity of Conclusions
Using Circle Diagrams

---

1. Write out each premise and the conclusion of the syllogism.
2. Next to each statement, draw all correct diagrams, using the diagrams shown in Fig. 4.1.
3. Systematically combine all diagrams for Premise #1 with all diagrams for Premise #2. Try Premise #1a (the first diagram for Premise #1) with Premise #2a (the first diagram for Premise #2). Continue combining Premise #1a with all Premise #2 diagrams, then go on and combine all Premise #1b with all Premise #2 diagrams. Continue in this manner (Premise #1c with all Premise #2 diagrams, then Premise #1d with all Premise #2 diagrams) until
4. You find *one* diagram in which the conclusion is invalid or
5. You have tried all combinations of Premise #1 and Premise #2 diagrams.

Note: Sometimes, there will be more than one way to combine diagrams from the two premises. Be sure to try all combinations. When trying out all combinations, remember that there are five possible ways to combine two circles: (a) A inside B; (b) B inside A; (c) A and B overlapping partially; (d) A and B with no overlap (two separate circles); and (e) A and B represented by one circle (A and B are the same circle). These five possibilities are shown thus:

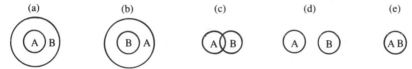

Let's try this method with Syllogisms #2, #7, and #12. I've drawn below the possible correct interpretations of each premise and the conclusion.

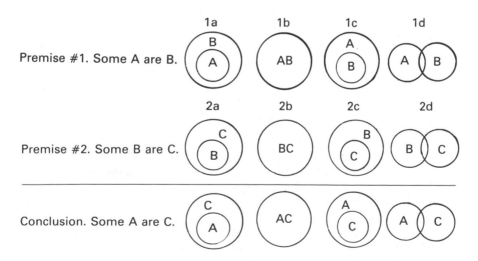

As you can see, a major problem will be considering all possible combinations that correspond to Premise #1 plus Premise #2 to check the validity of the conclusion. Let's start trying combinations in a systematic manner. First, draw combinations of Premise #1a with Premise #2a.

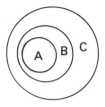

1a. The A circle is in the B circle.

2a. The B circle is in the C circle.

Is this drawing consistent with the conclusion that ''Some A are C?'' Because the A circle is inside the C Circle, the answer is ''yes.'' Let's go on and try Premise #1a with Premise #2b.

1a. The A circle is in the B circle.
2b. B and C are the same circle.

Is this drawing consistent with the conclusion that ''Some A are C?'' Again, the answer is yes, because the A circle is inside the C circle. Continue by combining Premise #1a with Premise #2c.

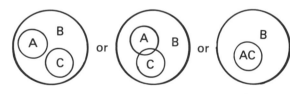

1a. The A circle is in the B circle.
2c. The C circle is in the B circle.

Notice that there is more than one way of combining these two diagrams in which the A circle is inside the B circle and the C circle is inside the B circle. The A and C circles can have no overlap, some overlap, or complete overlap (i.e., be the same circle) and still be inside the B circle. Look at these diagrams. Are they all consistent with the conclusion that ''Some A are C?'' Fortunately, no. The first diagram shows a situation in which the A circle is not inside the C circle, is not the same as the C circle, the C circle is not inside the A circle, and the A and C circle do not overlap. Why did I say, ''fortunately?'' Because we can stop here and decide that the conclusion is invalid. We found one combination of the two premises in which the conclusion does not follow from the premises; therefore, the conclusion is invalid.

As you will see when you work through Syllogisms #3, #8, and #13, the solution turns out to be identical to the preceding one. Let's try it. I've diagrammed the premises and the conclusion as follows:

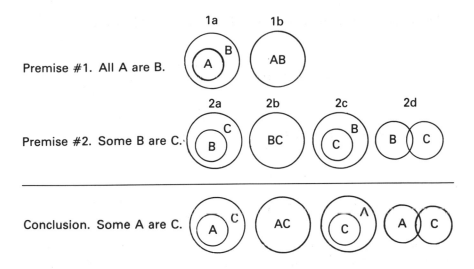

Premise #1. All A are B.

Premise #2. Some B are C.

Conclusion. Some A are C.

Now let's try all combinations of Premise #1 diagrams with Premise #2 diagrams, stopping at each step to check if the conclusion is valid.

Premise #1a
+ Premise #2a

1a. The A circle is in the B circle.
2a. The B circle is in the C circle.

Conclusion is OK; go on to next step.

Premise #1a
+ Premise #2b

1a. The A circle is in the B circle.
2b. B and C are the same circle.

Conclusion is OK; go on to next step.

Premise #1a
+ Premise #2c

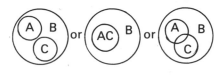

1a. The A circle is in the B circle.
2c. The C circle is in the B circle.

Stop here!

Again, fortunately, we found one combination of the premises in which we cannot conclude that "Some A are C." We can stop here and decide that the conclusion is invalid.

Here is the same combination process for Syllogisms #4, #9, and #14.

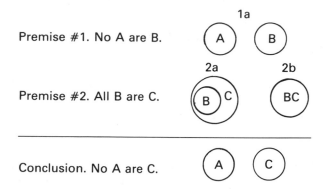

Premise #1. No A are B.

Premise #2. All B are C.

Conclusion. No A are C.

In order for the conclusion to be valid, there must be no combination of Premise #1 and Premise #2 in which A and C overlap. Let's combine Premise #1a with Premise #2a and see what happens.

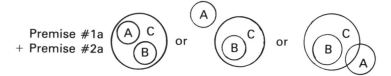

Premise #1a
+ Premise #2a

1a. A and B do not overlap.
2a. The B circle is in the C circle.

As you can see, when I combine Premise #1a with Premise #2a, I can draw a diagram in which A and B do not overlap, B is inside C, but A and C overlap. Therefore, the conclusion is invalid and I can stop here. These diagrams get easier with practice. I hope that you're enjoying thinking about ways the premises can combine. Try Syllogisms #5, #10, and #15.

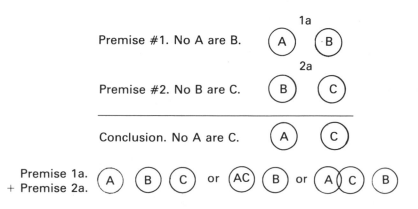

Premise #1. No A are B.

Premise #2. No B are C.

Conclusion. No A are C.

Premise 1a.
+ Premise 2a.

1a. A and B do not overlap.
2a. B and C do not overlap.

As you can see in the combination step, there are four different possible combinations of Premise #1 (no overlap of A and B) and Premise #2 (no overlap of B and C) in which A and C overlap, thus the conclusion is invalid.

Five Rules of Categorical Syllogisms

It's a peculiar thing about circle diagrams; some people love working on them and others seem to hate them. The problem in working with them is trying all possible combinations of representations for both premises. People who prefer to think spatially seem to "see" the combinations with apparent ease, whereas those who prefer verbal modes of representation seem to have more difficulty with this. For those of you who have difficulty combining premises into circle relationships, take heart, because there are verbal rules for determining if the conclusion of a syllogism is valid. These rules will work just as well as circle diagrams. Sternberg and Weil (1980) found that verbal and spatial strategies draw on different abilities and that the effectiveness of a given strategy depends on one's preferred mode of thought.

There are five rules that can be used to determine the validity of a conclusion. In order to use these rules, there are two additional terms that need to be learned.

There are three categories named in syllogisms, the A, B, and C, or whatever category names we substitute for them in more concrete examples. One of these categories is called the **middle term.** To determine which is the middle term, go to the conclusion. There are two categories in the conclusion; one is the subject of the sentence, the other is in the predicate. The category that is not mentioned in the conclusion is the middle term. It is called the middle term because it links the other two terms in the premises. Look back at Syllogism #13. The conclusion is "Some judges are liberals." "Judges" is the subject of this sentence, and "liberals" is the predicate adjective. The middle term is "wise." The middle term is in both premises, but it is not in the conclusion.

The second term that you need to know is **distributed.** A term is distributed if the statement applies to every item in the category (Govier, 1985). Consider the four types of category relationships shown in Table 4.2. I've indicated next to each one which terms are distributed and which terms are undistributed. As you can see in Table 4.2, categories that are modified by "all," "no," and "not" are distributed.

Look carefully at the statement "All A are B." B is undistributed in this statement, because there may be some B that are not A, so the statement is not about every B. On the other hand, consider "No A are B." In this case, B is

TABLE 4.2
Distributed and Undistributed Terms in the Four Moods of Syllogisms

All A are B.	A is distributed. (A is modified by "all.")
	B is undistributed. (B is undistributed because there may be some B that are not A.)
Some A are B.	Both A and B are undistributed.
No A are B.	Both A and B are distributed. (Both A and B are modified by "no.")
	(This is the same as saying that "No B are A.")
Some A are not B.	A is undistributed.
	B is distributed. (B is modified by "not.")

distributed because when we say "No A are B," we are also saying "No B are A." Thus, in the second case, the statement is about all B.

For a conclusion to be valid, the syllogism must pass all five of these rules. If it fails on any one of them, then it is invalid.

1. The middle term must be distributed in at least one premise.
2. Any term that is distributed in the conclusion must be distributed in at least one premise.
3. At least one premise must be affirmative. There are no valid conclusions with two negative premises.
4. If the conclusion is negative, one premise must be negative, and conversely, if one premise is negative, the conclusion must be negative.
5. If both premises are universal, the conclusion cannot be particular.

Let's apply these rules to the syllogisms we've already solved with circle diagrams.

Syllogism #1.
 All A are B.
 All B are C.
 All A are C.

The middle term for this syllogism is B. It is the one that is mentioned in both premises and that is missing from the conclusion. The first rule is that it must be distributed in at least one premise. It is. B is modified by "all" in the second premise, so it passes the first rule. The second rule is that any term that is distributed in the conclusion must be distributed in at least one premise. A is distributed in the conclusion and in the first premise, so it passes the second rule. The third rule is easily checked: At least one premise must be affirmative. In this syllogism, both premises are affirmative. The fourth rule only has to be checked if the conclusion is negative, so we can move on. The fifth rule is that if both premises are universal, the conclusion can't be particular. We have two universal premises and a universal conclusion, so this rule is passed. All five rules have been passed, so we conclude that the syllogism is valid. Not surprisingly, this is the same conclusion that was reached with the circle diagrams. Use the five rules to verify our answers with the circle diagrams for the other four syllogisms presented on pp. 129–130.

Syllogisms in Everyday Contexts

Somewhere during the last section, you may have said to yourself, "Why bother!" It may seem that syllogisms are artificial stimuli created solely to make work for students and teachers. If you did have this thought, you were questioning the **ecological validity** of syllogisms. Ecological validity concerns the real-world validity, or applications of a concept outside of the laboratory or classroom. In other words, do people use syllogistic reasoning in real-world contexts?

Syllogistic reasoning and the other types of reasoning (linear ordering and if, then statements) that are discussed later in this chapter are sometimes considered as a subset of problem solving. Often, when solving a problem, we begin with statements that we believe or know to be true (the premises) and then decide which conclusions we can logically infer from them.

Syllogisms also appear implicitly in normal English prose. Of course, in natural context, the premises and conclusions aren't labeled, but the underlying structure is much the same. They are especially easy to spot in legal and political arguments, and thus often appear on standardized tests for college, graduate, and law school admissions.

Here is an example of syllogistic reasoning that may seem more like the kind of syllogism you'd find in everyday contexts:

> The death sentence should be declared unconstitutional. It is the cruelest form of punishment that is possible, and it is also very unusual. The constitution specifically protects us against cruel and unusual punishment.

Can you conclude from these statements that the death sentence is unconstitutional? Try to formulate these sentences into standard syllogism form (two premises and a conclusion). Use circle diagrams or the five rules to check on the validity of the conclusion. Stop now and work on this natural-language syllogism. Your syllogism should be similar to this:

Premise #1: The death sentence is cruel and unusual punishment.
Premise #2: Cruel and unusual punishment is unconstitutional.
Conclusion: The death sentence is unconstitutional.

If we put this in terms of A, B, and C, this roughly corresponds to:

A = the death sentence
B = cruel and unusual punishment
C = unconstitutional

This then becomes:

All A are B.
All B are C.
All A are C.

In its abstract form, this becomes the same syllogism as Syllogism #1, which we've already established is valid. The point here is that syllogisms are often contained in everyday arguments. Often, we don't recognize them because they are not neatly labeled by premise and conclusion, but if you get in the habit of looking for them, you may be surprised how frequently they can be found.

Missing Quantifiers

When syllogisms are found in everyday use, the quantifiers are often missing. Sometimes this is done deliberately, in the hope that you will infer one particular quantifier (e.g., assume "all" instead of the more truthful "some.") Here is an example of categorical reasoning used in a recent presidential campaign. A presidential candidate (in the U.S. primaries) was questioned about his well-publicized extramarital affairs. He responded this way: I have not been perfect in my private life, but we have had other great presidents who were also not perfect in their private lives.

Let's convert this to a categorical syllogism:

Premise #1:   I am not perfect (in my private life).
Premise #2:   Some great presidents were not perfect (in their private lives).
Conclusion: I will be a great president.
(implied)

It its abstract form, this becomes:

A = I (the speaker)
B = people who are not perfect
C = great presidents

or

All A are B.
Some C are B.
All A are (will be) C.

The conclusion he wanted listeners to draw is that he would also be a great president. Check the validity of this conclusion either with circle diagrams or the five rules. Is the implied conclusion valid? Note, also, his choice of words to describe his extramarital affairs. This is the same reasoning that is being used in the Calvin and Hobbes cartoon shown on page 143.

In everyday language, the quantifiers may be somewhat different from those used here. "Every" and "each" may be used as substitutes for "all," and "many" and "few" may be used as substitutes for "some." It is a simple

matter to change them to the quantifiers used here and then check the conclusion for its validity (Nickerson, 1986).

Here is an example (with some editing) that I recognized in a recent conversation: "People who go to rock concerts smoke dope. John went to a rock concert. Therefore, John smokes dope." The validity of this everyday syllogism depends on whether the speaker believes that "All people who go to rock concerts smoke dope" or "Some people who go to rock concerts smoke dope." In understanding statements like these, it's important that you specify which missing quantifier is intended. If "some" is intended, then you quickly point out that it is not valid to conclude that John was among those who smoke dope. If "all" is intended, then you can question whether it is the appropriate quantifier.

Changing Attitudes With Syllogisms

The basic organization of two premises and a conclusion is frequently used to change attitudes. When used in this fashion, the first premise is a belief premise, the second premise is an evaluation of that belief or a reaction to the belief premise, and the conclusion is the attitude (Shaver, 1981). The basic structure is like this:

Belief premise
Evaluation premise
Attitude Conclusion

Consider how this works in the following example (Shaver, 1981):

Preventing war saves lives.
Saving lives is good.
Therefore, preventing war is good.

Over time, attitude syllogisms become linked so that the conclusion from one syllogism is used as the evaluation premise of another:

Defense spending prevents war.
Preventing war is good.
Therefore, defense spending is good.

In these syllogisms, the middle term (remember what this means?) becomes the reason for the conclusion. In general, the greater the number of syllogisms with the same conclusion that we believe are true, the greater the support for the conclusion. If I wanted you to conclude that defense spending is good, I'd also tell you that:

> Defense spending creates jobs.
> Creating jobs is good.
> Therefore, defense spending is good.

The quantifiers are implicit in these syllogisms, but the underlying organization is the same. It's a matter of determining if a conclusion follows from the premises.

Common Errors in Syllogistic Reasoning

> *At this point in the history of psychology, when it is claimed that machines can think, it seems strange to say that people cannot.*
> —Ceraso & Protivera (1971, p. 400)

© 1982, Sidney Harris, created for Discover.

Research has shown that some syllogisms are more difficult to solve than others. An analysis of the erroneous conclusions that people make has revealed that the errors fall into distinct types or categories. Categories of errors include confusing truth with validity, making illicit conversions, being misled by atmo-sphere effects, and using faulty strategies.

Confusing Truth With Validity

Earlier in this chapter, I said that the rules for deciding if a syllogism is valid are the same no matter what terms we use for A, B, and C. This probably bothered some of you. Suppose I said,

All students are lazy drunks.
You are a student.
Therefore, you are a lazy drunk.

You'd probably protest this conclusion. Given the premises, the conclusion is valid. Test it for yourself. But, that doesn't make it true. The next chapter addresses the issue of determining the truth or believability of the premises. So far, we've only considered the question of validity: whether a conclusion must be true if the premises are true. People very often have trouble separating truth from validity. This is particularly difficult when the conclusion runs counter to cher-ished beliefs.

Although the rules of logic dictate that content is irrelevant in the conclusions we formulate, the truth is that content does influence how we choose valid conclusions. It is possible to construct syllogisms so that the beliefs that most people maintain conflict with logical conclusions. **Belief bias** occurs when an individual's beliefs interfere with her or his selection of the logical conclusion. Here are some examples from a study by Morgan and Morton that was published in 1944. Obviously, most Americans in 1944 had very strong beliefs about World War II, which clearly influenced their reasoning process. Syllogisms like the following one were devised to investigate the way beliefs affected how people reason.

Some ruthless men deserve a violent death; since one of the most ruthless men was Heydrich, the Nazi hangman:
1. Heydrich, the Nazi hangman, deserved a violent death.
2. Heydrich, the Nazi hangman, may have deserved a violent death.
3. Heydrich, the Nazi hangman, did not deserve a violent death.
4. Heydrich, the Nazi hangman, may not have deserved a violent death.
5. None of the given conclusions seems to follow logically. (p. 48)

Again, in checking the validity of the conclusions, convert this to an abstract syllogism and then use either circle diagrams or the five rules

The logically correct answer is number 5. The authors presumed that response number 1 reflected the beliefs of American college students who served as subjects. When this syllogism was presented, 38% selected response number 1, as compared to 1% when the syllogism was presented in abstract terms, using the letters X, Y, and Z.

It should come as no surprise to you that human reasoning becomes illogical when we are discussing emotional issues. This is true for people in every all strata of society, even for Justices of the United States Supreme Court. When Justice William O. Douglas was new to the Supreme Court, Chief Justice Charles Evans Hughes gave him these words of advice, "You must remember one thing. At the constitutional level where we work, ninety percent of any decision is emotional. The rational part of us supplies the reasons for supporting our predilections" (Hunt, 1982, p. 129). Unfortunately, appellate legal proceedings are sometimes exercises in politics, with decisions changing as frequently as the political climate. Legal "reasoning" has sometimes served as a framework to persuade others that a conclusion is valid. If you understand how to formulate valid inferences, you'll be able to withstand and recognize its misuse by those who use it to their advantage.

Content Effects

The content, or topic, of the syllogism influences how we think, even when the topic is not an emotional one. In everyday reasoning, we use what we know about a topic to determine if a conclusion is logical. We don't rely (and probably should not rely) on the information given in the premises. Consider these two syllogisms (Bucci, presented in Braine, 1978, p. 2):

All football players are strong.
This man is strong.
Is this man a football player?

This is a simple syllogism. Most people will decide that they don't know.

All oak trees have acorns.
This tree has acorns.
Is it an oak tree? (p.2)

Most people will readily respond, "Yes," although this syllogism is identical in form to the one about football players. In their abstract form, both syllogisms become:

All A are B.
All C are B.
All C are A.

Braine (1978) concluded that "In general, then, the common fallacies of syllogistic reasoning can be seen as due to the intrusion into formal reasoning of habits characteristic of practical reasoning and ordinary language comprehension'' (p. 2). In other words, we use our knowledge about the world when we reason; we do not merely decide what logically follows from the premises we've been given.

The rules presented for determining if a conclusion is valid apply whether or not the premises are true (or believed to be true). In the next chapter, we consider how to evaluate premises and conclusions when the premises are not true.

Illicit Conversions

When most people read statements like, "All A are B," the representation they form in their mind is one in which it is also true that "All B are A," (Chapman & Chapman, 1959). As you should realize by now, "All A are B" is not the same as "All B are A." Transforming a premise into a nonequivalent form is a type of error known as an **illicit conversion.** Using circle diagrams to visualize illicit conversions, the premise "All A are B" is represented only by the diagram on the left, and the diagram on the right is not considered.

People tend to consider   People tend to ignore
this A–B relationship.   this A–B relationship.

It should be clear to you by now that either of these representations is correct, given that the mood of the premise is universal affirmative. (If you don't remember what these terms mean, you'll need to do some careful reviewing.) Many people interpret this statement to mean that A is the same as B, and thus illicitly convert or change the meaning. People do not reason the way logicians believe that they should. They systematically misinterpret the premises and/or fail to consider all possible interpretations.

Another common illicit conversion is the belief that "Some A are not B" also implies that "Some B are not A." The second statement is not equivalent to the first. What would circle diagrams of "Some A are not B" look like?"

Any of the three following diagrams is a correct depiction of this Particular Negative statement. Look closely at all of the diagrams.

   or

People tend to ignore   People tend to consider
these A–B relationships.   only this A–B relationship.

In the middle diagram, Some A are not B, and All B are A. Again, the conversion of "Some A are not B" to also mean that "Some B are not A" most likely occurs when people fail to consider all possible meanings of syllogism premises. In a study by Ceraso and Protivera (1971), subjects were given modified syllogisms that would help them to consider all possible interpretations of the premises. For example, the traditional form of the premise, "All yellow blocks are striped" was modified so that it became, "Whenever I have a yellow block, it is striped, but there are some striped blocks that are not yellow" (p. 403). People who were given the modified instructions made correct interpretations of the premises, and they did not make the illicit conversions. Stating the premise in its modified form helped them to improve their reasoning.

Atmosphere Effect

The **atmosphere effect** is an explanation of reasoning errors in syllogisms that was recognized for the first time in 1935 (Woodworth & Sells). The basic idea is that the logical terms "some," "all," "no," and "not" create an atmosphere or global impression that leads subjects to accept certain types of conclusions as valid. Certain terms predispose people to accept certain conclusions that may or may not be valid. Begg and Denny (1969) have listed three components of the atmosphere effect as exemplified in the following syllogisms:

1. No Smurfs live in Illinois.
   All people who live in Illinois are new wave.
   No Smurfs are new wave.
   Valid or Invalid?

Although the correct answer is "invalid," many people get this syllogism wrong. The atmosphere effect that occurs in this type of syllogism was described as: Whenever one or more of the premises is negative, people believe that the valid conclusion will also be negative (i.e., the conclusion will contain the words "no" or "not.")

2. Some politicians are dishonest.
   Some dishonest people are rich.
   Some politicians are rich.
   Valid on Invalid?

The correct answer is "Invalid." This is another example of a common error in syllogistic reasoning. Whenever one or more of the premises contains the word "some" (particular form), the most commonly accepted conclusion will contain the word "some."

3. All professors are intellectuals.
   All snobs are intellectuals.
   All professors are snobs.
   Valid in Invalid?

The correct answer is "Invalid." This is another common example of a common error. Whenever both premises contain the word "all" and are affirmative (universal affirmative), the most commonly accepted conclusions will contain "all" and be affirmative.

If you drew circle diagrams to depict these syllogisms, or used the five rules, you would have avoided falling prey to the atmosphere effect errors. I'll work through the first one for you:

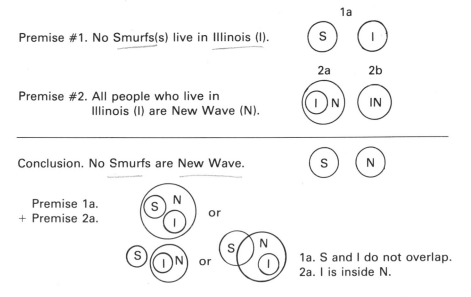

Premise #1. No Smurfs(s) live in Illinois (I).

Premise #2. All people who live in
Illinois (I) are New Wave (N).

Conclusion. No Smurfs are New Wave.

Premise 1a.
+ Premise 2a.

1a. S and I do not overlap.
2a. I is inside N.

Using the five rules for valid conclusions, you'll see that the middle term is "Illinois," because it is not mentioned in the conclusion and is mentioned in both premises. According to Rule #1, the middle term must be distributed in at least one premise. Illinois is distributed in both premises, so the conclusion passes the first rule. The second rule is that any term that is distributed in the conclusion must be distributed in at least one premise. Both "Smurfs" and "new wave" are distributed in the conclusion. The term "Smurfs" is distributed in the first premise, but the term "new wave" is not distributed in the premises. Because the conclusion did not "pass" this rule, it is invalid.

Check the last two syllogisms for yourself.

Research on the kinds of illogical conclusions that people are willing to accept as true has shown that people who have never had formal training in reasoning often make the kinds of mistakes predicted by the atmosphere effect. J. R. Anderson (1985) has suggested that people rely on the atmosphere effect for understanding difficult syllogisms. They rely on a few key words (all, some, not, no) without working through the problem. Furthermore, Anderson argued that, although the atmosphere effect will sometimes lead to erroneous conclusions, "used by itself, the atmosphere heuristic leads to performance more than 80 percent correct. This is not bad for such a crude heuristic'' (p. 277). (A heuristic is a ''rule of thumb'' or informal strategy for making decisions. For a discussion of the use of heuristics, see chapter 8, ''Decision Making.'') The term **paralogic** has been coined to denote that, although people are not strictly logical, they do utilize logiclike standards when interpreting statements. However, logiclike standards will sometimes lead to invalid conclusions, whereas logic standards ensure valid conclusions.

Research has shown that it is easy to learn to avoid errors that are caused by the atmosphere effect. Simpson and Johnson (1966) explained the atmosphere effect to their students, using an explanation similar to the one presented in this section, and, after only a few minutes of training, their students substantially reduced the number of atmosphere effect errors that they made.

Faulty Strategies

Johnson-Laird and Steedman (1978) have done much of the seminal work on understanding how people solve syllogisms. They proposed a theory to explain their results. What do people do when faced with syllogisms like this one?

No florists are bowlers.
Some bowlers are athletic.
No florists are athletic.

The psychologists' study indicated that people imagine a roomful of florists and bowlers, each wearing different hats to symbolize that ''No florists are bowlers.'' The bowlers are wearing hats that look like bowling balls and the florists are wearing flowers in their hats. Some of the bowlers are also wearing athletic clothing to symbolize that ''Some bowlers are athletic.'' People then use these imagerylike depictions to derive conclusions. Although this may be an adequate description of the way untrained subjects solve syllogisms, it is a fallible system that will sometimes lead to invalid conclusions. Because none of the imaginary florists are wearing athletic clothing, people tend to falsely conclude that ''No florists are athletic.'' If you use circle diagrams and remember to diagram all of the possible relations or use the five rules of syllogisms, you'll find a substantial improvement in your reasoning skills.

LINEAR ORDERING

Reasoning is simply a matter of getting your facts straight.
—B. F. Anderson (1980, p. 62)

Joel is stronger than Bill, but not as strong as Richard. Richard is stronger than Joel, but not as strong as Donald. Who is strongest and who is second strongest?

Although I'm sure that you've never met Joel, Donald, Richard, and Bill, I'm also sure you could answer this question. The premises or statements in this problem give information about the orderly relationship among the terms, hence it is called a **linear ordering** or **linear syllogism.** Like the syllogisms presented in the last section, the premises are used to derive valid conclusions; only this time we're concerned with orderly relationships instead of class inclusion and exclusion as denoted by terms like "all," "some," "no," and "not." How did you solve the problem about Joel, Donald, Richard, and Bill? Most people work line-by-line, ordering the people as specified in each line:

"Joel is stronger than Bill but not as strong as Richard" becomes:

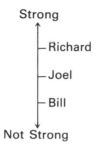

Strong

— Richard

— Joel

— Bill

Not Strong

"Richard is stronger than Joel, but not as strong as Donald" adds Donald to the previous representation:

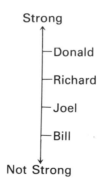

Strong

— Donald

— Richard

— Joel

— Bill

Not Strong

Thus, it is easy to "see" that Donald is strongest and Richard is second strongest.

Research with linear syllogisms has shown that people rely, at least in part, on spatial imagery or some sort of spatial representation to answer the question. Spatial imagery, however, is only part of the process.

According to a study by DeSoto, London, and Handel (1965), Mickey Mantle and Willie Mays were both having a bad day at an exhibition baseball game, which prompted a fan to shout, "I came to see which of you guys was better, Mantle or Mays. Instead I'm seeing which is worse" (p. 513). How did they know that they had been insulted? The term "better" conveys a neutral evaluation, whereas the term "worse" conveys a sense that both are bad. According to the laws of logic, "Mantle is better than Mays" should be equivalent to "Mays is worse than Mantle," but the two sentences clearly are not. As discussed in chapter 3, adjectives that connote a bias are called "marked" adjectives.

Work through the following pairs of linear syllogisms. Try to decide if one member of each pair is easier to solve than the other:

1. a. Julio is smarter than Diana.
        Diana is smarter than Ellen.
        Who is smartest? Julio, Diana, Ellen, or don't know.

                        or

    b. JoAnne is taller than Susan.
        Rebeccah is taller than JoAnne.
        Who is shortest? JoAnne, Susan, Rebeccah, don't know.

2. a. Pat is not taller than Jim.
        Jim is shorter than Tiffany.
        Who is tallest? Pat, Jim, Tiffany, don't know.

                        or

    b. Les is worse than Moshe.
        Harold is worse than Moshe.
        Who is worst? Les, Moshe, Harold, don't know.

3. a. Stuart doesn't run faster than Louis.
        Louis doesn't run slower than Dena.
        Who is slowest? Stuart, Louis, Dena, don't know.

                        or

    b. Howard is fatter than Ace.
        Ace is thinner than Kyla.
        Who is thinnest? Howard, Ace, Kyla, don't know.

As you worked through these problems, did some seem more difficult to you than others?

You probably found Problem 1a to be the easiest. Research has shown that, when the second term in the first premise is the first term in the second premise (Diana in Problem 1a), and when the comparison terms are congruent (smarter, smarter, smartest), the linear ordering is fairly easy to solve. Problem 1B does not follow this simple form. The comparisons are between JoAnne and Susan and Rebeccah and Susan. In addition, the comparison terms are not congruent (taller, taller, shortest). The correct answer for 1a is Julio. The correct answer for 1b is Susan.

Problem 2a contains the negation term "not," which adds to the complexity of the problem. In addition, information is given in terms of both taller and shorter, which makes this a difficult problem. The correct answer is Tiffany. (Pat could be the same height or shorter than Jim.) You can represent this relationship graphically as:

Tall
├─Tiffany

├─Jim   ┬
Short   ↓ Pat (same as or shorter than Jim)

Although Problem 2b contains all congruent comparison terms (worse, worse, worst), some people find it tricky because we don't know if Les or Harold is worst. In addition, research has shown that it is more difficult to comprehend terms like "worse" than it is to use terms like "better," because it denotes that all three are bad, whereas "better" is a more neutral term. Reasoning with marked adjectives is more difficult than reasoning with unmarked adjectives. (The correct answer is "don't know"). Problem 3a contains two negative terms as well as incongruent comparison terms (faster, slower, slowest). From the information given, we can't determine who is slowest. Problem 3b is somewhat easier, because it doesn't contain negatives, but it does contain incongruent comparison terms (fatter, thinner, thinnest). The answer as to who is thinnest is Ace.

Hopefully, as you worked through these problems, you discovered some of the following psychological principles of linear orderings:

1. Orderings are easiest to solve when comparison terms are congruent.
2. Solutions will be facilitated if the second term in the first premise is the first term in the second premise.
3. Negations make the problem more difficult.
4. Comparisons between adjacent terms (e.g., "Julio" and "Diana" in Problem 1a) are more difficult than comparisons between end terms ("Julio" and "Ellen") (Potts, 1972).
5. When you are faced with a difficult syllogism of any sort, a good strategy for solving it is to draw a spatial array. With a linear syllogism, draw a linear array, so that the relationships among the terms can be inspected visually.
6. Comparison terms that limit the meaning of a sentence, like "worse" and "dumber," are more difficult to process than more general and neutral terms like "better" and "smarter." The adjectives that connote a bias (e.g., "worse," "dumber") are called **marked adjectives,** and the neutral adjectives are called **unmarked adjectives.**

These summary remarks can be used as an aid for clear communication of linearly ordered information. When you want someone to understand a linear ordering, use congruent terms, make the second term in the first premise the first term in the second premise, and avoid negations and marked adjectives.

IF, THEN STATEMENTS

Reason, of course, is weak, when measured against its never-ending task. Weak, indeed, compared with the follies and passions of mankind, which, we must admit, almost entirely control our human destinies, in great things and small.

—Albert Einstein (1879–1955)

"If, then" statements, like the other examples of reasoning presented in this chapter, utilize premises that are known or believed to be true to determine if a conclusion validly follows. "If, then" statements are concerned with **contingency relationships**—some events are dependent or contingent upon the occurrence of others. If one of the premises is true, then a second premise must also be true. "If, then" statements are sometimes called **conditional logic** or **propositional logic.** Work through the four following "if, then" statements. Decide if the third statement is a valid conclusion.

1. If she is rich, she wears diamonds.
   She is rich.
   Therefore, she wears diamonds.
   Valid or Invalid?
2. If she is rich, she wears diamonds.
   She isn't wearing diamonds.
   Therefore, she isn't rich.
   Valid or Invalid?
3. If she is rich, she wears diamonds.
   She is wearing diamonds.
   Therefore, she is rich.
   Valid or Invalid?
4. If she is rich, she wears diamonds.
   She isn't rich.
   Therefore, she isn't wearing diamonds.
   Valid or Invalid?

In each of these problems, the first premise begins with the word "if"; the "then" is not explicitly stated ("then she wears diamonds"). The first part of this premise ("If she is rich") is called the **antecedent;** the second part ("she wears diamonds") is called the **consequent.**

Like the other types of deductive reasoning problems, conditional statements can be represented with a spatial display. Tree diagrams, which are used in several chapters in this book, can be used to determine validity. You begin by drawing the antecedent as the first event on the "tree" and add a second branch to represent the consequent. The validity of the conclusion can be determined by examining the branches. Let's try this with the first problem.

"If she is rich" becomes:

"She wears diamonds" is added as a second set of branches by showing that the "rich" node is always followed by "diamonds," but the "not rich" node may or may not be followed by "diamonds." We put both possibilities on the branches leading from "not rich," because we are not given any information about the relationship between being "not rich" and "wearing diamonds."

When we are told that "She is rich," we move along the branches from the "rich" node and conclude that she "wears diamonds."

Thus, the conclusion to Problem #1 is valid. The technical term for this problem is *affirming the antecedent.* In this case, the second premise affirms or indicates that the antecedent is true; therefore, its consequent is true.

Problem #2 also contains a valid conclusion. The tree diagram is exactly the same as in the first problem, because the same "if, then" statements are made. In determining the validity of the conclusion, we begin with "She isn't wearing diamonds" and trace this back to the "not rich" node. Because the second premise indicates that the consequent is not true, this sort of problem is technically called *denying the consequent.*

Many people are willing to conclude that Problem #3 is also valid when, in fact, it is not. Although it must be assumed to be true that if she is rich, she wears diamonds, it is also possible that poor people wear diamonds. I have found that intelligent college students have difficulty with this problem. Because the second premise states that the consequent has occurred, this sort of problem is called *affirming the consequent.* It is fallacious to believe that, because the consequent is true, the antecedent must also be true. "If," in these reasoning problems, doesn't mean "if and only if," which is how many people interpret it. Of course, she may be rich—it may even be more likely that she is rich,—but we cannot conclude that she is rich just because she is wearing diamonds. You can see this on the tree diagram. There are two different nodes labeled "wear diamonds," one connected to the "rich" node and one connected to the "not rich" node. We cannot determine which must be true, because either is possible.

The fallacy of affirming the consequent is similar to the syllogism error, illicit conversion, that was discussed earlier in this chapter. If you recall (if you don't, you'd better reread this section), illicit conversions occur when people think that "All A are B" also means that "All B are A." Illicit conversions, in "if, then" statements occur when people believe that "If A, then B" also means "If B, then A." In formal language, this error is called *affirming the consequent,* but you should be able to see that it is just another type of illicit conversion.

Problem #4 is also invalid, although it is tempting to conclude that if she isn't rich, she isn't wearing diamonds. Can you guess the technical term for this sort of problem? It is called *denying the antecedent,* because Premise #2 states that the antecedent is false. Again, by starting at the "not rich" node, you can see that it is connected to both "wears diamonds" and "doesn't wear diamonds," so either is possible.

A summary of these four kinds of reasoning, with examples of each, is shown in Table 4.3.

Several popular advertisements take advantage of people's tendencies to make invalid inferences from "if, then" statements. A highly successful yogurt commercial goes something like this:

> Some very old people from a remote section of the Soviet Union are shown. We're told that it is common for people in this remote region to live to be 110 years old. We're also told that they eat a great deal of yogurt. The conclusion that the advertisers want people to make is that eating yogurt will make you live 110 years.

Implicitly, we're being told that if we eat yogurt, then we'll live to be 110 years old. Of course, it's possible to live to be 110 without ever tasting yogurt, and we have no reason to believe that yogurt has added years to their lives. These remote Russians engage in strenuous physical labor most of their lives and do not come into contact with many outsiders who carry potentially contagious diseases. Either of these facts, or countless others, including heredity, could account for their longevity. (It is also possible that the longevity claim is subject to question.) The advertisers are obviously hoping that the viewers will fall prey to the fallacy of affirming the consequent and say to themselves, "If I eat yogurt, I will live to a very old age."

"If, then" statements, like syllogisms and linear orderings, appear implicitly in standard prose. Of course, we seldom find them neatly labeled "premise and conclusion." Yet, they are often the basis for many common arguments. The fallacies of denying the antecedent and affirming the consequent in everyday contexts are quite common.

TABLE 4.3
Four Kinds of Reasoning with If, Then Statements

	Antecedent	Consequent
Affirming	Affirming the Antecedent Valid Reasoning Example: If I am dieting, then I will lose weight. I am dieting. Therefore, I will lose weight.	Affirming the Consequent Invalid Reasoning Example: If Harry went to the supermarket, then the refrigerator is full. The refrigerator is full. Therefore, Harry went to the supermarket.
Denying	Denying the Antecedent Invalid Reasoning Example: If it is raining, then my hair is wet. It is not raining. Therefore, my hair is not wet.	Denying the Consequent Valid Reasoning Example: If Judy and Bruce are in love, then they are planning to marry. They are not planning to marry. Therefore, Judy and Bruce are not in love.

There is currently an acrimonious debate over the issue of providing junior and senior high school students with contraceptive information. The pro side argues that if students are given this information, then they will act responsibly when engaging in intercourse. Formally, this becomes: If students receive contraceptive information, then they will engage in "protected" intercourse. The con side argues that students should not engage in intercourse (whether protected or not); therefore, they should not receive contraceptive information. This is an example of the fallacy of denying the antecedent. It does not follow that if they are not given contraceptive information, then they will not engage in intercourse.

Content Effects

A point that has been made repeatedly throughout this chapter is that people often do not reason according to the laws of formal logic without instruction in reasoning. In everyday (practical) reasoning, we use information that is not stated in the premises in order to decide if the conclusion follows from the premises. One sort of knowledge we rely on is our knowledge about the content of the premises. The following two sentences demonstrate this point (Braine, 1978):

If Hitler had had the atomic bomb in 1940, he would have won the war.

and

If Hitler had had one more plane in 1940, he would have won the war. (p.19)

Many people would decide that the first sentence is probably valid and the second sentence is invalid because they confuse truth with validity. When we interpret, "if, then" statements in everyday contexts, we rely on our knowledge about the content to decide if a conclusion follows. According to the rules of formal logic, reasoning should be independent of content. We should all arrive at identical, logically correct conclusions no matter what the content is. Of course, humans are not perfect logic machines. We do and should determine if the premises are true before deciding if a conclusion follows. (This point is emphasized in the following chapter.)

If, and Only If

Certain contents seem to require that we understand them in a way that is inconsistent with the laws of logic. Suppose you are told: "If you mow the lawn, I'll give you five dollars" (Taplin & Staudenmeyer, 1973, p. 542). This statement invites the interpretation, "If you do not mow the lawn, I won't give you five dollars." In the everyday inference we make from language, this is a valid conclusion, although it is erroneous from the perspective of formal logic. In understanding statements of the "If p, then q" variety, the conclusions that we are willing to accept as valid depend very much on what p and q are. In this lawn-mowing example, the intended meaning is "if, and only if, you mow the lawn, then I'll give you five dollars." In dealing with real world "if, then" statements, you need to decide whether the intended message is "if p, then q" or "if, and only if, p, then q."

Negation

The use of negatives ("no," "not") in a reasoning problem makes it much more difficult to solve (Wason, 1969). These difficulties are apparent in the following example, in which the antecedent is negative.

> If the light is not green, I will go to Rome.
> *It is not true that the light is not green.*
> What, if anything, can you conclude?
> If the letter is B, then the number is not 4.
> *The number is not 4.*
> What, if anything, can you conclude?

These are difficult to deal with because of the use of negation and its affirmation or denial. The first statement denies the negative antecedent (not [not green]). This is called a **double negation.** You can't assume anything about the consequent when the antecedent is denied, even when the antecedent itself is negative. Look at the second example. Most people incorrectly decide that it is correct to conclude from the second example that "The letter is *B*." You should recognize this as an example of affirming the consequent.

I once heard a politician make a statement similar to these. He said, "It is not true that I do not favor the legislation." It took me a few seconds to realize that he implied that he favored the legislation. He could have meant that he was neutral with respect to the legislation, neither favoring nor opposing it, but in the context, I interpreted his statement to mean that he favored the legislation. This is an example in which I utilized context to clarify intended meaning. Recall that negation also makes linear orderings difficult to solve. In order to communicate clearly, avoid negations whenever possible.

Either/Or

Consider these two sets of premises:

Either Chuck is handsome, or else he is famous.
Chuck is not famous.
What can you conclude?

Either Chuck is handsome, or else he is not famous.
Chuck is famous.
What can you conclude?

The conclusions to both of these sets of premises is the same—Chuck is handsome. Most people find the second set of premises to be much more difficult to comprehend. "Either/or" premises are also used in reasoning. With either/or statements, only one of the two (or more categories) is true. The easiest way to deal with them is to draw two symbolic representations of what could be true, then see if you can eliminate one of them. The remaining one is the answer.

Let's try this with the preceding either/or statements. Either Chuck is handsome, or else he is famous.

Draw two circles, one representing each possible state, handsome and famous.

Now read the second sentence: Chuck is not famous. Cross out the circle labeled famous.

The remaining is "handsome." Therefore, he is handsome. Now, try this with the more difficult second example. Either Chuck is handsome, or he is not famous. Draw circles representing these two possible states.

Now read the second sentence: Chuck is famous. Because he can't be both famous and not famous at the same time, cross out the circle labeled "not famous."

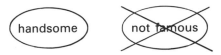

What is left? The circle labeled "handsome." This is the correct answer.
Either/or statements are frequently used in advertising. This is one of my favorites:

> Our low prices are guaranteed. If you can find a lower advertised price anywhere, we'll either match it or you get the item free!

Quite a deal. I doubt that they'll choose to give me the item free. What, then, is the alternative? The advertisement could have said: "We'll match any advertised price." Does it seem like a better deal to know that they'll either match the price *or* give it to you free? The issue here, of course, is who gets to choose. If it were my choice, I'd get the item free, but I doubt that the buyer will be the one to decide.

Confirmation Bias

Confirmation bias, the predilection to seek and utilize information that supports or confirms your hypotheses or premises, is a topic that has received a great deal of attention in recent years. It appears in several places in this text because it is seen in so many contexts. (See chapters 6 and 8, for related discussions.)
Demonstrate this effect for yourself (Johnson-Laird & Wason, 1970):

> Four cards are lying face up on a table in front of you. Every card has a letter on one side and a number on the other. Your task is to decide if the following rule is true, "If a card has a vowel on one side, then it has an even number on the other side." Which card or cards do you need to turn over in order to find out whether the rule is true or false? You may turn over only the minimum number necessary to determine if this rule is true. Please stop now and examine the cards below to determine which ones you would want to turn over. Don't go on until you have decided which cards you would want to turn over.

[handwritten at top: If I'm going to NY I always take a train (NY, PLANE)]

LA A	*NY* D	*TRAIN* 4	*PLANE* 7

Few people select the correct cards in this problem, which has become known as the **four-card selection task.** Most people respond "A only" or "A and 4". The correct answer is "A and 7." Can you figure out why?

The best way to determine the correct answer is to draw a tree diagram that corresponds to the statement, "If a card has a vowel on one side, then it has an even number on the other side." It should look like this:

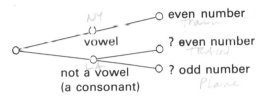

If A doesn't have an even number on the other side, the rule is false. Similarly, if 7 has a vowel on the other side, the rule is false. What about D and 4? D is a consonant. It doesn't matter if there is an even or odd number on the back, because the rule says nothing about consonants. Because 4 is an even number, it doesn't matter if there is a vowel or consonant on the back. The reason that this is such a difficult problem is that people interpret the rule to also mean "If a card does not have a vowel on one side, then it does not have an even number on the other side" or, without negatives, "If a card has a consonant on one side, then it has an odd number on the other side." These alternate interpretations are incorrect. Do you recognize the error as denying the antecedent? This is a robust (strong) effect. It is an extremely difficult task because of the crucial role of disconfirmation. People fail to appreciate the importance of a falsification strategy. This is exacerbated with the incorrect assumption that the converse of the rule is also true. The only correct way to solve this problem is to select only cards that can falsify the rule.

Part of the difficulty people have with this task may be related to the abstract nature of the problem. After all, there is very little we do in our everyday life that relates vowels and even numbers. Try out a more realistic and less abstract version of this task (adapted from Johnson-Laird, Legrenzi, & Legrenzi 1972):

In order to understand this task, you may need some background information (depending on your age). Many years ago, the United States Post Office had two different postage rates, known as first class and second class mail. You could pay full postage, which was 5 cents, if you sealed your letter (first class), or you could pay a reduced, 3-cent rate, if you merely folded the flaps closed and didn't seal them (second class). (First class mail had priority for delivery over second class mail.)

FIG. 4.2.   Which of these letters would you turn over to decide if the following rule is true: "If a letter is sealed, then it has a 5¢ stamp on it." (Adapted from Johnson-Laird, Legrenzi, & Legrenzi, 1972.)

Suppose you are a postal employee watching letters as they move across a conveyor belt. The rule to be verified or disconfirmed is: "If a letter is sealed, then it has a 5-cent stamp on it." Four letters are shown in Fig. 4.2. Which ones would you have to turn over to decide if the rule is true?

Stop now and work on this problem. Don't go on until you've decided which letters (at a minimum) you would have to turn over to test this rule. Be sure to draw a tree diagram that corresponds to the rule.

Did you notice that this is the same task that was posed earlier? The correct answer is the first sealed envelope and the last envelope (the one with the 3¢ stamp). This is an easier problem than the more abstract one, because people find it easier to understand that a letter that is not sealed could also have a 5¢ stamp on it than it is to understand that if the letter is not a vowel it could also have an even number on the back. Your tree diagram should look like this:

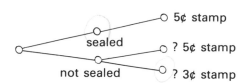

Johnson-Laird and Wason (1977) found that when the problem was presented in this realistic manner, 22 out of 24 subjects were able to solve the problem. Johnson-Laird and Wason concluded that our everyday experiences are relevant in determining how we reason. Cheng and Holyoak (1985) reached a similar conclusion. They found that, when they included a rationale for the rule, most of the people they asked to solve this problem had no difficulty with it. In the sealed envelope problem, they added the following rationale for the rule, "The country's postal regulation requires that if a letter is sealed, then it must carry a 20¢ stamp" (p. 400). Thus, the rule was extremely difficult to apply when it was presented in an abstract form, but when it was used in a familiar context with an explanation, it was easily used by most people.

Probabilistic Reasoning

> *The straight path of reason is narrow, the tempting byways are many and easier of access.*
>
> —Joseph Jastrow

In everyday reasoning, we don't view premises as "truths" that will necessarily require certain conclusions; instead, we think of premises as statements that either support or fail to support certain conclusions. Probabilistic reasoning occurs when we use the information we have to decide that a conclusion is probably true or probably not true. In everyday reasoning, we rely on notions of probability to assess the likelihood of a conclusion being true. Although probability is discussed in chapters 6 and 7, it is also a reasoning skill that should be considered in this context.

Suppose you learn that people who have untreated diabetes are frequently thirsty, urinate often, and have a sudden weight loss. You notice that you have these symptoms. Does it necessarily follow that you have diabetes? No, of course not, but these symptoms do make a diagnosis of diabetes more likely. In everyday contexts, much of our reasoning is probabilistic.

Consider this example presented by Polya (1957):

If we are approaching land, we see birds.
Now we see birds.
Therefore, it becomes more credible that we are approaching land. (p.186)

In a shorthand format, this becomes:

If A, then B.
B is true.
Therefore, A is more probable than it was before we knew that B is true.

Much of our everyday reasoning is of this sort, and although A is not guaranteed with probabilistic reasoning, it does become more probable after we've told the second premise. When viewed from the perspective of "if, then" reasoning, we would be committing the fallacy of affirming the consequent. But, in real life, we need to consider many variables and goals. Although seeing birds doesn't guarantee that land is near, I'd be getting happy if I saw birds while I was drifting and lost at sea. Probabilistic reasoning is often a good strategy, or "rule of thumb," especially because few things are known with absolute certainty in our probabilistic world. From the standpoint of formal logic, it is invalid to conclude that land is near. As long as you understand the nature of probabilities and the distinction between probabilistic and valid (must be true if the premises are true) reasoning, considering probabilities is a useful way of understanding and predicting events. When we reason in everyday contexts, we consider the strength and likelihood of the evidence that supports a conclusion and often decide if a conclusion is probable or improbable, not just merely valid or invalid. This point is explained more fully in chapter 7.

Our beliefs in the premises of syllogisms are not usually all-or-none. For example, consider this syllogism:

Premise 1: If a liberal candidate is elected to the school board, then the dress code will be abolished.

Premise 2: Jane Fonda, a liberal candidate, will be elected to the school board.

Conclusion: The dress code will be abolished.

Suppose that you believe that there is an 80% chance that the first premise is true and a 75% chance that the second premise is true. How would this affect your belief in the conclusion? It should seem clear that you would believe that, although the abolition of a dress code is likely, it is not a certainty. (Of course, you would also need to know the probability of a nonliberal being elected and the probability of a nonliberal abolishing the dress code.) The mathematical method for determining the actual probability of the conclusion occurring (in this case, abolishing the dress code), is given in chapter 7.

Because much of our reasoning is dependent on the rules of probability, McGuire (1981) has coined the term **probabilogical** to describe the joint effects of these disciplines on the way we think. Accordingly, we place greater faith in conclusions when we believe that the premises are highly probable than when we believe that the premises are unlikely.

REASONING IN EVERYDAY CONTEXTS

Reasoning is the only ability that makes it possible for humans to rule the earth and ruin it.

—Scriven (1976, p. 2)

Syllogisms, linear orderings, and "if, then" statements are commonly found in everyday conversation. Of course, they are embedded in discourse and not labeled by premise or conclusion. They are sometimes used in ways that seem to be either deliberately misleading, or at least to capitalize on the common reasoning errors that most people make.

If you pay careful attention to bumper stickers, you'll probably be surprised to find that many are simple reasoning problems. Consider the bumper sticker I recently saw on a pick-up truck:

> All (should be Some)
> Off-road users
> are not abusers.

The off-road users that this bumper sticker refers to are dirt bike riders who enjoy racing through open land (unpaved areas). Many people are concerned that this sport is destroying our natural resources by tearing up the vegetation. This bumper sticker is designed to present the opposing view. Notice how this is accomplished. The term "all" is implied in the first premise, when in fact "some" is true. You should recognize this as a syllogism with missing quantifiers.

Another popular bumper sticker that relies on missing quantifiers to make the point is:

> If guns are outlawed,
> only outlaws will have guns.

If A then B
A
∴ B

This is a standard "if, then" statement. The implied conclusion is "don't outlaw guns."

Suppose someone responded to this bumper sticker by suggesting that if guns are outlawed approximately 80% of the crimes of violence and 90% of the petty crimes that are committed with a gun would probably be committed with a less dangerous weapon. How does an argument like this refute the "if, then" statement and its implied conclusion on the bumper sticker?

Consider a common argument that often appears in a slightly disguised form:

If minorities are not as bright as Whites, then they will score lower on tests of intelligence. *A ... B*

Minorities score lower on tests of intelligence. *B   Affirm Consequent*

∴ A

Obviously, a conclusion is implied.

The implied conclusion is that it therefore follows that minorities are not as bright as Whites. I hope that you realize that this is an invalid conclusion. This is the fallacy of affirming the consequent. It is possible that minorities will score lower than Whites on intelligence tests for a host of other reasons (e.g., test bias, culture differences, etc.). Furthermore, only some minorities score lower than Whites. Many minorities score higher than Whites. The implied conclusion is invalid.

APPLYING THE FRAMEWORK

1. *What is the goal?* In deductive reasoning, the goal is to determine which conclusions are valid, given premises or statements that we believe are true. When you identify your goal as a deductive reasoning task, you will use the reasoning skills presented in this chapter.

2. *What is known?* In everyday prose, you will have to convert phrases and sentences into a reasoning format. You will have to determine what the premises are before you can decide whether they support a conclusion. Often, quantifiers are missing and conclusions are left unstated. Sometimes, you will have to consider context to decide if "if, then" really means "if, and only if, then." You will have to decide if you are reasoning with implied or explicit quantifiers, if there is a linear ordering, and whether an "if, then" statement is being made.

3. *Which thinking skill will get you to your goal?* The following skills to determine whether a conclusion is valid were presented in this chapter. Review each skill and be sure that you understand how and when to use each one.

- discriminating between deductive and inductive reasoning
- identifying premises and conclusions
- using quantifiers in reasoning
- solving categorical syllogisms with circle diagrams
- solving categorical syllogisms with the five rules
- understanding the difference between truth and validity
- recognizing when syllogisms are being used to change attitudes
- using linear diagrams to solve linear syllogisms
- watching for marked adjectives
- using the principles of linear orderings as an aid to clear communication
- reasoning with "if, then" statements
- using tree diagrams with "if, then" statements
- avoiding the fallacies of confirming the consequent and denying the antecedent
- using circles with either/or statements
- examining reasoning in everyday contexts for missing quantifiers and use of fallacies
- recognizing and avoiding belief bias, confirmation bias, and illicit conversions

4. *Have you reached your goal?* This is an accuracy check on your work. When determining valid conclusions from categorical syllogisms, did you get the same answer with both the rules for syllogisms and the circle diagrams? Did you consider all combinations of representations when drawing your diagrams? Did you consciously consider common fallacies and biases so as to be sure to avoid them? Does your answer make sense?

CHAPTER SUMMARY

1. Deductive reasoning (the type of reasoning considered in this chapter) is the use of premises or statements that we accept as true to derive valid conclusions.

2. People don't approach reasoning problems according to the laws of formal logic. Instead of determining whether a conclusion logically follows from the premises as they are stated, there is a tendency to alter the premises according to one's own beliefs and then decide whether a conclusion follows from the altered statements.

3. Quantitative syllogisms indicate which terms belong in the categories that are specified. Statements in syllogisms can take one of four different moods: universal affirmative, particular affirmative, universal negative, and particular negative.

4. When syllogisms involve meaningful terms and categories, people often use their knowledge of the categories and their beliefs about the topics to determine which conclusions are valid.

5. Circle diagrams are useful aids for understanding relationships and checking inferences in syllogisms. The extent to which circles overlap depicts category inclusion and exclusion. An alternative to circle diagrams that many people prefer is to check conclusions for validity using the five rules of syllogisms.

6. The greatest difficulty in using circle diagrams is being certain that all combinations of the two premises have been represented.

7. Illicit conversions are common errors in syllogisms. The most frequent illicit conversion is to interpret "All A are B" as also meaning that "All B are A."

8. The atmosphere effect leads to erroneous conclusions, because the quantifiers in premises (e.g., "all," "some," "no") predispose people to consider conclusions that contain similar terms.

9. Human reasoning is often biased by beliefs about emotional issues.

10. People often confuse truth with validity. Validity refers to the form of an argument and is unrelated to content. If a conclusion necessarily follows from the premises, then it is valid. The topic of truth and believability of premises is addressed in chapter 5.

11. In linear orderings, we use premises to establish conclusions about ordered relationships. A good strategy for solving linear orderings is to utilize a spatial representation with the items arranged in an ordered manner.

12. In "if, then" statements, a conditional relationship is established. As in syllogisms and linear orderings, the premises that are given are used to determine valid conclusions.

13. "If" is frequently interpreted as "if, and only if" in "if, then" statements. Although this conversion is an error according to the rules of formal logic, sometimes it is justified by the context in which it is embedded.

14. Confirmation bias is the predilection or tendency to seek and utilize information that supports or confirms the hypothesis or premise that is being considered. The "four-card selection task" is a demonstration of this robust bias.

Terms to Know

Check your understanding of the concepts presented in this chapter by reviewing their definitions. If you find that you're having difficulty with any term, be sure to reread the section in which it is discussed.

Reasoning. Has two forms: deductive and inductive. When reasoning deductively, we use our knowledge of two or more premises to infer if a conclusion is valid. When reasoning inductively, we collect observations and formulate hypotheses based upon them.

Conclusion. An inferential belief that is derived from premises.

Logic. A branch of philosophy that explicitly states the rules for deriving valid (correct) conclusions.

Illogical. Reaching conclusions that are not in accord with the rules of logic.

Failure to Accept the Logical Task. In every day reasoning, we alter the statements we're given according to our personal beliefs and then decide if a conclusion follows from the altered statements. We reject the logical task of deciding if a conclusion follows from the statements as they are given.

Inductive Reasoning. Observations are collected that suggest or lead to the formulation of a conclusion or hypothesis.

Deductive Reasoning. Use of stated premises to formulate conclusions that can logically be inferred from them.

Syllogistic Reasoning. A form of reasoning that involves deciding whether or not a conclusion can be properly inferred from two or more statements.

Quantifiers. Terms like "all," "some," "none," and "no" that are used in syllogisms to indicate category membership.

Categorical Reasoning. A type of syllogistic reasoning in which the quantifiers "some," "all," "no," and "none" are used to indicate category membership.

Syllogism. Two or more premises that are used to derive a valid conclusion or conclusions.

Premises. Statements that allow the inference of logical conclusions.

Mood. Used to classify the premises and conclusions of a categorical syllogism. There are four moods that are dependent on the quantifiers used in the statements. The four moods are: universal affirmative (all A are B); particular affirmative (some A are B); universal negative (no A are B); and particular negative (some A are not B).

Universal Affirmative. The mood of statements in a categorical syllogism with the format, "All A are B."

Particular Affirmative. The mood of statements in a categorical syllogism with the format, "Some A are B."

Universal Negative. The mood of statements in a categorical syllogism with the format, "No A are B."

Particular Negative. The mood of statements in a categorical syllogism with the format, "Some A are not B."

Circle Diagrams. A spatial strategy for determining the validity of a conclusion in a categorical syllogism. Circles are used to represent category membership.

Middle Term. In a categorical syllogism, it is the term that is omitted from the conclusion and is mentioned in both premises.

Distributed. In a categorical syllogism, a term is distributed when it is modified by "all," "no," or "not."

Ecological Validity. Concerns the real-world validity, or applications of a concept outside of the laboratory.

Belief Bias. The interference of one's personal beliefs with the ability to reason logically.

Illicit Conversions. Transformations of the premises in a syllogism into nonequivalent forms (e.g., converting "All A are B" into "All B are A").

Atmosphere Effect. When reasoning with syllogisms, the quantifiers create a set that causes people to accept certain conclusions as valid. Whenever one or more of the premises is negative, people tend to accept a negative conclusion; whenever one or more of the premises contains the word "some," people tend to accept conclusions that contain the word "some;" whenever both premises contain the word "all," people tend to accept conclusions that contain the word "all."

Paralogic. Although people do not behave according to the laws of formal logic, they do utilize logic-like standards when interpreting premises. These logiclike standards are called paralogic.

Linear Ordering (Also known as linear syllogism). Reasoning that involves the inference of orderly relationships (e.g., size, position) among terms.

Linear Syllogism. See linear ordering.

Marked Adjectives. Adjectives that connote a bias when they appear in a question (e.g., "poor," "dumb," or "small"). When asked "How poor is he?", it is presumed that the response will be toward the poor extreme and not toward the rich extreme.

Unmarked Adjectives. Adjectives that are neutral, in that they don't connote a particular direction when they appear in a question (e.g., "big," "smart," "tall"). When asked "How big is he?", the response could be a large or a small number. Compare with marked adjective.

If, Then Statements. Statements of a contingency relationship such that if the antecedent is true, then the consequent must be true.

Contingency Relationships. Relationships that are expressed with "if, then" statements. The consequent is contingent or dependent on the antecedent.

Conditional Logic (Also known as propositional logic). Logical statements that are expressed in an "if, then" format.

Antecedent. In "if, then" statements, it is the information given in the "if" clause.

Consequent. In "if, then" statements, it is the information given in the "then" clause.

Double Negation. The denial of a negative statement.

Probabilogical. Term coined to label the joint influences of probability and logic on the way we think.

Confirmation Bias. The predilection to seek and utilize information that supports or confirms one's hypothesis or premises while ignoring disconfirming information.

Four-Card Selection Task. A task that is often used to demonstrate confirmation biases. Subjects are required to indicate which of four cards they need to turn over in order to verify a rule about the contents of each side of the card. Overwhelmingly, subjects only select cards that will confirm the hypothesis that they are considering instead of seeking information that would disconfirm their hypothesis.

Content Effect. When we reason, we do not automatically accept the given premises as true. We use our knowledge about the topic (content) to judge the veracity of the premises and to supply additional information that influences which conclusion we will accept as valid.

Chapter Questions

Be sure that you can answer the following questions:

1. Are the psychological processes that people use in formulating conclusions the same ones that are specified by the laws of formal logic? How do they differ? (This should provide a helpful hint for the first question.)

2. Why is the legal process described as an "exercise in reasoning?"

3. What is a syllogism? State the mood for each of the following premises:
No drugs are good.
Some dogs can't bark.
All birds have feathers.
Some junk food is good.

4. Explain what circle diagrams are. Why are they used?

5. What are the five rules of syllogisms?

6. Define the terms "middle term" and "distributed."

7. How does content affect the way we reason with syllogisms? How does this differ from the rules of logic?

8. List and describe five common errors in the way people interpret syllogisms. How can circle diagrams be used to prevent these errors?

9. How are linear orderings similar to syllogisms? What are some factors that determine the ease with which we solve linear orderings?

10. What are the common errors that occur when people reason from "if, then" statements?

11. How do probability and logic interact to influence our belief in the validity of conclusions?

12. Confirmation bias is a ubiquitous effect. What is it? How is it demonstrated in the "four-card selection task?" Explain the correct answer to this problem.

Exercises

Try out the reasoning skills you've learned in this chapter.

I. Use circle diagrams to select the valid conclusion in these syllogisms: (Check your work with the rules for syllogisms.)

A. Some baseball players are scholars.
No blondes are baseball players.
Therefore:
1. All blondes are scholars.
2. Some blondes are scholars.

3. No blondes are scholars.
4. All of the above are invalid.

B. All cats are animals with nine lives.
All animals with nine lives are mammals.
Therefore:

1. All cats are mammals.
2. Some cats are mammals.
3. No cats are mammals.
4. All of the above are invalid.

C. Some accountants are honest.
Some honest people are dancers.
Therefore:

1. All accountants are dancers.
2. Some accountants are dancers.
3. No accountants are dancers.
4. All of the above are invalid.

D. No presidents are young.
All young people like LaVerne and Shirley.
Therefore:

1. No presidents like LaVerne and Shirley.
2. All presidents like LaVerne and Shirley.
3. No people who like LaVerne and Shirley are presidents.
4. All of the above are invalid.

E. Some poor people do not own houses.
All homeowners have assets.
Therefore:

1. Some poor people have assets.
2. No poor people have assets.
3. Some people with assets are poor.
4. All of the above are invalid.

II. Solve these linear orderings:

A. Carl is smarter than Abby.
Dan is smarter than Bruce.
Carl is smarter than Dan.
Who is smartest? *Carl*
Who is dumbest? *Can't Tell*

B. The dog is to the left of the rooster.
The newt is to the right of the rooster.
The hyena is to the left of the giraffe.
The newt is to the left of the hyena.
Which animal is on the right? *giraffe*

III. Which of these conclusions is valid?

A. If gun control reduces violent crime, then people will vote for it.
People are voting against gun control. *Not B Deny the conseq.*
Therefore:

1. Gun control reduces violent crimes.

2. Gun control does not reduce violent crime.

3. No definite conclusion.

B. If the Lakers were second, the 76ers came in first.   *If A ∴ B*
   The Lakers were second.   *A*
   Therefore: *Affirm Antec.*

   1. The 76ers came in first.

   2. The 76ers did not come in first.

   3. No definite conclusion.

C. If Robin doesn't phone home, her parents worry.
   Her parents are worried.   *affirm conseq.*
   Therefore:

   1. Robin didn't phone home.

   2. Robin phoned home.

   3. No definite conclusion.

D. If Edna doesn't practice, she won't play well.
   She doesn't play well.   *affirm conseq.*
   Therefore:

   1. Edna doesn't practice.

   2. Edna does practice.

   3. No definite conclusion.

E. Curly threw the pie or Larry didn't eat it.
   Larry ate it.   *deny conseq.*
   What can you conclude?

F. If you pass the English exam, you may take either Freshman Composition or Contemporary Literature, but not both. You passed the exam. Contemporary Literature is filled. What should you take?   *affirm antec.*

G. Either goats eat grass or elephants fly.
   Goats do not eat grass.
   What can you conclude?

H. Paula, Lee, Charlie, and Botwa are cousins. Paula is older than Lee, and younger than Charlie. Botwa is older than Charlie. Who is youngest?

I. Every man is an animal.
   No book is a man.
   Can I conclude that no book is an animal?

IV. "Mrs. Cooke had studied home economics in college. 'Youth is a time of rapid growth and great demands on energy,' she said. 'Many youngsters don't get enough vitamins in their daily diet. And since some vitamin deficiencies are dangerous to health, it follows that the health of many of our youngsters is being endangered by inadequate diet.' (Does it follow that the health of many youngsters is being endangered by inadequate diet? Give your reasoning)" (Henle, 1962, p. 371).

V. Consider the four cards below (adapted from Wason, 1969).

Every card has a triangle on one side and a circle on the other. Every card that has a black triangle on one side has a black circle on the other side. Your task is to indicate which of the cards you need to turn over in order to find out whether this rule is true.

VI. Present the four-card selection task to your family and friends. Keep track of the percentage of people who select the correct answer as well as other combinations of answers. Explain the correct answer to them.

VII. Find examples of valid and invalid reasoning from the newspaper, television, billboards, and conversations. If the reasoning is invalid, explain what is wrong with it. Use circle diagrams to check on the conclusions in syllogistic arguments.

SUGGESTED READINGS

The literature on reasoning dates back, at least, to Aristotle's time, and probably earlier. Currently, reasoning texts are written either by philosophers or psychologists, and each field has a different perspective on the area. The philosophical approach tends to be more prospective or concerned with what reasoning should be, whereas the psychological approach tends to be more descriptive or concerned with the way people actually reason. There is, however, considerable overlap between these two disciplines.

Some recommended texts that assume a philosophical viewpoint are Kelley's (1988) *The Art of Reasoning,* Wright's (1982) *Better Reasoning,* Salmon's (1973) *Logic,* Hitchcock's (1983) *Critical Thinking: A Guide to Evaluating Information,* Copi's (1986) *Informal Logic,* and Ruggiero's (1984) *The Art of Thinking.* My favorite of all of the texts in this area is Govier's (1985) *A Practical Study of Argument.*

Among the texts with a psychology perspective, my favorite is Nickerson's (1986) *Reflections on Reasoning.* It's interesting reading, filled with thought-provoking examples and excellent questions. Other recommended books in psychology are Revlin and Mayer's (1978) *Human Reasoning,* Wason and Johnson-Laird's (1972) *Psychology of Reasoning,* and Evans' (1982) *The Psychology of Deductive Reasoning.* An old classic text in psychology with a good basic section on reasoning is Bruner, Goodnow, and Austin's (1956) *A Study of Thinking.* A recent addition to this area is an edited book by Sternberg and Smith (1988). There is a good chapter on reasoning in Anderson's (1985) text *Cognitive Psychology and Its Implications.* There are also several good chapters in Galambos, Abelson, and Black's (1986) edited book *Knowledge Structures.* Especially recommended from this collection is a chapter by McGuigan and Black entitled, "Creation and Comprehension of Arguments."

If you are interested in the development of reasoning skills in children, you will want to consult Piper's (1985) article entitled "Syllogistic Reasoning in Varied Narrative Contexts: Aspects of Logical and Linguistic Development." He has presented several interesting examples of reasoning from text.

A useful and clever guide to logical pitfalls is Thouless' (1932) *Straight and Crooked Thinking.* The back section of the book contains a wealth of everyday examples of faulty logic. It may help you win arguments.

If you're looking for additional reasoning problems to practice and sharpen your skills, you'll enjoy Summers' (1968) *New Puzzles in Logical Deduction* and Summers' later book (1972) *Test Your Logic: 50 Puzzles in Deductive Reasoning.* Some of the material presented in Summers' books is similar to the topics covered in chapter 9 of this book "The development of Problem Solving Skills." This shouldn't be surprising to you, because early in the chapter, reasoning was described as one kind of problem solving. Two edited volumes with good collections of articles on this topic are Wason and Johnson-Laird's (1968) *Thinking and Reasoning* and Johnson-Laird and Wason's (1977) *Thinking: Readings in Cognitive Science*.

5 Analyzing Arguments

Contents

Eat All Day and Still Lose Weight

Trade your old body for a new one now through an amazing scientific break-through. Doctors and medical technicians have made it possible for people like you and me to lose weight **quickly** and permanently. Tested at university labs, retested at clinics and major hospitals and acclaimed by doctors all over the world, finally there is something that helps you lose weight. If years of stubborn fat build up have been your problem, **NOW AT LAST THERE IS A WAY TO ELIMI-NATE FAT, A WAY TO LOSE WEIGHT FAST AND EASILY.** We call it XXXXXXX because it totally attacks excess fat and fluids that have plagued most people for years. . . . Everyday you will feel stronger and full of pep and energy as the excess weight you have carried for so long is carved off your body. . . . **DON'T LET THIS GOLDEN OPPORTUNITY AND CHANCE OF A LIFE-TIME PASS YOU BY.** Just fill out the coupon below and let it be the ticket to a slimmer you. So, what are you waiting for?

I hope that you weren't looking for a coupon for this marvelous weight loss product. The preceding paragraph was taken verbatim from a full page advertise-ment in a popular fashion magazine. The only change that I made was to omit the name of this ''miracle'' diet. The name has a chemical sound to it. It's multi-syllabic and ends with a number. The name sounds like a chemical formula. I had trouble selecting which advertisement I wanted to use here, because there were so many that made numerous unsupported claims. Advertisements like this one can be found in most magazines and newspapers. I refer back to this adver-tisement later in this chapter, when I talk about analyzing arguments and recog-nizing fallacies. Hold onto your money until you've read these sections.

THE ANATOMY OF AN ARGUMENT

Neither a closed mind nor an empty one is likely to produce much that would qualify as effective reasoning.

—Nickerson (1986, p. 1)

The technical meaning of the word **"argument"** is somewhat different from its everyday meaning. When we use the word "argument" in everyday language, it means a dispute or a quarrel. We say two people "are having an argument" when they disagree about something in a heated or emotional way. More technically, an argument consists of one or more statements that are used to provide support for a **conclusion.** The statements that provide the support for a conclusion are called the **reasons,** or **premises,** of the argument. The reasons, or premises, are presented in order to persuade the reader (or listener) that the conclusion is true or probably true. Let's consider an example. Suppose that I want to convince you to stay in college until graduation. Here are some reasons that I could give:

Premise #1: College graduates earn more money than college dropouts or people who have never attended college.

Premise #2: College graduates report that they are more satisfied with their lives than people who have not graduated from college.

Premise #3: College graduates are healthier and live longer than people who have not graduated from college.

Premise #4: College graduates have jobs that are more interesting and more responsible than people who have not graduated from college.

Conclusion: You should graduate from college.

Arguments are sometimes called "the giving of reasons." Harman (1986) has called this process "a change in view," because the objective is to change an "old view" or belief into a "new view" or belief with reasoning.

Reasoning

Old View   ---------→   New View
or Belief   or Belief

Every argument will have one or more premises (or reasons) and one or more conclusions. Usually, there will be several premises for one conclusion, but other combinations (one premise for several conclusions and several premises for several conclusions) are possible. If you cannot identify at least one premise *and* at least one conclusion, then it is not an argument. Of course, in everyday, natural-language arguments, the premises and conclusions are not labeled. They are usually embedded in extended prose. The extended prose could be a paragraph, a section or chapter of a book, or even an entire book.

Here are some examples that are *not* arguments:

- I like my critical thinking course better than my chemistry course. (No reasons are given for this preference.)
- We drove up to the mountains, went skiing, then drove home. (This is just a descriptive list of activities linked together. There are no reasons or conclusions.)

- Buy your burgers at Burgerland. (No reasons given, but see the following section, because reasons are often inferred from context in statements like this one.)
- We saw the Martians land. (This is simple description.)
- Never trust a communist. (This is an opinion without reasons.)
- Is dinner ready? (simple question)

It may seem that it should be fairly simple to determine whether or not a statement or set of statements contains an argument, but, in everyday language, most arguments are incomplete. Sometimes the premises aren't stated, but are inferred, and other times the conclusion is unstated. Consider the popular automobile advertisement that goes something like this:

> More people have bought LaBaroness automobiles than any other American car.

At first glance, this seems like a straightforward declarative sentence, with no reasons and no conclusion. But, the advertisers expect consumers to convert this sentence into an argument. When you hear this sentence, you presumably start generating your own reasons for the popularity of LaBaroness. If more people are buying it, it must be best. And shouldn't you also buy the best? This is an example in which the listener supplies both the reasons and the conclusion. Statements very similar to this one can be found in advertisements for a diverse assortment of products, including beer, beauty supplies, fitness clubs, and airlines. (The use of the comparative term ''more'' is discussed later in this chapter.)

If an advertiser wants to be sure that you supply the missing reasons and conclusion, the advertisement could be altered slightly so that it now reads:

''More people have bought LaBaroness automobiles than any other American car. There must be some very good reasons.''

Notice that a second sentence was added, but no reasons were given. It is expected that the second sentence will cue listeners (or readers) to start supplying their own reasons.

Premises

The premises are the reasons that support a conclusion. They are the ''why'' part of an argument. In everyday language, they can appear anywhere among a set of statements. Sometimes, the conclusion will be stated first, followed by its premises. (Here is what I believe, and the reasons for this belief are . . .) Other times, the conclusion may be presented last or embedded in the middle of a paragraph or other text, with premises both before and after it. Premises are not always easy to recognize. There are certain key words, called **premise indicators** or **premise markers** that often signal that what comes after them is a premise. Although premise indicators aren't *always* followed by a premise, they often are, and for this reason, it is a good idea to check for these key words when identifying premises.

Premise Indicators

because

for

since

if

given that (or being that)

as shown by

as indicated by

the reasons are

it may be inferred (or deduced) from

the evidence consists of

in the first place (suggests that a list of premises will follow)

secondly

seeing that

assuming that

it follows from

whereas

Here are some simple examples of the use of premise indicators:

- You should graduate from college **because** you will earn more money with a college degree.
- The need for the U.S. to send troops to Central America is **indicated by** the build up of armed rebels in countries neighboring those with civil wars.
- **Seeing that** the current policy of supplying organ transplants is benefitting the rich, a new program is needed.

Premises can be "matters of fact" or "matters of opinion" or both. Consider, for example, the following two sentences:

All teenagers should be taught safe sex practices because of the risk of AIDS and other venereal diseases. (The reason is a matter of fact.)

All teenagers should be taught how to knit because this will provide them with an enjoyable hobby. (The reason is a matter of opinion.)

Conclusions

The conclusion is the purpose, or the "what," of the argument. It is the belief or point of view that is supported or defended with the premises. Some authors have identified the conclusion as the most important part of an argument, but I think that this is misleading. Both the premises and the conclusion are important, and both are essential components of any argument.

It is usually easier to identify the conclusion of an argument than the other components. For this reason, it is a good idea to start with the conclusion when you are analyzing arguments. There are **conclusion indicators, or conclusion markers,** that indicate that what follows is probably a conclusion. As with premise indicators, they do not guarantee that a conclusion follows them.

Conclusion Indicators
therefore
hence
so
thus
consequently
then
shows that (we can see that)
accordingly
it follows that
we may infer (conclude) (deduce) that
in summary
as a result
for all these reasons
it is clear that

Some simple examples of the use of conclusion indicators are:

- Based on all of the reasons just stated, we **can conclude that** the flow of illegal drugs must be stopped.
- **In summary,** postal rates must be increased because we can no longer afford to run the postal system with a deficit.
- We have had very little rain this season. **Consequently,** water will have to be rationed.

Has my use of the word "simple" to describe these examples made you feel uneasy? Have you begun to expect that things will soon get more complex? If so, you are right. Natural language is complex and so are natural-language arguments. (A natural language is a language that has evolved over time for the purpose of communication between people. Artificial languages are languages that are created for special purposes, such as computer languages.) Although all arguments *must* contain at least one premise and one conclusion, most arguments consist of additional components. Three additional components are presented here. They are assumptions, qualifiers, and counterarguments.

Assumptions

An **assumption** is a statement for which no proof or evidence is offered. Although assumptions can be either stated or unstated (implied), they are most often unstated. Advertisements and political rhetoric are good places to look for examples of stated and unstated assumptions. Let's go back to the example of the advertisement for LaBaroness that was presented earlier in this chapter. (I changed the name of the real car being advertised.)

> More people have bought LaBaroness automobiles than any other American car.

The implied statement is that if more people bought LaBaroness, it must be better (in some way) than its competitors. The unstated assumption is that, when large numbers of consumers make a choice, it is a good choice. There is no justification for this assumption. The implied conclusion is that you should also be making this wise choice. The advertisement could easily be altered so that the assumption is made explicitly:

> More people have bought LaBaroness automobiles than any other American car.
> When so many people agree, it must be the right choice.

Notice that, with the addition of the second sentence, the assumption is now stated explicitly. It is still an assumption, because it is stated without any justification. If I had supplied some justification for this belief, then it would no longer be an assumption.

Suppose I alter these statements so that they now become:

> More people have bought LaBaroness automobiles than any other American car.
> Recent research by several well-known social psychologists has shown that whenever a majority of people agree on something, they make the best choice.

Look carefully at the changes I just made. In this version, I provided a reason, or justification, for believing that whenever large numbers of people make a choice it is a good one. The research that I made up is phony, but suppose for now that it is true. The research findings become the premises, or reasons, for the conclusion that, whenever large numbers of people make a choice, it will be a good one. In this context, it is no longer an assumption, because there are now reasons supporting it. This new conclusion then becomes the premise for the unstated conclusion that you should also buy LaBaroness. If you read the previous chapter on reasoning, this should not be a new idea for you. The idea that the conclusion from one set of statements can then become the premise for another set of statements was demonstrated in the previous chapter. In extended (longer) arguments, the conclusion from one set of statements will often become the premise in another set of statements. The arguments that are used to build the main argument are called **subarguments.** The main argument in an extended passage is called the **main point.** The kinds of arguments that are often found in books, book chapters, and, sometimes, sections of chapters proceed in stages with subarguments linked to provide support for a main point.

Qualifiers

A **qualifier** is a constraint or restriction on the conclusion. It states the conditions under which the conclusion is supported. An example might be helpful:

> Historical evidence has shown that the buildup of the military in preparation for war is beneficial to the economy. Therefore, we should build a military that is ready for war as a means of improving the economy. The benefit to the economy by increasing the readiness of the military only applies to conventional warfare. If the buildup is based on preparing for total nuclear war, then the economy won't improve.

Let's dissect this paragraph into its component parts:

The conclusion is: Build up the military so that it is ready for war. (It's usually easiest to start with the conclusion.)

A premise is: Building the military is good for the economy. (This premise is, in turn, supported by the historical evidence.)

An unstated assumption is: A good economy is desirable.

A qualifier (or limiting condition) is: The conclusion is valid only when the type of buildup is with conventional weapons.

As you can see from this example, a qualifier states the conditions under which the conclusion is valid. It sets limits or constraints on the conclusion.

Counterarguments

Sometimes, an extended argument will state reasons that support a particular conclusion and reasons that refute the same conclusion. The set of statements that refute a particular conclusion is called a **counterargument.** Let's extend the previous argument so that it now also contains a counterargument:

> Historical evidence has shown that the buildup of the military in preparation for war is beneficial to the economy. Therefore, we should build a military that is ready for war as a means of improving the economy. The benefit to the economy by increasing the readiness of the military only applies to conventional warfare. If the buildup is based on preparing for total nuclear war, then the economy won't improve. Of course, we also have to consider that when we build up the military, we disrupt families, because we have to relocate our military personnel. But, this is a small price to pay, considering the great benefit to be gained from a good economy.

I hope that you're paying careful attention to the way the additions are altering the argument. As just presented, the conclusion, premise, assumption, and qualifier remain the same. The counterargument presents a reason for not building up the military. The reason presented (disruption of families) is counter to the conclusion that we should build up the military. That is why these statements are called counterarguments. Even with the addition of the counterargument, the conclusion remains unchanged. The argument was written in a way that suggests that the counterargument is weaker than the main argument. The point being made is that, despite the counterargument, we should still build up the military.

Does this particular example make you uneasy? Can you think of other premises that might support a different conclusion? If so, you have already begun to anticipate the content of the section on how to evaluate arguments.

DIAGRAMMING THE STRUCTURE OF AN ARGUMENT

In order to analyze or dissect an argument, we need to know not only its component parts, but also how the parts are related to each other. The parts that make up an argument are premise(s), conclusion(s), assumption(s), qualifier(s), and counterargument(s). The only restriction on arguments is that each must have at least one premise and one conclusion. Beyond this, any one of a large variety of arrangements is possible. A good way to understand the relationships among the parts of a prose passage is to draw a diagram. Diagrams are used in every chapter of this book, because they require the drawer to be specific about the relationships being depicted and to think about underlying relationships. Drawing a diagram is a good general thinking strategy. Let's consider the simplest argument, with only one premise and one conclusion:

Be sure to get plenty of exercise because exercise will help you build a strong cardiovascular system.

Conclusion #1 (C1): Get plenty of exercise. (I started with the conclusion because this is often the easiest part to identify.)

Premise #1 (P1): Exercise will build a strong cardiovascular system. (This is the "why" part of the argument.)

A diagram of this relationship shows the conclusion supported by the premise:

(C1)
↑
(P1)

Now let's consider an argument in which two different premises support one conclusion:

Be sure to get plenty of exercise, because exercise will help you build a strong cardiovascular system, and it will increase the density of your bones.

Conclusion #1 (C1): Get plenty of exercise.
Premise #1 (P1): Exercise will build a strong cardiovascular system.
Premise #2 (P2): Exercise will increase the density of your bones.

A diagram of this argument will look like this:

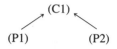

In this diagram, we have two premises supporting one conclusion. Both of the arrows point to the same conclusion. This is called a **convergent structure** because both premises converge onto the same conclusion. Longer arguments will often contain several premises that support a conclusion. Let's compare this argument structure to one in which two premises are linked to each other, so that instead of both premises supporting the same conclusion, the first premise is the reason for the second premise, which in turn becomes the reason for the conclusion:

Be sure to get plenty of exercise, because exercise will help you build a strong cardiovascular system. Research has shown that activities that raise your heart rate can increase your stamina.

In this example, we have two premises and one conclusion, but the relationship between the premises is different from that in the previous example.

Conclusion # 1 (C1): Get plenty of exercise.
Premise #1 (P1): Exercise will build a strong cardiovascular system. (This is a reason for the conclusion.)
Premise #2 (P2): Activities that increase heart rate increase stamina. (This is a reason supporting P1.)

A diagram of this argument will look like this:

Arguments in which the conclusion of one subargument becomes the premise of a second argument are called **chained** (or **linked**) **structures.** Can you see an important distinction between this type of argument and the previous one, in which two premises converge onto the same conclusion? Remember the old saying that a chain is only as strong as its weakest link? When arguments have a chained structure, the conclusion is only as strong as the weakest subargument. If P2 doesn't provide very much support for P1, then the conclusion is weakened. By contrast, when two or more premises converge onto the same conclusion, we only increase the strength of the conclusion by adding more premises.

Let's consider an example in which there are three premises and two conclusions.

Be sure to get plenty of exercise, because exercise will help you build a strong cardiovascular system, and it will increase the density of your bones. You can also increase the density of your bones by maintaining a diet that is rich in calcium.

Conclusion #1 (C1): Get plenty of exercise.

Conclusion #2 (C2): Maintain a diet that is rich in calcium.

Premise #1 (P1): Exercise will build a strong cardiovascular system.

Premise #2 (P2): Exercise will increase the density of your bones.

Premise #3 (P3): Calcium will increase the density of your bones.

A diagram of this argument will look like this:

(C1)   (C2)
(P1)   (P2)   (P3)

This is an example of two separate arguments in the same paragraph.

Let's try diagramming the more complex argument, containing a conclusion, a premise, an assumption, a qualifier, and a counterargument, that was presented earlier.

Historical evidence has shown that the buildup of the military in preparation for war is beneficial to the economy. Therefore, we should build a military that is ready for war as a means of improving the economy. The benefit to the economy by increasing the readiness of the military only applies to conventional warfare. If the buildup is based on preparing for total nuclear war, then the economy won't improve. Of course, we also have to consider that when we build up the military, we also disrupt families, because we have to relocate our military personnel. But, this is a small price to pay, considering the great benefit to be gained from a good economy.

Conclusion #1 (C1): Build up the military so that it is ready for war.

Premise #1 (P1): Building the military is good for the economy.

This premise was the conclusion of a subargument in which we concluded that building the military is good for the economy because this relationship was historically true. For the purpose of diagramming, we will call the reason for believing that building the military is good for the economy Premise #2. It doesn't matter how you assign numbers, as long as you keep the numbers in the correct position in your diagram.

Premise #2 (P2): In the past, building the military has been good for the economy. (This is the support for believing that P1 is true.)

Assumption #1 (A1): A good economy is desirable.

Qualifier #1 (Q1): The conclusion is valid only when the type of buildup is with conventional weapons.

Counterargument #1 (CA1): Building up the military will disrupt families.

A diagram of this argument looks like this:

$$
\begin{array}{ccc}
& (C1) \leftarrow \sim\!\!\sim\!\!\sim (CA1) \\
& \uparrow & \\
(A1) & (P1 + Q1) & \\
& \uparrow & \\
& (P2) &
\end{array}
$$

Notice that the relationship between the counterargument and the conclusion is indicated with a wavy line. This indicates that they are negatively linked. The counterargument works against the conclusion. The qualifier is added to the statement that it qualifies. P1 only supports the conclusion under the conditions stated in the qualifier, so they need to be considered together. The unstated assumption is shown supporting the conclusion in the same way that a premise does. It is a reason for the conclusion. Finally, the statement that the buildup of the military is good for the economy is supported by the historical evidence. This is represented by having P1 supported by P2. This is an example in which the conclusion of one argument becomes the premise of a second argument.

General Guidelines for Diagramming Arguments

In understanding complex arguments, it is a good idea to identify the conclusions, premises, assumptions, qualifiers, and counterarguments, and then diagram the structure of their relationship. This is a useful aid in determining how good a particular argument is. The major difficulty in using this procedure is that complex arguments have complex structures. Sometimes, there is more than one possible interpretation and, correspondingly, more than one possible diagram. Sometimes, the difficulty lies in deciding if a statement is really part of a subargument or part of the main argument. In longer text, you will often have to restate premises, conclusions, counterarguments, assumptions, and qualifiers in your own words. This can involve reducing whole chapters of books to single statements. Although this can be difficult, it is an excellent strategy for comprehension. Often, the process of diagramming will reveal what's wrong or right about a certain argument. If more than one diagram of an argument is possible, then you can consider each separately. Does one diagram provide stronger support for the conclusion? Is one diagram a "truer" representation of the statements being made? You won't want to diagram every argument you read or hear, but sometimes the issues are troublesome and important, and diagramming can be very useful in clarifying the underlying relationships among the statements. Writing and diagramming unstated premises, conclusions, and assumptions can also be very helpful in considering the strength or quality of an argument by making these components explicit and placing them in the argument framework.

EVALUATING THE STRENGTH OF AN ARGUMENT

> *Advertising persuades people to buy things they don't need with money they ain't got.*
>
> —Will Rogers

All arguments are not equally good or equally bad. Think about how your belief about an issue can be swayed or reinforced as each speaker in a debate presents the reasons and conclusions that support or refute a position. Some reasons for a particular conclusion are better than others, and sometimes good reasons don't seem to be related to the conclusion. In this section, we consider how to evaluate the quality of an argument.

Arguments are evaluated by how well they meet three criteria. The first criterion concerns the acceptability and consistency of the premises. The second criterion concerns the relationship between the premises and the conclusion. Do they support the conclusion? Does the conclusion follow from them? The third criterion concerns the unseen part of the argument. What's missing that would change your conclusion? Let's consider each of these criteria in turn.

Acceptable and Consistent Premises

The premises are the "why" part of an argument. The premises must be **acceptable.** A premise is acceptable when it is true or when we can reasonably believe that it is true. Let's consider what this means. If I say that the sun is hot, this is an acceptable premise. I have never touched the sun, but many experts in the field have said that the sun is hot. Much of what we believe to be true comes from experts' statements and personal and common or shared knowledge. Similarly, I have no direct, first-hand knowledge of bacteria, but it is reasonable to believe that they exist. They are commonly acknowledged "truths" of science. I believe that California is larger than New Jersey, even though I have never measured them. You could probably give a long list of "facts" that are commonly believed to be true. These are examples of acceptable premises.

Premises that are false are unacceptable. Examples of false premises include: Men can give birth to babies, whales can fly, all mammals are dogs, and Spanish is the primary language of Canada. I don't want to get into the philosophical considerations of how can we ever know "truth." Personal or common knowledge and expert testimony will be the guide for determining acceptability.

Unfortunately, acceptability is not an either/or proposition in which a premise is either acceptable or it is not. Sometimes, part of the job of analyzing an argument involves determining how acceptable a premise is. This may require research on your part. Suppose that you are listening to an argument about the safety of building a chemical warfare laboratory in your backyard. The corporation that wants to build the laboratory argues that the chemical warfare laboratory is safe; therefore, you have nothing to worry about. One way to decide about the acceptability of this premise is to spend some time in the library reading about the kinds of experiments conducted in such laboratories, the kinds of safety precautions that are used, and past accidents at other similar laboratories. You will also need to consider the statements of experts in this area. When you assess the acceptability of a premise, you will often have to determine the credibility of the experts who are asserting the premises.

Credibility

What makes an expert credible? In deciding who and what to believe, you need to consider the source of the information. Ask yourself the following questions about an expert who is presenting the reasons for a belief:

1. Is the "expert" a recognized authority in the *same field* in which she or he is providing testimony? Why should you believe an expert in computer graphics when the topic concerns chemical warfare?

2. Is the expert an *independent* party in this issue? If the expert who says the laboratory is safe was hired by the corporation that owns the laboratory, then her or his testimony is suspect. It may not necessarily be wrong, but you should be wary, because the motive for personal gain is involved.

3. What are the "expert's" *credentials?* Did she or he write several journal articles on the subject that were then published in respected journals, or is her or his expertise documented with a single night school course in the topic? Is the expert current in the field? Even a renowned expert on chemical warfare from World War II will have little knowledge of advances in the field over the last 40 years.

4. Does the expert have *specific and first-hand knowledge* of the issue? She or he could conclude that chemical warfare laboratories are generally safe, but have no direct knowledge of the one being proposed. Did she or he check the plans for safety features? Does she or he know exactly what sorts of experiments are being planned?

5. What *methods of analysis* were used by the expert? Are there standard safety assessments for laboratories that contain dangerous chemicals? Were these used?

Reread the advertisement presented at the beginning of this chapter that states that we can "eat all day and still lose weight." Who are the doctors and universities that support this claim? (No names are given. You should immediately begin to question the credibility of this information.) Was their expertise in weight loss? What are their credentials? Are they independent, or will they make money if you buy this product? What were the methods of analysis that were used to document the statement that it will make you feel stronger and full of pep? (None were mentioned.) Are the claims made in this advertisement credible?

Decisions about the acceptability of premises will often depend on how you evaluate the source of the information. When you have two experts who disagree, which is frequently the case, you need to understand the nature of the disagreement and their relative expertise. Are they disagreeing on research findings or the interpretation of those findings? Try to zero in on the specific points on which they disagree, so that you can scrutinize these points.

In a good argument, the premises are also **consistent.** When several premises are presented to support a conclusion, they must not contradict each other. For example, an argument in which one premise states that we have to reduce unemployment in order to improve the economy and another premise states that we have to increase unemployment in order to improve the economy is an argument that contains inconsistent premises.

When considering the premises of an argument, check for acceptability and consistency.

Premises That Support the Conclusion

Consider the following argument:

It is important that we elect a prime minister from the New Democratic Party (a political party in Canada), because the rain in Spain falls mainly on the plain.

I hope that your response to this was, "huh?" The premise or reason why we should support a candidate from the New Democratic Party had nothing to do with it. The rain in Spain is unrelated to political elections in Canada. In technical terms, the premise does not support the conclusion.

In determining the relevance, or relatedness, between the premises and the conclusion(s), I like to use an analogy to a table. The conclusion is the top of the table, and the premises are the legs. When the premises are unrelated to the conclusion, they are off somewhere in another room and cannot support it. It is easy to detect instances in which the premises are totally unrelated to the conclusion. Other examples are more difficult, because relatedness is a matter of degree. Premises can be more or less related to the conclusion.

Premises can deal with the same topic as the conclusion yet not support the conclusion. For example, suppose I were to argue that you should get plenty of exercise because athletes get plenty of exercise. Both the conclusion and the premise concern exercise, but the premise is not a *reason for* the conclusion. Even if it is true that athletes get plenty of exercise, it may not follow that you should therefore get plenty of exercise. Maybe you have a "weak" heart and would die from exercise. The conclusion does not follow from the premise. One way of checking for the relatedness of the premise(s) to the conclusion(s) is to ask yourself if the conclusion must be true or extremely likely if the premise is acceptable. If the answer is "no," then you have to question how well the conclusion is being supported by the premise.

Determining the relatedness between the premises and the conclusion can be difficult. This is exactly the sort of determination that judges are required to make all of the time. Consider a rape case in which the defense wants to show that the woman agreed to sexual intercourse. Is her previous sexual behavior related to this issue? Most of the time, the courts have ruled that a woman's past sexual history is unrelated to whether or not she was coerced at the time in question, but, under special circumstances, such evidence may be admissible because the judge decides that it may be related to a particular case.

The premises not only have to be related to the conclusion, they also have to be strong enough to support the conclusion. Some authors call this condition **adequate grounds.** When premises provide good support for the conclusion, we say that there are adequate grounds for believing that the conclusion is true or likely to be true.

Let's return to the table analogy. Think of the conclusion as a solid wooden table top. A solid wooden table top will topple over if we try to support it with a few toothpicks. The only way to support it is to use one or more strong legs or many weaker legs that, when used together, will form a strong base of support. These possibilities are depicted in Fig. 5.1.

Let's consider some examples of strength of support:

1. Marion and Engelbert have filed for divorce. Therefore, they plan to get a divorce.

C1: Marion and Engelbert plan to get a divorce.

P1: Marion and Engelbert have filed for divorce.

The unstated assumption that they are married will be omitted from the diagram because it is not relevant to the point being made; but, if it were included, it would point to P1, Graphically, this becomes:

$$(C1)$$
$$\uparrow \quad \text{Strong}$$
$$(P1)$$

2. Marion and Engelbert had eggs for breakfast. Therefore, they plan to get a divorce.

C1: Marion and Engelbert plan to get a divorce.

P1: Marion and Engelbert had eggs for breakfast.

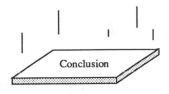

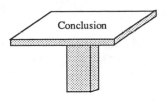

Premises Unrelated to Conclusion

Single Strong Premise
Supports Conclusion

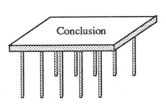

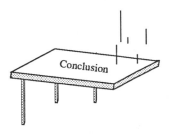

Many Weak Premises
Support Conclusion

Few Weak Premises
Fail to Support Conclusion

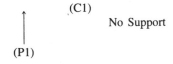

FIG. 5.1.   Table analogy for understanding the strength of an argument. The table top is the conclusion and the legs are the premises. Strong arguments have a firm base of support.

Because the premise is unrelated to the conclusion, it provides no support for the conclusion.

(C1)

No Support

(P1)

3. Marion and Engelbert had a fight this morning. Therefore, they plan to get a divorce.

C1: Marion and Engelbert plan to get a divorce.

P1: Marion and Engelbert had a fight this morning.

In this example, the premise is related to the conclusion, but the support is weak.

(C1)

↑

Weak Support

(P1)

4. Marion and Engelbert had a fight this morning. In fact, they fight everyday. Engelbert is moving out of their apartment and plans to move in with his mother. Marion made an appointment with a divorce attorney. Therefore, they plan to get a divorce.

C1: Marion and Engelbert plan to get a divorce.

P1: Marion and Engelbert had a fight this morning. (weak)

P2: They fight everyday. (weak)

P3: Engelbert is moving out. (moderate)

P4: Marion made an appointment with a divorce attorney. (strong)

In this example, there are multiple premises to support the conclusion. Taken together, they provide strong support.

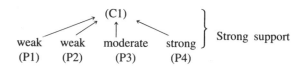

Look at the list of premises. With only the first one, the support for the conclusion was very weak. The addition of the second made the support somewhat stronger. As additional premises were added, support for the conclusion increased. This is another example of a convergent argument structure in which multiple premises point to (converge on) the same conclusion. Additional premises, even weak ones, increase the strength of the argument.

When analyzing the relationship between premises and a conclusion, you need to consider their relevance to the conclusion and the strength of the support that they supply. Using the table analogy, ask yourself if the table top has a sound base of support or is shaky and easy to topple over.

Missing Components

> *They will try to tell you to prove you are right; I tell you to prove you are wrong.*
>
> —Louis Pasteur

Most arguments are written to persuade the reader or listener that a conclusion is true or probably true. Good examples of this can be found in advertisements and political rhetoric. When you read or listen to advertisements and political claims, it is important to keep in mind the restrictions imposed on these arguments.

There are laws that punish false statements by advertisers; similarly, false political statements are likely to be detected by the press or opposition party. Therefore, false statements are not usually a factor in political and advertising argument analysis; nonetheless, you should remain wary of them. The bigger problem in attempts to persuade is missing and distorted claims. In other words, it is the missing parts of most arguments that are often the most important parts. In order to evaluate the quality of an argument, you need to consider what's been left out.

When evaluating an argument, consider each component separately and think about ways the statements could have been distorted and what has been omitted. Let's try this with an example that was used earlier in this chapter:

> Historical evidence has shown that the buildup of the military in preparation for war is beneficial to the economy. Therefore, we should build a military that is ready for war as a means of improving the economy. The benefit to the economy by increasing the readiness of the military only applies to conventional warfare. If the buildup is based on preparing for total nuclear war, then the economy won't improve. Of course, we also have to consider that when we build up the military, we disrupt families, because we have to relocate our military personnel. But, this is a small price to pay, considering the great benefit to be gained from a good economy.

One of the best ways to think about what's missing is to change your point of view so that you now become an advocate for the "other side." In this case, try to view the argument from the perspective of someone who does not want the military to be built up. What premises are missing or additional information is needed that would support an opposite conclusion? I would want more information about the nature of the relationship between the economy and military buildup. Do we need to prepare for a full war in order for the economy to increase, or does partial buildup also aid the economy? If the real goal is how to improve the economy, what are other possible solutions? Would increasing technology work as well to improve the economy? What is the nature of the historical evidence? Is it so out of date that it no longer applies to a modern economy? What additional qualifiers are needed? Think about additional counterarguments. The only one mentioned was disrupting some families. Are there others? Is the disruption of families a minor or major counterargument?

Although the consideration of missing components could theoretically go on forever, the extent to which we scrutinize an argument depends on its importance. I would spend a great deal of time and effort analyzing an argument in which the conclusion concerns the safety of building a chemical warfare laboratory near my home (or someone else's home). There are many arguments in life that should be carefully evaluated, and this includes seeking and considering missing and misleading statements.

Sound Arguments

A good argument is technically called a **sound argument.** An argument is sound when it meets the following criteria:

1. The premises are acceptable and consistent.
2. The premises are relevant to the conclusion and provide sufficient support for the conclusion.
3. Missing components have been considered and are judged to be consistent with the conclusion.

Satisfying each of these criteria is a matter of degree. Premises are usually acceptable on some continuum from unacceptable to totally acceptable. The nature of support that they provide for the conclusion also lies on some continuum from no support to complete support. Similarly, the missing components, especially counterarguments, may weaken the argument anywhere from completely to not at all. Because all of these assessments have to be combined to decide if an argument is sound, we usually think of soundness as ranging from unsound to completely sound. An argument is unsound if its premises are false or if they are unrelated to the conclusion. An argument is completely sound if the premises are acceptable and related to the conclusion in a way that guarantees the acceptability of the conclusion. Most real-life arguments fall somewhere between these two extremes. For this reason, conclusions are often preceded with probability terms like, "it is likely that," or "we can probably conclude that." Here are some examples of different degrees of soundness:

Completely Sound Argument (premises are acceptable and related to the conclusion in a way that guarantees the conclusion)

All mothers are women who have (or had) children. Suzi is a woman who has a son. Therefore, Suzi is a mother.

Unsound Arguments (either the premises are unacceptable or they are unrelated to the conclusion)

All fathers have given birth to a child. Norbert has a son. Therefore, Norbert has given birth to a child. (Premise is unacceptable.)

Norbert has a son; therefore, Norbert also has a daughter. (Premise is unrelated to the conclusion.)

Don't confuse the truth or acceptability of a conclusion with the soundness of an argument. A conclusion can be objectively true, even when the argument is unsound. The conclusion could be true for reasons that have nothing to do with the information stated in the argument. Here is an example of a conclusion that is objectively true embedded in an unsound argument:

The structure of the family has been changing rapidly, with more single parents now heading their own households. Consequently, the divorce rate has begun to level off and decline slightly.

The conclusion about the divorce rate is true (according to demographers), but the argument is unsound because the premise does not support the conclusion.

Complex issues rarely have one correct conclusion. More often, many conclusions are possible, and the task of analyzing an argument involves deciding which of two or more conclusions has the greater strength or support.

How To Analyze an Argument

1. The first step is to read or listen to the passage to determine if it contains an argument. Is there at least one premise and at least one conclusion? If not, no further analysis is needed.

2. Identify all the stated and unstated component parts: premises, conclusions, assumptions, qualifiers, and counterarguments.

3. Check the premises for the acceptability and consistency. If all of the premises are unacceptable, stop here, because the argument is unsound. If only some of the premises are unacceptable, eliminate them and continue with the acceptable premises. If the premises are inconsistent with each other, stop here. An argument cannot be sound if the premises are inconsistent or contradict each other.

4. Diagram the argument. Consider the strength of the support that each premise provides for the conclusion. Rate the strength of support as nonexistent, weak, medium, or strong. Look over the number of supporting premises. A large number of supporting premises can provide strong support for the conclusion in a convergent structure, even when, separately, each only provides weak support. Recall that, in a linked structure, a single weak link can destroy an argument.

5. Consider the strength of counterarguments, assumptions, and qualifiers (stated or omitted) and omitted premises. Do they destroy the support provided by the premises, or strengthen or weaken it?

6. Finally, come to a global determination of the soundness of the argument. Is it unsound, completely sound, or somewhere in between? If it is somewhere in between, is it weak, medium, or strong?

Here is a completed example. The following passage was edited and abstracted from a syndicated column by Jane E. Brody (1988):

With 1 in 10 women destined to get breast cancer, the National Cancer Institute had planned to study the possible link between breast cancer and dietary fat. But, as noted in the consumer newsletter *Nutrition Action,* the researchers were worried about the probability of the 16,000 women in the intervention group sticking to a diet as low in fat as the Japanese, with only 20% of the calories coming from fat.

There was also concern about a study by Harvard researchers who found no relationship between fat intake and breast cancer risk. But, other evidence suggests that such a link might exist. A study of diet and breast-cancer mortality conducted by the director of the American Health Foundation showed the higher the daily fat intake, the higher the death rate from breast cancer. Studies of migrants also showed that when women leave a country with one breast-cancer rate, they soon acquire the breast-cancer rate of their adopted country.

But, is fat the cause? Might total caloric intake be the answer since calories increase along with fat intake? Some of these difficulties can be resolved with animal studies in which diet and fat intake can be controlled. The animal studies are clear cut: Animals on high-fat diets are fare more likely to get mammary cancer and die of it than those consuming a low-fat diet.

Few women can afford to wait for definitive evidence.

Let's apply the steps for evaluating arguments, using this passage:

   1. It contains at least one premise and one conclusion, so it satisfies the minimal requirements for an argument.
   2. Identify the components.

(C1): Women should reduce dietary fat. I think that it is fair to represent the author's conclusion this way. The conclusion is found in the last sentence.

(P1): Low-fat diets reduce the risk of cancer. This is the reason for the conclusion.

(CA1): In the study mentioned, Harvard researchers found no effect of dietary fat on the risk of breast cancer. (They are a credible source of information.)

(CA2): Controlled studies with humans have not been conducted. (These counterarguments work against the conclusion.)

(P2): (reason for P1) Cross-cultural research shows a link between dietary fat and breast cancer.

(P3): (reason for P1) Migration studies show that risk of cancer changes when people move from one country to another.

(A1): (assumption for P3) Immigrants change their eating habits so that their diets become like those in their new country. (This is an unstated assumption.)

(P4): (reason for P1) Controlled animal studies show an association between dietary fat and breast cancer.

(CA3): (counterargument for P4) Results found with other animals may not apply in the same way to humans. (unstated counterargument)

(Q1): Fat levels may have to be reduced to less than 20% of caloric intake in order to get reduced risk of cancer. (unstated)

(A2): (assumption for CA2) Controlled research with humans may never be possible.

(P5): (Missing premise) There are many other health benefits to a low-fat diet (e.g., weight reduction and reduced risk of coronary disease).

Now, go back over the list of component parts and rate the premises for acceptability. There are no absolute standards here, except for the two extremes of "must be true" and "must be false." Unfortunately, few things in life fall into these categories. At this step, I rate P2, P3, P4, and P5. I do not rate P1 at this step, because it is the conclusion of a subargument that is built on P2, P3, and P4. I rate P1 after all the premises that support P1 have been considered. You are really on your own at this point in how you assign ratings. There are no absolute standards for rating strength of support.

P2—weak (This is my assessment of the cross-cultural data. I gave it a weak rating because so many variables are different in different cultures that it is impossible to know if other variables are responsible for the reduced risk of cancer. I talk more about this in chapter 6.)

P3—moderate

P4—strong

P5—strong

At this point, I will diagram the relationships and rate the strength of the counterarguments.

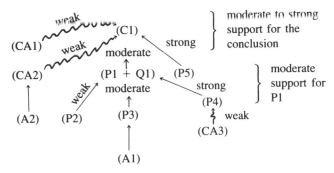

Looking over the diagram of the argument, I see that there are three premises that support the belief that low-fat diets reduce the risk of cancer (P2, P3, P4) and two counterarguments (CA1, CA2). The strength of support that the premises provide for the statement that low-fat diets reduce the risk of cancer (P1) has been rated as weak, moderate, and strong. The strongest premise is modified by a weak counterargument. Although the assumption pointing to P3 wasn't rated, it was considered and found to be acceptable. With all of these components considered, I rate the support that P1 supplies to the conclusion as moderate. Now looking at the premises supporting the conclusion that women should reduce their dietary fat, I see that it is moderately supported by the premise that low-fat diets reduce cancer and strongly supported by the premise that there are other health benefits associated with a low-fat diet. The counterarguments weaken the support for the conclusion, but don't destroy it. I rate this argument as moderate-to-strong in the strength that it supplies to the conclusion.

You may be thinking that this was a lot of work. You are right. Diagramming and evaluating complex arguments can be as demanding as deriving a long proof in mathematics or comprehending a complex novel. But, before you decide to make life-long changes in your diet or some other decision concerning an important belief or action, you want to be sure that the decision is based on sound reasoning. In this case, the conclusion is based on acceptable premises that provide good support for the conclusion.

I realize that few people will formally diagram an argument in real life; however, it is a powerful and useful tool for comprehending complex arguments. Practice with diagramming arguments will aid in the analysis of other arguments even when, for time or other reasons, actual diagramming is not feasible. It will help you distinguish among the components of an argument and make judgments about its strength. When the issue is important and complex, making a diagram of its structure can be well worth the time and effort required.

It is important to note that, when you evaluate arguments, you are also evaluating your own knowledge about the subject matter. There may be other counterarguments that are quite strong but are unknown to you. Similarly, your ratings of the strength of the components may be biased in ways that support a conclusion that you favor. Nickerson (1986) made an important distinction between reasoning and **rationalizing.** When we rationalize, we attend to information that favors a conclusion that is preferred. We may selectively gather information that supports a preferred conclusion or rate counterarguments as weak because they detract from a preferred conclusion. The nature of the missing components that we supply is also affected by a type of bias. When we add to an argument, the information that we supply is information that is readily recalled. If you've already read chapter 2 (memory), then you are well aware of the many ways that memory can be biased. Rationalizing is usually not a deliberate process to distort the analysis of arguments, which makes it difficult to recognize and guard against. It is easier to recognize rationalizing when someone else is doing it. Perhaps the best we can do is realize that rationalizing does occur and try to be especially vigilant for rationalizing when there is a preferred conclusion.

FALLACIES

Persuasion and Propaganda

> *Through clever and constant application of propaganda, people can be made to see paradise as hell, and also the other way round, to consider the most wretched sort of life as paradise.*
>
> —Adolf Hitler
> *Mein Kampf*

Whenever we are confronted with an argument, it is important to keep in mind that the material we are reading or hearing has been written to persuade us to do something or to believe something. Much of the communication that we receive is concerned with getting us to act or think in a certain way. The American Heritage Dictionary of the English Language (Morris, 1969) defines **propaganda** as "material disseminated by the proselytizers of a doctrine" (p. 1048). In other words, it is material that is written or spoken by people who want others to believe that what they are saying is true. This broad definition is applicable to a great variety of situations. Propaganda, like beauty, is in the eyes of the beholder. It does not require that the information be false or misleading, but it does, at least, imply less concern for truth or rigorous argument than the sort of arguments found in scholarly journals or presented by independent parties. Frequently, the information provided is charged with appeals to emotion rather than reason.

Humans are very clever in using techniques that aim to influence others' thinking. The cleverest way to influence how someone thinks is with a well-crafted argument. As you now realize, an argument requires the use of reasons, and we like to have reasons for our beliefs, even when the reasons are not very good and the argument itself is weak.

The Psychology of Reasons

Three psychologists conducted a study in which they examined how people respond to the appearance of reasons (Langer, Blank, & Chanowitz, 1978). In this study, they had a confederate (someone working with the experimenters whose identity is not known to the subjects) try various combinations of requests and reasons for barging ahead of people waiting in line to use a copier machine. There were three different conditions: (a) Request alone ("Excuse me, I have five pages. May I use the Xerox machine?"), (b) Request plus reason ("Excuse me, I have five pages. May I use the Xerox because I'm in a rush?"), and (c) Request plus the appearance of a reason ("Excuse me, I have five pages. May I use the Xerox machine because I have to make some copies?").

The results of this study are very interesting. In the request alone condition, 60% of the people waiting said that it was okay for the confederate to make the copies. In the request plus reason condition, this figure jumped to 94%. What about the request plus appearance of a reason? In this condition, 93% of the people waiting to use the machine let the confederate go ahead. The use of the word "because" suggested that there was a reason. Remember the section on premise indicators? "Because" was listed as a word that is frequently followed by a reason. The statement "because I have to make some copies" is not a reason to let someone ahead of you in line at the copier machine. Everyone standing in line has to make some copies. It seems that we like to believe that our actions and beliefs are reasonable—that is, based on reasons. Unfortunately, even nonreasons, poor reasons, and reasons that are unrelated to the action or belief will often suffice. People who want to change how we think often rely on this human tendency and will deliberately use unsound reasoning to convince us that a conclusion is true. Unsound reasoning techniques used for the purpose of persuasion are called **fallacies.** As you go through the list of fallacies presented in the next section, you can classify each as violating one or more of the criteria for sound arguments.

It is impossible to list every fallacy that has been employed to change how people think. The list would be too long to be useful, with only subtle differences among several of the techniques. Accordingly, only the most common and representative techniques are discussed. If you understand how fallacies work in general, you'll be better prepared to recognize and defend against them. Toulmin, Rieke, and Janik (1979) called the ability to recognize fallacies "a kind of sensitivity training" because they train the reader to be sensitive to common tricks of persuasion.

Twenty Common Fallacies

1. Association Effects

One of the oldest principles in psychology is the notion that, if two events occur close together in time and/or space, the mind will form an association between them. Thereafter, when one occurs, the other is expected to occur. This principle has become widely used in the political arena, especially to create **guilt by association.** Suppose you read in the newspaper that a violent mass murderer endorsed a presidential candidate. This endorsement would be detrimental to the candidate, even if she or he did not desire it and had done nothing to promote it.

An example of the propagandistic use of association came from a political group called "California Tax Reduction Movement." Their 1983 literature stated: "This court, dominated by Jerry Brown appointees, and having radical views close to those of Jane Fonda and Tom Hayden, has twisted the words until we don't even recognize them!" You might be wondering what Jane Fonda and Tom Hayden are doing in a sentence about the California Supreme Court. In the jargon of analyzing arguments, the premise is unrelated to the conclusion. Fonda and Hayden had no connection with the court. This literature was written with the belief that people who favor tax reductions will also be opposed to Jane Fonda and Tom Hayden. The court is being made guilty by association with them. The actual association is somewhat convoluted. When Jerry Brown was governor of California, he appointed judges to the state supreme court. Jane Fonda and Tom Hayden were supporters of Jerry Brown. Although it is implied, it does not logically follow that the Supreme Court therefore has views that are similar to those of Jane Fonda and Tom Hayden. It may or may not have had such views. (Note, also, the use of the emotion-laden word "radical.") Whenever you see examples of associations with no justifiable connection like this one, be wary of the rest of the message. It is likely to contain an appeal to your emotions rather than to your cognition.

Just as one can have guilt by association, it is also possible to have **virtue by association.** In this instance, the names or label attached to the person are "good" ones. Perhaps this is why certain political offices tend to run in families. People expected the Kennedy brothers to be similar as politicians because of their obvious association with each other. This expectation is being passed onto their children, many of whom are now involved in or considering political careers. Would you vote for or against an unknown Kennedy simply because he or she is in the Kennedy family?

A wary recipient of messages that rely on association will ask about the nature of the association. If a leader is a member of the Ku Klux Klan, then associating the doctrine of the Klan with this individual is reasonable. If, on the other hand, a friend of the candidate's mother is a member of the Klan, the association is ludicrous.

2. Arguments Against the Person

Arguments against the person is the formal term for name calling or, in its Latin form, *argumentatum ad hominem*. This form of persuasion or propaganda attacks the people who support a cause, and not the cause itself. As an example of this, the Nazis believed that the theory of relativity was wrong, because its discoverer was a Jew named Albert Einstein. They never considered the evidence for or against the theory, just the religion of its originator. It is basically another form of the association effect. In this case, the association that is being made is between an idea and a person. The underlying principle is that if you don't like the person who supports an idea, then you should also oppose the idea itself, because the idea and the person are associated.

Suppose you were serving on a jury that had to decide which of two witnesses was telling the truth. Would you be swayed if one attorney told you to disregard one man's testimony because he had been divorced twice? Presumably not, because the man's marital status is irrelevant to the issue. Suppose you were told that one of the men had two previous convictions for lying to a jury. Would this argument against the person be relevant? I would think so. In this case, the information provided about the witness is relevant to the question of whether or not he is lying. Consider the strength and relevancy of the argument and the purpose for which it is used, and don't be misled by irrelevant attacks on the supporters or detractors of any position.

3. Appeals to Pity

An **appeal to pity** is easy to spot. "Support this position" or "buy that product" because it needs your help. A rental car agency has made it well known that they're number 2 in their business and therefore will try harder. They hope that consumers will root for the "underdog" and support the company that is number 2. Does this conclusion logically follow from the fact that they're number 2? No! You could also logically conclude that the number 1 company will try harder to retain their lead or that the number 2 company would have been number 1 if it had tried harder. Appeals to pity are often found in legal pleadings. A defendant's poor background or turbulent home life will often be brought up during a trial. These appeals to pity have nothing to do with the question of whether a defendant is guilty or innocent, although they may be persuasive appeals for leniency in sentencing if the defendant is found guilty.

4. Popularity and Testimonials

The **popularity** technique (also known as the "bandwagon") relies on the need for conformity for its persuasive power. It is persuasive because it explains that everyone supports a position or buys a certain product. It is expected that the message recipients will adopt the belief or buy the product in order to feel as if she or he belongs to the groups mentioned. Implicitly, the message is, "if everyone is doing it, it must be right." This fallacy was presented earlier in this chapter, when we considered the advertisement for LaBaroness, the car that more people are buying than any other American car.

A variation of the popularity technique is **testimonials.** Respected politicians or movie stars endorse a belief or product. It is believed that, because people will want to be similar to the people they respect, they will choose to use the same deodorant or hair spray or support the same causes. The recipients of testimonials are expected to infer a conclusion from the information stated. It is expected that they will reason along these lines: Christie Brinkley is a gorgeous model. She uses the advertised beauty product. If I use this beauty product, I will look like Christie Brinkley. Of course, this conclusion does not follow from the first two sentences, but many people believe that it does or, at least, that it might. This fallacy is worsened when the testimonial is not even in the area in which the personality has expertise. Christie Brinkley also endorses a national newspaper. As far as I know, this is an area in which she has no expertise. She is not a credible expert in the area of journalistic quality. Yet, advertisements like these do sell products.

Consider this classic television commercial:

She's lovely.
She's engaged.
She uses Ponds.

Of course, it is never stated that she became engaged *because* she uses Ponds. This is an implied conclusion. It is also implied that everyone who uses Ponds will get engaged.

Sometimes, however, the popularity technique and testimonials can be valid persuasive techniques. If, for example, all of the members of any unbiased expert panel that is established to study the effects of a drug decide that the drug is unsafe, I would consider this information relevant to the question of the drug's safety, because it passes the test of credibility. Similarly, if a leading educator endorses a reading text, this might properly have an impact on your evaluation of the text. Both of these examples presume that the "experts" have no personal motives for their endorsements—that is, they're not being paid for saying these things, and their expertise is relevant to the position or product that they're supporting. In this case, they are credible sources of information.

5. False Dichotomy

Don't give him two sides to a question to worry him. Give him one; better yet, give him none!

—Ray Bradbury
Farenheit 451

There are very few political or social decisions that have simple answers or that can be solved with simple choices. Yet, simple slogans are the **prototype,** or most common and representative form, of persuasive techniques. **False dichotomy** is sometimes called *simplification* or the **Black or White Fallacy,** because readers are asked to decide between two positions, without allowing other alternatives or "gray areas" that would combine aspects of both choices.

The following question appeared in a questionnaire that was sent by an assemblyman to his constituents (Assemblyman Montjoy Needs Your Views, 1983):

"Would you prefer that government cut spending or increase taxes?"
cut spending   increase taxes

Does this question bother you? It should. The answers to our fiscal problems are not this simple. You should ask where and how the cuts would be made and how and how much taxes would be increased. Perhaps "cuts" could be combined with small or temporary increases in taxes. Can you guess which answer the assemblyman prefers? Given this choice, I believe that most people would prefer to "cut spending," yet, for many, an entirely different response would result from a question that was worded differently.

When you are faced with a false dichotomy or the simplification of a complex issue, don't ask yourself if the ideas are good or bad. Ask instead what is good about the ideas and what is bad about them. Consider other alternatives and combinations of ideas. Remember that one of the steps in analyzing arguments calls for supplying missing components—omitted premises, assumptions, qualifiers, and counterarguments.

6. Appeals to Pride or Snobbery

Speech was given to man to disguise his thoughts.

—Talleyrand

An **appeal to pride or snobbery** usually involves praise or flattery. A blatant and humorous example can be found in an advertisement that was mailed to me at home. (Notice that it begins with my name, a sure attention-getting technique.)

> Dear Dr. Halpern,
>
> You may just be the solution.
> Here is the problem: How do you find the right subscribers for an extraordinary magazine that is about to be published—BUT, a magazine that isn't for everyone? A magazine that is, in fact, for only a handful of bright, literate people, people who still in this world of instant communication love to sit down with a good book.

I'd love to believe that the publishers know me personally, and have written a magazine just for the kind of person I'd like to be. The truth is, this letter went to thousands of people whose names were bought as part of various mailing lists. Clearly, they are attempting to persuade me to purchase their magazine by appealing to my pride or snobbery.

Consider the following question, which appeared as part of a ''1982 Congressional Questionnaire'' (Congressman Carlos J. Moorhead Reports, Summer, 1982):

> In an attempt to make federal social programs more responsive to citizens' needs, less wasteful and more efficient, the Administration has proposed a New Federalism where the programs and funds—in the form of block grants—are transferred to local government for management and administration. Do you think that you, your neighbors, and your local officials have the ability to handle this new responsibility?   yes   no

Do you think that this question is slanted toward a ''yes'' response? The appeal to pride and snobbery is less obvious in this question than in the first example, possibly making it even more potent. The question is really, ''Are you and your friends smart enough to handle X?'' It doesn't matter what X is; most people believe that they are smart. The congressman has also posed the wrong question. You may be able to ''handle this new responsibility'' without believing that block grants are a good idea. Responses to this question were subsequently used to support the idea of block grants. Be wary of persuasive communications that include flattery. Although flattery is not in and of itself wrong, it may be used to obscure real issues.

7. Card Stacking or Suppressed Information

Card stacking, or suppressed information, operates as a persuasive technique by omitting information that supports the unfavored view. An automobile company recently compared the car they were advertising on television with a competitor's. The advertisers stressed that their car got better mileage and cost less. What about the variables they omitted? Which car needed fewer repairs, had the more comfortable seating, or accelerated better? What about other makes of cars? Did a brand that was not mentioned exceed the advertised one on all of these dimensions? When considering persuasive information, be sure to consider what has not been stated along with the stated claims. This is another example of the need to consider the missing components in an argument.

8. Circular Reasoning

In **circular reasoning,** the premise is simply a restatement of the conclusion. If you were to diagram the structure of this sort of argument, you would get a circle, because the support for the conclusion is a restatement of the conclusion. Here is an example of circular reasoning:

We need to raise the speed limit because the current legal speed is too slow.

In this example, the reason given (current speed is too slow) is just another way of saying that we need to raise the speed limit. It does not support the conclusion. The conclusion would be supported with premises such as the assertion that there has been no change in the number or severity of automobile accidents with a lower speed limit or some similar statement that supports this conclusion.

9. Irrelevant Reasons

Arguments that utilize irrelevant reasons are fairly common. The Latin word for this sort of fallacy is *non sequitur,* which literally translates to "it doesn't follow." In other words, the reason or premise is unrelated to the conclusion. Of course, you recognize the importance of having relevant premises as one of the criteria for sound arguments. (If you don't, go back over the section of evaluating the strength of an argument.)

One example that comes to mind is a statement that a faculty member made at a curriculum committee meeting in which we were discussing whether or not we should require every student to take classes in a foreign language. The faculty member in favor of the proposal made this statement: "We should require every student to study a foreign language, because it is important that we provide our students with a quality education." Look carefully at the conclusion and the premise. Is the premise related to the conclusion? Everyone on the curriculum committee believed that all students should receive a quality education, but the issue was whether all students should be required to study a foreign language. There were no reasons given as to why studying a foreign language should be a required part of a quality education. The conclusion did not follow from the reason that was given.

10. Slippery Slope or Continuum

The **slippery slope** fallacy is best described by an example. One of the arguments against court-ordered desegregation of the schools was that, if we allow the court to determine which public schools our children will attend, the court will also tell us whom we have to allow into our churches, whom we have to invite into our homes, and even whom we should marry. In this example, the action (court-ordered desegregation) lies on a continuum, with the court ordering whom we should marry at an extreme end. The argument being made is that, if we allow the court to have jurisdiction over events at one end of the continuum, then it will take over the other events on the continuum. For that reason, this type of fallacy is called either *slippery slope* (once you start sliding down a slope you can't stop) or the fallacy of **continuum.**

Most of life's events can be ordered along a continuum. It does not necessarily follow that actions concerning some part of the continuum will also apply to other portions of the continuum. Let's consider a second example. The Irish believe that current U.S. immigration laws are biased against immigrants from Ireland. They have asked the U.S. immigration service to increase the quota for Ireland. Those who have argued against increasing the immigration quotas for Ireland have said that if we increase the quota for Ireland, then we'll have to increase the quota for every other country in the world, an action that they see as disastrous. Increasing the number of immigrants that we accept from Ireland does not mean that we would also have to increase the quotas for other countries. The immigration office may or may not decide to alter quotas from other countries; taking an action on behalf of one country does not mean that the other actions will follow. A more colorful name for this fallacy is "the camel's nose in the tent." It is based on the idea that if we let a camel stick its nose in the tent, the rest of the camel will soon follow (Kahane, 1980).

11. Straw Person

A **straw person** is weak and easy to knock down. With a straw person argument, a very weak form of an opponent's argument is set up and then knocked down. It occurs when an opponent to a particular conclusion distorts the argument in support of the conclusion and substitutes one that is much weaker. Again, an example is probably the best way to describe this sort of fallacy. In a discussion about whether students should be evaluating their professors, one opponent to this idea offered this straw person argument: "You say that students' evaluations of their professors should be included in decisions about which professors we should be promoting. Well, I certainly don't think that the decision as to which professors get promoted should be made by students." Notice how the original argument that "student evaluations should be included in the decision-making process" was changed to "students should not be deciding which professors get promoted." The original argument was for student evaluations to be *part of* the criteria used in the decision-making process. This is not the same as having students make the decisions. In its changed form, the argument is easier to knock down, just like a straw person.

12. Part–Whole

Part–whole fallacies are flip sides of the same error. A part–whole fallacy is made whenever a speaker (or writer) assumes that whatever is true of the whole is also true of all of its parts, and whatever is true of the parts is also true of the whole. Consider some outstanding, prestigious university. (Are you thinking about your own school?) As a whole, the student body is highly intelligent, but it would be wrong to believe that every student who attends that university is, therefore, highly intelligent. Similarly, think of several brilliant scientists. Just because they are each brilliant doesn't mean that if we put them on a committee together (made a whole out of them), the committee would be brilliant. They might never agree or perhaps spend so much time impressing each other with how smart they are that no work would get done.

13. Appeals to Ignorance

The peculiar thing about **appeals to ignorance** is that they can often be used to support two or more totally different conclusions. This should be a clue to you that the reasoning involved is fallacious. In appeals to ignorance, the premise involves something we don't know. Our ignorance is being used to argue that because there is no evidence to support a conclusion, the conclusion must be wrong. Our ignorance of a topic can also be used to support a conclusion by stating that, because there is no evidence that contradicts it, the conclusion must be right. I have heard both sides argue this way in a debate on the existence of God. Believers have argued that because no one can prove that God doesn't exist, He therefore must exist. Nonbelievers have argued that because no one can prove that God exists, He therefore doesn't exist. The absence of evidence doesn't support any conclusion.

14. Weak and Inappropriate Analogies

The topic of analogies was presented in chapter 3. It also appears later in the book, in chapters 9 and 10. Analogies are a basic thinking skill. We use analogies whenever we encounter something new and try to understand it by reference to something we already know. Although analogies can be extremely useful aids to comprehension, they can also be misused. Two objects or events are analogous when they share certain properties. When we argue with analogies, we conclude that what is true of one object or event is true of the other.

Consider the mother who decides that her child should not be given piano lessons because the child had dropped out of dance class. The mother formed the analogy that the child dropped out of one type of creative arts lessons and, because dance class and piano lessons were similar in some ways, the child would also drop out of piano lessons. The child may or may not have continued with piano lessons, but it was a weak sort of analogy that formed the support for this conclusion. Dance class and piano lessons are similar in certain respects, but they also have many distinct differences. When considering an argument by analogy, it is important to consider the nature and the salience of the similarity relationship. It is possible that the child would have stuck with piano.

15. Appeals to Authority

I already introduced this fallacy in an informal way earlier in this chapter, when I discussed expert credibility. Much of what we know and believe is based on what we learn from authorities. The fallacy of **appeals to authority** occurs when the authority we use to support the premises in an argument is the wrong one. If I wanted to sell you a stereo, it would be valid if I quoted from an article on stereos written by a professor of acoustics (who is an independent authority). It would be a fallacious appeal if I told you that Pee Wee Herman called it the best stereo system he had ever seen. Thus, the fallacy is not in appealing to an authority on a topic, but in appealing to someone who is not a credible authority.

16. Incomplete Comparisons

"More doctors agree that Dopeys can give you the fastest pain relief." Advertisements like this one are so common that it's almost impossible to open a magazine without seeing one. Two different comparisons are made in this statement, and both are incomplete. Whenever you see comparative terms, ask yourself "more than what," "fastest compared to what?" **Incomplete comparisons** are missing the other half of the equation.

Incomplete comparisons often contain evaluative terms like "better," "safest," and, of course, "cleanest." This is a special case of considering missing components in an argument. How was *better* defined? How was it measured? By whom? Compared to what? There is no way to interpret claims like, "Washo will make your whole wash cleaner" without additional information. An ice cream store that I pass on my way to work has a large sign outside it that states, "Voted the best ice cream." I presume that I am supposed to infer that their ice cream was voted the best, but by whom, compared to which other ice creams, what criteria were used to decide which was best, and how were the ice creams evaluated with these criteria? Every time you see a comparative claim, you should ask yourself these questions. If the answers aren't provided, then the comparison is incomplete.

17. Knowing the Unknowable

Sometimes, we are given information that it is impossible to know. This is the fallacy of **knowing the unknowable.** Suppose you read in the newspapers that we need to increase the size of the police force because the number of unreported rapes has increased dramatically. A little alarm should go off when you read this: How can anyone know about the number of unreported rapes? I don't doubt that many rapes are not reported to the police or that this is an important issue. What is at question is the increase or decrease in the number when the actual number in unknowable. There are numerous times when sources give precise figures when such figures are impossible. Child abuse is another example. This is a tragic and important issue for society to grapple with, but estimates about the number of children involved can never be very accurate, because much of it is undetected. Researchers can try to extrapolate from the number of child abuse cases that are treated in the emergency rooms of hospitals or that go to court, but there are no good methods of converting these known figures to unreported cases. An increase in the number of cases of rape or child abuse may be due to increased awareness and education about these crimes. An increase in reported cases could be associated with an increase, decrease, or no change in unreported cases. There is no way we can know the unknowable.

18. False Cause

The fallacy of **false cause** is discussed more completely in chapter 6, but it is also important to discuss in the context of reasoning fallacies. The fallacy of false cause occurs whenever someone argues that because two events occur together, or one follows the other closely in time, that one caused the other to occur. An example of this is an explanation of the finding that as the number of churches increase in a city so does the number of prostitutes. It would be false to conclude that churches cause an increase in prostitution or that prostitutes cause more churches to be built. In fact, as the size of a city increases so does the number of churches and the number of prostitutes, as well as the number of schools, dry cleaners, and volunteer agencies. Neither of them cause any of the others. They all result from a third factor—in this case, an increase in population.

19. Put-Downs

Only a fool would endorse this candidate! No patriotic American would disagree! You'd have to be stupid to believe that! These are all examples of **put-downs** (also known as belittling the opposition). An opposing viewpoint is belittled so that agreeing with it would put you in the class of people who are fools, or unpatriotic, or stupid. This technique is not so much a reasoning fallacy as it is an emotional appeal or dare. It is at least partly because of emotional factors that identifying the components of an argument and diagramming the structure of an argument is a good way to determine the strength of an argument. It allows you to strip away the more emotional portions and focus on the nature of the premises and the way they support the conclusion.

20.   Appeals to Tradition

''That's the way we've always done it.'' Anyone who has tried to change a policy has heard this sentence or its variant, ''If it ain't broke, don't fix it.'' In **appeals to tradition,** the unstated assumption is that what exists is best. It may be true that current policy is better than some suggested change, but it also may not be true. There is nothing inherent in the fact that ''that's the way we've always done it'' that makes it a good or best way to accomplish an objective. One of the attitudes of a critical thinker that was presented in the first chapter is flexibility. Appeals to tradition deny the possibility that a different way may be an improvement.

DISTINGUISHING AMONG OPINION,
REASONED JUDGMENT, AND FACT

Compare the following three statements:

- Computereasy is the best personal computer you can buy. I like it.
- Computereasy is the best personal computer you can buy for under $2000. It is easier to use than the five other leading brands and will run all of the software programs that I use.
- Computereasy comes with a 40 mb hard disk drive, a built-in laser printer, and is fully compatible with all software written for the IBM, Apple, and Apple Macintosh.

In the first example, I have expressed an **opinion.** It is a simple assertion of a preference. I like it; I think it's best. No reasons were given to support the evaluation. Opinion reflects how an individual or group has assessed a position or product—for example, ''Vote for Max Lake; he's the best man for the job!''

The second example also expresses a preference, but, in this example, the preference is supported by reasons. I prefer X because Y. This is an example of **reasoned judgment.** Other examples of reasoned judgment are provided throughout the chapter. Remember the extended argument concerning the relationship between low-fat diets and breast cancer? The premises supported the conclusion, which in this case was a statement about which type of diet is best.

The third statement concerns factual claims. **Facts** have a verifiable truth value—for example, ''Gravel-O's breakfast cereal has 100% of the recommended daily requirement of iron.'' Although I can't personally check the truth value of these facts, a credible authority (e.g., the Food and Drug Administration) has verified these claims for me. Often, the distinction among fact, opinion and reasoned judgment is a fine one. If we say that you should buy Gravel-O's because it has 100% of the recommended daily requirement of iron, this is a reasoned judgment, based, in part, on the unstated assumption that it is good to eat cereals that contain 100% of the recommended daily requirement of iron. The distinction becomes even more difficult when you recall that opinions can serve as the premises (reasons) in an argument. Thus, when I say that you should buy Gravel-O's because of its great nutty taste, I have a reason to support my conclusion. If I were to add that you should buy Gravel-O's because it has a great nutty taste and it supplies the recommended daily requirement of iron, this would increase the strength of the argument.

"Pure" facts that are untainted by opinion are often hard to come by. Take for example, your daily newspaper. Although news reporters are obligated to provide readers with facts, their opinions certainly color what they report and how they report it. Compare the way two different newspapers cover the same story. One newspaper could make it the headline on page 1, thus making it important news that will be read by many, whereas the other could place it in an inside section in smaller print; thus making sure that fewer people will read the story. Look at the words used to convey the same story. A quiet night in Poland during a period of martial law could be described as "Poland Enforces Martial Law" or as "All is Quiet in Poland." Both of these headlines could be factually correct, yet they clearly convey different ideas about Polish life.

You may be thinking that at least one source of honest facts is your textbooks. Although it is usually safe to assume that text authors do not set out deliberately to mislead students, the facts that they report are also subject to interpretation. Easily quantified and verifiable information, such as the number of soldiers sent to a South American country or the size of the national deficit, are probably correct or as close to correct as possible, presuming that there has been no deliberate attempt to lie. Other facts, such as the sequence of events and their importance in causing a war, or strategies at political conventions, or poverty in America, need to be interpreted by the text author who will decide how to describe them. The words she or he uses, the events included and omitted, and the amount of information given all contribute to the "factual" information that is printed. Personal bias can, of course, influence the way the ideas are presented.

It has been said that there is never just one war fought. Each side has its own version, and rarely do they agree. Unfortunately, there is always fighting somewhere around the world so that you can verify this statement for yourself. It is not unusual for each side to claim that the other fired first, or for both sides to claim victory in a battle. Obviously, in the absence of verifiable truth there is no way to know which, if either, side is presenting the facts. As before, the best way to assess the quality of the information provided is to consider the credibility of the reporter. I would prefer a report from an independent third party with firsthand and direct knowledge and appropriate credentials to a report from spokespersons from either of the sides involved in a dispute.

Advertisements make extensive use of opinions dressed up as fact. Consider the advertisements for headache remedies. Often, they will show an attractive man in a white laboratory coat, obviously selected to portray a physician. He tells you that, "Speedo works fast on headache pain." Although this may seem like a fact, it is an opinion. *Fast* is a vague term, and, therefore, it is a matter of judgment. If the appropriate tests with a large number of people had shown that, on the average, Speedo brings pain relief in 20 minutes, this information would be a fact. If you are in doubt as to whether information is fact or opinion, check for vague or evaluative terms (fast, better, lovelier, etc.), and ask yourself how the evaluative term was defined and what type of test was conducted to support the claim. This topic is covered in more detail in chapter 6.

HOW TO CHANGE BELIEFS

We are constantly surrounded by people and groups who want to change what we think and how we act. Advertising agencies want us to buy whatever product they are selling; political candidates want our votes; the Beef Council wants us to change what we eat. The list is endless. Some of these beliefs and actions are beneficial, but others are not. One of the best ways to understand the dynamics of changing beliefs is to consider the issues from the perspective of someone who wants to change the beliefs of someone else. You can use this knowledge to change beliefs or to resist change. The following list is adapted from a summary of the attitude-change literature by Dember, Jenkins, and Teyler (1984, p. 751).

1. Provide a credible source for the information you are presenting. The source of information should be a person or agency with the necessary expertise in the field who is independent with respect to the issue. Additional requirements for assessing the credibility of an information source are provided in this chapter.

2. Anticipate counterarguments, raise them, and provide counterexamples. This is a good technique when debating an issue before an audience. It can leave the opposition with few points to make. As you know, counterarguments weaken the support for a conclusion. This technique allows you to weaken the counterarguments.

3. Don't appear one-sided, especially when the audience may be predisposed to the opposite side. The willingness to use qualifiers and to consider counterarguments makes you position appear more credible.

4. Be direct. "Tell them what to believe." By explicitly stating the conclusion, you eliminate the possibility that the audience will arrive at a different conclusion or not "see" the support for the conclusion that you are advocating.

5. Encourage discussion and public commitment. These variables have not been discussed in this chapter, although they appear in other places in the book. The discussion

allows the audience to generate reasons and to "own" them or view them as reasons that they provided. Public commitment is a powerful motivator. If someone signs a document or speaks in favor of a position, a host of psychological mechanisms are brought into play. It is a kind of a promise to believe or act in a certain way. This technique was used extensively by Caesar Chavez and others in their attempt to get consumers to boycott grapes. (The motivation for the boycott was to protest the use of certain pesticides on the grapes.)

6. Repeat the conclusion and the reasons that support the conclusion several times. People prefer positions that are familiar to them. You can make the same points in several different ways. Repetition is a useful aid in recall. Thus, reasons that are easily remembered (i.e., more available in memory) are more readily used to assess the strength of an argument. (The potent effects of repeated exposure are presented in chapter 8.)

7. Provide as many reasons to support the conclusion as is feasible. As you already know, one way to increase the strength of an argument is by increasing the number of reasons that support it.

8. The message should be easy to comprehend. People are negatively affected by messages that they find incomprehensible (Fiske & Taylor, 1984).

9. You could use any of the 20 common fallacies presented in this chapter. But be wary, they are examples of unsound reasoning. If you want to persuade someone, your reasoning should be sound. Shoddy reasoning is detectable, and if detected, it could (and should) destroy your credibility.

APPLYING THE FRAMEWORK

Let's consider the steps in applying the general framework for thinking to analyzing arguments.

1. *What is the goal?* You'll want to use the skills for analyzing arguments any time you encounter attempts to persuade you or you attempt to persuade someone that a particular conclusion is either true or likely to be true. Once you become accustomed to "looking for arguments" (in its technical meaning, not in its everyday meaning) and looking at reasons, you'll be surprised how frequently you are bombarded by advertisements, political claims, and other attempts to "change your point of view."

2. *What is known?* This question is about starting points in the thinking process. In analyzing arguments, you begin with statements and determine if they contain an argument. The statements are then evaluated to assess the quality of the argument. The process proceeds by identifying the conclusion and premises and systematically applying the steps of argument analysis in order to reach the goal of making a determination about how good the argument is.

3. *Which thinking skill or skills will get you to your goal?* The skills of analyzing arguments involve the sequential application of "tests of goodness"—How acceptable are the premises, how much support do they provide for the conclusion, and which and how many components are missing? At a minimum, you should be able to apply the three criteria for sound arguments to any set of statements. Unlike most of the other chapters, the skills involved in analyzing arguments are ordered, with less emphasis on selecting the correct skill than on the systematic application of the entire set.

It is almost as important to be able to say why an argument is unsound as it is to be able to identify unsound arguments. You should be able to recognize the 20 fallacies presented in this chapter and explain how each of them violates one of the principles of sound arguments.

The following skills for analyzing arguments were presented in this chapter. If you are unsure about how to use any of these skills, be sure to reread the section in which it is discussed.

- identifying arguments
- diagramming the structure of an argument
- evaluating premises for their acceptability
- examining the credibility of an information source
- determining the consistency, relevance to the conclusion, and adequacy in the way premises support a conclusion
- remembering to consider missing components by assuming a different perspective
- assessing the overall strength of an argument
- recognizing, labeling, and explaining what is wrong with each of the 20 fallacies that was presented
- recognizing differences among opinion, reasoned judgment, and fact

4. *Have you reached your goal?* This is a particularly important question in analyzing arguments, because one of the steps involves considering components that are not there. Have you consciously tried to restructure the argument, using an opposite perspective? Are you able to make an overall judgment about the strength of the argument? It is important to review the way in which you weighted the supporting premises. Often, a decision to weight a premise as either weak or moderate will have very different effects on your overall assessment of the strength of the argument.

CHAPTER SUMMARY

1. An argument is an attempt to convince the reader (or listener) that a particular conclusion is true, based on the reasons presented.

2. All arguments must have at least one conclusion and one premise (reason). Arguments may also have assumptions, qualifiers, and counterarguments.

3. Arguments have structures that can be identified and diagrammed.

4. Sound (good) arguments meet three criteria: the premises are acceptable and consistent; the premises provide support for the conclusion by being relevant to the conclusion and sufficiently strong; and missing components of the argument (e.g., assumptions, counterarguments, qualifiers, premises, and rival conclusions) have been considered.

5. When analyzing the strength of an argument, the amount of support that each premise supplies to the conclusion is weighted along with the negative effects of counterarguments. Missing components are made explicit and are considered along with the stated components.

6. It is often necessary to assess the credibility of a source of information when deciding on the acceptability of a premise.

7. People like to believe that their beliefs and actions are "reasoned"; however, most people are not sensitive to poor or weak reasoning.

8. Twenty common techniques of propaganda were presented. Most can be categorized as types of unsound reasoning in which emotional appeals are often substituted for reasons.

9. A distinction was made among the terms "opinion," "reasoned judgment," and "fact." An opinion is an unsupported statement of preference. Reasoned judgment is a belief that is based on the consideration of premises that support that belief. Facts have a verifiable true value.

10. The beliefs of others can be changed with sound and unsound reasoning. Beware of attempts to manipulate your beliefs with shoddy reasoning techniques.

Terms to Know

Check your understanding of the concepts presented in this chapter by reviewing their definitions. If you find that you're having difficulty with any term, be sure to reread the section where it is discussed.

Argument. An argument consists of one or more statements that are used to provide support for a conclusion.

Conclusion. The belief or statement that the writer or speaker is advocating.

Reasons. The bases for believing that a conclusion is true or probably true. Note: This word may be singular or plural, because there may be one or more reasons for a conclusion. When we reason (singular only), we are following rules for determining if an argument is sound.

Premises. The formal term for the statements that support a conclusion.

Premise Indicators. Key words that often (but not always) signal that the statement or statements that follow them are premises.

Conclusion Indicators. Key words that often (but not always) signal that the statement or statements that follow them are conclusions.

Assumptions. In an argument, assumptions are statements for which no proof or evidence is offered. They may be stated or implied.

Subarguments. Arguments that are used to build the main argument in an extended passage.

Main point. The principal argument in an extended passage.

Qualifier. A constraint or restriction on the conclusion.

Counterargument. Statements that refute a particular conclusion.

Convergent Structures. A type of argument in which two or more premises support the same conclusion.

Chained (or Linked) Structures. Argument types in which the conclusion of one subargument becomes the premise of a second argument.

Acceptable. A standard for assessing the quality of a premise. A premise is acceptable when it is true or when we can reasonably believe that it is true.

Consistent. A standard for assessing the quality of an argument. When the premises that support a conclusion are not contradictory, they are consistent.

Adequate Grounds. A standard for assessing the quality of an argument. Occurs when the premises provide good support for a conclusion.

Sound Argument. Meets three criteria: (a) acceptable and consistent premises; (b) premises are relevant and provide sufficient support for the conclusion; and (c) missing components considered and evaluated.

Rationalizing. A biased analysis of an argument so that a preferred conclusion will be judged as acceptable or a nonpreferred conclusion will be judged as unacceptable. The process of rationalizing is usually not conscious.

Propaganda. Information presented by proselytizers of a doctrine or belief. The objective is to get the reader or listener to endorse the belief.

Fallacies. Unsound reasoning techniques that are used to change how people think.

Guilt by Association. The propaganda technique of associating a position or person with an undesirable position or person in order to create a negative impression.

Virtue by Association. The propaganda technique of associating a position or person with a desirable position or person in order to create a favorable impression. Compare with *guilt by association*.

Arguments Against the Person. A form of propaganda that attacks the people who support a cause and not the cause itself.

Appeals to Pity. A propaganda technique that asks for your compassion instead of appealing to your reason.

Popularity. A propaganda technique in which the only reason for the conclusion is that it is endorsed by "everyone."

Testimonial. An appeal in which the sole support for a conclusion is someone's unsupported opinion.

False Dichotomy. An argument in which two possible conclusions or courses of action are presented when there are multiple other possibilities. (Also known as *Black or White Fallacy*.)

Card Stacking. A propaganda technique that omits important information that might support an unfavored view.

Appeals to Pride or Snobbery. The use of praise or flattery to get its recipient to agree with a position.

Circular Reasoning. An argument structure in which the premise is a restatement of the conclusion.

Slippery Slope. Counterargument for a conclusion in which the premise consists of the idea that, because certain events lie along some continuum, it is not possible to take an action without affecting all the events on the continuum.

Continuum. Fallacy of the Continuum is the same as *Slippery Slope*.

Straw Person. A type of propaganda in which an opponent to a conclusion distorts the argument that supports the conclusion by substituting a weaker argument.

Appeals to Ignorance. An argument in which the premise involves something that is unknown.

Knowing the Unknowable. Fallacy in which numbers are provided for events that cannot be quantified.

False Cause. Fallacy in which one event is said to have caused the other because they occur together.

Put-Downs. Belittling an opposing point of view so that it would be difficult for a listener to agree with it.

Appeals to Tradition. A propaganda technique that utilizes the reason that what exists is best.

Chapter Questions

Be sure that you can answer the following questions:

1. Why did Harman call reasoning "a change in view"?
2. How do convergent argument structures differ from chained structures? What is the net effect on the strength of the argument if I add a weak premise to each of these argument structures?
3. How do you determine if a premise is acceptable? What standards should you be applying?
4. What do you need to consider when assessing the credibility of an expert? Why is the credibility of an expert an important factor in determining the acceptability of a premise?
5. Explain the concept of relatedness as it applies to the relationship between a premise and a conclusion.
6. What are the criteria for a sound argument?
7. Why is it important to consider what's missing from an argument when you evaluate its soundness?
8. Explain the experiment that was described in the section on the psychology of reasons. Under what circumstances were people willing to let someone go ahead of them when waiting in line?
9. The 20 common fallacies are based on unsound reasoning. Which ones are examples of premises that are unrelated to the conclusion?
10. How does *reasoned judgment* differ from *opinion?* Give an example in which an opinion serves as a premise in an argument.
11. How do you change someone's beliefs?

Exercises

Diagram and evaluate the soundness of the following statements, using the steps for analyzing arguments.

1. The reason we have so many juvenile delinquents is that there are too many working mothers.

2. She looked deep into his baby blue eyes and proclaimed, "I love you."

3. You really should consider becoming a physics major. The topic is interesting, and there are plenty of good jobs available.

4. You really should consider becoming a physics major. The topic is interesting, and there are plenty of good jobs available. With a wide range of available jobs, you probably could find a job near your home town. Of course, it will require lots of hard work. Physics is a particularly good choice for students who enjoy the sciences and mathematics. Students with math anxiety probably won't be happy as physics majors.

5. Eighteen-year-olds should not be allowed to drink, because they are too young.

6. The trade agreement between Mexico and the U.S. is needed in order to improve the skiing in Colorado.

7. There is too much violence shown on the network channels. Advertisers will only pay for shows that have large viewing audiences, and these tend to be shows with excessive sex and violence. For this reason, a public television station supported by tax dollars is needed. But is it fair to make all taxpayers contribute to public television stations when most don't watch them? We believe that it is. Without tax-supported public television, we will never be able to provide high-level television programming.

8. The classic books of Western civilization are the building blocks of our society. Very few college students will read them unless they are required to. For these reasons, these books should be required reading for all college students.

9. Are you tired of the way politicians are running this country? If so, vote for me. Remember, when you vote for Elvira Slick, you're voting for me.

For each of the following examples, indicate if a fallacy is being committed, and, if so, label it and explain why the reasoning is fallacious. (More than one fallacy may apply.) Whenever you decide that a line of reasoning is fallacious, you should be able to explain why.

1. How can the U.S. Supreme Court decide that high school newspapers can be censored when papers written by persons not in high school cannot be censored? Nothing magical happens the day someone graduates from high school. Students are only one day older. We can't have laws that apply to you one day and different laws that apply the next day.

2. "At last, four new residences designed to delineate a new level of luxury. Some visitors will find the opulence disturbing. Perhaps you will recognize a unique opportunity. From one-half million dollars . . ." (quote from an advertisement for condominiums, Los Angeles Times, 1983).

3. Of course, the new senator will be conservative. His father and mother are conservatives, and his brother-in-law is head of "Conservatives for Better America."

4. We can only conclude that there is no such phenomenon as extra sensory perception, because no one has been able to demonstrate that it exists.

5. "Your honor, the defendant came from a broken home."

6. California State University is the best school for you. It has a better computer major than Colorado State and is cheaper than Harvard.

7. This diet is doctor-tested and approved!

8. Over the past 50 years, all U.S. Wars occurred while we had a Democratic administration. ''I would ask [Senator Kennedy] to name one Republican president that led this country into war.'' (This sentence was spoken by Richard Nixon during a televised debate.)

9. Walter Cronkite buys his clothes at Snooty Brothers. He's a man who knows. Shouldn't you be shopping here too?

10. You'll get better tasting cake with Happy Homemaker Cake Mix.

11. We can either send troops to the Middle East or we can pull out entirely. Which course of action do you prefer?

12. What will I do to improve the union now that I've been elected president? Why, I'll do anything I can to make it better.

13. The committee to investigate the causes of Alzheimer's disease will surely be able to find the cause, because the committee is composed of leading researchers in the field.

14. The question of whether we should allow gay fraternities to meet on campus is easy to answer. How would you like it if your son joined a gay fraternity?

15. The problem of incest is a serious one for contemporary society. There has been a dramatic increase in the number of unreported cases in the last several years alone.

16. You want to change the way we do business around here. Well, I believe that if it ain't broke, don't fix it.

17. ''More Californians are choosing Bank of America because we have more automatic teller machines'' (taken from a television commercial).

18. The U.S. should not be sending troops to South America. We sent troops to Viet Nam and the outcome was very poor.

19. It is stupid to believe that the U.S. should stay out of South America.

20. We cannot believe that genetic engineering is safe, because the researchers are atheists.

21. We cannot believe that genetic engineering is safe, because the researchers have a substantial profit motive that may override their concern for safety.

22. Marijuana is a serious threat to society. College enrollment has declined at a rate that is the same as the rate of increase in marijuana consumption.

23. He is a poor writer, because his essays are badly written.

24. Wrinkle Away cream is the fastest way to reduce wrinkles around the eyes and mouth.

25. You really should take Professor Snodley's class, because enrollment in his class is low.

Carefully consider the following statements. For each statement, decide if it is an opinion, reasoned judgment, or fact. If it is a fact, decide if it is an important or relevant one.

1. Bold has a new and improved formula to get clothes even whiter.
2. The new formula in Soapies is effective in removing spinach and grass stains; therefore, Soapies' new and improved formula will get clothes even whiter than the previous formula.
3. Speedo is a faster acting cold remedy.
4. Tang has more vitamin C than plain orange juice.
5. Pearl Gray is the best candidate for the job!
6. Josh is the best pitcher on the team.
7. Josh hit more home runs than anyone else on the team.
8. Josh is the best pitcher on the team. He was the only pitcher to pitch a no-hitter.
9. Ray got 80% of the arithmetic problems correct.
10. Druggies hits a higher level of pain relief.
11. In a taste test with over 100 dogs, three out of every four dogs preferred the taste of Crunchies brand dog food. Doesn't your dog deserve the best?
12. Diamonds are a good investment.
13. Interest rates have dropped three percentage points since March.
14. The national debt must be reduced.
15. As free Americans, we have the right to bear arms.
16. George Washington had wooden teeth.
17. Historians who have examined photos of George Washington have concluded that he didn't have wooden teeth.
18. Vegetarian diets can reduce certain health risks.
19. Vegetarians have low cholesterol levels. It seems likely that vegetarian diets can reduce certain health risks.

Keep a record of the persuasive techniques that appear on billboards, radio, and television. A particularly good source for this material is the solicitations for political and charitable organizations that are mailed to your home. Letters to the editor in newspapers and cartoons also rely on common persuasive techniques to "make their point."

SUGGESTED READINGS

Many of the books that were suggested in chapter 4 also deal with the general topic of analyzing arguments. If you consult some of the recommended books, you will find some differences in the way certain terms are used. One common practice is to label the topics I've included in chapter 4 as "formal reasoning" and to use the label "informal reasoning" for the topics I include here. Many of the books published within the last few years have taken a more applied and practical approach than the older texts. My favorites among them include Damer's (1987) *Attacking Faulty Reasoning,* Fogelin's (1987) *Understanding Arguments, An Introduction to Informal Logic,* Thomas' (1986) *Practical Reasoning in Natural Language,* and Govier's (1985) *A Practical Study of Argument.* The book by Fogelin has particularly good sections on legal reasoning and scientific arguments.

Although much has been written over the past three decades about persuasion and propaganda, three classic texts that are still contemporary in their content are Flesch's (1951) *The Art of Clear Thinking* and an even older book by Thouless (1939), *Tests of Logical Reasoning: How to Think Straight*. Also recommended is Thouless' earlier book, written in 1932, entitled *Straight and Crooked Thinking*. The last chapter in this gem of a book is called "Thirty-Four Dishonest Tricks." It is a list of persuasive techniques that are as current as the day it was written. Most importantly, he tells us how to defend against them.

A colorful and well-illustrated source of information on persuasion and propaganda is Sparke, Taines, and Sidell's (1975) *Doublespeak: Language for Sale*. Billing itself as "a guide to propaganda for students of propaganda, for citizens generally who are objects of propaganda, and for propagandists" (p. vii), is Lee's (1953) worthwhile book, *How to Understand Propaganda*. Kahane's (1988) text, *Logic and Contemporary Rhetoric: The Use of Reason in Everyday Life,* also contains numerous examples of political and advertising techniques designed to sell goods and politics to consumers. Kahane's book is now in its fifth edition, which is a genuine tribute to its author. Hitchcock's (1983) *Critical Thinking: A Guide to Evaluating Information* lists and discusses a variety of persuasive techniques in a structured outlinelike format. It's a clearly written text that could also serve as an introduction to the general area of argument analysis. I also highly recommend a clever article by Jason (1987), entitled "Are Fallacies Common? A Look at Two Debates." In this article, he has presented and analyzed examples of irrelevant reasons, false cause, arguments against the person, and popularity that he gleaned from presidential debates. This is good reading for anyone who believes that the issues discussed in this chapter are not important. The presidential candidates freely used many of these fallacies to persuade the American public that they were the best candidate for the presidency.

6

Thinking as Hypothesis Testing

Contents

The conversation was getting heated. "Look, I know what I'm talking about," Kay said to Chris in an angry tone. "Busing school children for the purpose of integration works. My daughter is now close friends with both White and Black girls, and her grades have improved since busing was adopted in her district."

"Oh, yeah," Chris answered. "Well, my son has become more prejudiced since they forced him to be bused across town, and his grades are barely passing."

"Your son's grades were barely passing before he was bused," Kay responded, "And furthermore, my neighbor thinks that busing is good, too. You're just too pigheaded to look at the evidence."

"Pigheaded! My son is being bused to a school with dumb students. It's as plain as the large nose on your face. Busing is bad news."

Heated discussions like this fictional one between Kay and Chris have been taking place in large and small towns across the country as people argue for and against the issue of busing children from neighborhood schools to other schools in order to achieve desegregation. How did Kay and Chris arrive at their conclusions? How did each become so convinced that he or she is correct? What do you think about school busing, and how did you arrive at your conclusion?

UNDERSTANDING HYPOTHESIS TESTING

Research is an intellectual approach to an unsolved problem, and its function is to seek the truth.

—Leedy (1981, p. 7)

Much of our thinking is like the scientific method of **hypothesis testing.** A **hypothesis** is a set of beliefs about the nature of the world; it is usually a belief about a relationship between two or more variables. In order to understand the world around us, we accumulate observations, formulate beliefs or hypotheses (singular is hypothesis), and then observe if our hypotheses are confirmed or disconfirmed. Thus, hypothesis testing is one way of finding out the truth about the world. Formulating hypotheses and making systematic observations that could confirm or disconfirm them is the same method that scientists use when they want to understand events in their academic domain; thus, when thinking is done in this manner, it has much in common with the experimental methods used by scientists.

Explanation, Prediction, and Control

All . . . by nature desire knowledge.

—Aristotle

There is a basic need to understand events in life. Nisbett and Ross (1980) believe that, in our attempt to understand, we often function as "intuitive scientists." Like scientists, we have our own theories about the causes of social and physical events. It is important to be able to explain why people react in certain ways (e.g., He's a bigot. She's tired after work.) to predict the results of our actions (e.g., If I don't study, I'll fail. If I wear designer clothes, people will think I'm cool.) and to control some of the events in our environment (e.g., If I want to have a good job in business, I'll have to do well in my accounting course.).

The goal of hypothesis testing is to make accurate predictions about the portion of the world that we're dealing with (Holland, Holyoak, Nisbett, & Thagard, 1986). In order to survive and function with maximum efficiency, we must reduce the uncertainty in the environment. One way to reduce uncertainty is to observe sequences of events with the goal of determining predictive relationships. Children, for example, may learn that an adult will appear whenever they cry; your dog may learn that when he stands near the kitchen door, you will let him out; and teenagers may learn that their parents will become angry when they come home late. These are important predictive relationships, because they reduce the uncertainty in the environment. The process that we use in determining these relationships is the same one that is used when medical researchers discover that cancer patients will go into remission following chemotherapy or that longevity is associated with certain lifestyles. Because the processes are the same, some of the technical concepts in scientific methods are applicable to practical everyday thought.

In order to understand the parallels between scientific and everyday thought, let's examine an example of scientific thought from a study by a clinical psychologist (H. Halpern, 1983). As a clinical psychologist, Halpern wanted to understand the variables that contribute to positive and negative attitudes toward homosexuality. As you probably know, some people believe that homosexuality is a sin or a mental disorder; others believe that it is a legitimate alternative lifestyle. How can we explain these differences in people's attitudes? Halpern formulated several hypotheses. He hypothesized that people who never had a close friendship with a homosexual would, in general, tend to have negative attitudes toward homosexuals. He also hypothesized that people with strong sex-role stereotypes (beliefs that certain activities and behaviors are appropriate for females, whereas others are appropriate for males) would have negative attitudes toward homosexuals. He also believed that persons from urban areas would tend to hold more positive attitudes toward homosexuals than those from rural areas.

If you've never thought about this topic, give it some thought now. What do you think about Halpern's hypotheses? If they were your own, how would you go about collecting the information that would confirm or disconfirm them? If your observations confirmed these hypotheses, then you would have, at least, a partial explanation of the way people feel toward homosexuals. You could use this information to predict someone's attitude. If you met a man from a rural area who had never met a homosexual and who believed in traditional sex-role stereotypes, what would you guess about his attitudes toward homosexuals? You would predict that they would not be favorable. Of course, sometimes you'd be wrong—he may even be homosexual himself—but, if the relationships among sex-role stereotypes, where a person lives, the lack of positive interactions with homosexuals, and attitudes toward homosexuals were as hypothesized, it would allow you to predict the attitudes of people you've never met. This information could also be used to improve attitudes toward homosexuals. You could provide opportunities for homosexuals to meet with other members of the community. You could attempt to change people's attitudes about traditional sex roles, and you could provide rural populations with some of the experiences of urban life. In this way, you could use your understanding of the concepts involved in improving attitudes toward homosexuals. (Of course, if you are interested in worsening attitudes toward homosexuals, you could also use your information to provide experiences that are opposite to the ones just discussed. This section is not concerned with the issue of whether homosexuality is good or bad; it is simply being used as an example to compare and discuss the similarity between scientific research and everyday thought.)

Inductive and Deductive Methods

Sometimes, a distinction is made between inductive and deductive methods of hypothesis testing (see chapter 4). In the **inductive method,** you observe events and then devise a hypothesis about the events you observed. To take a trivial example, you might notice that Joan, an attractive woman whom you know, seems to have many dates. Then you note that Minnie and Sue Ann, who are also attractive women, also seem to have many dates. On the basis of these observations, you would hypothesize (invent a hypothesis or explanation) that attractive women go out on many dates. In this way, you would work from your observations to your hypothesis. The inductive method is sometimes described as "going from the specific to the general." In an excellent book, entitled *Induction,* (Holland et al., 1986), the authors argued that the inductive process is the primary way in which we learn about the nature of the world. They stated, "The study of induction, then, is the study of how knowledge is modified through use" (p. 5).

In the **deductive method,** you begin with a hypothesis that you believe to be true and then make systematic observations to see if your hypothesis is correct. You might logically infer that, because beauty is a valued asset for women in our society, attractive women will be popular and thus be asked out on many dates. After coming up with this hypothesis, you'd look around to find out which women are attractive and then determine if they date often. You'd also want to compare them to their less comely friends to see if women who are not attractive go out on fewer dates. When you begin with a hypothesis and then collect evidence that would confirm or disconfirm it, you are using the deductive method. The deductive method is sometimes described as "going from the general to the specific."

Although a distinction is usually made between these two types of reasoning, in real life they are just different phases of the hypothesis testing method. Often, people observe events, formulate hypotheses, observe events again, reformulate hypotheses, and collect even more observations. The question of whether the observations or the hypothesis comes first is moot, because our hypotheses determine what we choose to observe, and our observations determine what our hypotheses will be. It's like the perennial question of what came first, the chicken or the egg. Each process is dependent on the other for its existence. In this way, observing and hypothesizing recycle, with the observations changing the hypotheses and the hypotheses changing what gets observed.

If you are a Sherlock Holmes fan, you'll recognize this process as one that was developed into a fine art by this fictional detective. He would astutely note clues about potential suspects. For example, Sherlock Holmes could remember that the butler had a small mustard-yellow stain on his pants, although it is well known that you don't serve mustard with wild goose. He would use these clues to devise hypotheses like, "the butler must have been in the field where wild mustard plants grow." The master sleuth would then check for other clues that would be consistent or inconsistent with this hypothesis. He might check the butler's boots for traces of the red clay soil that surrounds the field in question. After a circuitous route of hypotheses and observations, Sherlock Holmes would announce, "The butler did it." When called on to explain how he reached his conclusion, he would utter his most famous reply, "It's elementary, my dear Watson."

Many of our beliefs about the world were obtained with the use of inductive and deductive methods, much like the great Sherlock Holmes. Do you see the parallels between the way Sherlock Holmes determined that "the butler did it" and the way Kay and Chris, in the opening paragraph of this chapter, decided if busing was beneficial or harmful? Think about the arguments that were presented by Kay and Chris at the beginning of this chapter. Both of them gathered information, devised hypotheses about relationships, gathered more data, and then processed the data into a conclusion about the truth of their hypotheses. Arthur Conan Doyle's fictional detective was invariably right in the conclusions that he drew. Unfortunately, it is only in the realm of fiction that mistakes are never made. Let's examine the components of the hypothesis testing process to see where mistakes can occur.

Operational Definitions

An **operational definition** tells the reader how to recognize and measure the concept that he or she is interested in. For example, if you believe that nerds study all the time, you'll need to provide an operational definition for the concepts "nerds" and "study all the time." How will I recognize a nerd when I meet one? If you've already read chapter 3, then you should recognize the need for operational definitions as being the same as the problem of vagueness. You'd need to provide some statement, like, "Nerds are students who wear unfashionable clothes and hairstyles and are the teachers' pets.'' You'll find that it is frequently difficult to provide good operational definitions for terms. I can think of several people who more or less fit this description, yet don't fit any other stereotype of nerds (i.e., they are popular, athletic, and engage in many sorts of activities). Thus, this would seem to be an unsatisfactory operational definition. Suppose, for purposes of illustration, that this is our operational definition to classify people into ''nerds'' and ''non-nerds'' categories.

How would you operationally define ''studies all the time?'' Suppose you decided on ''spends at least 40 hours a week on homework.'' Once these terms are operationally defined, you could go around finding out whether nerds and non-nerds differ in how much they study. Operational definitions are important. Whenever you hear people talking about ''our irresponsible youths,'' ''knee-jerk liberals,'' ''bleeding hearts,'' ''rednecks,'' ''reactionaries,'' ''fascists,'' or ''feminists,'' ask them to operationally define their terms. You may find that the impact of their argument is diminished when they are required to be precise about their terms.

Many arguments hinge on operational definitions. Consider, for example, the debate over whether or not alcoholism is a disease. The issue turns on the answer to operational definitions. What defines a ''disease?'' Does alcoholism possess the defining characteristics? If so, it is a disease: if not, it isn't.

In Halpern's study on attitudes toward homosexuals, how should he operationally define his terms? What is a negative or positive attitude toward homosexuals? He answered this question by using a scale that consisted of statements about homosexuals. Respondents had to agree or disagree with statements like ''Homosexuality is unnatural.'' Individual responses to these statements served as a way of measuring attitudes towards homosexuals in order to operationalize this concept. Another scale was used to measure sex-role stereotypes. He was still faced with the task of providing operational definitions for his other variables—the urban/rural distinction and the establishment of a close friendship with a homosexual. The urban/rural distinction was based on the size of the town in which respondents lived. He operationalized the close friendship with a homosexual variable by asking people if they had ever had such a relationship. Thus, by using operational definitions, he improved the precision of his study.

When you use operational definitions, you avoid the problems of ambiguity and vagueness. Try, for example, to write operational definitions for the following terms: love, prejudice, motivation, good grades, sickness, athletic, beautiful, and maturity.

Independent and Dependent Variables

A **variable** is any measurable characteristic that can take on more than one value. Examples of variables are gender (female and male), height, political affiliation (Republican, Democrat, Communist, etc.), handedness (right, left), and attitudes toward homosexuals (could range from extremely negative to extremely positive). When we test hypotheses, we begin by choosing the variables we're interested in. In their argument over school busing that was presented at the start of this chapter, Kay and Chris were interested in the relationships among school busing, prejudice, and classroom performance. Kay argued that busing is beneficial because it reduces prejudice and improves academic performance. Chris' argument was opposite to Kay's: School busing is harmful because it increases prejudice and decreases school performance.

The variable that they're arguing about is busing. It is the one that they decided on before they collected their observations. In this case, they could decide to compare children who are bused with children who walk to their neighborhood schools. Busing is their **independent variable,** because they decided on its measurement before they collected their observations. Any variable whose change (busing or no busing) is expected to affect the event that is being studied is called the independent variable. Ideally, if you want to know if busing *causes* changes in prejudice, you must be able to assign children at random to either the busing or no-busing group. In this way, any other differences among the children (e.g., differences in socioeconomic status, sex, age, or neighborhood of residence) should "cancel out" so that the two groups differ only in whether or not they are bused to school.

The behaviors they want to measure as they relate to busing are prejudice and school achievement. These are their **dependent variables.** In general, the behaviors you want to measure are called dependent measures. The question they want to answer is: "Do children's prejudice and their academic performance depend on whether or not they are bused?"

The next step in the hypothesis testing process is to define the variables operationally. Suppose we decide to define "busing" as riding a school bus 2 or more miles from a segregated neighborhood to an integrated school for at least a year and "not busing" as never having ridden a school bus. With these definitions, we can decide which children will be in the "busing" group and which children will be in the "not busing" group. (Note also that, with these definitions, children who have ridden a school bus less than a year or over distances less than 2 miles or who have not gone from segregated neighborhoods to integrated schools won't be studied.)

How did you define prejudice? Would you be happy with a definition that separated people into two groups—prejudiced and not prejudiced—or would you prefer a definition that measured the amount or degree of prejudice—a measure that allowed people to be measured as more or less prejudiced? Because I believe that prejudice is an attitude that exists in varying degrees, I'd prefer an operational definition that would allow me to quantify this variable. One way to operationalize this variable is to ask children how many close friends they have whose race differs from their own. In this way, a child who has no close friends of other races would be classified as more prejudiced than a child with one close other-race friend, and so on. Academic performance could be operationalized with grade point average. The higher the grade point average, the better the academic achievement.

It is important to think critically about operational definitions for your variables. If they are not stated in satisfactory terms, the conclusions that you draw from your study may be wrong. In this example, the number of other-race friends that a child has is a poor measure of prejudice. Suppose that the children who walk to school attend schools that are either 100% Black or 100% White. These children may have very few other-race friends, not because they are prejudiced, but because they simply don't have the opportunities to meet children of other races. If this is so, then you're not measuring prejudice, but some other variable, like the availability of other-race friends. Variables that we're not interested in, but that affect our results, are called **extraneous variables.** They are extraneous to the purpose of our study.

Measurement Sensitivity

When we measure something, we systematically assign a number to it for the purpose of quantification. Someone who is taller than you are is assigned a higher number of inches of height than you are. If not, the concept of height would be meaningless.

When we think as scientists and collect information in order to understand the world, we need to consider how we measure our variables. For example, suppose you believe that love is like a fever, and that people in love show feverlike symptoms. To find out if this is true, you could conduct an experiment, taking temperatures from people who are in love and comparing your results to the temperatures of people who are not in love. How will you measure temperature? Suppose that you decide to use temperature headbands that register body temperature with a band placed on the forehead. Suppose further that these bands measure temperature to the nearest degree (e.g., 98°, 99°, 100°, etc.). If being in love does raise your body temperature, but only raises it one-half of a degree, you'd never know this if you used headband thermometers. They just wouldn't be sensitive enough to register the small increment in body temperature. You would incorrectly conclude that love doesn't raise body temperatures, when in fact it may have. As far as I know, this experiment has never been done, but it is illustrative of the need for sensitive measurement in this and other situations.

Populations and Samples

In order to decide whether or not Kay's or Chris' hypothesis about the effects of busing is correct, we need to decide which children we want to study. What we really want to know about is the effect of busing on all children in North America. The group we want to know about is called a **population.** Because we obviously can't study every child, we'll need to study a subset of this population. A subset of a population is called a **sample.** How do we decide who will be in our study?

Biased and Unbiased Samples

We want our sample to be representative of our population. The problem then becomes one of finding a group of children that would be representative of all children in North America. To be representative, the children in our sample would need to be both female and male, from all socioeconomic levels, all intellectual levels, rural and urban areas, and so on. We need **representative samples** so that we can generalize our results. **Generalization** refers to using the results obtained with our sample to infer that similar results would be obtained from the population if everyone in the population had been measured.

What happens when the sample is not representative of the population? Suppose we bus children from the Ozark Mountains, or Chicago, or any other single location and then use their scores on our measures of prejudice and grade point average to make conclusions about the effect of busing on all children in North America. You would rightly be concerned about any conclusions drawn from this study. If you used only children from the Ozark Mountains or only children from Chicago, you would have a **biased sample.** Because it is not representative or unbiased, you could not use it to draw conclusions about the population.

The biggest fiasco in sampling history probably occurred in 1936, when the *Literary Digest* mailed over 10 million straw ballots to people's homes in order to predict the winner of the presidential election that was to be held that year (Kimble, 1978). The results from this large sample were clear cut: The next president would be Alf Landon. What, you don't remember learning about President Landon? I'm sure that you don't, because Franklin Delano Roosevelt was elected president of the United States that year. What went wrong? The problem was in how they sampled voters. They mailed ballots to subscribers to their literary magazine, to people listed in the phone book, and to automobile owners. Remember, this was 1936, and only the affluent belonged to the select group of people who subscribed to literary magazines, or had phones, or owned automobiles. They failed to sample the large number of poorer voters, many of whom voted for Roosevelt instead of Landon. Because of biased sampling, they could not generalize their results to the voting patterns of the population. Even though they sampled a large number of voters, the results were wrong because they sampled in a biased way.

Another pitfall in sampling is the possibility of **confounding.** Suppose you study two groups of children—those who are bused and those who are not bused. The children in the bused group are all from middle-class and wealthy homes, whereas the children in the "not bused" group are all from poorer homes. These groups differ in two ways. They differ with respect to the variable you're interested in (busing) and with respect to a second variable that you're not interested in (family income). If you found that the children who were bused had higher grades, you wouldn't know if this were due to busing or the differences in family income between the groups. Because you can't separate these effects, you have a confounded experiment.

Usually, scientists use **convenience samples.** They study a group of people who are readily available. The most frequent subjects in psychology experiments are college students. The extent to which you can generalize from these samples depends on your research question. If you want to understand how the human visual system works, college students should be useful as subjects. If, on the other hand, you want to understand sex-role stereotyping in adults, college students would not be a representative sample, because college students tend to be less stereotyped than other adults. In this case, you could only generalize about college students.

Sample Size

> Given a thimbleful of facts, we rush to make generalizations as large as a tub.
>
> —Gordon Allport (1954, p. 8)

The number of subjects you include in your sample is called the **sample size.** Refer back to Kay and Chris' argument. What was their sample size? Kay used only one subject, her daughter. Chris also used only one subject, his son. (A subject is a person, animal, or entity who participates in an experiment.) When scientists conduct experiments, they often use large numbers of subjects. If, for some reason, they cannot use a large number of subjects, they may need to be more cautious or conservative in the conclusions that they derive from their research. Although a discussion of the number of subjects needed in an experiment is beyond the scope of this book, it is important to keep in mind that, for most everyday purposes, we cannot generalize about a population by observing how only a few people respond.

Suppose this happened to you: After months of deliberation, you finally decided to buy a Chevrolet Citation. You found that both Consumer Report and Road and Track magazines have given the Citation a good rating. The Citation is priced within your budget, and you like its racing stripes and "sharp" appearance. On your way out the door to close the deal, you run into a close friend and tell her about your intended purchase. "A Citation!" she shrieks. "My brother-in-law bought one and it's a tin can. It's constantly breaking down on the freeway. He's had it towed so often that the rear tires need replacing." What do you do?

Most people would have a difficult time completing the purchase, because they are insufficiently sensitive to sample size issues. The national magazines presumably tested many cars before they determined their rating. Your friend's brother-in-law is a single subject. You should place greater confidence in results obtained with large samples than in results obtained with small samples (assuming that the "experiments" were equally good). Yet, many people find the testimonial of a single person more persuasive than information gathered from a large sample.

We tend to ignore the importance of having an adequately large sample size when we function as intuitive scientists. If you asked just one woman from Little Town, Iowa how she felt about homosexuals and compared her response with that of a single woman in Boston, would you consider this a fair test of the hypothesis that rural inhabitants maintain different attitudes toward homosexuals than their urban counterparts? I hope not. Everyone in Little Town or in Chicago doesn't think the same way about complex issues. People are variable in the attitudes that they maintain.

Variability

The term **variability** is used to denote the fact that all people are not the same. Just by chance, you could have picked someone with unusual attitudes for either Little Town or Boston. What we really want to know is whether people in Little Town are, on the average, more negative in their attitudes toward homosexuals than people in large cities like Boston. To answer this question, we'd ideally take a large **random sample** (a sample in which everyone in the population has an equal chance of being selected) of residents from rural and urban areas and compare the average attitudes from each group.

A few years ago, there was much excitement over the use of laetrile, an extract from apricot pits, as a cure for cancer. Although the United States medical establishment found that it was worthless in the fight against cancer, many people continued to believe that it could be used as a cure. Suppose you read about a woman who was diagnosed as having cancer, and she then took laetrile. Later, this lucky individual recovered from her cancer. What can you conclude? Would you be willing to conclude that, at least for some people, laetrile can cure or help to cure cancer? This conclusion is unwarranted. Some people recovery from cancer, and others do not. Just as people are variable in beliefs and attitudes that they maintain, they are also variable in the way they respond to disease. With a sample size of one, we cannot conclude that the laetrile contributed to her cure. Large-scale studies are needed that compare the survival rates of groups of people on laetrile with groups of people who used other forms of cancer treatments to decide if laetrile can be beneficial in the treatment of cancer. When these tests were conducted by the United States government, laetrile was found to be worthless. It's easy to see how desperate cancer patients can be misled into believing results obtained with a very small number of people.

People's willingness to believe that results obtained from a few subjects can be generalized to the entire population is called the **law of small numbers** (Tversky & Kahneman, 1971). In fact, we should be more confident when predicting to or from large samples than small samples (Kunda & Nisbett, 1986). In an experimental investigation of this phenomenon (Quattrone & Jones, 1980), college students demonstrated their belief that if one member of a group made a particular decision, then the other members of that group would make the same decision. This result was especially strong when the college students were observing the decisions of students from other colleges. Thus, it is easy to see how a belief in the law of small numbers can maintain prejudices and stereotypes. The actions of a single group member are indicative of the actions of the entire group. Have you ever heard someone say, "_____s (fill in your group) are all alike?" An acquaintance once told me that all Jamaicans are sneaky thieves. She came to this conclusion after having one bad experience with a person from Jamaica. Expressions like this one are manifestations of the law of small numbers. Can you see how the law of small numbers can also explain the origin of many prejudices like racism? A single memorable event involving a member of a group with which we have little contact can color our beliefs about the other members of that group. Generally, when you collect observations about people and events, it is important to collect a large number of observations before you reach a conclusion.

There is one exception to the general principle that we need large samples in order to make valid generalizations about a population. The one exception occurs when everyone in the population is exactly the same. If, for example, everyone in North America responded exactly the same way to any question (e.g., Do you approve of the death penalty?) or any treatment (e.g., had no "heart attacks" when treated with a single aspirin), then sample size would no longer be an issue. Of course, all people are not the same. You may be thinking that this was a fairly dumb statement, because everyone knows that people are different. Unfortunately, research has shown that most of us tend to underestimate the variability of groups with which we are unfamiliar. Several investigators have found that college students perceive students at their own college as highly variable; whereas, they perceive students from other colleges as being highly similar (Nisbett, Krantz, Jepson, & Kunda, 1983). They are quick to generalize with statements like, "Everyone who goes there is snobby and rich" or "They're all brains" (or jocks or whatever). By contrast, they see the students at their own college as variable, with the student body made up of various ethnic groups and a broad mix of brains, jocks, and so on.

Minority members of any group often report that the leader or other group members will turn to them and ask, "What do Blacks (or women or Hispanics, or Asians, or whatever the minority is) think about this issue?" It's as though the rest of the group believe that the few minority members of their group can speak for the minority group as a whole. This is a manifestation of the belief that groups other than the one to which we belong are much more homogeneous (less variable) than the groups to which we belong.

The ability to make accurate predictions depends, in part, on the ability to make accurate assessments of variability. It is important to keep the concept of variability in mind whenever you're testing hypotheses either formally in a research setting or informally as you try to determine relationships in the everyday environment.

DETERMINING CAUSE

Do you believe that children who are neglected become teenage delinquents?
Does jogging relieve depression?
Will a diet that is low in fat increase longevity?
Do clothes make the man?
Will strong spiritual beliefs give you peace of mind?
Does critical thinking instruction improve how you think outside the classroom?

All of these questions concern a causal relationship in which one variable (e.g., neglect) is believed to cause another variable (e.g., delinquency). What sort of information do we need to determine the truth of causal relationships?

Isolation and Control of Variables

Stop and think for a minute about the way you would go about deciding if neglecting children causes them to become delinquent when they are teenagers. You could decide to conduct a long-term study in which you would divide children into groups—telling some of their parents to cater to their every need, others to neglect them occasionally, and still others to neglect their children totally. You could require everyone to remain in their groups, catering to or neglecting their children as instructed until the children reach their teen years, at which time you could count up the number of children in each group who became delinquents—remembering, of course, that you have to define operationally the term "delinquent." This would be a good, although totally unrealistic, way to decide if neglect causes delinquency. It's a good way because this method would allow you to control how much neglect each child received and to isolate the cause of delinquency, as this would be the only systematic difference among the people in each group. It's unrealistic to the point of being ludicrous, because very few people would comply with your request to cater to or neglect their children. Furthermore, it would also be unethical to ask people to engage in potentially harmful behaviors.

In some experimental settings, it is possible to isolate and control the variables you're interested in. If you wanted to know if grading students for course work will make college students work harder and therefore learn more, you could randomly assign college students to different grading conditions. Half of the students could be graded as pass or fail (no letter grades), whereas the other students would receive traditional letter grades (A, B, C, D, or F). At the end of the semester, all students would take the same final exam. If the average final exam score for the students who received grades was statistically significantly higher than for the students in the pass/fail condition, you could conclude that grades do result in greater learning. (See chapter 7 for a discussion of significant differences.)

Can you see why it's so important to be able to assign students at random to either the graded or pass/fail conditions instead of just letting them pick the type of grading they want? It is possible that the students who would pick the pass/fail grading are less motivated or less intelligent than the students who would prefer to get grades, or vice versa. If the students could pick their own grading condition, we wouldn't know if the differences we found were due to the differences in grading practices or due to differences in motivation or intelligence, or some other variable that differs systematically as a function of which grading condition the students select.

Let's return to the question of whether child neglect causes delinquency. Given the constraint that you cannot tell parents to neglect their children, how would you go about deciding if child neglect causes delinquency? You could decide to find a group of parents and ask each about the amount of care he or she gives to each child. Suppose you found that, in general, the more that children are neglected, the more likely they are to become teenage delinquents. Because you lost the control over your variables by not assigning parents to catering and neglecting groups, it is not possible, on the basis of this experiment alone, to conclude that neglect causes delinquency. It is possible that parents who neglect their children differ from caring parents in other ways. Parents who tend to neglect their children may also encourage drug use, or engage in other lifestyle activities that contribute to the development of teenage delinquency. Because parents couldn't be assigned to groups, it would take many different studies to establish conclusively this relationship. A point that is made in several places in this book is that just because two variables occur together (neglect and delinquency), it doesn't necessarily mean that one caused the other to occur.

Three-Stage Experimental Designs

When researchers want to be able to make strong causal claims, they use a three-stage experimental design (Kimble, 1978). An experimental design is a plan for how observations will be made.

1. *The first stage* involves creating different groups that are going to be studied. In the example about the effect of pass/fail grading on how much is learned, the two groups would be those who receive a letter grade and those who

receive a grade of either "pass" or "fail." It is important that the two groups differ only on this dimension. You wouldn't want all the students in the letter grade group to take classes taught by Professor Longwinded, while those in the pass/fail group take classes taught by Professor Mumbles. One professor may be a better teacher, and students may learn more in one condition than the other because of this confounding variable. One way to avoid this confound is to assign half of the students in each class to each grading condition, with the assignment of students to either group done at random. Strong causal claims will involve equating the groups at the outset of the experiment.

2. *The second stage* involves the application of the "experimental treatment." If we were conducting a drug study, one group would receive the drug and the other group would not receive the drug. Usually, the "nondrug" group would receive a **placebo** that would look and/or taste like the drug, but would be chemically inert. The reason for a placebo is to avoid any effects of subjects' beliefs or expectancies. The topic of expectancies and the way they can bias results is discussed later in this chapter. As discussed in an earlier section, when these sorts of controls were used to determine the effectiveness of laetrile, it was found to be worthless against cancer.

In the grading example, the term "treatment" doesn't fit well, but it corresponds to taking the course under the two different grading conditions.

3. *Evaluation is the final phase.* Measurements are taken and the two (or more) groups are compared on some outcome measure. If the study involved a new drug for headaches, the two groups would be compared on measures of headache frequency and severity. In the grading example, final examination scores for students in the letter grade group would be compared to the scores for students in the pass/fail group. If students in one group performed significantly better than the students in the other group, then we would have strong support for the claim that one grading method *caused* students to study harder and learn more than the other.

Of course, we are not always able to equate groups at the outset and randomly assign subjects to groups, but when we can, results can be used to make stronger causal claims than in less controlled conditions.

Prospective and Retrospective Research

Consider a medical example: Some health psychologists believe that certain stressful experiences can cause people to develop cancer. If this were your hypothesis, how would you determine its validity? One way would be to ask cancer patients if they had anything particularly stressful happen to them just before they were diagnosed as having cancer. If the stress caused the cancer, it would have to precede (come first in time) the development of cancer. When experiments are conducted in this manner, they are called **retrospective experiments.** Retrospective experiments look back in time to understand causes for later events. There are many problems with this sort of research. As discussed in chapter 2, memories are selective and malleable. It is possible that knowledge of one's cancer would change how one's past is remembered. Moderately stressful events, like receiving a poor grade in a college course, may be remembered as being traumatic. Happier events, like getting a raise, may be forgotten. It's even possible that the early stages of the cancer were causing stress instead of the stress causing the cancer. Thus, it would be difficult to determine if stress causes cancer from retrospective research.

A better method for understanding causative relationships is **prospective research.** In prospective research, you identify the causative factor when it occurs and then look forward in time to see if the hypothesized result occurs. In a prospective study, you would have many people record stressful life events when they occur (e.g., death of a spouse, imprisonment, loss of a job) and then see which people develop cancer. If the people who experience more stressful events are more likely to develop cancer, this result would provide support for your hypothesis.

Most of the research that we conduct as intuitive scientists is retrospective. We often seek explanations for events after they have occurred. How many times have you tried to understand why a long-running marriage ended in divorce, or why a star rookie seems to be losing his touch, or why the underdog in a political race won? Our retrospective attempts at explanations are biased by selective memories and lack of systematic observations. (See the section on hindsight in chapter 8 for a related discussion.)

Correlation and Cause

What you are about to read is absolutely true: As the weight of children increases, so does the number of items that they are likely to get correct on standardized tests of intelligence. In other words, heavier children answer more questions correctly than lighter ones. Before you start stuffing mashed potatoes into your children in an attempt to make them smarter, stop and think about what this means. Does it mean that gaining weight will make children smarter? Certainly not! Children get heavier as they get older, and older children answer more questions correctly than younger ones.

In the preceding example, the variables *weight* and *number of questions answered correctly* are related. An increase in one variable is associated with an increase in the other variable—as weight increases, the number of questions answered correctly concomitantly (at the same time) increases. **Correlated variables** are two or more variables that are related. If you've already read chapter 5, then you should recognize this concept as the fallacy of False Cause.

People frequently confuse correlation with cause. Consider the following example: Wally and Bob were arguing about the inheritance of intelligence. Wally thought about everyone he knew and concluded that, because smart parents tend to have smart children and dumb parents tend to have dumb children, intelligence is an inherited characteristic. Bob disagreed with Wally's line of reasoning, although he concurred with the facts that Wally presented. He agreed that if the parents score high on intelligence tests, then their children will also tend to score high, and if the parents score low on intelligence tests, then their children will also tend to score low. When two measures are related in this way—that is, they tend to rise and fall together—they have a **positive correlation.** Although parents' intelligence and their children's intelligence are positively correlated, we cannot infer that parents caused their children (through inheritance or any other means) to be intelligent. It is possible that children affect the intelligence of their parents, or that both are being affected by a third variable that hasn't been considered. It is possible that diet, economic class, or other lifestyle variables determine intelligence levels, and because parents and children eat similar diets and have the same economic class, they tend to be similar in intelligence.

Let's consider a somewhat different example. Many people have taken up jogging in the belief that exercise will help them to lose weight. The two variables in this example are *exercise* and *weight.* I've heard people argue that because there are no fat athletes (except perhaps sumo wrestlers), exercise must cause people to be thin. I hope that you can think critically about this claim.

It does seem to be true that exercise and weight are correlated. People who tend to exercise a great deal also tend to be thin. This sort of correlation, in which the tendency to be high on one variable (exercise) is associated with the tendency to be low on the other variable (weight) is called a **negative correlation.** Let's think about the relationship between exercise and weight. There are several possibilities: (a) It is possible that exercise causes people to be thin; or (b) It is possible that people who are thin tend to exercise more because it is more enjoyable to engage in exercise when you are thin; or (c) It is possible that a third variable, like concern for one's health, or some inherited trait, is responsible for both the tendency to exercise and the tendency to be thin. Perhaps there are inherited body types that naturally stay thin and also are graced with strong muscles that are well suited for exercise.

If you wanted to test the hypothesis that exercise causes people to lose weight, then you would use the three design stages described earlier. If the subjects who were assigned at random to the exercise group were thinner after the treatment period than those in a no-exercise condition, then you could make a strong causal claim for the benefits of exercise in controlling weight.

Actually, the question of causation is usually complex. It is probably more accurate to use the word "influence" instead of cause, because there is usually more than a single variable that causes the occurrence of another variable. A colleague suggested the following example to clarify this point (Dr. Richard Block at Montana State University): When a man is being hanged for having committed a crime, is it because someone gave him money to buy the weapon he used in the crime, or is it because someone saw him commit the crime, or is it because no one stopped him?

In summary, when considering the relationship between variables, there are several possible explanations. Of course, it is also possible that they are unrelated or not correlated. Some examples of variables that are not correlated are typing speed and hat size, number of hairs on your head and grade point average, and height and reaction time on a drive test.

Some positive correlations are: height and weight, number of churches and number of prostitutes in a city (both increase with increases in population), and the number of ice cream cones sold and number of reported rapes (both increase with increases in temperature). Two negative correlations are: amount of fluoride children consume and number of cavities they get and hours spent studying and number of courses failed. In understanding the relationship between two correlated variables, it is possible that variable A caused the changes in variable B ($A \rightarrow B$), or that variable B caused the changes in variable A ($B \rightarrow A$), or that both A and B caused changes in each other ($A \rightarrow B$ and $B \rightarrow A$) or that both were caused by a third variable, C ($C \rightarrow A$ and $C \rightarrow B$).

Illusory Correlation

An amusing anecdote of attributing cause to events that occur together was presented by Munson (1976):

> A farmer was traveling with his wife on a train when he saw a man across the aisle take something out of a bag and begin eating it. "Say, Mister," he asked, "What's that thing you're eating?"
>
> "It's a banana," the man said. "Here, try one."
>
> The farmer took it, peeled it, and just as he swallowed the first bite, the train roared into a tunnel. "Don't eat any, Maude," he yelled to his wife. "It'll make you go blind!" (p. 277)

Do blondes really have more fun? A popular advertisement for hair dye would like you to believe that having blonde hair will cause you to have more fun. Many people believe that they see many blondes having fun; therefore, blondes have more fun than brunettes, for example. The problem with this sort of observation is that there are many blondes who are not having more fun (a term badly in need of an operational definition) than brunettes, but because they are at home or in other places where you are unlikely to see them, they don't get considered. The term **illusory correlation** has been coined for the erroneous belief that two variables are related when, in fact, they are not (Chapman & Chapman, 1967, 1969).

Professionals and nonprofessionals alike maintain beliefs about relationships in the world. These beliefs guide the kinds of observations they make and how they determine if a relationship exists between two variables.

Let's try another example. Do you believe that you often see fat people overeating? Most people believe that they do; yet, research has shown that overweight adults tend to eat less in public places than normal-weight people. We expect to see overweight people overeating; and therefore, we believe that we see the world according to our beliefs.

Beware of illusory correlations when you function as an intuitive scientist. This phenomenon works to maintain stereotypes (e.g., redheads are hot-tempered; Scots are cheap; women can't understand math; etc.). Our beliefs about relationships between variables guide the observations we make and the way we utilize this information to formulate conclusions.

Validity

The **validity** of a measure is usually defined as the extent to which it measures what you want it to measure. If I wanted to measure intelligence and measured the length of your big toe, this would obviously be invalid. Other examples of validity are less obvious. A popular radio commercial, touting the benefits of soup, points out that tomato soup has more Vitamin A than eggs. This is true, but it is not a valid measure of the goodness of tomato soup. Eggs are not a good source of Vitamin A. Thus, the wrong comparisons were made, and the measure does not support the notion that soup is an excellent food. If you've already read chapter 5, then you should realize that the claim that tomato soup has more Vitamin A than eggs does not support the conclusion that "soup is good food." It may well be true that soup is an excellent source of vitamins, but claims like this one don't support that conclusion.

How would you react to this claim: "The Baroness is a sleek new luxury car that will provide its owner with dependable transportation for many years to come. In fact, in a recent laboratory test, the Baroness went from zero to 60 miles per hour in 7 seconds flat, beating out the six other cars in the competition." Is the acceleration speed of a car a valid index of its dependability? Probably not. Even if the figure is accurate, it is not a valid measure of dependability. If you want to know about dependability, you'll want to know about the frequency of repairs, average number of miles the car can be expected to be driven before it gets turned into scrap metal, and how it performs on impact.

Convergent Validity

When several different measures all converge onto the same conclusion, the measures are said to have **convergent validity.** If, for example, you wanted to measure charisma—the psychological trait that is something more than charm that people as diverse as John F. Kennedy, Liza Minelli, and Laurence Olivier are said to possess, you'd need convergent validity for your measure. People who scored high on your charisma test should also be the ones who are selected for leadership positions and have other personality traits that are usually associated with charisma. If the class wallflower scored high on your test of charisma, you'd need to rethink the validity of your test.

People outside the laboratory also need to be mindful of the need for convergent validity. Before you decide that your classmate, Joyce, is shy because she hesitates to talk to you, you need to determine if she acts shy with other people in other places. If she frequently speaks up in class, you wouldn't want to conclude that she is a shy person, because this inconsistency in her behavior would signal a lack of convergent validity.

The idea of convergent validity is very similar to the topic of convergent argument structures that was presented in chapter 5. If you have already read chapter 5, then you should recall that the strength of an argument is increased when many premises support (or converge on) a conclusion. This is exactly the same situation as when several sources of evidence support the same hypothesis. The language used in these two chapters is different (support for a conclusion versus support for a hypothesis), but the underlying ideas are the same: The more reasons or evidence we can provide for believing that something is true, the greater the confidence we can have in our belief.

Illusory Validity

> Everyone complains of his memory and no one complains of his judgement.
>
> —La Rochefoucauld

Both professionals and nonprofessionals place great confidence in their conclusions about most life events, even when their confidence is objectively unwarranted. Overconfidence in judgments is called **illusory validity.** In an experimental investigation of this phenomenon, Oskamp (1965) found that, as clinicians were given more information about patients, they became more confident in the judgments they made about patients. What is interesting about this result is that they were not more accurate in judgment, only more confident that they were right. Why do people place confidence in fallible judgments? There are several reasons why we persist in maintaining confidence in our judgments. A primary factor is the selective nature of memory. Consider this personal vignette: As a child, I would watch Philadelphia Phillies baseball games on television with my father. As each batter would step up to home plate, my father would excitedly yell, "He's going to hit a home run, I just know it!" Of course, he was usually wrong. (Phillies fans had to be tough in the 1950s and 1960s). On the rare occasions when a Phillies batter actually did hit a home run, my father would talk about it for weeks. "Yep, I knew as soon as he stepped up to home plate that he would hit a home run. I can always tell just by looking at the batter." In this instance, and in countless others, we selectively remember our successful judgments and forget our unsuccessful ones. This tends to bolster confidence in the judgments we make.

A second reason for the illusion of validity is the failure to seek or consider disconfirming evidence. (See chapter 8 for an additional discussion of this phenomenon.) This is the primary reason why people tend to believe that variables are correlated when they are not correlated. Suppose that you have the job of personnel officer in a large corporation. Over a period of a year, you hire 100 new employees for your corporation. How would you go about deciding if you're making good (valid) hiring decisions? Most people would check on the performance of the one hundred new employees. Suppose that you did this and found that 92% of the new employees were performing their jobs in a competent, professional manner. Would this bolster your confidence in your judgments? If you answered yes to this question, you forgot to consider disconfirming evidence. What about the people you didn't hire? Have most of them gone on to become vice presidents at General Motors? If you found that 100% of the people you didn't hire are superior employees at your competitor's corporation, you would have to revise your confidence in your judgmental ability.

Part of the reason that we fail to utilize disconfirming evidence is that it is often not available. Personnel officers don't have information about the employees they don't hire. Similarly, we don't know much about the person we chose not to date, or the course we didn't take, or the house we didn't buy. Thus, on the basis of partial information, we may conclude that our judgments are better than they objectively are.

Reliability

The **reliability** of a measure is the consistency with which it measures what it's supposed to measure. If you used a rubber ruler that could stretch or shrink to measure the top of your desk, you'd probably get a different number each time you measured it. Of course, we want our measurements to be reliable.

Researchers in the social and physical sciences devote a great deal of time to the issue of reliable measurement. We say that an intelligence test, for example, is reliable when the same person obtains scores that are in the same general range whenever she or he takes the test. Few of us even consider reliability when we function as intuitive scientists. When we decide if a professor or student is prejudiced, we often rely on one or two samples of behavior without considering if the individual is being assessed reliably.

Suppose that you learn that your friend Ricardo failed a college course which all others easily passed. Could you conclude that his teacher is prejudiced? You'd need to collect many other observations of the same teacher to see how consistently or reliably Hispanic males failed that teacher's class. If there is an unusually high failure rate among Hispanic males (or whatever group you're interested in) in that class compared to their failure rate in other classes, then you'd have a strong case for the inference that the teacher is prejudiced. Without careful measurement and, in this case, a larger sample size, you cannot infer that the professor is prejudiced.

THINKING ABOUT ERRORS

To a scientist a theory is something to be tested. He seeks not to defend his beliefs, but to improve them. He is, above everything else, an expert at "changing his mind."

—Wendell Johnson

When we try to understand relationships by devising and testing hypotheses, we will sometimes be wrong. This idea is expanded on more fully in chapter 7, which concerns understanding probabilities. For now, consider this possibility: Suppose that you drive into work every day with a male friend. Every morning you stop at a drive-up restaurant window and buy coffee. You decide that instead of hassling every morning with who will pay (I'll get it—No, no let me"), he will flip a coin. When the outcome is heads, he will pay; when the outcome is tails, you will pay. Sounds fair enough, but on 9 of the last 10 days, the coin landed with tails up. Do you think that your friend is cheating?

The truth is that your friend is either cheating or he is not cheating. Unfortunately, you don't know which is true. Nevertheless, you need to make a decision. You will decide either that he is cheating or he is not cheating. Thus, there are four possibilities: (a) He is cheating and you correctly decide that he is cheating; (b) He is not cheating and you correctly decide that he is not cheating; (c) He is cheating and you incorrectly decide that he is not cheating; and (d) He is not cheating and you incorrectly decide that he is cheating. With these four possibilities, there are two ways that you can be right and two ways that you can be wrong. These four combinations are shown in Table 6.1. As you can see from Table 6.1, there are two different ways that we can make errors in any hypothesis-testing situation. These two different errors are not equally "bad." It is far worse to decide that your friend is cheating when he is not (especially if you accuse him of cheating) than it is to decide that he is not cheating when he is. Because of this, you would want stronger evidence to decide that he is cheating than you would want to decide that he is not cheating. In other words, you need to consider the relative "badness" of different errors when testing hypotheses.

If you take a course in statistics or experimental design, you'll find that the idea of error "badness" is handled by requiring different levels of confidence for different decisions. The need to consider different types of errors is found in many contexts. A basic principle of our legal system is that we have to be very certain that someone has committed a crime (beyond a reasonable doubt) before we can convict him or her. By contrast, we don't have to be convinced beyond a

TABLE 6.1
Four Possible Outcomes for the "Who Buys the Coffee" Example

	You Decide	
	He is Cheating.	*He is Not Cheating.*
The Truth is:		
He is cheating.	He is cheating and you decide that he is cheating. Correct Decision!	He is cheating and you decide that he is not cheating. An Error!
He is not cheating.	He is not cheating and you decide that he is cheating. A Serious Error!	He is not cheating and you decide that he is not cheating. Correct Decision!

Note. that the error associated with deciding that he is cheating is more serious than the error associated with deciding that he is not cheating. Because of the difference in the severity of the errors, you will want to be more certain when deciding that he is cheating than when deciding that he is not cheating.

reasonable doubt that he or she is innocent, because wrongly deciding that someone is innocent is considered a less severe error than wrongly deciding that someone is guilty. Similarly, when you are testing hypotheses informally, you also need to be aware of the severity of different types of errors. Before you decide, for example, that no matter how hard you study, you'll never pass some course or that the medicine you're taking is or isn't making you better, you need to consider the consequences of right and wrong decisions. Some decisions require that you should be more certain about being correct than others.

SELF-FULFILLING PROPHECIES

Robert Rosenthal, a well-known psychologist, and his colleague (Rosenthal & Fode, 1963) had their students train rats to run through mazes as part of a standard course in experimental psychology. Half of the students were told that they had rats that had been specially bred to be smart at learning their way through mazes, whereas the other half of the students were told that they had rats that had been specially bred to be dumb at this task. As you probably expected, the students with the bright rats had them out-performing the dull rats in a short period of time. These results are especially interesting, because there were no real differences between the two groups of rats. Rosenthal and Fode had lied about the rats being specially bred. All of the rats were the usual laboratory variety. They had been assigned at random to each group. If there were no real differences between the groups of rats, how do we explain the fact that students who believed they had been given bright rats had them learn the maze faster than the other group?

The term **self-fulfilling prophecies** has been coined as a label for the tendency to act in ways that will lead us to find what we expected to find. I don't know what the students did to make the rats learn faster in the "bright" group or slower in the "dull" group. Perhaps the bright group was given extra handling or more food in the goal box. (When rats learn to run through mazes, they are given a food reward when they reach the goal box to keep them motivated.) Maybe the students given the "dull" rats dropped them harshly into the maze or were not as accurate in the records that they kept. Whatever they did, somehow, they influenced their experimental results so that the results were in accord with their expectations.

If self-fulfilling prophecies can influence how rats run through mazes, what sort of an effect will they have on everyday thinking and behavior? Earlier in this chapter, illusory correlations were defined as the tendency to believe that events that you are observing are really correlated because you believe that they should be. Psychologists are becoming increasingly aware of the ways that personal convictions direct our selection and interpretation of facts. When you function as an intuitive scientist, it is important to keep in mind the ways we influence the results we obtain.

One way to eliminate the effects of self-fulfilling prophecies is with **double-blind procedures.** Let's consider a medical example. There are probably 100 home remedies for the common cold. How should we decide which, if any, actually relieve cold symptoms? Probably, somewhere, sometime, someone gave you chicken soup when you had a cold. Undoubtedly, you got better. Almost everyone who gets a cold gets better. The question is: Did the chicken soup make you better? This is a difficult question to answer, because if you believe that chicken soup makes you better, you may rate the severity of your symptoms as less severe even when there was no real change. This is just another example of self-fulfilling prophecies. The only way to test this hypothesis is to give some people chicken soup and others something that looks and tastes like chicken soup and then have each group rate the severity of their cold symptoms. In this example, all of the subjects are blind to the nature of the treatment they are receiving. It is important that the experimenters also be unaware of which subjects received the "real" chicken soup so that they don't inadvertently give subtle clues to the subjects. Experiments in which neither the subjects nor the experimenters know who is receiving the treatment are called double-blind experiments.

Although the chicken soup example may seem a little far-fetched, the need for double-blind procedures is critical in deciding whether any drug or treatment is working. Formal laboratory research on drugs that may be effective against AIDS or cancer always use double-blind procedures. Most people, however, do not apply these same standards when making personal decisions, such as which type of psychotherapy is effective or whether massive doses of a vitamin will improve some aspect of their lives. Before you decide to see a therapist who claims to be able to improve your diabetes by manipulating your spine or to engage in screaming therapy to improve your self-confidence, look carefully for double-blind studies that support the use of the proposed therapy.

THINKING AS AN INTUITIVE SCIENTIST

One theme that has followed throughout this chapter is that everyday thinking has much in common with the research methods used by scientists when they investigate phenomena in their academic domains. Many of the pitfalls and problems that plague scientific investigations are also common in everyday thought. If you understand and avoid some of these problems, you will be a better consumer of research and a better intuitive scientist.

When you are evaluating the research claims of others or when you are asserting your own claims, there are several questions to keep in mind:

1. What was the nature of the sample? Was it large enough? Was it biased?
2. Are the variables operationally defined? What do the terms mean?
3. Were the measurements sensitive, valid, and reliable? Are the appropriate comparisons being made to support the claims?
4. Were extraneous variables controlled? What are other plausible explanations for the results?
5. Do the conclusions follow from the observations?
6. Are correlations being used to support causative arguments?
7. Is disconfirming evidence being considered?
8. How could the experimenter's expectancies be biasing the result?

If you scrutinize your own conclusions and those of others with these questions in mind, you should be able to defend yourself against invalid claims and improve your own ability to draw sound conclusions from observations.

APPLYING THE FRAMEWORK

In applying the general thinking skills framework to thinking as hypothesis testing, consider the following questions:

1. *What is the goal?* You should use the skills developed in this chapter whenever you are devising hypotheses about the relationships among events and then collecting observations to test the validity of your hypotheses. There is a virtually endless number of examples of when these skills are applicable. They should be used when considering

social relationships (e.g., She likes it when I compliment her), physical relationships (e.g., The mercury in the tube rises when the temperature increases), treatment effects (e.g., Laughter therapy can improve the recovery rate from some dread diseases), and when functioning as a consumer of research.

2. *What is known?* This question is about how to plan the thinking process. When thinking like an intuitive scientist, you need to begin by explicitly deciding on the nature of the hypothesis that you're testing and the way you will go about making observations. You also need to consider the relative severity of different kinds of errors. The knowns include how you will operationalize your variables and how confident you want to be before you decide if your hypothesis is correct. In short, this step involves becoming explicit about your starting point in the thinking process.

3. *Which thinking skill or skills will get you to your goal?* The selection of the appropriate skill depends on how you've answered the previous questions. If you've decided that the hypothesis that you're testing is important enough to require a formal test, then you'll want to sample subjects in an unbiased manner and be certain that the number of subjects is sufficiently large and that measurement was accurate. Of course, I don't expect you to be testing lethal drugs based on the hypothesis testing skills presented in this chapter. This sort of testing needs to be conducted by researchers with extensive knowledge of research and experimental design. But, you should know how to be a consumer of this sort of research and look for evidence of good hypothesis testing methods. The skills involved when thinking as an intuitive scientist include:

- recognizing the need for and using operational definitions
- understanding the need to isolate and control variables in order to make strong causal claims
- checking for adequate sample size and unbiased sampling when a generalization is made
- being able to describe the relationship between any two variables as positive, negative, or unrelated
- understanding the limits of correlational reasoning
- seeking converging validity to increase your confidence in a decision
- being aware of the bias in most estimates of variability
- considering the relative ''badness'' of different sorts of errors
- determining how self-fulfilling prophecies could be responsible for experimental results or everyday observations

These skills should be used in your own thinking and in critiquing the thinking of others. After reading this chapter, you should be able to use these skills in any context in which they are appropriate.

4. *Have you reached your goal?* The final question to consider is whether you have reduced uncertainty: Can you predict the results of certain actions, or can you make better decisions because you used the hypothesis testing skills presented in this chapter? The ubiquitous concern for accuracy is always the final test of the quality of the decision you've arrived at. When you function like an intuitive scientist, you will sometimes make

wrong decisions, because we never know "truth." But, you can minimize wrong decisions by carefully using the hypothesis testing skills presented in this chapter.

CHAPTER SUMMARY

1. Much of our everyday thinking is like the scientific method of hypothesis testing. We formulate beliefs about the world and collect observations to decide if our beliefs are correct.

2. In the inductive method, we devise hypotheses from our observations. In the deductive method, we collect observations that confirm or disconfirm our hypotheses. Most thinking involves an interplay of these two processes so that we devise hypotheses from experience, make observations, and then, on the basis of our observations, we redefine our hypotheses.

3. Operational definitions are precise statements that allow the identification and measurement of variables.

4. Independent variables are used to predict or explain dependent variables. When we formulate hypotheses, we want to know about the effect of the independent variable on the dependent variable(s).

5. When we draw conclusions from observations, it's important to utilize an adequately large sample size, because people are variable in the way they respond. Most people are too willing to generalize results obtained from small samples.

6. In determining if one variable (e.g., smoking) causes another variable (e.g., lung cancer) to occur, it is important to be able to isolate and control the causal variables. Strong causal claims require the three-stage experimental design that was described in this chapter.

7. In everyday contexts, we often use retrospective techniques to understand what caused an event to occur. These are not good techniques because our memories tend to be selective and malleable and because we have no objective systematic observations of the cause. Prospective techniques that record events when they occur and then see if the hypothesized result follows are better methods for determining cause–effect relationships.

8. Variables that are related so that changes in one variable are associated with changes in the other variable are called *correlated variables*. Correlations can be positive, as in the relationship between height and weight (taller people tend to weigh more, whereas shorter people tend to weigh less), or negative, as in the relationship between exercise and weight (people who exercise a great deal tend to be thin, and those who exercise little tend to be heavy).

9. A common error is to infer a causative relationship from correlated variables. It is possible that variable *A* caused variable *B*, or that variable *B* caused variable *A*, or that *A* and *B* influenced each other, or that a third variable caused them both.

10. The belief that two variables are correlated when they are not (*illusory correlation*) is another type of error that is common in human judgment.

11. It is important that you use measurements that are sensitive, valid, and reliable or the conclusions you draw may be incorrect. Few people consider the importance of measurement issues when they draw everyday conclusions about the nature of the world.

12. Although many of our judgments lack validity, people report great confidence in them. This is called *illusory validity*.

13. Inadvertently, we may act in ways that will lead us to confirm or disconfirm hypotheses according to our expectations. These are called *self-fulfilling prophecies*.

Terms to Know

Check your understanding of the concepts presented in this chapter by reviewing their definitions. If you find that you're having difficulty with any term, be sure to reread the section in which it is discussed.

Hypothesis. A set of beliefs about the nature of the world, usually concerning the relationship between two or more variables.

Hypothesis Testing. The scientific method of collecting observations to confirm or disconfirm beliefs about the relationships among variables.

Inductive Method. A method of formulating hypotheses in which you observe events and then devise a hypothesis about the events you observed.

Deductive Method. A method of testing hypotheses in which you formulate a hypothesis that you believe to be true and then deduce consequences from it. Systematic observations are then made to verify if your hypothesis is correct.

Operational Definition. An explicit set of procedures that tell the reader how to recognize and measure the concept in which you're interested.

(A) Variable. A quantifiable characteristic that can take on more than one value (e.g., height, gender, age, race).

Independent Variable. The variable that is selected (or manipulated) by the experimenter who is testing a hypothesis to see if changes in the independent variable will result in changes in the dependent variable. For example, if you want to know if people are more readily persuaded by threats or rational appeals, you could present either a threatening message or a rational appeal to two groups of people (message type is the independent variable), and then determine how much their attitudes toward the topic have changed (the dependent variable).

Dependent Variable. The variable that is measured in an experiment to determine if its value depends on the independent variable. Compare with independent variable.

Extraneous Variables. Variables that you're not interested in that can influence hypothesis testing results.

Population. For statistical and hypothesis testing purposes, a population is the entire group of people (or animals or entities) in which one is interested and about which one wishes to generalize.

Sample. A subset of a population that is studied in order to make inferences about the population.

Representative Sample. A sample that is similar to the population in important characteristics, such as the proportion of males and females, socioeconomic status, and age.

Generalization. Using the results obtained in a sample to infer that similar results would have been obtained from the population if everyone in the population had been measured. (When used in the context of problem solving, it is a strategy in which the problem is considered as an example of a larger class of problems.)

Biased Sample. A sample that is not representative of the population from which it was drawn.

Confounding. When experimental groups differ in more than one way, it's not possible to separate the effects due to each variable. For example, if you found that teenage girls scored higher on a test of verbal ability than preteen boys, you wouldn't know if the results were due to sex differences or age differences between the two groups.

Convenience Samples. The use of a group of people who are readily available as participants in an experiment. Such samples may be biased, in that they may not be representative of the population from which they were drawn.

Sample Size. The number of people selected for a study.

Subject. A person, animal, or entity who serves as a participant in an experiment.

Variability. Term to denote the fact that people (and animals) differ in the way they respond to experimental stimuli.

Random Sample. A sample in which everyone in a population has an equal chance of being selected.

Law of Small Numbers. The willingness to believe that results obtained from a few subjects can be generalized to the entire population.

Retrospective Research. After an event has occurred, the experimenter looks backward in time to determine its cause.

Prospective Research. A method of conducting research in which possible causative factors of an event are identified before the event occurs. Experimenters then determine if the hypothesized event occurs.

Correlated Variables. Two or more variables that are related. See negative correlation and positive correlation.

Positive Correlation. Two or more variables that are related such that increases in one variable occur concomitantly with increases in the other variable, and decreases in one variable occur with decreases in the other.

Negative Correlation. Two or more variables that are related such that increases in one variable are associated with decreases in the other variable.

Illusory Correlation. The belief that two variables are correlated when, in fact, they are uncorrelated.

Sensitive Measures. Measures that are able to detect small changes in the dependent variable.

Validity. The extent to which a measure (e.g., a test) is measuring what you want it to.

Convergent Validity. The use of several different measures or techniques that all suggest the same conclusion.

Illusory Validity. The belief that a measure is valid (measures what you want it to) when, in fact, it is not. This belief causes people to be overconfident in their judgments.

Reliability. The consistency of a measure (e.g., a test) on repeated occasions.

Double-Blind Procedures. An experimental paradigm in which neither the subjects nor the person collecting data know the treatment group to which the subject has been assigned.

Self-Fulfilling Prophecy. The tendency to act in ways that influence experimental results so that we obtain results that are consistent with our expectations.

Chapter Questions

Be sure that you can answer the following questions:

1. How is every day thinking like the experimentation used by scientists?

2. What is the difference between inductive and deductive methods? How are they used in a cyclical fashion?

3. Why do we need operational definitions?

4. What are hypotheses, and how are they tested?

5. What are some mistakes that we can make when generalizing from a sample to a population? Describe a better sampling technique than the one used by the *Literary Digest*.

6. Explain how confounding can lead to erroneous conclusions.

7. List three pairs of variables that you would expect to be positively correlated, three that you would expect to be negatively correlated, and three that you would expect to be uncorrelated.

8. Why can't we determine cause from correlated variables? Why is the three-stage experimental design a better method than correlation for making strong causal claims?

9. Why do people persist in believing in the validity of their conclusions even when their confidence is unwarranted?

10. Why is prospective research preferable to retrospective research?

11. We can be more confident in our conclusions when there is convergent validity. Why?

12. Explain why people sometimes believe that variables are correlated when, in fact, they are not.

13. How can experimenter and subject biases affect the results obtained from experiments? How do double-blind procedures protect against these biases?

Exercises

Using the questions for evaluating research claims that are summarized at the end of this chapter, critically discuss each of the following:

1. According to Einhorn and Hogarth (1978), Benjamin Rush, a professor at the first medical school in the United States, believed that "blood-letting" (bleeding) of patients would cure a variety of illnesses. When his patients recovered from their illnesses, he would attribute their recovery to the practice of blood-letting. (Sometimes leeches were

used to draw the blood.) When his patients died, he concluded that the nature of their illness was so severe that not even blood-letting could help them. Using your hypothesis testing skills, comment on Rush's observations and conclusions.

2. Whenever someone celebrates his or her 100th birthday, newspaper reporters ask him or her to reveal the secret of longevity. Suppose that you read in the newspaper that a 100-year-old man attributed his long life to drinking a bottle of gin a day. Can you conclude that drinking gin will help you to live long?

3. Although research has shown that salt-free diets reduce blood pressure, Mike doubts that this is true. Mike's father has been on a salt-free diet for over a year, and his blood pressure has remained high. What would you say to Mike about his conclusions?

4. Jim is very superstitious. He believes that when a black cat crosses his path, something bad happens. What would you tell Jim about his superstition?

5. You've probably heard a commercial that goes something like this: "Seven out of ten dentists recommend Chewsy Gum for their patients who chew gum." Comment on this commercial. What would you want to know in order to evaluate this research claim?

6. A conservative group of politicians attempted to persuade the local school board to eliminate its kindergarten program. A study conducted in a rural area of Montana showed that children who went to kindergarten did not score higher on an achievement test than children who did not attend kindergarten. How would you refute or prove their claim that kindergarten is a useless year?

7. The question of whether joint custody (custody of the child shared between both parents) is the best arrangement for children following the divorce of their parents has been a topic of considerable concern. Legal hearings on this topic will frequently have one or two families for whom joint custody either worked or didn't work testify about their experiences. Comment on this practice. How would you go about deciding whether or not joint custody is a generally good idea?

8. How would you decide if a new reading program should be implemented in your elementary schools?

9. Rosenthal and Jacobson (1968) told teachers that some of the children in their classrooms were ready to "bloom" intellectually. As you might expect, the children who were identified as bloomers did show large increases in intelligence. This is especially interesting in light of the fact that there were no real differences between the "bloomers" and other children. They had, in fact, picked the "bloomers" at random. What phenomenon discussed in this chapter can describe this result? How did it happen?

10. In a study by Pickren and Gamarra (1975, p. 188), the following relationship was found between histiocytes in lung tissues and people's smoking histories:

	Total Cases	No. of Cases with Histiocytes
nonsmokers	31	0 (0%)
former smokers	38	10 (27%)
smokers	43	40 (93%)

What can you conclude about the relationship between histiocytes and smoking history? Can you claim that smoking causes histiocytes? Why or why not? (Don't worry if you don't know what histiocytes are. It's not important in answering the question.)

11. A mad scientist taught his pet fly to "fetch" a small stick whenever a whistle was blown. The scientist then found that after he cut off the fly's wings, the fly didn't "fetch" the stick. He concluded that flies hear with their wings and that the fly had become deaf as a result of losing its wings. How would you convince the scientist that his experiment doesn't prove that flies hear with their wings?

12. Your friend just returned from a trip to a foreign country. During his trip he became ill, and a friendly family helped him to find a doctor and get the medicine he needed. Now he can't stop talking about the friendliness of the people he met there. In fact, he plans to drop out of school, sell his home, and move to this country. Interpret his experience and his conclusion about the people of this country, using the hypothesis testing skills developed in this chapter. Comment on his hypothesis, sample size, measurement, perception about "other group" variability, error "badness," and so on.

13. How would you apply double-blind procedures to test the claim that biofeedback can reduce the severity and frequency of migraine headaches?

14. A television commercial for a brand of cheese claims that their cheese is best for use in microwaves because it melts quickly. To demonstrate their point, the actors show that the cheese melts faster than a frozen popsickle. Comment on this "experiment."

15. A colleague (Dr. Gregory Kimble at Duke University) had a conversation with a taxi driver in New York. The driver told him that he trusted the weather predictions in the Farmer's Almanac because whenever it predicted rain, it would usually rain either on the predicted day or a few days before or after the predicted day. What do you think about the nature of this evidence?

16. Think about the television, radio, and magazine advertisements that bombard our daily existence. Collect some "choice" advertisements, and question their claims and conclusions. How should they have tested their product?

SUGGESTED READINGS

A good basic text on the topic of hypothesis testing is Leedy's (1981) *How to Read Research and Understand It*. It takes the perspective of a research consumer as opposed to that of the researcher. Three recommended books that discuss research methods are Drew's (1976) *Introduction to Designing Research and Evaluation*, Kerlinger's (1987) *Behavioral Research: A Conceptual Approach*, and Lewin's ((1979) *Understanding Psychological Research*. All three are lucid text that describe experimentation, correlation, and related research topics.

If you're interested in the development of scientific thinking through childhood and adolescence, see Siegler's (1978a) chapter, entitled "The Origins of Scientific Reasoning." It appears in an edited volume with other interesting chapters. The volume is Siegler's (1978b) *Children's Thinking: What Develops?*

A somewhat strange and iconoclastic book is *Against Method* by Feyerabend (1975). He argued against the use of scientific methods. Although this book is not easy reading, it is interesting. As an example that supports the notion that we don't need scientific methods, he argued that Galileo's views were eventually accepted, not on their scientific merit, but because Galileo "was clever in techniques of persuasion" (p. 13), wrote in Italian instead of Latin, and appealed to people who prefer new ideas to old ones.

The notion that we function as "intuitive" or everyday scientists is developed in *Human Inference: Strategies and Shortcomings of Social Judgment* by Nisbett and Ross (1980). This is an excellent text, filled with interesting examples and concisely reviewed research on the way people utilize research principles in everyday life. A recent and advanced treatise on the topics discussed in this chapter can be found in Holland et al.'s, (1986) book, entitled *Induction: Processes of Inference, Learning, and Discovery*. They take the position that induction is the primary thinking process by which we learn about the nature of the world. The authors are, by training, two psychologists, a computer scientist with expertise in artificial intelligence, and a philosopher with a common interest in how we think. It is highly recommended for advanced students.

7

Likelihood and Uncertainty (Understanding Probabilities)

Contents

The jury was facing a difficult decision in the case of *People v. Collins,* 1968 (cited in Arkes & Hammond, 1986). The robbery victim could not identify his assailant. All he could recall was that the robber was a woman with a blond pony tail who, after the robbery, rode off in a yellow convertible driven by a Black man with a moustache and a beard. The suspect fit this description, but could the jury be certain "beyond a reasonable doubt" that the woman who was on trial was the robber? She was blond and often wore her hair in a pony tail. Her codefendant "friend" was a Black man with a moustache, beard, and yellow convertible. If you were the attorney for the defense, you would stress the fact that the victim could not identify this woman as the robber. What strategy would you use if you were the attorney for the prosecution?

The prosecutor produced an expert in probability theory who testified that the probability of these conditions "co-occurring (being blond *plus* having a pony tail *plus* having a Black male friend *plus* his owning a yellow convertible and so on) was 1 in 12 million. The expert testified that this combination of characteristics was so unusual that the jury could be certain "beyond a reasonable doubt" that she was the robber.

The jury returned a verdict of "guilty."

PROBABILISTIC NATURE OF THE WORLD

The theory of probabilities is nothing more than good sense confirmed by calculation.

—La Place

As seen in the preceding example, the legal system recognizes that we can never have absolute certainty in legal matters. Instead, we operate with various degrees of uncertainty. Juries are instructed to decide that someone is guilty of a crime when they are certain "beyond a reasonable doubt." This standard was adopted because there is always some small amount of doubt that the accused may be innocent. Jurors are instructed to operate under a different level of doubt when they are deciding about guilt or innocence in a civil case. In civil cases, they are told to deliver a verdict of guilty when the "preponderance of evidence" supports this decision. Thus, jurors are instructed to operate under two different levels of uncertainty when the case before them is either criminal or civil. They need to be more certain when deciding that an accused party is guilty in a criminal case than in a civil case.

Probability is the study of likelihood and uncertainty. It plays a critical role in all of the professions and in most everyday decisions. All medical diagnoses and treatment decisions are inherently probabilistic, as are decisions made in business, college admissions, advertising, and research. Probability is the cornerstone of science; the laws of probability guide the interpretation of all research findings. Many of our leisure activities also rely on the principles of probability, most notably horse racing and card games. Every time you decide to take an umbrella, invest in the stock market, buy an insurance policy, or bet on a long shot in the Kentucky Derby, you are making a probability judgment. Other than the proverbial death and taxes, there is very little in life that is known with certainty. Because we live in a probabilistic world, critical thinking requires an understanding of probability.

There is good evidence that training in the use of probability will improve your ability to utilize probability values in appropriate manner. In a study of the use of statistical thinking in everyday reasoning tasks (Nisbett et al., 1983) researchers found that "Training increases both the likelihood that people will take a statistical approach to a given problem and the quality of the statistical solutions" (p. 339). In other words, although the thinking skills presented in this chapter will require the use of basic arithmetic, it's likely that you'll be a better thinker for having worked through the problems.

Likelihood and Uncertainty

If I flip a coin into the air and ask you to guess the probability that it will land heads up, you would say that the probability of a head is 50% (or .50). This means that the coin is expected to land heads up half of the time. In this chapter, we consider several different definitions of the term **probability,** including uncertainty, degrees of belief, and utilization of past frequencies. The definition of probability that is most useful in the present context is the number of ways a particular outcome (what we call a success) can occur divided by the number of possible outcomes. It is a measure of how often we expect an event to occur **in the long run.** Success may seem like a strange word in this context, but you can think of it as the outcome you're interested in. In this case, a success is getting the coin to land heads up. There is only one way for a coin to land heads up, so the number of ways a success can occur in this example is 1. What are all the possible outcomes of flipping a coin in the air? The coin can either land heads up or tails up. (I've never seen a coin land on its edge, nor have I ever seen a bird come along and carry it off while it's in the air, so I'm not considering these as possible outcomes.) Thus, there are two possible outcomes. To calculate the probability of getting a coin to land heads up, compute the number of ways a head can occur (1), divided by the number of possible outcomes (2), or ½, the answer you already knew. Because many people find it easier to think in percentages than in fractions, ½ is sometimes changed to 50%.

Let's try another example. How likely are you to roll a 5 in one roll of a die? As there is only one way for a 5 to occur, the numerator of the probability fraction is 1. A die is a six-sided (cube) figure; thus, there are six possible outcomes in one roll. The probability of rolling a 5 is ⅙, or approximately 17%.

What is the probability of rolling an even number in one roll of a die? To find this probability, consider the number of ways a success can occur. You could roll a 2, 4, or 6, all possible even numbers. Thus, there are three ways a success can occur out of six possible outcomes, so the probability of rolling an even number is $\frac{3}{6} = \frac{1}{2}$.

What is the probability of rolling a whole number less than 7? If someone asked me to bet on this happening, I'd put up my house, my children, and my meager savings account to make this bet. In other words, I'd bet that this *will* happen. Let's see why. The number of ways a whole number less than 7 can occur in one roll of a die is six (1, 2, 3, 4, 5, or 6), and the number of possible outcomes is six. Thus, the probability is $\frac{6}{6}$, or 1. When a probability is equal to 1 (or 100%), it must happen; it is certain to occur.

What is the probability of rolling an 8 in one roll of a die? Again, I'd put up everything I own, but this time I'd bet against this occurrence. The number of ways an 8 can occur is 0. Thus, the probability of this occurring is 0; it cannot occur. This situation also reflects absolute certainty. Probabilities range from 0 (can never happen) to 1 (must happen), (or 0% to 100%). Probability values close to 0 or 1 represent events that are almost certain not to occur or almost certain to occur, whereas probabilities near .5 (50%) represent maximum uncertainty, because either outcome is equally likely, and, thus, there is no basis for predicting either one. This relationship is depicted in Fig. 7.1.

The Laws of Chance

The most important phrase in the last section was "in the long run." Except for those special cases when the probability of an outcome is either 0% or 100%, we cannot know with certainty what will happen. I cannot know when I roll a die whether I will roll a 5, but, if I keep rolling a die for many, many trials, I do know that about 17% of the time I will roll a 5. I cannot know which trials will produce a 5, but I do know approximately how many. This is an important point. When we speak of the **laws of chance** (or laws of probability), we are referring to the ability to predict the number or percentage of trials on which a particular outcome will occur. With a large number of trials, I can be very accurate about the number of times a particular outcome will occur, but I cannot know which trials will yield a particular outcome. This means that I can make good "long run" predictions and poor "short run" predictions.

Let's consider insurance as an applied example of this distinction. When you buy a life insurance policy (or any other type of insurance policy), you are making a bet with the insurance company. You agree to pay a certain amount of money to the insurance company each year. They agree to pay your beneficiary a certain amount of money when you die. There are many different types of life insurance policies available, but for the purposes of this chapter, let us consider the simplest. Suppose that you are 30 years old and that you agree to pay the

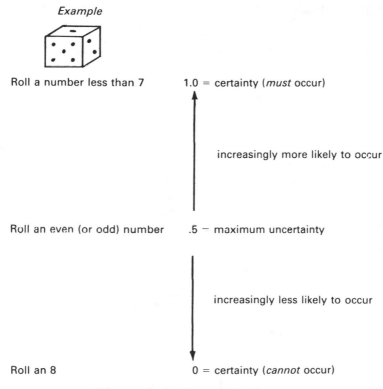

FIG. 7.1. Probability and Likelihood.

insurance company $1000 per year. When you die, your beneficiary will receive $20,000. You are betting with the insurance company that you will die at a fairly young age (a bet that you hope to lose) so that you will have paid them only a small amount of money and your beneficiary will receive a larger amount of money. If you die before the age of 50, you win the bet. Ignoring complications like inflation and interest, you will have paid less than the $20,000 that your beneficiary will receive if you die at a young age. The insurance company, on the other hand, will win the bet if you live to a ripe old age. If you die when you are 70 years old, you will have paid them $40,000 and your dearly beloved will receive only $20,000.

Insurance companies can make money because of the laws of chance. No one knows when you or anyone else will die, but we do know how many people aged 30 (the age at which you bought your policy) will die before they reach their 50th birthday. Thus, although we cannot predict accurately for any single individual, we can use the laws of chance to predict how many people will live to be any particular age.

Degrees of Belief

Probability is sometimes used to express the strength of a belief about the likelihood of an outcome. This is the second definition for the term **probability.** For example, if you apply for a job and believe that the interview went well, you might assess the probability that you will be offered the job as 80%. This probability value was not mathematically derived by calculating the number of ways a success could occur divided by the number of possible outcomes. Instead, it indicates your degree of belief that the job will be offered. It suggests a moderate-to-high likelihood. If someone else interviewed for the same job and believed that his or her chance of being offered the job was 50%, it would be obvious that he or she was less confident about getting the job than you were.

The use of probability to express one's degree of belief in the likelihood of an outcome is particularly prevalent at election time. Political analysts will often attach probability values to the likelihood of a candidate's election. If a political analyst gives a candidate a 30% chance of winning, she or he is predicting that, although the candidate might win, she or he believes that the candidate is more likely to lose. Probability values are handy ways of quantifying confidence in an outcome.

Factors That Affect Judgments About Degrees of Belief

An oft-repeated theme in the research that has examined how people utilize probability when making judgments about degrees of belief is that we are imperfect in our use of probability values. Consider the following two situations (adapted from Beyth-Marom et al., 1985, p. 39):

> The chances of war are equal to the chances of rolling a six with a fair die.

On a scale from 0 to 100, with 0 equal to "IT CANNOT HAPPEN" and 100 equal to "IT DEFINITELY WILL HAPPEN" select the number that best describes the likelihood of war.

Stop now, and actually select a number that reflects your assessment of the likelihood of war given this information.

> Mr. Baker has a minor medical problem, the presence of which affects his daily life only slightly. The problem can be solved with a complicated operation. The chances for its success (removing the problem) are equal to the chances of rolling a six with a fair die.

On a scale from 0 to 100, with 0 equal to "IT CANNOT HAPPEN" and 100 equal to "IT DEFINITELY WILL HAPPEN" select the number that best describes the likelihood of the operation being successful.

Stop now, and actually select a number that reflects your assessment of the likelihood of a successful operation given this information.

This is probably an unfair test of how you determine degrees of belief, because you just read about the probability of rolling a particular number with a fair die. If you reacted like most people, you would have rated the likelihood of war as being higher than the likelihood of a successful operation for poor Mr. Baker. You can try this out for yourself by asking different people to respond to either the war situation or the operation situation. (If you've already read chapter 6, then you'll remember to consider sample size and bias issues.)

It should be clear that the probability of rolling a 6 with a fair die is always 17%, so the best answer to both scenarios is 17. But, when people use probabilities in their everyday assessments, these numbers become distorted. It does not seem like a good idea for Mr. Baker to undergo the proposed operation, because his ailment is minor, and the surgery is described as "complicated." People consider the desirability of the surgery when they consider its probability for success. Whether the surgery is a good idea or not depends on many factors, but the probability of its success doesn't change (in this situation). By contrast, people often believe that an outcome such as a war is likely, and they use their belief to interpret probability claims. More simply put, when people use probability to express degrees of belief, the values that they select are affected by numerous factors that are unrelated to probability, such as the desirability of the event.

Overconfidence

By definition, there is always some uncertainty in probabilistic events. Yet, research has shown that people tend to be more confident in their decision about probabilistic events than they should be. Consider an example that Daniel Kahneman, a researcher in this area, likes to use. When he and his coauthors began working on a text on decision making, they were fairly confident that they would have it completed within a year, despite the fact that they knew that most books like the one they were writing take many years to complete. They believed that they would beat these "odds." In fact, it took them several years to complete the text.

A similar phenomenon is at work whenever we consult investment advisors. The probability of making money by investing in stocks is such that we would often make more money if we left our money in a low-interest passbook account. Yet, most people believe that they will defy these odds and make a winning investment.

In an experimental investigation of the **overconfidence phenomenon,** people were asked to provide answers with a specified degree of confidence to factual questions (Kahneman & Tversky, 1979). Try it with this question: "I feel 98% certain that the number of nuclear plants operating in the world in 1980 was more than ___0___ and less than __3 000__." Fill in the blanks with numbers that reflect 98% confidence. The researchers investigating this effect found that nearly one third of the time, the correct answer did not lie between the two values that reflected a 98% level of confidence. (The correct answer to this question is 189.) This result demonstrates that people are often highly confident when their high degree of confidence is unwarranted.

Have you ever bought a lottery ticket? Do you know what the odds are against your hitting the jackpot? The laws of probability dictate that you should expect to lose, yet countless numbers of people expect to win.

People tend to be most confident in uncertain situations when they believe that they have control over the uncertain events. Many state lottery advisors are familiar with this principle of human nature and now have a lottery plan that allows the buyer to select his or her own number. People prefer to select their own numbers over being given a number at random, because it gives them an illusion of control. The winning number is still selected randomly, but people believe they are more likely to win in the self-selection lottery.

Odds

It is often convenient to discuss probabilities in terms of **odds.** If a friend gives you 3-to-1 odds that his school's championship tiddly-winks team will beat your school's tiddly-winks team, this means that if 4 games were played, he would expect his team to win 3 of them. Authorities on organized sports (announcers, sports page editors, and almost everyone else) usually express their degree of belief in the outcome of a sporting event in terms of odds. (Betting odds like those posted at race tracks and boxing matches refer to the amount of money that has been bet on each contender and, thus, have a slightly different meaning from the one described here.)

USING PROBABILITY

Without giving it much thought, we utilize probabilities many times each day. Let's start with one of the few examples where probability values are made explicit. Many people begin each day by reading the weather forecast in the morning paper. What do you do when you read that the probability of rain is 90% today? Most people will head off to school or work toting an umbrella, because they interpret this statement as, "It probably will rain." What this statement objectively means is that on 90% of the previous days when the weather conditions (atmospheric pressure, humidity, etc.) were like today's, it rained. A 90% probability of rain has nothing to do with how much it will rain, just how likely we are to get rain.

The number of instances in which we are given explicit probability values that have been computed for us is relatively small. One area where this practice is growing is in the use of medicine inserts that are designed to help patients understand the risks and benefits of taking a particular drug. The Food and Drug Administration now requires that all oral contraceptive medications (birth control pills) be packaged with statistical information about the health risks associated with them. In order to arrive at an intelligent decision based on the information provided, potential oral contraceptive users must be able to understand the statistical summaries that are presented in the medicine inserts.

The following excerpt from an oral contraceptive packaged insert provides an example: "For women aged 20 to 44, it is estimated that about 1 in 2,000 using oral contraceptives will be hospitalized each year because of abnormal clotting. Among nonusers in the same age group, about 1 in 20,000 would be hospitalized each year" (Ortho Pharmaceutical Corp., 1979, p. 16). Although consumers can readily assess that clotting is more likely for pill users, this information is of little practical value unless an oral contraceptive consumer can decide if 1 in 2,000 is a large or small number, that is, "Is it a danger to me if I am taking the pill?"

Two related experiments (Halpern & Blackman, 1985; Halpern, Blackman, & Salzman, in press) have shown that most people find information like this to be relatively meaningless.

Consider the following: Suppose you read that the risk of developing heart disease is 10.5 times more likely for oral contraceptive users than for nonusers. Most people will conclude from this information that oral contraceptives present a substantial risk of heart disease. Suppose now that you are told that only 3.5 women out of 100,000 users will develop heart disease. You probably would interpret this sentence as meaning that there is little risk associated with oral contraceptive use. Consider the "flip side" of this information and think about how you would assess safety if you read that 99,996.5 women out of 100,000 users will *not* develop heart disease. Does it seem even safer?

Another way of presenting the same information is to convert it to a percentage. There is only a .0035% chance that oral contraceptive users will develop heart disease. Most people would now consider the risk associated with oral contraceptive use to be minuscule.

Which of these statements is correct? They all are. The only way they differ is the way in which the statistical information is presented, and different ways of presenting the same statistical information lead to very different assessments of safety (Halpern, Blackman, & Salzman, in press). It is important to keep this in mind when interpreting statistical information. There is a trend to provide consumers with statistical risk information so that they can make informed safety judgments about a diverse assortment of topics, including how to treat a particular type of cancer and the safety of nuclear energy. When you are confronted with risk probabilities, the best way to convert them to a meaningful value is to write out all of the mathematically equivalent values (i.e., X out of Y occurrences, number of times greater risk than a meaningful comparison event, number that will die, number that will not die). Graphic representations of relative risks can also be helpful when there are many values that need to be compared simultaneously. The use of spatial arrays is touted throughout this book (e.g., circle diagrams when interpreting syllogisms, graphic organizers to comprehend complex prose, tree diagrams for use in making sound decisions). One advantage that they confer in this situation is that they reduce the memory load in working memory and allow us to consider several different alternatives "at a glance."

Implicit Use of Probability

Although we are rarely given explicit, objectively determined probabilities to deal with, we are frequently required to derive our own subjective estimates of probability for use in making decisions. There are numerous everyday examples in which people tacitly utilize rough estimates of probability. Most students use probabilities in deciding how to study for exams. It may surprise you to learn that some students put off studying until a few nights before the exam, even though they know that they can learn more if they keep up with their work. Suppose Geraldine has 10 chapters to study for a final exam that she will have to take tomorrow. She can't possibly read all 10 chapters in one night. She could try to cut down on her reading by concentrating on the chapters she believes that her professor is most likely to emphasize on the exam. Of course, if she's wrong, the results could be disastrous. If Geraldine decides to skip chapters 2 and 6 in her text, and the exam draws heavily from these chapters, she'll most likely fail the exam.

Every time you drive your car, you make implicit probability estimates about what other drivers will do next. For example, accidents frequently occur when large trucks signal for a right-hand turn from the left-hand lane. Large trucks need the extra room to turn. Many drivers ignore the turn signal, thinking that the truck driver will probably continue straight, because he or she is in the left-hand lane. Too often, a collision is the unfortunate result.

Games of Chance

Cards

We are a country of people who love to play games. From Las Vegas to Atlantic City, and in all of the small towns in between, people spend countless hours and dollars playing games of chance, skill, and semi-skill. Card playing is a ubiquitous pastime, with small children playing "fish" and "old maid," and their older counterparts playing canasta, bridge, poker, pinochle, blackjack, hearts, and too many others to mention. The uncertainty that is inherent in card games adds to the pleasure of playing (although the comraderie and pretzels and beer also help).

Good card players, regardless of the game, understand and utilize the rules of probability. Let's apply the definitional formula for probability to card games. For example, how likely are you to draw the ace of spades from a deck of cards? The probability of this happening is $\frac{1}{52}$, or approximately 2%, because there is only one ace of spades and 52 possible outcomes. How likely are you to draw an ace of any suit from a full deck of cards? If you've been following the probability discussion so far, you'll realize that the answer is $\frac{4}{52}$, or approximately 8%, because there are four aces in a 52-card deck. Some professional card players have worked out careful plans that will help them change the odds of winning in their favor. Some people have reportedly been denied access to gambling casinos because their systems are so effective that the casino ends up losing money to them. This is especially true of blackjack "counters." It is difficult to tell to what extent these stories are hype. (Professional gamblers often enjoy bragging about their winnings.) In any case, it is possible to improve the odds or probability of winning most card games if the player is willing to spend some time figuring the relevant probabilities and keeping track of the cards that have already been played. In determining the likelihood of getting an ace, a player needs to "count" the number of aces that already have been played. If all four aces have been played, then a good player will realize that there is no possibility of getting the desired ace. On the other hand, if half of the deck has been played and no aces have shown up so far, then the probability of now being dealt an ace is $\frac{4}{26}$—considerably higher than the earlier probability.

One of the biggest problems in "beating the house" is remembering which cards have been played. Top professionals have devised systems to help them remember. The most obvious system and cheapest mnemonic (memory) device is pen and paper. This is usually not permitted in casinos or in most home games. Elaborate counting methods often use body positions to keep track of played cards. For example, players will cross their legs when two aces have been played, tuck their left leg behind the chair leg when all the kings have been played, and cross their index and third finger of their left hand when a queen is played. Then, when betting on a hand, trained players can "read" their body positions to determine relevant probabilities. The systems themselves are intricate and difficult to learn and use; and, although they may slightly improve a player's odds, they do not constitute a sure-fire scheme to quick riches. As you probably guessed, casino owners have responded to these schemes by tilting the odds back in their favor. Most blackjack games now use several decks simultaneously, making it extremely difficult to count effectively.

According to Gunther (1977), Vera Nettick (who is a real person) is a lucky lady. While playing a game of bridge, she was dealt a hand that contained all 13 diamonds. Breathlessly, she won a grand slam with the once-in-a-lifetime card hand. Any statistician will be quick to point out that every possible combination of cards will be dealt to somebody sooner or later. Thus, Vera Nettick's hand was no more unusual than any other card hand, although it certainly is more memorable. Can you guess how often such a hand would occur? Gunther (1977) figured this out as follows:

> There are roughly 635 billion possible bridge hands. Of these, eight might be called 'perfect' hands, though some are more perfect than others. To begin with, there are four perfect no-trump hands. Such a hand would contain all four aces, all four kings, all four queens, and one of the four jacks. Any of these four hands would be unequivocally perfect, because no bid could top it. Slightly less perfect, in descending order, are hands containing all the spades, all the hearts, all the diamonds, and all the clubs. If there are eight of these perfect hands in a possible 635 billion, the statistical probability is that such a hand will be dealt one in every 79 billion tries, give or take a few.
>
> Now all we have to do is estimate how many games of bridge are played every year and how many hands are dealt in each game. Using fairly conservative estimates, it turns out that a perfect hand should be dealt to some lucky bridge player, somewhere in the United States, roughly once every three or four years. (p. 30)

Actually, Gunther's figures are too low, because new decks of cards are organized in ascending order by suits so that one or two "perfect" shuffles will produce "perfect" bridge hands (Alcock, 1981). (A perfect shuffle occurs when, following a "cut," there is a one-to-one interleaving of cards from each half of the deck.

Consider the two card hands shown in Fig. 7.2. Which is more likely to be dealt from a well shuffled deck of cards. If you are following the logic in this section, you will realize that they are equally likely. Every possible combination of cards is equally likely when the cards are dealt at random. This topic is also discussed in chapter 8 ("Decision Making").

Roulette

Roulette is often thought of as an aristocratic game. It is strange that it has gained this reputation, because it is a pure game of chance. Unlike most card games, there is no skillful way to play roulette. As you probably know, roulette is played by spinning a small ball inside a circular array of numbered and colored pockets. Eighteen of the pockets are red; 18 are black; and 2 are green. Players can make a variety of bets. One possible bet is that the ball will land in a red pocket. What is the probability of this event? There are 18 red pockets out of 38 pockets (possible outcomes); therefore, the probability of the ball landing in a red pocket is $\frac{18}{38}$. Because this is a number less than .5, we know that it will land in a red pocket slightly less than half of the time. Thus, if you kept betting on red,

FIG. 7.2. Which of these two card hands are you more likely to be dealt from a well shuffled deck of cards?

you would lose slightly more often than you would win. Suppose now that you bet on black pockets. Again, the probability would be $^{18}/_{38}$; and again, if you continue to bet on black pockets, you will lose more often than you win. Of course, sometimes you will win, and at other times you will lose, but after many spins—in the long run,—you will lose at roulette.

The odds, or probability of winning, at any casino game are always favorable to the "house," otherwise, casinos could not stay in business. Actually, there is one person who has been able to "beat" the roulette odds. One of my heros is Al Hibbs, a scientist who gained fame for his work at the Jet Propulsion Laboratory in Pasadena, California, where most of the work on the United States space program is done. When he was a student, he used his knowledge of probability to run his original stake of $125 up to $6,300 at the Pioneer Club in Reno. Here's how he did it: Hibbs knows that, although every number in a roulette wheel should be equally likely to occur, all man-made devices have imperfections. These imperfections make some numbers more likely to occur than others. Hibbs and a friend recorded the results of 100,000 spins of the roulette wheel to find the numbers that occurred most often. Accordingly, they bet on these numbers. Unfortunately, none of us can duplicate his success, because the wheels are now taken apart and reassembled with different parts each day. Thus, although each wheel is still imperfect, the imperfections differ from day to day.

Computing Probabilities in Multiple Outcome Situations

We are often concerned with the probability of two or more events occurring, such as getting two heads in two flips of a coin or rolling a 6 at least once in two rolls of a die. These sorts of situations are called **multiple outcomes.**

Using Tree Diagrams

Although it is relatively easy to understand that the probability of getting a head on one flip of a coin is ½, it is somewhat more difficult to know intuitively the probability of getting four heads in four flips of a coin. Let's figure it out.

On the first flip, only one of two possible outcomes can occur; a head (H) or tail (T). What can happen if a coin is flipped twice? There are four possible outcomes; a head on the first flip and a head on the second (HH); a head on the first flip and a tail on the second (HT); a tail on the first flip and a head on the second (TH); and a tail on the first flip and a tail on the second (TT). Because there are four possible outcomes and only one way to get two heads, the probability of this event is ¼. There is a general rule, the "and rule," for calculating this value in any situation. When you want to find the probability of one event *and* another event (a head on the first *and* second flip), you multiply their separate probabilities. By applying the "and rule," we find that the probability of obtaining two tails when a coin is flipped twice is equal to ½ × ½, which is ¼. Intuitively, the probability of both events occurring should be less likely than either event alone, and it is.

A simple way to compute this probability is to represent all possible events with **tree diagrams.** On the first flip, either a H or T will land facing up. The probability of a head is equal to the probability of a tail, which is equal to .5. Let's depict this as follows:

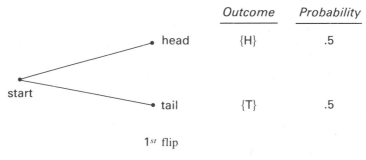

	Outcome	Probability
head	{H}	.5
start		
tail	{T}	.5

1st flip

When you flip a second time, either a H on the first flip will be followed by a H or T, or a T on the first flip will be followed by a H or T. The probability of a head or tail on the second flip is still .5. Outcomes from a second flip are added as "branches" on a tree diagram.

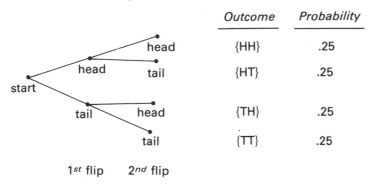

	Outcome	Probability
head	{HH}	.25
tail	{HT}	.25
head	{TH}	.25
tail	{TT}	.25

1st flip   2nd flip

As you can see from this tree, there are four possible outcomes. You can use this tree to find out the probability of other events. What is the probability of getting exactly one H in two flips of a coin? Because there are two ways for this to occur, (HT) and (TH), the answer is ¾, or ½ When you want to find the probability of two *or* more different outcomes, add the probability of each outcome. This is called the "or rule." Another way to ask the same question is, "What is the probability of getting either a head followed by a tail (¼) *or* a tail followed by a head (¼)?" The correct procedure is to add these values, which equals ½. Intuitively, the probability of two or more events occurring should be higher than the probability of any one of them occurring, and it is.

We can only use the "or rule" and the "and rule" when the events we're interested in are **independent.** Two events are independent when the occurrence of one of them does not influence the occurrence of the other. In this example, what you get on the first flip of a coin does not influence what you get on the second flip.

Tree diagrams are general ways of representing events that are useful in many situations. Let's extend this example. Suppose a man with a long handlebar moustache, shifty, beady eyes, and pinstripe suit stopped you on the street and asked you to bet on a coin-flipping game. He always calls heads. On the first flip, the coin lands heads up. On the second flip, the coin lands head up. On the third flip, the coin lands heads up. When would you begin to suspect that he wasn't using a fair coin? Most people would get suspicious by the third or fourth flip. Calculate the probability of a fair coin (probability of heads = .5) landing heads up in three and four tosses.

To calculate the probability of three heads in three flips, you would draw a probability tree with three sets of "nodes" with two "branches" coming off each node.

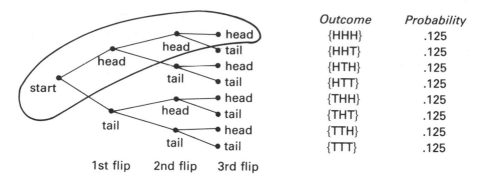

Outcome	Probability
{HHH}	.125
{HHT}	.125
{HTH}	.125
{HTT}	.125
{THH}	.125
{THT}	.125
{TTH}	.125
{TTT}	.125

Because there is only one way to get 3 Hs, multiply the probabilities along the HHH branch (circled in the previous drawing), which are $.5 \times .5 \times .5 = .125$. A probability of .125 means that if the coin is fair, it would, on the average, land heads up three times in a row 12.5% of the time. Although this is unlikely to happen, most people would be willing to conclude that the coin is fair if it landed heads up to three times in a row.

To calculate the probability of four heads in four flips, add another branch to the tree.

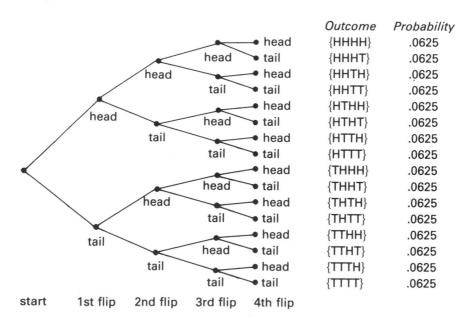

Outcome	Probability
{HHHH}	.0625
{HHHT}	.0625
{HHTH}	.0625
{HHTT}	.0625
{HTHH}	.0625
{HTHT}	.0625
{HTTH}	.0625
{HTTT}	.0625
{THHH}	.0625
{THHT}	.0625
{THTH}	.0625
{THTT}	.0625
{TTHH}	.0625
{TTHT}	.0625
{TTTH}	.0625
{TTTT}	.0625

The probability of 4 Hs is $.5 \times .5 \times .5 \times .5 = .0625$; or about 6.25% of the time. As most of you already know, this is mathematically equal to $(.5)^4$, that is, multiplying a number by itself four times is the same as raising it to the fourth power. If you work this on a calculator with the ability to raise numbers to the fourth power, you'll get the same answer, 6.25%. Although this is a possible outcome, one that will sometimes occur, it is an unlikely outcome. In fact, it is so unlikely or unusual that most people would be willing to say that he is probably cheating by using a biased coin. Certainly, by the fifth flip, it would seem reasonable to conclude that the coin is not fair. For most scientific purposes, an event is considered "unusual" if it would be expected to occur by chance less than 5% of the time. (In probability jargon, this is $p < .05$.)

Let's get away from coin flipping, because this is an artificial example, and use the same logic in a different context. I'm sure that every student has, at some time or other, taken a multiple-choice test. (Some students like to call them multiple-guess tests.) Most of these tests have five alternative answers for each question. Only one of these is correct. Suppose also that the questions are so difficult that all you can do is guess randomly at the correct answer. What is the probability of guessing correctly on the first question? If you have no idea which alternative is the correct answer, then you are equally likely to choose any of the five alternatives. Because the sum of all possible alternatives must be 1.0, the probability of selecting each alternative is .20. One alternative is correct, and four are incorrect, so the probability of selecting the correct alternative is .20. A tree diagram of this situation is shown here:

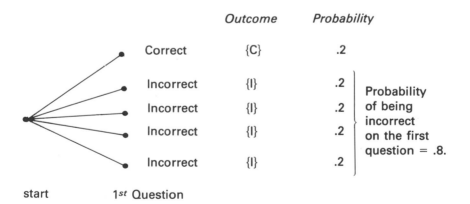

	Outcome	Probability	
Correct	{C}	.2	
Incorrect	{I}	.2	Probability
Incorrect	{I}	.2	of being
Incorrect	{I}	.2	incorrect
Incorrect	{I}	.2	on the first question = .8.

start   1ˢᵗ Question

What is the probability of getting the first two multiple-choice questions correct by guessing? We'll have to add a second branch to a tree that will soon be very crowded. To save space and to simplify the calculations, all of the incorrect alternatives can be represented by one branch labeled "incorrect." The probability of being incorrect on any single question is .8.

	Outcome	Probability
Correct	{CC}	.04
Incorrect	{CI}	.16
Correct	{IC}	.16
Incorrect	{II}	.64

The probability of two correct questions by guessing is .2 × .2, which equals .04. That means that this would happen by chance only 4% of the time. Suppose we extend our example to three questions. I won't draw a tree, but you should be able to see by now that the probability is .2 × .2 × .2 = .008. This is so unusual that it would occur less than 1% of the time by chance. What would you conclude about someone who got all three of these questions correct? Most people (professors are people, too) would conclude that the student wasn't guessing, and that she or he really knew something. Of course, it is possible that the student was just lucky, but it is so unlikely that we would conclude that something other than luck was responsible for the outcome that he or she obtained.

Let me point out a curious side to this kind of reasoning. Consider the plight of Sara. She took a 15-question multiple-choice test in which every question had five alternatives. Sara got all 15 questions wrong. Can you determine the probability of this happening by chance? I won't draw the tree diagram to depict this situation, but it is easy to see that the probability of being wrong on one question is .80; therefore the probability of being wrong on all 15 questions is $(.80)^{15}$. This is .80 times itself 15 times, which equals .0352. Because this would happen by chance only 3.52% of the time, can Sara present the argument to her professor that something other than chance determined this unusual result? Of course, Sara can make this argument, but would you be willing to believe her if you were her professor? Suppose she argued that she must have known the correct answer to every question. How else could she have avoided selecting it in all 15 consecutive questions? I don't know how many professors would buy her assertion that getting all 15 questions wrong demonstrates her knowledge, even though identical reasoning is used as proof of knowing correct answers when the probability of getting all the questions correct is about the same. (In this example, the probability of getting all 15 questions correct is $(.20)^{15}$, which is a number less than .0001.) Personally, if I were the professor, I'd give Sara high marks for creativity and for her understanding of statistical principles. It is possible that Sara did know ''something'' about the topic, but that ''something'' was systematically wrong. I'd also point out to her that it is possible that she was both dumb and unlucky enough to guess wrong 15 times. After all, unusual events do happen sometimes.

Before going on to the next section, be sure that you understand how tree diagrams are used to compute probabilities and to consider all possible outcomes. I return to these diagrams later in this chapter. Once you learn how to use them, you'll be surprised at how many possible applications there are for tree diagrams.

Cumulative Risks—Applying the "Or" Rule

It should be obvious that the probability of getting three questions correct by chance when there are five alternatives will be much smaller than the probability of getting just one question correct by chance and that the probability of getting at least one question correct by chance out of three questions will be higher than the probability of getting one question correct when there is only one question. These probabilities follow from the "and" and "or" rules. The kinds of examples presented so far were deliberately simple. Let's see how this principle applies in real-world settings.

Most real-life risks involve repeated exposure to a risky situation. Consider driving. The probability of having an accident in one car ride is very low. But what happens to this probability when you take hundreds or thousands of car rides? According to the "or" rule, this is the probability of an accident on the first *or* second *or* . . . nth car ride. In an interesting study of how people understand the concept of cumulative risk, Shaklee (1987) gave subjects different probability values that supposedly corresponded to the yearly risk of a flood. Subjects then had to estimate the likelihood of a flood in 1 month, 5 years, 10 years, and 15 years. Only 74% of her subjects knew that the likelihood of a flood increased with intervals over 1 year. Among those who gave higher probability values for intervals over one year, most seriously underestimated the **cumulative probability.**

Let's consider a similar example. In the case of contraception, a method that is 96% effective per year will result in an average of four pregnancies per 100 couples per year. Assuming a constant failure rate over time, we would expect 19 of the 100 women to become pregnant over a period of 5 years, 34 over 10 years, and 46 over 15 years of use (Shaklee, 1987). In a study with college students, only 52% realized that the number of expected pregnancies would increase over time, and most of these students significantly underestimated the number of pregnancies.

The message here should be clear: When you are determining risk, it is important to understand whether the value you are being given is per some unit of time (e.g., 1 year) and how cumulative risks increase with repeated exposure. It seems that many people do not understand the concept that cumulative risks are greater than one-time risks.

Conjunction Error—Applying the "And" Rule

The following problem was posed by Tversky and Kahneman (1983):

> Linda is 31 years old, outspoken and very bright. She majored in philosophy. As a student, she was deeply concerned with issues of discrimination and social justice, and also participated in anti-nuclear demonstrations.
>
> For the following list of statements estimate the probability that it is descriptive of Linda.
>
> A. Linda is a teacher in elementary school.
> B. Linda works in a bookstore and takes yoga classes.
> C. Linda is active in the feminist movement.
> D. Linda is a psychiatric social worker.
> E. Linda is a member of the League of Women Voters.
> F. Linda is a bank teller.
> G. Linda is an insurance salesperson.
> H. Linda is a bank teller and is active in the feminist movement. (p. 297)

Stop now and estimate the probability for each statement.

The short paragraph about Linda was written to be representative of an active feminist, which is statement C. Look at statements F (bank teller) and H (feminist *and* a bank teller). How did you rank these two sentences? Most people believe that H is more probably true than F. Can you see why F must be more likely than H? There are some bank tellers who are not active in the feminist movement. When determining the probability of both of two events occurring, you multiply the probabilities of each one occurring (the "and" rule). Thus, the probability of two events *both* occurring must be less likely than the probability of one of these events occurring. In Tversky and Kahneman's study, 85% of the subjects judged statement H to be more probable than statement F. The error of believing that the occurrence of two events is more likely than the occurrence of one of them is called the **conjunction error.**

Now that you understand the conjunction error, try the next question (also taken from Tversky & Kahneman, 1983).

> A health survey was conducted in a sample of adult males in British Columbia, of all ages and occupations.
> Please give your best estimate of the following values:
> What percentage of the men surveyed have had one or more heart attacks?
> _____ 20
>
> What percentage of the men surveyed both are over 55 years old and have had one or more heart attacks? _____ 10 (p. 308)

Stop now and fill in the blanks with your best estimate of these values.

Over 65% of the respondents believed that a higher percentage of the men would be both over 55 and have had a heart attack than the percentage of men who reported that they had a heart attack. Do you recognize this as another example of a conjunction error? The probability of two uncertain events both occurring cannot be greater than the probability of just one of them occurring.

EXPECTED VALUES

Place Your Bets

Which of the following bets would you take if you could only choose one of them?

1. The Big 12
It will cost you $1 to play. If you roll a pair of dice and get a 12, you'll get your $1 back, plus another $24. If you roll any other number, you'll lose your $1.

2. Lucky 7
It will cost you $1 to play (same cost as #1). If you roll a "lucky 7" with a pair of dice, you'll get your $1 back, plus another $6. If you roll any other number, you'll lose your $1.

Stop now and select either #1 or #2.

Most people choose #1, reasoning that $24 if a 12 is rolled is four times more than they can win if a 7 is rolled, and the cost is the same for each bet. Let's see if this thinking is correct.

In order to decide which is the better bet, we need to consider the probability of winning and losing and the corresponding value of each. There is a formula that will take these variables into account and yield the **expected value** (EV) for each gamble. An expected value is the amount of money you would expect to win on each bet if you continued playing over and over. The formula for computing an expected value (EV) is:

$$EV = \text{(probability of a win)} \times \text{(value of a win)} +$$
$$\text{(probability of a loss)} \times \text{(value of a loss)}$$

Let's consider the EV for Choice #1. We'll begin by computing the probability of rolling a 12 with a pair of dice. There is only one way to roll a 12, and that is with a 6 on each die. The probability of this happening is $\frac{1}{6} \times \frac{1}{6} = \frac{1}{36} = .028$. (Because we are interested in finding the probability of a 6 on the first *and* the second die, we use the "and rule," and multiply.) Thus, we'd expect to roll a 12 about 2.8% of the time. What is the probability of not rolling a 12? Because we are certain that you will either roll a 12 or not roll a 12 (this covers all possible events), you can subtract .028 from 1.00. The probability of not rolling a 12 is .972. (You could also arrive at this figure, with some small rounding differences, by calculating the probability of each of the 35 other possible outcomes—each will be $\frac{1}{36}$—and adding them together.) All possible outcomes from rolling a pair of dice are shown in Fig. 7.3.

Using these probability values, the EV formula for Choice #1 becomes:

EV (Choice #1)	= (Probability of a 12) × (Value of a 12) + (Probability of *not* getting a 12) × (Value of *not* getting a 12)
EV (Choice #1)	= [(.028) × ($24)] + [(.972) × (−$1)]
EV (Choice #1)	= $.672 − .972
EV (Choice #1)	= −$.30

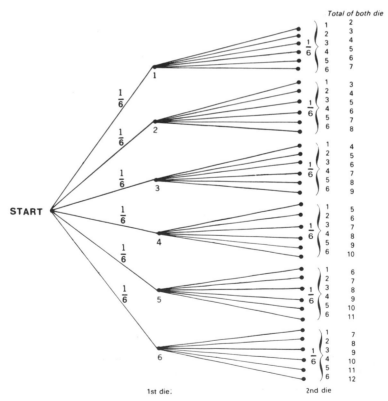

FIG. 7.3. A tree diagram depicting all possible outcomes of rolling a pair of dice.

Let's review what happened in this formula. If you rolled a 12, you'd win $24, which is the value associated with this win. If you rolled a number other than a 12, you'd lose the $1 you paid to play this game, thus -$1 is the value associated with this loss. The probability of a win was multiplied by the value of a win. The probability of a loss was multiplied by the value of a loss. Then, these two products were added together. The EV of this bet is -$.30. This means that, in the long run, if you continue playing this game many times, you could expect to lose, on the average, $.30 for every game played. Of course, on any single game, you'd either lose $1 or win $24, but after many, many games you would have lost an average of $.30 per game. If you played 1,000 games, making the same bet each time, you'd be $300 poorer.

How does this compare with Choice #2? To calculate the EV of Choice #2, we'll begin by computing the probability of rolling a 7. How many times is it possible to role a 7 with a pair of dice? You could get a 1 on the first die and a 6 on the second; a 2 and a 5; a 3 and a 4; a 4 and a 3; and a 5 and a 2; or a 6 and a 1. Thus, there are six possible ways to roll a 7 out of 36 possible outcomes. The probability of any one of these outcomes is $\frac{1}{6} \times \frac{1}{6}$, which equals $\frac{1}{36}$. (This is the probability of rolling, for example, a 1 on the first dic and a 6 on the second die.) Thus, to determine the probability of one number followed by a second number, you would apply the "and" rule. Because you are now concerned with the probability of a 1 followed by a 6 *or* a 2 followed by a 5 *or* a 3 followed by a 4 *or* a 4 followed by a 3 *or* a 5 followed by a 2 *or* a 6 followed by a 1, you should recognize the second step as a case where the "or rule" is needed. Because there are six possible combinations, you would add $\frac{1}{36}$ six times (which is, of course, the same as multiplying it by 6). Thus, the probability of rolling a 7 with a pair of dice is $\frac{6}{36}$ ($\frac{1}{6}$ or .167). The probability of not rolling a 7 is $1 - .167$, which equals .833. Now we calculate the EV of Choice #2.

$$\begin{array}{ll} \text{EV} & - \text{ (Probability of a 7)} \times \text{(Value of a 7)} + \text{(Probability of not} \\ \text{(Choice \#2)} & \text{getting a 7} \times \text{(Value of not getting a 7)} \end{array}$$

$$\begin{array}{ll} \text{EV} & = [(.167) \times (\$6)] + [(.833) \times (-\$1)] \\ \text{(Choice \#2)} & \end{array}$$

$$= (\$1.002 - .833)$$

$$= \$.169, \text{ or approximately } \$.17$$

This means that if you continued to gamble on Choice #2, you would win an average of $.17 for every game played. Thus, after 1,000 games, you could expect to be $170 richer. Of course, as in Choice #1, you would never actually win this amount on any single game; this is what would result if you continued playing many, many games.

Even though you might have originally thought otherwise, Choice #2 is the better choice, because of the relatively high probability associated with rolling a

7. Seven has a high probability, because there were six possible combinations that would add up to a 7.

There is a party game that is based on the principle that the more ways an event can occur, the more likely it is to occur. Suppose you get a random sample of 40 people together in a room. Estimate the probability that two of them share the same birthday. You may be surprised to learn that the probability is approximately .90. Can you figure out why it is so high? There are many, many ways that any 2 out of 40 people can share the same birthday. To figure out the exact probability, you would take all combinations of 40 people, 2 at a time. Thus, we'd have to start with the combination of person 1 with person 2, then person 1 with person 3, and so on until person 1 is matched with person 40, then we'd begin again matching person 2 with person 3, 2 with 4, and so on until 2 is matched with 40. This whole process would have to be repeated until everyone of the 40 people is matched with every other one. Because there are so many possible combinations of any two people sharing any birthday in the year, this "coincidence" is more probable than it may have seemed at first. The probability of two people sharing a common birthday is over .50 when there are 23 people and over .75 when there are 32 people (Loftus & Loftus, 1982). You can use this knowledge to make wagers at parties or at any gathering of people. It's a fairly good bet when the number of people is close to 40. Most people find it hard to believe that the probability is so high.

You can also use your knowledge of probability to improve your chances in other situations. Take, for example, Aaron and Jill, who have been arguing over who should take out the garbage. Their mother agrees to help them settle this matter by picking a number from 1 to 10. The one whose number comes closer to the one selected by their mother will win the dispute. Aaron goes first and picks 3. What number should Jill select to maximize her chances of winning? Stop now and decide what number she should select.

The best number for Jill to pick is 4. If her mother was thinking of any number greater than 3, Jill would win with this strategy. Thus, she can change the probability of winning in what seems like a chance situation.

SUBJECTIVE PROBABILITY

We rarely deal directly with known or objective probabilities, such as the probability of rain on a given day or the probability of developing heart disease if oral contraceptives are taken. Yet, every day we make decisions, using our best estimate of the likelihood of events. **Subjective probability** refers to personal estimates of the likelihood of events. This term is in distinction from **objective probability,** which is a mathematically determined statement of likelihood about known frequencies. Psychologists who have studied subjective probability have found that human judgments of probability are often fallible, yet we rely on them to guide our decisions in countless situations.

An Experimental Example

As a college statistics teacher, I can assert with some authority that, without specific training in the laws of probability, people have naive beliefs about probability. Suppose that you could choose one of the following:

1. There are 10 tickets in Box 1. One of them is the "winning ticket." You can close your eyes and pick one ticket from this box.

2. There are 100 tickets in Box 2. One of them is the "winning ticket." You can close your eyes and pick a total of 10 tickets, one at a time, returning each ticket to Box 2 before making the next selection. (Returning the tickets after each selection is called replacement.)

Did you make your choice? Cohen (1973) found that ⅘ of the subjects who were asked to make this choice preferred taking the single draw from a box of 10 tickets. In fact, the probability of drawing the winning ticket is exactly the same in these two choices. The probability of a success is $1/10$ for Box 1 and $10/100$, which equals $1/10$, for Box 2. Overwhelmingly, people report that Box 1 seems like a better deal. Consider now a third choice:

3. There are 10 separate boxes with 100 tickets in each. You may draw 10 tickets from each of these boxes (with replacement). Does this seem more likely to yield the winning ticket than the previous two choices?

Overwhelmingly, the subjects in Cohen's experiment preferred this situation to the earlier ones. Let's calculate the objective probability of drawing a winning ticket. As always, the probability of an event is equal to the number of ways a success can occur divided by the total number of possible outcomes. How many ways can a success occur? Because you would be selecting 10 tickets from 10 boxes, there are 100 ways a success can occur. Because there are 10 boxes with 100 tickets in each, there are 1,000 possible outcomes. Thus, the probability of drawing the winning ticket is $100/1000$, which is equal to $1/10$, the identical objective probability for Choices #1 and #2. It seems clear that most people are poor at assessing probabilities. Furthermore, they are wrong in consistent ways. Although terms like "probably" and "likely" are part of our everyday speech, few people can make accurate or even "ballpark" quantitative estimates of likelihood of the event they're discussing.

Gambler's Fallacy

The "Wheel of Fortune" is a popular game at fairs, casinos, amusement parks, and on television game shows. It consists of a large wheel that can be spun; the wheel is divided into many numbered sections, much like a roulette wheel. A rubber marker indicates the winning number.

Suppose that your friend, Vanna, decides to approach the Wheel of Fortune in a scientific manner. She sits at the Wheel of Fortune and records when each number comes up as the winning number. Suppose Vanna has recorded the following series of winning numbers: 3, 6, 10, 19, 18, 4, 1, 7, 7, 5, 20, 17, 2, 14, 19, 13, 8, 11, 13, 16, 12, 15, 19, 3, 8. After examining these numbers very carefully, she proclaims that a 9 has not appeared in the last 25 spins; therefore, she plans to bet heavily on number 9, because it is now much more likely to occur. Would you agree with her that this is a good bet?

If you responded, "Yes," you have committed a very common error in understanding probability. The Wheel of Fortune has no memory for which numbers have previously appeared. If the wheel had been built so that each number is equally likely to win, then a 9 is equally likely on each spin, regardless of how frequently or infrequently it appeared in the past. People believe that chance processes like spinning a Wheel of Fortune should be self-correcting so that if an event has not occurred in a while it is now more likely to occur. This misconception is called **Gambler's Fallacy.**

Gambler's Fallacy can be found in many settings. Consider a sports example. A "slumping" batter who hasn't had a hit in a long while is sometimes believed to be more likely to have a hit because he is "due" one. A sports enthusiast, who is a friend of mine, told me the following story about Don Sutton, a pitcher for the Dodgers. One season, Sutton gave up a great many runs. He predicted that this "slump" would be followed by a "correction" so that he would end up the season at his usual average. Unfortunately, there is no correction for chance factors and, because he had such a poor start to the season, he ended the season below his usual average.

Often, people will continue to believe in Gambler's Fallacy even after it has been explained to them. Students have told me that although they can understand on an intellectual level why Gambler's Fallacy must be wrong, on an intuitive or "gut" level, it seems that it ought to be right. Let's try another example.

Wayne and Marsha have four sons. Although they really don't want to have five children, both have always wanted a daughter. Should they plan to have another child, because they are now more likely to have a daughter, given that their first four children were boys? If you understand Gambler's Fallacy, you'll recognize that a daughter is as likely as a son on the fifth try, just as it was on each of the first four. (Actually, because slightly more boys than girls are born, the probability of having a boy baby is slightly higher than the probability of having a girl baby.)

Frequency and Relative Frequency

Consider the following:

Citing high housing costs, unemployment, and divorce among newlyweds, recent reports in the New York Times and U.S. News and World Report have proclaimed that more and more young adults are finding it necessary to live with their parents. Indeed, as the Times correctly reported, the number of people over 25 still living with their parents has jumped by 25% since 1970, to 4.5 million (Camer, 1983, p. 73).

Think carefully about this paragraph for a few minutes. Is there something wrong with the information it conveys? Obviously, there must be, or I wouldn't have raised the question. Assuming that the numbers cited are correct, and there are more young adults living with Mom and Dad than there were in 1970, these figures neglect the fact that there are more young adults now than there were in 1970. According to Camer (1983), "Since 1970, the proportion of young adults who haven't left the nest has only increased by 1 percent" (p. 73).

The figures cited in those prestigious news publications have failed to distinguish between frequency and **relative frequency.** Because there are more young adults now than in 1970, we could expect more of them to be doing almost anything, but if we want to talk about changing mores and patterns of behavior, relative frequencies are needed. Frequencies are obtained by counting the number of people who are doing what we're interested in. If you were in the housing business, this would be important to you, because you would know that more large houses are needed for the increased number of extended families, but the proportion of large to average-size houses that are needed hasn't changed much. If, however, you are interested in social change, then you would want to compare the relative frequencies or number of people doing what you're interested in relative to (or divided by) the total number of people available. This formula should sound familiar to you, because it is the same one that was used to calculate probabilities. Relative frequencies are used to make probability statements. Thus, if you found that the relative frequency (or percent if you multiply this number by 100) hasn't changed since 1970, you would conclude that there have been no real societal changes with respect to the variable that you're studying. People frequently make erroneous judgments based on frequency data instead of relative frequency data (Estes, 1976). Here is an example of some of the research used to support this statement:

In a recent Miss America pageant, Miss California's name appeared in 20 polls in which spectators were asked to select the most likely winner. She won 11 of these polls. Miss New York's name appeared in 8 different polls. She won 5 of them. The event went down to the wire, with a final run-off between these West and East coast beauties. Given the information presented, which one is more likely to win the key to Atlantic City?

Most people will predict that Miss California will win because she won 11 polls, whereas Miss New York only won 5. The frequency, or number of polls won, is the wrong comparison value, because they appeared in a different number of polls. What is needed is the relative frequency for each contestant.

$$\text{Relative frequency for Miss California} = \frac{11 \text{ polls won}}{20 \text{ polls entered}} = .55$$

$$\text{Relative frequency for Miss New York} = \frac{5 \text{ polls won}}{8 \text{ polls entered}} = .625$$

Thus, Miss New York is a better bet for those who wager on the outcomes of beauty pageants, because she won a greater portion, or relative frequency, of the prepageant polls.

The confusion of frequency with relative frequency is easier to spot in some contexts than in others. For example, this is an absolutely true statement: More people die in automobile accidents today than in 1928. Would you use this fact to conclude that the automobiles made today are not as safe as their 1928 counterparts? Most people would laugh at this statement, and realize there are many more drivers and automobiles today than there were in 1928. If however, you read that there are 10.3 million people unemployed today compared to 7.6 million in 1970, would you realize that these numbers are not comparable, because there have been dramatic changes in the number of people between the ages of 20 and 65 in the intervening years? Whenever you are given data like this, decide whether the frequency or relative frequency is needed, and then be sure that you are considering the correct one.

Judgments About Risks

The notion of frequency, or how often an event occurs, is inherent in the definition of probability. If an event is frequent, then its occurrence is highly probable. In order to determine the risk involved with a disastrous event, we need to first determine the frequency with which it occurs. Thus, in order to understand how people make judgments involving risks, we need to understand how they determine the frequency of real-life risky events. Several researchers (Lichtenstein et al., 1978) have focused on the way people judge the frequency of lethal (deadly) events. They studied this by asking college students and members of the League of Women Voters to decide which of two possible causes of death is more probable for several pairs of lethal events. In order to understand their experiment and their results, let's try a few examples. For the following pairs of items, indicate which is the more likely cause of death, and then estimate how much more likely your choice is than the other event:

A. asthma   or   tornado

B. excess cold   or   syphilis

C. diabetes   or   suicide

D. heart disease or   lung cancer

E. flood   or   homicide

F. syphilis   or   diabetes

G. asthma ✓   or   botulism
H. poisoning by vitamins   or   lightning ✓
 I. tuberculosis   or   homicide ✓
 J. all accidents ✓   or   stomach cancer

Researchers found that although, in general, people were more accurate as the differences in the true frequencies of occurrence between the events increased, they made a large number of errors in estimating the relative frequencies of the events. Their subjects overestimated the frequencies of events that occurred very rarely and underestimated the frequencies of those events that occurred very often. In addition, lethal events that had received a great deal of publicity (e.g., airplane crashes, flood, homicide, tornado, botulism) were overestimated, whereas those that were undramatic, silent killers (e..g, diabetes, stroke, asthma, tuberculosis) were underestimated. It seems that publicized events were more easily brought to mind, and this biased judgments of their frequency. Hazards that are unusually memorable, such as a recent disaster or an event depicted in a sensationalized film like "Jaws" or "The China Syndrome," distort our perceptions of risk. In chapter 2, I made the point that memory is an integral component of all thinking processes. What we remember is a major influence on how we think. The importance of being mindful of possible biases in memory when evaluating thought processes is seen in this quote (Lichtenstein et al., 1978):

> our society most often makes judgments about hazardous activities for which adequate statistical data is lacking, such as recombinant DNA research or nuclear waste disposal. We suspect that the biases found here (overestimation of rare events, underestimation of likely events, and an undue influence of drama or vividness) may be operating, indeed, may even be amplified in such situations. (p. 577)

Answers to the questions about the probability of lethal events are presented along with the true frequency of each event (rate per 1,000,000,000).

More Likely	Rate	Less Likely	Rate
A. Asthma	920	Tornado	44
B. Syphilis	200	Excess Code	163
C. Diabetes	19,000	Suicide	12,000
D. Heart Disease	360,000	Lung Cancer	37,000
E. Homicide	9,200	Flood	100
F. Diabetes	19,000	Syphilis	200
G. Asthma	920	Botulism	1
H. Lightning	52	Poisoning/Vitamins	.5
I. Homicide	9,200	Tuberculosis	1,800
J. All Accidents	55,000	Stomach Cancer	46,600

In general, most people believe that they are personally immune to common hazards. Rethan (1979, cited in Slovic, Fischoff, & Lichtenstein, 1986) found that most people believe that they are skillful drivers and that they are less likely to experience disastrous events than other people are. Over 97% of Rethan's respondents said that they were average or above average in their ability to avoid bicycle and power-motor accidents. Why does almost everyone believe that he or she is so skilled and careful? The reason for this belief lies in what we think about when we are asked to make these judgments. Even bad drivers have many accident-free trips. When deciding if we are careful or not, we search our memory and retrieve many accident-free trips. By comparison, even a few accidents seem like a small number; therefore, even relatively poor drivers decide that they are skilled at avoiding accidents. This phenomenon is similar to the belief that many people have about the lottery. When we believe that we are exercising some control (by selecting our own lottery number or driving our own car), we believe that the probability values that apply to the rest of the world no longer apply to us. This distorted view of the probability of risks has important consequences. For example, many people who live in areas that flood regularly do not purchase flood insurance because they perceive the likelihood of a flood affecting their home as less likely than a flood "somewhere else."

A major difficulty in interpreting low probability risks like flood or a nuclear accident is that the figures involved are not readily meaningful. Knowing that a particular risky event occurs in 1 in 10,000 individuals is difficult to interpret. We need to be able to convert this information into an answer to the question, "Is this likely to happen to me?" One suggestion for making this sort of information more meaningful is to convert all such risks to a standard "risk per hour" metric (Slovic et al., 1986). For example, suppose you learned that the risk involved in taking a motorcycle trip is the same as the risk of being 75 years old for 1 hour. Would this type of information be helpful in interpreting the risk of a motorcycle trip in a meaningful way? Although information of this sort might be useful for judging comparative risk (motorcycle trip compared to hang gliding), it may not be useful by itself because it is still difficult to understand what is meant by the risk of being 75 years old for 1 hour.

Base-Rate Neglect

Predicting Two (or More) Uncertain Events

Charlie is anxious to experience his first kiss. If he asks Louise to go to the movies with him, he's only 10% sure that she'll accept his invitation, but if she does, he's 95% sure that she'll kiss him goodnight. What are Charlie's chances for romance?

Initial or a priori probabilities are called the **base rate.** In this problem, the first hurdle that Charlie has to "get over" is getting Louise to go out with him.

The probability of this occurring is 10%. He wants to know the probability of two uncertain events occurring—she both goes out with him *and* she kisses him. Before we start to solve this problem, think about the kind of answer you would expect. Will it be greater than 95%, between 95% and 10%, or less than 10%?

To solve this problem, we'll use a tree diagram to depict the possible outcomes and the probability associated with each. We'll start with a tree diagram that first branches into Louise accepts his date and Louise declines. A second branch will be drawn from the Louise accepts his date node, indicating whether he gets kissed or not. Each branch should have the appropriate probability labels. Of course, if Louise declines his invitation, Charlie definitely won't get kissed. The branch from the "Louise declines" node is thus labeled 1.00 for "Charlie doesn't get kissed."

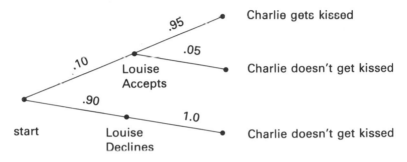

According to the *and* rule for finding the probability of two (or more) events, the probability that Louise will kiss Charlie goodnight is:

$$.10 \times .95 = .095$$

Are you surprised to find that the objective probability is less than the low base rate of 10% and much less than the higher secondary or subsequent rate of 95%? Most people are. Hopefully, you recognized that any value greater than 10% would have been indicative of a conjunction error. Recall from the earlier section on conjunction errors that the probability of two uncertain events both occurring (Louise accepts *and* kisses Charlie) must be less than the probability of either event alone. Most people ignore (or underestimate) the low base rate and estimate their answer as closer to the higher secondary rate. In general, people tend to overestimate the probability of two or more uncertain events occurring. This type of error is known as **base-rate neglect**.

Making Probabilistic Decisions

Most of the important decisions that we make in life involve probabilities. Although decision making is discussed more fully in chapter 8, let's consider how tree diagrams can be an aid for decision making.

Edith is trying to decide on a college major. She attends a very selective university that has independent admissions for each of its majors. She is seriously thinking about becoming an accountant. She knows that the accounting department accepts 25% of the students who apply for that major. Of those accepted, 70% graduate, and 90% of those who graduate pass the national accounting examination and become accountants. She would like to know what her chances are of becoming an accountant if she pursues the accounting major.

To answer this question, draw a tree diagram with branches that represent the ''path'' for success in accounting.

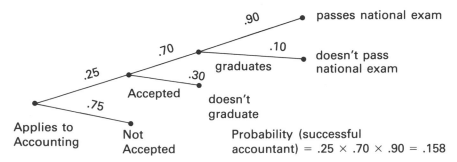

From the diagram, you can see that the probability of becoming a successful accountant is equal to .25 × .70 × .90, which is .158. At this point, Edith should consider other options. For example, she could consider applying to both the accounting major and to the education major. She could recalculate her chances for success in one of these majors, both of these majors (if this is a possible option for her), and neither of these majors.

This example assumes that we have no additional information on which to base Edith's chances of success. Suppose, instead, that we know that Edith has excellent math skills. Shouldn't this sort of information change the probabilities involved and make it more likely that Edith be admitted, graduate, and succeed in a math-related occupation? Intuitively, the answer is ''yes.'' Let's see how the problem changes by considering José's probability for success in the following example.

Combining Information to Make Predictions

José has always wanted to be an actor. Accordingly, he plans to sell his worldly possessions and head for a career in the ''Big Apple'' (the loving nickname for New York). Suppose that you and José both know that only about 4% of all actors ever ''make it'' professionally in New York. This value is the base rate; it is based on information that is known before we have any specific information about José. José tells you not to worry, because 75% of those who are successful have curly hair and can sing and tell jokes well. Because he has curly hair, is a good singer, and a hilarious comedian, he feels confident that he will soon be sending 8×10 glossy pictures of himself to his fan club members. This second value is called the conditional or secondary or posterior rate; it is the probability value that relates specific information about characteristics that are associated with José and with an outcome. We'll use these two probability values to decide if José's optimism is warranted. Exactly how likely is he to succeed? Before you continue, make a probability estimate for his chance of success. Remember, probabilities range from 0 to 1, with 0 meaning he will definitely fail and have to return to Peoria, and 1 meaning he will definitely succeed on Broadway. Stop now and make a subjective probability judgment of his chance for success.

Can you think of a way of objectively finding his chance of success? In order to arrive at an objective probability, you'll need to know the percentage of those who fail and have curly hair, can sing, and tell jokes. Few people realize that they need to consider this value in assessing the probability of success. For ease of reference, I call the attributes that are associated with success (curly hair, ability to sing and tell jokes) "curly hair," and the absence of these attributes I call "not curly hair." Suppose that 50% of those who fail have these attributes. Once again, tree diagrams can be used to determine probabilities in this context. Let's begin at a starting point and consider all possible outcomes. In this case, he will either succeed or fail, so we'll label the first branches "succeed" and "fail." As before, we'll put the probability of each event along the appropriate branch:

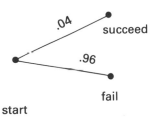

Notice that these two probabilities (.04 and .96) sum to 1.0, because they include all possibilities. One of these two possibilities must occur, so they will add up to 1.0 to indicate absolute certainty.

José knows that 75% of those who succeed have curly hair. What we are trying to find in this example is the probability of a certain outcome (success) *given that* we already have information that is relevant to the probability of that outcome. The phrase "given that" is indicated with a vertical bar (|). Let's add a second branch to the tree diagram, branching off from the succeed node and the fail node. There are four different probabilities involved in this example: the probability of succeeding given that a person has curly hair, the probability of succeeding given that a person does not have curly hair, the probability of failing given that a person has curly hair, and the probability of failing given that a person does not have curly hair. These four possibilities are shown in the next tree diagram:

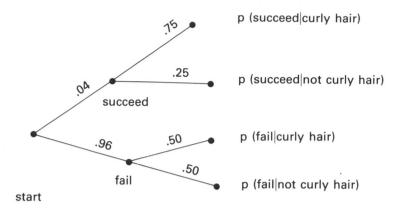

Note that 75% (.75) of those who succeed have curly hair, and 25% (.25) do not have this attribute, because one of these two attributes must occur. Similarly, 50% of those who fail have curly hair, and 50% of those who fail do not possess this attribute. Because we are considering everyone who fails, these values must also sum to 1.0.

Once the tree diagram is drawn, it is a simple matter to compute José's objective probability of success. As before, multiply along each branch to find the probabilities. In this case, we would multiply the values along each branch of the tree diagram and compile the information in a chart:

P[Succeed|Curly Hair]   = .04 × .75 =   .03
P[Succeed|Not Curly Hair]   = .04 × .25 =   .01
P[Fail|Curly Hair]   = .96 × .50 =   .48
P[Fail|Not Curly Hair]   = .96 × .50 = ____.48
                                            1.0000

To determine José's true chance of success, we need to divide the proportion who succeed and have curly hair by the total proportion who have curly hair. The reason we want to do this is so that we can find the proportion of all people who have curly hair and who are successful. We are trying to *predict* José's success, based on the knowledge that he has curly hair and that some proportion of all people with curly hair are successful. We are combining two different pieces of information; the success base rate that applies to everyone, regardless of whether or not they have curly hair, and the success rate for people with curly hair. The real question is: Given that José has curly hair, how likely is he to succeed?

$$\frac{\text{Proportion who succeed}|\text{curly hair}}{\text{Total proportion of people with curly hair}} = \frac{.03}{.03 + .48} \approx .06$$

Thus, José's chances for success are only slightly better (6% versus 4%) than they are for any unknown, aspiring actor. Knowing that he has certain attributes that are associated with success improved his probability of success above the base rate, but the improvement was very small.

Are you surprised to find that his chance of success is so low, given that the posterior or secondary probability value was so high (75%)? Most people are. The reason that José has such a slim chance of becoming an actor is because so few people, in general, succeed. The probability value José obtained was close to the a priori, or base rate, of success among all aspiring actors. Because so few actors, in general, succeed, José, and any other would-be thespian, has a low chance for success. Research has shown that, in general, most people overestimate success when base rates are low and underestimate success when base rates are high. In the earlier example concerning Edith, we had only base-rate information to use in predicting success. By contrast, we had additional information about José that allowed us to improve on the base rate when predicting his success, although because of the low rate of success for actors in general, the improvement was slight.

For those of you who prefer to think spatially, think about a large group of people, 4% of whom are successful actors and 96% are not. This group is shown in Fig. 7.4. Four percent of the people depicted are smiling—these represent the successful actors. If you had no other information to use to predict success for José, you would use this base-rate information and give him a 4% probability for success.

Now let's consider the additional information. Seventy-five percent of those who are successful have curly hair, whereas 50% of those who are not successful have curly hair. This information is combined with the base-rate information. It is depicted in Fig. 7.5 with the addition of curly hair to the successful and unsuccessful actors.

By examining these figures, it should be easy to see that what we are doing mathematically is finding the proportion of smiling faces with curly hair relative to all of the faces with curly hair in order to use this information about José to predict his success.

Let's briefly try another example of making predictions by combining information. Suppose that 1% of all children become juvenile delinquents. Two sociologists have developed a test that can predict who will become a juvenile delinquent. It correctly predicts delinquency for 80% of all delinquents. Unfortunately, your daughter has been identified by her score on this test as a future juvenile delinquent. What is the probability that this prediction is correct? Because we are interested in predicting one variable (delinquency), using our knowledge of a second variable (test score), this problem is similar to José's problem. As before, you'll need to know the probability that the test will incorrectly predict delinquency. Let's say that it is 10%.

Please stop now and work this problem before going on.

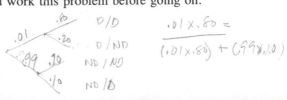

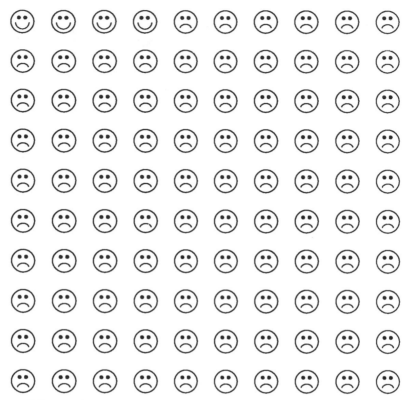

FIG. 7.4. Pictorial representation of a 4% success rate. Note that 4% of the faces are smiling.

Your answer should look like this:

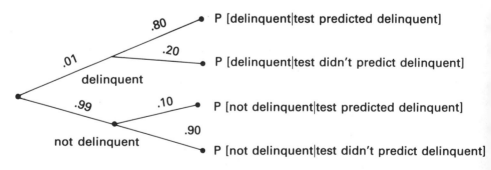

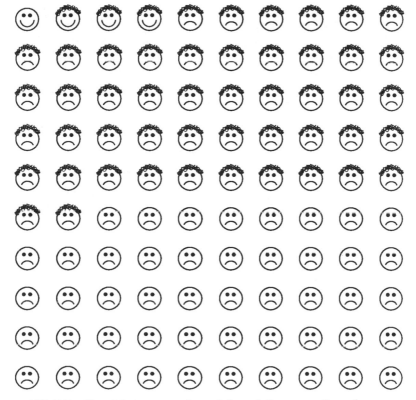

FIG. 7.5. Pictorial representation of the relative proportion of successful and unsuccessful actors who have the same attributes as José. These are depicted by the addition of curly hair.

We'll need to compute the probabilities in each branch:

P[delinquent|test predicted delinquent]   = .01 × .80 = .008

P[delinquent|test didn't predict delinquent] = .01 × .20 = .002

P[not delinquent|test predicted delinquent]   = .99 × .10 = .099

P[not delinquent|test didn't predict delinquent] .99 × .90 = .891
                                                        1.000

As before, we'll need to form the appropriate ratio:

proportion [delinquent|test predicted delinquent] =   .008
total proportion test predicted delinquent   = .008 + .099

                    = .008/.107 = .07

That is, this test will correctly predict future delinquents about 7% of the time. The other 93% of the time that the test predicts that a child will become a juvenile delinquent, it will be wrong! Because of the low base rate for juvenile delinquency and because of the more than negligible probability of an inaccurate prediction of delinquency in nondelinquents, a test like this one is of little value. Knowing that your daughter tested as a future delinquent made it more likely that she would become delinquent than not knowing this, but the probability that she becomes a delinquent is still fairly close to the base rate of .01.

To review, when you are calculating the probability of an outcome, given that you have information that is relevant to its probability, you will:

1. Draw a complete tree diagram, with the base-rate information (e.g., succeed or fail or become delinquent or not become delinquent) as the first set of nodes. Use the conditional information (the "given that" information) to draw the second set of nodes.

2. Make a chart with all combinations of the base-rate information and conditional information as the rows in the chart.

3. Multiply probabilities across each of the branches of the tree diagram, and fill in each row of the chart with these values.

4. Form a ratio (fraction) with the probability value from the branch that you are interested in (e.g., succeed given that he has curly hair or becomes delinquent given that the test predicted delinquent) as the numerator and the sum of this value and the other branch that contains the same conditional statement (e.g., fail given that he has curly hair or not become delinquent given that the test predicted delinquent).

5. Check your answer. Is the final probability value greater than the base rate value? It should be, because you have improved in your ability to make predictions with the conditional information, although the improvement will often be quite small.

There are many diseases that occur with low base rates in the population. Medical test results must be interpreted in light of the relevant base rates for each disease. Medicine, like most other disciplines, is a probabilistic science, yet few physicians receive training in understanding probabilities. Failure to utilize base-rate information can lead to improper diagnoses. Base-rate neglect is a pervasive error in thinking about probabilistic outcomes. Consider Dreman's (1979) summary of a large body of research on this effect:

> The tendency to underestimate or altogether ignore past probabilities in making a decision is undoubtedly the most significant problem of intuitive predictions in fields as diverse as financial analysis, accounting, geography, engineering, and military intelligence. The implications of such consistent errors and cognitive biases are enormous, not only in economics, management, and investments, but in virtually every area where such decision-making comes into play (cited in Myers, 1986, p. 278).

Nonregressive Judgments

Harris is a new student at Rah-Rah State University. The average grade point average (GPA) for all students at Rah-Rah is 2.8. Harris is new to this college and has not yet taken any exams. Although we have no information about Harris specifically, what would be your best guess that his grade point average will be? *2.8*

After his first set of midterm exams, Harris has a midterm GPA of 3.8. Given this new information, what would you now predict for Harris' GPA at the end of the school year? Most people readily answer the first question with 2.8, the *3.3* average GPA for all students at Rah-Rah. This is a correct answer, as in the absence of any specific information, the average for all students, the population at Rah-Rah, is the best estimate for anyone.

Most people answer the second question with 3.8. Unfortunately, this is not the best answer. Although it is true that someone who scores high on midterms will also tend to score high on finals, the relationship is not a one-to-one or perfect relationship. In general, when someone scores extremely high on some scale, she or he will score closer to the average the second time. Thus, the best prediction for Harris' GPA at the end of the school year will be less than 3.8 and greater than 2.8. (The actual value can be mathematically determined, but the calculations are beyond the scope of this book.) This is a difficult concept to understand, because most people find it to be counterintuitive. Yet, it is true.

It may be useful to think about a sports example. Consider your favorite athletes. Although they may have a truly exceptional performance one day, most often they will perform closer to average, but still above average on other days. After all, no one bowls all perfect games or bats 1.000. Sports enthusiasts will recognize this principle as the ''sophomore slump.'' After an outstanding first *authors* year at a sport, the star will usually perform closer to average during his or her *1st novel-* second year. Another example that may help to clarify the concept is an often- *excellent.* used one about fathers' and sons' heights. In general, very tall fathers will have sons that are closer to average height (although still above average) than the fathers are. This phenomenon is called **regression toward the mean.** (Mean is just another term for average—it is computed by adding up all the values you're interested in and dividing by the number of values.)

Earlier in this chapter, I talked about the laws of chance. No one can predict accurately the height of any particular individual. But, in the long run, that is with many, many extremely tall fathers, most of their son's heights will show regression toward the mean. Thus, as before, we can make better predictions by knowing about the laws of chance, but we won't always be accurate. It is important to understand this concept whenever dealing with probabilistic events.

Kahneman and Tversky (1973) studied what can happen when regression toward the mean is not understood by professionals. Israeli flight instructors were told that they should praise their students when they successfully performed difficult flight patterns and maneuvers and that they should criticize exceptionally poor performance. Based on what you've just learned about regression toward the mean, what, in general, should happen after a pilot performs extremely well? Subsequent maneuvers should be closer to average, or less than exceptional, because the performance moved or regressed toward the mean (average). Conversely, what should you expect to happen following very poor performance? Again, subsequent maneuvers should tend to be more average, or in this case, they would improve, although they may still be less than average. The Israeli flight instructors did not understand regression toward the mean and erroneously concluded that praise led to poorer performance and criticism improved it.

Desirability of Outcome

Suppose that you are waiting to find out if you've been accepted to law school. Do you think that the fact that you really want to be the next Perry Mason or Arnie Becker will influence how you assess your probability of acceptance?

For most people, the desirability of an outcome will influence its judged probability. In general, the true probability of an event will be overestimated if it is desirable and underestimated if it is undesirable. In experimental demonstrations of this effect, Morlock (1967) found that subjects required less information to decide that evidence was favorable to them than to decide that it was unfavorable. Halpern and Irwin (1973) found that college students would begin a problem-solving task by testing hypotheses that, if true, would earn them financial payoffs instead of testing alternative hypotheses that, if true, would cost them money. Furthermore, they would continue to look for evidence to support desirable hypotheses even when they were given information that clearly showed that these hypotheses were wrong. Nisbett and Ross (1980) have called the belief that the desired outcome is correct even after receiving evidence to the contrary the **perseverance phenomenon.** People tend to persevere in their optimistic prediction that events that are favorable to them are more likely to occur than is warranted. This phenomenon was mentioned in several other places in this chapter. The failure to purchase flood insurance in high-probability flood areas and the willingness to spend money for extremely low probability lottery tickets are other examples of the belief that desirable events are more likely to occur and undesirable ones are less likely to occur. Evidence of this effect can be found in the thinking of some of our most respected scientists. In a large-scale study of NASA scientists, Mitroff (1974) found that many research scientists continued to believe that their hypotheses about outer space were correct, despite accumulating evidence that supported a rival hypothesis.

STATISTICAL ABUSE

There are three kinds of lies: lies, damned lies, and statistics.
—Disraeli

When we want to find out something about a group of people, it is often impossible or inconvenient to ask everyone in the group. Suppose you want to know if people who donate blood to the Red Cross are, in general, kind and generous people. Because you can't examine everyone who donates blood to determine how kind and considerate she or he is, you would examine a portion of the population, which is called a **sample.** A number calculated on a sample of people is called a **statistic.** ("Statistics" is also the branch of mathematics that utilizes probability theory to make decisions about populations.)

Statistics are found everywhere, from baseball earned run averages to the number of war casualties. Many people are rightfully suspicious of statistics. A small book by Huff (1954) humorously illustrates many of the possible pitfalls of statistics. The book is entitled *How to Lie With Statistics.* In it, he rhymed the following message: "Like the 'little dash of powder, little pot of paint,' statistics are making many an important fact look like what she ain't" (p. 9).

On the Average

What does it mean to say that the average American family has 2.1 children? This number was computed by finding a sample of American families, adding up the number of children they have, and dividing by the total number of families in the sample. This number could provide an accurate picture of American families, as most may have about two children, with some having more and others less, or it could be very misleading. It is possible that half of the families had no children and half had four or more children, thus misleading the reader into believing that most families had "about" two children, when in fact none did. This is like the man who had his head in the oven and feet in the freezer and reported that, on the average, he was quite comfortable. It is also possible that the sample used to calculate this statistic was not representative of the population—in this case, all American families. If the sample consisted of college students or residents in Manhattan, the number obtained would be too low. On the other hand, if the sample was taken in rural farm areas, the number obtained may be too high. When samples are not representative of the population, they are called **biased samples.** The statistics calculated on biased samples will not yield accurate information about the population.

Averages can also be misleading, because there are three different kinds of averages. Consider Mrs. Wang's five children. The oldest is a successful corporate executive. She earns $200,000 a year. The second is a teacher who earns $25,000 a year. Child 3 is a waiter who earns $15,000 a year. The other two are starving artists, each earning $5,000 a year. If Mrs. Wang wants to brag about how well her children turned out, she could compute an arithmetic average, which is called the **mean.** The mean is what most people have in mind when they think about averages. It is the sum of all of the values divided by the total number of values. The mean income for Mrs. Wang's children is $250000/5 = $50,000. Certainly, anyone who is told this figure would conclude that Mrs. Wang has very successful and wealthy children.

The reason that the mean income for Mrs. Wang's children was so high is because there is one extreme score that inflated this type of average. Averages are also called **measures of central tendency.** A second kind of measure of central tendency is the **median.** It is not affected by a few extreme scores. To compute the median, the values are lined up in ascending or descending order. The middle value is the median. For Mrs. Wang's children, this would be:

$5,000; $5,000; $15,000; $25,000; $200,000.

The middle value, or median, is the third value of $15,000. Thus, she could also claim that her children earn, on the average, $15,000. (When there is an even number of values, the median is equal to the mean of the middle two values.)

A third type of average, or measure of central tendency, is the **mode.** The word "mode" comes from the French meaning fashionable. It is really the most fashionable value. Mathematically, it is the number that occurs most often. Because two of Mrs. Wang's children earn $5,000, this is the modal income for her children. When there are no values that occur more than once, there is no mode. There also may be two or more modes.

Mrs. Wang can honestly claim that her children earn, on the average, $50,000 or $15,000 or $5,000. The point of this discussion is that you should be wary of average figures. To understand them, you need to know whether the average is a mean, a median, or a mode as well as something about the variability of the data.

Precision

Suppose I tell you that a scientific survey was conducted on the length of workdays for office workers. Furthermore, this study found that the mean work day is 8.167 hours long. Does this sound impressive and scientific? What if I told you that most office workers work about 8 hours a day? Most of you would say, "I know that. Why did they bother?" The point is that we are often impressed with precise statistics, even when the precision is unwarranted.

Let me give you an example from a prestigious weekly news magazine. It is important that the magazine readers accept the articles as truthful and authoritative. A few years ago, a news magazine ran an article about the health hazards associated with dog droppings in New York City. To give the reader an idea of the magnitude of the problem, they presented the daily weight of New York City dog droppings, accurate to two decimal places. I have no idea how they arrived at that figure, nor do I even want to think about how they collected their data. I do know that they could not measure it that accurately. Of course, the impression that is created with such precise statistics is that the news magazine is a carefully researched journal that can be trusted for the information it provides.

A more humorous example of overprecision comes from one of America's most famous authors, Mark Twain. He once reported that the Mississippi River was 100 million and 3 years old. It seems that 3 years earlier, he had learned that it was 100 million years old.

Significant Difference

If you wanted to know the mean height of all women, you could select a sample of 100 women, measure their height, and compute the mean. Suppose you took another sample of one hundred women and computed their mean height. Would you expect the means of these two samples to be exactly the same? No, of course not, because there could be expected to be small differences or fluctuations between these values. Each value was computed on different women, and each will yield a slightly different mean value.

If someone measured a sample of women who belong to sororities and found that their mean height is 5′5″ and then measured women who don't belong to sororities and found their mean height to be 5′4½″, would you conclude that sorority sisters are taller than nonsorority women? I hope not, because small differences between groups can be expected to occur just by chance, especially when the **sample size,** or number of people in the sample, is small. There are statistical procedures to determine if a difference computed on two or more samples is likely to have happened by chance. If it is very unlikely to be a chance occurrence, it is called a **significant difference.**

The question of whether a change is meaningful also applies to populations. If your college enrollment went from 15,862 to 15,879, would the administrators be justified in concluding that the increase in enrollment is meaningful? The answer to this question depends on many other variables. If the enrollment figure has been edging up slowly every year for the last 5 years, then these figures may represent a slight, but steady, trend. On the other hand, the relatively small increase could be due to chance fluctuations and may not represent a meaningful trend. Because of chance factors, it could have just as easily gone down. Similarly, a change in the unemployment rate from 10% to 9.9% may be nothing more than random fluctuation, or it may be signaling the end of an economic quagmire. You can expect that Democrats and Republicans would interpret these figures differently, depending on who is in office at the time.

Extrapolation

Extrapolation occurs when a value is estimated by extending some known values. If the number of psychology majors over the last 5 years at Podunck University was approximately 150, 175, 200, 225, and 250, respectively, then most people would feel comfortable about the prediction that the number of psychology majors next year will be approximately 275.

Extrapolation can be wrong, and sometimes even ridiculous. An example of the latter was proved by Fischer (1970). The Census Bureau estimated that the size of the average American family increased from 3.54 to 3.65 in the decade between 1950 and 1960. If we assumed that family sizes would continue to increase at the same rate, then we would find that the average American family in the year 2070 would have 228.52 persons! This is, of course, an inconceivable idea! This is like saying that if the times for the 100-meter dash keep decreasing, eventually someone will run it in zero seconds.

The Psychic Fallacy

Have you ever wondered how psychics are able to predict future events? The answer does not lie in their secret mystical abilities, but in the laws of probability. The notion that some people can predict the future is sometimes called the **Psychic Fallacy.** Numerous popular self-proclaimed psychics make annual predictions about events that they believe will occur. In a study of the new year's predictions published in the *National Enquirer* between 1978 and 1984, the psychics' predictions were accurate 2% of the time (Strentz, 1984). None predicted significant unusual events, like the fact that a woman would run for the vice presidency of the United States. Furthermore, most of the accurate predictions were not very surprising (e.g., a famous rock star will get divorced), and some, like Pee Wee Herman running for president, were way off base.

Next time you are reading about a psychic, take a good look at the type of predictions being made. You'll find that most are quite vague (e.g., some economic decline). Just by chance, some of the numerous predictions will be true. When psychics talk about their successes, they "forget" their failures and boast about a correct prediction. Remember the "or" rule that was presented earlier. If you want to determine the probability of Prediction #1 *or* Prediction #2 *or* Prediction #3 being correct, you would add the individual probability values. If I, or some psychic, made numerous predictions, the likelihood that any one of them would be correct will increase with the number of predictions made. Thus, if you want to impress your friends with your psychic ability, make many vague predictions.

APPLYING THE FRAMEWORK

Let's consider the steps in applying the general framework for thinking to understanding and using probabilities.

1. *What is the goal?* Whenever you are making decisions about uncertain events, you will need to consider the skills developed in this chapter. This is particularly true when-

ever you are given probability values or when degrees of belief are presented or implied.

2. *What is known?* In setting up the problem, you need to know if the probability values you are being given were derived objectively or subjectively. You need to look for ways that these values could be biased. Has the desirability of an outcome influenced the probability values assigned to it? Although the topic of considering the credibility of a source of information was presented in chapter 5, it is also relevant in this context. Before you begin the process of using probabilities, you need to assess the quality of the information that you have. Because we frequently persuade others with probability values, you need to consider how the numbers that are being presented relate to the argument that is being offered.

When determining what is known, look for information that can be used in computing probability estimates. For example, if a probability of a risk is given, is it per year, per exposure (e.g., x-ray), or per lifetime? Are relative or absolute frequencies being given, and which is more meaningful for your purposes? Is there additional information available that can be combined with base rates so that a more accurate prediction can be made?

3. *Which thinking skill or skills will get you to your goal?* Numerous thinking skills have been presented for use when working with probabilistic events. One of the most useful is drawing a tree diagram, complete with probability values on each branch. This method allows you to "see" and objectively compute the likelihood of multiple outcomes. When you are combining information with base-rate information, it is important to form the appropriate ratios so as to avoid the problem of base-rate neglect. Other skills require recognition of the type of error that frequently occurs (e.g., conjunction error, failure to consider cumulative risks) and use of the "or" and "and" rules to improve probabilistic decision making.

Because there are so few things in life that are known with certainty, the skills for understanding and using probabilities should be used frequently. After reading this chapter, you should be able to:

- compute expected values in situations with known probabilities
- understand the difference between frequency and relative frequency and know which value is needed in a given situation
- recognize when regression to the mean is operating and adjust predictions to take this phenomenon into account
- use the "and" rule to avoid conjunction errors
- use the "or" rule to calculate cumulative probabilities
- recognize and avoid gambler's fallacy
- utilize base rates when making predictions
- use tree diagrams as a decision-making aid in probabilistic situations
- adjust risk assessments to account for the cumulative nature of probabilistic events
- understand the differences among mean, median, and mode
- avoid overconfidence in uncertain situations
- understand the limits of extrapolation
- use probability judgments to improve decision making

4. *Have you reached your goal?* The reason for considering probabilities is to quantify and reduce uncertainty. You will have reached your goal when you can attach more accurate probability values to uncertain events.

CHAPTER SUMMARY

1. Because few things are know with certainty, probability plays a crucial role in many aspects of our lives.

2. Probability is defined as the number of ways a particular outcome (what we call a success) can occur divided by the number of possible outcomes. It is also used to indicate degrees of belief in the likelihood of events with unknown frequencies and previous frequency of occurrence.

3. In general, people tend to be more confident about uncertain events than the objective probability values allow.

4. Mathematically equivalent changes in the way probability information is presented can lead to dramatic changes in the way it is interpreted.

5. Tree diagrams can be used to compute probabilities when there are multiple events (e.g., two or more flips of a coin). When the events are independent, the probability of any combination of outcomes can be determined by multiplying the probability values along the tree "branches."

6. Expected values can be computed that will take into account the probabilities and values associated with a loss and a win in betting situations.

7. Subjective probabilities are our personal estimates of how often events with unknown frequencies will occur. These values are distorted systematically when people believe that they have some control over probabilistic events.

8. Most people fail to consider the cumulative nature of the likelihood of risky events.

9. A common probability error is the confusion of frequency with relative frequency. You need to consider the number of people in the population at the time the statistic was computed in order to make meaningful comparison about two statistics collected at different times.

10. People judge events that are dramatic and more publicized to be more likely than events that are less dramatic or less well known. In general, people overestimate frequent events and underestimate infrequent ones.

11. There is a tendency to ignore base-rate information, especially when making predictions that involve combining information.

12. Few people realize that if a person scores extremely high or low on one measure, she or he will tend to score closer to average on the second measure.

13. If an outcome is desirable, we are more likely to believe that it will occur than if it is undesirable.

14. There are three measures of central tendency—the mean, median, and mode. Each is computed with a different mathematical formula.

15. Many people erroneously believe that statistics that are expressed in precise numbers (e.g., many decimal places) are highly credible.

16. Extrapolation occurs when a value is estimated by extending a trend from known values.

Terms to Know

Check your understanding of the concepts presented in this chapter by reviewing their definitions. If you find that you're having difficulty with any term, be sure to reread the section where it is discussed.

Probability. The number of ways a particular event can occur divided by the number of possible outcomes. It is a measure of how often we expect an event to occur in the long run. The term is also used to express degrees of belief and previous frequency of occurrence.

In the Long Run. Refers to the need for numerous trials in order to derive estimates of the proportion of outcomes that will be a "success."

Laws of Chance (or Probability). The ability to predict the number or percentage of trials on which a particular outcome will occur.

Overconfidence Phenomenon. The tendency for people to be more confident in their judgments of probability than the objective probability values allow.

Odds. A mathematical method for indicating probability that is commonly used in sporting events.

Multiple Outcomes. Refers to the probability of an event occurring in two or more trials.

Tree Diagrams. Branching diagrams that may be used to compute probabilities by considering all possible outcomes in a sequence of events.

Independent Events. Two or more events are independent when the occurrence of one event does not affect the occurrence of the other events.

Cumulative Probabilities. The probability of an event occurring over many trials.

Conjunctive Error. Mistaken belief that the co-occurrence of two or more events is more likely than the occurrence of one of the events.

Expected Value. The amount of money you would expect to win in the long run in a betting situation. The mathematical formula for determining expected values is the probability of winning times the value of winning plus the probability of losing times the value of losing.

Subjective Probability. Personal estimates of the probability or likelihood of uncertain events.

Objective Probability. Mathematically determined statements about the likelihood of events with known frequencies.

Gambler's Fallacy. The mistaken belief that chance events are self-correcting. Many people believe that if a random event has not occurred recently, it becomes more likely.

Relative Frequency. How often an event occurs relative to the size of the population of events at the time of its occurrence.

Base Rate. Initial or a priori probability that an event will occur.

Base-Rate Neglect. Pervasive bias to ignore or underestimate the effect of initial probabilities (base rates) and to emphasis secondary probability values when deciding on the likelihood of an outcome.

Regression Toward the Mean. In general, when someone scores extremely high or low on some measure, she or he will tend to score closer toward the mean (average) on a second measurement.

Perseverance Phenomenon. The tendency to persist in optimistic predictions that favorable events are more likely to occur than unfavorable ones.

Sample. A subset of a population that is studied in order to make inferences about the population.

Statistic. A number that has been calculated on a sample. (In its plural form, it is the branch of mathematics that is concerned with probabilities and mathematical characteristics of distribution of numbers.)

Biased Sample. A sample that is not representative of the population from which it was drawn.

Measures of Central Tendency. Numbers calculated on samples or populations that give a single-number summary of all of the values. Three measures of central tendency are the mean, median, and mode.

Mean. A measure of central tendency that is calculated by taking the sum of all the values divided by the total number of values.

Median. A measure of central tendency that is calculated by finding the middle value in a set of scores.

Mode. A measure of central tendency that is calculated by finding the most frequent value in a set of scores.

Sample Size. The number of people selected for a study.

Significant Difference. A difference between two groups or observations that is so large that it probably didn't occur by chance.

Extrapolation. The estimation of a value from a trend suggested by known values.

Psychic Fallacy. Belief that psychics can predict the future. Successful predictions can be explained with the laws of chance.

Chapter Questions

Be sure that you can answer the following questions:

1. How certain can we be about the occurrence of an event if its probability is 0? .2? .5? .9? 1.0?

2. Explain how Al Hibbs was able to "beat the house" at roulette.

3. What is the logic of tree diagrams?

4. What principle explains why the probability of any 2 people in a group of 40 sharing a common birthday is as high as .90?

5. Explain Gambler's Fallacy. What is fallacious about it? Ask your friends what they

would expect on the next flip of a fair coin that had landed "heads up" on the last five flips.

6. When people were asked to judge the frequency of lethal events, what kinds of errors did they make?

7. If a disease is very rare (i.e., it has a very low base rate), how optimistic can we be about devising a test that will detect it? Why?

8. If a student gets the highest grade in his or her class on a psychology exam, what grade would you predict that he or she will get on the final? What is the name of the principle you used to make this prediction?

9. Explain why the Israeli flight instructors believed that praise led to poorer performance and criticism improved performance. What is a better explanation of these results?

10. How can confusing frequency with relative frequency lead to erroneous conclusions?

11. How does the desirability of an event influence our estimates of its probability?

12. Give two examples of situations in which tree diagrams can be used as decision-making aids.

13. Demonstrations of ESP depend on statistical notions of probability. Explain the position taken in this chapter that unusual results are bound to occur sometimes just by chance and do not necessarily support an ESP interpretation.

14. How are conjunctive errors evidence that many people don't understand the reasoning behind the "and" rule?

Exercises

Apply what you've learned about probability to answer the following problems:

1. If each of the letters in the word "PROBABILITY" was thrown separately into a hat and one letter is drawn from the hat, what is the probability that it is a vowel?

2. Your friend is willing to give you 5 : 2 odds that the Phillies will beat the Dodgers. Convert these odds to a probability value.

3. What is the probability of drawing a picture card (jack, queen, or king) from a full deck of cards? What is the probability of drawing two aces in a row from a full deck (without replacement)?

4. In a party game called "Spin the Bottle," the players form a circle with a bottle at the center. A spinner spins the bottle and then kisses the person to whom it points. Although five people are playing, the bottle has pointed to Marlene on each of its three spins. What is the probability of this occurring by chance?

5. Professor Aardvark gives such difficult exams that students can only guess at the answers. What is the probability of getting all five questions on his true/false test correct by guessing? What is the probability of getting all five wrong?

6. Rubinstein and Pfeiffer (1980) have suggested that, instead of reporting weather forecasts in terms of the probability of rain, a more useful index would be the Expected

Value (EV) of rain. Suppose the weather forecaster knows that there is a 30% probability of 5 inches of rain and a 70% probability of no rain on a given day. What is the EV for rain?

7. Comment on the following: Today, over 47 million homes have air conditioning, whereas only 23 million homes had air conditioning a decade ago. What additional information would you need to know to determine if people are more likely to have air conditioning today?

8. In one survey, 10 out of 12 people preferred the taste of Crunchies corn cereal to that of Munchies, Flakies, or Hefties. Another survey found that 6 out of 7 people preferred the new, improved taste of Crackles to that of Munchies, Flakies, or Hefties. Both Crunchies and Crackles will soon be available in supermarkets. Which cereal is more likely to be preferred by the cereal-eating public?

9. Officials at the suicide prevention center know that 2% of all people who phone their hotline actually attempt suicide. A psychologist has devised a test that can identify 80% of all future suicides. Unfortunately, this test incorrectly predicts that 5% of those who don't commit suicide will. If you get a positive identification from a caller on this test, what is the probability that he or she would actually attempt suicide?

10. Suppose that your friend belongs to two "singles" clubs. The Suaves have 500 members; 60% of them are good dancers, and 40% of them can't dance. The other club, the Chics, have only 100 members; 95% of them are good dancers and 5% can't dance. You saw her at a party with a terrific dancer. Was he more likely a Suave or a Chic? (In answering this question, first determine that the probability that he is a Suave, and then compare this value to the probability that he is a Chic to decide which is more likely.)

11. Every student in Mr. Weasel's class kept a record of the number of books read over a 3-month period. The data are: 15, 5, 8, 12, 1, 3, 1, 7, 21, 4. Compute the mean, median, and mode for these numbers. Which one seems best?

12. Moishe is deciding between applying to graduate school and applying to medical school. He knows that 70% of graduate school applicants get admitted. Of that number, 90% graduate, and among graduates, 50% earn above $75,000. Medical school, on the other hand, only accepts 40% of all applicants. Of these applicants, 90% graduate, and of these graduates, 90% earn above $75,000. Moishe wants to be successful and rich. Is he more likely to achieve these goals if he applies to graduate school or medical school? What is the probability if he applies to both medical school and graduate school?

13. Abby scored very low on her SAT's. Her score of 450 is well below the mean of 800. If she retakes the test, which of the following is most likely to occur, and why did you pick that answer?
a. She will probably score below 450.
b. She will probably score close to 450.
c. She will probably score between 450 and 800.
d. She will probably score near 800.
e. She will probably score above 800.

14. There is a "morning-after" pill available for contraception that has a one-time failure rate of 1.5%. Explain why the failure rate for 1 year would be 18%, assuming that it was needed and used once a month for 1 year. Why is the "or" rule used to determine this value?

SUGGESTED READINGS

The classic in the misuse of probability and statistics is Huff's *How to Lie with Statistics* (1954). You'll find this small paperback both entertaining and instructive. Two other books on this topic that also maintain an informal style are Campbell's (1974) *Flaws and Fallacies in Statistic Thinking* and Kimble's (1978) *How to Use (and Misuse) Statistics*.

A psychological approach to expected values can be found in Slovic and Lichtenstein's (1968) article, "Relative Importance of Probabilities and Payoff's in Risk Taking." This article is somewhat more advanced than the usual textbook coverage of these topics. Rubinstein and Pfeiffer's (1980) excellent text, *Concepts in Problem Solving,* contains an easy-to-read section on computing probabilities using tree diagrams and expected values.

If you're interested in chance and are lucky, or even if you're not, you'll probably enjoy Gunther's (1977) *The Luck Factor.* This is an enjoyable book, filled with vignettes about randomness, probability, and people's notions about them. Alcock's (1981) *Parapsychology: Science or Magic?* reviews probability interpretations of ESP, as does an interesting article by Ayer (1965), entitled "Chance."

The psychologist who is most noted for his research on the distinction between frequency and relative frequency data is Estes. A somewhat advanced treatment of this topic appears in his journal article (1976), "The Cognitive Side of Probability Learning." If you found the section on the ways people judge the frequency of lethal events interesting, you'll enjoy reading *Acceptable Risk* by Fischhoff, Lichtenstein, Slovic, Derby, and Keeney (1981). In their book, the authors have described the variables that people consider when deciding whether the risk associated with an event (e.g., X-rays, nuclear accident, motorcycle riding) is low enough to be considered acceptable.

Summaries of the literature on subjective probabilities can be found in the following five sources: Tversky and Kahneman's (1974) article, "Judgment Under Uncertainty: Heuristics and Biases"; Tversky and Kahneman's (1983) article, "Extensional versus Intuitive Reasoning: The Conjunction Fallacy in Probability Judgment"; Hogarth's (1988) *Judgment and Choice: The Psychology of Decision (2nd ed.)*; Dawes' (1988) *Rational Choice in an Uncertain World,* and Nisbett and Ross' (1980) *Human Inferences: Strategies and Shortcomings of Social Judgment.* The Nisbett and Ross work interprets much of the literature on subjective probability in a social psychology framework. A diverse collection of papers on probability (some of them are advanced readings) can be found in Kyburg and Smoker's (1980) *Studies in Subjective Probability.* An excellent collection of papers on real-world applications of these principles appears in an edited book by Arkes and Hammond (1986), *Judgment and Decision Making: An Interdisciplinary Reader.* Also recommended is Brehmer, Jungermann, Lourens, and Sevon's (1986) book, entitled *New Directions in Research on Decision Making.*

9.

$P(A/TC) .02 \times .80 = .016$

$P(A(IC) .02 \times .20 = .004$

$P(NC/TI) = .98 \times .05 = .49$

$P(NS/TC) = .98 \times .95 = .95$

305

8 Decision Making

Contents

Six doctors in white hospital coats approach your bed. No one is smiling. The results of the biopsy are in. One doctor explains that the cells were irregular in shape; they appeared abnormal. It seems that the tumor was not clearly malignant, but not clearly normal either. They probably removed the entire tumor. It's hard to be certain about these things. You have some choices. You could leave the hospital this afternoon and forget about this unpleasant episode, except for semiannual checkups. There is an above-average chance, however, that some abnormal cells remain and will spread and grow. On the other hand, you could choose to have the entire area surgically removed. While this would be major surgery, it would clearly reduce the risk of cancer.

How do you decide what to do? Your first response is probably to ask the doctors what they recommend. But if you do, it's likely that you won't receive a consensus of opinion. Often, physicians disagree about the best way to treat a disease, especially a controversial one like cancer. It is possible that some will believe that the risk of cancer is small enough to warrant the wait-and-see decision, whereas others believe that immediate surgery is the best decision. Ultimately, the decision is yours.

Of course, not all decisions are a matter of life and death. We are constantly making minor decisions without much thought, such as what to wear, what to eat for breakfast, which pen to buy, and when to go to sleep. Everyone is faced with a lifetime of decisions, and some of them have major and far-reaching consequences. In this chapter, we are concerned with life's major decisions. Major decisions include medical decisions like the one at the beginning of this chapter, whether to marry, whom to marry, if and when to have children, what kind of occupation to choose, how to spend your hard-earned dollars, and so on. These are all personal decisions. We also must decide on a host of political and business issues, like whether to support off-shore drilling for oil, when to increase a company's inventory, which stock to invest in, how to negotiate a contract, which party to support during political upheaval, and how to increase profits. In this chapter, you will learn skills designed to help you make sound decisions. To accomplish this, we look at the kinds of decisions made by professional decision makers, examine common pitfalls and fallacies in the decision-making process, consider the risks involved, and develop a general strategy or plan that you can use when faced with a major decision.

Decision making always involves making a choice among a set of possible alternatives. If you've read the previous chapters in this book, then you've already encountered several sections on how to make intelligent choices. In chapter 5, on analyzing arguments, for example, you considered the way in which reasons support or refute a conclusion. When analyzing arguments, you make many decisions about the relevance and accuracy of information and how well the reasons that are provided support an action or a belief. In chapters 6 and 7, on hypothesis testing and using probabilistic information, there were sections on drawing tree diagrams, collecting information, and computing likelihoods to make decisions. Because decision making is a central theme in critical thinking, different aspects of it are presented throughout this book.

MAKING SOUND DECISIONS

The decision-making process is frequently stressful. Ask anyone you know who has recently made an important decision and you will most likely be told about sleepless nights, loss of appetite (or excessive eating), irritability, and generalized feelings of anxiety. Autobiographical and biographical accounts of decision-making stress can be found in the books written by and about several past presidents. Theodore C. Sorensen (1965), in his book, *Kennedy,* told of the stress that John Kennedy faced during the Berlin blockade crisis, and a book written by Richard M. Nixon before his presidency, appropriately titled *Six Crises* (1962), tells about the stress caused by his early political decisions. It is not surprising that many people will avoid making decisions whenever possible. Although avoidance is one way of handling stressful decisions, it is seldom a good way. Every time you find yourself avoiding a decision, remember that, in most cases, avoiding a decision is, in fact, making one without any of the benefits of a carefully thought out consideration of the problem.

A decision always involves two or more competing alternatives of action. Usually, each alternative has several pros and cons associated with it. The decision maker has to choose the "best" alternative. Decisions also involve uncertainty, because we cannot know in advance the consequences of our actions. Although decision making starts with the awareness that a problem exists, it differs from traditional problem solving in that there is no single correct solution. The difficulty lies in judging which alternative is best. Usually, decisions have to be made with missing information, and they involve guesses and predictions about future events. In the medical scenario at the beginning of this chapter, the best decision must take into account the likelihood of developing cancer at some time in the future, the risks and pain of surgery, and the pros and cons of various treatment regimens. When you decide which stock to invest in, you must consider what the economy will be like in the years to come. Similarly, the decision whether or not to have children requires that you think about what your life will be like with children who don't even exist yet.

Decision making is an active process. The decision maker takes responsibility for her or his own future. After all, you are in the best position for determining how you want to spend your life and how you should make the business and professional decisions that will ultimately reflect on you. Good decision makers get the good jobs and make favorable decisions about their personal lives as well. Although many famous instances of good decisions (profitable investments, successful army maneuvers) and bad decisions (Watergate, the U.S. attempt to rescue American hostages in Iran, NASA's decision to launch the Challenger in bad weather) come to mind, it is important to realize that a decision is judged to be good or bad after the fact. For example, most Americans would have agreed that President Carter made a wise decision to rescue American hostages in Iran if it had been successful and no lives were lost. However, because it failed and eight Americans were killed, it is now seen as a bad decision. Thus, there is an important distinction between how good a decision is and its outcome. Decisions are made using the information available at the time, and because much of the information is probabilistic in nature, sometimes good decisions will have bad outcomes. Conversely, bad decisions will sometimes have good outcomes. Of course, good decisions will result in desirable outcomes much more frequently than poor decisions will.

Often, we will never know if the best decision was made. If you are a college senior who must decide between a lucrative career in accounting or a more personally rewarding career as a high school English teacher, you may never be sure if you picked the better option, because you can only speculate about the career that you didn't select. Robert Frost, the famous American poet, captured this feeling in his poem about a traveler who comes to a fork in the road. The traveler can never know about "the road not taken."

Before a decision can be made, the individual must realize that a problem exists and that there are several possible solutions to the problem. Let's consider an example with which many of you will be able to identify. Monica is taking several demanding college courses. She needs to supplement her income by working part time, and she has family obligations as well. Her free time is virtually nonexistent. Monica has a problem. She must decide how to juggle all of these commitments while still having some time left for herself. Monica has to realize that a problem exists. Too often, this first step is missed, and inertia sets in. People will continue doing what they have been doing without contemplating ways to improve a difficult situation. A clear definition of the problem is the first step in successful decision making. Simply stated, the problem is that Monica has too many responsibilities, and this is making her feel anxious and stressed. The best solution will give her more time for herself while still allowing her to fulfill her responsibilities. As these are essentially conflicting goals, the best decision will probably involve a compromise that will only partially satisfy each. It is not likely that she will find a course of action that will allow her to fill her days with leisure activities while maintaining high grades, earning money, and caring for her family.

The objective criteria for a good decision are that it is feasible and that it will, at least, help to alleviate the problem. Some possible good decisions for Monica include finding a higher paying job or reducing her expenses so she would need to work fewer hours, beginning a more efficient study program, taking a lighter course load, and visiting her family less frequently. You may be surprised to find that, with a little effort, several possibilities occur to you that you might otherwise never have considered.

Devoted "Trekkies," (fans of the television and movie series called "Star Trek") can recall many stories in which the plot involved particularly clever decision making. Consider, for example, the movie "Star Trek II: The Wrath of Khan." In the opening scene, an attractive, pointy-eared Vulcan is facing a serious problem. A sister spaceship has wandered into enemy territory and has sent a distress signal. If the Vulcan does not decide to go in to save them they will perish; if she does, she risks enemy attack. She nervously decides to follow them and is immediately apprised that her starship is under attack. We soon learn that this is a computer-simulated drill that was designed to test the decision-making skills of future starship commanders and that only one person has made the correct decision in this drill. Of course, it is Captain Kirk. The question of interest is whether he decided to attempt to save the sister ship and thus risk attack of his own spaceship or whether he decided to sacrifice the crew of the sister ship to save lives on his own spaceship. It seems that Captain Kirk did neither. Later, we find out that he redesigned the computer problem so that he would have additional choices with more favorable outcomes. For him, the problem was "how to change contingencies in a mock drill." For others, the problem had been "how to save the sister starship without being attacked." Captain Kirk made a superior decision, because he defined the problem in a unique way. Some may say that he cheated or "copped out" by redesigning the simulation, but perhaps, he would use his ability to define problems in a unique way if he were out in space, and that's what makes him an outstanding starship commander. The point being made here is that, often, there are alternative ways of formulating what the problem is, and some will result in more favorable outcomes than others. Different formulations will lead to different solutions.

DECISION MAKING AMONG
TRAINED PROFESSIONALS

Whenever there is a simple error that most laymen fall for, there is always a slightly more sophisticated version of the same problem that experts fall for.

—Amos Tversky (quoted in Gardner, 1985)

It seems logical that one way to understand how good decisions are made is by studying professional decision makers—doctors, judges, research scientists, and others who routinely make important decisions that affect society. In recent years, a comprehensive series of experiments by several leading psychologists has revealed an interesting fact about the decisions made by trained professionals. They are often wrong. Moreover, they are wrong in predictable ways. This finding is of great concern, because it is the professional decision makers in our society who determine, for example, whether a tissue sample is malignant, whether an individual has committed a crime, and whether a certain level of radiation is harmful. Because the unfortunate consequences of wrong decisions by professional decision makers are painfully obvious, an examination of the types of errors they make is an important initial step toward correcting them.

It seems that, despite the many years of education they receive, professionals make the same kinds of mistakes that are made by people without their specialized education. Although physicians learn medicine and lawyers learn jurisprudence, few are being trained in the essential skills of decision making. Not even those trained in formal disciplines such as logic and probability theory are free from certain flaws in thinking.

A **fallacy** is an error or mistake in the thinking process. An example of common thinking fallacies among trained professionals can be found in research conducted by Smedslund (1963). He presented trained nurses with a deck of cards that supposedly contained information gleaned from the files of 100 patients. Each card indicated whether a patient had a particular disease and whether a particular symptom was present or absent in the patient. Thus, there were four possible combinations for each patient. The patient (a) has the disease and has the symptom; (b) does not have the disease and does not have the symptom; (c) does not have the disease but has the symptom; or (d) has the disease but does not have the symptom. The task for the nurses was to determine if there is a relationship between the symptom and the disease. The number of cases in each of these four categories is shown in Fig. 8.1. Stop now and look over the data presented in Fig. 8.1. Do you think that there is a relationship between the symptom and the disease? Overwhelmingly, the nurses concluded that there was a symptom–disease relationship, basing their decisions on the fact that 37 patients had both the disease and the symptom, and 13 had neither the disease nor the symptom. They tended to ignore the 33 cases in which the symptom was present without the disease and the 17 cases in which patients had the disease but not the symptom. These trained nurses routinely ignored half of the available information. The correct decision should have been that there was no relationship, because there were numerous instances of the disease without the symptom and the symptom without the disease. Decision-making errors like the one described here are prevalent in the everyday thinking of people from all walks of life. We need to examine common decision-making fallacies, because a skilled decision maker will need to know what to avoid as well as what to do.

	HAS THE DISEASE	DOESN'T HAVE THE DISEASE
HAS THE SYMPTOMS	37	33
DOESN'T HAVE THE SYMPTOMS	17	13

FIG. 8.1. Number of patients within each disease/symptom category. Is there a relationship between the disease and the symptoms?

PITFALLS AND PRATFALLS IN
DECISION MAKING

. . . great moments in history all turned on someone's judgment as to what should be done and someone's decision to do it.
—Arkes and Hammond (1986b)

A pitfall is a danger or difficulty that is not easily avoided. If you've ever spent long afternoons at the beach, you've probably seen bratty kids creating pitfalls. They dig holes in the sand and cover them with newspaper so that unsuspecting sun lovers will fall into them. The word "pratfall" needs no formal definition for fans of the original *Saturday Night Live* television series. Chevy Chase became famous for his frequent pratfalls on this television program. He's been described as "the comedian who falls down a lot." The American Heritage dictionary defines a pratfall as "a fall on the buttocks." Put these terms together, and you will realize that unless common pitfalls in decision making are avoided, the decision maker will slip and fall on the part of the anatomy that is featured on blue jeans commercials without reaching the best decision. Let's examine some of the common fallacies or pitfalls in decision making.

Failure to Seek Disconfirming Evidence

Suppose you have a friend who is always working on crossword puzzles, anagrams, mazes, and other similar problems from puzzle books. He corners you one day with the following problem:

> I'm going to give you a series of numbers. This series conforms to a simple rule. You have to figure out what the rule is. The way to do this is by coming up with your own series of numbers. I'll tell you whether or not your own series conforms to this rule. You can give me as many series of numbers as necessary to discover the rule. When you believe that you know the rule, tell it to me and I'll let you know if you're right.
>
> Reluctantly, you agree to participate. You are given the following number series:
>
> $$2 \quad 4 \quad 6$$

Stop right now, and think how you would go about generating other number series to determine the correct rule. This problem was actually presented to many subjects in an experiment conducted by Wason (1960, 1968). He found that most people had difficulty with this task. Suppose that you believe that the rule is "any continuous series of even numbers." To test this rule, most subjects would try series like "14, 16, 18." The experimenter would respond that this series conforms to the rule. To be certain, most subjects would try again with another series, "182, 184, 186." Again, the experimenter would respond affirmatively.

Confidently, the subject would announce the rule, "Any continuous even series of numbers." The experimenter then informs the subject that this is not the correct rule.

Typically, subjects will try again, this time thinking up a new rule that will describe the correct number series. Suppose this time the subject decides to try out the rule "the middle number is halfway between the other two." Now the subject asks about the series "50, 100, 150." The experimenter answers that this series is correct. The subject tries again "1006, 1007, 1008" and is told that this also conforms to the rule. Even more confident this time, the subject announces that the correct rule is "the middle number is halfway between the other two." The experimenter tells him that this is not the correct rule.

Have you discovered the correct rule by now? It is "increasing whole numbers." After almost an hour of working on this problem, one of Wason's subjects came up with this rule: "The rule is that either the first number equals the second minus two, and the third is random but greater than the second, or the third number equals the second plus two, and the first is random but less than the second." You can imagine how this poor subject felt when he was told that this rule was incorrect.

Why is this problem so difficult? In all of the sample number series I've given and most of the ones people actually try, the number series conform to the rule they have in mind. There is an infinite number of possible number series that conform to the correct rule, "numbers in increasing order of magnitude." What subjects should have done is try out series that would disconfirm the rule they were trying out. For example, if you believed that the correct rule is "any continuous series of even numbers" you should try the series "1, 2, 4. If the experimenter tells you that you are correct, then you know that the rule "any continuous series of even numbers" must be wrong.

The tendency to seek information that agrees with the ideas we have is called **confirmation bias.** We have a bias or predilection to look for confirming information. Another interesting example of the confirmation bias, or failure to seek disconfirming evidence, is discussed in chapter 4. This is the same error that was described in the previous section in which the nurses failed to consider evidence that disconfirmed the hypothesis that the symptoms and disease were related. It is a pervasive error.

What are the implications of the bias to seek confirming evidence on decision making? Suppose someone confronts your best male friend with "the opportunity of a lifetime." A dynamic saleswoman offers him the chance to invest in a new corporation that will manufacture and sell small computers. It sounds good, but he's unsure. Prudently, he decides to do some investigating. He checks out 10 computer companies that are listed on the New York Stock Exchange. He finds that IBM is a large profitable corporation. If he had only invested in IBM when it was just being formed, he'd be a rich man today. He can already imagine himself lighting cigars with $10 bills. What advice would you give your friend?

Hopefully, you would point out to him that he only looked for evidence that supports the decision to invest in the corporation, as only substantial corporations are listed on the stock exchange. He also needs to seek evidence that would disconfirm this decision. He should find out how many small computer corporations have gone bankrupt and how many have not gone bankrupt in the last 10 years. He also should attempt to estimate the future market for small computers.

Another real-life (nonlaboratory) example can be drawn from medical decision making. Imagine a young physician examining a sick patient. The patient is complaining of a high fever and a sore throat. The physician must decide on a diagnosis from among myriad possible diseases. The physician decides that it may be the flu and asks the patient if he or she feels "achy all over." The answer is "yes." The physician asks if the symptoms began a few days ago. Again, the response is "yes." It should be clear to the reader that the physician should also be seeking evidence that would disconfirm the flu diagnosis. She or he should also ask about patterns of symptoms that are not usually associated with the flu, like a rash or swollen joints.

The confirmation bias is a pitfall in decision making. Wason has claimed that it is prevalent in the thoughts and research of scientists. In fact, a large-scale study of NASA scientists showed a strong confirmation bias (Mynatt, Doherty, & Tweney, 1978). We all need to be trained to seek and examine data that are inconsistent with the ideas we are considering.

Availability Heuristic

A **heuristic** is an "rule of thumb" that we use to solve problems. It won't always give us the right answer, but it is a helpful aid. Psychologists usually distinguish between heuristics and algorithms. An **algorithm** is a procedure that will always yield the correct answer if you follow it exactly. Let's try a simple example from mathematics to clarify these terms. Remember the procedures you learned in solving long division problems. Given a problem like 176 $\overline{)7019}$, you were first told to estimate about how often 176 would "go into" 7019, as it is unlikely that you ever learned the 176 tables. You might estimate it to be about 4 times. The problem thus far would look like this:

$$\frac{4}{176\overline{)7019}}$$

You would check out this estimate with the appropriate multiplication.

$$\frac{4}{176\overline{)7019}} \qquad \text{Oops, too large!}$$
$$\underline{704}$$

You would soon realize that 4 was too large and would probably try 3. This

procedure is a heuristic. It is a guide or aid to help you find the c[
but it doesn't always work perfectly, as seen in the preceding exa[
other hand, an algorithm always leads to the correct answer. If yo[
the area of a rectangle that is 3 feet long and 2 feet wide, you will always get the
correct answer if you use the formula: length × width, or in this case, 3 feet × 2
feet = 6 square feet.

There are many situations in which we use both heuristics and algorithms. In
cooking, for example, a recipe is an algorithm. If the recipe is followed exactly,
the result should always be the same dish that is described in the cookbook.
When cooks ad lib by adding additional seasoning or when they create a new
recipe, they are using their general knowledge about the types of flavors that go
together. This is an example of a heuristic. Heuristics, or "rules of thumb," are
frequently used by a decision maker without the realization by the decision
maker that they're being used.

Availability is a commonly used heuristic. The term "availability heuristic"
was coined by two prominent psychologists, Daniel Kahneman and Amos
Tversky (1973; Tversky & Kahneman, 1974), who have conducted numerous
experiments on decision making. In order to understand the availability heuristic,
consider the following questions:

1. Are there more words in the English language that begin with the letter *k* or have
   the *k* in the third position?
2. Would you expect the 1990 census to show that there are more librarians or farmers
   in the United States?
3. Are there more deaths due to homicide or due to diabetes-related diseases?

If you answer the first question like most people, you believe that there are
more words that start with the letter *k* than there are words with *k* in the third
position. In answering this question, most people find that they can think of more
words that start with *k* (kite, kitty, kill, kiss, kick, key, king, know, knife, koala,
kidney) than have *k* in the third position (make, take, like, lake). In the jargon of
psychology, words starting with the letter *k* are more available than words with *k*
in the third position. That is, they come to mind more easily. If you answered
"words that start with *k*," you were wrong. According to Kahneman and
Tversky, the English language contains many more words with *k* in the third
position than in the first position. It is just more difficult to think of them,
because it is easier to retrieve words from memory by the first letter than by the
third. Earlier in this book, I talked about the pervasive influence of memory in
every aspect of critical thinking. This is another example of the way in which the
kinds of memories we retrieve can determine how decisions are made.

Your answer to the second question probably depends on whether you live in
an urban or rural area. Most city dwellers believe that there are more librarians

than farmers in the United States. After all, few city dwellers have ever met a farmer, whereas they probably know, or at least know of, several librarians. Actually, there are many more farmers in the Untied States than there are librarians. This is another example of how the use of the availability heuristic can lead to the wrong decision.

Most residents of large cities probably believe incorrectly that there are more deaths due to homicide than to diabetes. The reason for this is not difficult to understand. Pick up any newspaper or watch television news on any day and there is likely to be a report of one or more homicides. Although you may know only a few people who have diabetes and may not know personally anyone who has been murdered, you've heard or read about many homicide victims, so there seems to be more of them.

The availability heuristic can be found in many applied settings. Its influence can best be understood with an example:

In a medical text written by Gifford-Jones (1977), the author discussed the difficult medical decision concerning whether women in their late 30s or early 40s should have their ovaries removed when they are having a hysterectomy. Like all difficult decisions, there are pros and cons associated with each alternative. In discussing how this decision is often made, Gifford-Jones (1977) wrote:

> I recall operating some time ago with a former professor of gynecology at Harvard. He was in a rather philosophical mood and was pondering the pros and cons of what to do with the ovaries, "Sometimes whether or not I remove the ovaries depends on what has happened to me in the last few weeks," he said. "If I've watched a patient die from cancer of the ovary, I often remove them. But if I've been free of this experience for a while, I'm more inclined to leave them in." (pp. 174–175).

As you can see from this candid account of how some medical decisions are made, the availability of information in memory will frequently determine the alternative that is selected. In situations like this one, in which the pros and cons are nearly equal, it is difficult to know if a good decision has been made.

Although the availability heuristic can sometimes lead to poor decisions, it can, under certain circumstances, be a valuable decision-making aid. Very few cases of Toxic Shock Syndrome were reported before 1978. As soon as the relationship between Toxic Shock Syndrome and tampon use in menstruating women became widely publicized, there was a dramatic increase in the number of reported cases. The most likely explanation for this dramatic increase is that the diagnosis became available, or more easily recalled, by physicians. For most United States physicians, Toxic Shock Syndrome was one of the many illnesses that they studied many years ago when they were still in medical school, and therefore was not a diagnostic category that was easily available for them to use. The publicity surrounding Toxic Shock Syndrome helped many women receive a correct diagnosis.

The availability heuristic is frequently seen in other medical examples. It is not unusual for a pediatrician whose own children suffer from severe allergies to be especially vigilant about possible allergic reactions in his or her patients. This may or may not be a good thing. The best physician is one who has a broad scope of experience with a large variety of illnesses so that he or she has a large number of medical diagnoses available to him or her.

Prejudice and stereotypes may also exist, at least in part, because of the human tendency to utilize readily available information. Although prejudice and stereotypes were discussed more fully in chapter 2, it is easy to see how availability plays a role in establishing and maintaining them. If a minority person is convicted of a heinous crime, many people will distrust other members of the same minority. The thousands of honest, hard-working minority persons are forgotten or overlooked. Their existence is overshadowed by the salient criminal.

Availability has been carefully studied in the laboratory by research psychologists, because it plays a role in decisions that are made in a wide range of settings. In another experiment by Tversky and Kahneman (1974), groups of college students were given one of the two following arithmetic problems:

$$8 \times 7 \times 6 \times 5 \times 4 \times 3 \times 2 \times 1 = ?$$
or
$$1 \times 2 \times 3 \times 4 \times 5 \times 6 \times 7 \times 8 = ?$$

The college students examined either the first or second row of numbers for 5 seconds. Their task was to estimate the product, because 5 seconds was not enough time to solve this problem. Students who were given the first problem, the one beginning with large numbers, gave an average estimate of the product to be 2,250. Students who were given the second problem, the one beginning with small numbers, gave an average estimate of the product to be 512. The correct answer is 40,320. Thus, when the problem began with large numbers, the estimated answer was large compared to the problem that began with small numbers. The estimate differences between the ascending and descending series demonstrates that judgments were systematically biased toward the most readily available information.

Representativeness Heuristic

Suppose that a young man in a pinstripe suit, black shirt, and white tie comes up to you and asks if you'd like to make some money by betting on whether a coin lands on "heads" or "tails." You look at him dubiously. He explains that it's really quite simple. He'll flip one coin six times. All you have to do is bet on the pattern of heads and tails that will result from six tosses of a coin. Although there are many sequences possible, you decide to concentrate on three of them. Using the letter "H" to represent heads and "T" to represent tails, which of the following three outcomes would you bet on?

H-T-H-T-T-H
H-H-H-T-T-T
H-T-H-T-H-T

If you responded like most other people, then you selected the first series of heads and tails, probably because it seemed more similar to a random or chance pattern of heads and tails. In fact, all three series are equally likely. If you've read chapter 7, you already knew this. Any series of heads and tails taken six at a time is as likely to occur as any other. The preceding example demonstrates the belief that an outcome of a random process should look like, or be representative of, randomness. Because our common-sense notion of randomness is that of a process without a pattern, we tend to think that H-T-H-T-H-T is not as likely to occur from six tosses of a coin as a more random-looking series. This, however, is not true. (What some people find even more surprising is that H-H-H-H-H-H is as likely as H-T-H-T-H-T.)

Of course, you're more likely to get approximately equal numbers of heads and tails after many coin flips than you are to get mostly or all heads or mostly or all tails, because there are more possible patterns that yield these outcomes. For example, there is only one pattern of outcomes that will correspond to six heads (H-H-H-H-H-H), whereas there are many ways to get three heads and three tails in six flips of a coin (e.g., H-H-H-T-T-T; H-T-H-T-H-T; T-T-T-H-H-H; H-T-T-T-H-H; etc.). Each series, or pattern, of heads and tails is equally likely. This concept is also discussed in chapter 7.

To clarify the **representativeness heuristic,** let's try another example. Suppose you get a letter from an old male friend from whom you haven't heard in many years. He tells you that he is the proud father of six children—three girls and three boys. After trying to consider what life is like with six children, you then wonder about their birth order. Which of the following orders do you think is more likely (with "G" standing for girls and "B" standing for boy): B-B-B-G-G-G or B-G-G-B-G-B? If you've followed the discussion so far, you will realize that, although the second series appears to be more representative of a random process, they are, in fact, equally likely (Khaneman & Tversky, 1972).

Wishful Thinking (Pollyanna Principle)

Quite often, people will overestimate their chances for success or the likelihood of a desired outcome. Halpern and Irwin (1973) found that when participants in an experiment wanted an event to occur (they would win money), they believed that it was more likely to occur than when its occurrence would have been unfavorable (they would lose money). It seems that humans are an optimistic species. The tendency to believe that pleasant events are more likely than unpleasant ones is a manifestation of **wishful thinking,** the idea that if we want something to happen, it will. This has also been called the Pollyanna Principle, in honor of the protagonist of a 1913 novel who always found something to be happy about, no matter how bleak the situation.

A large fast-food hamburger chain is basing a promotional gimmick on wishful thinking. The corporation that made golden arches an integral part of American life is offering a game that pays off with large sums of money. Some lucky Big Mac hamburger consumer will match up small game coupons for the grand prize. A blitz of television advertising shows lucky burger eaters exclaiming over the money they've won. Apparently, the lure of winning must sell more hamburgers, or it would have been discontinued. It must be assumed that people grossly overestimate their chance of winning the prizes. The actual estimated probability of winning the grand prize is less than a million to one. As required by law, these odds are posted (in fine print) on the posters that announce the game, yet they are routinely ignored and thought to be more favorable than they actually are. Few of us can appreciate astronomical odds like this one. You're probably more likely to find a needle in a haystack. Yet, because of wishful thinking, many people will line up for hamburgers and a chance to win.

Optimism may be a wonderful human trait, but not when it distorts the decision-making process. Good decisions rely on realistic assessment of likelihood, not optimistic ones. Failure to consider seriously unpleasant outcomes can lead to disastrous consequences. Currently, seismologists (people who study earthquakes) are predicting that a major earthquake will occur in Southern California within the next 50 years. Few people will be prepared, however, if an earthquake occurs, because they are duped by wishful thinking. Most believe that a major earthquake won't occur or, alternatively, if it does, it will be "somewhere else." Random "person on the street" interviews shown on television reveal that the Pollyanna Principle is alive and well and living in Southern California. Similar reactions have been found with people living in other regions that are plagued with flood, hurricanes, and other natural disasters.

Entrapment

Suppose you were offered the opportunity to bid on a $1 bill. You and some friends can make bids, and the highest bidder will pay the amount bid and get $1 in return. The only hitch is that both the highest bidder and second highest bidder must pay the amount they bid, but only the highest bidder will receive the dollar in return. Suppose that you agree to play and that you continue to raise your bid until you have offered 80 cents. Now a friend bids $1. What do you do? You will probably decide to bid $1.05 for the $1, because you'll certainly lose $.80 unless you continue to increase your bid. Shubik (1971) has found that people will continue to bid amounts over $1 to win the dollar bill in an attempt to keep their losses at a minimum in this game.

What has happened in this game is **entrapment,** a situation in which an individual has already invested money, time, or effort and decides to continue in this situation because of the initial investment. People commonly fall prey to entrapment. Consider Fred's decision about his automobile. He has already replaced the muffler, brakes, and ignition system when he finds out that his car needs a new transmission. Because he has already invested so much money into his car, he feels "trapped" into replacing the transmission instead of buying a new car. Or consider another common example. Almost everyone has had the frustrating experience of calling on the phone for some information and being put on "hold." After listening to the irritating strains of "elevator music" for several minutes, you need to decide whether to hang up or to continue waiting. Many people continue to wait because of the time they've already invested.

Making decisions in light of previous investments requires that the individual consider *why* the investment has been so high either in terms of money or time. Because Fred has been "pouring money" into his car for some time, it is likely that it will continue to need repairs, and thus, the purchase of a new automobile is probably the better choice if it is financially feasible. If you've waited on "hold" for several minutes without any indication or recognition of your call, it is likely that the secretary or whoever you were waiting for has forgotten about you. Eventually, he or she may notice that you are still on the line, but it is probably best to hang up and call again. On the other hand, if you have been waiting a long time for a bus, it should be more likely that one will come along, unless there's been a bus drivers' strike or heavy snow that may have shut down public transportation. You need to consider the other alternatives in deciding if you should continue waiting—the cost and availability of other means of transportation, time constraints, and so on.

Examples of entrapment are commonly found in government budget hearings (Fischer & Johnson, 1986). One argument in favor of continuing to support the development of the MX missile is that the millions of dollars that have already been spent on it would be lost if we decided to discontinue the project. Whenever you are faced with an entrapment argument, carefully consider why the costs have been so high, and examine the costs and benefits of other alternatives.

Psychological Reactance

Our emotional states have a major impact on the kinds of decisions that we make (Kavanaugh & Bower, 1985). We select alternatives that seem "best" to us, and our determination of what's best is not always based on sound rational criteria. One example of the effect of emotional states on the kinds of decisions people make has been labeled **psychological reactance**, which is resistance arising from restrictions of freedom. Consider this example of psychological reactance (Shaver, 1981): It's been a bitterly cold winter, and you can hardly wait for a much deserved spring break. One of your close friends is planning on basking in the Fort Lauderdale sun. Another friend can't wait to hit the slopes in Vail. Both friends have asked you to join them in their spring break revelry. As you consider the options, you begin to favor the bikini-clad vacation when your Florida-bound friend tells you that you *must* go to Florida with him or her. How does this loss of freedom affect your decision?

Logically, it seems that being told that you must do what you want to do would have no affect on your decision, but many people do not react in this manner. Some people would react to this loss of freedom by deciding to go skiing instead. The extent to which psychological reactance affects a decision depends on the number of freedoms that are being threatened and the source of the threat. There are also large differences among individuals in the extent to which they are prone to reactance. Consider how you will probably respond when you are told what to do in different situations. If you are likely to do the opposite, no matter what you are told to do, then you are demonstrating reactance and will sometimes make poor decisions because of this tendency. Whether you're dealing with your parents, an employer, or a foreign government, psychological reactance can interfere with the decision-making process by causing you to select a less desirable alternative.

Liking

It should seem obvious that people select alternatives that have been evaluated positively along some dimension. This point is made more explicitly later in this chapter; however, it is important to consider here some of the factors that influence positive evaluations. In other words, what are some factors that determine liking?

Reciprocity

When assessing the pros and cons of various alternatives, our subjective feelings about the alternatives play a large role in decision making. Simply put, we choose people and actions that we like. Reciprocity is one determinant of what and whom we like. We tend to like people who like us. In Cialdini's (1988) delightful book about myriad influences that affect our thoughts and actions, he told about the "World's Greatest Car Salesman." The super salesman seems to differ from other more mundane sellers in several ways, but the most interesting is his strange habit of correspondence. Super Salesman sends a card to each of his more than 13,000 former customers each month. Can you guess the message on this card? No, it's not a list of maintenance tips or repair coupons. In fact, every card every month contains the same message: "I like you." Twelve times a year, every former customer receives the same obviously impersonal message. It seems to work. When the time comes to decide where to purchase another car, these former customers are reminded of their "friend" who likes them. Reciprocity of liking apparently has a powerful effect on decision making in this context.

The psychological literature is full of other examples of the influence of reciprocity on decisions. For example, you are much more likely to buy a product if I give you a free sample than if I don't. People seem to feel that they owe something in exchange for the "free" sample. Political favors are blatant examples of reciprocity-induced liking, as are charitable requests that are accompanied by "gifts" like address labels, key rings, and stamped return envelopes.

Mere Exposure Effect

Suppose that you walked into a voting booth on a primary election day and were faced with the following choice:

County Solicitor (Choose One)
Myron Jones
John Adams
Victor Light

Unfortunately, you have not kept up with local politics, and are unfamiliar with the record of any of these candidates. Which candidate would you vote for? Studies indicate that you probably chose John Adams.

In a recent election in New Hampshire, John Adams, an unemployed cab driver who did not campaign, won the Republican nomination for the State's First Congressional District. Why did John Adams, a man who spent no money on his campaign and who never gave a speech, win his party's nomination? Psychologists believe that when voters were confronted with three names they didn't recognize, they picked the one linked in history with a political figure. Hence, prior exposure creates a sense of familiarity, which in turn can enhance your liking for the stimulus, a phenomenon known as the **mere exposure effect.**

Political commercials often operate on this principle. They repeatedly hark, "Vote for Brandon Lee, He's the One!" Such commercials give absolutely no information about the candidate. They rely on the well-documented effect that familiarity will enhance liking. Based on this principle, repetition was commonly used in Nazi Germany and North Korean prison camps during World War II in an attempt to make their political ideologies more palatable to the prisoners.

What should you do if you face unknown candidates' names in a voting booth? If you can't vote intelligently for an office, skip that section and vote for the offices that you're familiar with. Intelligent voters ask themselves, "What do

I know about these candidates?'' and do not fall prey to a familiar-sounding name.

UNCERTAINTY AND RISKS

Murphy's Law: Anything that can go wrong, will. Comment on Murphy's Law: Murphy was an optimist.

Decision making always involves uncertainty, and, for this reason, the principles involved in assessing likelihood and uncertainty are an integral part of the decision-making process. The decisions that we make have implications for the future, and the future inherently involves unknowns.

Research on how people typically deal with uncertainty has shown that, usually, the response is to ignore it (Hogarth, 1988). Although this may reduce the immediate complexity of a decision, it is obviously a maladaptive procedure that could lead to catastrophic results.

It is possible to reduce the number of unknowns in any situation. This will almost always involve some work by the decision maker, but if the decision is an important one, it will be time well spent. Let's consider a common example. Most of us will purchase several automobiles in our lifetimes. For a majority of Americans, this will represent the second largest expenditure that they will make, exceeded only by the purchase of a home. The quality of this decision can be improved with a little research. You can determine which automobile variables are important to you and gather relevant data about each car you are considering for possible purchase.

Almost any decision can be improved with a little research. For example, if you are uncertain about the safety of nuclear plants, an afternoon at the library reading both pro and con materials should allow you to make a much more informed decision about this important issue.

Assessing Desirable and Undesirable Consequences

The decision maker must always be aware of the risks and benefits associated with taking or not taking a particular course of action. If you live in an apartment near a college campus, you are well aware of the ''joys'' associated with apartment hunting. Rental units are often in short supply in college communities and are priced in a range that strains the typical student's budget. Students may find themselves considering an apartment that lacks the amenities they were hoping for at a price that is really above their income. The risk associated with turning the apartment down is that they might not find another apartment within walking distance to the college campus. The risks associated with renting the apartment must also be considered. What if they find that they really can't afford to keep up the monthly rental payments? The decision maker has to decide which risk is greater and the likelihood of each occurring. Obviously, both risks need to be assessed very carefully and additional alternatives considered. Perhaps a cheaper apartment can be found in another section of town with good public transportation to campus, or perhaps a roommate can be found to share the rent.

A poignant example of failure to assess risks adequately can be found in an analysis of the United States' military actions just prior to the attack on Pearl Harbor. Admiral Kimmel, Commander in Chief of Naval Operations in the Pacific, had received several warnings from Washington that a Japanese attack in the Southwest was possible. He decided to downplay the probability of an attack on Pearl Harbor, because he believed that other naval sites were more likely targets. Quite by accident, and almost an hour before the attack, two army privates spotted on a radar screen large unidentified aircraft flying toward Pearl Harbor. Realizing that these could be Japanese bomber planes, they reported the presence of the unidentified aircraft to the Army's radar center.

Let's consider the plight of the officer on duty at the radar center. The United States was not at war with Japan. He had never received the recent warning that a Japanese attack was imminent. He had to decide whether the unidentified objects on the radar screen belonged to the United States or Japan. There were costs and risks associated with either choice. If he had erroneously decided that they were Japanese planes, he would have been responsible for recalling personal "leaves" for large numbers of servicemen and women and creating havoc and panic on the military base. There were also large financial costs involved in preparing for anti-aircraft maneuvers. Because he assessed the possibility of a Japanese attack to be low, he told the two privates to forget about the objects detected by radar. He decided that they were probably the Army B-17's that were expected to arrive some time that day. With the unfortunate benefit of hindsight, it is clear that he failed to assess adequately the risks associated with each decision. The result was the worst naval disaster in United States history, with over 2,000 lives lost. Even though he believed that an attack was unlikely (wishful thinking), he should have realized that the risks were too great to justify his decision. Decisions made under extreme risks need careful scrutiny and not an off-hand dismissal. In this case, the risks associated with deciding that the plans belonged to the United States were many times greater than those associated with the decision that they were Japanese bombers.

Research has shown that the Pearl Harbor scenario is not unusual. Whenever extreme risk is associated with a course of action, there is a tendency to minimize the unfavorable consequences (Janis & Mann, 1977). This is sometimes called **biased discounting.** It is the bias or predilection to discount or reduce perceived risk or its probability. Thus, the radar officer could bolster his decision to ignore the unidentified objects by rationalizing either that even if they were Japanese bomber planes they probably would not do much damage or it was extremely unlikely that they were Japanese aircraft.

Risky Decisions

Every day we take risks and avoid others. It starts as soon as we wake up.
— Wilson and Crouch (1987)

How do the experts make decisions that involve potentially disastrous outcomes? How can we, as informed citizens and voters, make risky decisions? Questions like these are timely, but not easy to answer.

The goal of risk assessment is to find ways to avoid, reduce, or manage risks (Wilson & Crouch, 1987). Risk is associated with every aspect of life. For example, approximately 200 people are electrocuted each year in accidents involving home wiring or appliances, and 7,000 people die each year in U.S. homes as a result of falls (most of them are over 65). Yet, few of us would interpret these risks as great enough to either forgo electricity or to stop walking in our homes. Other risks are clearly too large to take. Few of us, for example, would decide to cross a busy freeway wearing a blindfold. And still other risks are largely unknown, such as the release of a new chemical into the environment or the development of a new technology. Wilson and Crouch (1987) have suggested several ways of estimating risks that voters and consumers should consider when deciding if an action or a technology is safe enough. One method of risk assessment involves examining historical data. For example, to understand the risk of cancer due to exposure to medical x-rays, there are data that indicate that for a given dose per year (40 mrem) there is an expected number of cancers (1,100). This sort of risk information can be compared to other known risks so that consumers can decide if the benefits of medical x-rays outweigh the risks.

The risk of a new technology for which there are no historical data can be computed by calculating the risk of separate components and multiplying along the branches of a decision tree. This method of calculating probabilities was presented in chapter 7. A well-known example is the probability of a severe accident at a nuclear energy plant. Risks can also be calculated by analogy. (The use of analogies as an aid to problem solving is discussed more fully in chapter 9.) When animals are used to test drugs, the experimenter is really using an analogy to extrapolate the risk to humans.

When objective risk information is not available, people rely on their own subjective estimates. As discussed earlier in this chapter, information that is highly available in memory is judged as more likely to occur than information that is difficult to recall. The availability heuristic is also at work when people make subjective risk estimates. Slovic (1987) has found that phenomena that are not observable and are associated with spectacular dreaded outcomes (DNA technology, radioactive waste, AIDS, and nuclear reactors) are believed to be riskier than phenomena that involve known risks and/or less dreaded outcomes (smoking, auto accidents, dynamite, and handguns). Experts, on the other hand, perceive risks based on annual mortality so that the event that results in the greater number of deaths is judged to be the greater risk. Experts, for example, ranked motor vehicles as riskier than nuclear power (because more people are expected to die from motor vehicle accidents); whereas, samples of college students and members of the League of Women Voters ranked nuclear power as the greater risk (because it is an example of a spectacular dreaded outcome).

As voters and consumers, we face countless decisions about a large and diverse array of topics, which include nuclear energy, food irradiation, surgical procedures, air and water quality, and drug use. An informed decision will always require a careful consideration of the information that is relevant to risk assessment (e.g., historical data, risk by analogy, and risks of separate components), as well an understanding of the way subjective estimates of risk are biased in favor of unobservable events with spectacular outcomes.

ELIMINATION BY ASPECTS

Let's return to the earlier problem of deciding which automobile to buy, because it is a decision that most of us will make several times. With so many automobiles on the market, where do you begin? Most people begin decision-making processes of this sort with a strategy known as **elimination by aspects,** although few people know it by this name (Tversky, 1972). An individual who is concerned about unemployment in the United States car industry would begin by eliminating cars that are not manufactured in the United States. In this instance, the aspect under consideration is the place in which the automobile is manufactured. At this point, most people will decide which features (or aspects) of automobiles are important to them. Suppose that you are on a limited budget so that cost is an important feature to you. You would probably determine the cost of various models of Fords, Plymouths, Chevrolets, and other United States autos. Models that cost more than your price ceiling would be eliminated. Let's suppose further that frequency of repair is another important variable. Of course, no one can tell you how frequently the car you choose will need repair, but you can reduce some of the uncertainty associated with this variable by finding out how often other models similar to the ones you are considering have needed repair in the past. This information is available in consumer periodicals in every library. If some of the models that you are still considering are judged as ''worse than average'' on the frequency of repairs, then, presumably, these would be eliminated from further consideration. The elimination by strategy would be recycled repeatedly until the decision maker is left with a few possible models from which to choose. Typically, small and seemingly insignificant differences will come into play to complete the process—for example, ''I'm tired of shopping,'' or ''Let's take this one,'' or ''The dealer will include at no extra cost furry dice to hang from the rear view mirror if I buy this model," or "I can drive this one home today."

The method of elimination by aspects can be used in many contexts. Political candidates, for example, can be thought of as choices that vary along several criteria. If you decide that the issues that are important to you include a strong military defense, reduction of taxes, and school prayer, then you could rank each of these candidates along these aspects and eliminate the candidates who don't share these views with you. You would have to determine which of these aspects is most important if you find that none of the candidates shares all of your views about these important issues.

MULTIDIMENSIONAL COMPARISONS

The overwhelming majority of decisions involve **multidimensional comparisons.** The concept of multiple dimensions is best understood with an example adapted from research conducted by Tversky (1969). Think for a moment about how you would decide which one of three students should be admitted to a university. Most likely, you would want to know something about the intelligence of these three applicants. You learn that Student A's (Anne's) high school grade average (on a scale from 0 to 100) is 92, Student B's (Bruno's) is 85, and Student C's (Clarence's) is 81. If you only considered intelligence, you would decide that Anne should be admitted, because she appears to be most intelligent. In this case, you have made only a **unidimensional comparison.** Although scores on intelligence can range from low to high, it is only one dimension. Most people would object to considering only intelligence in determining who is best suited for a university education. Certainly, other variables, like emotional stability and sociability (the ability to get along with others), are important considerations. Suppose you are now given additional information about the three applicants. You're told that Anne's rating on emotional stability is 71 (also on a scale from 0 to 100), Bruno's is 93, and Clarence's is 80. Given this additional information, would you switch your choice to Bruno or Clarence?

Stop now and decide whom you would select at this point.

What would you decide if you now learned that the sociability score (also on a scale from 0 to 100) for each prospective student is: Anne, 89, Bruno, 73, and Clarence, 96? A summary table of this information appears as follows:

Dimensions	Anne	Bruno	Clarence
Intelligence	92	85	81
Emotional Stability	71	93	80
Sociability	89	73	96

If you based your decision on information about intelligence, emotional stability, and sociability, then your decision involved multidimensional comparisons. If any student had scored highest on all of the dimensions, the task would be easy; however, this is rarely true. Tversky, who conducted this experiment, found that subjects used more than one of the relevant dimensions when making decisions of this sort. In other words, people take into consideration which comparisons are most important and the distances among applicants on each dimension.

Transitivity

How can we determine when subjects are utilizing multidimensional comparisons? The answer to this question involves the mathematical concept of **transitivity.** Somewhere back in elementary school, you should have learned that:

> if $A > B$ (A is greater than B)
> and $B > C$ (B is greater than C)
> then $A > C$ (A is greater than C)

Applying transitivity to decision making is straightforward. If you considered only intelligence as the criterion for university admission, then you would have ranked the applicants:

> Anne > Bruno (Anne is preferred over Bruno)
> Bruno > Clarence (Bruno is preferred over Clarence)

Thus, your first choice for admission would be Anne (she has the "most" intelligence), then Bruno, then Clarence. If you had to choose between Anne and Clarence you would select Anne, because Anne > Clarence by the rules of transitivity. This demonstrates transitivity in decision making and may seem obvious and logical.

If, after receiving the information about emotional stability and sociability, you are asked to choose between Anne and Clarence, you might look at the composite information and combine what you've learned about the three candidates overall and select:

> Anne > Clarence,

and when choosing between Clarence and Bruno you might select

> Clarence > Bruno.

Suppose that you are now asked to choose between Anne and Bruno. If the decisions were transitive, then you would select Anne > Bruno. Many people, however, would find the difference in emotionality scores too large to ignore (Bruno has 93, Anne has 71) and decide

Bruno > Anne

This preference for Bruno over Anne represents intransitivity (a violation of transitivity). Whenever intransitivity occurs, experimenters infer that multidimensional comparisons have been made. Thus, it is not necessarily true that logical or good decisions obey the mathematical principle of transitivity. (Note: It is possible for a set of decisions to obey the law of transitivity even when multidimensional comparisons have been made. If one applicant scored highest on all dimensions, a second was consistently in the middle, and a third was always lowest, decisions would still be transitive. However, only when decisions are intransitive can experimenters assert that multidimensional comparisons were made.)

PREPARING A WORKSHEET

Researchers have found that the best way to make an important decision involves the preparation and utilization of a decision worksheet. The purpose of a worksheet is to optimize decision making. Psychologists who study **optimization** compare the actual decision made by a person to a theoretical "ideal" decision to see how similar they are. Proponents of the worksheet procedure believe that it will yield optimal (best) decisions. Although there are several variations on the exact format that a worksheet can take, they are similar in their essential aspects. Worksheets require defining the problem in a clear and concise way, listing all possible solutions to the problem, listing the relevant considerations that will be affected by the decision, determining the relative importance of each consideration, and mathematically calculating a decision. The end product of the worksheet procedure is a single numerical summary of each possible solution or alternative. The alternative with the highest number of points emerges as the best decision.

Most important problems are multifaceted, with several alternatives to choose from, each with unique advantages and disadvantages. One of the benefits of a pencil-and-paper decision-making procedure is that it permits us to deal with more variables than our immediate processing ability would allow. If you've already read the chapter on utilizing memory (chapter 2), you'll recall (I hope) that working memory is limited in the number of pieces of information it can deal with at one time. On the average, we can keep about seven ideas in our mind at once (Miller, 1956). A worksheet can be especially useful when the decision involves a large number of variables with complex relationships.

Let's consider the worksheet procedure with a realistic example for most college students: "What will I do after graduation?" A hypothetical student,

Evan, has several postgraduation opportunities. He is contemplating the following: (a) a job in a large fashionable department store where he will train to be a buyer; (b) a teaching position in an inner-city school, probably a 5th- or 6th-grade class; (c) a graduate school degree in business administration; (d) a law school degree; and (e) a year off to "bum around" Europe. A decision-making worksheet will be very important in helping him choose the best alternative.

Defining the Problem

The first step is the realization that a decision needs to be made. A decision-making worksheet begins with a succinct statement of the problem that will also help to narrow it. Thus, the problem for Evan becomes "What will I do after graduation that will lead to a successful career?" If Evan words his decision this way, he has already decided that his decision will involve long-range goals and not immediate ones. It is important to be clear about this distinction because, most often, long-range goals will involve a different decision than short-range ones. Thus, the options of attending graduate or law school are really statements about working in business or as a lawyer and not decisions about school per se.

The importance of this first step cannot be overemphasized. The entire decision-making process depends on the way the problem is defined. If Evan had posed the problem as "How can I best earn a good living?", he would find that the process would focus on monetary considerations. Similarly, the process would change if he posed the problem as, "Should I go to graduate school?" Recent research with business managers has shown that the ability to redefine business problems is an important characteristic of good decision making in management (Merron, Fisher, & Torbert, 1987).

Generating the Alternatives

The next step is to write out, in separate columns across the top of the worksheet, all possible alternatives that could solve the problem. You'll need a large sheet of ruled paper, because it would make no sense to cut the worksheet process short because you ran out of space on your paper. It is important that you don't evaluate the alternatives at this stage; however, this is not the place for fiction, either. If you are tone deaf, this is not the time to fantasize about a career in the opera. Allow room for two columns under each alterative that will be used later for calculations. Thus far, Evan's worksheet would look something like this (Table 8.1).

Evan notices, while drawing up his worksheet, that these alternatives are not all mutually exclusive. There's no reason why he can't decide to travel around Europe for a year and then select a career goal; besides, a vacation in Europe is not a long-range plan, and the decision currently being made is for life career goals. He decides at this point to erase the fifth alternative, because it seems to

TABLE 8.1
What Will I Do After College That Will Lead to a Successful Career?

Alternatives	Dept. Store buyer	Teacher—inner city school	Graduate School— Business	Law School	"Bum" in Europe for a year

require a separate decision from the other four. He also remembers at this point that his father always hoped that Evan would want to run the family-owned lumber business after his graduation from college. Although this is not an appealing idea to Evan, he substitutes it as an additional choice, because the rules for this step of the process do not allow for evaluation.

Listing the Considerations

The decision Evan makes will have multiple effects. His feelings about making a personal contribution to society, his income and his future lifestyle, his parents' and friends' opinions of him, the quality of his workday, and many other variables are at stake. If Evan were married with children, the impact of each decision on his spouse and children would also need to be considered. At this point, Evan should cover the alternatives and list on the left-hand side of his worksheet the considerations or variables that will be affected by his decision. The worksheet would now look like this (Table 8.2).

Before proceeding, Evan should now put the worksheet away and mull over the problem: the alternatives and the considerations. Often, people find that in the course of worksheet preparation they think of new alternatives and discover which considerations are important to them. It is also a good idea to ask other people that you trust if they can think of additional alternatives and considerations. Considerations and alternatives that are not listed on the worksheet will not be considered, so it is extremely important to list all the relevant alternatives and considerations.

TABLE 8.2
What Will I Do After College That Will Lead to a Successful Career?

Alternatives	Dept. Store Buyer	Teacher— Inner City School	Graduate School— Business	Law School	Run Family Lumber Business
Considerations					
Desire to Help Society					
Income					
Parents' Opinions					
Friends' Opinions					
Interest in the Work					

TABLE 8.3
What Will I Do After Graduation That Will Lead to a Successful Career?

Alternatives	*Dept. Store Buyer*	*Teacher— Inner City School*	*Graduate School— Business*	*Law School*	*Run Family Lumber Business*	*Jazz Musician*
Considerations						
Desire to Help Society						
Income						
Parents' Opinions						
Friends' Opinions						
Interest in the Work						
Prestige of Occupation						
Employment Security						
Amount of Vacation and Free Time						
Likelihood of Success						

Be sure, however, that you don't let other people make the decision for you. Suppose that Evan's friend suggests that Evan seriously pursues his interest in music and becomes a jazz musician. In addition, Evan thinks up several additional considerations, which he lists on his worksheet. He also decides that as he is planning for his future, he should realistically consider his chances for success at each alternative. (See Table 8.3.)

Listing all relevant considerations is an important part of the worksheet process. Janis and Mann (1977) believe that poor decisions often result from failures to think through all of the relevant considerations. They suggest that considerations be listed under four categories—gains and losses for self, gains and losses for significant others, self-approval and disapproval, and social approval and disapproval, to avoid overlooking important considerations.

Weighing the Considerations

It is almost always true that the considerations are not equally important to the decision maker and therefore need to be weighed accordingly. A five-point scale in which 1 = of slight importance, 5 = of great importance, and the numbers 2, 3, 4, reflect gradations of importance between these end points can be used to quantify the relative importance of each consideration. Weighing considerations is a personal matter. It is likely that each of us would assign weights somewhat differently. If Evan felt that his desire to help society was moderately important to him, he would rate it a "3." Similarly, if he believed that income was more than moderately important to him, but less than "of great importance" he would rate it a "4." The appropriate weights are placed alongside each consideration.

Weighing the considerations is an important part of the worksheet process. After assigning numbers (the weights) to each consideration, you should stop to survey the weights. If Evan rated "friend's opinions" with a larger number than "parents' opinions," this reflects how he feels about their relative opinions. This is a good way to clarify which considerations are most important to you.

Weighing the Alternatives

Now is the time to think carefully about each alternative and determine how well each satisfies the considerations listed. The alternatives will be weighed using the numbers -2, -1, 0, $+1$, and $+2$. A positive number indicates that it is favorable, or "pro," the consideration, with $+2$ indicating that it is highly favorable and $+1$ indicating that it is somewhat favorable. A negative number will be used if an alternative is incompatible with, or "con," a consideration, with -2 indicating that it is a highly incompatible and -1 indicating that it is somewhat incompatible. Zero will be used when an alternative is neither favorable nor unfavorable to a consideration.

We'll use Evan's worksheet to demonstrate how to weigh alternatives. First, Evan has to contemplate how becoming a department store buyer will satisfy his desire to help society. Certainly it won't hurt society, but it probably won't help it either. Evan believes that, although it may create additional jobs in related industries (fashion, sewing, etc.), this is not really what he had in mind when he thought about helping society; therefore, he rates it a zero on this consideration. This number is placed under "Department Store Buyer" in the left-hand column on the first row. Subsequent ratings will be placed directly below this number. If he does eventually become a buyer for a large department store, he probably will earn a satisfactory income. He certainly won't be rich, but it will be enough money to allow him to live comfortably; therefore, he gives it a $+1$. Both his parents and friends will consider it to be a moderately good job, so he rates it a $+1$ on both these considerations. He believes that it should be very interesting work and rates it a $+2$ on "interest in the work." It should be a moderately prestigious occupation and thus rates a $+1$ in this category. Unfortunately, it probably won't offer much employment security, because department store sales are tied to the economy, which seems to fluctuate erratically; he therefore rates it -1 on "employment security." A department store buyer is required to work a 40-hour or more work week with only a few weeks a year for vacation, thus rating a -2 on vacation and free time. He notes that he is moderately likely to succeed as a department store buyer, so he rates it $+1$ on this consideration.

It is usually necessary to gather more information at this stage of the decision-making process. Evan may need to phone the local school district to find out what the median salary is for school teachers. He also might seek the advice of his college advisor to determine if he has the math skills needed to succeed in business administration.

Each alternative is rated in a similar manner by thinking how well it satisfies the objectives of each consideration. When he has completed weighing the alternatives, Evan's worksheet looks like this (Table 8.4.)

TABLE 8.4
What Will I Do After College That Will Lead to a Successful Career?

Alternatives		Dept. Store Buyer	Teacher— Inner City School	Graduate School— Business	Law School	Run Family Lumber Business	Jazz Musician
Considerations							
Desire to Help Society	(3)	0	+2	0	+1	0	0
Income	(4)	+1	−1	+2	+2	0	−1
Parents' Opinions	(2)	+1	0	+1	+2	+2	−1
Friends' Opinions	(3)	+1	+2	0	+1	−1	+2
Interest in the Work	(5)	+2	+2	+1	0	−1	+1
Prestige of Occupation	(1)	+1	−1	+2	+2	−2	+1
Employment Security	(3)	−1	−2	0	+1	+2	−2
Amount of Vacation and Free Time	(2)	−2	+2	−2	−2	+1	+2
Likelihood of Success	(5)	+1	+1	−1	−1	+2	−2

Calculating a Decision

If you have carefully followed the worksheet procedure this far, you've realized that it requires numerous decisions before even coming close to yielding the one you want to make. By now, Evan has decided what type of decision he's making (long range), listed all the alternatives and all the considerations that he believes to be necessary, and decided how important each consideration is to him and how well each alternative satisfies the objectives of each consideration.

There are three different strategies for calculating a decision at this point. They are overall assessment, dimensional comparison, and the "⅔ Ideal Rule." Each utilizes a different criterion for selecting the best decision from a worksheet.

Overall Assessment

An **overall assessment** is obtained by determining how well each alternative satisfies the considerations taken as a whole or overall. This is calculated by multiplying the weight previously assigned for each consideration by the value assigned to how well an alternative satisfies that consideration. For example, Evan has rated his desire to help society a "3" and the department store buyer alternative a "0" on this consideration. The first cell of the worksheet is 3 × 0 = 0. This result, 0, is placed in the right-hand column under "department store buyer." Continuing down to the next consideration, we see that Evan rated income as "4" and the department store buyer alternative "+1" on income. Because 4 × 1 = 4, he would place a "4" in the right-hand column below Department Store Buyer and next to "Income." This procedure is repeated for each alternative. The right-hand column for each alternative is then added,

TABLE 8.5
What Will I Do After College That Will Lead to a Successful Career?

Alternatives		Dept. Store Buyer		Teacher— Inner City School		Graduate School— Business		Law School		Run Family Lumber Business		Jazz Musician	
Considerations													
Desire to Help Society	(3)	0	0	+2	6	0	0	+1	3	0	0	0	0
Income	(4)	+1	4	−1	−4	+2	8	+2	8	0	0	−1	−4
Parents' Opinions	(2)	+1	2	0	0	+1	2	+2	4	+2	4	−1	−2
Friends' Opinions	(3)	+1	3	+2	6	0	0	+1	3	−1	−3	+2	6
Interest in the Work	(5)	+2	10	+2	10	+1	5	0	0	−1	−5	+1	5
Prestige of Occupation	(1)	+1	1	−1	−1	+2	2	+2	2	−2	−2	+1	1
Employment Security	(3)	−1	−3	−2	−6	0	0	1	3	+2	6	−2	−6
Amount of Vacation and Free Time	(2)	−2	−4	+2	4	−2	−4	−2	−4	+1	2	+2	4
Likelihood of Success	(5)	+1	5	+1	5	−1	−5	−1	−5	+2	10	−2	−10
			18		20		8		14		12		−6

yielding a total score for each alternative. This is demonstrated in Table 8.5.

Perusal of the worksheet now shows that, based on an overall assessment, the alternative with the highest total score is "Teacher—Inner City School." You will also notice that the alternative to become a department store buyer obtained a fairly high score that was close to a winning alternative. Thus far, it seems that Evan should seriously be thinking about a career as a teacher.

Dimensional Comparison

In a **dimensional comparison** strategy, each consideration (the "dimensions") is examined to find which alternative has the highest score. For example, if "Desire to Help Society" is examined, you will see that "Teacher—Inner City School" had the highest rating among all the other alternatives; therefore, it would "win" on this consideration and get one point. Looking at "Income," you will see that both "Graduate School—Business" and "Law School" were assigned +2 on this dimension. In the event of ties, each of the winning tied alternative is awarded one point. If each consideration is examined in a similar manner, the following number of considerations won for each alternative will result:

Number of Considerations Won

Dept. Store Buyer	Teacher Inner- City School	Graduate School— Business	Law School	Run Family Lumber Business	Jazz Musician
1	4	2	3	3	2

As seen here, the alternative "Teacher—Inner City School" scored highest among the alternatives on four considerations. Thus, the results of the dimensional comparison strategy agree with the overall assessment results. Notice that both "Law School" and "Run Family Lumber Business" won three considerations each, yet scored fairly low on the overall assessment.

⅔ Ideal Rule

The "⅔ **Ideal Rule**" was suggested by Carkhuff (1973). It requires the decision maker to calculate an overall assessment total for a perfect or ideal alternative. If an ideal alternative were added to Evan's worksheet, it would rate +2 on each consideration, because it would be highly favorable to each consideration. A total overall score for an ideal alternative can be arrived at by adding all of the consideration weights and multiplying the total by 2, as seen here:

$$3 + 4 + 2 + 3 + 5 + 1 + 3 + 2 + 5 = 28$$

$$28 \times 2 = 56$$

The reasoning behind the ⅔ Ideal Rule is that a best alternative may not be good enough if it fails to measure up to ⅔ of an ideal solution. Thus, according to this rule, a minimally acceptable alternative would score an overall 37.5 (⅔ × 56 = 37.5). If you turn back to the completed worksheet, you'll see that the highest total was for the teacher alternative and it rated, by the overall assessment method, a 20 (considerably less than the 37.5 required by this rule). Evan has several choices at this point. He can disregard the ⅔ Ideal Rule (which is likely if he is pleased with the decision to become a teacher), or he can expand and recycle the process by generating additional considerations and alternatives until he reached a consensus with all three calculating procedures.

The "⅔ Ideal Rule" is based on the idea that some alternatives are "good enough," whereas others are not. Searching for alternatives that are good enough is called **satisficing** (Marsh & Shapira, 1982; Tversky & Kahneman, 1981). Satisficing refers to terminating the decision-making process when an alternative that is "good enough" to satisfy most of the important considerations is found. The decision-making process cannot go on forever, so at some point, the decision maker will have to decide that one alternative is "good enough." The problem really is *when* to terminate the process, and there are no simple answers to this question. Important decisions, like the one considered in this example, should be given the time and effort that they deserve. Often, better decisions are possible if the decision maker would invest more time and effort into generating alternatives and listing considerations.

Dilemmas in Decision Making

The decision maker will often encounter dilemmas in calculating a decision. It is not unusual for two or more alternatives to have exactly the same high score or for one alternative to obtain the highest total with the overall assessment and a different one with the dimensional comparison. This can always be remedied by generating additional considerations and repeating the process until an alternative emerges as best. It is also possible to combine two or more alternatives. For example, Evan could become a buyer in a department store and volunteer to tutor children on weekends. This would allow him to realize his desire to help society while maintaining the benefits of the buyer alternative. Sometimes, the decision maker will abandon the worksheet before it's completed because the process helped to clarify the issues and led directly to a decision without the calculations.

Certainly, the worksheet procedure requires a great deal of work, as its name implies. You might be wondering if there is any evidence to suggest that it's worth the extra effort — that it actually leads to better decisions. Yes, there is. In a study by Mann (1972), he randomly selected 30 high school seniors (15 females and 15 males) from a college preparatory program to participate in an experimental investigation of the worksheet procedure. He taught them how to prepare a worksheet that would help them make decisions about college. The procedure he used was similar to the one presented here, but not identical to it. He also employed a "control group" of 20 students who were not taught the worksheet procedure. Mann contacted the students approximately 6 weeks after they notified the college about their decision concerning which college they planned to attend. The group that had received worksheet training (the experimental group) had less postdecision stress and anxiety and were happier about the decisions they had made than the control group. Mann also reported that they had considered possible unfavorable consequences of their decision more carefully than the control group. Thus, if something does go wrong, they will more likely be prepared for it than those in the group without worksheet training.

Additional evidence that supports the validity of the worksheet procedure comes from a study by Wanous (1973). He conducted an experiment to study the employment decisions of telephone operators. One group of prospective telephone operators was shown a film that portrayed both the positive and negative aspects of the job, whereas a control group was shown the standard training film that stressed only the positive aspects. All subjects in both groups decided to accept the employment offer to become telephone operators. One month later, subjects who had viewed the "balanced" presentation reported that they were happier with their decision than the other telephone operators, who had viewed the standard one-sided film. In addition, significantly fewer subjects from the experimental group were thinking about quitting their jobs than from the control group. In a similar vein, Janis and Mann (1977) reported several studies in which the worksheet procedure has been utilized in health decisions (e.g., elective surgery) with beneficial outcomes. One of the benefits of the worksheet procedure is that it allows people to feel more confident about difficult decisions.

POSTDECISION COMMITMENT AND EVALUATION

To begin with it was only tentatively that I put forward the views that I have developed . . . but in the course of time they have gained such a hold upon me that I can no longer think in any other way.

—Sigmund Freud (1930)

The decision-making process doesn't end with the decision. Once a course of action has been selected, the decision maker must make detailed plans to carry it out and needs to remain committed to the decision. However, if a major change occurs in the evaluation of the consideration, then the process should be repeated. For example, if Evan were unexpectedly offered a lucrative contract to become a jazz musician, he would be wise to reconsider this alternative. Success at this alternative would now seem much more likely, and a large income would be assured. Decision making is not a static process. Our major life decisions will have to be reconsidered whenever a major variable changes.

Cognitive Dissonance

Most of the time, people find that they are pleased with their decisions. This finding has been of considerable interest to research psychologists. Leon Festinger (1957), a famous research psychologist, proposed a theory to explain this phenomenon. It is called the theory of **cognitive dissonance.** It is based on the idea that people like their beliefs, attitudes, and actions to be consistent, and, when they are not consistent, an unpleasant internal state arises—dissonance. Dissonance needs to be reduced. If you believe that it is wrong to smoke marijuana, and you attend a party where you smoke marijuana, you will feel uncomfortable because your actions and beliefs are not in agreement. They are not consistent with each other. In order to reduce the discomfort of cognitive dissonance, the unpleasant internal state, you will generally change your beliefs and conclude that you did the right thing, because "marijuana probably isn't so bad after all." In general, the theory of cognitive dissonance has received considerable experimental support. In one study (Brehm, 1956), subjects rated the desirability of several gifts (e.g., toaster, coffee maker). They were then asked to choose between two gifts that they had rated as equally desirable. After a decision had been made, subjects rated the rejected gift as being much less desirable than the one they chose. The theory of cognitive dissonance would have predicted this result, because subjects would now believe that they must like the selected object much more than the rejected one in order to maintain consistency. It seems that, once a decision is made, the alternatives that were not selected will seem much less attractive than the one that was.

The theory of cognitive dissonance can be applied in a number of situations. It can be used to explain the famous fable The Fox and the Sour Grapes. The story

338

goes something like this: A hungry fox spies grapes hanging high overhead. After repeated unsuccessful attempts to reach them, he decides that they were probably sour and walks away. Like the human subjects described in this section, he downplayed the desirability of the object he didn't obtain.

The theory of cognitive dissonance only applies when a conscious decision has been made. If you were coerced in some way, there would be no dissonance. Suppose that you were required to write an essay on some topic that you are opposed to, like the inferiority of a racial or ethnic group, or why drugs should be available to elementary school children. If you were coerced into doing this, there would be no need to change your attitudes to keep them consistent with this behavior. However, if you voluntarily decided to write such an essay, then cognitive dissonance theory would predict a change in your attitude toward the position you took in the essay. This is a major theory in social psychology that explains why people are usually satisfied with the decisions they make.

Hindsight and Forethought

The term **hindsight** is probably not a new one for you. After a decision has been made and the relevant events occur, well-meaning friends will often tell you that they could have predicted the consequences of your decision. If you have ever been divorced (or have exchanged confidences with someone who has), there were probably several acquaintances who claimed to have known all along that, "he (or she) was no good for you." Events appear different with the benefit of hindsight. Forethought is the opposite of hindsight. There should be fewer unfortunate consequences if decisions are carefully thought out before they are made.

In experimental investigations of hindsight, most participants erroneously believed that they could have predicted the consequences of historical and personal decisions before they occurred. In our earlier analysis of the Pearl Harbor disaster, it seemed obvious that the only possible decision was to assume that the aircraft belonged to the Japanese. It should be remembered that we analyzed the disaster with the full knowledge of the ensuing events. Hindsight occurs only when poor or wrong decisions have been made. It is seldom that good decisions are analyzed after the fact. Forethought and hindsight are qualitatively different. At the time of the decision (forethought), there is doubt and deliberation, but following the unfavorable consequences of the decision (hindsight), there is often a great sense of certainty that the future should have been predicted more accurately.

An example of the power of hindsight occurred in 1974, when an editorial in a Eugene, Oregon newspaper called on the local prison warden to resign. A "convicted murderer, bank robber, and all-around bad actor" had been given a 4-hour pass to leave the state penitentiary (Fischhoff, 1975). Instead of returning, he kidnapped and murdered an Oregon couple. With the benefit of hindsight—that is, with the full knowledge of the result—does it seem that the warden should

psychiatrist

have known that this would happen? Given the disastrous outcome, it was a wrong decision, but was the result obvious, or even likely, before the pass was granted? The convict had been a model prisoner before the pass was granted. Do you think that the warden should have been required to resign?

Hindsight is of little value in the decision-making process. It distorts our memory for events that occurred at the time of the decision so that the actual consequence seems to have been a "forgone conclusion." Thus, it may be difficult to learn from our mistakes. Retrospective (after the fact) review, on the other hand, can be a valuable aid in improving future decisions. Unlike hindsight, it does not involve a faulty reconstruction of the information available at the time of the decision so that the consequence appears obvious.

It is a good idea to determine what went wrong if a poor decision has been made. Look for the kinds of fallacies discussed earlier in the chapter. If you can find the weaknesses in earlier decisions, you'll know what to watch out for in subsequent ones. With practice and hard work, you can actively plan for your future and make good decisions that will affect your whole life.

APPLYING THE FRAMEWORK

In applying the general thinking skills framework to decision making, consider the following questions:

1. *What is the goal?* The skills involved in decision making should be used whenever you are faced with selecting the best alternative among a set of alternatives. Examples of situations that require the use of these skills include personal, professional, and political decisions.

2. *What is known?* The entire decision-making process is predicated on the belief that you are selecting from among a set of alternatives. If you have no alternatives, then there is no decision. Thus, a starting point for the process is a careful consideration of all possible alternatives. A decision can only be as good as the information that it is based on. If you do not know much about a problem, then you cannot select intelligently from a set of solutions. Probably, the greatest difficulty with making decisions is the failure to consider alternatives that aren't listed on a worksheet or aren't made conscious in some other way. Good decisions will require information gathering and assessment *before* the selection of alternatives begins.

3. *Which thinking skill or skills will get you to your goal?* The kind of skill you select when you are confronted with an important decision depends on the nature of the problem. Some of the skills involve avoiding common fallacies like the failure to seek disconfirming evidence or the reliance on available information to assess the likelihood of an outcome. If the decision has potentially negative consequences, then the positive and negative results of a course of action have to been compared to each other and to those associated with other alternatives. The weighing of considerations to calculate relative importance and likelihood is helpful whenever there are multiple alternatives and the decision is an important one.

The following decision-making skills were developed in this chapter:

- listing alternatives and considering the pros and cons of each
- restating the problem so as to consider different types of alternatives
- recognizing the need to seek disconfirming evidence
- understanding the way that information that is readily recalled or appears representative of a random process can influence how decisions are made
- considering how overly optimistic assessments bias the selection of alternatives
- recognizing arguments that are based on entrapment and considering why the costs have been high
- being mindful of the way emotional states like psychological reactance can lead us to select less desirable alternatives
- evaluating positive assessments of alternatives that are based on reciprocity or familiarity
- seeking information to reduce uncertainty when making risky decisions
- preparing a decision-making worksheet for important decisions
- understanding the distinction between the quality of a decision and its outcome
- estimating unknown risks with historical data, analysis of component risks, and analogy with similar known risks
- recognizing that hindsight analysis of a decision is usually biased and of limited value

4. *Have you reached your goal?* The process of making a decision could, theoretically, go on forever. Most decisions, however, have deadlines. After you have carefully considered various outcomes, you need to take an overview of your decision and then follow through and act on it. Does the decision seem right? Are you satisfied with the process and outcome? As stated in the chapter, because of the uncertainty inherent in decisions, sometimes good decisions will have poor outcomes. When this happens, scrutinize the nature of the outcome. Was there a consideration that you failed to consider at the time the decision was made? Can you learn from the negative outcome?

CHAPTER SUMMARY

1. Decision making is an active process that begins with a clear definition of the problem and a set of alternative solutions from which to choose.

2. One way to improve on the way in which decisions are made is to phrase the problem in several ways. Additional alternatives can emerge by changing the focus of the problem.

3. Because few people have ever received formal instruction in thinking skills, even trained professionals commit common decision-making fallacies.

4. A common error in decision making is the failure to seek disconfirming evidence.

5. People often rely on heuristics, or "rules of thumb," to help them make decisions. The availability heuristic, or reliance on events that are readily recalled, is a common decision-making heuristic.

6. Because of the widespread but erroneous belief that the laws of chance are self-correcting, many people believe that "random-looking" sequences of outcomes are more probable outcomes of a random process than orderly sequences of outcomes.

7. Unwarranted optimism can also lead to poor decisions, because it prevents realistic assessment of both desirable and undesirable consequences of a decision.

8. People often fall prey to entrapment. They find it difficult to reverse their decision after having invested large amounts of time or money.

9. Decisions are often biased by emotional states, like psychological reactance (the resistance to a loss of freedom) and liking induced by reciprocity and familiarity.

11. Risky decisions require special care. There is often a tendency to downplay the likelihood of a disastrous outcome.

12. When you are making decisions that involve risk, assess the degree of risk by seeking historical data. If no historical data are available, find information about the risks associated with the component parts of an alternative, or try to determine degree of risk by analogy to a similar and known phenomenon.

13. When the alternatives vary along several dimensions, decisions are sometimes made by eliminating alternatives until only one or two choices remain.

14. Important decisions can be optimized by preparing a worksheet in which alternatives and considerations are listed and weighed in a table format.

15. People are most often satisfied with the decisions that they make, possibly because cognitive dissonance works to maintain consistency between actions and beliefs. Thus, we reason that if we decided on a course of action it must have been the best one.

16. After the consequences of a decision have occurred, there is a great sense of certainty that the consequences should have been obvious. Hindsight is a ubiquitous phenomenon that distorts how we perceive the information that was available before the decision was made.

17. There is an important distinction between a good decision that is based on the information that is available when the decision is being made and its outcomes. Sometimes, good decisions will have undesirable outcomes, because of the inherent uncertainty in most important decisions.

18. When experts consider relative risks, they rely on the expected number of deaths per year to make their assessments. By contrast, nonexperts rate phenomena that are unobservable and have disastrous outcomes as most risky.

Terms to Know

Check your understanding of the concepts presented in this chapter by reviewing their definitions. If you find that you're having difficulty with any term, be sure to reread the section in which it is discussed.

Fallacy. An error or mistake in the thinking process.

Confirmation Bias. The predilection to seek and utilize information that supports or confirms one's hypothesis or premises while ignoring disconfirming information.

Heuristic. A general "rule of thumb" or strategy that we use to solve problems and make decisions. Although it doesn't always produce a correct answer, it is usually a helpful aid. Compare with algorithm.

Algorithm. A problem-solving procedure that will always yield the solution to a particular problem if it is followed exactly. Compare with heuristic.

Availability Heuristic. A decision-making "rule of thumb" that is used when estimates of frequency or probability are made based on the ease with which instances come to mind; for example, many college students believe that there are more professors in America than farmers because they can think of more professors whom they know than farmers.

Representativeness Heuristic. A decision-making "rule of thumb" in which the determination of a sample's likelihood is made by noting its similarity to a random process. If it "looks like" a random process, it is judged to be more probable than if it appears orderly or patterned.

Wishful Thinking. People tend to overestimate their chances of success or the likelihood of a desirable outcome.

Entrapment. A situation in which an individual has already invested much money, time, or effort and therefore decides to continue in this situation because of the initial investment.

Psychological Reactance. Resistance arising from restrictions of freedom. Some people will select a less preferred alternative if they are told that they must select the preferred alternative.

Mere Exposure Effect. Very often, repeated exposure to a stimulus will enhance your liking for it.

Biased Discounting. Predilection to discount or reduce the magnitude or probability of risk.

Elimination by Aspects. A decision-making strategy in which choices are sequentially eliminated if they fail to meet one or more considerations.

Multidimensional Comparison. When the choices in a decision-making task vary in many different ways, people compare them on all of their differences and combine all of the information to make their decisions. For example, if three homes differed in price, size, and location, the information about these three considerations would be combined when making a choice.

Unidimensional Comparison. When the choices in a decision-making task vary in only one way, the decision is straightforward and relies only on the differences on this dimension. For example, if three hats were identical, varying only in price, then price alone would dictate the choice.

Transitivity. The property of numbers such that if $A > B$ and $B > C$, then $A > C$.

Optimization. In decision making, it refers to making the best possible decision in any situation.

Overall Assessment. A method of calculating a decision from a worksheet. The choice with the highest worksheet total would be selected. Compare with dimensional comparison and ⅔ Ideal rule.

Dimensional Comparison. A method for calculating a decision from a worksheet. The choice that has "won" the greatest number of considerations would be selected. Compare with overall assessment and ⅔ Ideal rule.

⅔ Ideal Rule. A method for calculating a decision from a worksheet. Only choices whose worksheet totals are at least ⅔ as large as the ideal choice would be chosen. Compare with dimensional comparison and overall assessment.

Satisficing. Terminating the decision-making process when an alternative that is "good enough" to satisfy most of the important considerations is found.

Cognitive Dissonance. A theory based on the notion that people want their beliefs, attitudes, and actions to be consistent. When they are not consistent, an unpleasant internal state arises—dissonance—which needs to be reduced. We reduce dissonance by changing our beliefs and attitudes so that they are in accord with our actions.

Hindsight. Reevaluation of a decision after it has been made and its consequences have occurred, with the belief that the consequences should have been known before the decision was made.

Chapter Questions

Be sure that you can answer the following questions:

1. Describe some experimental studies that support the validity of the worksheet procedure.

2. What are heuristics? How do they differ from algorithms? Describe two examples of heuristics. Are they necessarily bad?

3. List and describe the steps in preparing a decision worksheet.

4. How does the theory of cognitive dissonance explain why people are usually satisfied with the decisions they make?

5. Explain how the "elimination by aspects" strategy can be applied to deciding where to live.

6. What should a decision maker do if one alternative "wins" by the overall assessment method, and a different one "wins" by the dimensional comparison method?

7. How can the "failure to seek disconfirming evidence" lead to wrong decisions in research?

8. Justify all of the effort involved in making a worksheet.

9. How could a decision worksheet be a valuable aid to people in psychotherapy?

10. How does the mathematical concept of transitivity apply to decision making? If your friend was deciding which university to attend and told you that she preferred Ohio State over Penn State, and Penn State over California State, but preferred California State over Ohio State, what could you conclude about her decision?

11. Explain how psychological reactance can cause people to select a less desirable alternative.

12. How does reciprocity influence the kinds of choices we make?

13. Why is hindsight a detrimental process? Why does the author state that sometimes good decisions will have detrimental outcomes? If the outcome is bad, doesn't that mean that the decision was bad?

14. What sort of information should you have when making a decision about a potential risk?

Exercises

Try out the decision-making skills you've learned in this chapter.

1. Think of a major decision that you will be facing in the near future. Use the worksheet procedure to help you reach a decision.

2. Study a major political decision that was made in the last 25 years (e.g., The Bay of Pigs decision, Watergate, President Ford's decision to pardon former President Nixon, the decision to offer arms to Iran in exchange for hostages). Look for the role that fallacies and heuristics played. Analyze the decision. Based on the information that was available at that time, would you have made the same one? If not, what would you have done?

3. Look for instances of the confirmation bias, availability heuristic, representativeness heuristic, wishful thinking, cognitive dissonance, and hindsight, in the everyday decisions made by yourself and others around you.

4. Reread the hospital scenario presented at the beginning of this chapter. Based on what you've learned about how to make sound decisions, what would you do if you were the protagonist in this story?

5. Try out some of the examples presented in this chapter on your friends (e.g., the ascending number series, the multiplication series, the information about a symptom and disease, the head–tail sequence). If they make the usual errors, explain to them why the errors occurred and how to avoid these errors in the future.

6. Consider the political candidates that are running in a current election, or select a past election. Use the process of elimination by aspects to decide which candidate is best. Explain the process.

7. Comment on the following:

"We've already invested over $2 million of taxpayer funds in this project. If we pull out now, all that money will be wasted."

"Of course Ngyuen will make a fine class president. He always says nice things to me."

"No, we're not prepared for a flood. Although we had a serious flood last year, another one is not likely to happen."

"Italians are naturally musical. After all, where do you think Frank Sinatra came from?"

"I'm sure that their next child will be a girl. After all, they already have six boys."

"It's a good idea to use 'Goniffs Are us' for investment advice. Last year they recommended that their clients invest in Bob's Bank, and that turned out to be an excellent investment."

"I think that there is no reason to require motorcycle riders to wear a helmet, but I do believe that we should have strict laws regarding recombinant DNA, because it's so risky"

"After all the work Loren put into selecting the right phone company, the company he selected was subject to a corporate takeover, and now we're stuck with poor phone service. He would have been better off if he'd just flipped a coin."

8. The following problem was suggested by a colleague (Dr. George Marsh at California State University, Dominguez Hills). If a therapist found that 80% of the women clients she treats who have sexual problems were abused as children can she decide that

345

child abuse causes sexual dysfunction later in life? Why or why not? What additional information does she need to make this decision?

SUGGESTED READINGS

A comprehensive and moderately easy-to-read coverage of the decision-making process can be found in a book appropriately named *Decision Making* by Janis and Mann (1977) and in *A Practical Guide for Making Decisions* by Wheeler and Janis (1980). Both have an extensive section on the worksheet procedure, as does *The Art of Problem-Solving* by Carkhuff (1973).

Several excellent papers on heuristics and biases appear in a volume edited by Johnson-Laird and Wason, entitled *Thinking: Readings in Cognitive Science* (1977). A book that is fun to read because the examples of decision strategies are humorous and current is *Decisions Decisions: Game Theory and You* by Bell and Caplans (1976). An interesting multidisciplinary approach can be found in *Making Decisions: A Multidisciplinary Introduction* by Hill et al. (1979). This book begins with the problem of "What to do with dear Aunt Sarah?" It discusses the ethical, economic, psychological, and philosophical problems that a family is faced with in planning the future of an aging aunt. A collection of interdisciplinary papers appears in *Decision Making: An Interdisciplinary Inquiry,* edited by Ungson and Braunstein (1982) and in Arkes and Hammond (1986) book entitled, *Judgment and Decision Making: An Interdisciplinary Reader.*

Advanced treatments of decision making can be found in *Human Judgment and Decision Making: Theories, Methods, and Procedures* by Hammond, McClelland, and Mumpower (1980), *Human Judgment and Decision Processes,* edited by Kaplin and Schwarts (1975), and *Decision Methodology* by White (1975). An excellent new text in this area that is highly recommended is Baron's (1988) *Thinking and Deciding.* A collection of papers that deal with a variety of topics in the field of decision making can be found in *Cognitive Processes in Choice and Decision Behavior,* edited by Wallsten (1980). Fischhoff has tackled some of the most difficult issues in decision making in a volume edited by Sternberg and Smith (1988), entitled *The Psychology of Human Thought.* Fischhoff has discussed how certain safety decisions reflect inherent beliefs about the worth of a human life. It is fascinating reading, no matter what your level of expertise in this area is.

If you're interested in learning more about the theory of cognitive dissonance, you can consult the classic in this area, *A Theory of Cognitive Dissonance* by Festinger (1957). Some of the experimental literature on cognitive dissonance appear in a volume edited by Festinger (1964), called *Conflict, Decision and Dissonance.* An interesting study of dissonance with a group of people who believed that the world would end on a given day, and their reactions when it didn't, appear in *When Prophecy Fails* by Festinger, Riecken, and Schacter (1956). For a contemporary update on these issues, see Cialdini's (1988) book on *Influence.* This book is so well written that it's the sort of book you would read even if you didn't have to.

The literature on decision making has always been applied to real-world problems. Two examples of this are *The 19th Annual Symposium on Cognition: Political Cognition,* edited by Lau and Sears (1986) and Elstein, Shulman, and Sprafka's (1978) volume,

Medical Problem Solving: An Analysis of Medical Reasoning. Both books examine how the skills and fallacies described in this chapter operate in real-world settings.

Those of you who are concerned with the way in which risky decisions are made will want to consult volume 236 of *Science* (April 1987), which is devoted to risk assessment. For a critical review of the research in the use of heuristics, see Anderson's chapter in an edited book by Brehmer, Jungermann, Lourens, and Sevon (1986), *New Directions in Research on Decision Making.* Finally, an award-winning book by Neustadt and May (1986), *Thinking in Time: The Uses of History for Decision Makers,* is highly recommended. These authors have proposed that political leaders use lessons from the past to tackle current problems.

9 Development of Problem-Solving Skills

Contents

Suppose you're driving alone at night on a long, dark stretch of freeway that is infrequently traveled, when you suddenly hear the familiar ''thump-thump'' of a very flat tire. You pull onto the shoulder of the road and begin the unpleasant task of changing a tire, illuminated only with the light of the moon and a small flashlight. Carefully, you remove the lug nuts and place them in the hubcap by the roadside. A speeding motorist whizzes past you, hitting the hubcap and scattering the lug nuts across the dark freeway and out of sight. Here you sit, a spare tire in one hand, a flat tire propped against the car, and no lug nuts, on a dark night on a lonely stretch of freeway. To make matters worse, a cold rain is beginning to fall. What would you do?

One of my students told me that this incident actually happened. He went on to elaborate that the flat tire occurred alongside a large mental institution near our college. While the hapless motorist sat pondering his problem, he attracted the attention of several ''residents'' of the institution, who gathered near the motorist along the chain-link fence that separated them. One resident offered this solution to the motorist's problem: Remove one lug nut from each of the other three tires and use them to attach the spare. Each tire should hold securely with three lug nuts until the motorist reaches a gas station. The grateful motorist thanked the institution resident and then asked, ''How'd you think of such a good solution to this problem?'' The resident replied, ''I'm not dumb, I'm just crazy!''

I doubt if this exchange ever really occurred. After this problem appeared in the first edition of this book, students from all over the country wrote to tell me that they heard the same story, but with the poor motorist breaking down near their school. In any case, virtually everyone agrees that the resident offered a good solution to the motorist's predicament. Why was it so difficult for the motorist to solve the problem? Why did the solution seem so easy and obvious after it was revealed? How did the resident come up with such a good solution?

ANATOMY OF A PROBLEM

Finding the right answer is important, of course. But more important is developing the ability to see that problems have multiple solutions, that getting from X to Y demands basic skills and mental agility, imagination, persistence, patience.

—Mary Hatwood Futrell, President, NEA
(cited in Heiman & Slomianko, 1986, p. 18)

Consider this mundane problem: Keith has to catch a 9:00 AM plane for Philadelphia, and he's already behind schedule. The freeway route to the airport is the quickest, except when the traffic is heavy. The traffic is almost always heavy with commuters during the morning rush hour. There is a back-roads route that might be a good one, if the road along the river isn't flooded. The road is frequently closed because of flooding after heavy rains. As you can probably guess by now, it rained last night. The surface street route is the longest. If Keith chooses this route, he may miss his plane. Of course, if he spends too much time pondering this problem, he'll surely miss his plane. Which route should he take?

In their classic book, Newell and Simon (1972) have conceptualized all problems as being composed of the same basic parts or structures. Their idea is that problems can be understood by reducing them to their anatomical parts. According to this view, the **anatomy of a problem** can be thought of as having a starting or **initial state** (Keith's home) and a final or **goal state** (the airport). Hayes (1978) used this framework when he asked: "What is a problem? . . . The problem is the gap which separates where you are from where you want to be" (p. 177). All of the possible **solution paths** from the initial state to the goal state comprise the **problem space.** In more general terms, all possible alternative solutions to a problem are called the problem space. In solving a problem, people search through the problem space to find the best path from the initial state to the goal; that is, they consider the alternatives that would lead to the goal and select the best one.

In addition to an initial state, a goal state, and the paths that connect them, there are givens, or information and rules that place constraints on the problem. The givens are the knowledge needed to reach the goal. They can be explicitly stated or implicitly assumed. Two implicit givens in the problem presented earlier were the knowledge that Keith would drive a car to the airport and that he would take either the freeway route, back-roads route, or surface-street route. When solving a problem, the given information is used to select the best solution. This anatomy or framework for understanding problems has proven useful in understanding the process of problem solving. We are all faced with countless problems, and surely know one when we see one. Yet, like most of the topics in this book, the word "problem" remains a difficult one to define. Polya (1962), a pioneer in this area, has offered the following definition: "Solving a problem means finding a way out of a difficulty, a way around an obstacle, attaining an aim that was not immediately understandable." The anatomy of the airport problem is schematically shown in Fig. 9.1. We return to the airport problem later in the chapter as different problem solving strategies are considered.

Problems differ in difficulty. In the airport problem, the difficulty lies in choosing which of the three paths (routes) would get Keith to the goal in the shortest time. In the lug nut problem, the difficulty was in generating any solution path. The initial state was a spare tire and no lug nuts; the goal was a spare tire attached to the car securely enough to drive the car. The problem was the apparent absence of paths to the goal.

Consider Rubik's cube as a difficult problem. The goal for a Rubik's cube is to align each small colored square so that each of the six sides of the cube will be

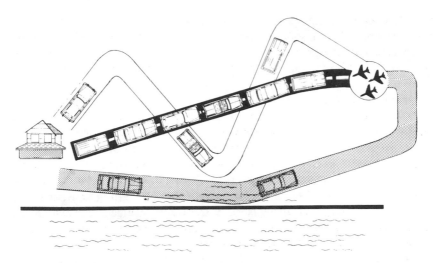

FIG. 9.1. The anatomy of the airport problem. *Givens:* Keith will drive to the airport. He will take one of these routes. He must take the fastest route.

a uniform color. This is a prohibitive problem, because there are millions of combinations of possible moves (paths to the goal). The "trick" is to determine which combination of moves will lead to the goal. In this sort of problem, the difficulty lies in reducing the number of possible paths so that only potentially correct ones will be chosen. Newell and Simon (1972) calculated that the average 40-move chess game has 10^{120} paths. This is a number that is hugely greater than the national debt! Perhaps this is why we view great chess masters with such awe. They have the knowledge to avoid blind paths (bad moves) that won't lead to the goal (winning) and to select the best combination of moves.

Although problem solving, decision making, and creativity are discussed in separate chapters in this book, there is considerable overlap among these topics. Many decisions are involved in solving a problem, and generating satisfactory solution paths often requires considerable creativity. The division among these topics is for ease of presentation. All of the chapters in this text are interrelated, in that they represent somewhat arbitrary ways of "cutting up the thinking pie." The information presented in the other chapters will also contribute to your understanding of problem solving.

STAGES IN PROBLEM SOLVING

The aim of heuristics is to study the methods and rules of discovery and invention. . . . Heuristic, as an adjective, means "serving to discover."
—G. Polya (1945, pp. 112–113)

In 1926 Graham Wallas examined anecdotal accounts of creative scientists and concluded that problem solving progresses in a series of stages. Although there is disagreement among psychologists as to whether all problem solving is done in qualitatively different stages, a brief review of the hypothesized stages may prove useful to problem solvers.

The first stage is **preparation, or familiarization.** This includes the time spent in understanding the nature of the problem, the desired goal, and the givens. This is a crucial part in problem solving, because a correct solution cannot be generated without an adequate understanding of the problem. This point is reiterated in chapter 11, when I discuss mathematical problem solving. The second stage is the **production stage.** During this stage, the problem solver produces the solution paths that define the problem space. **Judgment, or evaluation,** is the third stage. During this stage, individuals evaluate the solution paths in order to select the best one. The fourth stage is a strange one that may or may not occur, depending on the problem. Sometimes, when we can't find a solution path, we stop working on the problem. The period when we're not actively considering the problem is called the **incubation stage.** There are many reports from famous scientists that a solution came to them during the incubation phase—seemingly "out of the blue." Because of the fascination that incubation holds for most people, it deserves separate consideration.

Incubation

The idea of an incubation phase is attractive to most people. It represents one of the few instances in which we may get something for nothing. An oft-cited example of incubation comes from the writings of the famous French mathematician Poincare (1929):

> Then I turned my attention to the study of some arithmetical questions apparently without much success and without a suspicion of any connection with my preceding researches. Disgusted with my failure, I went to spend a few days at the seaside, and thought of something else. One morning, walking on the bluff, the idea came to me, with just the same characteristics of brevity, suddenness and immediate certainty, that the arithmetic transformations of indeterminate ternary quadratic forms were identical with those of non-Euclidean geometry. (p. 388)

Have you ever had the experience of working unsuccessfully on a problem, then having the solution come to you sometime later when you were not consciously thinking about it? If so, then you have experienced incubation effects first-hand. The term *incubation* suggests a mother hen sitting on great ideas that are about to hatch.

Incubation is a poorly understood phenomenon. If your employer found you sitting with your feet propped on your desk, gazing out the window, she or he would be unlikely to be pleased to learn that you were "incubating" on company time. A familiar experience is having a correct answer come to someone immediately after turning in an exam or paper. This is most likely the result of incubation. It's a good idea to work well ahead of deadlines to allow ample time for incubation effects to occur. We don't know how people are able to produce solutions during time-outs. There is no evidence that people continue to work on the problem at an unconscious level, although some people have suggested that this is how incubation effects occur. Most likely, the time-out period serves to dissipate fatigue and allow individuals to get out of sets or ruts in their thinking processes so that they can view the problem from a different perspective.

Herbert A. Simon (1977), the Nobel Prize-winning psychologist, has attempted to explain incubation as due, in part, to selective forgetting. He suggested that when we are working on a problem, we rely on a relatively small number of concepts held in a limited-capacity short-term memory. (See chapter 2 for a detailed discussion of this concept.) When we're not working on a problem, the information held in short-term memory is quickly forgotten. If this information was not productive for discovering a solution, then having forgotten it will be beneficial to finding a good solution. Simon regards scientific discovery as a form of problem solving. He goes on to say that selective forgetting may be one of the processes that underlies the incubation effect, famous examples of which are Galileo's discovery of uniform acceleration, Newtonian notions of gravity, and Einstein's theory of relativity.

It's a good idea to put aside a problem that you're having difficulty solving and return to it at a later time. This is especially good advice during an exam. At least you'll be sure of getting credit for the easier problems, but watch your time limits carefully so that you can correctly finish as many problems as possible in the allotted time. (Of course, it's also a good idea to work on the problems worth the most points first to maximize your exam score.)

Insight

Did you ever have the solution to a problem come to you "in a flash?" Sudden knowledge of the solution is called **insight,** or the Aha! experience. Insightful solutions can occur during periods of incubation or while actively working on a problem. It is metaphorically referred to as a light bulb in the head that is suddenly switched on. Interestingly, the earliest studies of insight were conducted with chimpanzees, not humans (Kohler, 1925). It seems that when chimpanzees are confronted with problems such as reaching food that can only be obtained by putting two sticks together to form a rake, a period of seemingly random behavior is followed by what appears to be sudden insight into the problem.

Insight experiences are common. I have found them to occur frequently in the statistics classes that I teach. Often, students will ponder over a problem or listen attentively to a lecture, then suddenly they'll break into a broad grin and exclaim, "Now I understand." A law school student once told me that she spent the first three fourths of her first year in law school in an intellectual fog. She really felt that she understood very little about the basic concepts. Then, something "clicked," and she suddenly understood the legal principles. It's as if a little light went on that illuminated the concepts. In fact, what happened was that she "saw" the structure and the logic of the law. Her insight paid off into a successful legal career.

It should be noted that the insight follows a period of concentrated effort. It occurs after the problem solver has become familiar with the problem and has considered possible solutions. A review of the problem-solving strategies presented later in this chapter provides some thinking guides that serve to direct the thinking processes in ways that will increase the likelihood of insightful solutions.

WELL-DEFINED AND ILL-DEFINED PROBLEMS

Here is Edward Bear, coming downstairs. Now, bump, bump, bump, on the back of his head, behind Christopher Robin. It is, as far as he knows, the only way of coming downstairs, but sometimes he feels that there really is another way, if only he could stop bumping for a moment and think of it.

—A. A. Milne (*Winnie the Pooh*)

Problems come in all shapes and sizes. Consider the following two problems:

1. The parallelogram problem (after Wertheimer, 1959). Some time back in fifth or sixth grade, you learned that, in order to find the area of a rectangle, you should multiply the height by the length. Now you are given the following parallelogram that is 4″ long and 2 ″ high. What is its area?

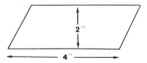

2. Write a poem expressing the joy you feel when spring flowers bloom.

Do these problems seem qualitatively different to you? Have you figured #1 out? Wertheimer suggests that the correct answer lies in **perceptual reorganiza-**

tion, or seeing the problem in a new way. The new way consists of seeing the parallelogram in terms of a rectangle and two triangles. Thus, the parallelogram becomes:

Once the problem is restructured this way, it is only a short leap to figure out that the area of the parallelogram can be found with the same formula for the area of a rectangle, because the two triangles can be fit together so that a new rectangular figure is formed with a 4″ length and a 2″ height. In the present example, the area of the parallelogram is 2″ × 4″ = 8 square inches. There is no other correct answer. The goal (correct answer) is **well defined,** as is the path to the goal.

Writing a poem is a different sort of problem. The goal (a beautiful poem) is **ill defined,** as there are many forms a poem can take. There are countless ways to write a poem. The greatest difficulty in this case lies in evaluating the quality of the end product. The goal is uncertain in ill-defined problems, thus part of the difficulty lies in determining if the problem has been solved (Dorner, 1983).

Most of the problems that confront people outside of the laboratory are ill defined, in that the problem solver must decide how to define the goal and then evaluate how well the goal has been attained. Other examples of ill-defined problems are: creating a way to increase sales for a business; finding more effective ways to study; writing a clear, easy-to-read textbook; saving money for college tuition; building a better mousetrap; deescalating the nuclear arms race, and improving the environment. In ill-defined problems, the goal may be vague or incomplete, which makes the generation of solution paths difficult and their evaluation even more difficult.

One of the best ways to approach ill-defined problems is to make the goal explicit. It is usually possible to state the goal in several different ways for ill-defined problems. For example, the problem of increasing sales can be reidentified as the problem of increasing profits, because the real goal is to find ways to make more money. When asked in this form, the problem changes from its initial conceptualization. Solution paths can now include ways to cut losses, reduce inventories, or collect bad debts. The best way to approach ill-defined problems is to specify multiple goals in objective terms so that a variety of solution paths can be considered.

Sometimes, the distinction between well-defined and ill-defined problems blurs. Consider again the problem of getting Keith to the airport on time. If the problem is selecting among the three routes to the airport, it is well defined, but if other solution paths and goals are possible, for example, fly to the airport, take a different plane from a nearer airport, or take the subway, then the problem becomes somewhat more difficult to define.

PROBLEM PLANNING AND REPRESENTATION

In the mathematics and science courses I took in college, I was enormously irritated by the hundreds of hours that I wasted staring at problems without any good idea about what approach to try next in attempting to solve them. I thought at the time that there was no educational value in those "blank" minutes and I see no value in them today.

—Wickelgren (1974, p. ix)

Recent research in problem solving has focused on the importance of devising a plan for finding and selecting solutions (Friedman, Scholnick, & Cocking, 1987). Planning is a higher order thinking skill that is used to direct and regulate behavior (Pea & Hawkins, 1987; Scholnick & Friedman, 1987). A plan provides a structure that problem solvers can use in a step-by-step manner to help them reach the desired goal. Most programs designed to improve problem solving skills stress the importance of a "planful approach" (Covington, 1987).

Although plans for solving problems can vary in complexity, most will consist of five basic steps: (a) recognition that a problem exists; (b) construction of a representation of the problem that includes the initial and goal states; (c) generation and evaluation of possible solutions; (d) selection of a possible solution; and (e) execution of the possible solution to determine if it solves the problem. Unfortunately, some or all of the steps will have to be repeated if the goal is not attained. This could include changing the representation or redefining the goal as well as generating additional possible solutions and reevaluating the possible solutions.

Bransford and Stein (1984) used the acronym IDEAL to stand for these five steps:

I (Identify the problem); D (Define and represent the problem); E (Explore possible strategies); A (Act on the strategies); L (Look back and evaluate the effects of your activities). (p. 12)

One of the major goals of The Productive Thinking Program (Covington, Crutchfield, Davies, & Olton, 1974), a popular program designed to help children "learn to think," is to develop the habit of planning a solution strategy. Figure 9.2 shows a few sample frames from this program that emphasize the need to approach problems in an orderly manner.

The best way to solve a problem is to devise the best representation, This forces the problem solver to be explicit about the desired goal and to plan carefully the steps necessary to reach the goal.

The representation of a problem is often a good index of how well it is understood (Greeno, 1973, 1977). A good representation will contain all of the relevant information or givens and display the relationships among the givens in

Work on the problem In a planful way.

FIG. 9.2.   Advice for children on how to devise a problem-solving plan. (From *The Productive Thinking Program* by Covington, Crutchfield, Davies, & Olton, 1974, Lesson 6, p. 17).

a way that will facilitate progress toward the goal. A good problem representation is a critical element in finding a solution. In discussing the way good representations are constructed, Newell (1983) said that "Memory must be tickled." What he meant by this remark is that the individual's knowledge about the problem must be accessed and utilized. The problem solver must be able to make inferences from problem statements in order to build an adequate problem representation—one in which missing and conflicting information is made obvious.

Of course, when you begin solving a problem, it is difficult to determine which of the possible solution paths will ultimately lead to the goal. The givens need to be transformed in ways that will generate solution paths with **operations.**

Every time an operation is applied, the problem space changes. Different representational systems can be thought of as strategies or "plans of attack." The following section contains suggestions for devising good representations and demonstrates the intimate relationship between the representation and the solution to the problem. Let's try some examples of ways to represent problems.

Write It Down

All problems are initially represented in your head. It is a good idea to get the paths and goals on paper or into some other concrete form. This will reduce the memory load and allow you to view the problem visually. The simplest example of the aid provided by a pencil and paper is a straightforward multiplication problem. Solve the following problem without writing anything:

$$76$$
$$\times\ \underline{89}$$

Of course, you would consider this a ridiculous request, because it is a simple problem with paper and pencil and a difficult one to perform in your head because of the memory demands. Whenever there are several facts to keep track of, it is a good idea to use a paper and pencil.

Draw a Graph or Diagram

"A bear, starting at point P, walked one mile due south. Then he changed direction and walked one mile due east. Then he turned again to the left and walked one mile due north, and arrived exactly at the point P he started from. What was the color of the bear?" (Polya, 1957, p. 234).

Does this problem seem strange or even impossible to you? If you draw a simple "map" of the bear's route, it will be a pie-shaped wedge. Where on earth is this possible? Think about a globe. Did you just say "Why, of course, point P must be the North Pole" to yourself? Once you realize that you're at the North Pole, this problem becomes easy to solve. The bear must be white, because only polar bears live at the North Pole.

Consider the following problem: A venerable old monk leaves the monastery at exactly 6:00 AM to climb a winding mountain trail to the solitude of the mountain peak. He arrives at exactly 4:00 PM. After spending the night in sleep and prayer, he leaves the mountain peak at exactly 6:00 AM and arrives at the monastery at exactly 4:00 PM. There are no constraints on the speed at which he walks. In fact, he stops several times along the way to rest. Is there some point on the mountain trail that he passes at exactly the same time each day?

Stop and think about this problem for a moment. Does it seem like a difficult one? There are two ways to consider this problem that will make the answer seem simple, but before you go on, decide how you would go about solving this problem, then solve it.

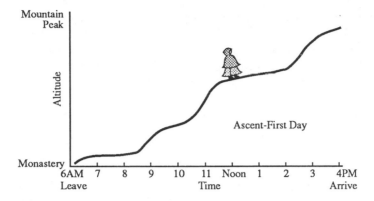

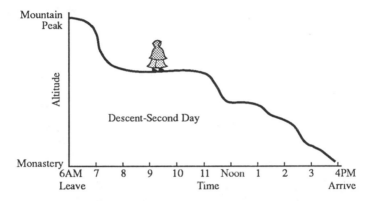

FIG. 9.3. Graphs of the monk's ascent and descent. The graphs can take any shape, because the monk can rest as often as he wishes.

One solution is to draw a graph of the monk's ascent and descent. The graph can take any shape, because you know nothing about his hourly progress. The graphs of the ascent and descent should appear as in Fig. 9.3.

Now, superimpose the two graphs and see if there must be some point where the graphs intersect. If there is, then there is some time when the monk passed the same point at the same time on each day. This is shown in Fig. 9.4. Drawing a graph provides a clear picture of the results. Actually, an easier way of solving this problem involves changing the representation and restating the facts in the problem in an equivalent, but different, form. Assume two people traverse the same mountain path at the same time on the same morning. If one starts at the monastery and the other starts at the mountain peak, both leaving at 6:00 AM and both arriving at their opposite destinations at 4:00 PM, it is obvious that they must meet somewhere along the path no matter how often each chooses to rest

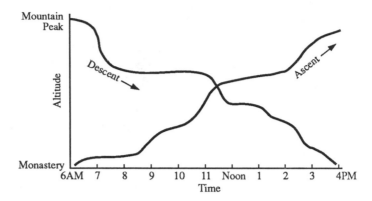

FIG. 9.4. By superimposing the ascent and descent graphs, it is easy to see that there must be some place at which the graphs intersect. Thus, there must be a place on the mountain trail that the monk crosses at the same time each day.

and reflect. Thus, with a change in representation, a difficult problem can become trivial.

Drawing a graph is often an excellent strategy for solving problems. Several years ago, I taught a laboratory course in experimental psychology. In that course, college students were required to conduct experiments, gather data, and interpret their data in a meaningful way. Although the students were taught the statistical methods needed for data analysis, I found that when they graphed their results they obtained a much better understanding of the phenomenon they were investigating. They were able to use their experimental results to formulate sound conclusions, because they understood the nature of their findings. The students found that a simple graph was a more valuable tool for comprehension than the elaborate statistical procedures that they were required to use.

Graphs and other kinds of diagrams are especially useful comprehension strategies in mathematical and scientific problem solving. For example, a common problem in undergraduate statistics courses requires finding the area between two points under a certain kind of curve called a "normal" or "bell-shaped" curve. This can be a difficult or confusing problem for students, but it becomes easy if they draw the curve and shade in the area they want to find. In fact, I don't give my statistics students the algebraic rules for finding the appropriate area. Students find it easier to figure it out for themselves from the diagrams they draw. Mathematical and scientific problem solving are discussed in more detail in chapter 11.

Graphs and diagrams are also useful in solving spatial problems. The blueprints of architects and engineers are their problem-solving tools. Problems in geometry and trigonometry usually require carefully labeled diagrams for their correct solution.

Consider the geometry problem that was posed by Köhler in 1969. You are given only the information in Fig. 9.5 and the fact that the radius of the circle is 5 inches. Can you find the length of line L in inches?

One of the reasons that this is a difficult problem is that, in the pictorial representation, line L appears most saliently as the hypotenuse of two right triangles, the triangle with sides LDX, and the triangle with the other two sides defined by the intersecting horizontal and vertical radii. How can you change this diagram so that the solution can be obtained?

Consider the information given. Because the only length given in this diagram is the radius of the circle, it is likely that this will be needed in solving the problem. Try drawing in additional radii around the circle, as shown in Fig. 9.6. Does this help to suggest the solution?

Look carefully at the quadrant containing L. Can you find another line equal in length to L? If you think of L as the diagonal inside a rectangle with sides D, X, and the unlabeled sides formed by the intersection of the horizontal and vertical radii, the other diagonal in the rectangle must be the same length as L. The other diagonal must be the radius; thus line L, like the radius, is also 5 in. long. Although the initial representation of the problem was somewhat misleading, a solution was found with the appropriate operations.

Of course, there was no way of knowing at the outset that moving the radii around the circle would lead to the answer. It was obvious, however, that the answer would depend on the radius in some way, because it was the only measurement given, and the goal was to find the length of line L. The operations

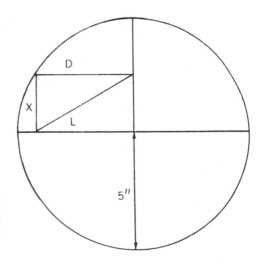

FIG. 9.5. Using only the information given in this figure, can you determine the length of line L? (Problem adapted from Köhler, 1969.)

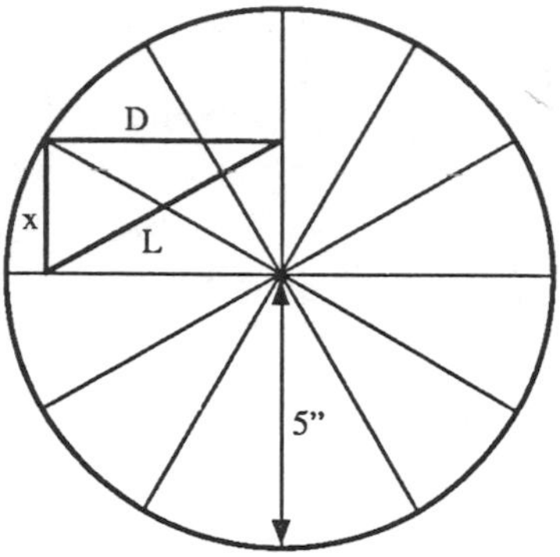

FIG. 9.6. Additional radii have been drawn over Fig. 9.5 as an intermediate step toward a solution. Can you use the additional radii to find the length of the line L?

used to transform the givens into solution paths involved the knowledge that you brought with you to the problem. If you did not know that the two diagonals in a rectangle must be equal, then you could not have solved the problem. Good problem solvers utilize a solid knowledge base that is built up over a lifetime of educational experiences—ones that are accumulated both inside and outside of the classroom. The best strategy for solving problems is to know a great deal about a great many topics.

Let's try another example in which graphs or diagrams will simplify the search for a solution path.

In order to save money and their sanity, Melvin, Brock, Marc, and Claire decide to form a baby-sitting cooperative. They agree to baby-sit for each other's children, with the understanding that when one of them stays with another's children, the recipient will repay the sitter with an equal number of baby sitting hours. They decide to tally baby-sitting hours at the end of the month. During the month, Melvin sat with Brock's children 9 hours, Marc sat with Melvin's children 3 hours, and Claire stayed with Melvin's children 6 hours. Marc baby-sat 9 hours with Claire's children and Brock baby-sat 5 hours with Claire's children. Which of these people has 12 hours of baby-sitting time due to him or her?

A good diagram of the relationship among these four people is clearly needed. The relevant givens will involve the four people and the number of hours owed to each. Let's start with the first sentence, "Melvin sat with Brock's children 9 hours." Thus, Brock owes Melvin 9 hours of baby sitting at the end of the month. The operation being used is the transformation of number of hours spent baby sitting into number of hours owed to each sitter. A simple diagram of this relationship is:

$$\underset{\text{Brock} \qquad\qquad \text{Melvin}}{\xrightarrow{\hspace{1cm}\text{9 hours}\hspace{1cm}}}$$

The next sentence translates into "Melvin owes Marc 3 hours and Melvin owes Claire 6 hours."

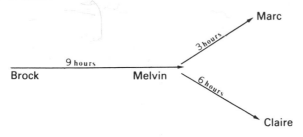

Then, changing the third sentence so that it reflects what is owed, Claire owes Marc 9 hours and Claire owes Brock 5 hours.

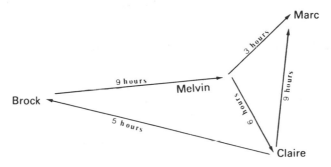

It is easy to see from this diagram that only Marc is owed 12 hours of baby sitting, 3 hours from Melvin and 9 hours from Claire. A diagram of the hours owed is essential in finding the solution to this problem.

There are several other ways of representing the information in the baby-sitting co-op problem that will display all of the essential relationships, and thus also give the correct answer. When a colleague (Dr. Susan Nummedal at California State University, Long Beach) posed this problem to her students, she found that they devised a variety of representations to solve the problem. One student used a simple bar graph to keep track of the number of hours sat by each participant. This representation is shown in Fig. 9.7.

Other students used a variety of table formats. One listed the number of hours "gave" as a positive number and "received" as a negative number because it was owed. Another student split the information into "sitter" and "sat for" categories, then filled in a table of information, summing across the columns for the total number of "sat for" hours for each participant, and summing down the rows for the total number of "sitter" hours for each participant. These representations are offered in Tables 9.1 and 9.2, respectively.

As a baby-sitting co-op problem demonstrates, there are often many ways of

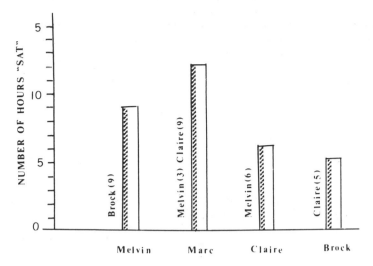

FIG. 9.7. Alternative form of representation for solving the co-op problem.

TABLE 9.1
A Table Format for Representing the Information
in the Babysitting Co-op Problem

	Gave	*Received*	*Total Due*
Melvin	+9	−3, −6	0
Marc	+3, +9		12
Claire	+6	−9, −15	−8
Brock	+5	−9	−4

TABLE 9.2
An Alternative Table Format That Can Be Used
to Represent the Information in the Babysitting Co-op Program

	Sitter				*Total Number of Hours Sat For*
	Melvin	*Marc*	*Claire*	*Brock*	
Sat For *Melvin*		3	6		9
Marc					0
Claire		9		5	14
Brock	9				9
Total Number of Hours Sat	9	12	6	5	

representing a given problem. As you work through the problems in this chapter, try a variety of representations. A good representation will present all of the relevant information in a way that it can be readily understood and assimilated. Good representations provide the necessary solution paths to the goal.

Try a Hierarchical Tree

Hierarchical trees are branching diagrams. They are most frequently used to assess mathematically the probability or likelihood of uncertain outcomes. In this context, they are called decision trees. (See chapter 7 for the use of decision trees in determining probabilities.) Hierarchical trees, or tree diagrams, can be useful aids in the context of problem solving. (As stated earlier in this chapter, the distinction between problem solving and decision making is somewhat artificial, because they are closely related concepts.)

If the problem you're working on is fairly complex, with each possible solution path requiring subsequent additional paths, a hierarchical tree or tree diagram should be considered.

Here is a classical problem first presented by Duncker (1945). Although the problem is a medical one, no specialized knowledge is needed to solve it:

A patient has an inoperative tumor deep within her stomach. The problem is to devise a way of treating the tumor with X-rays without damaging the healthy tissue that surrounds the tumor on all sides. Stop and think for a few minutes how you would go about solving this problem.

Most of Duncker's subjects went about reaching a solution in several steps. Although a variety of solutions were attempted, the best solution is to use several weak rays, each coming from different places outside the body focused so that they would meet and summate at the tumor site. In this manner, the healthy tissue won't be hurt by the weak rays and the tumor will receive a high level of radiation. This solution was formulated from a broader category of solutions that included having each ray grow stronger as it reached the tumor.

One subject's search for solution paths is shown in Fig. 9.8 in a hierarchical tree diagram. Note that the goal is explicitly stated at the top of the tree. General broad strategies are listed one level below the goal, with more specific ways of satisfying each strategy on lower levels.

Tree diagrams are particularly useful when the given information has a natural hierarchical organization. For example, all living things are classified into a hierarchical organization by biologists. If you ask a child if a bee is an animal, he or she will probably respond that it isn't an animal because it is an insect. The problem can be made clear to him or her by drawing a biological classification tree like the one shown in Fig. 9.9.

Another example of using trees to solve problems is the familiar use of family

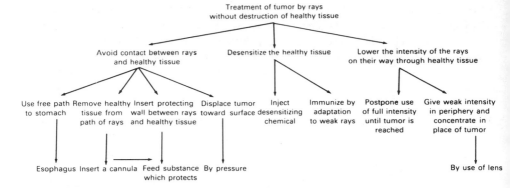

FIG. 9.8. A hierarchical three diagram of one subject's attempted solutions to Duncker's X-ray problem. (After Duncker, 1945.)

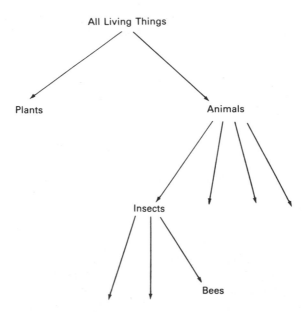

FIG. 9.9. A hierarchical three diagram that can be used to answer the question, "Are bees animals?"

trees. Estate lawyers, who often face a tangled web of family relationships, need to be able to determine the relations among family members in order to handle wills and estate taxes. Multiple spouses, cohabitation, step-children, half-siblings, and out-of-wedlock births can make the difficult matter of inheritance a legal nightmare. A carefully drawn family tree that places each member on the appropriate generation branch is an invaluable aid in solving tangled inheritance claims.

Make a Matrix

A **matrix** is a rectangular array of facts or numbers. It is really just a fancy word for a chart. When the givens in a problem can be broken down into categories, a matrix may be a good method of representation. Consider the problem posed by Whimbey and Lochhead (1982):

> Three men—Fred, Ed, and Ted—are married to Joan, Sally, and Vickie, but not necessarily in that order. Joan, who is Ed's sister, lives in Detroit, Fred dislikes animals. Ed weighs more than the man who is married to Vickie. The man married to Sally breeds Siamese cats as a hobby. Fred commutes over 200 hours a year from his home in Ann Arbor to his job in Detroit. Match up the men with the women they married. (p. 67)

What are the categories of information given in this problem? The givens concern husbands and wives. Set up a three-by-three matrix and fill in as much of it as you can with the information:

	Joan	*Sally*	*Vickie*
Fred			
Ed			
Ted			

Because Joan is Ed's sister, she cannot be his wife, so fill in a "NO" in the Joan—Ed cell of the matrix. Skip the next two statements for the time being and go on to the statement that Ed weighs more than the man married to Vickie; therefore, Ed is not married to Vickie. Ed must be married to Sally. So far, the matrix appears as follows:

	Joan	*Sally*	*Vickie*
Fred		NO	
Ed	NO	YES	NO
Ted		NO	

Peruse the problem for more clues. Have you found the important one? Fred lives in Ann Arbor and Joan lives in Detroit; therefore, we'd conclude that they're probably not married. Because Fred is not married to Joan or Sally, he must be married to Vickie. Who's left for Ted? Joan must be married to Ted. The completed matrix:

	Joan	*Sally*	*Vickie*
Fred	NO	NO	YES
Ed	NO	YES	NO
Ted	YES	NO	NO

Let's try another example. This problem is from a delightful book by Phillips (1961), called *My Best Puzzles in Logic and Reasoning*. This one should seem easier, because you are now familiar with the technique.

"My four granddaughters are all accomplished girls." Canon Chasuble was speaking with evident self-satisfaction. "Each of them," he went on, "plays a different musical instrument and each speaks one European language as well as—if not better than—a native."

"What does Mary play?" asked someone.

"The cello."

"Who plays the violin?"

"D'you know," said Chasuble, "I've temporarily forgotten. Anno Domini, alas! But I know it's the girl who speaks French."

The remainder of the facts which I elicited were of a somewhat negative character. I learned that the organist is not Valerie; that the girl who speaks German is not Lorna; and that Mary knows no Italian. Anthea doesn't play the violin, nor is she the girl who speaks Spanish. Valerie knows no French; Lorna doesn't play the harp; and the organist can't speak Italian.

What are Valerie's accomplishments?

Stop now and work on solving this problem. Don't go on until you've actually worked through this problem.

You'd begin by realizing that, because the relevant information is categorical, a matrix is a good form of representation. There are four granddaughters, musical instruments, and languages. Thus, the matrix can be set up as:

Granddaughter	*Musical Instrument*	*Language*
Mary	Cello	
Valerie		
Lorna		
Anthea		

Because most of the information we have is negative, let's list the possible combinations of granddaughters, instruments, and languages.

Granddaughter	Musical Instrument	Language
Mary	Cello	Spanish or French or German
Valerie	Violin or Harp	Spanish or Italian or German
Lorna	Violin or Organ	French or Italian or Spanish
Anthea	Harp or Organ	Italian or German or French

Because the girl who plays the violin speaks French, this must be Lorna. Anthea is the organist who speaks German. This means that only Mary can speak Spanish. The only combination left for Valerie is the harp and Italian.

Admittedly, these are artificial problems, not much like the ones we encounter in real life. Let's consider a more practical application of the matrix form of problem representation.

There is considerable controversy over the issue of vitamin C as a deterrent for the common cold. How would you decide if vitamin C prevents colds? Most probably, you'd give vitamin C to some people and not others and count the number of colds in each group. Suppose you found the following results: 10 people who took vitamin C did not catch a cold; 4 people who took vitamin C caught a cold; 8 people who didn't take vitamin C didn't catch a cold and 6 people who didn't take vitamin C caught a cold. What would you conclude?

Because we have categories of information (took or didn't take vitamin C and caught or didn't catch a cold), a matrix displaying the appropriate values will help us understand the givens:

		Vitamin C		
		Took Vitamin C	Didn't Take Vitamin C	
	Caught a Cold	4	6	Total number who caught a cold 10
Cold	Didn't Catch a Cold	10	8	Total number who didn't catch a cold 18

By examining every cell of the matrix, you can determine if vitamin C prevented colds. To see if vitamin C worked, you need to consider how many of those who caught a cold had taken vitamin C. The answer is 4 out of 10, or 40%. You also need to consider how many of those who didn't catch a cold had taken vitamin C. The answer is 10 out of 18, or 55.5%. Few would be willing to conclude from these data that vitamin C helped to prevent colds. (Research concepts are discussed more fully in chapters 6 and 7.) The point being made here is that, by representing the information in a matrix, the results can be more easily understood.

Manipulate Models

It is often a good idea to make a concrete representation for abstract problems. You've probably seen an architect's model for a planned complex like a shopping center, office building, or college campus. The miniature buildings and walkways are not made because architects love doll-sized buildings. Although they are often made to communicate architectural plans to others who are not skilled at reading blueprints, the miniature models also help the architect solve problems. With the movable parts, she or he can move the buildings to find the best way to place them before construction begins.

Let's try a problem where making a model will help in finding a solution. The problem I want you to solve has an interesting history. It was originally known as the Missionaries and Cannibals Problem, with the cannibals as the ''bad guys.'' In response to possible racist overtones, other versions have made the missionaries the ''bad guys.'' (They converted the cannibals against their will). A later version calls the two groups Hobbits and Orks, because there is no racial identification with either mythical group:

There are two groups of beings on a mythical planet in a far-away galaxy: They are Hobbits and Orks. One day, three Hobbits got lost while exploring the homeland of the Orks. The Hobbits could get home safely if they could cross the river that separates their two homelands. The Orks agreed to help the Hobbits cross the river, but the only boat they had could hold only two beings at a time, and the Hobbits could not let themselves ever be outnumbered by the Orks or the Orks would eat them.

Your problem is to figure out a sequence of moves that will carry all three Hobbits to the other side of the river and return all three Orks to their own side. The constraints are that only two beings can fit in the boat at one time, and if, at any time, the Orks on one shore outnumber the Hobbits, you'll have to start over.

This would be an impossible problem to solve without some external form of representation. Use some small objects to represent the Hobbits and Orks and move them across an imaginary river. Three large paper clips for the hobbits and three small paper clips for the Orks will work well. You'll have to imagine that you are transporting them in a boat. Be sure to write down all of your moves. Plan to take as long as 10 to 15 minutes to solve this problem. As you work toward the solution, be aware of how you're thinking about the moves. Don't go on until you've worked through the problem.

The complete sequence of moves needed to move the Hobbits is shown in Fig. 9.10. One of the greatest difficulties with this problem is the need to move all three Orks across the river, a situation that is not desired, in order to move the

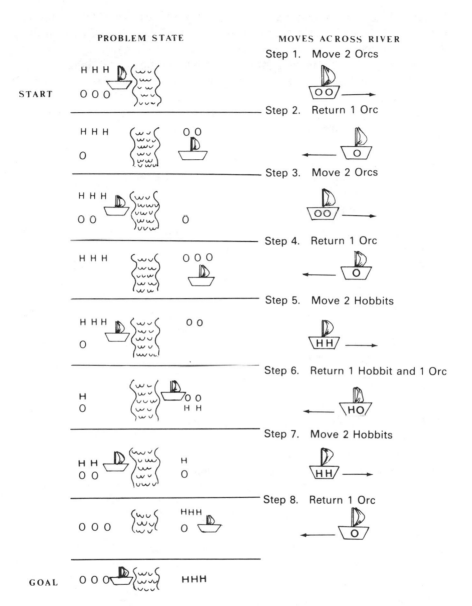

PROBLEM STATE	MOVES ACROSS RIVER

Step 1. Move 2 Orcs

START H H H / O O O

Step 2. Return 1 Orc

H H H / O   O O

Step 3. Move 2 Orcs

H H H / O O   O

Step 4. Return 1 Orc

H H H   O O O

Step 5. Move 2 Hobbits

H H H / O   O O

Step 6. Return 1 Hobbit and 1 Orc

H / O   O O / H H

Step 7. Move 2 Hobbits

H H / O O   H / O

Step 8. Return 1 Orc

O O O   H H H / O

GOAL O O O   H H H

FIG. 9.10. Steps needed to move three hobbits across the river using a boat that will hold only two beings without allowing the orks to ever outnumber the hobbits.

Hobbits without allowing them to become outnumbered. Problems of this sort have come to be known as **detour problems,** because the path to the goal is not a direct linear one. Intermediate steps are required that seem directly opposite to the goal—in this case, moving all three Orks to the opposite side of the river when the desired goal is to have all of them on the side from which they originated. It is important to recognize that the route to a goal will often involve detours. As a more realistic example, consider Leon's goal to become very wealthy. One solution path to the goal may involve going deeply into debt in order to finance his education. Although going deeply into debt is seemingly antagonistic to becoming wealthy, it may be a necessary detour. Be sure to consider solution paths that involve detours when faced with difficult problems.

Select the Best Representation

It's a good idea to utilize an external form of representation (e.g., paper and pencil) whenever there are more than a few givens that need to be manipulated. The immediate or working memory span can quickly become overloaded. An external form of representation will help to alleviate this problem. Experimental results, or almost any other pattern of numbers, should always be graphed.

If your problem is mathematical or spatial, a diagram is likely to be helpful. Diagrams can help to disentangle any situation in which the givens have many complex interrelationships. Diagrams can make important relationships explicit, a fact that can often lead directly to the goal. Hierarchical trees are a natural form of representation when the material itself forms a hierarchically arranged structure. Matrices are likely to be useful when the givens can be grouped into categories for meaningful comparisons. "Mock-ups," or miniature models, can aid in problem solving when movement and placement of the givens determine the solution. Often, the way a problem is represented can mean the difference between a solution or nonsolution (Posner, 1973). If you find that one form of representation isn't fruitful, try a different one.

PROBLEM-SOLVING STRATEGIES

Solving problems can be regarded as the most characteristically human activity.

—Polya (1962)

It does no good to tell someone who is faced with a problem that he or she should plan a solution, if the person has no idea how to plan. The steps look deceptively simple—generate and evaluate possible solutions. But, what if you can't think of any solutions? There are several strategies that can be used in a systematic manner to help you generate solutions. Although no single strategy can guarantee perfect solutions every time, learning how to use several different strategies can give you direction and confidence when presented with a new problem.

Schoenfeld (1979) found that many mathematicians and scientists claimed to use specific strategies and rules when solving problems in their academic disciplines. Many of the scientists and mathematicians believed that their students would solve problems better if they learned some basic skills for attacking problems. In addition, several researchers have found that instruction in general problem-solving skills can improve problem-solving ability (e.g., Klein & Weizenfeld, 1978; Wickelgren, 1974). You can think of the following strategies or problem solving aids as ways to plan a solution.

Means–Ends Analysis

Most often, progress toward the goal is not made along a single, well-paved road. When the goal is not immediately attainable, we often need to take detours or break the problem down into smaller problems, called **subproblems,** each with its own goal, called **subgoals.**

Like all of the strategies for solving problems, selecting and utilizing subgoals requires planning. The procedure by which people select subgoals and use them to progress toward the goal is called **means–ends analysis.** This is a general, often powerful method for problem solving. The problem is first broken down into subgoals. Operations that will reduce the distance between the problem solver's current state and each subgoal are then used. In this manner, the problem solver will move closer and closer to the goal. Work through the following examples in order to clarify this concept.

The first step in means–ends analysis is to enumerate appropriate subgoals and to select the most promising one. Suppose that, during a game of chess, you decide that a good subgoal is to put the opposing king in check. The goal, of course, is to win the game, but it will be necessary to work toward subgoals to attain the goal. Putting the opposing king in check is the immediate "end" toward which you're working. You now need to select the "means" for obtaining that end, hence the term "means–ends analysis." In order to achieve your subgoal, determine the current state (i.e., the current position of your pieces). Then, identify any difference between where your pieces are and where you want them to be. Operations would be selected that would reduce this difference and place the opposing king in check. Suppose no single move can achieve this subgoal. The means–ends analysis procedure would recycle, this time selecting a smaller subgoal, perhaps moving another piece out of the way. The constant recycling of these two processes—setting subgoals and reducing distances—will allow you to make progress toward the goal.

A favorite problem of psychologists that can be used to demonstrate means–

ends analysis is the Tower of Hanoi problem. The name of this puzzle is derived from an interesting legend. Suppose that there are three pegs and 64 disks, each one a different size, stacked on one of the pegs in size order. It may help to think of the disks as 64 different size doughnuts that can stack one on top of each other on the pegs. The task is to transfer all of the disks from the first peg to the third peg, using the middle peg as an intermediary. The rules for moving disks include moving only one disk at a time and never placing a disk on top of a smaller one. The legend around this task is that there are monks in a monestary near Hanoi who are working on this puzzle, and when they complete it the world will come to an end. Even if this legend were true, you would have little cause for worry, because if they were to make perfect moves at the rate of one per second, it would take close to a trillion years to complete this task (Raphael, 1976).

Because you probably don't want to spend quite that much time solving the Tower of Hanoi, you can try a simplified version of it, using only three disks. You can easily work this problem using any three coins of different sizes (a quarter, penny, and dime will work well) and three small sheets of paper. Stack the coins with the smallest on top and largest on the bottom on one sheet of paper. The task is to move the coins from the first piece of paper to the third so that they will be in the same size order. You may move only one coin at a time. All three pieces of paper may be used in solving the problem. Write down all of the moves you make in solving this problem. The initial and goal states are shown in Fig. 9.11.

In a means–end analysis of the Tower of Hanoi problem, one obvious subgoal is to get the quarter on the third piece of paper. This cannot be done immediately, because the dime and penny are on it; therefore, a second subgoal needs to be considered. A second subgoal is to end up with the penny on the quarter. This can be accomplished when the penny is on the second paper and the quarter is on the third paper. This subgoal cannot yet be pursued, because the dime must be moved first. In this manner, subgoals, or ends, are considered along with the means to accomplish them. A complete solution with all of the moves is shown in Fig. 9.12. If you try the problem with four or five coins instead of three, you'll find that it gets much more complicated, although the strategy remains the same.

Means–ends analysis is a general strategy that is applicable to a wide variety

FIG. 9.11. Start state and goal for the Tower of Hanoi problem. Use the strategy of means-ends analysis to solve this problem.

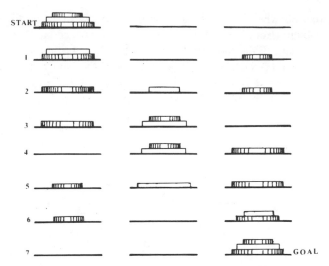

FIG. 9.12.   Solution to the Tower of Hanoi problem. Notice how subgoals are planned and obtained in reaching the goal.

of problems. There is a general-purpose computer program called the **General Problem Solver** that was developed in 1972 by Newell and Simon. The program is given specific information about the problem to be solved, for example, a proof in geometry. The General Problem Solver uses this knowledge and the means–ends analysis strategy to solve the problem. With a little practice with this strategy, people can also become general problem solvers.

Working Backward

Means–ends analysis is a **forward-looking strategy,** which means that all of the planning is done by considering operations that move you closer to subgoals and, ultimately, the final goal. Sometimes, it is a better strategy to plan your operations by **working backward** from the goal to your present or initial state. The simplest example of this can be found in the paper-and-pencil mazes that many children love to solve.

Some of these mazes have several possible paths leading away from the start box and only one correct path ending in the goal box. Even young children realize that they can solve the maze more quickly if they work the maze backward, beginning from the goal and drawing their path to the start box. An example of this type of maze is shown in Fig. 9.13.

Working backward is a good strategy to use whenever there are fewer paths leading from the goal than there are leading from the start. Of course, mazes aren't the only situation when working backward is a good strategy. Consider the following problem (from Fixx, 1978): "Water lilies on a certain lake double in area every 24 hours. From the time the first water lily appears until the lake is completely covered takes 60 days. On what day is it half covered?" (p. 50).

The only way to solve this problem is to work backward. Can you solve it? If the lake is covered on the 60th day and the area covered by the lilies doubles

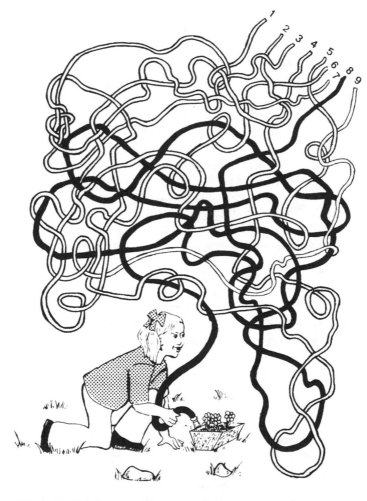

FIG. 9.13. Working backward is a good strategy when there are fewer paths from the goal than from the start.

every day, how much of the lake is covered on the 59th day? The answer is half. Thus, by working backward, the problem is easy to solve. A forward-looking strategy with this problem will insure insanity.

It is often a good idea to combine forward and backward strategies. If you are faced with the task of solving proofs in geometry and trigonometry, a combination of forward and backward strategies may often prove most useful. You can start from the goal, transforming expressions on each line and then alternate operations between the start state and the goal until the solution path meets somewhere between the two.

Simplification

> You turn the problem over and over in your mind; try to turn it so it appears simpler. . . . Is the problem as simply, as clearly, as suggestively expressed as possible?"
> —Polya (1962)

Problems that are difficult to solve are often complex in nature. A good way to approach such problems is to strip away as much of the complexity as possible in order to reduce it to a simple form. Often, the best form of representation can perform the task of **simplification** because it will allow you to "see" the solution in an efficient way.

Suppose you are faced with the classic cat-in-the-tree problem. According to common folklore, cats can climb up trees, but not down. (There is no more truth to this than to the notion that elephants are afraid of mice.) Suppose that you are faced with the task of retrieving a cat from the top branch of a 10-foot-tall tree. The only ladder you have is 6 feet long. You'll need to place the base of the ladder 3 feet from the trunk of the tree to steady it. Will you be able to reach the cat?

Like most problems, a good way to approach this problem is to diagram the given facts. A diagram of this problem has been drawn in Fig. 9.14. Once the information is presented in a diagram format, it is easy to perceive the problem as a simple geometry problem: What is the hypotenuse of a triangle whose two other sides are 10 feet and 3 feet long? At this point, you'd need to rely on previously acquired knowledge about triangles to recognize and solve this problem. When the topic is thinking, there is no substitute for a good education to provide the foundation and raw materials for thought.

The formula for finding the hypotenuse of a right triangle is:

$$a^2 + b^2 = c^2$$

FIG. 9.14.   The cat-in-the-tree problem. Once the information is drawn in a diagram format, it is easy to see that it is a simple geometry problem. (See text for details.)

Substituting the appropriate values in the above equation:

$$10^2 + 3^2 = c^2$$
$$100 + 9 = c^2$$
$$\underline{109} \qquad = c^2$$
$$\sqrt{109} \qquad = c$$
$$10.4 \qquad = c$$

Thus, the ladder would need to be 10.4 feet long to reach the top. But wait, could you redraw the problem, using the information given to find out if you could still use the 6-foot ladder to reach the cat? See Fig. 9.15 for a slightly different diagram of the problem.

The same formula can be used, but now the unknown is not the hypotenuse, but another one of the sides of the right triangle.

FIG. 9.15.   If the cat-in-the-tree problem is changed so that the un-known value is how high a 6-foot ladder will reach if it is placed 3 feet from the trunk, a different answer is obtained. (See text for details.)

Rearranging the terms will yield:

$$a^2 + b^2 = c^2$$
$$a^2 = c^2 - b^2$$
$$a^2 = 6^2 - 3^2$$
$$a^2 = 36 - 9$$
$$a^2 = 27$$
$$a = \sqrt{27}$$
$$a = 5.2$$

Thus, the top rung of the ladder will touch the tree 5.2 feet above the ground. Will you be able to reach the cat? Draw yourself near the top rung of the ladder. If you are over 5 feet tall, you should have no trouble reaching the cat if you are standing on the top or second rung. In fact, you won't even have to reach up.

Simplification is a good strategy when the problem is abstract or complex or contains information that is irrelevant to finding a solution. Often, simplification will work hand-in-hand with selecting the optimal form of representation, because a good representation will often simplify a problem.

Generalization and Specialization

When confronted with a problem, it is sometimes helpful to consider it as an example of a larger class of problems (**generalization**); or to consider it as a special case (**specialization**).

The form of problem representation that is most compatible with the generalization and specialization strategy is the tree diagram. Most goals can be classified as both a subset of a larger category and as a heading for a smaller one. Let's work an example to clarify what this means. As a furniture designer, you are given the problem of designing a chair that will be especially well suited for reading. How would you go about solving this problem?

As you probably realized, this is an ill-defined problem. The difficulty is largely centered on evaluating which of several possible chairs will best satisfy the goal. Use a tree diagram to classify chairs in general, and "chairs for reading" in particular. Although there are many possible diagrams, one example is presented in Fig. 9.16.

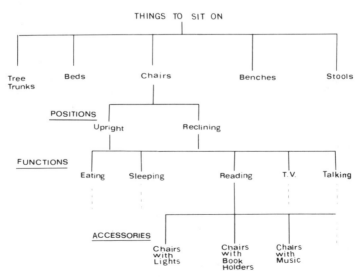

FIG. 9.16.   Possible tree diagram for problem of designing a chair for reading.

I hope that you worked through this problem and drew your own tree diagram. As you can see in Fig. 9.16, thinking about "chairs for reading" as a subset of the category "chairs" can help you to incorporate other features of chairs in your design while custom tailoring the chair with some of the possibilities that are unique to "chairs for reading."

Thus, the process of generalization and/or specialization can help you to consider your problem from both broad and narrow perspectives.

Random Search and Trial-and-Error

Recall that the anatomy of a problem consists of a start, or initial state, a goal, and solution paths leading from the start state to the goal. One strategy for searching among possible solution paths is **random search.** Although this probably seems like a nonstrategy or "un-strategy," in some cases it will work quite well. When there are very few possible solution paths, random search will lead to the goal in a short time. A truly random search would mean that there is no systematic order to which the possible paths are explored and no memory for paths already tried. A systematic **trial-and-error** search through the problem space (contains the paths, goal, and start state) is preferable. Trial-and-error search is best applied to well-defined problems with few possible solution paths. Simple, short anagrams are good candidates for these search methods. Unscramble the following letters to form an English word:

THA

Because there are only six possible orders for these three letters (THA; TAH; HTA; HAT; ATH; AHT), trying each one until a solution is found is fairly straightforward and simple strategy. If you used a truly random search, you would not keep track of which letter orderings you used and would repeat some until the correct order was found. Systematic trial-and-error is almost always superior to random search, although only slightly better when there are very few possibilities.

Both trial-and-error and random search are poor strategies when the number of possible paths increases, because of the sheer number of possible combinations. Often, in larger problems, it is helpful to eliminate some of the paths and then search among a smaller subset with a trial-and-error strategy.

Rules

Some kinds of problems, like series problems, depend on **rules.** Once the underlying principles are established, the problem is solved. Most problems in mathematics and the physical sciences follow rules. Look back at the tower of Hanoi problem presented earlier in the section on Means–Ends Analysis. The solution is quite easy, once the rule that "a larger circle should never be placed on top of a smaller circle" was discovered. A good way to discover rules is to look for patterns in the givens or subgoals. Problems requiring rule discovery are often used on tests of intelligence.

Complete the following pattern:
ABBACCCADDDDA-----
This is a fairly simple series problem. The next six letters are EEEEEA. Certain patterns are common in problems of this sort. To detect them, count the number of repeating symbols, look across the series for repetitions at long intervals, try simple additions and subtractions, and so on. This is not a trivial problem. The decoding of enemy war messages during World War II was a major factor contributing to our victory. The United States and British governments employed many professional decoders whose job it was to find rules that could be used to decipher German and Japanese military messages.

Suppose for a minute that there is intelligent life in outer space, and that they are also wondering about us. How would they let us know that they exist? Some scientists, science fiction authors, and members of the general public believe that they would make their presence known by sending messages. No one believes that these messages would be in English, or Chinese, or Samoan, or any other Earth language. They would send messages in their own native tongue or native whatever if they don't have tongues. How would we on Earth recognize such messages? The United States military has decided that, if we are being sent messages from outer space, the one distinguishing characteristic of these messages would be a rule-governed "grammar" or patterned repetition. As strange as this may seem, the military does monitor outer space for anything that seems like a patterned communication. So far, they haven't received any and we can continue to believe, for the time being at least, that we are the most intelligent beings in space (or that the more intelligent beings do not want us to know they are out there, or that they can't reach us, or they don't want to reach us.)

Hints

Hints are additional information that is given after an individual has begun to work on a problem. Often, the hint provides additional information that is important to your solution. Sometimes a hint will require that you change the way you have been approaching the problem. A common example of the use of hints is the "hot–cold" game played by children. An object is hidden in a room. The child who is "it" wanders around the room while the other children yell "hotter" if she or he is moving closer to the hidden object and "colder" if she or he is moving away from the hidden object. In this problem, the child who is "it" should take one small step at a time, continuing in the same direction when the hint is "hotter" and trying a slight change in direction when the hint is "colder."

Research on the way people use hints has shown that general hints, like "think of new ways of using objects," don't facilitate the problem solution (Duncan, 1961). The more specific the hint, the greater the benefit derived from it.

One of psychology's favorite problems is the two-string problem. Imagine walking into a room with two strings hanging from the ceiling. The strings are too far apart for you to reach both at the same time, yet your task is to do exactly that. This situation is depicted in Fig. 9.17.

The best solution to the two-string problem involves setting one string in a swinging motion, usually by tying a heavy object to the end of one string to serve as a weight, so that the problem solver can reach the string as it swings toward him or her. When researchers provided hints for the problem solver by pretending to accidentally bump against one string to get it swinging, most of the problem solvers hit on this solution, but few were consciously aware that they utilized this hint (Maier, 1931).

In one experimental investigation of how people use hints, researchers had subjects learn pairs of words so that if the experimenter said one word, the subject would respond with its pair. (This is called paired-associates learning.) One of the pairs that the subjects learned was ''candle–box.'' After learning the list of paired associates, subjects were given Duncker's (1945) candle problem, which involved affixing a candle to a wall by using a box as the candle holder (see Fig. 1.1 in chapter 1). Did this hint help to solve this problem? In general, their performance on this task was improved only if they were told by the experimenter to think about the pairs of words they had learned as a problem-

FIG. 9.17. The two-string problem. How could you reach both strings at the same time? (After Maier, 1930.)

solving aid (Weisberg, DiCamillo, & Phillips, 1978). They did not spon-taneously use this hint to solve the problem, most likely because they were unaware that it was a hint. Recent research has confirmed these results with other types of problems (Perfetto, Bransford, & Franks, 1983). In general, it seems that hints are helpful only when the problem solver perceives the hint as a possible solution aid.

Good problem solvers will seek out hints. Gathering additional information can be thought of as hint-seeking behavior. It is almost always a good strategy to get all of the information that you can about your problem. The additional givens will help to restructure the problem space and provide direction so that solution paths may be found more easily.

Split-Half Method

The **split-half method** is an excellent search strategy when there is no a priori reason for selecting among a sequentially organized set of possible solution paths. Suppose, for example, that there is a stoppage in the plumbing system that prevents water from coming out of your kitchen sink. The stoppage is some-where between the place where your pipes connect with the other pipes on your street and your kitchen faucet. How would you search for the pipe stoppage while making as few holes as possible in the pipe?

In this example, the solution (the place where the pipe is stopped) lies some-where along a linear route. The best way to search in this problem is the split-half method. Because this problem requires that you break the pipe each place you search, you want to search as efficiently as possible. Begin halfway between the street connection and your kitchen sink. If you find that water can still run freely at this point, you know that the stoppage is between this point and your sink. If this happens, look again half-way between this point and your kitchen sink. If the water is still running freely at this point, then you'll know that the stoppage is closer still to the sink, and you'll look again midway between that point and your sink.

Suppose that, on your first attempt, you find that the water is not running at this point. Then the stoppage must be between the street and this midpoint. Your next search would be midway between the current search point and the street connection. In this manner, you would continue searching until the stoppage is found. This is a good method anytime you have a similar problem, such as trying to locate a break in the electrical wiring in your home or auto.

You can use the split-half method to play a party game called "Guess Your Age." (I made this game up.) Your friends can pretend to be any age. You can guess the age of anyone between 0 and 100 with only 7 guesses. How would you do it? Begin with the age that is midway between 0 and 100, which, of course, is 50. The player would have to respond by telling you if the age that he or she is thinking of is older or younger than 50. Thus, he or she would respond with "younger" or "older." Suppose that the response was "younger." What age should you guess next? You'd pick the age midway between 0 and 50, which is 25. Suppose your friend now responds, "older." Your third guess should be halfway between 25 and 50. Because we're only concerned with whole numbers, your next guess would be 38. If he or she now responds "younger," you'd guess 32, as this number is midway between 25 and 38. If the next response is "older," you'd guess 35 (midway between 32 and 38). If the response is "younger," you'd guess 33. At this point, you know that the player is pretending to be either 33 or 34. Thus, any age can be guessed with, at most, seven guesses. Try this method out with some friends. It will be good practice in using the split-half strategy. Consider this strategy whenever there are several possible equally likely solutions.

Brainstorming

The best way to have good ideas is to have lots of ideas.
—Linus Pauling

Brainstorming is fun. It was originally proposed by Osborn (1963) as a method for group problem solving, but it's also useful for individuals working alone. Brainstorming is useful in generating additional solution paths, and thus should be considered whenever the difficulty involves finding solution paths.

The goal of brainstorming is to produce a large number of possible solutions. Problem solvers are encouraged to think up wild, unusual, imaginative ideas and to write them all down, no matter how silly they seem. The underlying principle is that the greater the quantity of ideas, the greater the likelihood that at least one of them will be good. In order to foster creative use of imagination, rules include no criticism or ridicule, even when the ideas may appear ridiculous. Judgments about the worth of the ideas are deferred until a later evaluation phase. Sometimes parts of the various ideas are combined or refined to improve on them.

Brainstorming can be done in large or small groups or alone. After the brainstorming session, the list of possible solutions can be perused to find ones that will solve the problem in light of the problem constraints, which often include financial and time limitations and/or ethical considerations.

Brainstorming was used effectively by a food manufacturer faced with the problem of finding a better way to bag potato chips. The problem solvers (corporate executives) were asked to think up the best packaging solution they had ever seen. Someone said that bagging wet leaves was the best packaging solution he had ever seen. If you attempt to bag dry leaves they crumble and don't fit into trash bags well, but if you hose them down before bagging them, you can use fewer bags and fill them more easily with less empty space in each bag. Following this lead, they tried wetting potato chips and then putting them into bags. The result was disastrous—the potato chips dried into tasteless crumbs. But, this idea ultimately led to the popular potato chip that comes stacked in a can. The identical chips are formed from a liquid potato mixture that is cooked into chip-shaped molds. In this manner, a wild and not-too-good solution (wetting potato chips) was parlayed into a highly successful solution.

Contradiction

According to Wickelgren (1974), the method of **contradiction** works by showing that "the goal could not possibly be obtained from the givens, since it is inconsistent with the givens" (p. 109). A simple example of the use of contradiction is the problem of finding out if it is snowing, given that you're indoors and a large overhanging roof prevents you from looking up. If it is snowing, then there will be snow on the ground, so look down to solve this problem. If you find that there is no snow on the ground, then by the method of contradiction, you can conclude that it is not snowing.

Contradiction can be used in a variety of contexts. You may want to know if a democratic country is politically conservative or liberal. Given that all liberal candidates were recently elected, the country cannot be conservative (assuming, of course, that conservative candidates were running for the election, their political views were well known, etc.).

Wickelgren (1974) has suggested that contradiction is a good strategy when the population of alternative goals is small, or when alternative goals can be classified and thus reduced to a smaller number of mutually exclusive possibilities. This method is well suited for certain kinds of mathematical problems, a topic that is discussed in chapter 11.

Restate the Problem

Restating the problem is a most useful strategy for ill-defined problems. In well-defined problems, the goal is usually explicitly stated in unambiguous terms that leave little room for restatement.

Consider the problem that faces virtually every adult I've ever met: "How can I save money?" Countless families around the world shop in discount markets, eat peanut butter sandwiches, and spend their Saturday evenings at home in an attempt to solve this problem. Suppose you restate this problem so that it becomes, "How can I have more money?" Additional solutions would now include finding a better paying job, moving to a less expensive apartment, marrying a rich man or woman, investing in high-paying stocks, winning the Irish Sweepstakes, and so on. Whenever you are faced with an ill-defined problem, try to restate the goal. This is often a very good strategy, because a different goal will have different solution paths. The greater the number of solution paths you have to consider, the more likely you are to obtain the goal.

Analogies and Metaphors

> *We can scarcely imagine a problem absolutely new, unlike and unrelated to any formerly solved problem; but if such a problem could exist, it would be insoluble. In fact, when solving a problem, we should always profit from previously solved problems, using their result or their method, or the experience acquired in solving them.''*
>
> —Polya (1945)

Gick and Holyoak (1980) asked, "Where do new ideas come from?" Many scientists and mathematicians respond that their ideas or solutions to problems come from recognizing **analogies** and **metaphors** drawn from different academic disciplines (Hadamard, 1945). In fact, it seems that the most common form of inference is made by noting similarities (analogies and metaphors) between two or more situations. Like hints, the analogy must be recognized as relevant to the problem being considered and then modified for the particular situation.

Consider the following problem (from Gick & Holyoak, 1980):

A small country fell under the iron rule of a dictator. The dictator ruled the country from a strong fortress. The fortress was situated in the middle of the country, surrounded by farms and villages. Many roads radiated outward from the fortress like spokes on a wheel. A great general arose who raised a large army at the border and vowed to capture the fortress and free the country of the dictator. The general knew that if his entire army could attack the fortress at once it could be captured. His troops were poised at the head of one of the roads leading to the fortress, ready to attack. However, a spy brought the general a disturbing report. The ruthless dictator had planted mines on each of the roads. The mines were set so that small bodies of men could pass over them safely, since the dictator needed to be able to move troops and workers to and from the fortress. However, any large force would detonate the mines. Not only would this blow up the road and render it impassable, but the dictator would then destroy many villages in retaliation. A full-scale direct attack on the fortress therefore appeared impossible. (p. 351)

To help you solve this problem, I'll also give you a hint. The solution is analogous to one discussed earlier in this chapter, although the context is entirely different. Stop for a few minutes and attempt to work on this problem. Think about the problems presented earlier.

The solution to this problem is analogous to the one used in the inoperable stomach tumor problem. In that problem (Duncker, 1945), the best solution involved sending weak rays through the body simultaneously from several different points so that they would converge on the tumor. Similarly, the army could be divided into small groups that would attack the fortress from all sides. Did you recognize that these problems were essentially similar in form and could be solved with the same solution?

Analogies and metaphors are useful strategies in many situations. They are considered again in chapter 10, "Creativity," and in chapter 11, "Applications of Critical Thinking Skills," where they are discussed in the context of solving mathematical problems.

Gordon (1961), originator of a group called "Synectics," has presented guidelines for the use of analogies in solving problems. The term "Synectics" was taken from the Greek. It means joining together of different and apparently unrelated elements. Gordon has suggested that we consider four different types of analogies when faced with a problem:

1. **Personal Analogy**

If you want to understand a complex phenomenon, think of yourself as a participant in the phenomenon. For example, if you want to understand the molecular structure of a compound, think of yourself as a molecule. How would you behave? What other molecules would you want to attach yourself to? Get away from reliance on scientific notations and actually pretend to be a molecule bouncing in a compound. You may see relationships from this perspective that you were blind to when acting as a scientist.

2. **Direct Analogy**

Compare the problems you're working on with several problems in other domains. According to Gordon (1961), this method was used by Alexander Graham Bell: "It struck me that the bones of the human ear were very massive indeed, as compared with the delicate thin membrane that operated them, and the thought occurred that if a membrane so delicate could move bones relatively so massive, why should not a thicker and stouter piece of membrane move my piece of steel. And the telephone was conceived" (p. 41).

A particularly fertile area for analogies is biology, where many solutions to biological problems have been evolving since the first life form appeared on Earth. When a Synectics group was faced with the problem of devising a bottle closure that could be used with glue or nail polish, the analogy they used was the biological closure of the anus (rectum). Apparently, this solution worked quite well. (You can think about this the next time you use a bottle of LePage's mucilage.)

3. **Symbolic Activity**

This solution strategy utilizes visual imagery. Its goal is to get away from the constraints of words or mathematical symbols. Students who utilized imagery to visualize the tumor problem and the fortress problem were most likely to notice spontaneously that the two problems were analogous. If you work on generating a clear image of a problem, you may "see" a solution that had been overlooked.

4. **Fantasy Analogy**

In your wildest dreams, what would you want of a solution? An example of this is to imagine two small insects that would automatically zip your jacket or a silk worm that would spin silk rapidly to keep you warm when the temperature drops. These are fantasy analogies. Like brainstorming, a fantasy analogy can result in wild, impractical solutions that can later be modified to practical, workable ones.

Analogies and metaphors are useful problem-solving strategies; however, difficulties can arise when analogies are misapplied. Consider this problem, posed by DeBono (1967b):

Place three bottles upright on a table or on the floor. Position them so that each bottle forms the corner point of a triangle of equal sides. The distance between the bases of any two bottles should be slightly more than the length of a knife.

Using only [the] four knives, construct a platform on top of the bottles. No part of any knife may touch the ground. The platform must be strong enough to support a full glass of water. (p. 7)

The solution to this problem involves forming a triangle by interweaving three of the knives. The fourth isn't used. Now that I've told you how to solve the three-bottle problem, try this one (from DeBono, 1967b):

This time use only two bottles. Place these upright, their bases separated by the length of a knife handle added to the length of a knife.

Using only [the] four knives, erect between the two bottles a bridge which will support at its center the weight of a full glass of water. The ends of the bridge rest on the top of the bottles. No part of any knife may touch the ground. (p. 31)

Stop now, and work on this problem.

The solution entails interweaving the four knives so that they form a square area with only two of the knives resting on a bottle. This is a difficult problem to solve. An analogy can be used from the earlier problem, but it needs to be adjusted so that each knife is no longer resting on a bottle. You can use the analogy of folding two tops of a carton by sliding the corner of the fourth side under the corner of the first one. People often find that the change in the way the second problem is solved is a source of difficulty. DeBono (1967b) concluded:

There is a limit to the usefulness of re-examining old experiences in this way. Sometimes it is more efficient to approach the problem as a fresh one than to spend a long time seeking a parallel in past experience. It depends on how similar the other problems are, but that depends on how good one is at detecting similarities. . . (p. 37)

Consult an Expert

If at first you don't succeed, try, try, again. Then quit. No use being a damned fool about it.

—W. C. Fields (quoted in Teger, 1979, p. XIV)

Often in life, we don't have to solve problems alone. Sometimes, the best way to solve a problem is to let experts do it for us. People seek accountants for help with their tax problems, attorneys for their legal problems, physicians for their health problems. We elect officials to handle the problems of running our country and rely on military experts to wage wars. These people became experts in their field by obtaining the appropriate knowledge in their subject area and through repeated applications of this knowledge to real-world problems. Consulting an expert is often an excellent solution strategy. Their greater experience and knowledge will allow them to solve many problems in their area of expertise much more efficiently than a novice. If you decide to consult an expert, the problem becomes: (a) how to know somebody who is an expert; and (b) how to select which "expert" to use. Once you've passed these hurdles, your problems still aren't over. You need to be sure that the expert has all of the facts and has considered all of the relevant alternatives. Listen carefully to the expert's analysis of the risks and alternatives, but make the decision yourself. An expert is a problem-solving aid, not the solution.

Select the Best Strategy

Thirteen different strategies have been presented as aids in problem solving. When confronted with a problem, how do you know which to use? It is important to keep in mind that these strategies are not mutually exclusive. It will often be best to use them in combinations. The best strategy or strategies depends on the nature of the problem. After all, if you are taking an exam, you could be expelled if you consult the paper of an "expert" student sitting next to you.

Along with each strategy, I presented some guidelines for its appropriate use. In general, a few higher level "strategies for selecting strategies" include:

1. If the problem is ill defined, try to restate the goal or the problem.
2. When there are very few possible solutions, a trial-and-error approach will work well.
3. If a problem is complex, try simplification, means–ends analysis, and generalization and specialization.
4. When there are fewer paths leading away from the goal than there are from the start state, work backward.
5. If you can gather additional information, do it. Look for and utilize hints.
6. If there is an ordered array of equally likely alternatives, try the split-half method and seek rules.
7. If the problem is a lack of possible solution paths, brainstorm to generate alternative solution paths.
8. Problems in mathematics and logic are especially amenable to a solution by contradiction.
9. Using analogies and metaphors and consulting an expert are widely applicable to all sorts of problems.
10. Remember that these are only guidelines to solving problems. The best way to be an expert problem solver is to solve lots of problems.

PROBLEM-SOLVING PROBLEMS

Problems are our most important product.
—Beardsley

Functional Fixedness and Mental Set

Recall the two-string problem presented earlier in this chapter. The task was to grasp, simultaneously, two strings that hung from the ceiling. The correct solution involved setting one string into motion, perhaps by tying a heavy object like a pair of pliers to its end to serve as a weight. One reason why this was such a difficult problem is **functional fixedness.** Subjects were fixated, or "stuck," on the usual function of a pair of pliers and had difficulty thinking of them as having a different function.

Another example of functional fixedness was presented in the Introduction (chapter 1). In a classic problem, subjects were asked to attach a candle to the wall so that it could be burned, using only a box of thumbtacks and some matches. Subjects had difficulty thinking of the box as a candle holder, because they saw it in terms of its usual function—a container for thumbtacks.

Functional fixedness is one kind of **mental set.** I think of these terms as "ruts in one's thinking." They are predispositions to think and respond in certain ways. To demonstrate how powerful some sets can be, work on the nine-dot problem in Fig. 9.18. Stop now and work on this problem.

The difficulty posed by the nine-dot problem comes from a perceptual set imposed by the square arrangement. Most people attempt to solve the problem by staying within the imaginary boundary formed by the outer dots. If you extend your lines beyond this imaginary boundary, you'll find that the problem is easy to solve. In addition, most people attempt solutions in which the line goes through the center of each dot. One solution to the nine-dot problem is shown in Fig. 9.19.

FIG. 9.18. The nine-dot problem. Using no more than four straight lines and without lifting your pencil from the paper, draw a line through all nine dots.

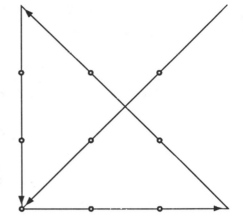

FIG. 9.19. One possible solution to the nine-dot problem. Note that the solution involves breaking "set." Most people assume that the lines must form a square and that each line must pass through the center of each dot.

There are several other solutions to the nine-dot problem. Each of them involves set-breaking in some way. Two solutions (Adams, 1979, pp. 25–26) are presented in Fig. 9.20. A few other, more exotic solutions, including one submitted by a 10-year-old girl, which consists of one very fat line drawn through all nine dots can be found in Adams' (1979) gem of a book, *Conceptual Blockbusting*. The set of staying within the rectangular area is pervasive and difficult to break. Strategies that get you to view problems in novel ways, like the personal analogy strategy, are good ways to work on set-breaking solutions.

Misleading and Irrelevant Information

My father used to love this riddle:

> Suppose you are a bus driver. On the first stop, you pick up 6 men and 2 women. At the second stop, 2 men leave and 1 woman boards the bus. At the third, stop 1 man leaves and 2 women enter the bus. At the fourth stop, 3 men get on and 3 women get off. At the fifth stop, 2 men get off, 3 men get on, 1 woman gets off, and 2 women get on. What is the bus driver's name?

Could you answer this question without rereading the problem? The bus driver's name is, of course, your name, because the riddle began, "Suppose you are a bus driver." All of the information about the rest of the passengers was irrelevant. Often, information that is irrelevant to the problem serves to mislead problem solvers down dead-end paths.

Real-life problems often involve deciding what information is relevant. To avoid being misled by information, be clear about the goal state. Simplification will sometimes help in separating the relevant from the irrelevant givens.

Let's try another example (from Fixx, 1978):

One possible solution is to fold the paper as indicated so that the dots line up in a straight line.

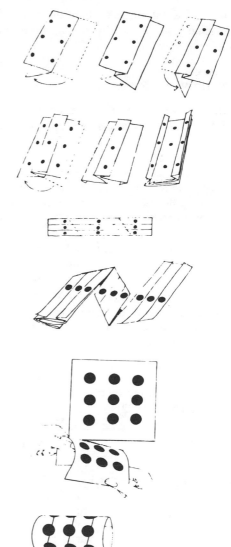

It is also possible to roll up the puzzle and draw a spiral through the dots, and otherwise violate the two-dimensional format.

FIG. 9.20. Two possible solutions to the nine-dot problem. (from Adams, J. L. (1979), *Conceptual blockbusting.* N.Y.: W. W. Norton, pp. 25–26).

If you have black socks and brown socks in your drawer mixed in the ratio of 4 to 5, how many socks will you have to take out to make sure of having a pair of the same color?

Think about this problem. What is relevant? What is irrelevant? The answer is three socks, because any two must match if there are only brown and black socks. The information about the ratio of socks is irrelevant and misleading. Imagine yourself actually picking socks from a drawer, and this problem will be easier to solve.

World-View Constraints

Often we fail to solve problems because of the **world-view constraints** placed on us by our social class, nationality, or political views. Consider the following problem:

> A ping pong ball 1″ in diameter falls into a 3″ length of pipe that is 1⅛″ in diameter. The pipe is firmly affixed to the concrete pavement. It is extremely important to remove the ball. You and some friends are faced with this task. All you have is some fine wire and your collective abilities to solve this problem. What do you do?

Most people approach this task by attempting to bend fine wire into tweezers to pluck it up. A better solution is to urinate into the pipe so that the ball will float to the top. This probably never occurred to you, because it is not an acceptable thought for most people in our society. Although this has never been verified, it would probably be an easier task for people in other societies where urination is not considered as private an act as it is in our society.

Mechanization

Using jars with the following capacities, measure the amount of water desired (after Luchins, 1942):

	Jug A	Jug B	Jug C	Desired
1	14	163	25	99
2	18	43	10	5
3	9	42	6	21
4	20	59	4	31
5	23	49	3	20

STOP NOW, and solve these five problems. Keep a record of how you went about solving them.

The first four problems can be solved by filling Jug B, then filling Jug A from it once and then filling Jug C from it twice. The water left in Jug B will be the desired amount. In algebraic terms, it's B-A-2C.

Look at how you solved the fifth problem. Did you use this formula? Most people do, although it's much simpler to fill Jug A, then pour from it into C to get the answer. People overlook the simpler solution because their approach to the problem has become mechanized. You can guard against this by rethinking occasionally about the way you are solving a problem. **Mechanization** can be helpful, in that it saves solution times when we don't have to stop and rethink each problem, but it can also blind us to better solutions.

APPLYING THE FRAMEWORK

The general thinking skills framework that we've been using throughout the book is particularly applicable to problem solving.

1. *What is the goal?* One of the first steps in solving a problem is to be explicit about the goal. This is relatively easy for well-defined problems (e.g., How many ounces are in a pound?). Most problems, however, are ill-defined and can have multiple goals. Being explicit about the goal or considering goals will force you to cast the problem in the thinking skills framework and to begin goal-directed thinking.

2. *What is known?* This is part of the preparation or familiarization process. The knowns, or "givens," determine the nature of the problem. It is often possible to improve on what is known by gathering additional information. Once you have a clear determination of the knowns, you can use that information as a guide to selecting the best representation and best problem-solving strategy.

3. *Which thinking skill or skills will get you to your goal?* Thirteen different kinds of strategies or skills were presented in this chapter. You need to select the ones most likely to solve the problem. A trial-and-error approach to selecting a strategy is, itself, a poor strategy. Guidelines were presented for evaluating strategies, depending on the nature of the problem.

The skills for planning and solving problems that were presented in this chapter are applicable to almost any problem. After reading this chapter, you should be able to:

- plan and monitor a strategy for finding a solution
- identify any problem as either well defined or ill defined, and adjust your solution plan according to the type of problem
- use graphs, diagrams, hierarchical trees, matrices, and models as solution aids
- devise a quality representation of a problem
- select the problem-solving strategies that are appropriate for the problem
- use all of the following strategies: mean–ends analysis; working backward; simplification; generalization and specialization; random search and trial-and-error; rules; hints; split-half method; brainstorming; contradiction; restate the problem; analogies and metaphors; and consulting an expert
- be aware of functional fixedness so as to avoid it
- distinguish between relevant and irrelevant information
- understand how world views can constrain the problem-solving process

4. *Have you reached your goal?* The final step in problem solving is an assessment of the quality of the solution. In well-defined problems, this question becomes: Is your

solution the correct one? In ill-defined problems, the solution has to be evaluated qualitatively both in an absolute sense (Does it alleviate or reduce the problem?) and in a relative sense (Is it the best alternative?).

CHAPTER SUMMARY

1. All problems can be conceptualized as being composed of "anatomical" parts that include a start state, a goal state, and paths leading from the start to the goal. This entire structure is called the problem space.

2. It is common to divide the problem-solving process into four stages: preparation or familiarization; production; judgment or evaluation; and incubation. Incubation is an optional stage that does not always occur.

3. Problems can be classified along a continuum ranging from well defined to ill defined. Well-defined problems have explicit paths and goals. Ill-defined problems are subject to multiple interpretations. Most of the problems encountered in life are ill defined.

4. Solution strategies need to be planned. A plan for solving a problem will include the construction of a representation and the generation and evaluation of possible solutions.

5. An invaluable aid in solving problems is to devise an external form of representation. The best representation to choose will depend on the type of problem.

6. Thirteen different strategies for generating and evaluating solutions were presented. Often, several will be used together in solving a problem. General guidelines were offered for the appropriate use of each.

7. There are four common sources of difficulty that problem solvers encounter. Functional fixedness refers to the failure to utilize items in unusual ways. Mental set refers to the predisposition to respond to any situation in a fixed way. Misleading and irrelevant information can "derail one's trail of thought" and can lead you down blind paths. The constraints imposed on us by our society cause us to view problems from our own narrow experiences. Mechanization refers to the rote unthinking applications of previous solutions without stopping to think about improving our strategies.

Terms to Know

You should be able to define or describe the following terms or concepts. If you find that you're having difficulty with any term, be sure to reread the section in which it is discussed.

Anatomy of a Problem. Newell and Simon (1972) have conceptualized all problems as consisting of parts or components—an initial state, a goal state, and solution paths that link the initial state to the goal state.

Initial State. The starting or beginning place in a problem. A problem is solved when the problem solver can find "paths" from the initial state to the goal.

Goal State. The desired end state in a problem. When a problem solver finds "paths" to the goal, the problem is solved.

Solution Paths. Methods or means for solving problems. Routes that lead from the initial state to the goal state in a problem.

Problem Space. All possible paths from the initial state to the goal state in a problem.

Preparation or Familiarization Stage. The first stage in problem solving, which includes the time spent in understanding the nature of the problem, the desired goal, and the givens.

Production Stage. The second stage in problem solving. During this state, the problem solver produces the solution paths that define the problem space.

Judgment or Evaluation Stage. The third stage in problem solving, during which time the problem solver evaluates the solution paths in order to select the best one.

Incubation. A period in problem solving when the problem solver is not actively working on the problem. Sometimes people report that a solution comes to them during this "time out" period.

Insight. Sudden knowledge of a solution to a problem. Also known as the Aha! experience.

Well-Defined Problems. Problems with a single correct answer.

Ill-Defined Problems. Problems with many possible correct answers. The difficulty with these problems lies in evaluating possible solutions to decide which is best. Often the goal in these problems is vague or incomplete.

Perceptual Reorganization. Seeing or restructuring a problem in a new way so that attempts to find a solution will be facilitated. Perceptual reorganization is one way to break mental sets or predispositions to respond to fixed ways.

Operations. The transformations of the "givens" in a problem into solution paths that will solve the problem.

Hierarchical Trees. Branching diagrams that serve as a representational aid in solving problems. Instances of categories provide the "nodes" of the trees.

Matrix. A rectangular array of numbers that is used as a means of representing problems that contain categories of information.

Detour Problems. Problems in which the path to the goal is not a direct linear one. Intermediate steps are required that seem directly opposite the goal.

Subproblems. When difficulty is encountered in solving a problem, it can be broken down into several smaller problems or "subproblems."

Subgoal. When difficulty is encountered in solving a problem, it can be broken down into several smaller problems, called "subproblems." Each subproblem has its own goal, called a "subgoal."

Means–End Analysis. A general problem-solving strategy in which operations are used to reduce the distance between the problem solver's current state and the nearest possible subgoal or goal.

General Problem Solver. A generally applicable computer program developed by Newell and Simon that can solve a wide variety of problems. It utilizes means–ends analysis as its problem-solving strategy.

Working Backward. A problem-solving strategy in which operations are planned that move from the goal to the present or initial state. This method is usually contrasted with the forward-looking strategy.

Forward-Looking Strategy. A problem-solving strategy in which all of the planning is done by considering operations that move the problem solver closer to subgoals and the goal. This method is usually contrasted with working backward from the goal.

Simplification. A problem-solving strategy in which as much of the complexity as possible is removed from the problem in order to facilitate a solution.

Generalization. A problem-solving strategy in which the problem is considered as an example of a larger class of problems.

Specialization. A problem-solving strategy in which the problem is considered as a special case drawn from a larger set of problems.

Random Search. A problem-solving strategy in which all possible solution paths from the initial state to the goal are considered in an unsystematic (random) manner. This method is usually contrasted with trial-and-error search.

Trial-and-Error. A problem-solving strategy in which all solution paths from the initial state to the goal are searched systematically. This method is usually contrasted with random search.

Rules. The principles that underlie some problems. For example, solutions to problems that require a prediction of the next element in a series depend on the discovery of their rules.

Hints. Additional information that is given after an individual has begun to work on a problem.

Split-Half Method. A problem-solving strategy that is useful when there is no a priori reason for selecting among a sequentially organized set of possible solution paths. The method consists of continually selecting a point that is halfway between the present state and the goal as a systematic means for "guessing" at the solution.

Brainstorming. A group or individual method for generating solution paths for problems. Problem solvers are encouraged to think up wild, imaginative solutions and to defer judgment on these solutions until a later time when they may be modified or combined. The goal is to produce a large number of possible solutions.

Contradiction. A problem-solving strategy with which the problem solver shows that a goal cannot be obtained from the givens because of inconsistencies.

Restating the Problem. A problem-solving strategy that is best suited for ill-defined problems. It is sometimes easier to find a solution to a problem when it is expressed in different words.

Analogies. (in problem solving) Problem-solving strategies in which similarities are noted between two or more situations, while simultaneously discerning that there are also differences; for example, by noting similarities between two different problems, the problem solver may discover that similar solutions are applicable.

Personal Analogy. A problem-solving strategy suggested by Gordon (1961) in which you think of yourself as a participant in the phenomenon that you want to understand.

Direct Analogy. A problem-solving strategy suggested by Gordon (1961) in which you note similarities between your problem and related problems in other domains.

Symbolic Activity. The deliberate use of visual imagery or other symbolic representation as a problem-solving aid.

Fantasy Analogy. A problem-solving strategy suggested by Gordon (1961) in which problem solvers utilize their imagination to conceptualize ideal solutions.

Functional Fixedness. A type of mental set in which individuals only consider the usual use (function) of objects.

Mental Set. Predispositions to think and respond in a certain way.

World-View Constraints. Limitations on the way we approach problems placed upon us by our social class, nationality, or political views.

Mechanization. A routinized approach to solving commonly encountered problems.

Chapter Questions

Be sure that you can answer the following questions.

1. Identify and explain the "anatomical" parts of all problems.

2. What are the four stages in problem solving? How does each stage contribute to the solution?

3. Give an example of a well-defined and an ill-defined problem. In general, how do they differ?

4. How are external forms of representation (e.g., graphs, diagrams) helpful in solving problems?

5. List five different problem representations, and explain when each is most likely to be useful.

6. Explain how the General Problem Solver is able to solve a wide variety of problems.

7. Compare and contrast the 13 problem-solving strategies presented in this chapter. Provide an example in which each might be used.

8. Four different kinds of analogies were suggested for use. Describe each, and give an example when each would be useful.

9. How does each of the problem-solving problems relate to the anatomical parts of a problem? For example, irrelevant information causes people to consider solution paths that don't lead to the goal. How do the other problem-solving problems interfere with obtaining a direct route to the goal?

10. There are good and bad aspects to mechanization. What are they?

Exercises

Try out the problem-solving skills you've learned in this chapter.

1. A frog fell into a 5-foot-deep well and needs to begin the arduous task of hopping out. Every hour, he jumps 2 feet, but then slides back one foot. How long will it take him to get out of the well? (Hint: Draw a diagram.)

2. Irvin has begun a jogging program. He jogs 2 miles north, then turns right and jogs 3 miles, then heads left 1 mile, then turns and jogs 2 miles to the right, then he jogs 3 miles south, and finally 5 miles west. How far is he from his starting point? (Hint: Draw a map.)

3. You agree to be a contestant on a silly television show. There are 24 gift boxes lined up in four rows of 6 boxes each. One of these boxes contains the grand prize (a weekend in San Bernardino, California). You can ask your television host any question that has a "Yes" or "No" answer. What questions would you ask him? How many questions would you need to definitely identify the box containing the grand prize? (Hint: Use the strategy that works best with an organized array of equally likely choices.)

4. There are four dogs sitting in front of their dog houses. The dogs, in left-to-right order, are Pizza, Tiger, Lady, and Sancho. Based on the following information, figure out which dog eats Crunchy Blend dog food:

- Pizza lives in a blue dog house.
- The dog who lives in a red house eats Yummies.
- Sancho eats Butcher Boy dog food.
- Lady lives next to the dog with the green house.
- Tiger lives next to the dog who eats Crunchy Blend.
- The dog in the white house is next to the dog who eats Butcher Boy.
- The dog who eats medium-rare steak is farthest away from the dog who eats Butcher Boy.

(Hint: Use the form of representation that is recommended when the givens are taken from categories of information.)

5. Solve the following anagrams:

CRA   ETA

NIK   NTU

(Hint: Use the strategy that is recommended for problems with few solution paths.)

6. Design an automobile that can drive across land and water.

7. Using Fig. 9.21, place the cowboys on their horses so that they can ride properly. (After Scheerer, 1963). (Hint: You will have to break set to answer this problem.)

FIG. 9.21. Can you figure out how to place the cowboys on their horses so that they could ride them properly? (From Scheerer, M. Problem solving. © 1963 by Scientific American, Inc. All rights reserved) (Solution is presented on p. 402, see Fig. 9.23.)

FIG. 9.22. The notched check-erboard problem. (After Wick-elgren, 1974, p. 29.)

8. Using only six short sticks, arrange them to form four equilateral triangles. (Hint: This problem will also require that you break a mental set.)

9. The notched-checkerboard problem (from Wickelgren, 1974):

You are given a checkerboard and 32 dominoes. Each domino covers exactly two adjacent squares on the board. Thus, the 32 dominoes can cover all 64 squares on the checkerboard. Now suppose two squares are cut off at diagonally opposite corners of the board [see Fig. 9.22]. Is it possible to place 31 dominoes on the board so that all of the 62 remaining squares are covered? If so, show how it can be done. If not, prove it impossible. (p. 29)

(Hint: Specialize and consider which squares can be covered by each domino.)

10. The Jealous-Husbands Problem (from Reed, 1982).

Three jealous husbands and their wives, having to cross a river at a ferry, find a boat. However, the boat is so small that it can hold no more than two people. Find the simplest schedule of crossings that will permit all six people to cross the river so that no woman is left in company with any of the men unless her husband is present. It is assumed that all passengers on the boat unboard before the next trip and that at least one person has to be in the boat for each crossing. (p. 308)

(Hint: This problem is directly analogous to another one solved in this chapter.)

11. A favorite of Newell and Simon's (1972) is this crypt arithmetic problem:

        D O N A L D
    +   G E R A L D
        R O B E R T

The problem is to substitute a digit (0 through 9) for each letter so that the letters follow the usual rules of addition. (Hint: D = 5). I'll demonstrate the first step:

```
5 O N A L 5
G E R A L 5
R O B E R O
```

I'll give you a second hint: *R* must be an odd number. Complete this problem.

12. Complete the following letter series. (This problem has been used in intelligence tests for English school children.)
OTTFFSS———
What are the next three letters? (Hint: Thinking about repeating sequences of letters will lead to blind paths.)

13. An anxious mother wanted to send a T-square (a rigid drafting instrument) to her son in college. The T-square is 13″ long. Unfortunately, the express mail service won't accept any packages more than 12″ long. How was she able to send the T-square by express mail. (No, she didn't cut or fold it. Hint: Draw boxes around an imaginary 13″ T-square.)

14. A penny gum machine is filled with red and white gumballs. There is no way of knowing the color of the next ball. If Mrs. Jones wants to be sure of getting a matching pair of gumballs, how many pennies must she be prepared to spend (Gardner, 1978)? (Hint: This problem is analogous to another one presented in this chapter.)

15. A man bought a horse for $60 and sold it for $70. Then he bought it back again for $80 and sold it for $90. How much money did he gain or lose in these transactions? (Hint: Think about different ways to rephrase the problem.)

16. "If one greyhound can jump over a ditch two meters wide, about how wide a ditch can six greyhounds jump across?" (Bereiter, 1984).

17. The alphabet is presented hereafter in two rows. What is the rule that determines whether a letter belongs in the top or bottom row?

```
A     EF  HI  KLMN        T  VWXYZ
   BCD   G   J          OPQRS  U
```

18. Find problems of your own, and apply the strategies you've learned in this chapter.

FIG. 9.23. Solution to the problem shown in Fig. 9.21. This is a difficult problem because it requires that we break a mental set by rotating the horses 90° to a vertical position and switching heads for each horse. (From Scheerer, M. Problem solving. © 1963 by Scientific American, Inc. All rights reserved.)

SUGGESTED READINGS

There are many excellent books and articles on problem solving. My personal favorites are Sternberg's (1986a) *Intelligence Applied,* Bransford and Stein's (1984) *The Ideal Problem Solver,* Adam's (1979) *Conceptual Blockbusting: A Guide to Better Ideas* (3rd ed.), Levine's (1988) *Effective Problem Solving,* and Gardner's (1978) *Aha! Insight.* They provide many examples of clever solutions to problems as well as helpful guidelines for those who want to be better problem solvers.

A classic in the field of problem solving is Rubinstein's (1975) text, *Patterns of Problem Solving.* This text is heavily mathematical and requires serious concentration. His coauthored undergraduate text (Rubinstein & Pfeiffer, 1980), *Concepts in Problem Solving,* is highly recommended. Another classic is Wickelgren's (1974) text, *How to Solve Problems.* Like Rubinstein's 1975 book, this is not easy reading because of its heavy reliance on mathematics.

Hayes' (1981) *The Complete Problem Solver* and Whimbey and Lochhead's (1982) *Problem Solving and Comprehension* (3rd ed.) are easy-to-read, interesting books in this area. Both are written for undergraduate audiences. If you don't have enough problems in life, you can always purchase books filled with them. Virtually every book stand has several to choose from. Some thought-provoking problems can be found in Phillips' (1961) *My Best Puzzles in Logic and Reasoning.* Fixx, the author of *The Complete Book of Running,* has written several delightful books filled with problems to solve. I especially recommend his 1978 book *Solve It!*

Polya's (1957) book, *How to Solve It,* gives helpful advice about understanding problems, devising plans, carrying them out, and then looking back. I am a great fan of Polya's work. He was the first to offer explicit advice on what to do when you're staring at a problem that you can't solve. If you'd like some empirical evidence that people can, in fact, improve the way they solve problems by learning general strategies, see Klein and Weizenfeld's (1978) journal article, "Improvement of Skills for Solving Ill-Defined Problems," and Schoenfeld and Herrmann's (1982) journal article, "Problem Perception and Knowledge Structure in Expert and Novice Mathematical Problem Solvers." Schoenfeld and Herrmann found that, after college students took a general problem-solving course, they demonstrated a marked improvement in their problem-solving performance.

The literature on problem solving for children has been proliferating in recent years. Much of the advice given to children's books is useful for adults as well, and often it is better written and easier to understand than the adult counterparts. *The Productive Thinking Program* (Covington, Crutchfield, Davies, & Olton, 1974) is a delightful series designed for children in the upper elementary school years. Also recommended among the children's books are Walberg's (1980) *Puzzle Thinking* and Kohl's (1981) *A Book of Puzzlement.*

10 Creative Thinking

Contents

The history of civilization is essentially the record of man's creative ability.

—Osborn (1963, p. ix)

I recently spent a morning at a special summer program for "mentally gifted" kids, the ones who score within the top one or two percent of all children in their age group on intelligence tests. Every morning, the 2nd- to 10th-graders gather in a small auditorium to contemplate a "thought for the day," work on a puzzle, plan activities, and gripe about the usual things all kids gripe about. The puzzle for the day was "How can you take one away from 9 and get 10?" The kid sitting next to me whispered, "Do you know the answer?" After a few seconds' thought, I gloated with a "Yes" response, pleased as punch that I could keep up with this elite group of short people.

Many hands went up in response to the puzzle. The first child to answer was a tiny, redheaded girl, reminiscent of Charlie Brown's heartthrob. "It's easy," she said as she walked confidently to the chalkboard. "If you take away a negative one, the effect will be the same as addition." As she spoke, she wrote the following on the board:

$9 - (-1) = 9 + 1 = 10$

I was amazed. Why hadn't I thought of that? A second hand shot up, and a young boy on the verge of adolescence explained another answer: "In Roman numerals, nine is written 'IX,' so if you take 'I' (one) away, you'll end up with 'X,' the Roman numeral for 10."

Another child responded with a sheepish grin, saying that, "This is a little silly, but, if you write '9' and take the one, or vertical line, away and place it in front of the changed number, you'll have '10.'" I don't know why this was a silly answer—it was the one I had been thinking of.

Still more hands were up, anxious to demonstrate more ways to answer the puzzle. One child wrote out the word "NINE," then erased the second letter (the i that looked like a one), which left her with a "N NE." If you count the number of straight lines left in these letters, there are 10 (three in each "N" and four in the "E").

Actually, there were even more answers, but I lost track as I sat with my mouth gaping open, trying to follow each explanation. The director of this summer program for gifted children is Dr. Barbara Clark from California State University, Los Angeles. Their usual summer curriculum includes activities designed to encourage creative thinking. Watching the children work on their daily puzzle made me keenly aware of the great creative potential in this small group of children.

DEFINING CREATIVITY

A psychology of man is impossible without understanding man's ability to create.

—Arasteh & Arasteh (1976, p. 3)

Creativity is a difficult word to define. We say that someone "is creative" when she or he has produced an outcome or a product that is both unusual and appropriate (or meaningful or useful). Thus, the creative process is defined by its outcome. It's probably most useful to conceptualize creative thinking within the framework that was developed in the chapter on problem solving (chapter 9). A problem exists when there is a discrepancy between where the problem solver is and the desired end state, or goal. A solution is a plan for attaining the goal. Consider the simple problem of garbage: When it's in my house, I want it somewhere else. If I take my garbage out to the curb every Thursday morning for collection, few people would be willing to claim that is a creative solution to my garbage problem. Yet, somewhere in the past, some unsung hero must have come up with the idea for curbside garbage pickup. This may have been a real breakthrough in how to handle the garbage problem. The originator of this idea was creative; the rest of us who trudge out weekly with our heavy tin cans are not. Thus, a definition of creativity must include a sense of originality, uniqueness, or unusualness as well as an evaluation of how well the solution solves the problem. Guilford (1977) described the relationship between problem solving and creativity:

> as closely related with the very definitions of those two activities showing logical connections. Creative thinking produces novel outcomes, and problem-solving produces a new response to a new situation which is a novel outcome. Thus, problem-solving has creative aspects.

Both the unusualness and appropriateness criteria require judgments: How unusual is the idea and how well does it solve the problem? Because both of these criteria vary along some quantitative dimension, creativity exists in degrees (Perkins, 1981). Creativity is not a single trait that people either have or don't have. It is a set of processes that occurs in a context. These processes involve novel ways of defining a problem, generating and evaluating possible solutions, and judging how uniquely and how well they solve the problem.

Suppose that you are invited to supper at your friend Hazel's house. You know that she is an adventuresome cook, and therefore you look forward to the meal with relish. The main dish is an original concoction of hot dogs and fruit salad in a cold mustard sauce. (This part is a true story. I was once served this at a friend's house.) The coup de grace is a dessert that she made on her new ice cream maker—liver-flavored ice cream. Although these are unusual dishes, few people would be willing to eat them. Most of us would not judge these culinary delights as creative, because they do not satisfy the criterion that the idea or product be good or useful.

One problem with our working definition of creativity concerns the terms "unusual," "good," and "useful," because satisfaction of these criteria is a matter of judgment, and people will often disagree. Imagine that you are given the task of discovering which students have musical creativity. One way to do this would be to amass musical experts and have them judge the student's performance. Suppose that you got together with Itzhach Perlman, the great violinist, "Benny Goodman—The King of Swing" type musicians, the rock star Keith Sweat, and the well-known country music singer, Willie Nelson. Do you think that they would be able to agree on what constitutes musical creativity? Probably not!

It's easy to see why creativity has been an elusive topic to deal with. Someone or some group must judge an act or idea as unusual and good or useful before it can be labeled creative, and there will often be disagreement on the way these attributes are judged. The usual way in which a product is judged to be creative is by consensual agreement among recognized experts in the field. Thus, we would probably rely on expert rock musicians to judge rock music, expert classical musicians to judge classical music, and so on. Although there may be little agreement across the various fields of music, research has shown that there is fairly good agreement about what constitutes a creative product when the judging is being done by experts within the field.

Prince (1970) offered a somewhat poetic definition of creativity, which, I believe, is itself creative. Consider this definition:

> CREATIVITY: an arbitrary harmony, an expected astonishment, a habitual revelation, a familiar surprise, a generous selfishness, an unexpected certainty, a formidable stubborness, a vital triviality, a disciplined freedom, an intoxicating steadiness, a repeated initiation, a difficult delight, a predictable gamble, an ephemeral solidity, a unifying difference, a demanding satisfier, a miraculous expectation, an accustomed amazement. (p. i)

However we choose to define creativity, we need it, and we all possess it to some extent. Our everyday life is more pleasurable because of our creative actions; the arts depend on it for their existence; and the sciences and mathematics could not progress without it. Every time we express a complex thought or fill a blank piece of paper with our words, we are creating.

Lateral and Vertical Thinking

> *Vertical thinking is concerned with digging the same hole deeper. Lateral thinking is concerned with digging the hole somewhere else.*
> —DeBono (1977, p. 195)

The distinction between lateral and vertical thinking was first made by DeBono (1968). It is best illustrated with a short story:

Many years ago when a person who owed money could be thrown into jail, a merchant in London had the misfortune to owe a huge sum to a money-lender. The money-lender, who was old and ugly, fancied the merchant's beautiful teenage daughter. He proposed a bargain. He said he would cancel the merchant's debt if he could have the girl instead.

Both the merchant and his daughter were horrified at the proposal. So the cunning money-lender proposed that they let Providence decide the matter. He told them that he would put a black pebble and a white pebble into an empty money-bag and then the girl would have to pick out one of the pebbles. If she chose the black pebble she would become his wife and her father's debt would be cancelled. If she chose the white pebble she would stay with her father and the debt would still be cancelled. But if she refused to pick out a pebble her father would be thrown into jail and she would starve.

Reluctantly the merchant agreed. They were standing on a pebble-strewn path in the merchant's garden as they talked and the money-lender stooped down to pick up two pebbles. As he picked up the pebbles the girl, sharp-eyed with fright, noticed that he picked up two black pebbles and put them into the money-bag. He then asked the girl to pick out the pebble that was to decide her fate and that of her father.

What would you do if you had been the girl? If you think about this problem in a careful, logical, straightforward way, you're using **vertical thinking,** a type of thinking that will not be much help in this situation. Typical "vertical thinking" answers are: Let the girl sacrifice herself or expose him for the crook he is. Consider DeBono's suggested solution: The girl should fumble when she draws the pebble from the bag, dropping it onto the pebble-strewn path. She should then tell the villain that they can determine the color of the pebble she took by seeing the color of the one left in the bag. Because the remaining pebble must be black, the money-lender will be forced to admit that she had chosen the white pebble or expose himself as a crook.

Virtually everyone agrees that this is a good answer to the girl's dilemma. **Lateral thinking** is a way of thinking "around" a problem. "Lateral thinking generates the ideas and vertical thinking develops them" (DeBono, 1968, p. 6). Lateral thinking, then, is like creative thinking, or idea discovery, whereas vertical thinking is the refinement and improvement of existing ideas.

The world's most famous fictional detective, Sherlock Holmes, often exhibited lateral thinking. One of my favorite examples was Holmes' response to an idea by his faithful assistant, the good Dr. Watson. Watson pointed out that a certain dog would not be at all helpful in solving a mystery, because the dog had done nothing the night of the murder. Sherlock cleverly noted that the dog was extremely important in solving the mystery, precisely because he had done nothing on the night of the murder, because dogs would be expected to bark or become excited at the sight of strangers or of violent struggles.

Lateral thinking, or "thinking around a problem" is really just another term for "redefining the problem." In the story about the clever girl, she didn't conceptualize the problem as "What should I do when I pick the black pebble?" Instead, she redefined the problem as "How can I avoid picking the black pebble?" It's not so much "thinking around the problem" as it is redefining the problem so that it can be solved in a favorable way. This point was also made in chapter 9, on problem solving. In a recent review article of research and theory on creativity, Mumford and Gustafson (1988) noted that creativity is related to "information that is seemingly irrelevant to solution of the problem at hand" (p. 30). By focusing on the fact that the pebbles on the path were black and white and therefore she could drop one without its being identified, the heroine of this short story was able to generate a novel solution.

Redefining the Problem and Selecting Relevant Information

Virtually every creative act involves a novel way of defining the problem and the selection of information that is relevant to reaching the goal. We usually think of creativity in the arts and sciences, but it can and should exist in a host of everyday settings.

Consider a couple seeking marriage counseling. The wife complains that her husband spends too much time at work, and if he really loved her he would spend more time at home. The husband complains that he has a great deal of pressure at the office and that he has to work long hours to "get ahead." If his wife loved him more, she would understand. There are multiple possible ways to define their problem. They could pose the problem as: "Should we get a divorce?" But, other possible problem definitions include (a) How can we find ways to spend more time together? (b) How can we assure each other that we are still in love? (c) How can the husband "get ahead" while spending less time at work? (d) How can they learn to adjust to the present situation? (e) Is "getting ahead" an important goal? and (f) What can the wife do so that she doesn't feel lonely and resentful when her husband is at work?

If you consider the problem for a few more minutes, you can come up with many other problem definitions. The nature of the solution will change every time the problem is redefined.

The selection of relevant information to help you reach a goal is related to your knowledge of the problem space (topic). In this example, you would need to know more about the couple to help them find a good solution. Suppose that you know that the wife is an aspiring artist. You could suggest that she pursue her art interests so that she would feel less lonely and deserted. Alternatively, if you know about the availability of other jobs for the husband, you could suggest that he change jobs.

There is no substitute for knowledge about a topic. If you want to be more creative in the sciences, for example, you would need to acquire knowledge about the field so that relevant information will be available for solving problems.

Sensitivity, Synergy, and Serendipity

> *Creative thought is innovative, exploratory, venturesome.*
> —Kneller (1965, p. 6)

Creativity has been described as the three *S*'s: sensitivity, synergy, and serendipity (Parnes, Noller, & Biondi, 1977). **Sensitivity** is the use of our senses, our "windows to the world" that we use to touch, smell, taste, and see. It has been suggested that highly creative people may experience the physical world with greater intensity than the rest of us, although I don't know of any data to support this possibility. One of the benchmarks of a creative person is the ability to find problems and not just solutions to them. Look at Fig. 10.1. This is called "Boring's Wife and Mother-in-Law." Can you guess why? Look closely. Can you see an old woman and a young woman in the picture? Count the prongs on

FIG. 10.1.   Boring's Wife and Mother-In-Law. Can you see both an old woman and a young woman in this picture?

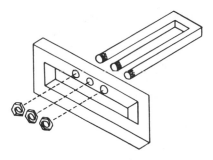

FIG. 10.2. An impossible figure. Try to count the prongs.

Fig. 10.2. Do they disappear as you count them? This is an impossible figure—impossible because it can't ever exist, except in the artist's mind. In creating each of these figures, the artists displayed a sensitivity to details that is both unusual and appropriate.

All of our great inventors were problem finders. They recognized problems that the rest of the world never saw. We all studied the great inventors of the past, people like Benjamin Franklin, George Washington Carver, and Thomas Edison. Present-day inventors also find problems. An "Invention Convention" is held annually in the United States to highlight the creative talents of current inventors. Some of the items displayed at this year's convention are a double-headed toothbrush that can brush both sides of the teeth at the same time, a portable hot water shower that can be used for camping because it is lightweight and relies on the sun to heat the water, and an electric box that makes and bakes a loaf of bread—all you do is pour in the ingredients.

Synergy is the bringing together of seemingly disparate parts into a useful and functioning whole. It is close to Koestler's notion of **bisociative thinking,** in which two previously unconnected "frames of reference" are amalgamated. If you can take ideas from different domains and bring them together so that they work successfully in a new context, you have demonstrated synergy. Gordon (1961) has suggested that one way to promote creativity is to bring people from diverse fields together to find problems and to create solutions, the two mainstreams of the creative process. Consider modern surgery to unclog clogged arteries. A thin tube is threaded into the artery. When the clog is reached, a small "balloon" is inflated in the artery to open the clogged area. This is the same technique that has been used by plumbers to open clogged pipes. Thus, a common problem-solving technique in plumbing is being used by surgeons to save lives. Many creative acts involve adapting solutions from one field for use in an unrelated field.

According to von Oech (1983), Johannes Gutenberg conceived of the printing press by combining two previously unconnected ideas—wine and the coin punch. The purpose of the coin punch was to leave an impression on a small area, such as a coin. By contrast, the wine press applied pressure over a large area in order to squeeze the juice out of grapes. One day, Gutenberg put the coin punch under the wine press and found that he could get images on paper. This simple, but original, combination resulted in the printing press.

Serendipity is a happy, unexpected discovery that occurs when you least expect it. Biographies of great scientists often contain accounts of serendipitous events, some of them seemingly preposterous. I have often felt that focusing on serendipity did the scientist a great injustice. A new miracle drug may have been the result of an accidental spill, but it was the prepared scientist who could appreciate the results of the accident that created the drug. The scientist was able to select the relevant information from the accident so that it could be used in a novel way instead of simply labeling it a mistake and forgetting about it. Although serendipity may have contributed to a creative act, the persistence, motivation, and hard work on the part of the creator allowed the serendipitous event to occur. Serendipity may play a role in great scientific discoveries, but such pleasant ''accidents'' seem most likely to occur in the laboratory at 2:00 A.M.

Consider how an artist friend of mine combined sensitivity, synergy, and serendipity to create a new form of art. Robert Perine, a San Diego artist, decided to incorporate the glass that is used to cover pictures into the pictures themselves. He cut odd-shaped glass coverings and placed them over his watercolor paintings to see how the beveled edges in the glass would refract the paint beneath it and give it a glossy, shimmering appearance. It was a simple idea that brought together the framing process and the picture itself in a new art form that incorporates the picture and the glass used to protect it. Creative ideas often seem simple and surprising.

Jokes, puns, and witticisms could also be considered as a form of creative expression. A joke brings together two ideas that are not usually combined.

Did you hear the one about the two former school mates who met unexpectedly for the first time in 25 years? As they caught up on the details of their lives, one asked the other if he had any children. Sorrowfully, he replied, ''Yes, one living and one married.'' The listener was expecting the phrase ''one living and one dead,'' and the surprise juxtaposition of ''living and married'' is the humorous element in this joke. Laughter is often the response to original ideas also. The surprising combination of elements (synergy) makes for good jokes and creative ideas.

MEASURING CREATIVITY

The man with a new idea is a crank until the idea succeeds.
—Mark Twain

If you are very, very lucky, and if you've worked very hard, you could one day find yourself the recipient of the John D. and Catherine MacArthur Award.

Grants of up to $300,000 are given to people to do exactly whatever they wish with the money. No strings attached. Of course, the coveted prize doesn't go to just anyone. It's given to people who are believed to possess special creative talents. The MacArthur Foundation believes that a wise way to help humanity is by allowing its most talented members to pursue their creative bent. The foundation selects their recipients based on an individual's past accomplishments and their own intuitive "hunch" as to who will continue to make creative contributions. Whereas the MacArthur Foundation can afford to use the intuition of their advisers in these matters, psychologists have had to develop a more systematic and scientific approach to the question of creativity.

A problem for psychologists has been both to recognize and to quantify creativity. If we could devise reliable and valid tests of creativity, we could utilize this information in a variety of ways. **Psychometrics** is the branch of psychology that is concerned with the measurement of psychological traits such as creativity, intelligence, aggressiveness, androgyny, and so on. Many tests have been devised to measure creative ability. Two of the most popular ones are described here.

Divergent Production Test

> *When all think alike, no one is thinking.*
> —Walter Lippmann

Guilford (1967) made a distinction between convergent and divergent thinking. Consider the different types of thinking required by these questions:

What is the capital of Nebraska?
How many different uses can you think of for a carrot?

The first question has a single correct answer. Any answer other than "Lincoln" is incorrect. When you are required to come up with a single correct answer, you are engaging in **convergent thinking.** You are converging onto the correct answer. What is the correct answer to the second question? Obviously, there is no single correct answer. **Divergent thinking** is required when a person needs to generate many different responses to the same question. According to Guilford, divergent thinking is the essence of creativity. If you can produce several solutions to a given situation by thinking divergently and avoiding solutions you've relied on in the past, you are a creative thinker. Guilford hypothesized that the human intellect comprises 120 different mental abilities. About one fifth of these are creative or divergent thinking abilities. Guilford devised a test known as the Divergent Production Test to assess creative abilities. Three sample test items are presented in Fig. 10.3.

Another test of creativity that was devised by Guilford (1962, p. 159) to

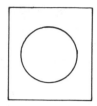

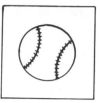

Example 1.   Given a simple, familiar form, e.g., a circle, the examinee is to make as many objects as he can with a minimum of additional lines, as in the Sketches test.

Example 2.   In the Make a Mark test, the examinee is to make as many simple line figures as he can, keeping within a class specification. The examples given were in response to the instruction: make different simple, open figures in dotted lines.

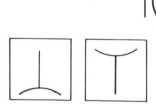

Example 3.   In Make a Figure, given two line elements, the examinee is to combine them in a great variety of ways to make figures.

FIG. 10.3. Sample items from the Divergent Production Test (Guilford, 1967).

assess divergent thinking is the Plot Titles Test. The test taker is to come up with as many different titles to a story that she or he can. One of the stories is about a missionary captured by cannibals who immediately placed him in a pot to boil. The cannibal princess intervenes and promises to save his life if he will marry her. He refuses and is boiled to death. Some examples of titles that were judged as not particularly creative are:

Defeat of a Princess
Eaten by Savages
The Princess
Boiled by Savages

Examples of creative titles are:
Pot's Plot
Potluck Dinner
Stewed Parson
Goil or Boil
A Mate Worse than Death
He Left a Dish for a Pot
Chaste in Haste
A Hot Price for Freedom

Remote Associations Test

> *The creative act owes little to logic and reason.*
> —Gardner (1978)

Creativity can be thought of as the ability to form new combinations of ideas to fulfill a need. Mednick and Mednick (1967) have created a test to tap this dimension of creativity. It is called the Remote Associations Test or RAT for short. Test takers are given three words and are asked to come up with a fourth word that relates to all three. As an example, what word relates to:

RIVER   NOTE   BLOOD

Can you come up with the relational word? (The answer is *bank*—river bank; bank note; blood bank.) Try these other remote associations that are similar to the ones on the RAT.

1.	BOARD	DUCK	DOLLAR	*Bill*
2.	FILE	HEAD	TOE	*nail*
3.	BOILED	LID	FLOWER	*pot*
4.	BALL	MALARIA	BUTTER	*fly*
5.	CLASS	STAGE	SOCCER	*coach*

(The answers are on page 437.)

Do creative people come up with remote associations when they think creatively? It seems that some do. An invention by Michael Reynolds of Taos, New Mexico, seems to epitomize this type of thinking. He combined his knowledge of the high cost of housing with the problem of soda cans littering the countryside, and the proverbial light bulb went on. He made these remote associations and constructed a house of aluminum soda cans. For his second house, he is filling the cans with water so that the solar heated cans of water can supplement his home energy needs.

Validity Issues

One of the objections I hear to setting forth creativity as a goal for higher education is, "We can't all be Einsteins." This is undeniable; it is also irrelevant.

—Hutchings (1986, p. 14)

You are probably wondering if either of these tests (Divergent Production and the RAT Test) can actually predict or assess creativity. There have been hundreds of studies using these and many other tests, showing mixed results. Some studies have found very little relationship between the scores that individuals get on these tests and their creative accomplishments in life, whereas others have found a low-to-moderate relationship. In addition, the scores that individuals get on both tests may not agree very well with each other.

The relative lack of success at predicting or measuring creativity seems to be inherent in the nature of creativity itself. First, remember that creativity is defined by its products. Creative thinkers are identified when the thinking is completed and their products are judged as worthy or not. People in art, science, or industry often cannot agree about which products are creative. Thus, any attempt to measure creativity is at least partially doomed, because we have no clear-cut, universal standard for comparison.

A second problem concerns the kinds of activities we are willing to label creative. A successful homemaker with limited financial means may be quite creative in the ways that she feeds her family or furnishes her home. Yet, the products of her creativity are likely to go unnoticed.

Third, creativity is a **multidimensional concept.** A multidimensional concept is one that varies in many qualitatively different ways. Creative thoughts can help us to understand past civilizations, solve pollution problems, or visualize futuristic societies. It is difficult to imagine a single test that could predict success in every possible area.

ENCOURAGING CREATIVITY

Natural Abilities

Discovery consists of looking at the same thing as everyone else and thinking something different.
—Albert Szent-Gjorgyi (Nobel Prize Winner in Medicine)
(Quoted in von Oech, 1983, p. 7)

It is clear that creativity is not something that exists in an all-or-none fashion. People are more or less creative, just as they are more or less athletic or good-looking or prejudiced. The question of whether there is some inborn or inherited trait that is associated with high creativity has been difficult to answer. Most of the research has centered on the relationship between creativity and intelligence. Are intelligent people the most creative ones?

In general, people with above-average scores on intelligence tests tend to be creative, whereas those with low IQ scores tend not to be; but the relationship is not a perfect one. It just isn't true that the very smartest people are always the most creative. It seems best to conclude that there is a certain minimum intelligence that is needed to be creative, but beyond the minimal level, IQ doesn't seem to matter much. Even if you're not a particularly intelligent person, you may have great creative potential.

Environmental Factors

Amabile and her colleagues (Amabile, 1983; Amabile, Hennessey, & Grossman 1986; Hennessey & Amabile 1987) have studied the environmental factors that can encourage or discourage creativity. Unfortunately, they concluded that much of what happens in school and work settings is not conducive to the development of creativity. They found that creative individuals view their work as a labor of love. They work long hours because they are impelled by their curiosity and their own desire to achieve a goal. This sort of motivation is called **intrinsic motivation,** because it comes from within the individual. By contrast, much of the motivation provided at school and work is **extrinsic motivation,** that is, motivation that comes from others, such as promise of a good grade or money. According to Amabile and her colleagues, the best way to promote creativity is to arrange the environment so as to maximize intrinsic motivation. Six conditions that tend to kill intrinsic motivation are (a) constant evaluation, (b) surveillance, (c) reward, (d) competition, (e) restricted choice (e.g., choice of materials to use), and (f) an extrinsic orientation toward work. These six restrictions are often present in school settings.

Schank and Childers (1988) agreed that the academic environment is often hostile to innovative ideas. They believe that the tendency to discourage new ideas is best seen in the grant review process that is part of academic life for university researchers. Colleagues often turn down funding requests for ideas that haven't been proven. Thus, risk taking, an essential component of creativity because of its reliance on the unusual, is punished even in those institutions that are supposed to encourage creative efforts.

Most school and work environments tend to be heavily weighted toward extrinsic motivators; teachers and supervisors watch while students and employees work, and the workers receive grades or payment for their efforts. It is impossible to avoid extrinsic motivators completely, as there will always be deadlines, competition, and choice restrictions, for example. Despite these realities, it is possible to design school and work environments to foster creativity by reducing the focus on extrinsic motivators and emphasizing the intrinsic rewards of the creative process. Of course, in addition to these changes in the environment, creativity training also needs a skills component. No one can become a creative scientist or great author or talented artist without the factual knowledge and technical skills that are relevant to their chosen field. If you want to promote creativity, there is no substitute for subject matter knowledge (Snow, 1986). This point is elaborated in the next chapter, which is entitled "Varieties of Thinking."

Environmental factors are important. A quality education (both inside and outside of school) will give you the basis for the remote associations or divergent thoughts or novel ideas. You need a head that is filled with thoughts and facts in order to create them. The inferences from Amabile's work are clear: Cultivate a love of learning; reward your own creative efforts; take the college courses that will fill your mind with new thoughts (and not just the easiest courses offered). Creative endeavors result from hard, intellectual work that is self-motivated and self-monitored. Don't be afraid to engage in it.

Personality Factors

There are certain personality factors that are consonant with creativity. Because creativity (as we have defined it) requires an unusual or novel act, the creative individual must not be swayed by a need for conformity nor be resistant to change. Perhaps there is some validity to the notion of the "eccentric" artist or scholar.

The creative person must be self-motivated. Sometimes, school experiences tend to favor the noncreative students, as many traditional assignments don't call for creative response. Creative people may have to create their own rewards for their actions and find satisfaction in the creative process itself.

The ability and willingness to take risks and to tolerate ambiguity is also needed for creative acts. When we try to do things differently, we sometimes fail. Most of the great discovers in modern times were initially met with ridicule and repeated failure (a horseless carriage, a machine that could fly, etc.). We need to teach children that failure is an important part of life and that every great success was built upon previous failures.

In a study of creative people (Barron, 1958), writers, artists, musicians, and mathematicians were given a battery of tests to determine if they had any personality traits in common. In general, these highly creative individuals were nonconforming, unconventional, and generally less concerned with "making a good impression." Of course, this does not mean that if you become nonconforming and unconventional, you'll then become highly creative, but it suggests that a more open-minded and less structured approach to life's problems can pay off.

STRATEGIES FOR CREATIVE THINKING

Basic Principles

The nation that neglects creative thought today will assuredly have its nose ground into the dust of tomorrow.

—Fred Hoyle

Creativity has never been given the attention it deserved in standard educational settings. Lowenfeld (1962) has called creativity "education's stepchild." There seems to be no place in the traditional school curriculum for creativity training. There have been many programs developed with the specific goal of training people to be creative in order to fill this gap. Although there are considerable differences among these programs, they all share some basic common principles:

1. Teach students to think of different ways to accomplish an objective and then how to select the best one.

2. Provide plenty of examples and exercises to model and practice creative skills.

3. Teach students how to ask relevant questions and how to discover when a problem exists.

4. Evaluate the quality of an idea by its consequences.

5. Reward original and relevant ideas. Let students know that their ideas are valuable. Help them enjoy the creative process.

6. Provide unstructured situations. Teach them the value of persistence when they fail.

7. Provide students with a tangible plan for finding solutions. Plans include recognizing puzzling facts, seeking information, generating possible solutions, changing perspectives, and restating the goal.

You may be thinking that there is no such thing as "strategies for creative thinking," because creativity involves breaking rules, not following them—a sort of a free activity. Bailin (1987) has argued against this notion of creativity. As she noted, most creative actions take place within a framework of rules. Even the most beautiful sonnet contains 14 lines of specified metre and rhyme, all great ballets performed with the principles and techniques of dance, and all scientific discoveries are made by experts who are knowledgeable in their field. In order to depart from a framework or to bend the usual rules, the creative individual must have some knowledge of convention as well as some guidelines for unconventional thinking.

Productive Thinking Program

The most famous creative training program was developed by Covington, Crutchfield and Davies in 1971 for fifth and sixth graders. The program consisted of a workbook in which the brother-and-sister team of Jim and Lila had to solve a series of detective stories. The reader, along with Jim and Lila, had to formulate hypotheses, gather evidence, and ask questions in order to solve the crime. If you've already read chapter 6 ("Thinking as Hypothesis Testing"), you'll recognize this sequence as the steps used in experimental methods of discovery. All along, Jim and Lila were guided by a wise "Uncle John," who would provide hints and explain their mistakes. This program was discussed briefly in chapter 9.

party, they brought wrapped gifts for the wealthy hostess. Suddenly, the lights went out, and, when they went on again, a valuable jewel was missing. Lila and Jim had to determine what had happened to the jewel. No one could have left or entered the room, as the door had remained locked. The window was opened, but there were no footsteps in the fresh snow that covered the ground. Later, we learned that there was a feather on the floor and that one of the boxes had a hole in the bottom. Have you solved the crime by now? A trained pigeon was taken from a wrapped box and used to transport the jewel to an accomplice.

It took Lila and Jim a while to find and put together the clues in order to solve this crime. Crutchfield (1966) believes that, with direct training with stories like this one, children can learn to think more creatively. The reader engages in the discovery process along with the protagonists, and may even solve the problem before Lila and Jim. Figure 10.4 demonstrates how the program attempts to encourage creative thinking.

There have been several evaluations of Covington, Crutchfield, and Davies'

FIG. 10.4. An excerpt from Covington, Crutchfield, Davies and Olton's (1974) program of creativity training. (Reprinted by permission of Charles E. Merrill Publishing Co.).

program, most of them positive. However, it is important to keep in mind that the children are evaluated with material that is similar to the type used in training (detective stories). There is no good evidence that children trained with this method actually grow up to be more creative adults or that they ever apply these skills in real-life settings. This is, of course, the real goal of any thinking skills program—use of the skills in unrelated situations. It was also found that the teacher was an important variable in the program's success. Children with rigid, uninterested teachers did not improve as much as those with involved teachers, underscoring once again the importance of environmental variables in the development of creativity.

Other creativity training programs have offered similar evidence of success. One of the more spectacular successes is attributed to a creativity training program at Sylvania Electric Company that resulted in "double profit; 2,100 new products; increased patent applications five-fold; saved $22 million" (Edwards, 1968). Although these claims seem fantastic, we really have no idea what these figures should be compared to, and, therefore, a more restrained enthusiasm is probably prudent.

Although any single study or method may have its limitations and qualifications, numerous experimental programs indicate that creativity can be stimulated under proper conditions. It is not an inborn gift for a lucky few. We all can become more creative. Instead of attempting to review each of the training programs, let's examine some of the strategies and methods they've used so that you can apply them in your own life in an attempt to increase your creativity.

Quantity Breeds Quality

The notion that if you have lots of ideas, some of them will be good is the major thrust of **brainstorming.** Brainstorming was discussed in chapter 9 (on the "Development of Problem Solving Skills") as a way to find solution paths that solve problems. It is a creative way to generate solution paths and is often used in creative problem solving. Brainstorming is a way of producing a list of ideas that can subsequently be evaluated. Although brainstorming can be done individually, it is more commonly considered a group activity. The only rule of brainstorming is that all judgment be deferred until some later time so that no one hesitates to offer unusual or off-beat ideas. Osborn (1963) has offered many examples in his book, *Applied Imagination.* For example, Osborn reported that a 15-minute brainstorming session at American Cyanamid Corporation produced 92 ideas, or more than 6 ideas per minute. This was an average of 8 ideas per participant.

The quantitative advantages of brainstorming are without question. But do more ideas necessarily imply better ones? Often, the best ideas result from the combination (synergy) and alteration of the ideas listed. The atmosphere of deferred judgment is clearly consistent with the discussion on environment presented earlier in the chapter. It encourages risk taking and unconventionality, both of which are prerequisites to creative thinking. At the very least, brainstorming is fun. It is a recommended strategy for enhancing creative thought.

Osborn had a group of parents brainstorm on how to get their children to watch less television and read more books. Read carefully through the list of ideas that the parents came up with. It seems to me that some combination of these ideas would surely be effective. (In fact, I used them at home with my own children.)

1. Pull plug on TV set.
2. Break up the set.
3. Set a definite time for looking at TV.
4. Arouse interest in books.
5. Acquire a bad horizontal tube.
6. Reorient antenna in order to get bad reception.
7. Select a book that has been seen on TV.
8. Set example by reading yourself.
9. Buy a portable radio for children.
10. Evaluate TV programs.
11. Encourage visits to library.
12. Have the children write book reports.
13. Give money for movies.
14. Donate a TV to library.
15. More outdoor companionship with parents.
16. As a result of seeing TV story (say, Robinson Crusoe), children given same book to read and do research on.
17. Start reading aloud to them when young.
18. Read them good books.
19. Make reading as convenient as TV.
20. Give them their own bookcase in room.
21. Give records for hi-fi.
22. Give subscriptions to children's magazines.
23. Select books suitable to age.
24. Get them interested in daily newspapers, even if only the comics.
25. Help them with their homework.
26. Select type of news they read.
27. Discuss with them the books they have read.
28. Have them read to you.
29. At PTA meeting, have subject discussed with teachers; get teachers to recommend books.
30. Encourage group reading.

31. Buy them a good dictionary.
32. Always answer questions if you can.
33. Buy a good children's encyclopedia.
34. Institute games requiring the use of words and general knowledge.
35. Get local schools to have course in fast reading and good reading.
36. Have children checked physically—there may be some reason why they are unable to read.
37. In addition to their allowance, give them a fee for each good book that they read.

Creative Ideas Checklist

Another method for producing creative ideas is to present people with a checklist of diverse categories or adjectives or questions that could conceivably apply to the question or problem at hand. These lists are called **creative ideas checklists.**

In one study of the use of lists to stimulate creative ideas, Davis and Roweton (1968) gave students the following list, which was labeled "Aids in Thinking of Physical Changes":

a. Add or Subtract Something
b. Change Color
c. Change the Materials
d. Change by Rearranging the Parts
e. Change Shape
f. Change Size
g. Change Design or Style

Students who were given this list were told, "List as many physical changes as you can for a thumbtack." Davis and Roweton reported that the group that had received the checklist produced a greater number of ideas and more creative ideas than a control group that had not been given the checklist. Recently, a cookie manufacturer began making "reverse" chocolate chip cookies—chocolate cookies with white chocolate chips. They have become an overnight financial and taste success. You should recognize this simply as "d" in the preceding list—a change by rearranging the parts. This simple creative act has paid well for its innovator.

Perhaps the most famous checklist is a generalized one that can be applied in a variety of situations. Whiting (1958) attributed this list to Osborn.

Put to Other Uses? New ways to use as is? Other uses if modified?

Adapt? What else is like this? What other idea does this suggest? Does past offer parallel? What could I copy? Whom could I emulate?

Modify? New twist? Change meaning, color, motion, odor, form, shape? Other changes?

Magnify? What to add? More time? Greater frequency? Stronger? Larger? Thicker? Extra value? Plus Ingredient? Duplicate? Multiply? Exaggerate?

Minify? What to substitute? Smaller? Condensed? Miniature? Lower? Shorter? Lighter? Omit? Streamline? Split Up? Understate?

Substitute? Who else instead? What else instead? Other ingredient? Other material? Other process? Other power? Other place? Other approach? Other tone of voice?

Rearrange? Interchange components? Other pattern? Other layout? Other sequence? Transpose cause and effect? Change pace? Change schedule?

Reverse? Transpose positive and negative? How about opponents? Turn it backward? Turn it upside down? Reverse roles? Change shoes? Turn tables? Turn other cheek?

Combine? How about a blend, an alloy, an assortment, an ensemble? Combine units? Combine purposes? Combine appeals? Combine ideas? (p. 62)

Although there are many such lists, a third one worth considering is from Parnes (1967), who suggested that you ask yourself these idea-spurring questions when you're looking for new ideas:

1. Effects on objective?
2. Individuals and/or groups affected?
3. Costs involved?
4. Tangibles involved (material, equipment, etc.)?
5. Moral or legal implications?
6. Intangibles involved (opinions, attitudes, feelings, aesthetic values, etc.)?
7. New problems caused?
8. Difficulties or implementation and follow-up?
9. Repercussions of failure?
10. Timeliness?, etc. (p. 231)

Although the purpose of creative ideas checklists is to create novel ideas, it is also possible that they could have an inhibiting effect. If you only considered the possibilities on a small checklist, you could miss other ideas by narrowing your search to ones that are suggested by the list.

We've all had the experience at one time or another of being "stuck," when ideas don't seem to flow. If you go through these checklists, pondering each item, you're bound to get your thoughts flowing again.

Attribute Listing

In **attribute listing,** every characteristic or quality of the item or situation is listed and then examined for possible modification or recombination. Let's try an example.

Suppose you want to make something really different for dinner tonight. In fact, you want to make a food that no one else in the world has ever tasted before. How would you go about doing this? First, you could list many different foods:

eggs
hot dogs
baked alaska
stewed tomatoes
steak tartare
chocolate pudding
etc.

Alongside each food, you would list several of its attributes, such as shape, consistency, color, texture, odor, temperature, and so on. You'd then randomly pair attributes to come up with a new food. You might think of the "soft and shimmery" attribute of jello and the cold, hard attribute of ice cream and combine the two so that you'd freeze the jello or whip the ice cream.

Attribute listing is a good procedure for fashion design. You could list every part of a dress, for example, and every attribute of that part. A partial example is:

Dress Part	Attribute
collars	pointed, rounded, none, Nehru
sleeves	raglan, short, rolled, long
waist	cinched, gathered, dropped, loose
skirt	full, straight, ruffled, pointed

A talented dress designer could combine possible dress attributes, coming up with thousands of unique designs (e.g., a dress with a Nehru collar, short sleeves, gathered waist, and ruffled skirt.)

Crovitz's Relational Algorithm

Those of you who have already read chapter 8 (on the "Development of Decision Making Skills") know that an algorithm is a step-by-step guide that leads to a solution. Crovitz's **Relational Algorithm** is a solution guide that relies on changing the relations among items. Crovitz (1970) listed 42 "relational words." They are:

about	at	for	of	round	to
across	because	from	off	still	under
after	before	if	on	so	up
against	between	in	opposite	then	when
among	but	near	or	though	where
and	by	not	out	through	while
as	down	now	over	till	with (p. 100)

When you are in need of a creative solution, you have only to try different ways of "relating" the elements. Crovitz used Duncker's classic X-ray problem as an example. Although this problem was described in chapter 9 I'll present it again briefly. The problem is to get rid of an inoperable stomach tumor with X-rays without harming the healthy tissues. However, when the radiation is intense enough to destroy the tumor, it will also harm the healthy tissue surrounding it. The best solution involves using several weak rays through different parts of the body so that they will summate on the tumor. Crovitz demonstrated how the relational algorithm can be used to find a solution to this and other problems. The procedure is fairly simple. Form a sentence with each relational word using it as it might relate to the tumor. For example (Crovitz, 1970):

1. Take the rays **through** the esophagus.
2. Take the sensitivity **from** the tissues.
3. Take tissue **off** the tumor.
4. Take strong rays **after** weak rays.
5. Take a shield **on** stomach walls.
6. Take the tumor **across** the stomach.
7. Take a cannula **through** the stomach wall.
8. Take the power **from** the rays.
9. Take the tumor **to** the exterior. (p. 102)

Crovitz has claimed that this method works well because it forces the individual to consider new relationships among the parts of the problem.

Plus, Minus, Interesting

Plus, Minus, Interesting (PMI) is a plan for beginning the problem-solving process that was suggested by DeBono (1976). When you are searching for a solution to an intractable problem, one way to begin is to list all of the "givens" in a problem and all possible solutions (even ones that are unrealistic) and to consider for each what is positive about it, what is negative about it, and what makes it interesting. The idea behind this process is that a careful and methodic consideration of various components of different solutions and other aspects of the problem will help the problem solver to find new solutions by highlighting positive aspects and eliminating negative ones. The use of the "interesting" category will help the problem solver to consider what makes a solution interesting, and thereby lead to the consideration of additional alternatives. It is a plan for seeking information that may be relevant to a solution.

Activating Inert Knowledge

All of the strategies for creative thinking are designed to increase the "flow of ideas." Psychologists call this improving **"ideational fluency."** In PMI, for example, the problem solver is given a plan for generating ideas. She or he is told the kind of information to consider (givens and possible solutions) and how to evaluate them. Earlier in this book, I talked about the importance of tickling memory. This is particularly important when you seem to have "run out of ideas." There are several simple plans that can be employed when this happens. For example, in a study described by Perkins (1985), children were instructed to list words that they might use when writing a composition about a selected topic. The children were given a few minutes to complete this prewriting task. The researchers reported that, after only a few sessions of training with this method, the children were writing longer and better passages. Let's consider the simple elegance behind this procedure. By listing topic-relevant words, the students were required to think about their knowledge of the topic *before* they began to write. They made their knowledge about the topic more available for use in their composition. It forced them to plan their response.

Writing is one of the most creative tasks that we can be asked to do. Students and even prolific authors often complain about "writer's block." This simple method, which is applicable at all levels, should help to eliminate writer's block, because it is a way of activating one's knowledge of the topic so that it can be used.

Browsing

In our society, we have great institutions that function as repositories for ideas. They are called libraries. Wicker (1981) suggested that we "probe library sources" to generate new ideas. Pick up newspapers and magazines, case histories and biographies, scholarly journals, joke books, and even children's literature. Use a broad range of sources. You can't make "remote associations" or borrow ideas from other fields if your own knowledge is confined to a narrow discipline.

Use qualitative and quantitative information. Census reports can suggest new problems because they succinctly state what people are doing, where they are doing it, what they are eating, how they are living, and how they are dying. Learn something new every day. If you pick up a journal at random and read one new article a day, you'll be surprised at how the newly acquired information crops up in everyday contexts. Libraries are a great source for new ideas. You can also browse with quality television shows like Nova, 60 minutes, and National Geographic. They contain a wealth of fascinating information on almost any topic of interest. Don't forget to go to museums, art galleries, theater, and the opera. If you feel that you can't afford these outings, remember that many have a "free day" once a month and offer reduced rates for students, the elderly, and groups.

Analogies and Metaphor

Analogy is inevitable in human thought.
—Oppenheimer (1956, p. 129)

Analogies underlie much of our everyday thinking, our artistic expressions, and scientific achievements. Sternberg (1977) noted:

> . . . reasoning by analogy is pervasive in everyday experience. We reason analogically whenever we make a decision about something new in our experience by drawing a parallel to something old. When we buy a new goldfish because we liked our old one, or when we listen to a friend's advice because it was correct once before, we are reasoning analogically. (p. 353)

Thinking involves the ability to note resemblances or correspondence between two objects while simultaneously discerning that there are also differences. When you use analogies, you observe that two entities are similar with respect to some property, and dissimilar with respect to others. You'll find that analogies are discussed in several chapters in this book, because they are pervasive in human thought.

We utilize analogies to make sense out of the world. They help us to understand new events by relating them to ones already known; they allow us to communicate our thoughts; they are the foundations of creative thinking. Analogies are one way of making the unfamiliar known.

Analogies are always imperfect because they imply a similarity between objects and events that are not identical. In evaluation and category analogies, carefully consider the nature of the comparison. If I say that you are like your brother because you both have two eyes, you would certainly object, because the number of eyes one has is not a relevant dimension for comparison. However, if I say that you are like your brother because you are both passive and stingy, you might still object, but the nature of the comparison is a relevant one.

A **metaphor** is an analogy that notes similarities between things that are basically dissimilar. (The English grammatical distinction between metaphor and simile is not being considered here, because it is irrelevant to this discussion.) When Shakespeare wrote, ''My love is like a red, red rose,'' he was speaking metaphorically, because roses and love are basically dissimilar. Analogies enhance the creative process by encouraging the problem solver to recombine elements from two concepts that are initially perceived as dissimilar (Gilhooly, 1987; Halpern, 1987a, 1987b). For example, if I tell you that the atom is like a miniature solar system, you can use your knowledge of the solar system to infer information about the atom. To use analogies and metaphors creatively, practice forming them, extending familiar ones, changing common ones, or reversing the process and seeking differences instead of similarities.

The most famous creative use of analogy is seen in the story of Archimedes. He was given the task of determining if the King's crown was pure gold—the only kind of crown worthy of a king. According to the legend, Archimedes did not know how to solve this problem because of the irregular shape of the crown. One day, while lowering himself into a bathtub full of water, the tub overflowed.

The answer was immediately obvious. Like his body, a solid gold crown would displace a volume of water identical to that displaced by a bar of gold that was equal in weight to that of the crown. The story goes on to say that, in his excitement, he ran naked through the street yelling, "Eureka, I have found it!" He had a true creative insight mediated by the analogy of his body displacing his bathtub water and the knowledge that a gold crown would displace a predetermined volume of water. In case you're interested, the crown was pure gold, and the king was very happy.

Analogies appear on most tests of intelligence, because the ability to infer similarities is considered a high-level cognitive skill. They usually involve four terms. The test taker has to infer the nature of the similarity between the first two terms and then verify if the same relationship exists between the last two. Some examples of analogies are:

thermometer : temperature	: :	clock : time
dog : bark	: :	cat : meow
tennis : racket	: :	baseball : bat
kitchen : eat	: :	bedroom : sleep
pharmacist : drugs	: :	grocer : food

In each of these analogies, there is a relationship between the first two terms that also exists between the last two terms (instrument of measurement, type of sound, type of sporting good, function of the room, and items sold).

Making the Familiar Strange

Although the usual function of analogies is to make the unfamiliar familiar, Gordon (1961, 1976), the founder of a creative technique known as synectics suggests that we reverse the process for creative results. Gordon (1976) has suggested that we use analogies and metaphors by trying "strange new contexts in which to view a familiar problem" (p. 251). Gordon suggested, as an example, that we consider a naive student examining a fish's heart for the first time. Because the student knows nothing about anatomy, the context is strange, yet the flow of blood through the heart may remind the student of a filter system for a local swimming pool. The student's analogy is a creative contribution to his or her understanding of anatomy.

Gordon has suggested four specific types of analogies for use when attempting to solve a problem creatively. They are personal analogy, direct analogy, symbolic analogy, and fantasy analogy. Each is described in chapter 9. Analogies can also be used creatively to find problems. For example, executives at Bradford Associates (Westport, Connecticut) spent an afternoon sipping martinis and brainstorming about possible new products that would be marketable. As they were enjoying their own liquid refreshments, they decided that the time had come "for a six-pack that a dog could ask for by name." They are now marketing a chicken-flavored soft-drink for dogs known as "Arf'n'Arf." Here is a clear example of the use of analogies to find problems (the need for a doggie soft drink). Similarly, a popular dog product is now being developed for people. Many dogs enjoy munching on bone-shaped biscuits that help to keep their teeth and gums healthy. A similar biscuit that will help humans keep their gums and teeth healthy will soon appear on market shelves.

Bionics

Bionics is a special type of analogy. It relies on analogies from nature that can be adapted to human problems. For example, special properties of the eyes of beetles have suggested a new type of ground-speed indicator for airplanes, and the principles of adhesion used by cockleburs have served as the prototype for Velcro-type closures. Bionics is also concerned that the broad impact of solutions be considered because, borrowing another analogy from nature, small changes in our ecological system can result in disastrous consequences to other life forms in the food chain. Papanek (1977) called this the "total-chain-of-design idea." It requires the creative consideration of entire systems and interrelationships of parts.

Visual Thinking

> When Mozart was asked where he got his ideas he said, "Whence and how they come I know not; nor can I force them."
> —(quoted in Vernon, 1970, p. 53)

Creative thinking often calls for images. The musician must first "hear" the sounds before he or she places the notes on paper; the poet must hear the rhyme before it is written; the painter must see the forms before his or her first brush stroke; and the chef must "taste" the combination of ingredients before the new recipe is created. It does seem that there are certain creative acts for which words are inadequate. Most people report that, at least some of the time, they think in images. An **image** is a picturelike representation in the mind. (See chapter 2 for discussion of imagery.)

Shaw and de Mers (1986–87) examined the relationship between imagery and creativity. They gave children three tests of creativity—the Remote Associations Test, which was described earlier, the Circles Test, which requires the individual to draw unique figures from circles, and the Just Suppose Test, in which children describe the consequences of improbable circumstances (e.g., suppose a great fog fell over the earth so that all we could see of people were their feet)—and three tests of visual imagery. They found a stronger relationship between imagery and creativity for children with high IQs than for children who score within the average range on intelligence tests. A relationship between creativity and imagery has been suggested by other researchers. The rationale behind this proposed relationship is that good imagers should be able to "see" problems in ways that should help them to generate solutions that are different from their peers who are low in the ability to create images. A suggested method for solving problems is to draw a diagram, thus transforming a verbal problem into a visual one. Adams (1979) called visual thinking an "alternative thinking language." It is an alternative to verbal-based thought. Adams suggested that we each take a drawing course to improve our ability to see and, in turn, to think creatively. He claimed that we can improve our visual thinking with practice.

Imagine the following (Adams, 1979):

1. A pot of water coming to a boil and boiling over;
2. Your Boeing 747 being towed from the terminal, taxiing to the runway, waiting for a couple of other planes, and then taking off;
3. Your running cow changing slowly into a galloping racehorse;
4. An old person you know well changing back into a teenager;
5. A speeding car colliding with a giant feather pillow;
6. The image in (5) in reverse. (p. 91)

McKim's (1972) *Experiences in Visual Thinking* provides a series of guided exercises designed to enhance your ability to utilize visual modes of thought.

It seems that how well we visualize a problem may depend on the medium in which it is presented. In a study reported in a recent newspaper article (TV Linked, 1988), both imagery and memory were enhanced when children listened to stories on the radio, compared to when they saw the same stories on television. Greenfield and Beagles-Roos, the psychologists who conducted this study, believe that the audio version helped students to create dynamic visual images, a process that was not enhanced in the video condition in which the children are presented with the images. It may be that Marshall McLuhan was right when he said, "The medium is the message."

Putting It All Together

Several different strategies or methods to produce creative thoughts have been presented. It would be naive to believe that if you can recite each of these methods, you will automatically have creative thoughts. They are merely guidelines for hard work, and some of us will have to work harder than others.

It is clear that creative thinking is a skill that can be cultivated (Edwards & Baldauf, 1987). The strategies presented in this chapter are the plans for developing that skill. You may be wondering, "Where do I begin?" You begin with a problem or a need. For some, creative ideas will immediately seem to flow; for others it will be more like pulling teeth. If you find yourself "out of fresh new ideas," try the techniques listed. Visualize the situation, use analogies and metaphors, consider relations, list attributes, mull checklists, and brainstorm. The creative process within you should ignite with some help from these strategies.

APPLYING THE FRAMEWORK

In applying the general thinking skills framework to decision making, consider the following questions.

1. *What is the goal?* The creative process is defined by its outcome. The goal in thinking creatively is the production of a novel and appropriate response.

2. *What is known?* A point that was made in this chapter, and that is the basis for the next chapter, is that one cannot be creative in a vacuum. You need the knowledge and skills of a domain to be creative. There is no substitute for information about the problem. You may have the potential to become a truly great architect or writer, but without knowledge of these fields, it is unlikely that you will design an innovative structure or write a truly great novel. In the problem about the merchant's daughter that was told in this chapter, there would have been no creative answer if she had not used her knowledge about the dishonest money lender to watch closely when he picked up the pebbles. Similarly, a careful consideration of the particular aspects of any problem is needed for finding problems and for finding solutions. Begin the creative process by listing the "givens."

3. *Which thinking skill or skills will get you to your goal?* This is really the question of how can we be creative. Numerous skills were suggested to guide the creative thinking process. The skill you select will depend on the nature of the problem. For example, visualizing the problem is more likely to be helpful with problems that have a spatial aspect to them, such as geometry problems or terrain problems. The skill of generating a list of topic-relevant words can be helpful in a variety of situations, but seems particularly well suited for writing and composing. Creative thinking checklists are useful in design problems; whereas "plus, minus, interesting" can be used anytime you find that you don't know how to begin finding a solution.

The following creative thinking skills were developed in this chapter. Review each skill and be sure that you understand how to use each one.

- defining a problem in multiple ways
- brainstorming to increase the number of ideas produced
- working with people from different backgrounds in order to increase probability of bisociative thinking
- considering the physical changes listed in the creative ideas checklist
- arranging the environment to maximize intrinsic motivation
- encouraging an attitude of risk taking
- evaluating possible solutions using the questions suggested by Parnes (1967)
- listing and combining attributes to devise a novel product

- forming sentences about the problem using relational words
- evaluating solutions and other aspects of the problem along the dimensions of plus, minus, interesting
- listing terms that are related to the problem before you attempt a solution
- gathering additional information
- using analogies to make the unfamiliar known and distorting analogies to make the familiar unknown
- visualizing the problem

4. *Have you reached your goal?* Because the creative process is judged by its outcome, the solution or product will need to be evaluated along the twin dimensions of originality and appropriateness. If it fails on either of these dimensions, then the thinking process will have to begin again until a creative outcome is produced.

CHAPTER SUMMARY

1. Creativity involves the dual notion of unusual or unique and good or useful. It always involves judgment, and people may not agree on which actions or outcomes deserve to be labeled "creative."

2. DeBono has made a distinction between vertical thinking and lateral thinking. Vertical thinking is logical and straightforward, whereas lateral thinking is a creative way to think "around" a problem.

3. Virtually all creative acts will involve novel ways of defining a problem and the selection of relevant information.

4. Creativity has been described as a blend of sensitivity, synergy, and serendipity. It is as if a fortuitous event brings together remote ideas in a person who is sensitive to their combination.

5. The Divergent Production Test and Remote Associations Test are the two most popular tests of creativity. Both have had low-to-moderate success in identifying creative individuals. Individuals who score high on one of these tests do not necessarily score high on the other.

6. Creativity is not a single trait. It is a set of processes that operate within a context.

7. Although it is true that, in general, intelligent people are more creative than less intelligent people, it seems that a minimal level of intelligence is all that is needed for creative expression.

8. A proper environment is important in encouraging creativity.

9. Intrinsic motivation seems to be one of the best predictors of creative behavior. In order to encourage the production of creative outputs, the environment needs to support intrinsic motivation.

10. Creative people tend to be self-motivated, tolerant of ambiguity, and willing to take risks.

11. Several strategies to foster creative thinking were presented. Brainstorming is

based on the supposition that, if you have many ideas, some of them will be good. Each item on a checklist of creative ideas can be applied to a problem to see if a creative spark is struck. Crovitz's relational algorithm relies on changing the relations among the parts of a problem to arrive at a solution. The PMI strategy encourages novel solutions by requiring the problem solver to evaluate the various aspects of the problem. Analogies and metaphors tune us in to similarities and differences that can be valuable in creating novel solutions. Visual thinking seems to be involved in many sorts of creative endeavors—especially the arts and sciences.

Terms to Know

You should be able to define or describe the following terms and concepts. If you find that you're having difficulty with any term, be sure to reread the section in which it is discussed.

Creativity. The act of producing something that is original and useful.

Lateral Thinking. Thinking "around" a problem. Used to generate new ideas. Compare with vertical thinking.

Vertical Thinking. Thinking that is logical and straightforward. Used in the refinement and development of ideas. Compare with lateral thinking, which is sometimes considered to be more creative.

Sensitivity. Responsiveness to the information we perceive through our senses.

Synergy. The bringing together of seemingly disparate parts into a useful and functioning whole. Creative thinking often seems to involve such combinations.

Bisociative Thinking. Bringing together two previously unassociated ideas or "frames of reference."

Serendipity. A happy, unexpected discovery that occurs when you don't expect it.

Psychometrics. The branch of psychology that is concerned with the measurement of psychological traits such as creativity, intelligence, and so on.

Convergent Thinking. The kind of thinking you engage in when you are required to come up with a single correct answer to a question or a problem. Compare with divergent thinking.

Divergent Thinking. The kind of thinking required when a person needs to generate many different responses to the same question or problem. Compare with convergent thinking.

Multidimensional Concept. A concept that varies in many qualitatively different ways.

Intrinsic Motivation. Inherent desire to engage in a task for its own sake and without regard for reward or punishment.

Extrinsic Motivation. Engaging in a task in order to receive reward or to avoid punishment.

Brainstorming. A group or individual method for generating solution paths for problems. Problem solvers are encouraged to think up wild, imaginative solutions and to defer judgment on these solutions until a later time, when they may be modified or combined. The goal is to produce a large number of possible solutions.

Creative Ideas Checklists. Lists that suggest ways to generate creative ideas by varying a problem's components and relationships among the components.

Attribute Listing. A method of generating creative solutions in which every characteristic or quality of the item or situation is listed and then examined for possible modification or recombination.

Relational Algorithm. A method for generating creative ideas that relies on changing the relations among items using relational words such as *on, between, under,* and *through.*

Analogies. (in problem solving) Problem-solving strategies in which similarities are noted between two or more situations while simultaneously discerning that there are also differences; for example, by noting similarities between two different problems, the problem solver may discover that similar solutions are applicable.

Ideational Fluency. The process of generating many ideas in order to solve problems.

Metaphor. Formed when we note similarities between things that are basically dissimilar. Often used in creative thinking.

Bionics. The use of analogies from nature that can be adapted to human problems.

Image. A picturelike representation in the mind.

Chapter Questions

Be sure that you can answer the following questions:

1.   Why is creativity difficult to define?

2.   Contrast the terms "vertical" and "lateral" thinking. Give an example of each. How is lateral thinking similar to redefining the problem?

3.   What does it mean to say that it takes a prepared mind to recognize a serendipitous event?

4.   Why is it so difficult to design valid tests of creativity?

5.   What is the relationship between intelligence and creativity?

6.   What kind of environment will foster creativity? How can intrinsic motivation be promoted in the classroom and the workplace?

7.   Describe Crutchfield's program to foster creativity in children.

8.   Why is it important to defer judgment during brainstorming?

9.   How are creative ideas checklists used? Compare them with the strategy of attribute listing.

10.   What is the principle behind "plus, minus, interesting?"

11.   Describe the program in which children had to list topic-relevant words before writing. What was the effect on the outcome? Why?

12.   Why are analogies always imperfect? How are they used in creative thought?

13.   Why should we try to "make the familiar strange?"

Exercises

Using the strategies for creative thinking presented in this chapter, give creative solutions to the following problems. Notice which of the creativity strategies you try for each problem and which one seems to work.

1. The 1958 Rockefeller Report on "The Pursuit of Excellence: Education and the Future of America" raised a number of still timely problems in need of creative solutions. Select one of the problems listed here:
   a. How can we improve conditions for "giving free expression to creativity" within the realms of science, government, business, and education?
   b. In what ways can colleges and universities provide the best climate for the creativity of the individual without sacrificing the benefits of group organization?
   c. How can we more quickly and surely identify the creative person and enhance his or her individuality?

2. Morale is low on the automobile assembly line. There is a heat wave that is affecting everybody's work, causing the employees to slow down and destroy the pace on the assembly line. Generate possible solutions to this problem.

3. An architectural firm has been given a difficult contract. They must build an essentially rectangular building to keep construction costs down, yet they want it to be aesthetic and match its colonial surroundings. What are some possible approaches?

4. If you've ever had the distasteful experience of trying to get a young child to take unpleasant-tasting medicine, you'll know that this is a difficult task. How can you get a young child to take unpleasant-tasting medication?

5. When college students move away from home and into the dorms, they often feel homesick. Because this seems like a childish problem, few will admit to it. What can be done to alleviate this problem?

6. Some young women literally starve themselves to death in order to gain the "super-thin" look that modern society endorses for women. What can we do about this problem?

7. You have been commissioned to create stained glass windows that depict the American Revolutionary War. What should you depict? How will you select your colors, etc.?

8. Your boss just called and is on his way over for dinner. Using only the ingredients you have in your house, what would you make for dinner?

9. How would you design a costume to represent what the well-dressed young man or woman will wear in the year 2000?

10. The headquarters of a large corporation is faced with rising costs and declining profits. In order to remedy this problem they could:
   a. fire six employees
   b. discontinue their new line of designer underwear
   c. cheat on their taxes
   d. require each employee to take a pay cut
   e. ask each employee to work an extra hour each day

f. borrow money at high interest rates.

Evaluate the impact of each of these solutions, and recommend additional ones.

11. Find a problem and suggest a solution. It can be something as silly as putting headlights on bedroom slippers so that the wearer can see where he or she is going at night or as serious as designing a better cane for the blind.

12. Apply your problem-solving skills to a contemporary social issue, such as eliminating racism, reducing pollution, or deescalating the arms race. You may use any of these suggestions or find a different contemporary problem.

13. Read the biography of a famous creative person. How did he or she arrive at creative solutions? Can you discern anything notable in the individual's background or personality that can help to explain the nature of creativity?

14. Find poems and other forms of artistic expression that have used analogies. How does the analogy convey the meaning that is implied by the artist?

Exercise your creative abilities in some of the following:

15. Write captions for cartoons.

16. Doodle.

17. Integrate principles learned in one class into another entirely different subject area.

18. Keep an idea file. Jot down ideas as they come to you. Review them periodically and use them.

19. Think of ways to improve on a favorite toy—like a teddy bear.

20. Enjoy your creative thoughts.

Answers to remote associations presented on page 415: 1. Bill   2. Nail
3. Pot   4. Fly   5. Coach

SUGGESTED READINGS

If you're seriously interested in increasing your creative potential, Parnes, Noller, and Biondi's (1977) *Guide to Creative Action: Revised Edition of Creative Behavior Guidebook* contains detailed instructions for 225 hours of creativity training, complete with practice exercises, an annotated bibliography, and articles on other creativity programs. An older edited volume filled with classic articles is Parnes and Harding's (1962) *A Source Book for Creative Thinking.*

Osborn (1963) outlined the concept of brainstorming and other creativity strategies in his classic text *Applied Imagination: Principles and Procedures of Creative Problem Solving.* Another book that is filled with very good "self-help" creativity ideas is Davis and Scott's (1971) *Training Creative Thinking.*

The concepts of vertical and lateral thinking are developed in two books by DeBono, (1967a) *The Use of Lateral Thinking* and (1968) *New Think.* Stein (1974, 1975) has a two-book series that comprises an excellent overall review of the topic. They are appropriately titled *Stimulating Creativity: Individual Procedures (Vol. I)* and *Stimulating Creativity: Group Procedures (Vol. II).*

Adams' (1979) *Conceptual Blockbusting* is a very good little book on a big topic. Even if you find the area dull, you'll find this book entertaining. I also recommend Adams' (1986) book *The Care and Feeding of Ideas: A Guide to Encouraging Creativity.* If you're interested in the life-span development of creativity, Arasteh and Arasteh's (1976) *Creativity in Human Development* will fit your needs. It is divided into three sections that mirror human development—the young child, adolescence, and adult. The relevant literature for each portion of the life span is reviewed. Regretfully, old age is missing, possibly because we don't know much about creativity in old age. A new book edited by Sternberg (1988), *The Nature of Creativity,* takes a contemporary and scholarly look at the multifaceted creature we call creativity.

Biographies of famous creative people always make fascinating reading. Ghiselin (1952) has compiled biographies from 38 brilliant women and men, entitled *The Creative Process.* You may find some of their stories inspirational. Arieti's (1978) book, *Creativity: The Magic Synthesis,* is fairly heavy reading, although it's worth consulting because of the fascinating art it contains. Amabile's (1983) *The Social Psychology of Creativity* contains a wealth of information on the environmental influences that can either promote or discourage the development of creativity. One of the most recent books about creativity is Weisberg's (1986) *Creativity, Genius, and Other Myths. What You, Mozart, Einstein, and Picasso Have in Common.* Who can resist a book with a title like that? The serious student of creativity will want to consult any of several books by Gardner, a psychologist who has spent much of his lifetime studying the creative process. I particularly suggest Gardner's (1982) *Art, Mind, and Brain.* Finally, there is a journal that is dedicated to research and theory concerning creativity, called *The Journal of Creative Behavior.*

11

Applications of Critical Thinking

Contents

Cora Anne's hands grew sweaty as she waited in the dean's outer office for what seemed like an eternity. Finally, the efficient and unsmiling secretary told her, "You may go in now. The dean will see you."

After shaking hands with the person behind the desk, whom she surmised was the dean of undergraduate programs, Cora Anne took a seat across from the dean's desk. "I really need your help," she began. "I'm a good student—see, I brought my transcript, but I must get out of the university's math requirement. I just can't do math. I'm willing to substitute anything you want, if you will just waive the requirement in mathematics. I'll take two additional courses; I'll give money to the scholarship fund; I'll do anything, but please help me get out of math."

Unlike the opening scenarios in the other chapters, this one is a true story that is repeated many times a year as countless students from all sorts of backgrounds try to find a way to avoid a particular subject that is required for graduation. Usually, students are trying to avoid coursework in mathematics, but the sciences and foreign languages also rank high among the academic disciplines that students most want to avoid. The students whom I've met this way are most often good students with high grade point averages and an unshakable belief that they cannot "do math" or whatever the dreaded subject is.

GENERIC THINKING SKILLS

Let us endeavor then to think well; therein lies the principle of morality.
—Blaise Pascal (1623–1662)

Stop for a minute and consider all of the times and places that you are required to think critically. If you are in school, then you should be thinking about your classes. Whether or not you are in school, you have to budget your money, decide which political candidate you will support, deal with car repair problems, assemble the VCR you recently bought, make decisions at your place of employment, make lifestyle choices for you and your family, and select health care professionals. The list of times and places when critical thinking is needed is virtually endless. The basic thinking skills that have been presented in this book are useful in all of these situations.

Whoever you are, however you live, you need to know how to retrieve information from memory so that it will be available when you need it, test hypotheses in order to predict and control your environment, evaluate evidence and assess claims, monitor comprehension, solve problems, estimate likelihoods, and make decisions. The skills that are used to analyze the arguments that are presented in history texts (e.g., Communism isn't working.) are also

Reprinted with special permission of NAS, INC.

used to analyze political and commercial appeals (e.g., Sam Ysidro favors big business; Timid gets your whole wash whiter.), scientific claims (e.g., Pollution is causing the earth to grow warmer.), and personal arguments (e.g., The fact that all of your friends wear Brandname Jeans is irrelevant.). The errors in thinking that were discussed in each chapter also reappear in myriad contexts. Examples of typical errors include assuming that events that follow other events are caused by the prior ones, drawing conclusions based on nonrepresentative or small samples, and believing that random differences represent significant effects.

Although there are generic thinking skills that can be utilized in a wide variety of situations, some skills are used more often that others in different academic disciplines and in different out-of-school contexts. Psychologists call the thinking skills that are used most often in a particular academic area **domain-specific thinking skills** (Nickerson, in press). Students who are poor in mathematics, for example, may have particular difficulty with the types of thinking skills that are most often needed to solve mathematical problems, such as translating words into symbols and symbols into words, devising multiple representations, and planning goal-directed behaviors. On the other hand, students who are weak in the social sciences and humanities may have particular difficulty in abstracting information from text and using the kinds of graphic organizers that were discussed in chapter 3.

We each have areas of specialization in which we are most proficient. Students become more proficient thinkers within their areas of academic specialization as they advance in their education. Much of the improvement is due to the growth of their knowledge in that area. As we learn more about a particular topic, it becomes easier to identify types of problems within that domain of knowledge and to recognize the distinction between information that is relevant and information that is irrelevant to finding a solution. Consider a skilled auto mechanic. He is better able to diagnose and repair a problem than is a novice auto mechanic, because he knows what sorts of problems are likely, given the situation, and because he has a richer array of available information for finding the problem and fixing it. Context-specific knowledge and experience separates the novices from experts in any field.

Thinking in the Disciplines

Recent research has focused on the development of thinking skills within academic disciplines (e.g., Chi, Glaser, & Rees, 1982). Some psychologists have argued that thinking skills instruction should concentrate on domain-specific problems, because these skills are more likely to be used when the conditions for their use are easily identified (Bransford, Sherwood, Vye, & Rieser, 1986). There is a considerable body of work on the development of thinking skills in the sciences and mathematics and in selected professions such as medicine, law, and auto repair. Although other areas of knowledge are equally important, we know less about the application of specific thinking skills in the humanities and social sciences, for example, because there are fewer opportunities to obtain funding in order to study these areas. For this reason, the following disciplines are considered in this chapter: mathematics; natural sciences; and selected professions.

MATHEMATICAL THINKING

"Amy Lowell goes out to buy cigars. She has 25 coins in her pocket, $7.15 in all. She has 7 more dimes than nickels, and she has quarters too. How many dimes, nickels, and quarters does she have?" (Tobias, 1978, p. 66).

STOP now and work on this problem. It's important that you actually try to solve this problem before going on.

How did you go about working on this mathematical word problem? If you are like most people, you started by looking for a formula that would help you to solve for the unknowns. A better approach is to consider the information given before proceeding with the solution phase. If you began this way, you would quickly realize that this problem is unsolvable. I hope that you can determine that if all of the 25 coins were quarters, the highest value coin, the total would be $6.25. It is not possible for the 25 coins to be worth $7.15. Most students continue for a long time, often in a frustrated manner, to look for an equation that will lead them to the correct answer without realizing that the problem is unsolvable.

The conclusion from several national studies is that "There is a crisis today in mathematics and science education" (Tucker, quoted in McDonald, 1987, p. A-1). In a recent article in *Science,* Steen (1987) reported that mathematical achievement among the top 5% of 12th graders is lower in the United States than in any other industrialized nation in the world and that 8th graders in the United States are below international norms in solving problems that require higher order thinking skills. "Indeed, as the 'back-to-basics' movement has flourished in the last 15 years, the ability of U.S. students to think (rather than just to memorize) has declined accordingly" (Steen, 1987, p. 251). The conclusion is obvious: There is a critical need for specialized instruction in mathematical thinking.

Cognitive psychologists and mathematics educators have begun to respond to this need by designing instructional programs that focus on the types of thinking skills that are needed to solve mathematical problems. Most of these programs have broken the task of solving mathematical problems into component parts and have designed instruction to correspond to each of the components.

Ask any student what she or he dreads the most about mathematics and the answer is most likely to be "word problems." Word problems are almost always more difficult than solving a formula or computing an arithmetic calculation, because word problems require the student to select or generate the appropriate formula or problem-solving procedure and then correctly calculate the answer. They are also more like real-world problems, which never come neatly labeled by type of problem or with directions regarding which formula to use. For this reason, we deal with word problems in this chapter.

The Components of Mathematical Problem Solving

According to Mayer (1986; 1987), the process of solving mathematical word problems proceeds in four stages: (a) problem translation; (b) problem integration; (c) solution planning and monitoring; and (d) solution execution. Let's consider each of these stages separately.

Problem Translation

The first stage of mathematical problem solving is comprehending the problem. Using the problem space terminology developed in chapter 9, this step involves understanding the information that is given and recognizing the goal, or desired end state. The problem is comprehended when you are able to (a) restate the information that is given and (b) specify the goal in your own words. As an example of these two skills, Mayer (1987, p. 348) provided the following questions:

1. Floor tiles are sold in squares 30 centimeters on each side. How much would it cost to tile a rectangular room 7.2 meters long and 5.4 meters wide if the tiles cost $.72 each?

Which of the following sentences is not true?

(a) the room is a rectangle measuring 7.2 meters by 5.4 meters
(b) each tile costs 30 cents
(c) each tile is a square measuring 30 centimeters by 30 centimeters
(d) the length of the long side of the room is 7.2 meters

2. Floor tiles are sold in squares 30 centimeters on each side. How much would it cost to tile a rectangular room 7.2 meters long and 5.4 meters wide if the tiles cost $.72 each?

What are you being asked to find?

(a) the width and the length of the room
(b) the cost of each tile
(c) the cost of tiling the room
(d) the size of each tile (p. 348)

Exercises like these help students focus on the critical aspects of the problem. One technique that you can use to help you with the comprehension of mathematical problems is the thought-process protocol that was described in the first chapter. With thought-process protocols, you either "think aloud" or write down your thoughts as you attempt to solve a problem. Lochhead (1984) used this procedure in an experimental mathematics course at the University of Massachusetts and found that students become more organized and clearer in their reasoning when they are required to make the thought process explicit. Thus, the first step in mathematical problem solving is a clear statement about the information given and the desired goal. It should not surprise you to realize that these are the first two steps in the framework for thinking that appears at the end of every chapter. Explicit statements about the givens and the goal will allow the problem solver to work both backward from the goal and forward from the givens during the course of solving the problem.

Problem Integration

Problem integration involves three distinct processes—representing the problem, usually as a diagram or other pictorial display, identifying the type of problem that it is, and deciding which information is relevant to finding a solution.

Representing the Problem.   Try this example: Draw a representation and write an algebraic formula that corresponds to the following statement: "There are six times as many students as professors at this university."

If you are like many college students, you drew a diagram like this one:

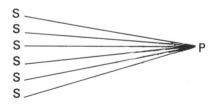

which then was translated into

$$6S = P$$

If I gave you the number of students, you could use this formula to find the number of professors, and vice versa. Can you see why the formula derived from this representation is wrong? The formula states that there are more professors than there are students, rather than the reverse! The reason that so many students have difficulty with this problem and others like it lies in the way in which the problem is stated. The juxtaposition of the words "six times the number of students" seems to automatically suggest that the number of students should be multiplied by six.

Mayer has found a significant improvement in the mathematical problem skills of college students after only three hours of training on how to derive correct representations (Lewis & Mayer, 1987; Mayer, 1988). He calls this type of training **representational training.** Students are taught to begin by drawing a simple number line:

low numbers   high numbers

In representational training, the student learns to begin working on the problem by locating the correct relationship among the variables that are used in the problem. To begin, the letter S (to stand for the number of students) is placed on the number line anywhere between the two end points.

low numbers   S   high numbers

The placement of the S is arbitrary in this example, because we were not given a value for it. The student now has to place the letter P (to stand for the number of professors) somewhere along the number line. At this point, the student must decide whether there are fewer professors than students, which would correspond to place the P to the left of the S, or whether there are more professors than students, which would correspond to placing the P to the right of the S.

The correct relationship between these two variables is shown as follows:

low numbers   P   S   high numbers

The beauty of relational training is that it requires problem solvers to consider the relative size of the variables used in the word problem before attempting a solution. If students gets an answer in which the number of professors is greater than the number of students, they would check it against their representation and find that there is an error. At this point, they would recheck both the representation and the obtained answer and, presumably, find the error.

Recognizing the Type of Problem.   The correct recognition of a problem as belonging to a class of problems also facilitates mathematical performance. If you can identify a problem as a "work" problem or "distance" problem, then selecting the relevant information and solving the problem is facilitated. You should label problems as you work on them as a way of practicing the identification of problem types. Mayer (1987) suggested that problems of mixed types (e.g., "time" problems, "work" problems) should appear in the same assignment or lesson. This will force problem solvers to identify problems with similar underlying principles as belonging to the same type of problem classification.

Selecting Relevant Information.   In real-world settings, the most difficult part of solving problems is often deciding which information is relevant to obtaining the goal. If mathematics were applied to the problem of calculating the various dimensions needed to build a bridge over a deep and rapidly moving river, the problem solver (probably an engineer) would have to seek information about the depth of the river, length of the bridge, desired height of the bridge, and so on. In most mathematics problems that are encountered in school, there is virtually no selection of information, because all of the relevant information is presented along with the problem. One suggestion for making school mathematics problems more like those encountered out of school is to include information than is not needed to solve the problem and to make students ask for needed information. This would force the problem solver to be selective about the information she or he believes will be needed.

Solution Planning and Monitoring

Schoenfeld (1985) taught college students five problem-solving strategies for use with mathematical problems. Three of these strategies are commonly used when solving problems in any context: (a) Draw a diagram, if at all possible; (b) Consider a similar problem with fewer variables; and, (c) Try to establish subgoals. These three strategies were discussed in chapter 9. The other two strategies are specific to mathematics. One concerns looking for patterns, and the other is a strategy that is useful in proofs. [I'm providing these last two strategies for those of you with a good background in mathematics. Don't worry if you're not able to understand these two mathematical problem-solving strategies: (d) If there is an integer parameter, look for an inductive argument. Is there an n or other parameter in the problem that takes on an integer value? List the integer parameters in order, and look for a pattern. Go beyond n objects and see what happens as you pass from n to $n + 1$; and (e) Consider arguing by contradiction or contrapositive. Contrapositive: Instead of proving the statement "If X is true, then Y is true," you can prove the equivalent statement, "If Y is false, then X must be false. Contradiction: Assume, for the sake of argument, that the statement you want to make is false. Using this assumption, go on to prove either that one of the given conditions in the problem is false, or that what you wish to prove is true.]

After only five training sessions practicing these strategies, the students who received this training were performing significantly better than a comparable control group who did not receive training with these general problem-solving strategies. You can apply this short list on your own when solving mathematical problems. Better yet, perhaps you can convince a mathematics teacher or a friend to use these strategies with you as you work through problems.

Solution Execution

The execution of a solution is the application of arithmetic procedures. Errors in the arithmetic stage can best be corrected with repeated practice with feedback and by diagnosing and correcting a particular "bug" (e.g., failure to carry correctly in long addition) using either problems you have worked out or thought-process protocols. Before you actually begin the calculations, make an estimate of the size of the answer. Is the answer you got "close to" the one you estimated? If not, why are the two figures so discrepant? Does the answer make sense? Check your answer with your representation. Does the magnitude of the variables show the relationship that you drew at the start of the problem-solving process?

Transfer of Training

The real goal of instruction in mathematics is transfer of training. Students trained on one set of problems should be able to apply what they've learned to a different set of problems. The little research that exists on this topic suggests that mathematical thinking skills that are developed with one set of problems will be applied to a novel set of problems (Mayer, 1988; Schoenfeld, 1985). Similarly, Catrambone and Holyoak (1987) found that when students receive explicit training in identifying subgoals in mathematical problems, they perform better on problems that are dissimilar to the ones they learned than a control group of students. Thus, the little research that is available on this topic suggests that students can learn how to think mathematically and that they can use this knowledge successfully when they encounter problems that are different from those they have previously encountered.

Applying the Research

Mathematics has two faces. Presented as a finished form, mathematics appears as a purely demonstrative science, but mathematics in the making is a sort of experimental science.

—Polya

What should you do when faced with difficult mathematical problems? First, restate the problem with explicit attention to identifying the givens and the goal. The next step is to draw a diagram, if possible. Before you write a formula or try to solve the problem, represent the variables on a number line so that you can check your answer with your representation. Try to identify the problem as belonging to a class of similar problems, and select information that you believe will be relevant to finding a solution. If you're still "stuck," use the problem-solving strategies suggested by Schoenfeld. Students have reported that simplification and setting subgoals seem to be the most valuable of Schoenfeld's strategies. Additional strategies for general problem solving are presented in chapter 9. After you find a solution, be sure to see if it makes sense. If not, check for errors in your calculations and in the way you set up the problem. If possible, discuss your solution strategy and answer with someone else. This last step will help you to explicitly identify the steps in your thinking, because it will force you to describe the solution process as well as provide another perspective on the process and outcome of solving mathematical problems.

THINKING IN THE SCIENCES

The Contributions of Jean Piaget

> *We recognize the gravity of the challenge to get our students to think, to think critically, and even to think scientifically. Certainly it is abundantly clear to me that science education fails if it doesn't tackle the matter of thinking.*
>
> —Munby (1982, p. 8)

One approach to enhancing thinking skills in the sciences is based on a model of intelligence that was proposed by the Swiss psychologist Jean Piaget. Piaget was primarily concerned with the way people acquire knowledge and the way cognitive processes change throughout childhood and early adulthood. According to Piaget, there are four broad developmental periods (each broken into stages). As people move from infancy into adolescence, their cognitive abilities mature in qualitatively distinct stages.

An advanced stage of cognitive development is **Formal Thought** or **Formal Operations,** which, according to Piaget, emerges at about 11 to 15 years of age and is characterized by logical thinking. It is a time when individuals can formulate hypotheses (What would happen if . . .) and manipulate abstract symbols, such as the ones needed to understand algebra and geometry. Piaget later acknowledged that formal thought may not be as universal as he had formerly believed (Piaget, 1977). Rather, individuals may be able to reason abstractly about some topics, but not others. As discussed earlier in this chapter, the expert in a domain of knowledge (e.g., auto repair, physics, bookkeeping, cooking) can differentiate relevant from irrelevant information more easily than a novice and is better at identifying types of problems and recalling successful solutions. It is therefore possible for an individual to be at the level of Formal Operations in one content area, but at a lower level in another.

There is considerable evidence that many people never progress to the mode of thought that is characteristic of Formal Operations (Neimark, 1975). Consider the intellectual abilities associated with Formal Thought (Sime, 1973):

> Very simply, it is the period in which most of us become able to reason abstractly—to hypothesize and work from the abstract to the particular, instead of the

other way round, or even to work from the abstract to the abstract. During this period we form and use concepts from abstractions, such as concepts of proportion (i.e., of a relation between relationships), of law, of justice, of infinity, and so forth. (p. 14)

Piaget's examples of abstract thought involve thinking skills that are needed to understand scientific concepts. Several researchers (e.g., Collea & Nummedal, 1980) have designed educational programs in which students learn the scientific thinking skills proposed by Piaget. The goal of these programs is to enhance the "level of thought" that each individual is able to attain and to enhance students' abilities in the sciences.

Here are some of the Piagetian scientific tasks to work on. They were originally reported in Inhelder and Piaget's book *The Growth of Logical Thinking From Childhood to Adolescence* (1958). Four skills that are particularly applicable to scientific thinking are: (a) combinatorial reasoning; (b) isolation and control of variables; (c) proportional reasoning; and (d) reciprocal implication. It's important that you actually work on these problems in order to develop the underlying skills.

Combinatorial Reasoning

Task 1: Mixing Colorless Chemicals.   This task involves mixing chemicals until a yellow color is obtained. Suppose that you were given four bottles of odorless, colorless liquids. They appear to be identical except for being labeled 1, 2, 3, and 4. You are also given a fifth beaker, labeled X, which is the "activating solution." The activating solution is always needed to obtain the yellow color, which results from a chemical reaction. How would you go about finding which of the chemicals in combination will yield the yellow color?
Some rules: The amount of each chemical is not important, nor is the order in which you combine them. It may help you in working on this problem to visualize the materials as presented in Fig. 11.1. Stop now, and think about how you would approach this problem. Do not go on until you have written down all of the tests you would perform.

Isolation and Control of Variables

Task 2: Bending Rods.   This task is to determine which of several variables affects the flexibility of rods. Imagine that you are given a long vertical bar with 12 rods hanging from it. Each rod is made of either brass, copper, or steel. The rods come in two lengths and two thicknesses. Your task is to find which of the variables (material, length, or thickness) influence how much the rods will bend. You can test this by pressing down on each rod to see how much it bends. You may perform as many comparisons as you like until you can explain what factors are important in determining flexibility. It may help you to visualize the setup as

FIG. 11.1.   Mixing colorless liquids. How would you determine which combinations of colorless liquids are needed to obtain a yellow color?

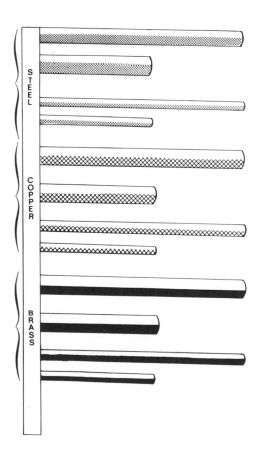

FIG. 11.2.   Bending rods. How would you determine whether material, length, or thickness affects rod flexibility?

presented in Fig. 11.2. What do you need to do to prove that length, or diameter, or the material rods are constructed from or some combination of these variables is important in determining flexibility? Stop now, and write out your answer to this problem. Don't go on until you have finished this problem.

Proportional Reasoning

Task 3: Me and My Shadow.   During a sunny afternoon at the beach, I noticed that your shadow was 10 feet long. A tree beside you cast a shadow of 24 feet. How tall is the tree? The variables in this problem are depicted in Fig. 11.3.

Reciprocal Implication

Task 4. Playing a Billiards-Type Game.   In this task, you are presented with a table that has a ledge or "buffer" around its edges so that a ball cannot roll off. A cue stick and a ball are placed at one corner of the table. There is a small toy figure on the table. Your task is to shoot the ball from the corner of the table so that it bounces off of the ledge and hits the toy figure. Consider the layout presented in Fig. 11.4. How would you go about positioning the ball and the cue stick so that you can hit the toy figure?

FIG. 11.3.   Me and My Shadow. Suppose that your shadow is ten feet long and that of a nearby tree is twenty-four feet long. How tall is the tree?

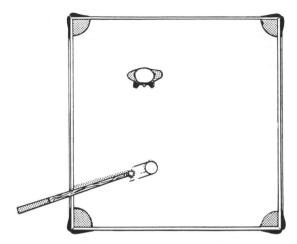

FIG. 11.4. Playing a billiards-type game. How would you position the cue stick so that the ball would bounce off the back wall and knock down the toy figure?

Solving the Piagetian Tasks

In all of these tasks, the process you used to arrive at your answer is as important as the answer itself. It's the way you find answers to these questions that will indicate whether you are functioning at the level of Formal Thought. Let's review how you solved the sample Piagetian tasks.

Task 1: Mixing Colorless Liquids.   How did you approach this problem? Did you realize that you needed an organized plan, or did you begin by randomly mixing the liquids? The best approach to this task is a very methodical one. It must include mixing each liquid separately with the activating solution (1+X, 2+X, 3+X, 4+X), then carefully mixing two liquids at a time with X (1+2+X, 1+3+X, 1+4+X, 2+3+X, 2+4+X, 3+4+X), then three at a time with X (1+2+3+X, 1+2+4+X, 1+3+4+X, 2+3+4+X), then all four at once (1+2+3+4+X), being careful to observe which combinations would yield the yellow color. If you carefully tested each combination, then you would score the Formal Operations level on this task.

Task 2: Bending Rods.   How did you go about exploring the effect of length, diameter, and material on rod flexibility? In order to solve this problem, you had to consider the possible factors that contribute to rod flexibility, and then systematically hold constant all of the variables except one. This is a basic concept in experimental methods. If you wanted to know if material was an important factor, which rods would you test? You would bend a brass rod, a copper rod, and a steel rod of the same length and diameter. This would hold constant the length and diameter variables while testing the material variable. Some possible tests of this would be to compare flexibility among the short and wide brass, copper, and steel rods. Similarly, if you wanted to find out if length is important, you would bend a short and a long rod of the same diameter that was constructed with the same material. An example of this would be to compare the short and wide copper rod with the long and wide copper rod.

How would you decide if diameter influences rod flexibility? By now, it should be clear that you would compare two rods of the same material and length and different diameters. You could test this by bending a short and wide steel rod with a short and thin steel rod.

Task 3: Me and My Shadow. The solution to this problem requires that you know your height and that you set up the correct ratios. Suppose that you are 63 inches tall. To keep units the same, change the length of the two shadows to inches. Your shadow becomes 120 inches, and the shadow of the tree becomes 288 inches. The correct ratios are:

$$\frac{\text{your height}}{\text{your shadow}} = \frac{\text{tree's height}}{\text{tree's shadow}}$$

Substituting numbers, this becomes:

$$\frac{63}{120} = \frac{X}{288}$$

$$151.2 = X$$

Converting inches back to feet, the tree is 12.6 feet tall. By the way, if you started with a representation of the variables, you would have drawn a number line and placed the height of the tree to the right of your height, because the tree is taller than you are. (Its shadow is also longer than yours.) If you got an answer that indicated that the height of the tree was less than your height, I hope that you would recheck both your representation and the proportion you calculated to determine why they didn't agree.

Task 4: Playing a Billiards-Type Game. This is a difficult task to conceptualize without actually trying to perform it. I was hoping that you've had enough experience with similar games (e.g., billiards) to formulate the answer or, at least, the way you would go about finding the answer. A trial-and-error approach to this problem does not qualify as Formal Thinking. You must first realize that the ball travels in a straight line and hits the ledge at an angle which is determined by the position of the cue stick. You should also come to realize that the angle at which the ball strikes the ledge is equal to the angle at which it is reflected from

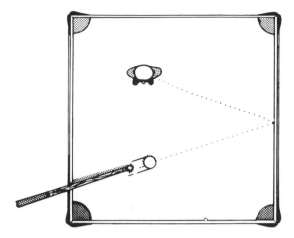

FIG. 11.5. Billiard game rebound diagram. The angle at which the ball strikes the ledge is equal to the angle at which it is reflected from the ledge.

the ledge. As in every context, there is no substitute for knowledge about the field. This is graphically demonstrated in Fig. 11.5.

All of these tasks require the individual to develop an organized approach to the problem—to generate hypotheses and perform all of the appropriate tests. The combinatorial reasoning in the chemical task is similar to that required for geometrical proofs (Sime, 1973). The isolation and control of variables needed to solve the rods task is essential for research in any area, and the ability to discover the path that a ball will take (called reciprocal implication) and the ability to reason about proportions are skills needed in all of the physical sciences.

Can You Learn to Function at the Level of Formal Thought?

Joe E. McKinnon, One of the leading advocates of incorporating Piaget's theories into school curricula, answers this question with an enthusiastic, "Yes." McKinnon has been particularly concerned with the intellectual development of college students. McKinnon administered Piagetian tasks like the ones presented in this chapter to college students at seven institutions. He found that approximately 50% of the students were not operating at the Formal Thought level. In response to the obvious need to teach thinking skills to college students, McKinnon (1976) developed an experimental curriculum that included "all the elements of inquiry—questioning, classifying, hypothesizing, verifying, restructuring, interpreting, and synthesizing" (p. 118). The success of this course was measured by comparing the number of students who had completed his experimental thinking course and had demonstrated that they were functioning at the Formal Thought level with the number of students who scored at this level without taking the course. Many more students from the experimental group (those who took the course) performed at the Formal Thought level than from the control group (those who didn't take the course). It seems clear that certain educational experiences can help students to think at an abstract level. Renner (1976) has concluded that "The research . . . leaves no doubt that intellectual development can be an outcome of education" (p. 190).

Reading Scientific Text

> *Science is not simply a collection of facts; it is a discipline of thinking about rational solutions to problems after establishing the basic facts derived from observations.*
>
> —Rosalyn S. Yalow
> (Distinguished Professor, City University of New York)

The growth of knowledge in the sciences is staggering. The number of scientific publications has been increasing at an unprecedented rate, with an estimated 8 to 10 million pages of printed material in the sciences and technology produced annually (Munby, 1982). It has been estimated that 90% of all scientists throughout history are alive today. Because the facts change as science advances, the only way to function as a scientist in modern society is to keep up with developments in one's field (Lesgold, 1988). Students and experts alike need to know how to extract information from scientific text. One reason that so many people have difficulty reading scientific text is that they lack a framework to guide them in selecting what's important and in organizing the information so that it can be recalled and used (Brooks & Dansereau, 1983).

Structure Training

> *The new basics include communication and higher problem solving skills and scientific and technological literacy—the thinking tools that allow us to understand the technological world around us.*
>
> —Linn (1986, p. 155)

Structure training is the name given to educational programs that provide specific instruction on the recognition of certain structures of scientific text. They provide students with strategies for comprehending and organizing the type of expository prose that is found in the sciences (Gagne, 1985; Kintsch & van Dijk, 1978; Mayer, 1989; Meyer, 1975). As the name implies, most scientific text has an organization or structure that students can be taught to recognize.

Macrostructure.   The **macrostructure** of a unit of text includes the main ideas that are presented and the most salient supporting and disconfirming evidence for the main ideas. It's like an outline of the text with only the major headings listed. Every text has one, or at most very few, **main ideas.** In chapter 5, I called the main idea of an argument the *conclusion.* Every time you read a scientific passage or any other expository text, you should be able to state the main idea(s) in one or two sentences and to list the supporting and disconfirming evidence (if any) for the main idea(s). If you cannot do this, you do not understand the information provided. You will not be able to "remember" the information at some later date, because it was never encoded (put into memory in a retrievable form).

It is important to develop the habit of monitoring your comprehension, especially when the text is highly technical. Stop at the end of every section of text (two to three pages is often a good size unit if the material is familiar to you, more often if the topic is unfamiliar) and either write a statement of the main ideas and supporting evidence or, at least, say it out loud. You should cover the text when you state the main idea so that it is abstracted and reconstructed from information that is in memory. It is too easy to think that you know the material when it is in front of you, only to find that it is "gone" as soon as you close the cover.

Sequences and Causal Relationships.   One typical structure in scientific prose concerns events that follow each other in time. Consider, for example, the life cycle of the butterfly. If you can identify a passage as descriptive of a **sequence,** then a simple list of events along a time line is the best way to abstract the information. One example that was presented in chapter 3 was the sequence of events that occur when food is digested.

Causal relationships also involve a sequence of events with some event occurring before some other event. The important difference between a sequence and a causal relationship is that in a causal relationship the prior event *caused* the later event to occur, such as the addition of a chemical to a solution, causing a chemical reaction to occur. If you can identify a passage as describing a causal relationship, then you will have to identify the antecedent and consequent events *and* look for evidence that the earlier event is responsible for the occurrence of the later event.

Enumeration.   Scientific passages sometimes contain a list of facts or examples that pertain to a topic. The type of structure that corresponds to an unordered list is **enumeration.** When you identify a passage as enumeration, you should be able to list the information that is provided. An example of this is a list of the duties that are performed by an astrophysicist or the types of weather conditions that are needed for a hurricane.

Comparison.   As the name implies, a passage that points out similarities and differences among topics is called **comparison.** Generating two or more lists that note the similarities and differences is a good strategy when you identify this type of information. An example of this type of structure is a passage that compares the planet Mars with Earth. You should be able to use the information to answer novel questions like whether life forms as we know them are able to exist on Mars (based on a comparison of temperature, composition of air, plant life, etc.) and what human exploration of Mars would be like.

Response.   Sometimes, scientific questions are posed in a text and then answered, a type of structure that has been called **response.** The actual response may have its own structure, depending on its length and complexity. Suppose a passage begins with, ''How can we satisfy the growing demand for energy?'' If a single answer is provided (e.g., solar energy), then the structure is a question and single response. A more complex version might pose the same question, but follow it with a list of possible energy solutions, and thus correspond more to an enumeration structure. Whatever the structure of the response, you should be able to identify the question and the answer(s) provided in the text.

Definitions.   Scientific jargon can be a foreign language, especially to novices in a field. **Definitions** need to be identified as such, and the essential components of the defining terms ''attached'' to the word that is being defined. Good strategies for learning definitions include putting the term in a meaningful context, visualizing the components, and using your knowledge of word origins and word parts (prefixes, suffixes, roots). For example, if you learn that anthropology is the study of human cultures, you should use it in a meaningful context, such as an explanatory paragraph. If you know that *anthro* means ''man,'' or mankind, and *ology* means the study of, then you can put the word together to arrive at ''the study of mankind.'' When learning definitions and other new vocabulary, it is better to elaborate the material, that is, add more information such as a context and knowledge of word parts, than it is to try to reduce the information about the word. The least effective strategy is to repeat the term and its definition until you can recite them verbatim. This sort of ''study'' does not build connected knowledge structures, and recall is more difficult because of the paucity of retrieval cues.

Applying the Research

The goal of structure training is to provide students with strategies for identifying different types of information so that they can abstract and outline information in a way that corresponds to the structure in the text.

How should you read and take notes from scientific text? Begin by stating the main idea and some supporting evidence for it. Then, identify the structure of separate passages using the types of structures listed in Table 11.1. Take notes by rephrasing the information in your own words and in a format that corresponds to the organization of the text. With the text covered, state the main ideas out loud or write them down. Check your summary of the material with the text to assure accuracy.

Recent research by Dee-Lucas and Larkin (1988) has shown that students in first-year science courses focus on definitions as being the most important portion of scientific text. Accordingly, students in beginning-level science courses spend more time learning definitions than other types of information and are somewhat better at recalling definitions than other facts that were presented in the text. Other researchers (Mayer, Dyck, & Cook, 1984) found that college students could be trained to recognize passages that describe cause-and-effect relationships and that comprehension and recall for the information in the passage is enhanced following a short training period. Additional support is pro-

TABLE 11.1
The Structure of Scientific Passages

Structure	Example	Activity
Macrostructure	"Prenatal hormones can affect the development of the immune system."	State the main idea(s), and list supporting and disconfirming evidence (if any).
Sequence	"Piaget's four stages of intellectual development are sensory-motor, preoperational, concrete and formal operations."	List the events in an ordered sequence.
Causal Relationship	"Obesity results from the consumption of more calories than the body expends."	Identify the cause(s) and the result(s) and evidence for the causal relationship.
Enumeration	"Galton's Laws of human heredity are the law of ancestral inheritance and the law of filial regression."	List the events without regard to order.
Comparison	"The cortex is the outer portion of the brain and is largest in primates. The brain stem is deep within the brain and is 'old' from the perspective of evolution."	List similarities and differences under topic headings (e.g., size, location, age, function for cortex and brain stem).
Response	"How do scientists study protoplasm? They use the techniques of staining, sectioning, and mounting."	Identify the question, and list the answers with it.
Definitions	"A burn is an injury that results from heat, chemical agents, or radiation."	Identify the essential components of the definition, and state them, using your own words.

vided by Heller and Reif (1984). They found that when beginning science students were required to describe science problems in terms of the concepts and principles involved before they attempted a solution, the students showed substantial improvement. Thus, by reviewing and using the types of scientific text structures presented in this section, you should be able to improve your own ability to abstract, retain, and apply information from scientific texts.

THINKING IN SELECTED PROFESSIONS

Just as different thinking skills are used more often in different academic disciplines, professionals in different fields tend to use some skills more than others. Researchers in this area study the thinking process of real people performing real on-the-job tasks as well as analyzing the tasks that are typically performed. This is a rapidly growing area of applied research. A sampler of some of the findings in three disparate professions is presented.

Medicine and Other Health Care Professions

Medical problem solving is governed by the same critical thinking principles as other types of problem solving and is susceptible to the same common errors. Perhaps the biggest difference between medical problem solving and problem solving in other domains is the high cost of errors. The old saying that physicians bury their mistakes is unfortunately sometimes true. Despite the importance of good thinking in medicine, the research literature on medical problem solving and decision making is relatively small, and the medical school curriculum rarely includes formal course work on how to arrive at diagnosis and treatment decisions.

The most comprehensive examination of medical problem solving was undertaken by Elstein, Shulman, and Sprafka (1978). They studied the thinking processes of experienced internists as they gathered information and made diagnoses and treatment decisions. The "patients" were actors who had rehearsed a set of symptoms that correspond to those that are typical patient complaints. The physicians were asked to "think aloud" so that their thought processes could be studied. Much of the information that is presented in this section comes from Elstein, Shulman, and Sprafka's (1978) book entitled, *Medical Problem Solving*.

Medical problems are among the most difficult kinds of problems, because they are almost always marked by high levels of uncertainty and ambiguity. Elstein, Shulman, and Sprafka (1978) described medical problem solving as "the process of making adequate decisions with inadequate information" (p. vii). Let's consider how some of the thinking skills that have been developed in other chapters in the book are applicable to medical settings.

Generating Hypotheses and Defining Problems

The usual scenario for medical practitioners begins with a patient with a symptom. In the simplest case, it could be an incisive wound that apparently needs some stitches to close it properly and to ensure rapid healing with minimal scarring. The information that is needed to determine that it is, for example, a knife wound, is fairly straightforward. The patient is asked, "How did you get this cut?", and the treatment decision is fairly obvious if the patient responds that it was done with a knife. At the other extreme is a patient brought into an emergency room in a coma with no other immediately apparent symptoms, such as blood loss. In this case, the ability to gather additional information is limited, time is critical, and there is a wide range of possible diagnoses.

In every case, the physician must begin to generate hypothetical diagnoses that will serve as a guide for further inquiry. Compare this sort of problem solving with the type of problem solving that students encounter in mathematics classes. The problems in mathematics classes and texts all have well-defined goals, and all of the information that is needed to solve the problem is presented. In fact, virtually all of the information that is given is needed to solve the problem, so students rarely have to select which information is relevant. By contrast, real-world medical problems, and most other real-world problems, are ill defined. The goal can often be stated in several ways, and the information that is needed for obtaining a solution has to be sought under very real time and money constraints.

Studies of medical problem solving have shown that physicians tend to consider a small number of possible hypotheses when exploring diagnostic categories. This is not a surprising finding if you've already read the chapter on memory (chapter 2). We all have limitations as to the number of topics we can consider at one time. Two ways to deal with these limitations are to keep careful notes, which can serve as an external memory aid during the information-gathering process, and to keep hypotheses very general (e.g., "abdominal infection" rather than "mesenteric adenitis") (Elstein, Shulman, & Sprafka, 1978). General hypotheses early in the information-gathering stage will allow for the possibility of many different types of abdominal infections. More specific hypotheses are useful later in the process.

Gathering Information

If you think back to your last visit to your physician, you'll probably recall that most of the time was spend gathering information. Think about the kinds of questions that your physician asked you. As discussed in chapter 8 ("Decision Making"), there is a large body of literature on the tendency to gather information that confirms the hypothesis that is being considered, rather than asking for information that might disconfirm the hypothesis. The tendency to seek confirmation evidence is called the **confirmation bias.** If a physician considers only a few disease categories and then proceeds to collect data that would confirm one of the categories, it is easy to see how other possible diseases would never be considered. The obvious remedy for the predilection to seek confirming information is a conscious attempt to gather evidence that would disconfirm the favored hypothesis. Clancey (1983, 1987) found that there was often a weak association between data and the conclusions because the physicians' tendency to focus on information that confirms a favored hypothesis. For example, if you show up at a physician's office with a scaly rash, the physician should begin by considering general categories of possible causes. If a favored hypothesis is that it might be a food allergy, the physician should ask questions that would *not* be indicative of food allergies. More specifically, instead of asking if you eat many foods that contain eggs, a better initial line of questioning might be about any unusual stress or whether you are also having difficulty sleeping or concentrating. The questions about foods in general, and more specifically eggs, would come later in the information-gathering process.

Encoding and Retrieving Information From Memory

Consider the following scenario: "You are a resident covering the out-patient clinic of a 400-bed hospital. A 45-year-old man has been brought into the clinic complaining of chest pains" (Frederiksen, 1986, p. 445). What do you do next?

The first step is to consider diagnostic possibilities. Symptoms suggest possible diagnostic categories with clusters of symptoms providing stronger evidence for any particular diagnosis than isolated symptoms. The physician needs to use the first few symptoms mentioned by the patient to begin testing hypotheses early in the information-gathering process. What seems critical at this stage is the ability to retrieve (i.e., remember) information about symptom–disease relationships. Gaps in medical knowledge or the inability to recall information when it is needed can mean disaster for the patient. Thus, information in memory needs to be organized in ways that will facilitate retrieval when the recall cues are symptoms.

Earlier in this chapter, I wrote about the structure of information in a passage. I suggested that the best way to comprehend and retain information from text was to identify the passage type and to study the information in a way that corresponds to the particular structure of the text. Thus, enumerated information would suggest list learning, comparisons would be learned best with a matrix array, and so on. There is a strong relationship between the way information is learned and the way it can later be recalled, such that different pieces of information that are learned together can serve as effective retrieval cues for each other. If, for example, you learn about George Washington while you are studying the Revolutionary War, you will more easily remember George Washington at some later time when someone is discussing the Revolutionary War than if you had learned about him in some other context (such as a list of great presidents).

Psychologists call this effect **encoding specificity.** We can apply this principle to learning medical information. The best way to optimize the probability of recalling a diagnostic category when presented with symptoms is to learn symptom–disease relationships, rather than studying diseases and symptoms separately.

Using Probabilities

Medicine is a probabilistic science. Unfortunately, few health care professionals receive formal training in using and understanding probabilistic information. Probabilities play a role in almost every aspect of medical problem solving. A good heuristic in testing hypotheses during the diagnostic phase of medical problem solving is to start with the most likely disease categories. Common diseases should be considered and eliminated before considering uncommon ones because, by definition, they are more likely to be the correct diagnosis. Of course, unusual diseases do occur sometimes, so they should not be ignored, but just postponed until more common diagnoses have been disconfirmed. Good health care professionals consider probabilities when deciding on possible diagnoses, ordering diagnostic tests, and determining a course of treatment.

Very often, patients have more than one disease; a set of symptoms could be indicative of more than one underlying cause. Depending on the likelihoods involved, a rare disease could be more likely than two fairly common diseases. (If you've read chapter 7, on understanding probabilities, you'll recall the "and" rule for determining the likelihood of two or more events.) Suppose you show up at a physician's office with a strange round rash and a runny nose. In testing hypotheses, the physician may need to consider that you have one rare disease that would be manifested with both of these symptoms or two more common ones (e.g., tick bites and a common cold). Suppose further that the tests to confirm the rare disease are expensive, painful, and pose a health risk. At this point, an accurate assessment of the various probabilities would be a useful guide in deciding what to do next.

Of course, probabilities aren't the sole determinants of diagnoses or courses of treatment. Physicians need to consider the possible consequences of delaying treatment. Suppose that you are bitten by a stray dog and that the dog can't be found. Although it may be unlikely that you will develop rabies, it is important to get medical injections to prevent this possibility, because there is no cure for rabies once the disease develops. Thus, a second heuristic is to rule out diseases most needing immediate treatment. Elstein, Shulman, and Sprafka (1978) suggested that a disease like Tay Sachs, which is rare, untreatable, and incurable, should not be given consideration early in the hypothesis-testing process, because there is no advantage to early detection. Other diseases or health problems that could be alleviated with early detection should be considered early in the process of generating hypotheses.

Disease probabilities are not static. Certain diagnoses become more probable as additional information is collected. Consider Tay Sachs. It is a rare disease, but it is more prevalent among infants born to Jewish parents of Eastern European ancestry. In the chapter on understanding probabilities, I talked about the importance of revising probabilities after collecting additional data. This is an important thinking skill for medical problem solving.

Communication

The doctor–patient relationship is based on the exchange of information. Patients often complain that their physician doesn't explain why certain tests are needed, how to take medications, or the prognosis or anticipated outcomes of treatment. Physicians, on the other hand, complain that patients don't listen well and tend to hear what they want to hear. Numerous guides for clear communication were presented in chapter 3, and many of the examples of miscommunication were taken from medical domains.

Medicine is often a foreign language, with many of the terms used by medical personnel misunderstood by people who are unfamiliar with the jargon. More attention must be paid to using terms that are more easily understood and on adjusting the level of the communication to the particular patient. For example, a uterus can be described as the "house for the baby" to a woman with little education or to someone with limited English proficiency. Communication also breaks down when there are distractions, and visits with physicians are often marred by distractions. A parent with a sick child may not be attending fully to the pediatrician's instructions about administering medication because the sick child is whimpering at the same time as the instructions are being given. This is easily remedied by ensuring that physician–patient conversations are relatively free of distractions. In the example of the sick child, a nurse could stay with the child in another room while the physician is discussing health care issues with the parent.

It is surprising how rarely health care information is written down. There is often a considerable amount of information that is conveyed, and the patient is expected to remember most or all of it. Written instructions that can be reviewed at a later time would alleviate some of the communication failures. The patient should also be asked to repeat the instructions as a check on communication. The elderly, for example, often take several different medications each day. Each medication has its own instructions. (Take two tablets with each meal; take a teaspoon of liquid whenever you feel dizzy; take a green pill every other day.) Complex medication instructions should be written and reviewed with each patient before he or she leaves the physician's office in order to avoid the potentially lethal consequences of confusing the instructions.

Law-Related Professions

Legal reasoning is the heart of the law professions. The components of legal reasoning are questions about facts, questions about laws that pertain to the facts, and the nature and strength of evidence. Legal reasoning usually occurs in an environment of advocacy in which the lawyers for each side in a dispute argue that their client's interpretation of the facts, laws, and evidence is the correct one. Emotions run high and sometimes seem to cloud the reasoning process. If you've already read chapter 5 (on analyzing arguments), you'll recognize the components of legal reasoning as a specialized list of topics that were discussed in that chapter.

Legal problems, like most other real-world problems, are difficult because they are so ill defined and because of the difficulty in determining which information is relevant. A legal professional will have to determine which legal principles apply to a set of facts and which facts are relevant to the principle that is being considered. The situation is even more complex because some relevant facts are not admissible in court because they may be considered prejudicial or inflammatory. As in medicine, where a patient may have two or more diseases, a set of facts may be governed by multiple laws. The situation gets even murkier when the laws themselves may be in conflict. Anyone preparing for a career in the law should review very carefully the guidelines for diagraming and evaluating arguments that were presented in chapter 5. These guidelines included techniques for identifying conclusions and premises, evaluating the strength of support for an argument, and the strength of counterarguments.

Arguing by Analogy

The legal system in Canada, the United States, and Great Britain is based on common law. Common law is a system of laws derived from previously decided cases in which a decision was rendered in connection with a given set of facts and circumstances. The outcomes of new cases are determined by their similarity to a previously decided case. Thus, arguments typically involve analogies with questions of law determined by deciding how similar a new case is to one that was previously decided. The lawyers for one side will typically argue that the case being tried is similar to an earlier one in all or most of the essential facts. The lawyer for the opposing side will argue that there are important differences between the case being tried and the earlier one. There will be differences of opinion about which case should apply to a given situation. Thus, reasoning by analogy is the principle mode of thinking in the legal profession.

Consider a hotly debated issue that surfaces at every election in the United States: Should churches and other religious agencies be required to pay taxes? One side argues that if churches had to pay taxes on their real estate, this practice would violate the principles of separation of Church and State. The other side argues that by not taxing churches, the state is supporting religion, and state support of religion violates the separation of Church and State. This is an issue about which people feel quite emotional. The problem is that the first amendment prohibits *both* the establishment of religion and interference with the exercise of religion, and sometimes these two rights are in conflict.

Another timely example of legal reasoning concerns the precedent-setting Supreme Court decision approximately 10 years ago that private schools cannot discriminate on the basis of race. Over 100 cases have been heard since then, with arguments based on the premise that racial discrimination in the private sector is therefore unconstitutional. Each side in these cases stresses either the similarity or dissimilarity between the case they are arguing and the Supreme Court decision regarding private schools. Consider a hypothetical case in which the issue is whether a private dining club can exclude members because of race. The plaintiff's side (usually a person denied membership) will attempt to show that a private dining club and a private school are similar in essential ways so the ruling from the Supreme court case would apply. The defendant's side (usually the club) will argue that there are essential differences between a private school and a private dining club, so the Supreme Court decision would not apply in this case. The judge or jury will ultimately decide if the circumstances are analogous to those in the original case or if they are too dissimilar to apply the earlier decision.

Using Statistical Information

Increasingly, statistics are being used in courts of law and in other aspects of legal practice. Consider a jury trial in which a man is being tried with a charge of burglary. A neighbor saw a very tall man with blond hair climbing through a window on the night of the burglary. The prosecutor will argue that this is strong evidence that the tall blond man on trial is indeed the burglar. The defense will argue that there are tens of thousands of tall blond men in the city and that the description is poor evidence that the accused was the burglar. Each side, in turn, will present information that will either make conviction more or less likely, depending on the side they represent. Additional information will be added during the course of the trial that will alter the probabilities, and the lawyers have to make the newly revised probabilities clear to the judge and jury.

Comprehending Language

The process by which language is comprehended is becoming increasingly important in legal proceedings. Legal arguments are often complex, and discerning the relationships among separate pieces of information can be difficult in the emotionally charged atmosphere of a courtroom. Information must be presented clearly, and the words used must convey the intended meaning. Because of the high load of information in many cases, lawyers should be using more overheads or flip-charts that outline their argument to be sure that the jurors perceive the relationship between the evidence being presented and arguments they support or refute.

Instructions to the jury is another area in which language comprehension can govern the outcomes of legal proceedings. Consider, for example, the charge to the jury. There are no objective definitions of what it means to be guilty "beyond a reasonable doubt." A good prosecutor will emphasize the fact that there will always be a small amount of doubt, but the jury is to decide if the doubt is reasonable. Suppose you entered your kitchen and found your son, covered with cookie crumbs, and the empty cookie jar on his lap. There may be some small doubt that he didn't take the cookies (there's always a monster possibility), but such doubt is not reasonable under normal circumstances. A discussion of what constitutes reasonable doubt can make a difference in how juries assess guilt and innocence.

Auto Repair

Auto repair is similar to medical problem solving with the exception that auto repair is much more difficult. The difficulty in repairing autos and other equipment (e.g., stereos, duplicating machines, dishwashers) lies in the fact that auto designs are often radically different, and mechanics have to repair models that they may never have seen before. By contrast, the physician's job is easy, because human bodies don't come in an almost infinite range of models, and the models don't change annually. The function, location, and design of the human liver, for example, will not change during the course of a physician's lifetime, but the function, location, and design of auto components can vary tremendously.

Wright (undated), in an article entitled, "Wanted: Old-style thinking mechanics" noted the need to change the way mechanics are taught from "knowing what" to "knowing why." Mechanics may know what a particular part does, but not why the part is designed in a particular way or why the component is needed. With auto parts rapidly changing in design, the more general "why" knowledge will help the mechanic diagnose and fix problems with components he or she has never seen before. Like experts in any field, the expert auto mechanic has organized his or her knowledge on the basis of concepts, principles, and abstractions (Nickerson, in press). A complex organization of knowledge with multiple connections between "pieces of knowledge" is essential for a deep understanding of the domain and for the successful transfer of knowledge to novel situations.

Most of the information presented in earlier chapters on hypothesis testing, problem solving, decision making, and understanding probabilities is useful in the context of auto and other equipment repair. One problem-solving technique that is particularly useful in auto repair is the use of fault trees. Like the physician, the auto mechanic sees "patients" with symptoms, and the major task is to diagnose and repair the problem. A fault-tree analysis begins with a list of possible hypotheses that would explain the symptoms. Listed under each hypoth-

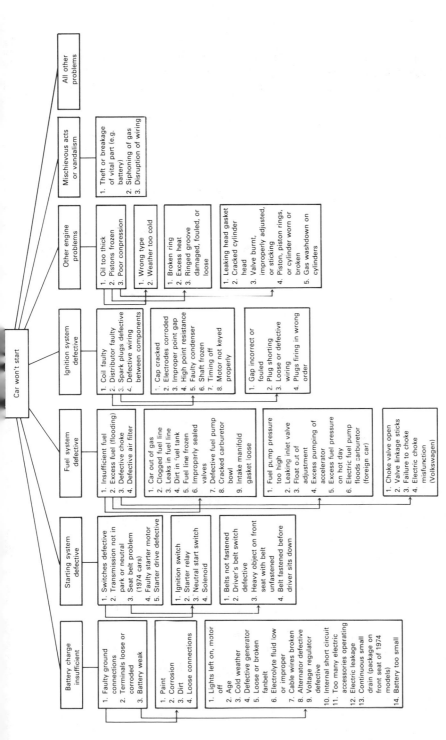

FIG. 11.6. A possible fault tree for discovering why a car won't start. From Fischhoff, Slovic and Lichtenstein, 'Fault trees: Sensitivity of estimated failure probabilities to problem representation.' Copyright © The American Psychological Association, 1978. Adapted by permission of the American Psychological Association.

esis are possible causes and, implicitly, ways to fix the problem. The initial level hypotheses are quite broad, with greater refinement later in the process. An example of a fault tree for diagnosing the problem "Car Won't Start" is presented in Fig. 11.6.

Although fault trees can be very useful, the biggest problem with them is the failure to consider hypotheses that are not listed on the tree. If entire branches are missing, the missing hypotheses will rarely be considered. Look carefully at Fig. 11.6. Suppose that the car won't start because the owner is using the wrong key. There is no branch that corresponds to this possibility, and many mechanics won't discover this problem until they've checked all the other possible branches.

Because of the similarity between medical problem solving and auto repair, many of the same thinking skills are used in both contexts. Mechanics, like physicians, should consider the most probable causes first. Utility is also important. A problem that may require hours of work to check out should be deferred until easier hypotheses are checked (e.g., is the key the right one?).

CHAPTER SUMMARY

1. Most of the thinking skills developed in the earlier chapters can be considered "generic," because they are applicable in a wide range of situations. Domain-specific thinking skills are those skills that are used most often in one academic domain (e.g., physics) or a particular situation.

2. The four stages of solving mathematical word problems are problem translation, problem integration, solution planning and monitoring, and solution execution.

3. When solving mathematical word problems, identify the givens and goal, locate the relative positions of variables on a number line, classify the type of problem being solved, seek relevant information, execute the solution, and check your answer for consistency with the diagram and meaningfulness.

4. Four Piagetian tasks that are commonly used in scientific thinking were presented. They are combinatorial reasoning, isolation and control of variables, proportional reasoning, and reciprocal implication.

5. In order to facilitate comprehension and recall of scientific text, readers should identify the structure of the text and abstract information from the text according to its structure. In addition to macrostructure, which is always present, common structures for scientific texts are sequences and causal relationships, enumeration, comparison, response, and definitions.

6. Medical professionals are urged to generate broad hypotheses early in the process of formulating a diagnosis. Information should be collected that would disconfirm the hypothesis being considered so as not to foreclose the search process too early. Diagnoses that are most probable should be considered before rarer ones and the utility of certain

diagnostic categories should help to guide the professional through the process of generating hypotheses.

7. Legal reasoning is primarily by analogy, with advocates for each side pointing out similarities and differences between a case being tried and an earlier one. Statistical information to determine probable guilt or innocence is increasingly being used in legal proceedings. As in all of the other professions, the ability to communicate effectively is essential in determining an outcome.

8. Because of the wide variety of auto and other equipment components, mechanics need to receive more training on why parts have a particular design so that they can work effectively with equipment they may never have seen before. The fault tree was suggested as a useful problem-solving technique for auto repair, but if a branch is missing from the tree, mechanics are unlikely to consider the missing information.

Terms to Know

Check your understanding of the concepts presented in this chapter by reviewing their definitions. If you find that you're having difficulty with any term, be sure to reread the section in which it is discussed.

Domain-Specific Thinking Skills. Thinking skills that are most often used in an academic domain (e.g., converting verbal statements to mathematical formulas).

Representational Training. Training in representing the relative size of variables in word problems by placing them on a number line.

Formal Thought (Also known as formal operations). The fourth stage in Piaget's theory of intellectual development. It emerges between 11 to 15 years of age, when people develop the ability to formulate hypotheses, reason logically, and deal with abstractions.

Structure Training. Training in the identification of the organization of text so that the reader can process the information provided in a way that corresponds to the particular structure.

Macrostructure. The main ideas of a passage, along with the most salient supporting and disconfirming evidence for the ideas.

Main Ideas. The conclusion of an argument and the premises or reasons that support the conclusion.

Sequence. A series of events that follow in an orderly fashion either in time or space.

Causal relationship. A relationship in which a preceding event is responsible for the occurrence of a subsequent event.

Enumeration. An unordered list. A list in which there is no assumption of causality or sequence.

Comparison. A type of text structure in which two or more events are contrasted along one or more dimensions.

Response. A question-and-answer text structure.

Definitions. The portion of text that introduces specialized terms or the jargon that is used in a field.

Confirmation Bias. The predilection to seek and utilize information that supports or confirms one's hypothesis or premises while ignoring disconfirming information.

Encoding Specificity. The idea that information can serve as a retrieval cue for other information if they were connected in some way during learning or acquisition.

Thinking Skills Presented in This Chapter

The following thinking skills were presented in this chapter. Review each skill and be sure that you understand when and how to use each one:

- translating mathematical problems
- drawing the relative placement of variables on a number line
- identifying types of problems
- selecting relevant information
- planning and monitoring a solution
- using combinatorial reasoning
- isolating and controlling variables to determine cause
- reasoning with proportions
- discerning structures in scientific text
- being aware (and avoiding) the bias to seek evidence that confirms a preferred hypothesis
- encoding two or more pieces of information together so that they can serve as retrieval cues for each other
- applying probability skills in several contexts
- understanding and using arguments by analogy
- using fault diagrams to diagnose problems

Chapter Questions

Be sure that you can answer the following questions:

1. Contrast the idea that there are generic thinking skills with the idea of domain-specific thinking skills. How could you reconcile the two concepts?

2. How are thought-process protocols useful in solving mathematical problems?

3. Compare the steps in solving mathematical problems with the general directions that were given in chapter 9. How are mathematical problems different from and similar to other types of problems?

4. What is the rationale behind representational training? Why is it important to mark the relative location of the variables on a number line before you solve the problem?

5. What sort of advice would you give someone who is ''stuck'' on a mathematical problem that would help her find the answer?

6. How can the ability to identify the structure of text help you to comprehend the information? What are common structures in the sciences?

7. Medical problem solving uses many of the skills that were presented in other chapters in this book. List four different skills, and explain how they are needed in medical settings.

8. Arguing by analogy was identified as a primary way of presenting arguments in the legal profession. What makes a strong argument by analogy?

9. Earlier in this chapter, I said that auto repair is more difficult that medicine. Explain that comment.

Exercises

1. A scientist is interested in determining the number of birds on a large island. One day she captured 40 birds and placed a band around the leg of each. She returned one week later and captured 60 birds. Twelve of these birds had a band on their legs. Can she use this information to estimate the total number of birds on the island?

If you answered yes to this question, what is the best estimate of the total number of birds? Explain how you arrived at this answer.

2. You have taken a space trip to the mythical planet of Xob. On Earth, you weigh 130 pounds. Your weight on Xob is 15 zerks. What is the weight in zerks of your 100-pound Earthling friend?

3. Several children want to play on a playground see-saw (also called a "teeter-totter") at the same time. They are all in kindergarten and are approximately the same weight. The see-saw is 6 feet long. Distances in 1-foot units have been marked off in the figures. Consider the situations in Fig. 11.7, both of which will keep the see-saw in

FIG. 11.7. These see-saws are in balance.

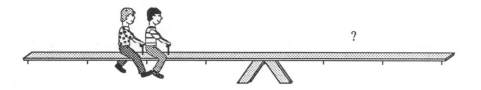

FIG. 11.8. Where should a third child sit to keep this see-saw in balance?

balance. Now consider the situation in Fig. 11.8. Two children are sitting on the left-hand side of the see-saw, at the positions indicated. If one child wanted to play with them, where should he sit to keep the board in balance? Explain your answer.

4.   This problem was presented to children in fourth through ninth grades by Karplus, Karplus, and Wollman (1974). You should recognize this as an easier version of Exercise #2.

Here is a picture of Mr. Short:

There is a figure called Mr. Tall who is similar to Mr. Short, but larger. Mr. Short's height was measured with large buttons. He is four buttons tall. When Mr. Tall was measured with the same buttons, he was found to be six buttons tall. When Mr. Short's height is measured with small paper clips, he was found to be nine paper clips tall. What is Mr. Tall's height in paper clips?

5.   Elliot is 5 feet tall. At 3:00 PM, his shadow is 2 feet long. E.T. is 2½ feet tall. How long would his shadow be at 3:00 PM?

6.   The Russians have a secret code. If you can break their code, you will have access to their defense secrets. You know that they can only use the digits 4, 7, 8, and 9 and that the code can be one, two, three, or four digits long. The same digit may not be used more than once in the code. How would you go about combining the digits 4, 7, 8, and 9 to break their code?

7.   The American Heart Association wants to know how diet (high and low fat), exercise (frequent and never), and blood pressure (high and low) contribute to heart disease. How should they study the effect of diet on heart disease?

8.   A physician believes that the patient he is seeing may have a rare disease that usually occurs after the patient ingests uncooked pork. What sort of questions should he ask early in the process of gathering information? Other than ''Have you eaten uncooked pork?'', what questions should he ask later in the information gathering process?

9.   Identify the text structures presented in this chapter in texts in other academic disciplines. Use these structures when you read texts in these fields.

10.   Select word problems from a mathematics text, and apply the skills that were presented in this chapter to those problems.

SUGGESTED READINGS

Several books and journal articles on domain-specific thinking skills have been published within the last few years. The all-time classic that has served as a prototype for much of the more recent work was written by Polya (1945) and is entitled, *How To Solve It: A New Aspect of Mathematical Method.* This gem has been translated in 17 languages and has been republished numerous times. Polya wrote this book soon after arriving in America. He had been told that America was the land of "how to" books, and he decided that a "how to" book that taught mathematical strategies, rather than basic concepts, was needed. I highly recommend that you look through a copy. You may be surprised at how many of today's modern discoveries about mathematical problem solving were known by Polya over four decades ago.

The collected papers of cognitive psychologists and mathematics educators appear in several edited volumes. If you want to know more about this area, consult Schoenfeld's (1987) *Cognitive Science and Mathematics Education,* Janvier's (1987) *Problems of Representation in the Teaching and Learning of Mathematics,* Silver's (1985) *Teaching and Learning Mathematical Problem Solving: Multiple Research Perspectives,* and Hiebert's (1986) *Conceptual and Procedural Knowledge: The Case of Mathematics.* A more general collection of papers on domain-specific thinking skills can be found in Dillon and Sternberg's (1986) *Cognition and Instruction.* This edited volume contains papers on thinking skills and in several disciplines, including reading, writing, music, and art.

If you notice researchers' names when you read, then you already know that Mayer is an important name in this area. He has written two books that address the topics discussed in this chapter. Both are extremely well written and contain a wealth of good advice that is backed by research. Mayer's (1983) *Thinking, Problem Solving, and Cognition* will soon be updated; a second edition is in the works. Mayer's (1987) *Educational Psychology: A Cognitive Approach* is written for practicing and prospective teachers. A colleague of mine remarked after reading this book that Mayer makes it seem that cognitive psychologists are doing important and useful work—the ultimate praise.

If you're looking for mathematical problems that you can use to practice the skills presented in this chapter, then you'll find that Whimby and Lochhead's (1982) *Problem Solving and Comprehension* (3rd ed.) will provide many good examples. For a collection of papers on the structure of text, consult Britton and Black's (1985) edited volume, *Understanding Expository Text.*

REFERENCES

Adams, A., Carnine, D., & Gersten, R. (1982). Instructional strategies for studying content area texts in the intermediate grades. *Reading Research Quarterly, 18,* 27–55.

Adams, J. F. (1986). *The care and feeding of ideas: A guide to encouraging creativity.* Reading, MA: Addison-Wesley.

Adams, J. L. (1979). *Conceptual blockbusting: A guide to better ideas* (2nd ed.). New York: Norton.

Adler, R. B., Rosenfeld, L. B., & Towne, N. (1980). *Interplay: The process of interpersonal communication.* New York: Holt, Rinehart & Winston.

Alcock, J. E. (1981). *Parapsychology: Science or magic?* Oxford: Pergamon Press.

Allport, G. W. (1954). *The nature of prejudice.* Cambridge, MA: Addison-Wesley.

Amabile, T. (1983). *The social psychology of creativity.* New York: Springer-Verlag.

Amabile, T. M., Hennessey, B. A., & Grossmann, S. (1986). Social influences on creativity: The effects of contracted-for-reward. *Journal of Personality and Social Psychology, 50,* 14–23.

American Association of Medical Colleges (1984). Report of the working group on fundamental skills. *Journal of Medical Education, 59,* 125–135.

Anderson, B. F. (1980). *The complete thinker: A handbook of techniques for creative and critical problem solving.* Englewood Cliffs, NJ: Prentice-Hall.

Anderson, J. R. (1985). *Cognitive psychology and its implications* (2nd ed.). New York: W. H. Freeman.

Anderson, N. H. (1986). A cognitive theory of judgment and decision. In B. Brehmer, H. Jungermann, P. Lourens, & G. Secon (Eds.), *New directions in research on decision making* (pp. 63–108). Amsterdam: North-Holland.

Arasteh, A. R., & Arasteh, J. D. (1976). *Creativity in human development.* New York: Schenkman Publishing Co.

Arieti, S. (1978). *Creativity: The magic synthesis.* New York: Basic Books.

Arkes, H. R., & Hammond, K. R. (Eds.). (1986a). *Judgment and decision making: An interdisciplinary reader.* Cambridge, MA: Cambridge University Press.

Arkes, H. R., & Hammond, K. R. (1986b). Law. In H. R. Arkes & K. R. Hammond (Eds.), *Judgment and decision making: An interdisciplinary reader* (pp. 211–212). Cambridge, MA: Cambridge University Press.

Arkes, H. R., & Hammond, K. R. (1986c). General introduction. In H. R. Arkes & K. R. Hammond (Eds.), *Judgment and decision making: An interdisciplinary reader* (pp. 1–10). Cambridge, MA: Cambridge University Press.

Arnheim, R. (1971). *Visual thinking*. Berkeley: University of California Press.

Atkinson, R. C. (1975). Mnemotechnics in second-language learning. *American Psychologist, 30,* 821–828.

Ayer, A. J. (1965). Chance. *Scientific American, 213,* 45–54.

Baddeley, A. D. (1972). Selective attention and performance in dangerous environments. *British Journal of Psychology, 63,* 537–546.

Baddeley, A. D. (1976). *The psychology of memory*. New York: Basic Books.

Bailin, S. (1987). Creativity and skill. In D. N. Perkins, J. Lochhead, & J. Bishop (Eds.), *Thinking: The second international conference* (pp. 323–332). Hillsdale, NJ: Lawrence Erlbaum Associates.

Baron, J. (1987). An hypothesis about the training of intelligence. In D. N. Perkins, J. Lochhead, & J. Bishop (Eds.), *Thinking: The second internal conference* (pp. 60–67). Hillsdale, NJ: Lawrence Erlbaum Associates.

Baron, J. (1988). *Thinking and deciding*. NY: Cambridge University Press.

Baron, J. B., & Sternberg, R. J. (Eds.). (1987). *Teaching thinking skills: Theory and practice*. NY: Freeman.

Barron, F. (1958). The psychology of imagination. *Scientific American, 199,* 151–166.

Barry, V. (1983). *Good reason for writing*. Belmont, CA: Wadsworth Publishing Co.

Bartlett, F. C. (1932). *Remembering: A study in experimental and social psychology*. England: Cambridge University Press.

Bartlett, F. C. (1958). *Thinking: An experimental and social study*. London: Allen & Unwin, Ltd.

Beardsley, M. C. (1950). *Practical logic*. Englewood Cliffs, NJ: Prentice-Hall, Inc.

Begg, I., & Denny, J. P. (1969). Empirical reconciliation of atmosphere and conversion interpretations of syllogistic reasoning errors. *Journal of Experimental Psychology, 81,* 351–354.

Bell, R., & Caplans, J. (1976). *Decisions decisions: Game theory and you*. New York: W. W. Norton.

Bereiter, C. (1984). How to keep thinking skills from going the way of all frills. *Educational Leadership, 42,* 75–77.

Berlin, B., & Kay, P. (1969). *Basic color terms: Their universality and evolution*. Berkeley: University of California Press.

Berliner, H. J. (1977). Some necessary conditions for a master chess program. In P. N. Johnson-Laird & P. C. Wason (Eds.), *Thinking: Readings in cognitive science*. England: Cambridge University Press.

Beyth-Marom, R., Dekel, S., Gombo, R., & Shaked, M. (1985). *An elementary approach to thinking under uncertainty*. Hillsdale, NJ: Lawrence Erlbaum Associates.

Black, H., & Black, S. (1985). *Book-3 Verbal building thinking skills*. Pacific Grove, CA: Midwest Publications.

Block, R. A. (1985). Education and thinking skills reconsidered. *American Psychologist, 40,* 574–575.

Block, R. A., & Taylor, S. V. (1984, August). Cognitive skills: Enhancement and assessment issues. In D. F. Halpern (Chair), *A psychological perspective on teaching thinking skills to college students*. Symposium conducted at the Annual Meeting of the American Psychological Association, Toronto, ON.

Bloom, B. S., & Broder, L. J. (1950). *Problem solving processes of college students*. IL: The University of Chicago Press.

Boring, E. G. (1932). Intelligence as the tests test it. *New Republic, 35,* 35–37.

Bourne, L. E., Ekstrand, B. R., & Dominowski, R. L. (1971). *The psychology of thinking*. Englewood Cliffs, NJ: Prentice-Hall.

Bousfield, W. A. (1953). The occurrence of clustering in the recall of randomly arranged associates. *Journal of General Psychology, 49,* 229–240.

Bower, G. H. (1970a). Analysis of a mnemonic device. *American Scientist, 58,* 496–510.

Bower, G. H. (1970b). Organizational factors in memory. *Cognitive Psychology, 1,* 18–46.

Bower, G. H. (1972). Mental imagery and associative learning. In L. Gregg (Ed.), *Cognition in learning and memory.* New York: Wiley.

Bower, G. H. (1981). Mood and memory. *American Psychologist, 36,* 129–148.

Bower, G. H. (1987). Commentary on mood and memory. *Behavior Research Therapy, 25,* 443–455.

Bower, G. H., & Cirilo, R. K. (1985). Cognitive psychology and text processing. In *Handbook of discourse analysis, Vol. 1* (pp. 71–105). New York: Academic Press, Inc.

Bower, G. H., & Clark, M. C. (1969). Narrative stories as mediators for serial learning. *Psychonomic Science, 14,* 181–182.

Braine, M. D. S. (1978). On the relation between the natural logic of reasoning and standard logic. *Psychological Review, 85,* 1–21.

Bransford, D. (1979). *Human cognition: Learning, understanding and remembering.* Belmont, CA: Wadsworth Publishing Company.

Bransford, J. D., Arbitman-Smith, R., Stein, B. S., & Vye, N. J. (1985). Improving thinking and learning skills: An analysis of three approaches. In J. W. Segal & S. F. Chipman (Eds.), *Thinking and learning skills: vol. 1. Relating instruction to research* (pp. 133–206). Hillsdale, NJ: Lawrence Erlbaum Associates.

Bransford, J. D., & Johnson, M. K. (1972). Contextual prerequisites for understanding: Some investigations of comprehension and recall. *Journal of Verbal Learning and Verbal Behavior, 11,* 717–726.

Bransford, J. D., & Johnson, M. K. (1973). Considerations of some problems of comprehension. In W. G. Chase (Ed.), *Visual information processing.* New York: Academic Press.

Bransford, J. D., Sherwood, R., Vye, N., & Rieser, J. (1986). Teaching thinking and problem solving: Research foundations. *American Psychologist, 41,* 1078–1089.

Bransford, J. D., & Stein, B. S. (1984). *The ideal problem solver: A guide for improving thinking, learning, and creativity.* New York: Freeman.

Brehm, J. W. (1956). Postdecision changes in the desirability of alternatives. *Journal of Abnormal and Social Psychology, 52,* 384–389.

Brehmer, B., Jungermann, H., Lourens, P., & Sevon, G. (1986). *New directions in research on decision making.* Amsterdam: North Holland.

Brim, O. G., Jr. (1966). High and low self-estimates of intelligence. In O. G. Brim, Jr., R. S. Crutchfield, & W. H. Holtzman (Eds.), *Intelligence: Perspectives 1965.* New York: Harcourt, Brace & World.

Britton, B. K., & Black, J. B. (Eds.). (1985). *Understanding expository text: A theoretical and practical handbook for analyzing explanatory text.* Hillsdale, NJ: Lawrence Erlbaum Associates.

Brody, J. E. (1988, March 30). Unresolved relationship: Breast cancer, dietary fat. *San Francisco Chronicle,* 2–3.

Brooks, L. W., & Dansereau, D. F. (1983). Effects of structural schema training and text organization on expository prose processing. *Journal of Educational Psychology, 75,* 811–821.

Brooks, L. W., Simutis, Z. M., & O'Neil, H. F., Jr. (1985). The role of individual differences in learning strategies research. In R. F. Dillon (Ed.), *Individual differences in cognition* (Vol. 2, pp. 219–251). New York: Academic Press, Inc.

Bross, I. D. J. (1973). Languages in cancer research. In G. P. Murphy, D. Pressman, & E. A. Mirand (Eds.), *Perspectives in cancer research and treatment* (pp. 213–221), New York: Alan R. Liss.

Brown, R. (1958). *Words and things.* New York: The Free Press.

Bruner, J. S. (1957). On going beyond the information given. In *Contemporary approaches to cognition* (pp. 41–69). Cambridge, MA: Harvard University Press.

Bruner, J. S., Goodnow, J. J., & Austin, G. A. (1956). *A study of thinking.* New York: Wiley.

Bugliosi, V. (1978). *Till death do us part.* New York: Bantam Books.

Camer, R. (1983). Dubious fact. *Psychology Today, 17,* 73.

Campbell, S. K. (1974). *Flaws and fallacies in statistical thinking.* Englewood Cliffs, NJ: Prentice-Hall.

Carey, J., Foltz, K., & Allan, R. A. (1983, February 7). The mind of the machine. *Newsweek.*

Carkhuff, R. R. (1973). *The art of problem solving.* Amherst, MA: Human Resource Development Press.

Carpenter, E. J. (1981). Piagetian interviews of college students. In R. G. Fuller, et al. (Eds.), *Piagetian programs in higher education* (pp. 15–22). Lincoln: University of Nebraska.

Carroll, D. W. (1986). *Psychology of language.* Belmont, CA: Brooks/Cole.

Catrambone, R., & Holyoak, K. J. (1987, November). Procedural variability and transfer in problem solving. Paper presented at the Twenty-eighth Meeting of the Psychonomic Society, Seattle, Washington.

Cattell, R. B. (1971). *Abilities: Their structure, growth and action.* Boston: Houghton-Mifflin.

Ceraso, J., & Protivera, A. (1971). Sources of error in syllogistic reasoning. *Cognitive Psychology, 2,* 400–410.

Chance, P. (1986). *Thinking in the classroom: A survey of programs.* Columbia University, NY: Teachers College Press.

Chapman, L. J., & Chapman, J. P. (1959). Atmosphere effect reexamined. *Journal of Experimental Psychology, 58,* 220–226.

Chapman, L. J., & Chapman, J. P. (1967). The genesis of popular but erroneous psychodiagnostic observations. *Journal of Abnormal Psychology, 72,* 193–204.

Chapman, L. J., & Chapman, J. P. (1969). Illusory correlation as an obstacle to the use of valid psychodiagnostic signs. *Journal of Abnormal Psychology, 74,* 271–280.

Chase, S. (1948). *The proper study of mankind.* New York: Harper & Row.

Cheng, P. W., & Holyoak, K. J. (1985). Pragmatic reasoning schemas. *Cognitive Psychology, 17,* 391–416.

Cherry, E. C. (1953). Some experiments on the recognition of speech with one and two ears. *Journal of the Acoustical Society of America, 25,* 975–979.

Chesler, P. (1972). *Women and madness.* NY: Doubleday.

Chi, M. T. H., Glaser, R., & Rees, E. (1982). Expertise in problem solving. In R. S. Sternberg (Ed.), *Advances in the psychology of human intelligence* (Vol. 1, pp. 7–75). Hillsdale, NJ: Lawrence Erlbaum Associates.

Cialdini, R. B. (1988). *Influence: Science and practice* (2nd ed.). Glenview, IL: Scott, Foresman & Company.

Clancey, W. J. (1983). Guidon. *Journal of Computer-Based Instruction, 10,* 8–15.

Clancey, W. J. (1987). *Knowledge-based tutoring: The GUIDON program.* Cambridge, MA: MIT Press.

Clark, H. H., & Clark, E. V. (1977). *Psychology and language: An introduction to psycholinguistics.* New York: Harcourt Brace Jovanovich.

Clark, H. H., & Haviland, S. E. (1977). Comprehension and the given–new contract. In R. O. Freedle (Ed.), *Discourse production and comprehension.* Norwood, NJ: Ablex Publishing.

Clarkson-Smith, L., & Halpern, D. F. (1983). Can age related deficits in spatial memory be attenuated through the use of verbal coding? *Experimental Aging Research, 9,* 179–184.

Cohen, J. (1973). *Psychological probability or the art of doubt.* Cambridge, MA: Schenkman Publishing Co.

Collea, F. P. & Nummedal, S. (1980). *Development of reasoning in science (DORIS): A course in abstract thinking* (Tech. Rep.). School of Mathematics, Science and Engineering: California State University, Fullerton.

Copi, I. M. (1986). *Informal logic.* New York: Macmillan.

Cordes, C. (1983, April). Search goes on for "best" ways to learn science. *American Psychological Association Monitor,* pp. 7–8.

Covington, M. V. (1987). Instruction in problem solving and planning. In S. L. Friedman, E. K. Scholnick, & R. R. Cocking (Eds.), *Blueprints for thinking: The role of planning in cognitive development* (pp. 469–511). Cambridge, MA: Cambridge University Press.

Covington, M. V., Crutchfield, R. S., Davies, L. B., & Olton, R. M., Jr. (1974). *The productive thinking program.* Columbus, OH: Charles E. Merrill.

Crovitz, H. F. (1970). *Galton's walk: Methods for the analysis of thinking, intelligence and creativity.* New York: Harper & Row.

Crutchfield, R. S. (1966). Creative thinking in children: Its teaching and testing. In O. G. Brim, Jr., R. S. Crutchfield, & W. H. Holtzman (Eds.), *Intelligence: Perspectives 1965, The Terman-Otis memorial lectures.* New York: Harcourt, Brace & World.

Cyert, R. M. (1980). Problem solving and educational policy. In D. T. Tuma, & F. Reif (Eds.), *Problem solving and education: Issues in teaching and research.* Hillsdale, NJ: Lawrence Erlbaum Associates.

Damer, T. E. (1987). *Attacking faulty reasoning* (2nd ed.). Belmont, CA: Wadsworth.

d'Angelo, E. (1971). *The teaching of critical thinking.* Amsterdam: B. R. Gruner.

Dansereau, D. F., Collins, K. W., McDonald, B. A., Holley, C. D., Garland, J., Diekoff, G., & Evans, S. H. (1979). Development and evaluation of a learning strategy training program. *Journal of Educational Psychology, 71,* 64–73.

Davis, G. A., & Roweton, W. (1968). Using idea checklists with college students: Overcoming resistance. *Journal of Psychology, 70,* 221–226.

Davis, G. A., & Scott, J. A. (Eds.). (1971). *Training creative thinking.* New York: Holt, Rinehart and Winston.

Dawes, R. (1988). *Rational choice in an uncertain world.* New York: Harcourt, Brace, Jovanovich.

DeBono, E. (1967a). *The use of lateral thinking.* Great Britain: Ebenezer Bayles and Son, Limited.

DeBono, E. (1967b). *The five day course in thinking.* New York: Basic Books.

DeBono, E. (1968). *New think: The use of lateral thinking in the generation of new ideas.* New York: Basic Books.

DeBono, E. (1976). *Teaching thinking.* London: Temple Smith.

DeBono, E. (1977). Information processing and new ideas—lateral and vertical thinking. In S. J. Parnes, R. B. Noller, & A. M. Biondi (Eds.), *Guide to creative action: Revised edition of creative behavior guidebook.* New York: Charles Scribner's Sons.

deGroot, A. A. (1983). Heuristics, mental programs, and intelligence. In R. Groner, M. Groner, & W. F. Bischof (Eds.), *Methods of heuristics* (pp. 109–129). Hillsdale, NJ: Lawrence Erlbaum Associates.

deGroot, A. D. (1966). Perception and memory versus thought: Some old ideas and recent findings. In B. Kleinmuntz (Ed.), *Problem solving: Research, method and theory.* New York: Wiley.

Dee-Lucas, D., & Larkin, J. H. (1988). Attentional strategies for studying scientific texts. *Memory and Cognition, 16,* 469–479.

Dember, W. N., Jenkins, J. J., & Teykler, T. (1984). *General psychology* (2nd ed.). Hillsdale, NJ: Lawrence Erlbaum Associates.

DeSoto, C. G., London, M., & Handel, S. (1965). Social reasoning and spatial paralogic. *Journal of Personality and Social Psychology, 2,* 513–521.

Detterman, D. K., & Sternberg, R. J. (1982). *How and how much can intelligence be increased?* Norwood, NJ: Ablex Publishing.

Dewey, J. (1933). *How we think.* New York: D. C. Heath.

Dillon, R. F., & Sternberg, R. J. (Eds.). (1986). *Cognition and instruction*. San Diego, CA: Academic Press.

Dorner, D. (1983). Heuristics and cognition in complex systems. In R. Groner, M. Groner, & W. F. Bischof (Eds.), *Methods of heuristics* (pp. 89–107). Hillsdale, NJ: Lawrence Erlbaum Associates.

Dremen, D. (1979). *Contrarian investment strategy: The psychology of the stock market success*. New York: Random House.

Drew, C. J. (1976). *Introduction to designing research and evaluation*. Saint Louis: C. V. Mosby Co.

Duncan, C. P. (1961). Attempts to influence performance on an insight problem. *Psychological Reports, 9*, 35–42.

Duncker, K. (1945). On problem solving. *Psychological Monographs*, (Whole No. 270) 1–113.

Edwards, J., & Baldauf, B., Jr. (1987). The effects of the CoRT-1 thinking skills program on students. In D. N. Perkins, J. Lockhead, & J. Bishop (Eds.), *Thinking: The second international conference* (pp. 453–473). Hillsdale, NJ: Lawrence Erlbaum Associates.

Edwards, M. W. (1968). A survey of problem solving courses. *Journal of Creative Behavior, 2*, 33–51.

Einhorn, H. J., & Hogarth, R. M. (1978). Confidence in judgment: Persistence of the illusion of validity. *Psychological Review, 85*, 395–416.

Elstein, A. S., Shulman, L. S., & Sprafka, S. A. (1978). *Medical problem solving: An analysis of clinical reasoning*. Cambridge, MA: Harvard University Press.

Erickson, J. R., & Jones, M. R. (1978). Thinking. *Annual Review of Psychology, 29*, 61–91.

Estes, W. K. (1976). The cognitive side of probability learning. *Psychological Review, 83*, 37–64.

Evans, J., St. B. T. (1982). *The psychology of deductive reasoning*. London: Routledge & Kegan Paul.

Ferguson, G. (1981). Architecture. In N. L. Smith (Ed.), *Metaphors for evaluation: Sources of new methods*. Beverly Hills, CA: Sage Publications.

Festinger, L. (1957). *A theory of cognitive dissonance*. CA: Standford University Press.

Festinger, L. (Ed.). (1964). *Conflict, decision and dissonance*. CA: Stanford University Press.

Festinger, L., Riecken, H. H., & Schacter, S. (1956). *When prophecy fails*. Minneapolis: University of Minnesota Press.

Feyerabend, P. (1975). *Against method*. London: Verso.

Fischer, D. H. (1970). *Historians' fallacies*. London: Routledge & Kegan Paul.

Fischer, G. W., & Johnson, E. J. (1986). Behavioral decision theory and political decision making. In R. R. Lau & D. O. Sears (Eds.), *The 19th Annual Carnegie Symposium on Cognition: Political Cognition* (pp. 55–65). Hillsdale, NJ: Lawrence Erlbaum Associates.

Fischhoff, B. (1975). Hindsight ≠ foresight: The effect of outcome knowledge on judgment under uncertainty. *Journal of Experimental Psychology: Human Perception and Performance, 1*, 288–299.

Fischhoff, B., Lichtenstein, S., Slovic, P., Derby, S. L., & Keeney, R. L. (1981). *Acceptable risk*. Cambridge, England: Cambridge University Press.

Fiske, S. T., & Taylor, S. E. (1984). *Social cognition*. New York: Random House.

Fixx, J. F. (1978). *Solve it*. New York: Doubleday.

Flesch, R. (1951). *The art of clear thinking*. New York: Harper & Row.

Fogelin, R. J. (1987). *Understanding arguments, an introduction to informal logic* (3rd ed.). New York: Harcourt Brace Jovanovich.

Fox, L. S., Marsh, G., & Crandall, Jr., J. C. (1983, April 30). *The effect of college classroom experiences on formal operational thinking*. Paper presented at the 1983 Annual Convention of the Western Psychological Association, San Francisco, CA.

Frederiksen, N. (1986). Toward a broader conception of human intelligence. *American Psychologist, 41*, 445–452.

Friedman, S. L., Scholnick, E. K., & Cocking, R. R. (Eds.). (1987). *Blueprints for thinking: The role of planning in cognitive development.* Cambridge, MA: Cambridge University Press.

Gagné, E. D. (1985). *The cognitive psychology of school learning.* Boston: Little, Brown.

Galambos, J. A., Abelson, R. P., & Black, J. B. (Eds.). (1986). *Knowledge structures.* Hillsdale, NJ: Lawrence Erlbaum Associates.

Gardner, H. (1982). *Art, mind and brain: A cognitive approach to creativity.* NY: Basic Books.

Gardner, H. (1983). *Frames of mind: The theory of multiple intelligences.* NY: Basic Books.

Gardner, H. (1985). *The mind's new science: A history of the cognitive revolution.* NY: Basic Books.

Gardner, M. (1978). *Aha! Insight.* New York: W. H. Freeman.

Geiselman, R. E., & Fisher, R. P. (1985, December). Interviewing victims and witnesses of crime. *Research in Brief, National Institute of Justice,* 1–4.

Gentner, D., & Gentner, D. R. (1983). Flowing water or teeming crowds: Mental models of electricity. In D. Gentner & A. L. Stevens (Eds.), *Mental models.* Hillsdale, NJ: Lawrence Erlbaum Associates.

Ghiselin, B. (Ed.). (1952). *The creative process.* Berkeley: University of California Press. (Reprinted in 1955, New York: Mentor Books)

Gick, M. L., & Holyoak, K. J. (1980). Analogical problem solving. *Cognitive Psychology, 12,* 306–355.

Gifford-Jones, W. (1977). *What every woman should know about hysterectomy.* New York: Funk & Wagnalls.

Gilhooly, K. J. (1987). Mental modeling: A framework for the study of thinking. In D. N. Perkins, J. Lochhead, & J. Bishop (Eds.), *Thinking: The second international conference* (pp. 19–32). Hillsdale, NJ: Lawrence Erlbaum Associates.

Gillette, R. (1987, December 4). Exotic ways to learn doubted by U.S. study. *Wall Street Journal,* pp. 1, 32.

Glaser, R. (1984). Education and thinking: The role of knowledge. *American Psychologist, 39,* 93–104.

Glucksberg, S., & Weisberg, R. W. (1966). Verbal behavior and problem solving: Some effects of labeling in a functional fixedness problem. *Journal of Experimental Psychology, 71,* 659–664.

Gordon, W. J. J. (1961). *Synectics.* New York: Harper & Row.

Gordon, W. J. J. (1976). Metaphor and invention. In A. Rothenberg, & C. R. Hausman (Eds.), *The creativity question.* Durham, NC: Duke University Press.

Gould, S. (1981). *The mismeasure of man.* New York: W. W. Norton.

Govier, T. (1985). *A practical study of argument.* Belmont, CA: Wadsworth.

Greeno, J. G. (1973). The structure of memory and the process of solving problems. In R. L. Solso (Ed.), *Contemporary issues in cognitive psychology.* Washington DC: Winston.

Greeno, J. G. (1977). Process of understanding in problem solving. In N. J. Castellan, Jr., D. B. Pisoni, & G. R. Potts (Eds.), *Cognitive theory* (Vol. 2). Hillsdale, NJ: Lawrence Erlbaum Associates.

Gregory, R. L. (1981). *Mind in science.* England: Cambridge University Press.

Griffiths, D. H. (1976). Physics teaching: Does it hinder intellectual development? *American Journal of Physics, 44,* 81–85.

Gruneberg, M. M., & Morris, P. E. (Eds.). (1979). *Applied problems in memory.* New York: Academic Press.

Guilford, J. P. (1962). Creativity: Its measurement and development. In S. J. Parnes, & H. F. Harding (Eds.), *A source book for creative thinking.* New York: McGraw-Hill.

Guilford, J. P. (1967). *The nature of human intelligence.* New York: McGraw-Hill.

Guilford, J. P. (1977). *Way beyond the IQ.* Buffalo, NY: Creative Education Foundation.

Gunther, M. (1977). *The luck factor.* New York: MacMillan.

Guyote, M. J., & Sternberg, R. J. (1981). A transitive-chain theory in syllogistic reasoning. *Cognitive Psychology, 13,* 461–525.

Hadamard, J. (1945). *The psychology of invention in the mathematical field.* NJ: Princeton University Press.

Halpern, D. F. (1985). The influence of sex role stereotypes on prose recall. *Sex Roles, 12,* 363–375.

Halpern, D. F. (1986). *Sex differences in cognitive abilities.* Hillsdale, NJ: Lawrence Erlbaum Associates.

Halpern, D. F. (1987a). Analogies as a critical thinking skill. In D. Berger, K. Peydek, & W. Banks (Eds.), *Applications of cognitive psychology: Computing and education* (pp. 75–86). Hillsdale, NJ: Lawrence Erlbaum Associates.

Halpern, D. F. (1987b). Thinking across the disciplines: Methods and strategies to promote higher-order thinking in every classroom. In M. Heiman & J. Slomianko (Eds.), *Thinking skills instruction: Concepts and techniques* (pp. 69–76). Washington, DC: National Education Association.

Halpern, D. F., & Blackman, S. (1985). Magazines vs. physicians. The influence of information source on intentions to use oral contraceptives. *Women and Health, 10,* 9–23.

Halpern, D. F., Blackman, S., & Salzman, B. (in press). Using statistical risk information to assess oral contraceptive safety. *Applied Cognitive Psychology.*

Halpern, D. F., & Irwin, F. W. (1973). Selection of hypotheses as affected by their preference values. *Journal of Experimental Psychology, 101,* 105–108.

Halpern, H. (1983). *Development and construct validation of a multidimensional scale of attitudes toward homosexuality.* Unpublished doctoral dissertation, University of Cincinnati, OH.

Hammond, K. R., McClelland, G. H., & Mumpower, J. (1980). *Human judgment and decision making.* New York: Praeger Publishers.

Hansen, C. C., & Halpern, D. F. (1987). *Using analogies to improve comprehension and recall of scientific passages.* Paper presented at the 28th Annual Meeting of the Psychonomic Society, Seattle, WA.

Hanson, N. R. (1958). *Patterns of discovery.* England: Cambridge University Press.

Harman, G. (1986). *Change in view: Principles of reasoning.* Cambridge, MA: MIT Press.

Harris, R. J. (1977). Comprehension and pragmatic implications in advertising. *Journal of Applied Psychology, 62,* 603–608.

Hayes, J. R. (1978). *Cognitive psychology.* Homewood, IL: Dorsey Press.

Hayes, J. R. (1981). *The complete problem solver.* Philadelphia: The Franklin Institute Press.

Hayes, J. R. (1982). Issues in protocol analysis. In G. R. Ungson & D. N. Braunstein (Eds.), *Decision making: An interdisciplinary approach.* Boston: Kent Publishing Co.

Heiman, M., & Slomianko, J. (1986). *Critical thinking skills.* Washington, DC: National Education Association.

Heller, J. I., & Reif, F. (1984). Prescribing effective human problem solving practices: Problem description in physics. *Cognition and Instruction, 1,* 177–216.

Henle, M. (1962). On the relation between logic and thinking. *Psychological Review, 69,* 366–378.

Hennessey, B. A., & Amabile, T. M. (1987). *Creativity and learning.* Washington, DC: National Education Association.

Herrnstein, R. J. (August, 1982). I.Q. testing and the media. *The Atlantic, 250,* 68.

Herrnstein, R. J., Nickerson, R. S., de Sanchez, M., & Swets, J. A. (1986). Teaching thinking skills. *American Psychologist, 41,* 1279–1289.

Hiebert, J. (Ed.), (1986). *Conceptual and procedural knowledge: The case of mathematics.* Hillsdale, NJ: Lawrence Erlbaum Associates.

Hill, P., Bedau, H., Checile, R., Crochetiere, W., Kellerman, B., Dunjian, D., Pauker, S., & Rubin, J. (1979). *Making decisions: A multidisciplinary introduction.* Reading, MA: Addison-Wesley.

Hitchcock, D. (1983). *Critical thinking: A guide to evaluating information.* Toronto, Canada: Methuen Publications.

Hogarth, R. M. (1988). *Judgment and choice: The psychology of decision* (2nd ed.). Chichester: Wiley.

Holland, J. H., Holyoak, K. J., Nisbett, R. E., & Thagard, P. R. (1986). *Induction: Processes of Inference, Learning, and Discovery.* Cambridge, MA: The MIT Press.

Holley, C. D., & Dansereau, D. F. (1984). Networking: The technique and the empirical evidence. In C. D. Holley & D. F. Dansereau (Eds.), *Spatial learning strategies: Techniques, applications, and related issues* (pp. 81–108). New York: Academic Press.

Holley, C. D., & Dansereau, D. F. (Eds.). (1984). *Spacial learning strategies: Techniques, applications, and related issues.* New York: Academic Press.

Holley, C. D., Dansereau, D. F., McDonald, B. A., Garland, J. D., & Collins, K. W. (1979). Evaluation of a hierarchical mapping technique as an aid to prose processing. *Contemporary Educational Psychology, 4,* 227–237.

Holt, J. (1964). *How children fail.* New York: Dell.

Hostetler, A. J. (1988, January). Army eyes novel learning methods. *The American Psychological Association Monitor, 19,* 7.

Huff, D. (1954). *How to lie with statistics.* New York: W. W. Norton & Company.

Hunt, M. (1982). *The universe within: A new science explores the human mind.* New York: Simon & Schuster.

Hutchings, P. (1986). Some late night thoughts on teaching creativity. *American Association for Higher Education, 39,* 9–14.

Inhelder, B., & Piaget, J. (1958). *The growth of logical thinking from childhood to adolescence.* New York: Basic Books.

Janis, I. L., & Mann, L. (1977). *Decision making: A psychological analysis of conflict, choice and commitment.* New York: The Free Press.

Janvier, C. (Ed.). (1987). *Problems of representation in the teaching and learning of mathematics.* Hillsdale, NJ: Lawrence Erlbaum Associates.

Jason, G. (1987). Are fallacies common? A look at two debates. *Informal Logic, 8,* 81–92.

Jensen, A. R. (1980). *Bias in mental testing.* New York: The Free Press.

Jensen, A. R. (1981). *Straight talk about mental tests.* New York: The Free Press.

Johnson, D. M. (1972). *A systematic introduction to the psychology of thinking.* New York: Harper and Row.

Johnson, M. K., & Raye, C. L. (1981). Reality monitoring. *Psychological Review, 88,* 67–85.

Johnson-Laird, P. N., Legrenzi, P., & Legrenzi, M. (1972). Reasoning and a sense of reality. *British Journal of Psychology, 63,* 395–400.

Johnson-Laird, P. N., & Steedman, M. (1978). The psychology of syllogisms. *Cognitive Psychology, 10,* 64–99.

Johnson-Laird, P. N., & Wason, P. C. (1970). A theoretical analysis of insight into a reasoning task. *Cognitive Psychology, 1,* 134–148.

Johnson-Laird, P. N., & Wason, P. C. (Eds.). (1977). *Thinking: Readings in cognitive science.* England: Cambridge University Press.

Kahane, H. (1980). *Logic and contemporary rhetoric: The use of reason in everyday life* (3rd ed.). Belmont, CA: Wadsworth Publishing Company.

Kahane, H. (1988). *Logic and contemporary rhetoric: The use of reason in everyday life* (5th ed.). Belmont, CA: Wadsworth Publishing Company.

Kahneman, D., & Tversky, A. (1972). Subjective probability: A judgment of representativeness. *Cognitive Psychology, 3,* 430–454.

Kahneman, D., & Tversky, A. (1973). On the psychology of prediction. *Psychological Review, 80,* 237–251.

Kahneman, D., & Tversky, A. (1979). Prospect theory: An analysis of decision under risk. *Econometrica, 47,* 263–291.

Kamin, L. J. (1974). *The science and politics of I.Q.* New York: Wiley.

Kaplin, M. F., & Schwartz, S. (Eds.). (1975). *Human judgment and decision processes.* New York: Academic Press.

Karplus, R., Karplus, E., & Wollman, W. (1974). Intellectual development beyond elementary school IV: Ratio, the influence of cognitive style. *School Science and Mathematics, 74,* 476–482.

Kavanagh, D. J., & Bower, G. H. (1985). Mood and self-efficacy: Impact of joy and sadness on perceived capabilities. *Cognitive Therapy & Research, 9,* 507–525.

Kelley, D. (1988). *The art of reasoning.* New York: W. W. Norton.

Kerlinger, F. N. (1987). *Behavioral research: A conceptual approach* (2nd ed.). New York: Holt, Rinehart & Winston.

Kimble, G. A. (1978). *How to use (and misuse) statistics.* Englewood Cliffs, NJ: Prentice-Hall.

Kintsch, W., & van Dijk, T. A. (1978). Toward a model of text comprehension and production. *Psychological Review, 85,* 363–394.

Klatzky, R. L. (1980). *Human memory: Structures and processes* (2nd ed.). San Francisco: Freeman.

Klein, G. A., & Weizenfeld, J. (1978). Improvement of skills for solving ill-defined problems. *Educational Psychologist, 13,* 31–41.

Kneller, G. F. (1965). *The art and science of creativity.* New York: Holt, Rinehart & Winston.

Koestler, A. (1964). *The act of creation.* London: Hutchinson.

Kohl, H. (1981). *A book of puzzlements: Play and invention with language.* New York: Schocken Books.

Köhler, W. (1925). *The mentality of apes.* New York: Harcourt, Brace & World.

Köhler, W. (1969). *The task of Gestalt psychology.* NJ: Princeton University Press.

Kunda, Z., & Nisbett, R. E. (1986). The psychometrics of everyday life. *Cognitive Psychology, 18,* 195–224.

Kyburg, H. E., & Smoker, H. E. (Eds.). (1980). *Studies in subjective probability* (2nd ed.). Melbourne, FL: Krieger.

Langer, E. J., Blank, A., & Chanowitz, B. (1978). The mindlessness of ostensibly thoughtful action: The role of "placebic" information in interpersonal interaction. *Journal of Personality and Social Psychology, 36,* 635–642.

Lau, D. R., & Sears, D. O. (Eds.). (1986). *Political cognition: The 19th Annual Carnegie Symposium on Cognition.* Hillsdale, NJ: Erlbaum.

Lee, A. M. (1953). *How to understand propaganda.* New York: Rinehart & Co.

Leedy, P. D. (1981). *How to read research and understand it.* New York: MacMillan.

Lesgold, A. (1988). Problem solving. In R. J. Sternberg & E. E. Smith (Eds.), *The psychology of human thought* (pp. 188–213). New York: Cambridge University Press.

Levine, M. (1988). *Effective problem solving.* Englewood Cliffs, NJ: Prentice-Hall.

Lewin, M. (1979). *Understanding psychological research.* New York: Wiley.

Lewis, A. B., & Mayer, R. E. (1987). Students' miscomprehension of relational statements in arithmetic words problems. *Journal of Educational Psychology, 79,* 363–371.

Lichtenstein, S., Slovic, P., Fischoff, B., Layman, M., & Combs, B. (1978). Judged frequency of lethal events. *Journal of Experimental Psychology: Human Learning and Memory, 4,* 551–578.

Lindsay, P. H., & Norman, D. A. (1977). *Human information processing: An introduction to psychology* (2nd ed.). New York: Academic Press.

Linn, M. C. (1986). Science. In R. F. Dillon & R. J. Steinberg (Eds.), *Cognition and instruction* (pp. 155–204). New York: Academic Press.

Lochhead, J., & Clement, J. (Eds.). (1979). *Cognitive process instruction: Research on teaching thinking skills.* Philadelphia, PA: Franklin Institute Press.

Lochhead, J. (1984, August). The use of writing for developing mathematical reasoning. In D. F. Halpern (Chair), *A psychological perspective on teaching thinking skills to college students.* Symposium conducted at the Annual Meeting of the American Psychological Association, Toronto, ON.

Loftus, E. F. (1975). Leading questions and the eyewitness report. *Cognitive Psychology, 7,* 560–572.

Loftus, E. F. (1979). *Eyewitness testimony.* Cambridge, MA: Harvard University Press.

Loftus, E. F. (1980). *Memory: Surprising new insights into how we remember and why we forget.* Reading, MA: Addison-Wesley.

Loftus, G. R., & Loftus, E. F. (1976). *Human memory: The processing of information.* Hillsdale, NJ: Lawrence Erlbaum Associates.

Loftus, G. R., & Loftus, E. F. (1982). *Essence of statistics.* Monterey, CA: Brooks/Cole Publishing Co.

Loisette, A. (1896). *Assimilative memory or how to attend and never forget.* New York: Funk & Wagnalls

Lopes, L. L. (1982). Doing the impossible: A note on induction and the experience of randomness. *Journal of Experimental Psychology: Learning, Memory & Cognition, 8,* 626–636.

Lorayne, H. (1975). *Remembering people.* New York: Stein & Day.

Lorayne, H., & Lucas, J. (1974). *The memory book.* New York: Stein & Day (Also published in paperback by Ballantine Books, 1975)

Lowenfeld, V. (1962). Creativity: Education's stepchild. In S. J. Parnes & H. F. Harding (Eds.), *A source book for creative thinking.* New York: Charles Scribner's Sons.

Luchins, A. S. (1942). Mechanization in problem solving: The effect of Einstellung. *Psychological Monographs, 54:6,* (Whole No. 248).

Luria, A. R. (1968). *The mind of a mnemonist.* New York: Basic Books.

Maier, N. R. F. (1931). Reasoning in humans II: The solution of a problem and its appearance in consciousness. *Journal of Comparative Psychology, 12,* 181–194.

Mandler, G. (1975). *Mind and emotion.* New York: Wiley.

Mann, L. (1972). Use of a "balance sheet" procedure to improve the quality of personal decision making: A field experiment with college applicants. *Journal of Vocational Behavior, 2,* 291–300.

Markle, S. M. (1977). Teaching conceptual networks. *Journal of Instructional Development, 1,* 13–17.

Marsh, J. G., & Shapira, Z. (1982). Behavioral decision theory and organizational decision theory. In G. R. Ungson, & D. N. Braunstein (Eds.), *Decision making: An interdisciplinary inquiry.* Boston, MA: Kent Publishing Co.

Mayer, R. E. (1983). *Thinking, problem solving, cognition.* New York: W. H. Freeman.

Mayer, R. E. (1986). Mathematics. In R. F. Dillon & R. J. Sternberg (Eds.), *Cognition and instruction* (pp. 127–154). New York: Academic Press.

Mayer, R. E. (1987). *Educational psychology: A cognitive approach.* Boston: Little, Brown.

Mayer, R. E. (1988, August). *Teaching for thinking: Research on the teachability of thinking skills.* G. Stanley Hall Lecture presented at the Annual Meeting of the American Psychological Association, Atlanta, Georgia.

Mayer, R. E. (1989, January). Teaching of thinking skills in the sciences and mathematics. In D. F. Halpern (Chair), *Development of thinking skills in the sciences and mathematics.* Symposium presented at the Annual Meeting of the American Association for the Advancement of Science, San Francisco, CA.

Mayer, R. E., Dyck, J. L., & Cook, L. K. (1984). Techniques that help readers build mental models from scientific text: Definitions pretraining and signaling. *Journal of Educational Psychology, 76,* 1089–1105.

McCormick, C. B., & Levin, J. R. (1987). Mnemonic prose-learning strategies. In M. A.

McDaniel & M. Pressley (Eds.), *Imagery and related mnemonic processes* (pp. 392–406). New York: Springer-Verlag.

McDaniel, M. A., & Pressley, M. (Eds.). (1987). *Imagery and related mnemonic processes*. New York: Springer-Verlag.

McDonald, K. (1987, November 4). Science and mathematics leaders call for radical reform in calculus teaching. *The Chronicle of Higher Education, xxxiv,* A-1, A-23.

McGuigan, S., & Black, J. B. (1986). Creation and comprehension of arguments. In J. A. Galambos, R. P. Abelson, & J. B. Black (Eds.), *Knowledge structures* (pp. 237–257). Hillsdale, NJ: Lawrence Erlbaum Associates.

McGuire, W. J. (1981). The probabilogical model of cognitive structure and attitude change. In R. E. Petty, T. M. Ostrom, & T. C. Brock (Eds.), *Cognitive responses in persuasion*. Hillsdale, NJ: Lawrence Erlbaum Associates.

McKim, R. (1972). *Experiences in visual thinking*. Monterey, CA: Brooks/Cole.

McKim, R. H. (1980). *Thinking visually: A strategy manual for problem solving*. Belmont, CA: Wadsworth.

McKinnon, J. W. (1976). The college student and formal operations. In J. W. Renner, D. G. Stafford, A. E. Lawson, J. W. McKinnon, F. E. Friot, & D. H. Kellog (Eds.), *Research, training and learning with the Piaget model* (pp. 110–129). Norman: University of Oklahoma Press.

McKinnon, J. W., & Renner, J. W. (1971). Are colleges concerned with intellectual development? *American Journal of Psychology, 39,* 1047–1052.

McTighe, J. (1986). Thinking about adolescent thinking. *The early adolescence magazine, 1,* 7–13.

Mednick, S. A., & Mednick, M. T. (1967). *Remote associates test: Examiners manual*. Boston, MA: Houghton Mifflin.

Merron, K., Fisher, D., & Torbert, W. R. (1987). Meaning making and management action. *Group & Organization Studies, 12,* 274–286.

Meyer, B. J. F. (1975). *The organization of prose and the effect on recall*. Amsterdam: North Holland.

Miller, G. A. (1956). The magical number seven plus or minus two: Some limits on our capacity for processing information. *Psychological Review, 63,* 81–97.

Miller, J. E., Jr. (1972). *Word, self, reality: The rhetoric of imagination*. New York: Dodd, Mead.

Mitroff, I. I. (1974). Norms and counter-norms in a select group of the Apollo moon scientists: A case study of the ambivalence of scientists. *American Sociological Review, 39,* 579–595.

Moray, N. (1959). Attention in dichotic listening: Affective cues and the influence of instructions. *Quarterly Journal of Experimental Psychology, 11,* 56–60.

Morgan, J. J. B., & Morton, J. T. (1944). The distortion of syllogistic reasoning produced by personal convictions. *Journal of Social Psychology, 20,* 39–59.

Morlock, H. (1967). The effect of outcome desirability on information required for decision. *Behavioral Science, 12,* 269–300.

Morris, W. (Ed.). (1969). *The American Heritage dictionary of the English language*. Boston: Houghton Mifflin.

Moss, J. (1950). *How to win at poker*. Garden City, NJ: Garden City Books.

Mumford, M. D., Gustafson, S. B. (1988). Creativity syndrome: Integration, application, and innovation. *Psychological Bulletin, 103,* 27–43.

Munby, H. (1982). *Science in the schools*. Toronto: University of Toronto.

Munson, R. (1976). *The way of words*. Boston, MA: Houghton Mifflin.

Myers, D. G. (1986). *Psychology* (1st ed.). NY: Worth.

Mynatt, C. R., Doherty, M. E., & Tweney, R. D. (1978). Consequences of confirmation and disconfirmation in a simulated research environment. *Quarterly Journal of Experimental Psychology, 30,* 395–406.

National Commission on Excellence in Education. (1983). *A nation at risk: The imperative for educational reform*. Washington, DC: Author.

Neimark, E. D. (1975). Intellectual development during adolescence. In F. D. Horowitz (Ed.), *Review of Child Development Research* (Vol. 4). Chicago: University of Chicago Press.

Neisser, U. (1982). *Memory observed: Remembering in natural contexts*. San Francisco: W. H. Freeman.

Neustadt, R. E., & May, E. R. (1986). *Thinking in time: The uses of history for decision makers*. New York: The Free Press.

Newell, A. (1983). The heuristic of George Polya and its relation to artificial intelligence. In R. Groner, M. Groner, & W. F. Bischof (Eds.), *Methods of heuristics* (pp. 195–243). Hillsdale, NJ: Lawrence Erlbaum Associates.

Newell, A., & Simon, H. A. (1972). *Human problem solving*. Englewood Cliffs, NJ: Prentice-Hall.

Nickerson, R. S. (1986). *Reflections on reasoning*. Hillsdale, NJ: Lawrence Erlbaum Associates.

Nickerson, R. S. (1987). Why teach thinking? In J. B. Baron & R. J. Sternberg (Eds.), *Teaching thinking skills: Theory and practice* (pp. 27–37). New York: W. H. Freeman.

Nickerson, R. S. (in press). On improving thinking through instruction. *Review of Research in Education*.

Nickerson, R. S., & Adams, M. J. (1979). Long-term memory for a common object. *Cognitive Psychology, 11*, 287–307.

Nisbett, R. E., Krantz, D. H., Jepson, C., & Kunda, Z. (1983). The use of statistical heuristics in everyday inductive reasoning. *Psychological Review, 90*, 339–363.

Nisbett, R. E., & Ross, L. (1980). *Human inference: Strategies and shortcomings of social judgment*. Englewood Cliffs, NJ: Prentice-Hall.

Nisbett, R. E., & Wilson, T. D. (1977). Telling more than we can know: Verbal reports on mental processes. *Psychological Review, 7*, 231–259.

Nixon, R. M. (1962). *Six crises*. Garden City, NY: Doubleday.

Norman, D. A. (1976). *Memory and attention: An introduction to human information processing*. New York: Wiley.

Oppenheimer, J. R. (1956). Analogy in science. *American Psychologist, 11*, 127–135.

Ortho Pharmaceutical Corp. (1979). *The pill—After your doctor prescribes . . .* Raritan, NJ: Author.

Orwell, G. (1949). *1984*. New York: Harcourt, Brace.

Osborn, A. F. (1963). *Applied imagination: Principles and procedures of creative problem solving* (3rd revised edition). New York: Charles Scribner's Sons.

Osgood, C. E. (1953). *Method and theory in experimental psychology*. New York: Oxford University Press.

Oskamp, S. (1965). Overconfidence in case-study judgments. *Journal of Consulting Psychology, 29*, 261–265.

Palincsar, A. S., & Brown, A. L. (1984). Reciprocal teaching of comprehension-fostering and comprehension-monitoring activities. *Cognition and Instruction, 1*, 117–175.

Papanek, V. J. (1977). Tree of life: Bionics. In S. J. Parnes, R. B. Noller, & A. M. Biondi (Eds.), *Guide to creative action: Revised edition of creative behavior guidebook*. New York: Charles Scribner's Sons.

Parducci, A. (1968). The relativism of absolute judgments. *Scientific American, 219*, 84–90.

Parnes, S. J. (1967). *Creative behavior workbook*. New York: Scribner.

Parnes, S. J., & Harding, H. F. (Eds.). (1962). *A source book for creative thinking*. New York: Scribner.

Parnes, S. J., Noller, R. B., & Biondi, A. M. (1977). *Guide to creative action: Revised edition of creative behavior guidebook*. New York: Charles Scribner's Sons.

Pea, R. D., & Hawkins, J. (1987). Planning in a chore-scheduling task. In S. L. Friedman, E. K.

Scholnick, & R. R. Cocking (Eds.), *Blueprints for thinking: The role of planning in cognitive development* (pp. 273–302). Cambridge, MA: Cambridge University Press.

Perfetto, G. A., Bransford, J. D., & Franks, J. J. (1983). Constraints on access in a problem solving context. *Memory & Cognition, 11*, 24–31.

Perkins, D. N. (1981). *The mind's best work: A new psychology of creative thinking.* Cambridge, MA: Harvard University Press.

Perkins, D. N. (1985). Postprimary education has little impact on informal reasoning. *Journal of Educational Psychology, 77*, 562–571.

Perkins, D. N., Lochhead, J., & Bishop, J. C. (Eds.). (1987). *Thinking. The second international conference.* Hillsdale, NJ: Lawrence Erlbaum Associates.

Phillips, H. (1961). *My best puzzles in logic and reasoning.* New York: Dover Publications.

Piaget, J. (1962). *Play, dreams, and imitation in childhood.* New York: W. W. Norton.

Piaget, J. (1977). Intellectual evolution from adolescence to adulthood. In P. N. Johnson-Laird & P. C. Wason (Eds.), *Thinking: Readings in cognitive science.* England: Cambridge University Press.

Pickren, J. W., & Gamarra, M. C. (1975). Effects of smoking. In G. P. Murphy, D. Pressman, & E. A. Mirand (Eds.), *Perspectives in cancer research and treatment.* New York: Alan R. Liss, Inc.

Piper, D. (1985). Syllogistic reasoning in varied narrative contexts: Aspects of logical and linguistic development. *Journal of Psycholinguistic Research, 14*, 19–43.

Pitt, J., & Leavenworth, R. (1968). *Logic for argument.* New York: Random House.

Poincare, H. (1929). *The foundations of science.* New York: Science House.

Pollio, H. F., Barlow, J. M., Fine, H. J., & Pollio, M. R. (1977). *Psychology and the poetics of growth.* Hillsdale, NJ: Lawrence Erlbaum Associates.

Polya, G. (1945). *How to solve it: A new aspect of mathematical method.* New York: Doubleday.

Polya, G. (1957). *How to solve it: A new aspect of mathematical method* (2nd ed.). Garden City, NY: Doubleday.

Polya, G. (1962). *Mathematical discovery* (Vol. 1). New York: Wiley.

Posner, M. I. (1973). *Cognition: An introduction.* Glenview, IL: Scott, Foresman.

Potts, G. R. (1972). Information processing strategies used in the encoding of linear orderings. *Journal of Verbal Learning and Verbal Behavior, 11*, 727–740.

Prince, G. M. (1970). *The practice of creativity.* New York: Harper.

Quattrone, G. A., & Jones, E. E. (1980). The perception of variability within in-groups and out-groups: Implications for the law of small numbers. *Journal of Personality and Social Psychology, 38*, 141–152.

Raphael, B. (1976). *The thinking computer: Mind inside matter.* San Francisco: Freeman.

Reed, S. K. (1982). *Cognition: Theory and applications.* Monterey, CA: Brooks/Cole Publishing Co.

Renner, J. S. (1976). What this research says to schools. In J. W. Renner, D. G. Stafford, A. E. Lawson, J. W. McKinnon, F. E. Friot, & D. H. Kellogg (Eds.), *Research, teaching, and learning with the Piaget model* (pp. 174–191). Norman: Oklahoma University Press.

Resnick, L. B. (Ed.). (1976). *The nature of intelligence.* Hillsdale, NJ: Lawrence Erlbaum Associates.

Resnick, L. B. (1983). Mathematics and science learning: A new conception. *Science, 220*, 477–478.

Resnick, L. B. (1985). Cognition and instruction. In B. L. Hammonds (Ed.), *Psychology and learning: The master lecture series* (pp. 127–186). Washington, DC: American Psychological Association.

Rethan, J. (1979). *An investigation of consumer perceptions of product hazards.* Unpublished dissertation, University of Oregon.

Revlin, R., & Mayer, R. E. (1978). *Human reasoning.* Washington, DC: Winston.

Reyes, R. M., Thompson, W. C., & Bower, G. H. (1980). Judgmental biases resulting from differing availabilities of arguments. *Journal of Personality and Social Psychology, 39,* 2–12.

Rips, L. J. (1988). Deduction. In R. J. Sternberg & E. E. Smith (Eds.), *The psychology of human thought.* (pp. 116–152). New York: Cambridge University Press.

Robinson, F. P. (1946). *Effective study.* New York: Harper.

Rokeach, M. (1960). *The open and closed mind.* New York: Basic Books.

Rosch, E. (1977). Human categorization. In N. Warren (Ed.), *Studies in cross-cultural psychology (Vol. 1).* New York: Academic Press.

Rosenthal, R., & Fode, K. L. (1963). The effect of experimental bias on the performance of the albino rat. *Behavioral Science, 8,* 183–187.

Rosenthal, R., & Jacobson, L. (1968). *Pygmalion in the classroom. Teacher expectations and pupils' intellectual development.* New York: Holt.

Ross, J., Laurence, K. A. (1968). Some observations on memory artifice. *Psychonomic Science, 13,* 107–108.

Rubinstein, J., & Slife, B. D. (1982). *Taking sides: Clashing views on controversial psychological issues.* Guilford, CT: Dushkin Publishing Group.

Rubinstein, M. F. (1975). *Patterns of problem solving.* Englewood Cliffs, NJ: Prentice-Hall.

Rubinstein, M. F. (1980). A decade of experience in teaching an interdisciplinary problem-solving course. In D. J. Tuma & F. Reif (Eds.), *Problem solving and education: Issues in teaching and research.* Hillsdale, NJ: Lawrence Erlbaum Associates.

Rubinstein, M. F., & Pfeiffer, K. R. (1980). *Concepts in problem solving.* Englewood Cliffs, NJ: Prentice-Hall.

Ruggiero, V. R. (1984). *The art of thinking: A guide to critical and creative thought.* New York: Harper & Row.

Sadler, W. A., Jr., & Whimbey, A. (November, 1985). A holistic approach to improving thinking skills. *Phi Delta Kappan, 67,* 199–202.

Salmon, W. (1973). *Logic* (2nd ed.). Englewood Cliffs, NJ: Prentice-Hall.

Samson, R. W. (1975). *Thinking skills: A guide to logic and comprehension.* Connecticut: Innovative Science, Inc.

Sapir, E. (1960). *Culture, language and personality.* Berkeley: University of California Press.

Schank, R. C., & Childers, R. C. (1988). *The creative attitude: Learning to ask and answer the right questions.* New York: Macmillan.

Scheerer, M. (1963). Problem solving. *Scientific American, 208,* 118–128.

Schoenfeld, A. H. (1979). Can heuristics be taught? In J. Lochhead & J. Clement (Eds.), *Cognitive process instruction: Research on teaching skills.* Philadelphia: Franklin Institute.

Schoenfeld, A. H. (1985). *Mathematical problem solving.* New York: Academic Press.

Schoenfeld, A. H. (Ed.). (1987). *Cognitive science and mathematics education.* Hillsdale, NJ: Lawrence Erlbaum Associates.

Schoenfeld, A. H., & Herrmann, D. J. (1982). Problem perception and knowledge structure in expert and novice mathematical problem solvers. *Journal of Experimental Psychology: Learning, Memory, and Cognition, 8,* 484–494.

Schonfeld, I. S. (1987). Evaluation issues in a quasi-experiment on teaching thinking skills. *American Psychologist, 42,* 958–959.

Scholnick, E. K., & Friedman, S. L. (1987). The planning construct in the psychological literature. In S. L. Friedman, E. K. Scholnick, & R. R. Cocking (Eds.), *Blueprints for thinking: The role of planning in cognitive development* (pp. 3–38). Cambridge, MA: Cambridge University Press.

Scriven, M. (1976). *Reasoning.* New York: McGraw-Hill.

Seamon, J. G. (Ed.). (1980). *Human memory: Contemporary readings.* New York: Oxford University Press.

Segal, J. W., Chipman, S. F., & Glaser, R. (Eds.). (1985). *Thinking and learning skills: Vol. 1. Relating instruction to research.* Hillsdale, NJ: Lawrence Erlbaum Associates.

Shaklee, H. (1987). *Estimating cumulative risk: Flood and contraceptive failure.* Paper presented at the 28th Annual Meeting of the Psychonomic Society, Seattle, WA.

Shaver, K. G. (1981). *Principles of social psychology.* Cambridge, MA: Winthrop Publishers, Inc.

Shaw, G. A., & de Mers, S. T. (1986–87). Relationships between imaginery and creativity in high-IQ children. *Imagination, Cognition & Personality, 6*(3), 247–262.

Shubik, M. (1971). The dollar auction game: A paradox in noncooperative behavior and escalation. *Journal of Conflict Resolution, 15,* 109–111.

Siegler, R. S. (1978a). The origins of scientific reasoning. In R. S. Siegler (Ed.), *Children's thinking: What develops?* (pp. 109–149). Hillsdale, NJ: Lawrence Erlbaum Associates.

Siegler, R. S. (Ed.). (1978b). *Children's thinking: What develops?* Hillsdale, NJ: Lawrence Erlbaum Associates.

Silver, E. A. (Ed.). (1985). *Teaching and learning mathematical problem solving: Multiple research perspectives.* Hillsdale, NJ: Lawrence Erlbaum Associates.

Sime, M. (1973). *A child's eye view: Piaget for young parents and teachers.* New York: Harper & Row.

Simon, H. A. (1977). The psychology of scientific problem solving. In H. A. Simon (Ed.), *Models of discovery.* Dordrecht, Holland: D. Reidel.

Simpson, M. E., & Johnson, D. M. (1966). Atmosphere and conversion errors in syllogistic reasoning. *Journal of Experimental Psychology, 72,* 197–200.

Skinner, B. J. (1968). *The technology of teaching.* New York: Appleton-Century-Crofts.

Slobin, D. I. (1974). *Psycholinguistics.* London: Scott, Foresman.

Slovic, P. (1987). Perception of risk. *Science, 236,* 280–285.

Slovic, P., Fischhoff, & Lichtenstein, S. (1986). In H. Arkes & R. Hammond (Eds.), *Judgment and decision making: An interdisciplinary reader.* Cambridge: Cambridge University Press.

Slovic, P., & Lichtenstein, S. (1968). Relative importance of probabilities and payoffs in risk taking. *Journal of Experimental Psychology Monograph, 78,* (3, Pt. 2).

Smedslund, J. (1963). The concept of correlation in adults. *Scandinavian Journal of Psychology, 44,* 165–173.

Snyder, M., & Uranowitz, S. W. (1978). Reconstructing the past: Some cognitive consequences of person perception. *Journal of Personality and Social Psychology, 36,* 941–950.

Solorzano, L. (1985, January 14). Think! Now schools are teaching how. *U.S. News & World Report.*

Snow, R. E. (1986). Individual differences and the design of educational programs. *American Psychologist, 41,* 1029–1034.

Sorensen, T. C. (1965). *Kennedy.* New York: Harper & Row.

Sparke, W., Taines, B., & Sidell, S. (1975). *Doublespeak: Language for sale.* New York: Harper's College Press.

Steen, L. A. (1987). Mathematics education: A predictor of scientific competitiveness. *Science, 237,* 251–252.

Stein, M. I. (1974). *Stimulating creativity: Individual procedures* (Vol. I). New York: Academic Press.

Stein, M. (1975). *Stimulating creativity: Group procedures* (Vol. II). New York: Academic Press.

Sternberg, R. J. (1977). Component processes in analogical reasoning. *Psychological Review, 84,* 353–373.

Sternberg, R. J. (1981). Intelligence and nonentrenchment. *Journal of Educational Psychology, 73,* 1–16.

Sternberg, R. J. (1982a). Who's intelligent? *Psychology Today, 16,* 30–33, 35–36, 37–39.

Sternberg, R. J. (1982b). Reasoning, problem solving, and intelligence. In R. J. Sternberg (Ed.), *Handbook of human intelligence* (pp. 225–307). New York: Cambridge University Press.

Sternberg, R. J. (Ed.). (1982c). *Handbook of human intelligence.* Cambridge, England: Cambridge University Press.

Sternberg, R. J. (1985a). *Beyond IQ: A triarchic theory of human intelligence.* New York: Cambridge University Press.

Sternberg, R. J. (1985b). Teaching critical thinking, part I: Are we making critical mistakes? *Phi Delta Kappan, 67,* 194–198.

Sternberg, R. J. (1985c). Teaching critical thinking, part II: Possible solutions. *Phi Delta Kappan, 67,* 277–280.

Sternberg, R. J. (1986a). *Intelligence applied: Understanding and increasing your intellectual skills.* San Diego: Harcourt Brace Jovanovich.

Sternberg, R. J. (1986b). Introduction: The nature and scope of intelligence. In R. J. Sternberg & R. K. Wagner (Eds.), *Practical intelligence: Nature and origins of competence in the everyday world* (pp. 1–10). Cambridge, MA: Cambridge University Press.

Sternberg, R. J. (1986c, October 15). In defense of "critical thinking" programs. *Education Week,* 19.

Sternberg, R. J. (Ed.). (1988). *The nature of creativity.* NY: Cambridge University Press.

Sternberg, R. J., & Detterman, D. K. (Eds.). (1979). *Human intelligence: Perspective on its theory and measurement.* Norwood, NJ: Ablex.

Sternberg, R. J., & Smith, E. E. (Eds.). (1988). *The psychology of human thought.* New York: Cambridge University Press.

Sternberg, R. J., & Weil, E. M. (1980). An aptitude-strategy interaction in linear syllogistic reasoning. *Journal of Educational Psychology, 72,* 226–234.

Stewart, J. K. (1985). From the director. *National Institute of Justice: Research in Brief.* Washington, DC: U.S. Department of Justice.

Strentz, H. (1984, December 25). The road to imbecility. *Cleveland Plain Dealer,* p. B23.

Summers, G. J. (1968). *New puzzles in logical deduction.* New York: Dover Publications, Inc.

Summers, G. J. (1972). *Test your logic: 50 puzzles in deductive reasoning.* New York: Dover Publications, Inc.

Taplin, J. E., & Staudenmayer, H. (1973). Interpretation of abstract conditional sentences in deductive reasoning. *Journal of Verbal Learning and Verbal Behavior, 12,* 530–542.

Teger, A. I. (1979). *Too much invested to quit: The psychology of escalation of conflict.* New York: Pergamon Press.

Thomas, S. N. (1986). *Practical reasoning in natural language* (3rd ed.). Englewood Cliffs, NJ: Prentice-Hall, Inc.

Thouless, R. H. (1932). *Straight and crooked thinking.* New York: Simon & Schuster.

Thouless, R. H. (1939). *Tests of logical reasoning: How to think straight.* New York: Simon & Schuster.

Tobias, S. (1978). *Overcoming math anxiety.* Boston: Houghton Mifflin.

Toulmin, S., Rieke, R., & Janik, A. (1979). *An introduction to reasoning.* New York: MacMillan Publishing.

Treisman, A. M. (1964). Verbal cues, language, and meaning in selective attention. *American Journal of Psychology, 77,* 206–219.

Tucker, T. W. (1987, November 4). (Cited in Kim McDonald, 1987). Science and mathematics leaders call for radical reform in calculus teaching. *The Chronical of Higher Education, xxxiv,* A-1, A-23.

Tuma, D. J., & Reif, F. (Eds.). (1980). *Problem solving and education: Issues in teaching and research.* Hillsdale, NJ: Lawrence Erlbaum Associates.

Turing, A. (1950). Computing machinery and intelligence. *Mind, 59,* 433–460.

TV linked to memory, radio to imagination. (1988, July 25). *Los Angeles Times,* Part II, p. 3.

Tversky, A. (1969). Intransitivity of preferences. *Psychological Review, 76,* 31–48.

Tversky, A. (1972). Elimination by aspects. A theory of choice. *Psychological Review, 79,* 281–299.

Tversky, A., & Kahneman, D. (1971). Belief in the law of small numbers. *Psychological Bulletin, 76,* 104–110.

Tversky, A., & Kahneman, D. (1974). Judgment under uncertainty: Heuristics and biases. *Science,* *185,* 1124–1131.

Tversky, A., & Kahneman, D. (1981). The framing of decisions and the psychology of choice. *Science, 211,* 453–458.

Tversky, A., & Kahneman, D. (1983). Extensional versus intuitive reasoning: The conjunction fallacy in probability judgment. *Psychological Review, 90,* 293–315.

Ungson, G. R., & Braunstein, D. N. (Eds.). (1982). *Decision making: An interdisciplinary inquiry.* Boston: Kent Publishing Co.

Vancouver Community Business Directory. (1987). *Pink Pages.* Advertising, Ltd.

Vaughan, J. L. (1984). Concept structuring: The technique and empirical evidence. In C. D. Holley & D. F. Dansereau (Eds.), *Spatial learning strategies: Techniques, applications, and related issues* (pp. 127–147). New York: Academic Press.

Vernon, P. (1970). *Creativity: Selected readings.* Harmondsworth, England: Penguin Books.

von Oech, R. (1983). *A whack on the side of the head.* New York: Warner Books.

Walberg, F. (1980). *Puzzle thinking.* Philadelphia, PA: The Franklin Institute Press.

Wallas, G. (1926). *The art of thought.* New York: Harcourt, Brace & World.

Wallsten, T. S. (1980). *Cognitive processes in choice and decision behavior.* Hillsdale, NJ: Lawrence Erlbaum Associates.

Walsh, J. (1981). A plenipotentiary for human intelligence. *Science, 214,* 640–641.

Wanous, J. P. (1973). Effects of a realistic job preview on job acceptance, job attitudes, and job survival. *Journal of Applied Psychology, 58,* 327–332.

Warren, R. M., & Warren, R. P. (1970). Auditory illusions and confusions. *Scientific American, 223,* 30–36.

Wason, P. C. (1960). On the failure to eliminate hypotheses in a conceptual task. *Quarterly Journal of Experimental Psychology, 12,* 129–140.

Wason, P. C. (1968). On the failure to eliminate hypotheses: A second look. In P. C. Wason & P. N. Johnson-Laird (Eds.), *Thinking and reasoning.* Baltimore: Penguin.

Wason, P. C. (1969). Structure simplicity and psychological complexity. *Bulletin of the British Psychological Society, 22,* 281–284.

Wason, P. C., & Johnson-Laird, P. N. (Eds.). (1968). *Thinking and reasoning.* Harmondsworth, England: Penguin Books.

Wason, P. C., & Johnson-Laird, P. N. (1972). *Psychology of Reasoning.* Cambridge, MA: Harvard University Press.

Weisberg, R. W. (1986). *Creativity, genius and other myths.* New York: W. H. Freeman.

Weisberg, R., DiCamillo, M., & Phillips, D. (1978). Transferring old associations to new situations: A nonautomatic process. *Journal of Verbal Learning and Verbal Behavior, 17,* 219–228.

Weizenbaum, J. (1966). ELIZA—A computer program for the study of natural language communication between man and machine. *Communications of the Association for Computing Machinery, 9,* 36–43.

Wertheimer, M. (1959). *Productive thinking* (2nd ed.). New York: Harper.

Wheeler, D. D. (1979). A practicum in thinking. In D. D. Wheeler & W. N. Dember (Eds.), *A practicum in thinking.* Cincinnati, OH: Department of Publications and Printing Services of the University of Cincinnati.

Wheeler, D. D., & Janis, I. L. (1980). *A practical guide for making decisions.* New York: The Free Press.

Whimbey, A. (1976). *Intelligence can be taught.* New York: Bantam.

Whimbey, A., & Lochhead, J. (1982). *Problem solving and comprehension: A short course in analytic reasoning.* (3rd ed.). Philadelphia: Franklin Institute Press.

White, D. (1975). *Decision methodology.* New York: Wiley.

Whiting, C. S. (1958). *Creative thinking.* New York: Reinhold.

Whorf, B. (1956). *Language, thought, and reality.* Cambridge, MA: MIT Press.

Wickelgren, W. (1974). *How to solve problems.* San Francisco: W. H. Freeman.

Wicker, A. W. (1981). *Getting out of our conceptual ruts: Strategies for generating new perspectives on familiar research problems.* Paper presented at the 1981 Annual Convention of the Western Psychological Association, Los Angeles, CA.

Wilson, R., & Crouch, E. A. C. (1987). Risk assessment and comparisons: An introduction. *Science, 286,* 267–270.

Wilson, T. D., & Nisbett, R. E. (1978). The accuracy of verbal reports about the effects of stimuli on evaluations and behavior. *Social Psychology, 41,* 118–131.

Woodworth, R. S., & Sells, S. B. (1935). An atmosphere effect in formal syllogistic reasoning. *Journal of Experimental Psychology, 18,* 451–460.

Wright, L. (undated). Wanted: Old style thinking mechanics. *Motor Trader.* Surrey, England.

Wright, L. (1982). *Better reasoning: Techniques for handling argument, evidence and abstraction.* New York: Holt, Rinehart & Winston.

Yates, F. A. (1966). *The art of memory.* London: Routledge & Kegan Paul.

Zechmeister, E. B., & Nyberg, S. E. (1982). *Human memory: An introduction to research and theory.* Monterey, CA: Brooks, Cole Publishing Co.

Author Index

Numbers in *italics* indicate pages with complete
bibliographic information.

Subject Index

Numbers in **bold** indicate pages with definitions
from the end of chapters.